AMERICAN HISTORY NOW

IN THE SERIES

CRITICAL PERSPECTIVES ON THE PAST,

edited by Susan Porter Benson, Stephen Brier, and Roy Rosenzweig

ALSO IN THIS SERIES

Michael Adas, ed., *Essays on Twentieth Century History*
Paula Hamilton and Linda Shopes, eds., *Oral History and Public Memories*
Tiffany Ruby Patterson, *Zora Neale Hurston and a History of Southern Life*
Lisa M. Fine, *The Story of Reo Joe: Work, Kin, and Community in Autotown, U.S.A.*
Van Gosse and Richard Moser, eds., *The World the Sixties Made: Politics and Culture in Recent America*
Joanne Meyerowitz, ed., *History and September 11th*
John McMillian and Paul Buhle, eds., *The New Left Revisited*
David M. Scobey, *Empire City: The Making and Meaning of the New York City Landscape*
Gerda Lerner, *Fireweed: A Political Autobiography*
Allida M. Black, ed., *Modern American Queer History*
Eric Sandweiss, *St. Louis: The Evolution of an American Urban Landscape*
Sam Wineburg, *Historical Thinking and Other Unnatural Acts: Charting the Future of Teaching the Past*
Sharon Hartman Strom, *Political Woman: Florence Luscomb and the Legacy of Radical Reform*
Michael Adas, ed., *Agricultural and Pastoral Societies in Ancient and Classical History*
Jack Metzgar, *Striking Steel: Solidarity Remembered*
Janis Appier, *Policing Women: The Sexual Politics of Law Enforcement and the LAPD*
Allen Hunter, ed., *Rethinking the Cold War*
Eric Foner, ed., *The New American History. Revised and Expanded Edition*
Collette A. Hyman, *Staging Strikes: Workers' Theatre and the American Labor Movement*

A list of additional titles in this series appears at the back of this book

AMERICAN HISTORY NOW

EDITED FOR THE

AMERICAN HISTORICAL ASSOCIATION BY

Eric Foner AND Lisa McGirr

TEMPLE UNIVERSITY PRESS
PHILADELPHIA

To the Memory of Susan Porter Benson
and Roy Rosenzweig

TEMPLE UNIVERSITY PRESS
Philadelphia, Pennsylvania 19122
www.temple.edu/tempress

Published 2011

Library of Congress Cataloging-in-Publication Data

American history now / edited for the American Historical Association by Eric Foner and Lisa McGirr.
p. cm. — (Critical perspectives on the past)
Rev. ed. of: The new American history. Philadelphia : Temple University Press, 1997.
Includes bibliographical references.
ISBN 978-1-4399-0243-1 (cloth : alk. paper) — ISBN 978-1-4399-0244-8 (pbk. : alk. paper) — ISBN 978-1-4399-0245-5 (e-book) 1. United States—Historiography. I. Foner, Eric. II. McGirr, Lisa, 1962– III. American Historical Association. IV. New American history (Temple University Press)
E175.A454 2011
973.072—dc22

2010050109

∞ The paper used in this publication meets the requirements of the American National Standard for Information Sciences—Permanence of Paper for Printed Library Materials, ANSI Z39.48-1992

Printed in the United States of America

2 4 6 8 9 7 5 3

CONTENTS

VOLUME EDITORS' PREFACE

First published in 1990, followed by a revised and expanded edition seven years later, *The New American History* introduced a generation of students, teachers, and members of the broader public to the ongoing transformation of the study of the American past. In the early twenty-first century, that transformation has continued apace. In embarking on a third edition, the editors decided to assemble an entirely new collection. First, we expanded the number of essays to eighteen, to allow us to incorporate emerging subfields not represented in the original editions. Second, we invited an entirely new group of historians to contribute. Each of the essays that follow is written by a young scholar at the forefront of current trends in his or her area of expertise. Eight deal with a specific time period, beginning with the colonial era; the remainder assess recent developments in historians' understanding of a major theme in the nation's past. To signal these substantive and generational changes, we gave the volume the new title *American History Now*.

It is worth noting at the outset that we have made no attempt to impose a uniform outlook or single interpretation on the contributors. We have given each author a free hand in defining his or her subject and developing an approach to it. Inevitably, therefore, there are overlaps, especially between chronological and thematic essays, as well as differences in emphasis and outlook. Nonetheless, certain themes recur with remarkable regularity.

The first editions of *The New American History* demonstrated, above all, the impact of the "new social history" on our understanding of the American past. Inspired initially by the social movements of the 1960s and 1970s, and influenced by methods and insights borrowed from other disciplines and from scholars of other national histories, American historians redefined the cast of characters who made up the nation's past. They devoted their energies to recovering the experience of previously neglected groups, not simply as an addition to a preexisting body of knowledge but as a fundamental redefinition of history itself. In the wake of that explosion of scholarship, our understanding of American history past was enormously enriched and expanded.

The scholars in this new edition build upon the work of that generation. Rather than seeking to debunk the interpretations of their forebears, these younger historians begin with the assumption that no narrative of American history can be considered complete that ignores the political, social, and cultural experiences of ordinary Americans and that fails to take into account the remarkable diversity that has always characterized American society. But they push this insight in dramatic new directions.

As these essays show, today's leading historians are less interested in developing new subfields or framing either/or dichotomies than in locating intersections and interactions. Categories like race and gender, touchstones of the new social history, are now considered essential to understanding major themes in American development, including the law, diplomacy, and public policy, rather than being limited to relations between blacks and whites or men and women. The distinction between "high" politics and that of ordinary folk has been jettisoned in favor of the study of the broad public sphere, defined so as to encompass many groups who were traditionally excluded from electoral participation yet who engaged in boisterous debates over issues such as economic justice and gender equality. Even national boundaries no longer delimit American history, as evidenced by the number of essays that touch on the history of "borderlands" where various national groups came into contact, as well as on the widespread interest in the global reach of the American experience. An age of globalization seems to demand embedding American history more powerfully than ever in a global framework.

One preoccupation of this new generation of scholars has been to link or reconnect previously fragmented studies of a diverse cast of characters into a new kind of synthesis, one quite different from the old "master narrative" in offering a richer and more complex view of the American past. The chronological essays, for example, devote attention to the importance of elites, established institutions, and public policy, but also place a strong emphasis on how less prominent groups responded to, and affected, constellations of power in the past. Women, Native Americans, workers, slaves, and others appear as important historical actors whose claims contested the shape of power relations. Some essays, like Woody Holton's on the revolutionary era, pointedly depart from the popular fascination with the founding fathers to emphasize the struggles of a broad array of distinct social groups. Others, including Seth Rockman's on the Jacksonian era, Robert Johnston's on Progressive America, and Kim Phillips-Fein's on the years since 1973, emphasize both national authority and the democratic aspirations of less powerful groups.

One theme of the essays that follow is the blurring of previously established scholarly boundaries, as subfields are redefined or abandoned in favor of broader new categories. The new history of capitalism, discussed by Sven Beckert, brings together older subfields such as labor history, business history, and economic history, all within a transnational framework. This new scholarship denaturalizes capitalism by making its emergence a subject of investigation rather than the result of some natural law standing outside of history. Environmental history, an emerging field mapped by Sarah Phillips, investigates human interactions with the natural universe and the conflicts in politics, society, economics, and the world of ideas over the relationship between human and nonhuman. Diplomatic history, as Erez Manela shows, has been revitalized by incorporating insights from cultural history and benefiting from the "transnational turn." The study of America in the world now includes not simply diplomacy but the activities of nongovernmental actors as well, from performing artists to missionaries and auto salesmen. Mae Ngai charts the recent remaking of immigration history from a field focused on the "assimilation" of European newcomers to a new emphasis on circular worldwide patterns of migration and concepts of cultural diaspora and hybridity. These essays offer vivid examples of what Lawrence Glickman describes as the broader "cultural turn" in historical analysis, which in the past generation has affected virtually every aspect of American history. Cultural historians seek to understand the evolution and hidden power relations within categories—race, class, and so on—that previous scholars took for granted.

Some of the essays cover fields that were ignored in previous editions but have emerged at the forefront of current scholarship. As John McGreevy points out, historians have long neglected the powerful impact of religious faith and religious institutions in the nation's past, but today, thanks in part to the prominent role of religion in contemporary American society, these attract the attention of increasing numbers of historians. Native American history, as Ned Blackhawk delineates, has in recent years become a flourishing enterprise. As Blackhawk shows (and Alan Taylor's essay on the colonial era underscores), attention to the Native American experience profoundly reshapes our understanding of key moments in American history.

"The only obligation we have to history," Oscar Wilde once quipped, "is to rewrite it." There is nothing unusual or sinister in the fact that each generation rewrites history to suit its own needs. Taken together, these essays portray a field characterized by remarkable diversity, vitality, and open-mindedness. They suggest that at its best, the study of history remains a mode of collective self-discovery. This generation is well on the way to fashioning a history of the United States that transcends boundaries rather than reinforcing or reproducing them, that offers a candid appraisal of our own society's strengths and weaknesses while engaging in a mutually illuminating dialogue with the entire world.

Eric Foner
Lisa McGirr

SERIES EDITOR'S PREFACE

It has been almost a quarter century since my late colleagues—Susan Porter Benson and Roy Rosenzweig—and I launched the Critical Perspectives on the Past series at Temple University Press, in close collaboration with Janet Francendese, our Temple editor for the entire series. Back then we were young(ish) scholars anxious to find ways to transform what we saw as a stodgy and hidebound profession far too interested in traditional historical subjects and traditional ways of recounting history. The first book in the series was our own *Presenting the Past: Essays on History and the Public*, which grew out of an issue of *Radical History Review* on public history that Roy, Sue, and I (along with Bob Entenmann and Warren Goldstein) had edited. We hoped in that collection and in the series which grew out of it to offer a fresh look at historical theory and practice. We ended up publishing thirty-nine monographs, edited collections, and public history books on diverse historical subjects and areas of the world over the next twenty-five years. In all our editorial choices, we tried to be especially attentive to issues of race, class, and gender and to the role of human agency in shaping historical events. We always sought books and collections that challenged the conventional historical wisdom of what was important for historians to write about while also focusing in on nontraditional ways in which historical ideas could be communicated to a broad public.

As the successor to two editions of *The New American History*, *American History Now*, edited by Eric Foner and Lisa McGirr, seems to be an appropriate place to cap the Critical Perspectives series and to bring our work on this series to a close. For this volume, Foner and McGirr have reached out to a younger generation of historians to summarize and reflect on the ongoing intellectual and conceptual transformations that have reshaped historical inquiry and academic life over the past decade. Those are the same kinds of intellectual questions and issues that originally piqued Roy's, Sue's and my interest in editing this series in the first place. Sue's untimely death from cancer in 2005 and Roy's death two years later from the same disease made me realize it was now time to pass the torch to the next generation of young scholars. This final book in the Critical Perspectives on the Past series is therefore dedicated to my old comrades, both of whom were wholly committed in their lives and careers to recapturing the histories of those left out of standard historical syntheses, to intellectual and pedagogical innovation, and to making history accessible to a broad democratic public. They are and will continue to be missed by me and hundreds of their colleagues and friends, as well as their families.

Steve Brier
New York City

AMERICAN HISTORY NOW

I

ERAS OF THE AMERICAN PAST

1

Squaring the Circles: The Reach of Colonial America

ALAN TAYLOR

In 1721 in South Carolina, the royal governor received a precious present: a deerskin map conveying a complex world of native peoples and their intricate interconnections. The gift came from Indian chiefs who met Governor Francis Nicholson at Charles Town (now Charleston), the colony's capital and leading seaport. The chiefs represented villages in the Piedmont, where the people spoke a Siouan language. Lumped together by the British (and subsequent historians) as "Catawbas," the people thought of themselves as belonging to a loose confederation of eleven villages named on the map: Casuie, Charra, Nasaw, Nustie, Saxippaha, Succa, Suttirie, Wasmisa, Waterie, Wiapie, and Youchine. The map also locates two more familiar native peoples—the Cherokee and Chickasaw—who had allied with the Catawbas and the British. Rather than represent natives as one, common mass of Indians, the map introduced the governor to a complex network of diverse peoples. Divided into hundreds of linguistically distinct peoples, the natives did not know that they were a common category until named and treated so by the colonial invaders. The Nasaw map warns us to beware of how much nuance we lose when lumping the many native peoples together as "Indians."

By giving the map, the Catawbas sought to educate the new governor to native diplomacy. Rather than depict geographical proportions, the map conveys social and political relationships between peoples, both native and colonial. The thirteen native peoples appear as circles of varying sizes and locations, with the largest and the most central—for the Nasaw—enjoying a pride of place. Asserting a hierarchy of power, the map defines the Nasaw as the pivotal and crucial people in a web of relationships that linked the British colonies of the coast with the Indians of the interior. Take us seriously, and treat us with a special generosity, the Nasaw mapmaker insisted.

A selective depiction of social space, the Nasaw map omits many of the peoples then dwelling between Charles Town, on the east, and the Chickasaws of the Mississippi Valley, to the west. Devoted to the Catawbas and their allies, the map excludes the powerful Creek and Choctaw confederations, who offered rival networks of native power. The map assured Nicholson that the Catawba peoples, and especially the Nasaw, were his special and indispensable friends, who served as his proper conduit into the wider native world of the vast interior. Of course, maps made by other native peoples altered the hierarchy and centrality of villages. In 1723, Nicholson collected a similar map made by the Chickasaws, who gave themselves centrality with strong links to the Choctaw and Cherokee and to the English at Charles Town but with only a marginal place allotted to the Catawbas.

The 1721 Catawba map also represents only two colonial polities: Charles Town appears on the left as a cross-hatching of lines at right angles, while a box named Virginia occupies the lower right-hand corner. The well-rounded natives thought of the newcomers as squares. Living in oval wigwams in circular villages surrounded by palisades, native peoples felt spiritually safest in rounded forms, which reflected the natural cycles of seasons and lives. Their conception of the world as a web of social circles derived from their ancestors who, as recently as the sixteenth century, had sustained the Mississippian culture, which featured many ceremonial mounds. In stark contrast, the Indians identified the colonists with their square and rectangular buildings in towns platted as grids: alien and unnatural forms that seemed ominous.

Rather than reject the strange newcomers, the map represents an Indian bid to incorporate them into a native nexus of diplomacy and trade in the hope that the colonists could learn how to coexist in a shared land. Parallel lines connect both Charles Town and Virginia to the native circles. The lines represented paths of safe conduct for traders and diplomats in a world that could otherwise turn violent. The map coaxed the British to approach the other Catawbas via the Nasaw, who claimed a primacy in trade and diplomacy. To contact the Nustie, for example, good manners demanded sending representatives (and presents of trade goods) first to the Nasaw. Far from accepting subordination to the Virginians or the Carolinians, the Nasaw cast themselves as the brokers of commerce and power in a world dominated by native peoples and conducted in native ways. In this map, Indians hold the center, while the colonists remain marginal.

The self-assurance of the map jars our conventional assumptions about Indians, for we usually narrate colonial history as a relentless and irresistible British drive to dominate and dispossess native peoples. Surely, we assume, natives must have quickly recognized an inferiority dictated by their smaller numbers and inferior technology. We do not expect to find them acting as the self-confident teachers of colonists cast as rather obtuse, but redeemable, students. The map offers an alternative vision of coexistence on native terms, thereby rejecting the colonizers' drive to dispossess native peoples and convert the survivors into Christian menials. Although the governor may not have grasped the intended lesson, the map can teach us more about native thoughts and ways than do the categorical statements of colonizers who lumped all Indians together as immutable primitives meant for eventual conquest.

In addition to the circles, squares, and paths, the map represents three animate beings. First, an especially large human figure wearing a skirt appears to float over the path between Nasaw and Virginia. Lacking a label, she apparently mattered more to the Nasaw mapmaker than to the British copyist. It is tempting to grant her a supernatural power in the minds of the Nasaw. A caption does identify the other, much smaller human figure as "An Indian a Hunting." Evidently male and armed with a musket, he faces an equally small deer. Long a staple of Indian subsistence, hunting deer had become essential to the new and expanding trade with colonists, who valued the hides for tanning to make clothing, especially gloves. By killing deer by the thousands for their hides, the Catawba paid for coveted British manufactures of cloth and metal—including guns and ammunition: goods the natives could not make for themselves. Both by its original material—a deer hide—and by representing a deer-hunting Indian, the map conveyed the trade at the heart of their relationship with the Carolinians.

Finally, in the lower left-hand corner, near Charles Town, the map seems to depict a deployed parachute. But modern eyes trick us into assuming that the English labels define a consistent up and down (or north and south). In fact, the Nasaw intended viewers to circle around the map to view it from every angle without privileging any one side. The apparent parachute is, instead, a ship with a central mast mounted by a pennant and linked by ropes to the deck. In addition to a grid of streets, Charles Town impressed natives as a harbor filled with ships capable of crossing the Atlantic.

The map offers a sophisticated reflection on a changing world where natives killed deer for a transatlantic market while hoping to preserve their traditional spirituality, including a sky woman. The mixed symbols mark the map as at the linkage between two different, but increasingly interpenetrated, networks: the native-made circles and paths of the interior and the Euro-American entrepots of transatlantic commerce.[1]

Two paper copies of the map survive because Governor Nicholson gave them to his patron in England, the Prince of Wales. To render the map meaningful to the prince (and, so, to us), the copyist added the English-language labels: translations and representations of the explanations orally conveyed by the chiefs when they delivered their gift. As a cherished curiosity, the copies enabled Nicholson to repay the favors that had promoted his career. That transatlantic career attests to the broad reach of the English empire (which became British in 1707). Born in Yorkshire in 1655, Nicholson was a veteran army officer, who, during the 1670s and 1680s, had led troops in Flanders in Europe, Tangier in Morocco, and Boston in New England. He subsequently governed the colonies of New York and Virginia before commanding a failed British bid to conquer French Canada in 1709. A year later Nicholson did capture French Acadia, which became British Nova Scotia, with Nicholson as the first governor. In 1720 he became the first royal governor of South Carolina. Returning to England in 1725, he died in London three years later after a life spent trying to increase the power of an empire along the Atlantic coast of North America.[2]

Histories

Brought together in 1721, the Nasaw mapgivers and the English governor jointly speak to the efforts by historians in recent years to grasp the interplay of the "Atlantic" and "Continental" networks of human movement, trade, diplomacy, and war in North America. "Atlantic historians" examine the complex interplay of Europe, Africa, and the Americas through the transatlantic flows of goods, people, plants, animals, capital, and ideas. American colonization derived from a global expansion of European exploration and commerce beginning in the fifteenth century. In cannon-armed sailing ships, Europeans created the first global nexus of trade by crisscrossing the Atlantic, Indian, and Pacific Oceans. Europe reaped windfall profits from the new global trade, especially in African slaves sent to the Americas to work new plantations devoted to sugar, tobacco, rice, and cacao. Atlantic history is a subset of the larger, global story of European expansion.

During the sixteenth century, the Portuguese led the way around Africa to India, while the Spanish crossed the Atlantic to explore and colonize the Americas. The Spanish took Mexico, to exploit the gold and silver mines, and the largest islands in the Caribbean, where they developed sugar plantations. Coming second, the French concentrated on harvesting the fish of the northern waters and the valuable furs of the northern forests drained by the St. Lawrence River. That left the intervening Atlantic Seaboard for belated exploitation by the English during the early seventeenth century. Disappointed in their hopes for finding precious minerals, the English compensated by creating profitable plantations and farms that attracted thousands of colonists. They also took over a Dutch attempt to create a New Netherland colony in the Hudson and Delaware valleys, between the English colonies in the Chesapeake to the south and New England to the north. In 1707 the English empire became British with the union of Scotland to England under one king and one parliament.

While necessary to assess the colonial era, an Atlantic approach is not sufficient. As Paul Mapp notes, North America was "where an Atlantic world interacted with multiple other worlds." To make sense of colonial North America we need to combine Atlantic and continental approaches. Mapp and other "continental historians" seek to restore the importance of native peoples to the colonial story. Rather than treat Indians as unchanging primitives doomed from the start to conquest and assimilation by the colonizers, the continental approach emphasizes the natives' ability to adapt to the newcomers and to compel concessions from them. Instead of lurking beyond the colonies in an ahistorical "wilderness," Indians have come back into the narrative as central and persistent protagonists who helped to shape every colony.

The new combination of Atlantic and continental history challenges the older orthodoxy that treated colonial America as a story of English cultural "seeds" first planted at Jamestown in Virginia in 1607 and at Plymouth in New England in 1620. According to the older view, "American history" began in the east in the English colonies and spread slowly westward, reaching only the Appalachian mountains by independence. In this story, the continent's Indian peoples and Spanish and French colonies seemed relevant only as enemies, as challenges that brought out the best in the English as they remade themselves into Americans.

According to our national origin myth, common English colonists escaped from the rigid customs, social hierarchies, and constrained resources of Europe into an abundant land of both challenge and opportunity. Rising to the challenge, they made the most of their frontier opportunities to prosper by turning the forest into farms. Thereby, they became entrepreneurial and egalitarian individualists who could only be ruled by their own consent. Inevitably, they rebelled against British rule to form an independent and republican union of states destined to expand to the Pacific. Known as "American exceptionalism," this interpretation casts the colonial period simply as an Anglophone preparation for the United States, defined as a uniquely middle-class society and democracy.[3]

American exceptionalism relies on some partial truths. Many British colonists did find more land, greater prosperity, and higher status than they could have achieved by remaining in the mother country. And (save for in the West Indies) British America did lack the aristocrats of the mother country, creating a social vacuum that enabled successful lawyers, merchants, and planters to comprise a colonial elite that favored commercial values. Historians long focused on the political participation of common colonists as voters and legislators in the British colonies. And those scholars scoured colonial events, including the revivals of the Great Awakening, for hints of the coming revolution.

But the traditional story of American uplift obscures the heavy costs of colonization. Especially during the seventeenth century in Virginia and the West Indies, thousands of colonists found only intense labor and early graves owing to diseases and Indian hostility. And those who succeeded bought their good fortune by taking lands from Indians and by exploiting the labor of indentured servants and African slaves. Few Indians and fewer Africans experienced colonial America as a world of attractive new opportunities. Between 1492 and 1776, North America lost population, as diseases and wars killed Indians faster than colonists could replace them. And, during the eighteenth century, most colonial arrivals were African conscripts forcibly carried to a land of slavery, rather than European volunteers seeking a domain of freedom. More than minor aberrations, Indian deaths and the African slaves were fundamental to the success of colonization and the prosperity of the free.

The traditional story also obscures the broad cultural and geographic range of colonial America, which extended far beyond the British colonies of the Atlantic Seaboard. Many native peoples encountered colonizers not as westward-bound Englishmen, but as Spanish heading north from Mexico, as Russians coming eastward from Siberia, or as French probing the Great Lakes and Mississippi River. Each of those colonial ventures interacted in distinctive ways with particular settings and Indians to construct varied Americas—which competed for the trade and alliance of the native peoples in the vast interior between the colonial enclaves.

In recent years, historians have paid greater attention to the broader continent, in general, and to the cultures of native peoples, in particular. These new approaches reveal that colonial societies *did* diverge from their mother countries—but in a more complex and radical manner than imagined within the narrow vision of American uplift for English men. Colonial conditions produced an unprecedented mixing of radically diverse peoples—African, European, and Indian—under stressful circumstances for all. The world had never known such a rapid and intense intermingling of peoples—and of microbes, plants, and animals from different continents. Everyone had to adapt to a new world wrought by those combinations. Thrown together in distant colonies, the diverse peoples from three continents had to find new ways to communicate and to coexist in North America.

The Indians also lived in a new world transformed by the intrusion of diverse newcomers bearing alien diseases, livestock, trade goods, weapons, and Christian beliefs. Ranging across the continent, those processes affected peoples and their environments far from the centers of colonial settlement. Reduced by disease and war, the Siouan peoples of the Carolina Piedmont began to consolidate their villages to form a loose confederation, which eventually became known as the Catawbas. Similar processes of ethnogenesis reshaped native peoples throughout the continent.

Despite the epidemics, the Indians of the interior remained sufficiently numerous and resourceful to slow (and sometimes to reverse) the colonial conquest. For example, on the Great Plains during the eighteenth century, the Indian peoples acquired large herds of horses that endowed them with a new mobility and prowess as buffalo hunters and mounted warriors. Better fed, clothed, and equipped than ever before, the mounted Indians could defy colonial intrusions and even roll back their settlements in Texas and New Mexico.

On the southern Great Plains, the Comanche were the big winners. During the seventeenth century, they had lived as hunter-gatherers in the foothills of the Rocky Mountains. During the early eighteenth century, they traded and raided to obtain horses, which enabled them to push south and east onto the plains to hunt buffalo. By procuring enlarged hunting territories, they improved their bargaining position as traders and their might as warriors. Preying upon the weaker Apaches, the Comanche took women and children captives for trade and for adoption. The many adopted captives and an improved diet of abundant buffalo meat fueled a population growth that starkly contrasted with the demographic decline afflicting most other native peoples. By 1800 the Comanche numbered about 20,000—twice as many as all other native peoples on the southern Great Plains.

Comanche expansion set off a domino effect, as their defeated rivals fled and came into conflict with new neighbors. Reeling from Comanche raids, Apache bands headed westward across the Rio Grande into western New Mexico or they pushed southward deeper into Texas. Many westering Apache refugees found a more secure haven in the canyons of northwest New Mexico. Along their way west, they raided the Pueblo peoples, taking horses, sheep, cattle, and captives. From their captives, the western bands learned weaving, pottery making, and the herding of domestic animals, especially sheep. These composite and increasingly prosperous western bands became known to the Hispanics as the Apache de Navihu—later shortened to Navajo.

Nowhere did the colonizers find a truly empty land free for the taking. However, by the eighteenth century, no natives lived in a primeval isolation from the impact of colonization. Disease epidemics, slave raids, and trade goods spread far beyond the colonies through Indian intermediaries. For example, few Indians lived farther from colonial power than did the Paiutes of the Great Basin: an arid region barely and rarely visited by the Spanish. And yet Ned Blackhawk reveals that hundreds of Paiutes became slaves in eighteenth-century New Mexico. They fell into captivity from raids by their Ute enemies wielding metal weapons obtained in trade from the Hispanics. That trade in Paiute slaves for manufactured goods sustained a Ute alliance that the Spanish desperately needed to protect New Mexico from other Indians. Such complications prevailed on every frontier as circles and squares overlapped, with both colonizers and natives jostling for an advantage over their rivals.

A hybrid work of cross-cultural translation and explanation, the Nasaw map simplifies to help the governor to grasp a part of the native world. The map focuses on native nations or tribes—the political units most familiar to a European governor. In the process, the map obscures the constituent clans, lineages, and villages—which, in fact, more fundamentally structured the lives of natives. A similar selectivity informs how we write about native peoples, for we remain saddled with a European-derived political vocabulary that casts empires and nations as advanced and complex. In this view, the colonists had coercive state structures with courts, gallows, standing armies, bureaucracies, and hierarchies of command—while Indians did *not*. Unwittingly, we cast their political arrangements as partial, simple, and immature by European standards, for we struggle to grasp their very different modes of complexity, where power derived from the forms and ties of kinship relations. Juliana Barr concludes, "We need to move away from the European constructions of power that are so familiar to us—those grounded in ideas of the state and of racial difference—and try to understand the world as Indians did—organized around kinship-based relationships."

In such a system, native women enjoyed more authority, within delimited realms, than did their colonial counterparts. In most native cultures, women owned the villages, their lands, and the crops—while men hunted, fished, and held the more conspicuous roles as orators, diplomats, and warriors. In that native world, so often at war, women enjoyed a special authority as the makers of peace: cherished and elusive. But they also served as the particular targets of raids to take slaves. In his study of natives and colonists in greater New Mexico, James Brooks reveals that female captives became kin with connections in multiple communities both native and colonial. Some even gained leverage from their cross-cultural expertise, becoming interpreters and brokers of trade and diplomacy between Hispanic settlements and native bands. In a constant cycle of trade and revenge, violence disrupted some families to enrich others as men, both colonial and native, tried to defend their own women and children and to take or buy those of other men. This "captive-exchange system" promoted a violent interdependence rather than peace.

Dependence

Every colonial empire depended on Indian peoples as guides to local plants, landscapes, and animals; as converts for missionary institutions; as trading partners; as slave catchers to retrieve runaway Africans; as raiders to make new slaves of other Indians; and as allies in wars with other empires. Through missions or trade, rival empires tried to build networks of native allies meant to counter those developed by their European rivals. Rather than imposing a pure colonial mastery, those alliances involved the mutual dependence of both colonists and natives. Although natives increasingly relied on European trade goods, they also compelled imperialists to accommodate to native protocols and alliances—often imposing heavy costs and great compromises on imperial visions.

Styling themselves fathers to Indian children, the French longed to dominate all of the natives of the continental interior. But they could never control the dispersed, decentralized, and shifting bands of natives. And in making allies of some, the French had to take on their enemies. Allying with the Algonkin and Huron embroiled the French in debilitating wars with the Haudenosaunee (also known as the "Iroquois") during the seventeenth century. A century later in the Great Lakes country, the Anishinaabe and Illinois manipulated their French allies into attacking the powerful Fox peoples. Brett Rushforth has shown that these native wars compromised the French dream of a universal trade empire engaging every native people in a vast alliance. Native allies repeatedly set limits to French ambitions by giving to them (or obliging them to buy) captives taken from native enemies—including the Fox. Rejecting those captives would wreck the alliance, but accepting them limited the alliance by alienating the raided peoples. The proliferation of enslaved Indians, known as Panis, in Montreal attested to the weakness, rather than to the strength, of the French empire in the Great Lakes watershed.

Savvy imperialists recognized that Indians determined the balance of power within North America. In 1755 an English trader observed,

> The importance of the Indians is now generally known and understood. A Doubt remains not, that the prosperity of our Colonies on the Continent will stand or fall with our Interest and favour among them. While they are our Friends, they are the Cheapest and Strongest Barrier for the Protection of our Settlements; when Enemies, they are capable of ravaging in their method of War, in spite of all we can do, to render those Possessions almost useless.

Despite their reduced numbers, the Indians were skilled guerrilla warriors who dominated the interior passages between the rival colonies. If alienated, the natives could obstruct the advance of their colonial enemy, and their raiders could terrify and destroy outlying settlements.

In regions where the colonizers arrived in relatively small numbers, they had to cultivate native goodwill. In the Great Lakes country during the seventeenth century, the French came by the dozen rather than the thousands. Dependent on Indian trade and protection, the French crafted an alliance based upon mutual accommodations. In the famous phrase of Richard White, the natives and the French found a "middle ground," where neither could dominate the other, so they had to deal with one another as allies.

Indians were even more powerful in eighteenth-century Texas, where colonial missions, presidios, settlements, and trading posts were few, isolated, and vulnerable oases in a native world. In colonial North America, such a native-dominated landscape was more common than, say, Massachusetts or Virginia, with their powerful concentrations of British colonists. Juliana Barr concludes that the native peoples of Texas treated the French and Spanish intruders as "just another collection of bands like themselves." To survive, the newcomers had to offer appealing trade goods, adopt the protocols of native diplomacy, and form kinship ties with the natives through marriage or ritual adoption. Readier to marry native women, the French gained an edge over their Spanish competitors.

Where colonists were few and Indians many, the colonizers tried to convert natives through the agency of missions run by priests. During the seventeenth century, Franciscan friars enjoyed remarkable success in Spanish Florida and New Mexico, founding dozens of missions that attracted thousands of native converts. At the same time, French Jesuits compensated for the small colonial population of Canada by building missions in the St. Lawrence Valley and among the Huron people of the Great Lakes.

The inability of traditional shamans to shield their people from the devastating new diseases induced many natives to seek spiritual protection from the missionaries. The ceremonial richness and sacred objects of Catholic worship also impressed the natives, who regarded the crucifixes, rosaries, Agnus Dei medals, and saint's relics as counterparts to the charms and *katsinas* long kept by Indians as sources of spiritual power.

The missions also proffered material and military incentives to entice native peoples. Many Indians coveted European manufactures including metal hoes, knives, fishhooks, hatchets, and cloth blankets—as well as the benefits of domesticated livestock, especially sheep and cattle. Missions often offered a more secure food supply through the seasons than did a traditional, mobile way of life. By converting, native peoples also hoped to secure a military alliance against their enemies. In Canada, the Montagnais, Algonkins, and Hurons sought French help against their Haudenosaunee foes to the south. In Florida, the Spanish promised protection against the Yamasee, Savannah, and Creek peoples to the north of their missions. In New Mexico, the Pueblo peoples needed allies to fend off the nomadic bands of Apache, Navajo, and Comanche who lived in the nearby mountains and Great Plains.

But the conversions were never as complete and irreversible as the priests initially believed, for native peoples regarded Christianity as a supplement, rather than as a substitute, for their traditional beliefs. Natives had long adopted and augmented their spiritual repertoire, clinging to a conceptual framework that regarded supernatural power as diverse and woven into their natural world. They accepted and adapted features of European culture, including Christianity, which they found useful or unavoidable, while privately maintaining their traditional spiritual beliefs. Above all, they tried to preserve a distinct identity and core culture derived from their ancestors. But the missionaries longed to believe that their native converts had forsaken their pagan ways once and for all, without compromise. When suddenly disabused of their illusions, the seventeenth-century missionaries felt betrayed, inflicting excessive punishments that sometimes provoked uprisings. In 1680, for example, the Pueblo peoples revolted, rousting the Spanish from New Mexico. At the end of that century, when the priests and soldiers returned, they behaved with greater circumspection, rebuilding the alliance on terms acceptable to the Pueblos.

Unlike the French and the Spanish, the English rarely developed missions, focusing instead on expanding their farms at Indian expense. Because the Chesapeake and New England colonies attracted many more immigrants than did New Mexico, Florida, and New France *combined*, the English colonists put greater pressure on native lands, provoking more frequent wars. During the late 1640s, a few Puritan clergymen belatedly created mission communities for the natives in New England. In permanent, compact "praying towns" the Indians could be pressured to change their beliefs, behavior, and appearance. By restricting Indians to fixed and limited towns, the Puritans hoped to free up additional lands for colonial settlement. But the Indians had their own reasons for joining the praying towns, which appealed primarily to smaller groups harder hit by disease and the settler intrusion. They saw the praying towns as their last hope for preserving their group identity on a part of their homeland. Indeed, the praying towns bore native names, including "Natick," which meant "my land."

By 1673 the colony of Massachusetts hosted fourteen praying towns with sixteen hundred inhabitants, but most of them collapsed two years later, when other Indians attacked the New English towns. Distrusting the missionized Indians, the colonial authorities sent them to cold and barren islands in Boston harbor, where hundreds died from exposure, malnutrition, and disease. During the spring and summer of 1676, the colonists suppressed the rebels with the help of scouts recruited from the surviving praying-town Indians. Some of the defeated rebels escaped northward to take refuge among the Indians in Canada. Nursing bitter memories, they helped the French to raid New England in subsequent wars between 1689 and 1760.

In Carolina, the English dispensed with missions, relying instead on trade to recruit Indian allies. Compared to their French and Spanish rivals, the Carolina traders offered especially prized trade goods at relatively good prices and on generous credit. Unlike their rivals, the English relied almost exclusively on their economic advantage, rather than on understanding (or converting) the culture of their customers. By offering guns in exchange for deer hides and native captives taken by their allies, the Carolinians secured their own frontier and wreaked havoc on natives who allied with the Spanish in nearby Florida or with the French in Louisiana. Slave raids enabled the Carolina allies to purchase more guns, compounding their military prowess. Raiding also crushed and dispersed rival peoples, opening up their deer-hunting grounds for exploitation by the victors.

The Carolina traders encouraged their allies to attack the Guale, Timucua, and Apalachee Indians who lived in the Spanish missions of Florida. Poorly armed by the Spanish, the mission Indians proved easy pickings for slave raids. Between 1704 and 1706 the Creek, Savannah, and Yamasee raiders destroyed thirty-two native villages and their missions, inflicting horrific casualties and enslaving about ten thousand people. The Carolina gun and slave trade had triumphed over the Spanish mission system as an instrument of colonial influence.

After the destruction of the Florida missions, potential captives became scarcer, and the raiders fell into arrears on their debts owed to the Carolina traders. In 1715 the Yamasees and the Cawtawbas sought to escape their debts by killing traders and attacking the Carolina settlements, killing about 400 and driving hundreds of refugees into Charles Town. But the Indian rebels lost momentum as they ran low on guns and gunpowder. They had counted on a continued supply from the British traders in Virginia, who competed with their counterparts in the Carolinas. Although the traders and leaders of Carolina and Virginia bickered almost constantly, during an Indian war their national and racial consciousness united them as English and white. Putting aside their rivalries, the Virginians assisted the Carolinians with weapons and troops and with an embargo on the trade in guns and gunpowder to the rebels. Aided by Tuscarora and Cherokee allies, the Carolinians forced the Catawbas to make peace and to help them subdue and enslave the Yamasees.

Threatened by the slave raids of Carolina's allies, the Indians in the Mississippi Valley sought an alliance with the French who founded Louisiana in 1699. From Carolina's success and Florida's failure, the French concluded that a commerce in guns better secured native support than did missionaries, so, in Louisiana, the French made gun trade, rather than missions, their priority in Indian relations. By uniting and arming the Mississippi Valley peoples, the French sought to stabilize them as enduring allies to keep the British away from Louisiana. But the French could not match the quantity, quality, and price of British manufactures, so they had to rely on bestowing trade goods as government-funded presents. Lacking the means to satisfy all the Indian nations on their periphery, the French had to settle for allying primarily with the numerous Choctaws. Unable also to supply the Chickasaws, the French accepted them as enemies who traded with the Carolinians. Indeed, during the 1720s the French encouraged the Choctaws to raid the Chickasaws for slaves.

The vast colony of Louisiana became two very different landscapes: a small plantation core around New Orleans, where settlers prevailed, and an immense hinterland dominated by Indians. In the interior, the French held only a few small and scattered forts hostage to the goodwill of the surrounding natives. French officials claimed that they had a particular gift for understanding and conciliating Indians, but their claim was only half true, for they conducted contrasting policies in Louisiana. In the hinterland, the French made a virtue of their weakness by cultivating some natives as their cherished allies (while treating others as necessary enemies). But, in the colony's core, where the colonists and their slaves were more numerous, the French treated natives as callously as did any other colonizers.

The Louisianans also worked to keep Indians and Africans apart lest they unite to destroy the plantations. To sow antipathies, the French conspicuously employed some trusted blacks in their militias sent to fight the Indians. A few particularly courageous and resourceful black soldiers won their freedom as a reward meant to inspire the exertions of their enslaved comrades. However, colonial leaders rewarded the Choctaw to hunt down runaway slaves and to punish rebel slaves by burning them to death. But the Louisiana elite also distrusted their own lower-class whites as little better, and sometimes worse, than Indians or enslaved Africans. Regarded as felons and vagrants, the common settlers and soldiers of Louisiana found that a white skin brought them far less privilege than it did to the common people of Carolina. In sum, the French relied on blacks and natives to control lower-class whites just as they employed Africans and Indians against one another.

That Louisiana balancing act contrasted with the British colonial tendency toward a greater formal equality and liberty for all white men, as they increasingly equated freedom with the white race and their property rights over Africans. Relative to the French, the British colonists enjoyed greater liberties from, and voice within, their government—and more shared power over slaves. As the British Americans grew even more numerous, prosperous, and confident, they developed their white racial solidarity and popular government.

Although commercially weaker than the British of Carolina, the French of Louisiana had the edge as Indian traders over the Spanish of New Mexico. The workshops in Spain were less productive, Spanish shipping more expensive, and trade more strictly regulated and heavily taxed by officials. Consequently, Spanish goods were more expensive and of lower quality than those offered by their French and British competitors. During the eighteenth century, that discrepancy had ominous consequences for security along the vast northern frontier of New Spain.

Although allies elsewhere, the French and Spanish became bitter rivals for sway with the native peoples in the immense Great Plains between French Louisiana and Hispanic New Mexico. Lacking guns to trade to the natives, the Spanish lost a trade war to the more accommodating French, who understood that trade bought influence and redirected Indian warfare against other natives in a rival trade orbit. During the 1710s and 1720s, the French-armed Comanche, Pawnee, and Wichitas raided the poorly armed villages of Apaches and Pueblos allied to the Spanish. The victorious raiders took captives to sell to the French traders in payment for more guns and ammunition. When facing east, the French opposed the English slave trade based in Carolina, but when facing west, the French encouraged their Great Plains clients to prey on poorly armed natives allied with the Spanish.

Beleaguered by French-armed raiders, the Spanish reformed their frontier policy during the late eighteenth century. Deemphasizing missions, the frontier officials sought to woo some Indian allies with presents of trade goods: the Louisiana French model. Partial success reduced the pressure on New Mexico, which had begun modestly, to prosper and grow, doubling its population from ninety-six hundred in 1765 to twenty thousand by 1800.

While New Mexico became more secure, the Spanish felt newly threatened on their northwestern flank, along the Pacific coast of California. During the mid-1760s, the Spanish belatedly learned of Russian explorers and fur traders active in the Aleutian Islands and along the southern coast of Alaska. The Spanish dreaded a Russian plot to strike south along the Pacific coast to attack precious Mexico. Spanish officials also exaggerated reports that British fur traders had crossed the northern Great Plains and the Rocky Mountains to approach the Pacific. The royal inspector general in New Spain, Jose de Galvez, concluded, "There is no doubt that in any case we have the English very close to our towns of New Mexico, and not very far from the west coast of this continent."

In 1768, to secure Mexico against both the Russian and the British phantoms, Galvez sent a small military expedition to occupy the Alta California coast with a system of forts, known as presidios, supported by missions run by Franciscan priests. For want of sufficient colonists, the Spanish revived in California a mission system that they had downplayed elsewhere as retrograde. By 1784, Alta California had only two towns, four presidios, and nine missions. The approximately nine hundred Hispanic colonists were stretched thin along a five-hundred-mile long coast from San Francisco to San Diego and scattered among thousands of Indians—twenty thousand of whom had joined the missions. As in other mission systems, the California Indians sought to preserve as much autonomy and land as possible "within an increasingly confining colonial order" (in the words of Steven Hackel).

Ends

While the Russians and Spanish jockeyed for an edge in the northwest, the British and the French escalated their warfare in the continent's northeastern quarter. Between 1689 and 1763, their empires waged four wide-ranging wars. Initially, the French and British concentrated their fighting in Europe, treating the colonies as a mere sideshow. That policy changed in the ultimate colonial conflict, the Seven Years War, which began in 1754, when the British invested men and money as never before to conquer New France.

Although divided into many tribes and subdivided into hundreds of villages, the Indian peoples of the Great Lakes and Ohio Valley shared a broad interest in prolonging their strategic middle position between the French and the British colonies. By exploiting the competition between the traders and officials of rival empires, the Indians sought favorable prices and abundant presents from both. By the 1750s, however, the chiefs felt alarmed by the growing British colonial population, which threatened to break through the Appalachian mountains into the continental interior. In 1754 the 1.5 million British colonists (and slaves) greatly outnumbered the seventy thousand French in North America.

Superior numbers emboldened the British to treat the Indians more arrogantly than did the French. British colonial officials could do little to stop their settlers from stealing Indian lands and taking Indian lives. The French, however, relied on Indian allies to hold the interior against encroaching British settlers, traders, and soldiers. Lightly built and garrisoned, the French forts depended on the natives for protection and paid for it with presents and mediation. In general, the Indians of the Great Lakes and Ohio Valley welcomed the French forts as assets instead of resenting them as threats. In sum, by 1750 the natives faced a greater threat from the numerous and aggressive British than from the few and more generous French.

In 1754 imperial war resumed between the French and the British, with North America as the prime stakes. During the early years of that war,

Indian allies helped the French to repel British attacks. But that native support softened as the British exploited their great countervailing advantage in offering superior trade goods in abundant quantities and at cheaper prices. The powerful British navy compounded that trade advantage by controlling the sea lanes and destroying French merchant shipping. Running out of trade goods, the colonial French could not supply their Indian allies, inducing many to make peace with the British. The defection of their native allies exposed Canada to a British invasion, which conquered Louisbourg in 1758, Quebec in 1759, and Montreal in 1760. Three years later the defeated French made a peace treaty that awarded Canada, the Great Lakes Country, and the Ohio Valley to the triumphant British.

British success threatened the Indian peoples of the interior, for they depended upon playing off rival empires to maintain their own autonomy. Deprived of a French counterweight, the British Empire could sweep settlements deep into the continent, pushing the Indians aside and transforming their land into farms and towns. But the Indians taught the British a bloody lesson by rebelling in 1763 to destroy most of the forts around the Great Lakes. To cut their losses, the British resumed giving presents to the Indians and tried to control the settler invasion of the Ohio Valley.

That British rapprochement with the Indians threatened colonial allegiance to the empire. After making such a major investment of money and lives to conquer Canada, the British were not about to resume their former policy of benign neglect. During the 1760s, Parliament and the Crown worked to tighten imperial management in an enlarged domain that threatened to spin out of control. Concluding that the empire was too weak and the colonists too insubordinate, the British tightened enforcement of the trade laws, kept a permanent garrison in North America, and imposed new taxes to pay for it. That shift in imperial policy shocked the colonial leaders, who felt a new confidence in their ability to defy the British Empire—if necessary—and to conquer and develop the continent for their own purposes. While securing the liberty of white men, their revolution would also build their own empire within the continent. By expanding westward during the following century, the new United States would dominate the continent by conquering Hispanics as well as the Indians.

From their colonial forebears, the citizens of the United States inherited an expansionist zeal driven by a defensive dread. During the wars of the 1750s and 1760s, the diverse British colonists had crafted a new, shared identity as "white people" and Americans by defining themselves against their Indian enemies. Particularly in the Middle Colonies of New York, Pennsylvania, and New Jersey, the German, Dutch, English, Welsh, Scots, and Irish immigrants set aside their old ethnic and religious differences by focusing on their new shared animosity for Indians. According to Peter Silver, the colonists imagined themselves as the innocent victims of brutal savages preying especially on women and children. By indulging in lurid depictions of scalping and torture, colonial men exhorted one another to live up to their patriarchal ideals by taking vengeance on native warriors.

And they cast as a race traitor anyone who defended Indians or faulted their killers. By downplaying denominational and ethnic difference, the rhetoric created an American nationalism that emphasized white and male supremacy as essential to defend their families.

Lumped together as a hostile enemy, Indians began to construct their own collective identity as "red people" who should unite against the invaders. In a process that paralleled the emerging racial identity of the white colonists, the most visionary Indians sought to submerge their traditional tribal enmities in a new pan-Indian confederation. In the Great Lakes country and Ohio Valley, that vision lay behind the native victory over the British in "Pontiac's Rebellion" of the mid-1760s. During the revolution and into the 1790s, those natives repeatedly defeated the forces of the United States. Thereafter, however, the new nation crushed the pan-Indian resistance, opening the continent up to American conquest.

Even in eventual defeat, the Indian enemy exercised a powerful hold over the cultural imagination of Americans, affecting even the domestic life of colonial women. In an innovative examination of cloth and cloth making, the historian Laurel Thatcher Ulrich demonstrates how the labor of white women helped to domesticate the lands taken from Indians: "cloth literally transformed the landscape as Algonkian beaver passed into the hands of English felt-makers and English sheep began to graze on American meadows." But Ulrich also refutes the mythic insistence that New England's Indians had vanished. She closely analyzes the nineteenth-century Indian baskets collected by the mythmakers, who remained oblivious to their testimony that the natives adapted and persisted long after their supposed disappearance. Often misinterpreted as timeless and primeval survivals, those baskets, in fact, employed new materials, techniques, and designs to appeal to nonnative consumers. In recent years, historians have broken with the essentialist notion of Indians as noble primitives capable of change only as a form of decay. Rejecting that ahistorical fantasy, historians now define "Indianness" as an adaptability that interweaves tradition with innovation in a struggle for cultural survival in a transformed land.

Employing war, treaties, and myths, the colonists worked to pin natives down within delimited reservations surrounded by settlements in a long process that triumphed during the nineteenth century. Reservations both enabled and depended upon a surrounding thicket of the private property lines for thousands of farms. A colony reaped allegiance from the speculators and settlers whose property depended on the land titles issued by the government and defended by its courts and militia. Energized by that grid of private property, settlers made farms by clearing the forest, depleting the wild animals, and fencing new fields. That environmental transformation alienated the land from the native peoples, who had relied on a wide-ranging mix of hunting, fishing, and horticulture. In sum, the making of private landholdings and the defining of Indian reservations were reciprocal processes. The colonial surveyors created a landscape of rectilinear tracts that obscures the native world of circles beneath and before.

Heirs to a world of square buildings and properties, we need to recall the very different cultural landscape of colonial America, where natives hoped to integrate the newcomers into a network of circles and paths. To understand the true sweep of colonial America and the pivotal importance of native peoples, multiply by a thousand the circles and the relational paths of the Nasaw map. Extend that array across the continent with links to British squares up and down the Atlantic seaboard; Spanish squares in Florida, Texas, New Mexico, and California; French squares in the Mississippi and St. Lawrence watersheds; and even Russian squares in the far northwest along the Aleutian Islands and the Alaska coast. That dense and complex picture belies the imperial fantasies of textbook maps where the claims of vast European empires cover the continent, prematurely submerging the many native peoples. Indeed, it took four centuries of trial and error, struggle and setback for Euroamericans to dominate the continent. During the long colonial era, the natives of the vast interior could oblige sojourning traders and soldiers to play by the rules of native diplomacy. Circles were not squares, but both had to share paths between them.

NOTES

1. White, "Nationalization of Nature," 978–979, urges attention to the overlap and connections of different scales of analysis: local, regional, national, and global.

2. Webb, "Strange Career." Although the deerskin original has long rotted away, two paper copies, with English labels, survive in British archives: the British Museum in London and the National Archives of the United Kingdom (in Kew).

3. For critiques, see Chaplin, "Expansion and Exceptionalism"; Tyrrell, "American Exceptionalism"; Bender, *Nation among Nations*, 15–60.

BIBLIOGRAPHY

The scholarly literature on colonial North America is so rich, diverse, and voluminous that the following bibliography offers only a selection, primarily recent works or relevant to the theme of this chapter.

Adelman, Jeremy, and Stephen A. Aron. "From Borderlands to Borders: Empires, Nation-States, and the Peoples in Between in North American History." *American Historical Review* 104 (1999): 814–841.

Anderson, Fred. *Crucible of War: The Seven Years' War and the Fate of Empire in British North America, 1754–1766*. New York: Knopf, 2000.

Axtell, James. *The Invasion Within: The Contest of Cultures in Colonial North America*. New York: Oxford University Press, 1985.

———. *The Indians' New South: Cultural Change in the Colonial Southeast*. Baton Rouge: Louisiana State University Press, 1997.

Barr, Juliana, *Peace Came in the Form of a Woman: Indians and Spaniards in the Texas Borderlands*. Chapel Hill: University of North Carolina Press, 2007.

Bender, Thomas. *A Nation among Nations*. New York: Hill and Wang, 2006.

Berlin, Ira. *Many Thousands Gone: The First Two Centuries of Slavery in North America*. Cambridge, MA: Harvard University Press, 1998.

Blackhawk, Ned. *Violence over the Land: Indians and Empires in the Early American West.* Cambridge, MA: Harvard University Press, 2006.

Bohaker, Heidi. "Nindoodemag: The Significance of Algonquian Kinship Networks in Eastern Great Lakes Region, 1600–1701." *William and Mary Quarterly*, 3rd. ser., 63 (2006): 23–52.

Braund, Kathryn E. Holland. *Deerskins and Duffels: The Creek Indian Trade with Anglo-America, 1685–1815.* Lincoln: University of Nebraska Press, 1993.

Brooks, James F. *Captives and Cousins: Slavery, Kinship, and Community in the Southwest Borderlands.* Chapel Hill: University of North Carolina Press, 2002.

Calloway, Colin G., ed. *After King Philip's War: Presence and Persistence in Indian New England.* Hanover, NH: University Press of New England, 1997.

———. *One Vast Winter Count: The Native American West before Lewis and Clark.* Lincoln: University of Nebraska Press, 2003.

Canny, Nicholas, and Anthony Pagden, eds. *Colonial Identity in the Atlantic World, 1500–1800.* Princeton, NJ: Princeton University Press, 1987.

Cayton, Andrew R. L., and Fredrika J. Teute, eds. *Contact Points: American Frontiers from the Mohawk Valley to the Mississippi, 1750–1830.* Chapel Hill: University of North Carolina Press, 1998.

Chaplin, Joyce. "Expansion and Exceptionalism in Early American History." *Journal of American History* 89 (2003): 1431–1455.

Coclanis, Peter A. "Atlantic World or Atlantic/World?" *William and Mary Quarterly*, 3rd ser., 63 (2006): 725–742.

Crosby, Alfred W., Jr. *The Columbian Exchange: Biological and Cultural Consequences of 1492.* Norman: University of Oklahoma Press, 1972.

———. *Ecological Imperialism: The Biological Expansion of Europe, 900–1900.* New York: Cambridge University Press, 1986.

Daniels, Christine, and Michael V. Kennedy, eds. *Negotiated Empires: Centers and Peripheries in the Americas, 1500–1820*, 1–14. New York: Routledge, 2002.

Delage, Denys. *Bitter Feast: Amerindians and Europeans in Northeastern North America, 1600–1664.* Vancouver: University of British Columbia Press, 1993.

Deloria, Philip. *Indians in Unexpected Places.* Lawrence: University Press of Kansas, 2004.

Dowd, Gregory Evans. *A Spirited Resistance: The North American Indian Struggle for Unity, 1745–1815.* Baltimore: Johns Hopkins University Press, 1992.

DuVal, Kathleen. *The Native Ground: Indians and Colonists in the Heart of the Continent.* Philadelphia: University of Pennsylvania Press, 2006.

Fenn, Elizabeth Anne. *Pox Americana: The Great Smallpox Epidemic of 1775–1782.* New York: Hill and Wang, 2001.

Gallay, Alan. *The Indian Slave Trade: The Rise of the English Empire in the American South, 1670–1717.* New Haven, CT: Yale University Press, 2002.

Games, Alison. "Beyond the Atlantic: English Globetrotters and Transoceanic Connections." *William and Mary Quarterly*, 3rd. ser., 63 (2006): 675–692.

Greer, Allan. *Mohawk Saint: Catherine Tekakwitha and the Jesuits.* New York: Oxford University Press, 2005.

Griffin, Patrick, *American Leviathan: Empire, Nation, and Revolutionary Frontier.* New York: Hill and Wang, 2007.

Gutierrez, Ramon A. *When Jesus Came, the Corn Mothers Went Away: Marriage, Sexuality, and Power in New Mexico, 1500–1846.* Stanford, CA: Stanford University Press, 1991.

Hackel, Steven W., ed. *Alta California: Peoples in Motion, Identities in Formation, 1769–1850.* Berkeley: University of California Press, 2010.

———. *Children of Coyote, Missionaries of Saint Francis: Indian-Spanish Relations in Colonial California, 1769–1850.* Chapel Hill: University of North Carolina Press, 2005.

Hall, Gwendolyn Midlo. *Africans in Colonial Louisiana: The Development of Afro-Creole Culture in the Eighteenth Century.* Baton Rouge: Louisiana State University Press, 1995.

Hämäläinen, Pekka. *The Comanche Empire.* New Haven, CT: Yale University Press, 2008.

Hijiya, James. "Why the West Is Lost." *William and Mary Quarterly*, 3rd. ser., 51 (1994): 276–292.

Hinderaker, Eric. *Elusive Empires: Constructing Colonialism in the Ohio Valley, 1673–1800.* New York: Cambridge University Press, 1997.

———. *The Two Hendricks: Unraveling a Mohawk Mystery.* Cambridge, MA: Harvard University Press, 2010.

Hinderaker, Eric, and Peter C. Mancall. *At the Edge of Empire: The Backcountry in British North America.* Baltimore: Johns Hopkins University Press, 2003.

Horn, James. *Adapting to a New World: English Society in the Seventeenth-Century Chesapeake.* Chapel Hill: University of North Carolina Press, 1994.

Hudson, Charles, and Carmen Chaves Tesser, eds. *The Forgotten Centuries: Indians and Europeans in the American South, 1521–1704.* Athens: University of Georgia Press, 1994.

Jacobs, Wilbur R., ed. *Indians of the Southern Colonial Frontier: The Edmond Atkin Report and Plan of 1755.* Columbia: University of South Carolina Press, 1954.

Knaut, Andrew L. *The Pueblo Revolt of 1680: Conquest and Resistance in Seventeenth-Century New Mexico.* Norman: University of Oklahoma Press, 1997.

Lepore, Jill. *The Name of War: King Philip's War and the Origins of American Identity.* New York: Knopf, 1998.

Liss, Peggy. *Atlantic Empires: The Network of Trade and Revolution, 1713–1826.* Baltimore: Johns Hopkins University Press, 1983.

Lockhart, James, ed. *Of Things of the Indies: Essays Old and New in Early American History.* Stanford, CA: Stanford University Press, 1999.

Mapp, Paul W. "Atlantic History from Imperial, Continental, and Pacific Perspectives." *William and Mary Quarterly*, 3rd. ser., 63 (2006): 713–724. (Quote on p. 718.)

Merrell, James. *The Indians' New World: Catawbas and Their Neighbors from European Contact through the Era of Removal.* Chapel Hill: University of North Carolina Press, 1989).

———. *Into the American Woods: Negotiators on the Pennsylvania Frontier.* New York: W. W. Norton, 1999.

Merritt, Jane T. *At the Crossroads: Indians and Empires on a Mid-Atlantic Frontier, 1700–1763.* Chapel Hill: University of North Carolina Press, 2003.

Murrin, John M. "Beneficiaries of Catastrophe: The English Colonies in America." In Eric Foner, ed., *The New American History*, 3–30. Philadelphia: Temple University Press, 1997.

Nobles, Gregory H. *American Frontiers: Cultural Encounters and Continental Conquest.* New York: Hill and Wang, 1997.

O'Brien, Jean M. *Dispossession by Degrees: Indian Land and Identity in Natick, Massachusetts, 1650–1790.* New York: Cambridge University Press, 1997.

Pestana, Carla Gardina. *The English Atlantic in an Age of Revolution, 1640–1661*. Cambridge, MA: Harvard University Press, 2004.

Piker, Joshua. *Okfuskee: A Creek Indian Town in Colonial America*. Cambridge, MA: Harvard University Press, 2004.

Pulsipher, Jenny Hale. *Subjects unto the Same King: Indians, English, and the Contest for Authority in Colonial New England*. Philadelphia: University of Pennsylvania Press, 2005.

Resendez, Andres. *Changing National Identities at the Frontier: Texas and New Mexico, 1800–1850*. New York: Cambridge University Press, 2005.

Richter, Daniel K. *Facing East from Indian Country: A Native History of Early America*. Cambridge, MA: Harvard University Press, 2001.

Rushforth, Brett. "'A Little Flesh We Offer You': The Origins of Indian Slavery in New France." *William and Mary Quarterly*, 3rd. ser., 60 (2003): 777–808.

———. "Slavery, the Fox Wars, and the Limits of Alliance." *William and Mary Quarterly*, 3rd ser., 63 (2006): 53–80.

Salisbury, Neal. *Manitou and Providence: Indians, Europeans, and the Making of New England, 1500–1643*. New York: Oxford University Press, 1982.

Saunt, Claudio, "Go West: Mapping Early American Historiography," *William and Mary Quarterly*, 3rd ser., 65 (2008): 745–778.

Seed, Patricia. *Ceremonies of Possession in Europe's Conquest of the New World, 1492–1640*. New York: Cambridge University Press, 1995.

Shoemaker, Nancy, ed. *Negotiators of Change: Historical Perspectives on Native American Women*. New York: Routledge, 1995.

———. *A Strange Likeness: Becoming Red and White in Eighteenth-Century North America*. New York: Oxford University Press, 2004.

Silver, Peter. *Our Savage Neighbors: How Indian War Transformed Early America*. New York: W. W. Norton, 2008.

Silverman, David J. *Faith and Boundaries: Colonists, Christianity, and Community among the Wampanoag Indians of Martha's Vineyard, 1600–1871*. New York: Cambridge University Press, 2005.

Sleeper-Smith, Susan. *Indian Women and French Men: Rethinking Cultural Encounter in the Western Great Lakes*. Amherst: University of Massachusetts Press, 2001.

Smith, Barbara Sweetland, and Redmond J. Barnett, eds. *Russian America: The Forgotten Frontier*. Tacoma: Washington State Historical Society, 1990.

Steele, Ian K. *The English Atlantic, 1675–1740: An Exploration of Communication and Community*. New York: Oxford University Press, 1986.

———. *Warpaths: Invasions of North America*. New York: Oxford University Press, 1994.

Sweet, John Wood. *Bodies Politic: Negotiating Race in the American North, 1730–1830*. Baltimore: Johns Hopkins University Press, 2003.

Taylor, Alan. *American Colonies*. New York: Viking/Penguin, 2001.

———. *The Divided Ground: Indians, Settlers, and the Northern Borderland of the American Revolution*. New York: Knopf, 2006.

Thornton, John. *Africa and Africans in the Making of the Atlantic World, 1400–1680*. New York: Cambridge University Press, 1992.

Tyrrell, Ian. "American Exceptionalism in an Age of International History." *American Historical Review* 96 (1991): 1031–1055.

Ulrich, Laurel Thatcher. *The Age of Homespun: Objects and Stories in the Creation of an American Myth*. New York: Knopf, 2001.

Usner, Daniel H., Jr. *Indians, Settlers, and Slaves in a Frontier Exchange Economy: The Lower Mississippi Valley before 1783*. Chapel Hill: University of North Carolina Press, 1992.

Vigil, Ralph H., Frances W. Kaye, and John R. Wunder, eds. *Spain and the Plains: Myths and Realities of Spanish Exploration and Settlement on the Great Plains*. Niwot: University Press of Colorado, 1994.

Warhus, Mark. *Another America: Native Maps and the History of Our Land*. New York: St. Martin's Press, 1997.

Waselkov, Gregory A. "Indian Maps of the Colonial Southeast." In Peter H. Wood, Gregory A. Waselkov, and M. Thomas Hatley, eds., *Powhatan's Mantle: Indians in the Colonial Southeast*, 320–324. Lincoln: University of Nebraska Press, 1989.

Webb, Stephen S. "The Strange Career of Francis Nicholson." *William and Mary Quarterly*, 3rd. ser., 23 (1966): 513–548.

Weber, David J. *Barbaros: Spaniards and their Savages in the Age of Enlightenment*. New Haven, CT: Yale University Press, 2005.

———. *The Spanish Frontier in North America*. New Haven, CT: Yale University Press, 1992.

West, Elliott. *The Way to the West: Essays on the Central Plains*. Albuquereque: University of New Mexico Press, 1995.

White, Richard. *The Middle Ground: Indians, Empires, and Republics in the Great Lakes Region, 1650–1815*. New York: Cambridge University Press, 1991.

———. "The Nationalization of Nature." *Journal of American History* 86 (1999): 976–986.

———. *Roots of Dependency: Subsistence, Environment, and Social Change among the Choctaws, Pawnees, and Navajos*. Lincoln: University of Nebraska Press, 1983.

Wood, Betty. *The Origins of American Slavery: Freedom and Bondage in the English Colonies*. New York: Hill and Wang, 1997.

Wood, Gordon S. *The Radicalism of the American Revolution*. New York: Knopf, 1992.

2

American Revolution and Early Republic

WOODY HOLTON

Books lavishing praise on the Founding Fathers or rehashing the traditional story of Patriots trouncing Redcoats still outsell all other treatments of the American Revolutionary era combined, but alternative histories of the founding period and the early republic have both multiplied and diversified. More and more people who were once ignored by scholars now seem worthy of attention, and historians have begun to study a wide range of topics that did not even exist thirty years ago—everything from hurricanes and smallpox to sensibility and sexuality. As the scope of the field radiates outward—as university courses called "The American Revolution" give way to those with titles like "The Revolutionary Atlantic"—one of the most cherished assumptions of earlier scholarship, that most early Americans agreed on most things, no longer seems tenable. And the conflicted nature of the founding years is reflected in their historiography, which looks less and less like a set of facts and increasingly like a series of debates.

Let us begin with the biographies of the Founding Fathers. Given their profitability, it seems appropriate to compare them to a stock exchange. Hamilton and Adams have both gained value in recent years, primarily on the strength of blockbuster biographies. Hamilton has also experienced a rise among many economists, who are so appreciative of his banking and tight monetary policies that they are perfectly willing to overlook his monarchism. John Adams's stock has risen even more dramatically, primarily on the strength of David McCullough's 2001 biography (which was felicitous not only in its prose but also in its timing, appearing as it did in June

2001, amid the bitter aftertaste of the Clinton-Lewinsky sex scandal) and the ensuing HBO miniseries.

Franklin remains a blue-chip investment with fairly stable value, David Waldstreicher's fascinating exposé of Franklin's deep involvement with slavery having been swamped by all the admiring tercentennial biographies (Franklin was born in 1706) penned by skillful writers like Walter Isaacson as well as such academic luminaries as H. W. Brands, Edmund S. Morgan, and Gordon S. Wood. Nor did Henry Wiencek's *An Imperfect God: George Washington, His Slaves, and the Creation of America* (2003) dent the first president's reputation; after all, Washington freed his slaves in his will.

In contrast, Thomas Jefferson's stock has lost considerable value. The primary reason, of course, is that he owned slaves even as he denounced slavery—and tried to deflect the charge of hypocrisy by depicting African Americans as innately unequal to whites. Some history buffs turned against the Virginian after a 1998 DNA study revealed that he was probably the father of his slave Sally Hemings's children. But many Jefferson lovers remain in denial, asserting—quite correctly—that the modern DNA evidence could have resulted from a relationship between Hemings and Jefferson's brother. But of course by that exalted standard, we cannot be sure that Jefferson's white descendants are actually his, either.

Most academic historians, however, now accept the Jefferson-Hemings relationship as fact. Indeed, such is the persuasive power of hard science among humanists that Andrew Burstein and Joseph J. Ellis, who had previously penned two of the sharpest critiques of the claim that Jefferson had fathered Hemings's children, responded to the DNA study by providing two of the most compelling explanations for why he became involved with her. Meanwhile, Kenneth Lockridge, Jack McLaughlin, and Jon Kukla further tarnished Jefferson's luster by describing his relationships with other women, and Anthony F. C. Wallace and other scholars provided unsparing descriptions of his Indian policies. Then in 2008, Gary B. Nash and Graham Russell Gao Hodges revealed that Jefferson failed not only to free his own slaves (except several Hemingses) but also to fulfill the dying wish of his friend Tadeusz Kościuszko (a Continental Army officer from Poland who had gone on to lead his own nation's failed bid for independence from Russia) that he use Kościuszko's estate to purchase slaves and free them. None of this debunking diminishes the majesty of the Declaration of Independence, but the author of that document increasingly seems to embody the truism that American history has been a constant struggle between the ideals of the Declaration and the circumstances of its creation.

Despite the overwhelming popularity of books about the Founding Fathers, the vast majority of academic historians studying the Revolutionary era now focus not on them but on Native Americans, African Americans, women of all races and ranks, and nonelite white men. In doing so, they have opened up a whole new series of debates—for instance, about whether to emphasize the ways in which white men oppressed women, Indians, and enslaved African Americans or, instead, on these groups' often-remarkable efforts to endure and overcome their oppression.

We are still waiting for a comprehensive survey of Indian involvement in the American Revolution. That none has yet appeared can no longer be ascribed to a lack of scholarly interest. Rather, Indians' experiences in the Revolution were so diverse—some Indians were loyal allies of the British, others enlisted in the Continental Army, while still others stood neutral or switched sides as circumstances dictated—that no one has tried to encompass all of them within the covers of a single volume. In 1995, Colin G. Calloway published *The American Revolution in Indian Country*, but he would be the first to admit that it was really a series of case studies aimed at casting a few flashes of light into the gloom. Other scholars of the topic have specialized to an even greater extent, producing biographies of individual Native Americans. But volumes devoted to Indians' involvement in the Revolutionary War are vastly outnumbered by those that barely mention it. For one category of historians this omission made particular sense, since their research interests drove them across the Mississippi and St. Lawrence Rivers to native villages that had little contact with Britain's thirteen rebel colonies. For instance, Juliana Barr, James Brooks, and Pekka Hämäläinen all won multiple academic prizes for their studies of interaction between Spanish settlers and the Indians of the American Southwest. Scholars also published innovative histories of the Native Americans of California, New France (later Canada), and the Great Basin.

Much of the new work analyzes native uprisings against European settlers. The first half decade of the twenty-first century saw the publication of no fewer than three studies of the wide-ranging 1763 Indian revolt that seems unable to shake off the misnomer *Pontiac's Rebellion*. Most work on Indian insurgency followed the lead of Gregory Evans Dowd in emphasizing its religious dimensions, many of the biggest attacks against the external enemy having begun as internal movements of spiritual regeneration. Other new studies of Native Americans concentrated on individual nations. While nonspecialists who discuss eighteenth-century America routinely refer to *Indians* and *slaves* as separate categories, several historians have recently drawn attention to Indian slavery, a reference both to Indians who held people captive and to those who were themselves enslaved. Allan Gallay discovered that the number of Africans imported into South Carolina as slaves before 1715 was actually eclipsed by the number of Indian slaves that the colony exported during this period.

Arguably the most influential discussion of eighteenth-century Indians to appear in the waning decades of the twentieth century was *The Middle Ground: Indians, Empires, and Republics in the Great Lakes Region, 1650–1815* (1991), by Richard White. Among White's breathtaking claims was that Indians, far from playing the role of helpless victim that earlier scholars—even sympathetic ones—had generally assigned them, often found ways to control their destinies and even to exert influence on the European invaders. Contending that interracial hatred and violence were by no means universal, White offered countless examples of Indians, Europeans, and African Americans not only trading with each other but also intermarrying and even exchanging religious and other ideas. In subsequent years White's thesis received support from works such as Charles A. Weeks's *Paths to a Middle Ground* and Stephen Aron's *American Confluence*, both published in 2005. One volume that was especially rich in evidence of Indian agency and interracial cooperation, Daniel H. Usner, Jr.'s *Indians, Settlers, and Slaves in a Frontier Exchange Economy: The Lower Mississippi Valley Before 1783* (1992), had actually appeared in dissertation form a decade before *Middle Ground*. But the opening of a new millennium brought something of a backlash against White's upbeat perspective, and the altered mood is plainly displayed in the title of one of the responses to *Middle Ground*, Alan Taylor's study of a nearby region, upstate New York, during a slightly later period, which he called *The Divided Ground* (2006).

Other scholars, however, continued to collect evidence of Indian agency and racial accommodation. Going White one better, Kathleen DuVal entitled her 2006 book on the Quapaws, Osages, and other Indians of the Arkansas River Valley *The Native Ground*, indicating that in this region Indians set "the terms of engagement"—at least until succumbing to the rising tide of white immigration into the region toward the middle of the nineteenth century, that is, and herein may lie a point of convergence between the supporters and critics of the *Middle Ground*. Traders, missionaries, and government officials who saw the Indians as potential customers, converts, and allies had every incentive to cooperate with them, but as these advance agents of empire gave way to settler families that simply wanted the Indians' land, the prospects for peaceful interaction diminished. Even Richard White finds an explosion of anti-Indian hatred in the Ohio Valley around the time of the American Revolution.

Meanwhile, historians have extended another of White's insights, charging that Indians and Europeans were not actually as different from each other as scholars had assumed. James Brooks found several similarities between southwestern Indians and the Europeans who settled on their land: Spanish and English men, like their Indian counterparts, believed they could avoid devastating shame only by successfully protecting and controlling their families, two imperatives that often depended upon their skill at negotiating with outsiders. Nancy Shoemaker also emphasized Indians' and Europeans' common traits. Indeed, in her view, it was often the two groups' surprisingly similar attitudes toward landownership that brought them into conflict. Shoemaker also shares White's belief that Native Americans could sometimes be the masters of their own destiny. Indeed, she argued that the fanciful notion that Indians have red skin may have originated not with Europeans but with Native Americans in the region that is now the southeastern United States.

Gregory Nobles draws attention (in a book he cowrote with Alfred F. Young) to a sure sign that the study of Native Americans in the Revolutionary era has come of age. From its inception in 1948 until 1989, the Bancroft

Prize, one of the highest honors in the profession, was never awarded to a book about Indians. James Merrell won it in 1990 for *The Indians' New World*, and by 2009, the Bancroft went to six additional books about Indians (including Merrell's *Into the American Woods*, which appeared in 1999).

In 2005, Washington College, the Mount Vernon Ladies' Association, and the Gilder Lehrman Institute of American History collaborated in establishing the George Washington Book Prize, which annually awards $50,000 to the author of the best book on the Revolutionary era. No one would be more surprised than President Washington to learn that for three years in a row—in 2007, 2008, and 2009—the prize went to books about the African Americans who made estates like Mount Vernon possible. Taken together, the three prizewinners sum up many of the key themes of eighteenth-century African-American history. Charles Rappleye's *Sons of Providence* (2006) focuses on the Brown family of Providence, Rhode Island, which made its fortune partly through transporting Africans to the Americas and went on to found Brown University. Moses Brown converted to the Quaker faith and freed his slaves in 1773, even as his brother John remained an enthusiastic investor in the African trade. In 2008, the Washington prize recognized a book that also described the African slave trade but shifted the emphasis to its victims: Marcus Rediker's *The Slave Ship* (2007). To an even greater extent than Rediker, the next winner, Annette Gordon-Reed's *The Hemingses of Monticello* (2008), drew attention to the ways that African Americans—in this case an African-American family that Thomas Jefferson inherited from his father-in-law in 1773—were able to shape their own destiny.

These works were part of a surge in scholarly interest in African Americans of the Revolutionary era. Rappleye's and Rediker's topic, the transatlantic slave trade, was also the focus of numerous other books, including several that described individual slaving voyages, reproduced traders' diaries, or chronicled and explained the campaign for the abolition of the trade. Scholars devoted particular attention to African-American abolitionists, some of whom, having themselves experienced the slave trade, brought peculiar authenticity to the campaign against it. Meanwhile the veracity of the most famous of the black abolitionists, Olaudah Equiano, was called into question on a crucial point. In *Equiano, The African* (2005), Vincent Carretta presented evidence that his subject was born in South Carolina, which would mean that the first part of Equiano's well-known *Interesting Narrative*, where he described his happy early life in Africa and then his kidnapping and subsequent torment during the voyage to America, was invented, presumably using information supplied by blacks who really had endured the Middle Passage. Carretta did not frame his findings as an exposé, instead depicting Equiano as bolstering his case against the slave trade by making it personal.

Gordon-Reed's *The Hemingses of Monticello* was only one of countless efforts to enter the world of enslaved African Americans. Some of these studies, such as Ira Berlin's *Many Thousands Gone* (1998), cover thousands of square miles and multiple centuries, while others, like Jon F. Sensbach's *Separate Canaan: The Making of an Afro-Moravian World in North Carolina, 1763–1840* (1998) and Lucia Stanton's *Free Slave Day: The African-American Families of Monticello* (2002) analyze individual slave communities. Few of these works devoted much attention to black involvement in the American Revolution itself, but several other books addressed that topic. Andrew Levy and Melvin Ely both published studies of Virginia slaveholders whose political and religious principles led them to free their slaves. Other historians showed that during the War of Independence, thousands of African Americans took advantage of a variety of opportunities to declare their own independence. Can anyone say that men like Jefferson and Washington derived more freedom from the Revolutionary War than did the slaves who used the conflict to become free (including several owned by Jefferson and Washington)?

South of the Potomac, where most slaves lived, they were not permitted to enlist in the Continental Army, but the British welcomed them. In November 1775, four score and seven years before Lincoln announced his Preliminary Emancipation Proclamation, Lord Dunmore, the last royal governor of Virginia, issued a proclamation that was not very different from Lincoln's, in that it offered freedom to any slave who was owned by a rebel, who was able and willing to bear arms against his insurgent owners—and who could make it to his lines. Several recent books describe the remarkable wartime alliance between the British and the blacks. Thousands of African Americans died during the war, some from battlefield wounds and many more from disease. But most of those who enlisted with the British and survived the war were able to claim their freedom, either in colonies like Nova Scotia that had remained loyal during the Revolutionary War or, as Cassandra Pybus has recently shown, in new British provinces ranging from Sierra Leone in Africa to New South Wales (Australia).

Although the stories of slaves who claimed their freedom during the War of Independence stir the imagination, historians point out that the conflict actually strengthened slavery in important ways. By setting in motion the dispossession of the Creeks, Choctaws, Cherokees, Chickasaws, and other Indians from the Old Southwest (the region bordered by the Atlantic Ocean, the Gulf of Mexico, and the Mississippi and Ohio Rivers), the Revolution opened up a vast new region for slavery. The slaveholders' victory was secured with the adoption of the United States Constitution, which turned a weak confederation into a nation powerful enough not only to drive the Indians from their land but also to quell rebellions by the bondsmen forcibly resettled there. Yet the word *slave* appears nowhere in the Constitution. Like the men who had gathered at the Pennsylvania statehouse to adopt the Declaration of Independence in the 1776, those who returned eleven years later to write the Constitution evinced their embarrassment regarding slavery by obscuring it in euphemism. Many modern historians replicate the Framers' reticence, but others examined the link between slavery and the Constitution. Robin Einhorn contended that the primary reason southern representatives at the Constitutional Convention (and later in the United States Congress) wanted to keep the government small and weak was that they feared it might someday become a threat to slavery. (It should be noted, however, that slaveholders did not want the federal government to be *too* weak: states' rights rhetoric notwithstanding, southern governors responded to all the major slave insurrections scares of the nineteenth century—in 1800, 1822, 1831, and 1859—by asking for federal troops.)

Historians once assumed that African Americans learned to love liberty by watching their white owners struggle for it during the War of Independence—a process that Bernard Bailyn described as the "contagion of liberty." Today most scholars acknowledge that black Americans had acquired their passion for freedom long before the American Revolution, which merely provided a language in which to express that desire and opportunities to act on it.

One region where slaves indisputably rebelled on a regular basis was the Caribbean, and the sugar islands are among the new territories into which historians of the American Revolution have expanded in recent decades. Like scholars who study African Americans and Indians of the North American mainland, those who focus on Caribbean slave revolts find them important not only in their own right but also as windows into these closed societies. As the twenty-first century opened, historians including David Geggus and Laurent DuBois, published new studies of the Haitian Revolution. In a forthcoming account of a 1763 uprising in Berbice (a Dutch colony on the northern coast of South America), Marjoleine Kars will employ a source that students of other slave revolts wish they had—letters written by the rebels themselves—to introduce further complexity into this topic, demonstrating, among other things, that one of the Berbice insurgents' demands was that they be permitted, once free, to own slaves.

Historians of the Caribbean addressed a wide variety of other topics as well. In *The Reapers' Garden* (2008), Vincent Brown analyzed white and black Jamaicans' attitudes toward one of their closest companions: death. In *Rebecca's Revival* (2005), Jon Sensbach described, in lyrical prose, the life of Rebecca Protten, a slave on the Dutch island of St. Thomas. After converting to the Moravian faith and leading a religious revival, Protten took the lead in gathering the first black Protestant church in the New World. Andrew Jackson O'Shaughnessy's *An Empire Divided* (2000) explained why whites in the Caribbean, who had joined their counterparts in British North America in objecting to imperial taxation without representation, nonetheless decided not to follow them into the movement for independence (it had to do with the fact that 90 percent of most sugar islands' inhabitants were slaves). In *Mastery, Tyranny, and Desire* (2004), Trevor Burnard described the almost unbelievable brutality of one Caribbean slaveholder, Thomas Thistlewood, who used his diary to record his 3,852 rapes of 138 enslaved women, and whose repertoire of punishments for recalcitrant slaves included sealing the offender's mouth shut for five hours after forcing another slave to defecate into it. Inevitably many of these and other authors found themselves trying to understand the white racial attitudes that made such unspeakable treatment possible. Most historians now agree that race, like beauty, is in the eyes of the beholder. Jennifer L. Morgan charts Englishmen's misperceptions of the bodies of Irish, Native American, and African women and goes on to show how their fanciful notions influenced their efforts to exploit black women's reproductive capacities. John Wood Sweet found that white Rhode Islanders distrusted blacks and Native Americans for opposite reasons—Indians because they were excessively autonomous and blacks because they were too dependent.

Like scholars who study Indians, historians of African Americans have delighted in disproving the old axiom that none of their subjects left behind sufficient evidence to assemble a biography, and in recent years we have seen, in addition to Carretta's biography of Equiano and Sensbach's of Protten, illuminating studies of Phillis Wheatley, Benjamin Banneker, Reverend Richard Allen, and numerous other African Americans. Many more such volumes are in the works, and the subtitle of Daniel L. Schafer's 2003 biography of a woman named Anna Madgigine Jai Kingsley hints at the range of possibilities: *African Princess, Florida Slave, Plantation Slaveowner.*

The publication of biographies of African-American women such as Rebecca Protten and Phillis Wheatley was not accompanied by an outpouring of similar studies of Native American women of the founding era. The study of white women in the Revolutionary era continues to be defined by two watershed books that appeared in 1980: Mary Beth Norton's *Liberty's Daughters* and Linda Kerber's *Women of the Republic*, both of which argued that for white women, the net effect of the Revolution was positive. Few historians before 1980 had tried to survey the revolutionary experience of American women and the publication of Kerber's and Norton's books led to a different kind of silence: they seemed so hard to top that during the subsequent decade and a half, no one attempted another synthesis. Then in 1996, Joan Gundersen came out with *To Be Useful to the World: Women in Revolutionary America, 1740–1790.* Did the Revolution help or hurt female Americans? It all depended, Gundersen argues, on race and class: most Indian women suffered (along with native men), while the impact of the war on black and white women was mixed. Gundersen accurately reflects the confusing reality of this period of social upheaval as well as the ambivalence of the academic community about its meaning for non-Indian women.

Several books published around the turn of the century argued that free women demonstrated a surprising ability to exert themselves in what Jürgen Habermas called "the bourgeois public sphere." The current thinking on the impact of the War of Independence on white women is summed up in the title of Rosemarie Zagarri's 2007 volume, *Revolutionary Backlash*, but eighteenth-century women of all ranks did experience long-term changes that mattered much more to them than political events. As Carole Shammas has noted, most women—along with most children, slaves, and servants—worried less about who ran their colony, state, or nation than about the man who governed their households. A high proportion of nearly every book about the founding mothers is focused on what Norton calls "the constant patterns of women's lives." Gundersen devoted only the last two of her ten chapters to the independence movement and Revolutionary War.

Paralleling (and outrunning) the recent uptick in biographies of African-American women, numerous volumes have focused on individual white women. The Patriot essayist, playwright, and historian Mercy Otis Warren, one of the few American women of the founding period to have achieved more fame than her husband during her lifetime, was the subject of three biographies. A fourth book compared Warren to the English historian Catharine Macaulay. Other familiar figures, from Martha Washington to Dolley Madison, also came in for fresh investigations. In *First Lady of Letters: Judith Sargent Murray and the Struggle for Female Independence*, Sheila Skemp revealed that Murray's feminism was fueled in part by the sense of entitlement that she inherited along with her exalted economic and social status.

Even as some biographers shed additional light on well-known founding mothers, others chose a different route, writing about women who had not previously been well known. The impact of Laurel Ulrich's *Midwife's Tale: The Life of Martha Ballard, Based on Her Diary, 1785–1812* has been huge. Alfred F. Young's *Masquerade* (2004) told the story of Deborah Sampson Gannett, who disguised herself as a man in order to enlist in the Continental Army—and then supported herself after the war partly by demonstrating her military prowess on stage. Another academic approach to women of the founding era has been to publish their letters and diaries, allowing readers to reach their own conclusions about what it did for them or to them.

Scholarly interest in eighteenth-century sex roles had scarcely been awakened when several younger historians, pointing out that men have gender, too, branched off to study them, and it almost seems that we now have more books on masculinity—among them *National Manhood*, *Republic of Men*, *Southern Sons*, and *Making Manhood*—than on women. Today masculinity studies embraces research on patriarchy, although that is actually the older of the two subjects. Calling a man a patriarch might seem to affirm his omnipotence, but historians of this topic tend to portray would-be patriarchs as barely able to maintain their sanity, much less their dominance. Four titles—Kenneth Lockridge's *On the Sources of Patriarchal Rage* (1992), Kathleen Brown's *Good Wives, Nasty Wenches, and Anxious Patriarchs* (1996), Rhys Isaac's *Landon Carter's Uneasy Kingdom* (2004), and my own *Forced Founders: Indians, Debtors, Slaves, and the Making of the American Revolution* (1999)—dispute the traditional description of the eighteenth-century Virginia gentry as proud and confident. Another offshoot of gender history has been the study of sexuality, where the volume with the greatest relevance to the American Revolution is also the most chilling: Sharon Block's *Rape and Sexual Power in Early America* (2006).

Several of the trends that have been observed in scholarship on founding-era Indians, African Americans, and women can also be seen in recent work on nonelite white men. For instance, many of these studies center on rebellions and on the backcountry regions where most, though not all, of them took place. The attraction of insurgency—on the part of tenants, draft resisters, food rioters, taxpayers, and the victims of any number of other exactions—is threefold: (1) rebellions are exciting, (2) they refute the widespread misconception that ordinary white men tended to defer to their social betters, and (3) friction generates sparks that illuminate everyone involved. Several uprisings, including the Regulator revolt in prerevolutionary North Carolina and Fries's Rebellion in northeastern Pennsylvania in 1798, came in for book-length treatment for the first time. A significant development in what might be called insurgency studies is a renewed emphasis on state power, especially in the form of onerous taxes levied on cash-strapped farmers. The trend is evident in a comparison between two histories of the 1786–1787 revolt in Massachusetts that seems to be stuck with the misnomer Shays's Rebellion. Leonard Richards's *Shays's Rebellion* (2002) differs from David Szatmary's *Shays' Rebellion* (1980) on whether the insurgent farmers were angrier at merchant-creditors and market capitalism (Szatmary's view) or at the Massachusetts assembly, which had imposed unprecedented taxes, primarily in order to service the war debt, much of which had been bought up by bond speculators, as Richards contends (a viewpoint that I endorse in *Unruly Americans and the Origins of the Constitution*, which came out in 2007). Historians like Szatmary, Terry Bouton, Christopher Clark, Marjoleine Kars, and Michael Merrill, who compile evidence of agrarian resistance to capitalism, must also contend with scholars such as Joyce Appleby, Winifred Rothenberg, and Gordon S. Wood, who claim ordinary farmers embraced it.

Most portrayals of backcountry farmers, especially those involved in rebellions, are sympathetic, but there are important exceptions, especially in scholarship focusing on white-Indian relations. In addition, Francis S. Fox showed, in his *Sweet Land of Liberty: The Ordeal of the American Revolution in Northampton County, Pennsylvania* (2000), that backcountry whites ruthlessly harassed everyone who refused to go along with the revolutionary program: not just Indians but Loyalists, Moravians, Mennonites, Quakers, and others.

One of the great challenges for historians who write about Americans other than the Founding Fathers is to weave their stories into the master narrative. Gary B. Nash's *The Unknown American Revolution* (2005) highlighted Indians, African Americans, women, and nonelite white men at the expense of the Founders, earning Nash harsh criticism from scholars accustomed to doing just the opposite. We are still waiting for a history of the American Revolution that is comprehensive enough to incorporate Indians, slaves, women, and ordinary farmers alongside the traditional tales of the Stamp Act Congress and the Battle of Bunker Hill. No one, perhaps, has come closer than Norman Risjord in the 2009 edition of his acclaimed *Jefferson's America, 1760–1815*. The prospects for a true synthesis brightend after the publication of two books conceived and coauthored by one of the most senior scholars in the field, Alfred F. Young. *Whose American Revolution Was It?* (cowritten with Gregory Nobles) offers a book-length historiography of the founding era. With Gary Nash and Ray Raphael, Young edited *Revolutionary Founders*, which contains biographies of twenty-two eighteenth-century Americans—most of them previously unknown outside of academia—who tried to make the independence movement truly revolutionary.

Not content merely to expand its ethnic and geographic reach, the current generation of founding-era historians has also begun to investigate a whole range of subjects that its predecessors had neglected or ignored. In the area of environmental history, Elizabeth Fenn's *Pox Americana: The Great Smallpox Epidemic of 1775–82* (2001) not only made bold and persuasive claims about the War of Independence (for instance, that the soldiers of the Continental Army might have failed in their mission if General Washington had not decided, midwar, to have them inoculated) but also traced the smallpox epidemic that coincided with the Revolutionary War as it spread to Indians and other Americans west of the Mississippi River. A few years later, describing a different sort of natural disaster, Matthew Mulcahy and Walter J. Fraser, Jr., observed the tendency of eighteenth-century hurricanes to lay bare many of a slave society's otherwise invisible mechanics.

Before about 1990, few historians gave much thought to how ordinary Americans remembered the Revolution, but that topic has since generated a great deal of interest. John Resch mined pension records to chronicle the soldiers' own efforts to affect how later generations perceived them. In a pair of well-received biographies, Alfred F. Young investigated the Revolutionary memories of two ordinary Americans, Deborah Sampson Gannett and shoemaker George Robert Twelves Hewes. Other scholars focused on the activities of museums and historical societies or on the contested memories of individual Founding Fathers.

Culture is by no means a new topic for historians of the American Revolution—after all, the preeminent journal in the field, *William and Mary Quarterly*, has billed itself as a "Magazine of Early American History and Culture" since its inception back in 1892—but historians have expanded their definition of the term and approached it from surprising new angles. The years around the turn of the century witnessed the publication of no fewer than three studies showing how Patriot sentiment was nursed and dispersed at the rough-hewn tables of America's public houses (taverns). Another cultural phenomenon that has come in for new scrutiny is the consumer revolution that was already in full gear when George III ascended the throne. Among this spate of fascinating studies, the one with the most bearing on the Revolution is T. H. Breen's *Marketplace of Revolution* (2004), which asserts that a motley band of Patriots found unity, the one indispensible element in any social movement, in the unlikeliest of places—their shared consumption of British "baubles." And then they further strengthened their bonds by jointly renouncing those same British manufactures.

Other cultural issues—from furniture and architecture to paintings and the theater—also receive considerably more attention today, but work on colonial culture continues to center in literature. Many scholars have made it their business to rediscover and relegitimize literary figures of the eighteenth and early nineteenth centuries, among them Thomas Paine, Susanna Rowson, and Lydia Maria Child. Others have taken on broader themes. Of particular interest to historians of the Revolution is the work of Cathy Davidson, Robert A. Ferguson, and the late Jay Fliegelman, whose *Prodigals and Pilgrims* (1982) describes a revolution in child-raising philosophy that preceded and influenced the political revolt of 1776. In Fliegelman's formulation, John Locke's *Second Treatise on Government* was less important to the revolutionaries than his *Some Thoughts on Education*, which advised parents to guide their children through persuasion rather than coercion. Judged against this standard, Great Britain seemed like a bad parent indeed. Fliegelman's *Declaring Independence* (1993) argues that the American revolutionaries shared the Scottish Enlightenment's most cherished preoccupations, including an emphasis on humans' ability to sympathize (a trait that Jefferson and others ominously declined to detect in African Americans) and a fascination with orators' ability to elicit involuntary emotional responses. Eighteenth-century oratory was also the subject of valuable studies by Christopher Grasso, Sandra Gustafson, and many others.

Members of the first generation of scholars to do all their writing on computers have also lavished attention on what they call "print culture." While much of this work focuses on that perennial favorite, eighteenth-century newspapers, dozens of scholars now pursue the history of the book. Although "sensibility," a term broad enough to embrace concepts ranging from genteel refinement (the subject of many recent studies) to "fellow feeling" (the notion that all humans naturally empathize—though that word was not invented until the end of the nineteenth century—with the joys and pains of others), has long interested scholars of English literature, Early Americanists' interest in it is relatively new. One of the first historians to link sensibility to the American Revolution was Garry Wills, who traced the intellectual origins of both the Declaration of Independence and the Constitution to David Hume, Adam Smith, and other Scottish Enlightenment thinkers who drew attention to the "moral sense." Emerging scholars—among them Nicole Eustace, in *Passion Is the Gale: Emotion, Power, and the Coming of the American Revolution*, and Sarah Knott and Sarah

M. S. Pearsall—have drawn their own connections between sensibility and the Revolution.

The history of the founding era has also expanded geographically. Alongside the new studies of Indians outside the orbit of the thirteen rebel colonies, we have dozens of volumes devoted to Britain's other thirteen American provinces—from Nova Scotia south to Bermuda, the Bahamas, the two Floridas, and such Caribbean islands as Barbados and Jamaica. Other historians have set their sights on non-British colonies like Quebec (which France ceded to Britain in 1763) and Louisiana. Scholars studying French and Spanish colonies have analyzed the same issues that interest those using English-language sources, such as gender and slavery, but also several subjects—like convents—that students of British America rarely confront.

Many of the volumes that fly under the flag of Atlantic History seem quite innovative, even if the field itself does not (scholars studying the Revolution have always been interested in its European roots and global impact). Notable examples of this genre include biographies of George Whitefield, the English evangelist who toured America a half dozen times between 1739 and his death in Newburyport, Massachusetts, in 1770, and of Joseph Priestley, who crossed the Atlantic and established an outpost of the Enlightenment in remote Northumberland County, Pennsylvania. Some of the most original work emphasizing transoceanic networks focuses on what historians call the Black Atlantic—the peregrinations (usually forced) of men like Thomas Peters, who greeted life in modern-day Nigeria, where he was kidnapped and sold to slave traders and then to a French colonist in Louisiana. Somehow Peters ended up in North Carolina, and in 1776 he escaped from his owner, fought on the British side during the Revolutionary War, and then settled with other Loyalists in Nova Scotia, only to join the black exodus to Sierra Leone in 1792. Almost as peripatetic as Peters was the black Patriot soldier at the center of Joyce Malcolm's *Peter's War: A New England Slave Boy and the American Revolution* (2009).

Other historians of the Atlantic world emphasized its polyglot and polychrome nature. In *The Many-Headed Hydra: Sailors, Slaves, Commoners, and the Hidden History of the Revolutionary Atlantic* (2000), Peter Linebaugh and Marcus Rediker compiled extensive evidence of laboring people of all races coming together to challenge merchant princes and high government officials, who compared them to the mythical hydra, a nine-headed serpent that grew a new head every time one was struck off. Critics accused Linebaugh and Rediker of portraying class relations in the seventeenth and eighteenth centuries as they ought to have been rather than as they were—and of doing so by ignoring the many cases where members of their "Atlantic working class" battled each other, generally under elite leadership. Their book nonetheless demonstrates that even if the hydra made few actual appearances, it instilled constant fear in its adversaries.

In addition to studying groups and topics that previous generations of scholars of the founding era had neglected or ignored, historians have revisited old topics from new perspectives. The very earliest books on the American Revolution linked it to the Enlightenment, and authors continue to explore that connection, but often with great skepticism. One particular aspect of Enlightened philosophy, its interest in natural history, has come in for particular scrutiny. For instance, in *American Curiosity* (2006), Susan Scott Parrish observes that by the time of the American Revolution, Europeans and their American descendants had ceased to distrust curiosity as a dangerous lusting after knowledge—at least when the curious person was male. She also points out that Europeans' desire for information about unique New World animals, plants, and geography inadvertently empowered the Americans who were their on-the-ground informants.

If the late eighteenth century was, as Thomas Paine declared it, an "age of reason," it also remained (to his chagrin) an age of faith, and numerous recent books on Early American religion bear directly on the Revolution. Many analyze the Great Awakening, the ill-defined series of religious revivals that stretched from the 1730s all the way up until the emergence of a Second Great Awakening at the end of the century, and most agree that it was an essential ingredient in the independence movement, fostering denominational unity across provincial boundaries and—more importantly—teaching individual Americans to question authority and trust their own consciences. A different link between religion and revolution was the colonists' anger at British officials for allegedly scheming to impose an Anglican bishop on them. Historians have also provided insight into religious movements that had little direct connection to politics, a striking example being Susan Juster's 2003 study of Revolution-era millennialists. She and other scholars emphasize that even Americans who sought a return to old-time religion were surprisingly successful at exploiting newspapers and other newfangled forms of mass communication.

Like the study of the founding era, economic history has extended its reach during the last three decades. Scholars have produced sensitive analyses—many of them comparative—of early manufacturing enterprises and small-time traders as well as merchant princes who dispatched their cargoes all over the world. Given economists' interest in production, Robert E. Wright deserves mention for having far surpassed all his fellow students of the founding era in scholarly output (while also providing plenty of insight and controversy). During the first decade of the twenty-first century, Wright wrote more than a dozen books and coauthored several others. In *Republic of Debtors* (2002), Bruce H. Mann contends that around the time of the Revolution, Americans ceased to see insolvency (the inability to pay one's debts) as a moral failing and began to accept it as simply the consequence of unfortunate or unwise business decisions. The new attitude was reflected in increased—and, for the first time, organized—opposition to the imprisonment of debtors.

It was not so long ago that labor historians only studied the labor movement, which barely moved at all before the middle of the nineteenth century, but scholars have recently published exciting work on the laboring classes of the founding era and the new republic. Seth Rockman describes his 2008 book *Scraping By: Wage Labor, Slavery, and Survival in Baltimore*, which covers the period from 1790 to 1840, as an early-nineteenth-century version of Barbara Ehrenreich's study of the modern workplace, *Nickel and Dimed: On (Not) Getting By in America* (2001), in that its subjects are working people of all races whose labor sustained the American economy but whose own survival was often in doubt. Many labor historians focus on sailors. When, many years ago, Samuel Eliot Morrison declared that merchant seamen were primarily drawn to the sea by their sense of adventure, he inaugurated a debate about their motivations that has only intensified in recent decades, with some historians describing them as simply desperate, others agreeing with Paul Gilje that they associated employment at sea with freedom, and still others endorsing Daniel Vickers's contention that working in the merchant marine was simply something that every young man in a seaport like Salem, Massachusetts (the setting of Vickers's 2005 book), was expected to do, at least for a few years. Julius S. Scott's widely read doctoral dissertation, "A Common Wind" (1986), and Jeffrey Bolster's book *Black Jacks* (1997) analyze African-American sailors, while Elaine Forman Crane, Lisa Norling, and others draw attention to the lives of female participants in the maritime world.

No aspect of the American Revolution is more traditional than its military history, yet even here, authors have made some remarkable new discoveries. Much of the recent scholarship shifts attention from the generals to common soldiers and other ordinary Americans caught up in the war. Harry Ward, whose many books include four biographies of Patriot generals, has recently turned his attention to such previously neglected topics as guerrilla warfare (also the subject of Mark Kwasny's 1996 *Washington's Partisan War*) and the Continental Army's military police. When Michael A. McDonnell researched military mobilization in Virginia, the colony and later state where earlier historians had perceived the greatest deference to gentry authority, he was stunned to find an ongoing pattern of determined, organized, and sometimes violent draft resistance. In *America Goes to War: A Social History of the Continental Army* (1996), Charles P. Neimeyer showed that nearly half the men at Valley Forge during the winter of 1777–1778 were immigrants and African Americans—and that most of the rest were landless or unskilled. Other scholars, however, disputed this depiction of the Revolutionary War as a poor man's fight.

Battlefield encounters might seem virtually impervious to historiographic revision, but historians have found ways to cast fresh light on several revolutionary battles. In *A Devil of Whipping: The Battle of Cowpens* (1998), Lawrence E. Babits used hundreds of pension applications, in which soldiers gave detailed accounts of their service, to reconstruct the initial positions and subsequent movements of every major unit engaged at Cowpens on January 17, 1781. David Hackett Fischer's *Washington's Crossing* took full account of common soldiers' experience (several froze to death on the way to Trenton) and also punctured some venerable myths (it turns out, for instance, that the Hessian garrison was not hung over that post-Christmas morning and did put up a fight).

Another arena where a superficial observer might plausibly assume that all the major questions raised by the American Revolution have been answered is politics. But here, too, scholars have kept the conversation lively by expanding it in countless directions. Dozens of founding-era historians transcended the simple narration of political events and trained their sights on what they called political culture. In *Affairs of Honor: National Politics in the Early Republic* (2001), Joanne Freeman investigated the Founding Fathers' obsession with their reputations (especially for veracity). In *Rebels Rising: Cities and the American Revolution* (2007), Benjamin Carp used the concept of political culture to show why colonial protests against imperial encroachments took very different turns in Boston, Newport, New York, Philadelphia, and Charleston. Political culture was also the focus of a feisty anthology, *Beyond the Founders: New Approaches to the Political History of the Early American Republic* (2004).

The current generation of founding-era scholars has also reopened a host of political issues that its predecessors thought they had settled. Most nonhistorians assume that the War of Independence led to a major transformation in American society, as Gordon S. Wood affirmed in *The Radicalism of the American Revolution* (1991) and again in *Empire of Liberty: A History of the Early Republic, 1789–1815*. Others, however—especially Jon Butler—insist that many of the changes that Wood and others attributed to independence actually preceded it. Historians have also offered startling new answers to such classic questions as why the Constitution was adopted. In *Redeeming the Republic*, Roger H. Brown drew attention to the intense battles over taxation that raged in the thirteen states during the Confederation era (1781–1789) and argued that the Federalists' principal objective was to create a federal government that would be impervious to popular demands for tax cuts. Like Brown, Swedish scholar Max Edling stressed taxation, but he argued in *A Revolution in Favor of Government* that the Constitution actually benefited taxpayers, since import tariffs allowed the federal government to meet all its demands without levying direct taxes on farmers (except for that little matter of the whiskey excise).

Another ancient debate that has intensified in recent years asks whether the Founders wanted America to be a Christian nation—more precisely, a white Protestant nation—or to erect (as Thomas Jefferson famously put it) "an eternal wall of separation between church and state." Some of the contributions have been startlingly original. In *One Nation under Law* (2005), Mark McGarvie, an attorney as well as a Ph.D. in history, insists that the First Amendment to the Constitution was less important to the disestablishment of religion than Article I, Section 10—the contracts clause. The Supreme Court repeatedly ruled—most famously in *Dartmouth College v. Woodward* (1819)—that the charters of private institutions such as churches and colleges were contracts and thus impervious to state interference. McGarvie sees the separation of church and state as part of a broader attempt at delineating the public and private spheres.

The Second Amendment has generated as much recent controversy as the First, the primary point of contention being whether the authors of the Bill of Rights intended to apply the "right to bear arms" to all individuals or just to state militias. Michael Bellesiles, in *Arming America: The Origins of a National Gun Culture*, undermined the case for an individual right to bear arms with its claim that surprisingly few Americans owned guns when the Second Amendment was adopted. Bellesiles's methods came under fire, first from gun rights advocates and later from his fellow scholars. But scholars continued to produce nuanced studies of the origins of the Second Amendment that did not quite fit anyone's modern political agenda.

Scholarship on the Federalist Era (1790–1800) continues to be dominated by Stanley Elkins and Eric McKitrick's eloquent—and pro-Federalist—*Age of Federalism*, but historians have offered fresh insight on topics as diverse as the Seneca sachem Red Jacket, the impact of the French Revolution on American politics, and Fries's Rebellion. Particularly noteworthy are a series of anthologies on the early sessions of Congress and the creation of Washington, DC, edited by Kenneth R. Bowling and Donald R. Kennon.

Taken together, new scholarship on the oldest founding-era questions makes it clear that historians cannot even reach a consensus about the fundamental nature of the American Revolution and the early republic. It was not always so. By the time of the bicentennial in 1976, most scholars, convinced that the Patriots were motivated by a set of ideas that nearly all Americans shared, firmly rejected Carl Becker's 1909 assertion that their struggle for home rule was accompanied by a dispute over "who should rule at home." It appears, however, that adherents to this ideological/consensus interpretation of the Revolution declared victory prematurely, for the subsequent decades have witnessed a surge in scholarship emphasizing conflict among Americans. Certainly if Indians and African Americans are to be counted as Americans, European settlers' struggles against them provide ample vindication of Becker's thesis. Many modern scholars also now affirm that conflict was intense among whites.

In 2005, when Jack Rakove claimed that his generation had "largely solved the major causal problems of explaining why the Revolution occurred," he likewise appears to have spoken too soon, for younger scholars have offered a wide variety of original and persuasive explanations for why the Revolution came about. Many of these alternative accounts are based on archival evidence of internal conflict and economic motivation—precisely the sorts of social data that Rakove and other senior scholars had assured the rising generation it would not find. As noted earlier, when slaves drew British officials into what was essentially an alliance, white colonists were furious, and for many of them, especially in the South, the Anglo-black alliance became a reason to rebel. Scholars have shown that Indians also played a role in white Americans' decision to declare independence. Even before the Continental Congress accused the British of inciting Indians as well as blacks, white colonists had grown furious at the crown for protecting Indians' right to their land (most notably in the Proclamation of 1763), an imperial policy that was motivated not by a passion for justice but by the government's desperate need to prevent additional insurrections like the one associated with the Ottawa chief Pontiac.

The independence movement was also fueled by social conflict among whites, and scholars who draw attention to these disputes can claim two renowned converts. Pauline Maier, in *American Scripture: Making the Declaration of Independence*, pointed out that the document approved by Congress on July 4, 1776, merely culminated a process that had begun at the grassroots level, ninety local and provincial gatherings having already adopted resolves either declaring independence on their own or demanding that Congress do so. Meanwhile three decades of scholarship on the indispensible role that common people played in the coming of the revolution—not only in town meetings but in unruly crowds as well—culminated in Breen's book *American Insurgents, American Patriots: The Revolution of the People* (2010).

Scholars found evidence that ordinary folk shaped the Founding Fathers' other famous decisions as well. Historians like David Szatmary, Terry Bouton, and me contended that the adoption of the Constitution was less an effort to construct a "more perfect union" than a response to the farmers' rebellions of the 1780s (of which Shays's Rebellion is only the most famous). Maier's next book, *Ratification* (2010), makes a similar argument about the Bill of Rights. Maier points out that the U.S. Constitution as adopted in Philadelphia on September 17, 1787, contained no Bill of Rights. It was only pressure from below—the refusal of delegates at state ratifying conventions to vote for the Constitution unless they were promised a Bill of Rights—that produced what is widely heralded as the most valuable section of the national charter. And the influence of putatively powerless people on the Founding Fathers did not end there. Catherine Allgor and Susan Branson showed that women in the nation's capitol—first in Philadelphia, then in Washington—contrived ways to influence both political discourse and public policy.

Scholarly interest in the impact of Indians, African Americans, small farmers, and women on grand political events has been accompanied by a renewed focus on how the revolution in turn affected all these subordinate groups. Just as Rosemarie Zagarri contended that white women's founding-era gains provoked a "revolutionary backlash," numerous historians believe that ordinary white men—especially the nation's agrarian majority—gained ground during the revolution but then lost it as a result of what Larry Tise calls an "American Counter-Revolution," a process neatly summed up in the title of Bouton's 2007 volume *Taming Democracy.*

Since 1990, scholarship on the revolution has branched out in every direction, and the expansion shows every sign of continuing as we head toward the nation's next big birthday in 2026.

BIBLIOGRAPHY

Allgor, Catherine. *Parlor Politics: In Which the Ladies of Washington Help Build a City and a Government*. Charlottesville: University Press of Virginia, 2000.

———. *A Perfect Union: Dolley Madison and the Creation of the American Nation*. New York: Henry Holt, 2006.

Anderson, Fred. *Crucible of War: The Seven Years' War and the Fate of Empire in British North America, 1754–1766*. New York: Knopf, 2000.

Archer, Richard. *As If an Enemy's Country: The British Occupation of Boston and the Origins of Revolution*. New York: Oxford University Press, 2010.

Aron, Stephen. *American Confluence: The Missouri Frontier from Borderland to Border State*. Bloomington: Indiana University Press, 2005.

Babits, Lawrence E. *A Devil of a Whipping: The Battle of Cowpens*. Chapel Hill: University of North Carolina Press, 1998.

Bailyn, Bernard. *The Ideological Origins of the American Revolution*, enlarged edition. Cambridge, MA: Harvard University Press, 1992.

Barr, Juliana. *Peace Came in the Form of a Woman: Indians and Spaniards in the Texas Borderlands*. Chapel Hill: University of North Carolina Press, 2007.

Becker, Carl Lotus. *The History of Political Parties in the Province of New York, 1760–1776*. Madison: University of Wisconsin, 1909.

Bellesiles, Michael A. *Arming America: The Origins of a National Gun Culture*. New York: Knopf, 2000.

Berkin, Carol. *Revolutionary Mothers: Women in the Struggle for America's Independence*. New York: Random House, 2005.

Berlin, Ira. *Many Thousands Gone: The First Two Centuries of Slavery in North America*. Cambridge, MA: Belknap/Harvard University Press, 1998.

Bernstein, R. B. *The Founding Fathers Reconsidered*. New York: Oxford University Press, 2009.

———. *Thomas Jefferson*. New York: Oxford University Press, 2003.

Blauvelt, Martha Tomhave. *The Work of the Heart: Young Women and Emotion, 1780–1830*. Charlottesville: University of Virginia Press 2007.

Block, Sharon. *Rape and Sexual Power in Early America*. Chapel Hill: University of North Carolina Press, 2006.

Bolster, W. Jeffrey. *Black Jacks: African American Seamen in the Age of Sail*. Cambridge, MA: Harvard University Press, 1997.

Bouton, Terry. *Taming Democracy: "The People," the Founders, and the Troubled Ending of the American Revolution*. New York: Oxford University Press, 2007.

Branson, Susan. *These Fiery Frenchified Dames: Women and Political Culture in Early National Philadelphia*. Philadelphia: University of Pennsylvania Press, 2001.

Breen, T. H. *American Insurgents, American Patriots: The Revolution of the People*. New York: Hill and Wang, 2010.

———. *The Marketplace of Revolution: How Consumer Politics Shaped American Independence*. New York: Oxford University Press, 2004.

Brewer, Holly. *By Birth or Consent: Children, Law, and the Anglo-American Revolution in Authority*. Chapel Hill: University of North Carolina Press, 2005.

Brooke, John L. *The Refiner's Fire: The Making of Mormon Cosmology, 1644–1844*. New York: Cambridge University Press, 1994.

Brooks, James. *Captives and Cousins: Slavery, Kinship, and Community in the Southwest Borderlands*. Chapel Hill: University of North Carolina Press, 2002.

Brown, Christopher Leslie. *Moral Capital: Foundations of British Abolitionism*. Chapel Hill: University of North Carolina Press, 2006.

Brown, Roger H. *Redeeming the Republic: Federalists, Taxation, and the Origins of the Constitution*. Baltimore: Johns Hopkins University Press, 1993.

Brown, Vincent. *The Reaper's Garden: Death and Power in the World of Atlantic Slavery*. Cambridge, MA: Harvard University Press, 2008.

Buel, Richard, Jr. *In Irons: Britain's Naval Supremacy and the American Revolutionary Economy*. New Haven: Yale University Press, 1998.

Burnard, Trevor. *Mastery, Tyranny, and Desire: Thomas Thistlewood and His Slaves in the Anglo-Jamaican World*. Chapel Hill: University of North Carolina Press, 2004.

Burstein, Andrew. *The Inner Jefferson: Portrait of a Grieving Optimist*. Charlottesville: University Press of Virginia, 1995.

———. *Jefferson's Secrets: Death and Desire at Monticello*. New York: Basic Books, 2005.

Burstein, Andrew, and Nancy Isenberg, *Madison and Jefferson*. New York: Random House, 2010.

Calloway, Colin G. *The American Revolution in Indian Country: Crisis and Diversity in Native American Communities*. New York: Cambridge University Press, 1995.

———. *One Vast Winter Count: The Native American West before Lewis and Clark*. Lincoln: University of Nebraska Press, 2003.

Carp, Benjamin L. *Defiance of the Patriots: The Boston Tea Party and the Making of America*. New Haven: Yale University Press, 2010.

———. *Rebels Rising: Cities and the American Revolution*. New York: Oxford University Press, 2007.

Carretta, Vincent. *Equiano the African: Biography of a Self-Made Man*. Athens: University of Georgia Press, 2005.

Chernow, Ron. *Washington: A Life*. New York: Penguin, 2010.

Conroy, David. *In Public Houses: Drink and the Revolution of Authority in Colonial Massachusetts*. Chapel Hill: University of North Carolina Press, 1995.

Crain, Caleb. *American Sympathy: Men, Friendship and Literature in the New Nation*. New Haven: Yale University Press, 2001.

Crane, Elaine Forman. *Ebb Tide In New England: Women, Seaports, and Social Change, 1630–1800*. Boston: Northeastern University Press, 1998.

Dixon, David. *Never Come to Peace Again: Pontiac's Uprising and the Fate of the British Empire in North America*. Norman: University of Oklahoma Press, 2005.

Doumlele, Ruth. *The Randolph Women and Their Men*. Bothell, WA: Book Publishers Network, 2010.

Dowd, Gregory Evans. *War under Heaven: Pontiac, the Indian Nations, and the British Empire*. Baltimore: Johns Hopkins University Press, 2002.

Dubois, Laurent. *Avengers of the New World: The Story of the Haitian Revolution*. Cambridge, MA: Belknap/Harvard University Press, 2004.

DuVal, Kathleen. *The Native Ground: Indians and Colonists in the Heart of the Continent*. Philadelphia: University of Pennsylvania Press, 2006.

Edling, Max M. *A Revolution in Favor of Government: Origins of the U.S. Constitution and the Making of the American State*. New York: Oxford University Press, 2003.

Egerton, Douglas R. *Death or Liberty: African Americans and Revolutionary America*. New York: Oxford University Press, 2009.

Ehrenreich, Barbara. *Nickel and Dimed: On (Not) Getting By in America*. New York: Metropolitan Books, 2001.

Einhorn, Robin L. *American Taxation, American Slavery*. Chicago: University of Chicago Press, 2006.

Elkins, Stanley, and Eric McKitrick. *The Age of Federalism: The Early American Republic, 1788–1800*. New York: Oxford University Press, 1993.

Ellis, Joseph J. *American Sphinx: The Character of Thomas Jefferson*. New York: Knopf, 1996.

———. *Founding Brothers: The Revolutionary Generation*. New York: Knopf, 2000.

———. "Jefferson: Post-DNA." *William and Mary Quarterly*, 3rd ser., 57 (January 2000): 125–138.

Eltis, David, et al., eds. *The Transatlantic Slave Trade*. Book and CD-ROM. New York: Cambridge University Press, 2000.

Ely, Melvin Patrick. *Israel on the Appomattox: A Southern Experiment in Black Freedom from the 1790s Through the Civil War*. New York: Knopf, 2004.

Eustace, Nicole. *Passion Is the Gale: Emotion, Power and the Coming of the American Revolution*. Chapel Hill: University of North Carolina Press, 2008.

Fenn, Elizabeth A. *Pox Americana: The Great Smallpox Epidemic of 1775–82*. New York: Hill and Wang, 2001.

Finkelman, Paul. *Slavery and the Founders: Race and Slavery in the Age of Jefferson*. Armonk, NY: M. E. Sharpe, 1996.

Fischer, David Hackett. *Washington's Crossing*. New York: Oxford University Press, 2003.

Fliegelman, Jay. *Declaring Independence: Jefferson, Natural Language & the Culture of Performance*. Palo Alto, CA: Stanford University Press, 1993.

Fox, Francis S. *Sweet Land of Liberty: The Ordeal of the American Revolution in Northampton County, Pennsylvania*. University Park: Pennsylvania State University Press, 2000.

Fraser, Walter J. *Lowcountry Hurricanes: Three Centuries of Storms at Sea And Ashore*. Athens: University of Georgia Press, 2006.

Freeman, Joanne B. *Affairs of Honor: National Politics in the New Republic*. New Haven, CT: Yale University Press, 2001.

Gallay, Alan. *The Indian Slave Trade: The Rise of the English Empire in the American South, 1670–1717*. New Haven, CT: Yale University Press, 2002.

Gates, Henry Louis. *The Trials of Phillis Wheatley: America's First Black Poet and Her Encounters with the Founding Fathers*. New York: Basic Civitas Books, 2003.

Geggus, David Patrick. *Haitian Revolutionary Studies*. Bloomington: Indiana University Press, 2002.

Gelles, Edith B. *Abigail and John: Portrait of a Marriage*. New York: William Morrow, 2009.

Gordon-Reed, Annette. *The Hemingses of Monticello: An American Family*. New York: W. W. Norton, 2008.

———. *Thomas Jefferson and Sally Hemings: An American Controversy.* Charlottesville: University Press of Virginia, 1997.

Grasso, Christopher. *A Speaking Aristocracy: Transforming Public Discourse in Eighteenth-Century Connecticut.* Chapel Hill: University of North Carolina Press, 1999.

Greene, Jack P., and J. R. Pole. *A Companion to the American Revolution.* Malden, MA: Blackwell Publishers, 2000.

Griffin, Patrick. *American Leviathan: Empire, Nation, and Revolutionary Frontier.* New York: Hill and Wang, 2007.

Gross, Robert A., ed. *In Debt to Shays: The Bicentennial of an Agrarian Rebellion.* Charlottesville: University Press of Virginia, 1993.

Gundersen, Joan R. *To Be Useful to the World: Women in Revolutionary America, 1740–1790,* revised edition. Chapel Hill: University of North Carolina Press, 2006.

Gustafson, Sandra M. *Eloquence Is Power: Oratory and Performance in Early America.* Chapel Hill: University of North Carolina Press, 2000.

Gutzman, Kevin R. C. *Virginia's American Revolution: From Dominion to Republic, 1776–1840.* Plymouth: Lexington Books, 2007.

Hämäläinen, Pekka. *The Comanche Empire.* New Haven, CT: Yale University Press, 2008.

Harms, Robert W. *The Diligent: A Voyage through the Worlds of the Slave Trade.* New York: Basic Books, 2001.

Haulman, Clyde A. *Virginia and the Panic of 1819: The First Great Depression and the Commonwealth.* London: Pickering and Chatto, 2008.

Haulman, Kate. *The Politics of Fashion in Eighteenth-Century America.* Chapel Hill: University of North Carolina Press, 2011.

Holton, Woody. *Abigail Adams.* New York: Free Press, 2009.

———. *Forced Founders: Indians, Debtors, Slaves, and the Making of the American Revolution in Virginia.* Chapel Hill: University of North Carolina Press, 1999.

———. *Unruly Americans and the Origins of the Constitution.* New York: Hill and Wang, 2007.

Howe, Daniel Walker. *What Hath God Wrought: The Transformation of America, 1815–1848.* New York: Oxford University Press, 2007.

Humphrey, Thomas J. *Land and Liberty: Hudson Valley Riots in the Age of Revolution.* Dekalb: Northern Illinois University Press, 2004.

Isaac, Rhys. *Landon Carter's Uneasy Kingdom: Revolution and Rebellion on a Virginia Plantation.* New York: Oxford University Press, 2004.

Isaacson, Walter. *Benjamin Franklin: An American Life.* New York: Simon and Schuster, 2003.

Isenberg, Nancy. *Fallen Founder: The Life of Aaron Burr.* New York: Viking, 2007.

Juster, Susan. *Doomsayers: Anglo-American Prophecy in the Age of Revolution.* Philadelphia: University of Pennsylvania Press, 2003.

Kamensky, Jane. *The Exchange Artist: A Tale of High-Flying Speculation and America's First Banking Collapse.* New York: Viking, 2008.

Kars, Marjoleine. *Breaking Loose Together: The Regulator Rebellion in Pre-Revolutionary North Carolina.* Chapel Hill: University of North Carolina Press, 2002.

Kastor, Peter J. *The Nation's Crucible: The Louisiana Purchase and the Creation of America.* New Haven, CT: Yale University Press, 2004.

Kelley, Mary. *Learning to Stand and Speak: Women, Education, and Public Life in America's Republic*. Chapel Hill: University of North Carolina Press, 2006.

Kennedy, Roger G. *Mr. Jefferson's Lost Cause: Land, Farmers, Slavery, and the Louisiana Purchase*. New York: Oxford University Press, 2003.

Kerber, Linda K. *Women of the Republic: Intellect and Ideology in Revolutionary America*. Chapel Hill: University of North Carolina Press, 1980.

Kern, Susan. *The Jeffersons at Shadwell*. New Haven, CT: Yale University Press, 2010.

Kierner, Cynthia A. *Beyond the Household: Women's Place in the Early South, 1700–1835*. Ithaca, NY: Cornell University Press, 1998.

———. *Scandal at Bizarre: Rumor and Reputation in Jefferson's America*. New York: Palgrave Macmillan, 2004.

Klepp, Susan E. *Revolutionary Conceptions: Women, Fertility, and Family Limitation in America, 1760–1820*. Chapel Hill: University of North Carolina Press, 2009.

Knott, Sarah. *Sensibility and the American Revolution*. Chapel Hill: University of North Carolina Press, 2009.

Kukla, Jon. *Mr. Jefferson's Women*. New York: Knopf, 2007.

———. *A Wilderness So Immense: The Louisiana Purchase and the Destiny of America*. New York: Knopf, 2003.

Kwasny, Mark V. *Washington's Partisan War, 1775–1783*. Kent, Ohio: Kent State University Press, 1996.

Lambert, Frank. *Inventing the "Great Awakening."* Princeton, NJ: Princeton University Press, 1999.

Larson, John Lauritz. *Internal Improvement: National Public Works and the Promise of Popular Government in the Early United States*. Chapel Hill: University of North Carolina Press, 2001.

Leamon, James S. *Revolution Downeast: The War for American Independence in Maine*. Amherst: University of Massachusetts Press, 1993.

Lepore, Jill. *A Is for American: Letters and Other Characters in the Newly United States*. New York: Knopf, 2002.

———. *The Whites of Their Eyes: The Tea Party's Revolution and the Battle over American History*. Princeton, NJ: Princeton University Press, 2010.

Levy, Andrew. *The First Emancipator: The Forgotten Story of Robert Carter, the Founding Father Who Freed His Slaves*. New York: Random House, 2005.

Linebaugh, Peter, and Marcus Rediker. *The Many-Headed Hydra: Sailors, Slaves, Commoners, and the Hidden History of the Revolutionary Atlantic*. Boston: Beacon Press, 2000.

Lockridge, Kenneth A. *On the Sources of Patriarchal Rage: The Commonplace Books of William Byrd and Thomas Jefferson and the Gendering of Power in the Eighteenth Century*. New York: New York University Press, 1992.

Lovell, Margaretta M. *Art in a Season of Revolution: Painters, Artisans, and Patrons in Early America*. Philadelphia: University of Pennsylvania Press, 2005.

Lyons, Clare A. *Sex among the Rabble: An Intimate History of Gender and Power in the Age of Revolution, Philadelphia, 1730–1830*. Chapel Hill: University of North Carolina Press, 2006.

Maier, Pauline. *American Scripture: Making the Declaration of Independence*. New York: Knopf, 1997.

———. *Ratification: The People Debate the Constitution, 1787–1788*. New York: Simon and Schuster, 2010.

Malcolm, Joyce Lee. *Peter's War: A New England Slave Boy and the American Revolution*. New Haven, CT: Yale University Press, 2009.

Mann, Bruce H. *Republic of Debtors: Bankruptcy in the Age of American Independence*. Cambridge, MA: Harvard University Press, 2002.

Mason, Matthew. *Slavery and Politics in the Early American Republic*. Chapel Hill: University of North Carolina Press, 2006.

McConville, Brendan. *The King's Three Faces: The Rise and Fall of Royal America, 1688–1776*. Chapel Hill: University of North Carolina Press, 2006.

———. *These Daring Disturbers of the Public Peace: The Struggle for Property and Power in Early New Jersey*. Ithaca, NY: Cornell University Press, 1999.

McCullough, David. *John Adams*. New York: Simon and Schuster, 2001.

McDonnell, Michael A. *The Politics of War: Race, Class, and Conflict in Revolutionary Virginia*. Chapel Hill: University of North Carolina Press, 2007.

McGarvie, Mark Douglas. *One Nation Under Law: America's Early National Struggles to Separate Church and State*. DeKalb: Northern Illinois University Press, 2004.

McGuire, Robert A. *To Form a More Perfect Union: A New Economic Interpretation of the United States Constitution*. New York: Oxford University Press, 2003.

McLaughlin, Jack. *Jefferson and Monticello: The Biography of a Builder*. New York: Henry Holt, 1988.

Meranze, Michael. *Laboratories of Virtue: Punishment, Revolution, and Authority in Philadelphia, 1760–1835*. Chapel Hill: University of North Carolina Press, 1996.

Merrell, James H. *The Indians' New World: Catawbas and Their Neighbors from European Contact through the Era of Removal*. Chapel Hill: University of North Carolina Press, 1989.

———. *Into the American Woods: Negotiators on the Pennsylvania Frontier*. New York: W. W. Norton, 1999.

Morgan, Edmund S. *Benjamin Franklin*. New Haven, CT: Yale University Press, 2002.

Morgan, Jennifer L. *Laboring Women: Reproduction and Gender in New World Slavery*. Philadelphia: University of Pennsylvania Press, 2004.

Morgan, Philip D. *Slave Counterpoint: Black Culture in the Eighteenth-Century Chesapeake and Lowcountry*. Chapel Hill: University of North Carolina, 1998.

Mulcahy, Matthew. *Hurricanes and Society in the British Greater Caribbean, 1624–1783*. Baltimore: Johns Hopkins University Press, 2005.

Nash, Gary B. *The Unknown American Revolution: The Unruly Birth of Democracy and the Struggle to Create America*. New York: Viking, 2005.

Nash, Gary B., and Graham Russell Gao Hodges. *Friends of Liberty: Thomas Jefferson, Tadeusz Kościuszko, and Agrippa Hull: A Tale of Three Patriots, Two Revolutions, and a Tragic Betrayal of Freedom in the New Nation*. New York: Basic Books, 2008.

Neimeyer, Charles P. *America Goes to War: A Social History of the Continental Army*. New York: New York University Press, 1996.

Nelson, John K. *A Blessed Company: Parishes, Parsons, and Parishioners in Anglican Virginia, 1690–1776*. Chapel Hill: University of North Carolina Press, 2001.

Nester, William R. *"Haughty Conquerors": Amherst and the Great Indian Uprising of 1763*. Westport, CT: Praeger, 2000.

Newman, Paul Douglas. *Fries's Rebellion: The Enduring Struggle for the American Revolution*. Philadelphia: University of Pennsylvania Press, 2004.

Newman, Richard S. *Freedom's Prophet: Bishop Richard Allen, the AME Church, and the Black Founding Fathers*. New York: New York University Press, 2008.

Newman, Simon P. *Embodied History: The Lives of the Poor in Early Philadelphia*. Philadelphia: University of Pennsylvania Press, 2003.

———. *Parades and the Politics of the Street: Festive Culture in the Early American Republic*. Philadelphia: University of Pennsylvania Press, 1997.

Norling, Lisa. *Captain Ahab Had a Wife: New England Women and the Whalefishery, 1720–1870*. Chapel Hill, NC: University of North Carolina Press, 2000.

Norton, Mary Beth. *Liberty's Daughters: The Revolutionary Experience of American Women, 1750–1800*. Boston: Little, Brown, 1980.

O'Shaughnessy, Andrew Jackson. *An Empire Divided: The American Revolution and the British Caribbean*. Philadelphia: University of Pennsylvania Press, 2000.

Parrish, Susan Scott. *American Curiosity: Cultures of Natural History in the Colonial British Atlantic World*. Chapel Hill: University of North Carolina Press, 2006.

Pasley, Jeffrey L. *"The Tyranny of Printers": Newspaper Politics in the Early American Republic*. Charlottesville: University Press of Virginia, 2001.

Pasley, Jeffrey L., Andrew W. Robertson, and David Waldstreicher. *Beyond the Founders: New Approaches to the Political History of the Early American Republic*. Chapel Hill: University of North Carolina Press, 2004.

Pearsall, Sarah M. S. *Atlantic Families: Lives and Letters in the Later Eighteenth Century*. New York: Oxford University Press, 2008.

Pybus, Cassandra. *Epic Journeys of Freedom: Runaway Slaves of the American Revolution and Their Global Quest for Liberty*. Boston: Beacon Press, 2006.

Ragosta, John A. *Wellspring of Liberty: How Virginia's Religious Dissenters Helped Win the American Revolution and Secured Religious Liberty*. New York: Oxford University Press, 2010.

Rakove, Jack. "An Agenda for Early American History." *Historically Speaking* 6 (March/April 2005): 4.

Raphael, Ray. *The First American Revolution: Before Lexington and Concord*. New York: New Press, Distributed by W. W. Norton, 2002.

——— *Founders: The People Who Brought You a Nation*. New York: New Press, 2009.

———. *A People's History of the American Revolution: How Common People Shaped the Fight for Independence*. New York: New Press, 2001.

Rappleye, Charles. *Sons of Providence: The Brown Brothers, the Slave Trade, and the American Revolution*. New York: Simon and Schuster, 2006.

Rediker, Marcus. *The Slave Ship: A Human History*. New York: Viking, 2007.

Resch, John, *Suffering Soldiers: Revolutionary War Veterans, Moral Sentiment, and Political Culture in the Early Republic*. Amherst: University of Massachusetts Press, 1999.

Richards, Leonard L. *Shays's Rebellion: The American Revolution's Final Battle*. Philadelphia: University of Pennsylvania Press, 2002.

Risjord, Norman K. *Jefferson's America, 1760–1815*, 3rd ed. Lanham, MD: Rowman and Littlefield, 2009.

Rockman, Seth. *Scraping By: Wage Labor, Slavery, and Survival in Early Baltimore*. Baltimore: Johns Hopkins University Press, 2008.

Schafer, Daniel L. *Anna Madgigine Jai Kingsley: African Princess, Florida Slave, Plantation Slaveowner*. Gainesville: University Press of Florida, 2003.

Schama, Simon. *Rough Crossings: Britain, the Slaves and the American Revolution*. London: BBC, 2005.

Scott, Julius S. "A Common Wind: Currents of Afro-American Communication in the Age of the Haitian Revolution." Ph.D. dissertation, Duke University, 1986.

Scully, Randolph Ferguson. *Religion and the Making of Nat Turner's Virginia: Baptist Community and Conflict, 1740–1840*. Charlottesville: University of Virginia Press, 2008.

Sensbach, Jon F. *Rebecca's Revival: Creating Black Christianity in the Atlantic World*. Cambridge, MA: Harvard University Press, 2005.

———. *A Separate Canaan: The Making of an Afro-Moravian World in North Carolina, 1763–1840*. Chapel Hill: University of North Carolina Press, 1998.

Shammas, Carole. "Anglo-American Household Government in Comparative Perspective." *William and Mary Quarterly*, 3rd ser. 52 (1995): 104–144.

Shoemaker, Nancy. *A Strange Likeness: Becoming Red and White in Eighteenth-Century North America*. New York: Oxford University Press, 2004.

Sievens, Mary Beth. *Stray Wives: Marital Conflict in Early National New England*. New York: New York University Press, 2005.

Silver, Peter. *Our Savage Neighbors: How Indian War Transformed Early America*. New York: W. W. Norton, 2008.

Simms, Brendan. *Three Victories and a Defeat: The Rise and Fall of the First British Empire, 1714–1783*. New York: Basic Books, 2009.

Skemp, Sheila L. *First Lady of Letters: Judith Sargent Murray and the Struggle for Female Independence*. Philadelphia: University of Pennsylvania Press, 2005.

Slaughter, Thomas P. *Exploring Lewis and Clark: Reflections on Men and Wilderness*. New York: Knopf, 2003.

Slauter, Eric. *The State as a Work of Art: The Cultural Origins of the Constitution*. Chicago: University of Chicago Press, 2009.

Smith, Barbara Clark. *The Freedoms We Lost: Consent and Resistance in Revolutionary America*. New York: New Press, 2010.

Smith, Merril D. *Women's Roles in Eighteenth-Century America*. Santa Barbara, CA: Greenwood, 2010.

Spangler, Jewel L. *Virginians Reborn: Anglican Monopoly, Evangelical Dissent, and the Rise of the Baptists in the Late Eighteenth Century*. Charlottesville: University of Virginia Press, 2008.

Stanton, Lucia. *Free Slave Day: The African-American Families of Monticello*. Chapel Hill: University of North Carolina Press, 2002.

Stoll, Ira. *Samuel Adams: A Life*. New York: Free Press, 2008.

Stuart, Nancy Rubin. *Muse of the Revolution: The Secret Pen of Mercy Otis Warren and the Founding of a Nation*. Boston: Beacon Press, 2008.

Sweet, John Wood. *Bodies Politic: Negotiating Race in the American North, 1730–1830*. Baltimore: Johns Hopkins University Press, 2003.

Szatmary, David. *Shays' Rebellion: The Making of an Agrarian Insurrection*. Amherst: University of Massachusetts Press, 1980.

Taylor, Alan. *The Civil War of 1812: American Citizens, British Subjects, Irish Rebels, & Indian Allies*. New York: Knopf, 2010.

———. *The Divided Ground: Indians, Settlers and the Northern Borderland of the American Revolution*. New York: Knopf, 2006.

———. *William Cooper's Town: Power and Persuasion on the Frontier of the Early American Republic*. New York: Vintage, 1995.

Thompson, Mary V. *"In the Hands of a Good Providence": Religion in the Life of George Washington*. Charlottesville: University of Virginia Press, 2008.

Tise, Larry E. *The American Counterrevolution: A Retreat from Liberty, 1783–1800*. Mechanicsburg, PA: Stackpole Books, 1998.

Ulrich, Laurel Thatcher. *A Midwife's Tale: The Life of Martha Ballard, Based on Her Diary, 1785–1812*. New York: Knopf, 1990.

Usner, Daniel H., Jr. *Indians, Settlers, and Slaves in a Frontier Exchange Economy: The Lower Mississippi Valley before 1783*. Chapel Hill: University of North Carolina, 1992.

Vickers, Daniel, with Vince Walsh. *Young Men and the Sea: Yankee Seafarers in the Age of Sail*. New Haven, CT: Yale University Press, 2005.

Waldstreicher, David. *In the Midst of Perpetual Fetes: The Making of American Nationalism, 1776–1820*. Chapel Hill: University of North Carolina Press, 1997.

———. *Runaway America: Benjamin Franklin, Slavery, and the American Revolution*. New York: Hill and Wang, 2004.

———. *Slavery's Constitution: From Revolution to Ratification*. New York: Hill and Wang, 2009.

Wallace, Anthony F. C. *Jefferson and the Indians: The Tragic Fate of the First Americans*. Cambridge, MA: Belknap/Harvard University Press, 1999.

Ward, Harry M. *The American Revolution: Nationhood Achieved, 1763–1788*. New York: St. Martin's Press, 1995.

———. *Between the Lines: Banditti of the American Revolution*. Santa Barbara, CA: Praeger, 2002.

———. *George Washington's Enforcers: Policing the Continental Army*. Carbondale: Southern Illinois University Press, 2006.

Weeks, Charles A. *Paths to a Middle Ground: The Diplomacy of Natchez, Boukfouka, Nogales, and San Fernando de las Barrancas, 1791–1795*. Tuscaloosa: University of Alabama Press, 2005.

West, Ellis M. *The Religion Clauses of the First Amendment: Guarantees of States' Rights?* Lanham, MD: Lexington Books, 2010.

White, Richard. *The Middle Ground: Indians, Empires, and Republics in the Great Lakes Region, 1650–1815*. New York: Cambridge University Press, 1991.

Wiencek, Henry. *An Imperfect God: George Washington, His Slaves, and the Creation of America*. New York: Farrar, Straus and Giroux, 2003.

Wilkins, Roger. *Jefferson's Pillow: The Founding Fathers and the Dilemma of Black Patriotism*. Boston: Beacon Press, 2001.

Wood, Gordon S. *The Americanization of Benjamin Franklin*. New York: Penguin, 2004.

———. *Empire of Liberty: A History of the Early Republic, 1789–1815*. New York: Oxford University Press, 2009.

Wright, Conrad Edick. *Revolutionary Generation: Harvard Men and the Consequences of Independence*. Amherst: University of Massachusetts Press, 2005.

Wright, Robert E. *One Nation under Debt: Hamilton, Jefferson, and the History of What We Owe*. New York: McGraw-Hill, 2008.

Young, Alfred F. *Liberty Tree: Ordinary People and the American Revolution*. New York: New York University Press, 2006.

———. *Masquerade: The Life and Times of Deborah Sampson, Continental Soldier*. New York: Knopf, 2004.

———. *The Shoemaker and the Tea Party: Memory and the American Revolution*. Boston: Beacon Press, 1999.

Young, Alfred F., and Gregory Nobles. *Whose American Revolution Was It? Historians Interpret the Founding.* New York: New York University Press, 2011.

Young, Alfred F., Ray Raphael, and Gary B. Nash. *Revolutionary Founders: Rebels, Radicals, and Reformers in the Making of the Nation.* New York: Knopf, 2011.

Zagarri, Rosemarie. *Revolutionary Backlash: Women and Politics in the Early American Republic.* Philadelphia: University of Pennsylvania Press, 2007.

3

Jacksonian America

SETH ROCKMAN

Only a decade ago, scholars despaired for the Jacksonian era. An outpouring of new research in social and cultural history during the 1980s and 1990s had multiplied the number of stories that could be told about the middle decades of the nineteenth century and left older political narratives of the Second Party System looking woefully incomplete. At the same time, historians working on the early national period had appropriated many of the developments that once defined the Jacksonian era: popular politics, an expanding franchise, liberal ideology, and intensified market relations. Even the most committed Jacksonian scholars wondered what, if anything, justified the study of the 1820s, 1830s, and 1840s as a discrete period. The declining reputation of Andrew Jackson as a national hero compounded these anxieties. In search of a more diverse past, scholars have identified many other Americans—Frederick Douglass or Margaret Fuller, for example—whose names might more convincingly convey the egalitarian aspirations of the era. In the phrasing of a predictable essay question: "Jacksonian Democracy was neither. Discuss."

Judging from the general public's continued fascination with presidents and high political history, however, Jacksonian America has withstood this crisis of confidence. Biographers continue to revisit the lives of Andrew Jackson, Henry Clay, and even James K. Polk, while scholars like Sean Wilentz, Daniel Walker Howe, and David Reynolds have produced new synthetic accounts that assimilate the work of social and cultural historians into narratives still fundamentally driven by the leading men of national politics. Prize committees have showered these books with the most prestigious awards in the profession, and publishers have made them available in digital, abridged, and audio formats to reach the largest possible audience. As traditional as this scholarship is in methodology and its privileging of the experiences of white men, these popular accounts readily convey the social dynamism and technological wonder of the era.

Scholars finishing doctorates and publishing monographs in the 1990s and 2000s have attempted to reorient the historiographical conversation by refusing the false choice between a political history of elections and legislative battles on the one hand, and a social and cultural history sensitive to minority and marginal perspectives on the other. The most exciting scholarship in the field has blurred these distinctions, whether in considering the role of dime novels and minstrel shows in the formation of American nationalism, or investigating the political claims that slaves, women, and other noncitizens made on the state. New work has borrowed theoretical insights from literary and cultural studies, political economy, and the burgeoning scholarship on modern empires. Divisions that once compartmentalized research into various subfields like women's history, African-American history, or labor history seem to carry less weight, especially as analytical categories of social difference like race, class, gender, and ethnicity are now studied for their "intersectionality." At the same time, calls for transnational history have destabilized the spatial parameters of Jacksonian America and have required scholars to consider the operations of Mexican federalism, the aspirations of Cuban sugar planters, the investments of British capitalists, the raiding strategies of Comanche warriors, and the trading cycles of the Pacific basin. The chronological bookends of the Jacksonian era have also been in flux. The primary professional organization for the field—the Society for Historians of the Early American Republic—has claimed the entirety of 1789–1861 as its domain, and as a result, scholars of the 1820s and 1830s have been inclined to see the continuities of historical processes that began in 1790s or 1800s; yet these same scholars struggle against the teleological label "antebellum" and resist the Civil War vortex that transforms every earlier development into a harbinger of disunion.

In light of shifting methodological, spatial, and temporal boundaries, it is no small challenge to capture recent developments in the historiography of Jacksonian America. This chapter focuses on four recent developments in the scholarship: the relocation of political history beyond elections into the broader realm of civil society, the transnational analysis of American geographical expansion, the recognition of slavery's centrality to the political, economic and cultural life of the nation as a whole, and newfound attention to the political economy of capitalism. If this chapter gives short shrift to Andrew Jackson himself, the core tensions of his presidency—the relationship of political democratization and economic development, of state power and local autonomy, of slavery and abolition, and of social inclusion and exclusion—receive sustained attention in the pages that follow.

The Politics of the Public

Political history remains a central concern for scholars of the Jacksonian period, but with particular attention to the 364 days a year when elections were *not* held. The privileges and constraints that shaped Americans' lives derived from many sources beyond the state and its legal apparatus, and scholars have emphasized the variety of public ways that power was exercised and contested outside the realm of formal politics. Daily interactions in parlors and plazas, as well as on plantations, are understood to be rife with political content. New research has stretched the ranks of the politically engaged to include the disfranchised men and women who laid claim to civic inclusion on the streets, at conventions, and through petitions sent to officials they themselves did not elect. The most crucial analytical concept in this new political history has been "civil society," or the expansive space of political engagement beyond the intimate domain of the family but distinct from the state. In *Democracy in America*, Alexis de Tocqueville had drawn attention to the American proclivity for joining voluntary associations, publishing newspapers, and declaiming political opinions no matter how ill-informed. For Tocqueville, the capacity of people to think and act politically without governmental interference not only made the United States an unusually free society but also served as the glue holding together an expansive monarchless nation. Recent historians have followed Tocqueville's observations into what the theorist Jürgen Habermas called the "public sphere," a figurative debate zone spanning physical space and the printed page. Indeed, print transformed solitary readers into members of a politicized public, one much larger—and much more diverse—than could assemble in any one place or cast ballots on election day.

"Public opinion" became contested terrain in American politics, as did the question of whose voices legitimately constituted "the public" in the first place. When white New England and Mid-Atlantic women petitioned Congress to oppose President Jackson's Indian removal policy in 1829, for example, many elected officials and political commentators disparaged the "Ladies' Circular" as originating from outside any recognizable constituency. But as Mary Hershberger has shown, the women's antiremoval campaign conveys many of the key concerns of an expanded political history: the role of print to constitute a reading public that could then be mobilized through everyday acts like signing petitions and attending public meetings; the critical leadership of those whose inability to vote in no way diminished their civic engagement; the ability of voluntary associations to transform philanthropic impulses into political action; and the ways in which all these developments destabilized the presumed boundary between public and private. Organizing in defense of the Cherokee nation galvanized a generation of women to involve themselves in abolitionism, temperance, women's rights, and other social reforms that were ultimately matters of public policy; their sustained political engagement owed less to formal citizenship rights than to the potent interplay of associational and print cultures.

For some historians, civil society was the most democratic aspect of the Jacksonian era, functioning in Kathleen McCarthy's words as the "stage on which men and women, rich and poor, black and white publicly contested for authority and power." Certainly, as scholars like Patrick Rael have documented, African-American political claims emanated from a network of African Methodist Episcopal churches, Masonic lodges, mutual aid and literary societies, temperance organizations, and a national convention movement that began in 1830 with delegates from seven states (including Maryland and Virginia) meeting in Philadelphia. Public meetings provided platforms to black orators like Maria Stewart and Henry Highland Garnet, whose speeches commercial publishers then brought into print alongside convention proceedings and a growing library of protest pamphlets. The nation's first black-edited newspaper, *Freedom's Journal*, began publishing in New York in 1827, and subsequent abolitionist newspapers like William Lloyd Garrison's *Liberator* provided column space to the opinions of black readers from states both slave and free. African-American public culture grew in importance precisely as black men faced new restrictions on voting under "democratizing" franchise reforms in New York, New Jersey, Pennsylvania, Connecticut, and Rhode Island between 1821 and 1842. Shane White has emphasized cultural expression as a powerful vehicle for black political claims, conveyed through the infrapolitics of a black theater troupe's subversive staging of Shakespeare's *Richard III* or the gait of black dandies on the streets of Manhattan.

Cities witnessed the most vibrant, if volatile, aspects of democratic public life. Urban plazas, markets, and promenades facilitated social interactions that, in Mary Ryan's words, "set the spatial stage, the limits and possibilities, for people to come together, to view both the differences and the commonalities through which a public might find itself." In her study of New York, New Orleans, and San Francisco, Ryan sees the cities of the 1830s and 1840s as crucibles of democratic diversity, especially as patrician politicians proved incapable of scripting civic celebrations into orderly rituals of deference. Given occasion to mark a national holiday, a groundbreaking, or a dignitary's visit with a parade, urban residents lay claim to "ceremonial citizenship" by marching in groups organized by trade, heritage, reform proclivities, and other affinities. The temperate and the tippling, the saved and the irreligious, the native born and the recent immigrant organized public life in ways that not only confounded the divisions of elite versus plebeian and Democrat versus Whig but that also, as David Henkin observes, "collapsed the distinction between imagining a community and participating in it." Perhaps the biggest winners in the boisterous arena of urban politics were working-class and immigrant white men, able both to vote as individuals and to affiliate by occupation and ancestry. If ethnic pluralism had been a hallmark of the American colonies and the new United States, the Jacksonian era catapulted ethnicity to an organizing category of public life and allowed Irish and German men in particular to reap the benefits of a democratized politics.

The same urban spaces and associational culture that promoted the democratic engagement of a diverse and fractious public could also facilitate illiberal efforts to exclude segments of the population from civic participation. Voluntary organizations brought together those intent on restricting the rights of immigrants, exiling free people of color, and vilifying religious sects, secret societies, and moral reformers. A meeting might convene to denounce abolitionists as readily as to contend for the end of slavery. The rhetoric of a democratic public served the antiabolitionist Rhode Islanders who identified themselves in 1835 as "a very numerous and respectable meeting of the citizens," as "a large majority of this community," and ultimately as "*We the People of Providence*" to condemn antislavery agitation. Perversely, the many mob actions of the 1830s transpired under the sign of democratic participation, as an already-empowered white male electorate reconvened in the streets as "the people" to attack prostitutes, nuns, medical students, gamblers, bankers, upstart religious sects, strikebreakers, and especially people of color, their institutions, and their allies.

Civil society allowed the era's most radical ideas—birth control, atheism, racial and sexual equality, and property redistribution—to gain a public hearing. While congressmen debated banks and tariffs, a much broader conversation about economic justice emerged from the meetings, newspapers, and protests of a flourishing labor movement. Trade unions activated laboring men and women to publicize the inadequacies of the wage system. Acting in association, laborers sometimes entered the realm of formal politics as workingmen's parties, but as Joshua Greenberg has shown, more commonly founded cooperatives, libraries, debating societies, and temperance organizations, each infused with a producerist ideology that championed those who made things with their hands. As with most social movements, labor organizing depended on print to circulate local convention resolutions, celebratory toasts, and fiery speeches to workers in distant locales waging their own struggles to shorten the workday and gain better pay. When seamstresses in New York staged a strike in 1831, they defended their right to unite against their employers in simple terms: "Is not this a free country?" Perhaps the most notorious female radical of the Jacksonian era was Frances Wright, who used the columns of *The Free Enquirer* to promote compulsory state-run boarding schools as a means of stemming economic inequality. Because Wright also equated Christianity with superstition and criticized women's subordination within marriage, the label "Fanny Wrightism" soon adhered to any social reform that threatened patriarchal authority.

Scholars like Nancy Isenberg have mapped the gendered terrain of civic participation. Those imagining the world as comprising dichotomous male (public) and female (private) realms had sharp words for women who transgressed these untenable boundaries. Attacks on abolitionism, for example, invariably drew attention to the impropriety of female speakers and the "promiscuous" audiences who heard them. But women's participation was deeply divisive in abolitionist circles as well, and the appointment of women to leadership positions in the American Anti-Slavery Society contributed to a schism in 1840. The "woman question" also rankled within African-American benevolent organizations, and as Martha Jones has observed, black women rightfully feared that greater visibility in public life could threaten the feminine respectability that projected their freedom to hostile whites. Black and white women's entrance into civil society elicited more elaborate explanations of why they did not belong there. The logic of women's exclusion had shifted radically between the colonial era and the Jacksonian era. If the eighteenth-century woman threatened to corrupt a refined republican political culture with her irrationality and passion, the nineteenth-century woman was too pure to risk corruption by the dirty world of competitive electoral politics. For a brief moment in the midst of that transformation, egalitarian arguments for women's citizenship gained traction, but ultimately conveyed fewer rights and more responsibilities on "republican mothers." By the 1830s, it was common to argue that nature never intended women for roles outside the home, a presumptively private site associated more with nurturing children and consuming manufactured goods than with household production and neighborhood sociability. Certainly, countless women invested their domestic responsibilities with a commensurate obligation to enter public life in the name of morality, Christianity, and benevolence, albeit without necessarily asserting their own equal rights as citizens. Women's public involvement was typically couched in the language of selflessness and community—a notable difference from masculine culture's valorization of the autonomous, self-interested individual.

Historians have long charted a path from women's benevolent activities to the assertion of legal citizenship claims at the end of the 1840s. Most famously, female abolitionists in the 1830s came to understand their own disfranchisement in the process of talking about slavery: if a slave was someone who could not vote, control property, gain equal education, or resist intimate violence, then white women must necessarily reconsider their status as free. Not surprisingly, abolitionist women predominated at the 1848 Seneca Falls convention renowned for proclaiming, "All men and women are created equal." Recent scholarship by Mary Kelley, Anne Boylan, and Elizabeth Varon has complicated the genealogy of the antebellum women's rights movement, reconsidering the intellectual history of its leaders and relocating its origins to female seminaries and academies, to the leadership experiences women gained running a host of benevolent organizations, and to the incontestably public, if utterly mundane, lives that women led in their own communities. The 1840 presidential campaign invested women in partisan identities as Whigs and Democrats, affiliations that involved Massachusetts and Virginia women in local electioneering rituals without undermining conventional femininity or generating demands for suffrage. The traditional gender roles of everyday communal life could nonetheless prompt bolder claims, as in the case of the six rural New York women who petitioned a state constitutional convention for voting rights in 1846. Having labored diligently to build farms and establish families on the northern frontier, these obscure women gained a "self-evident" entitlement to citizenship "from their daily concrete experience, not abstractions," as Lori Ginzberg puts it. In contrast, abstractions mattered a great deal to Elizabeth Cady Stanton, whose commitment to liberal individualism only began with the right to vote and extended to a critique of all social arrangements rendering women inferior to men.

A political history organized around the concept of civil society need not exclude the South, even as the slaveholding regime left minimal opportunity for the disfranchised to affect public policy through print and petitioning. Jonathan Wells has located a vibrant associational life in the cities and small towns of the South. National organizations like the American Bible Society and the American Colonization Society attracted a growing middle class of the South's merchants, lawyers, editors, and doctors, as well their wives, sisters, and daughters. By Timothy Lockley's recent count, the region boasted more than six hundred private societies devoted to the charitable relief of the indigent, insane, and incapacitated. As in the North, churches provided a steppingstone into benevolent organizations, which in the South might even seek to eradicate dueling, gambling, drinking, and other hallmarks of slaveholding culture (though not slaveholding itself); here was the bulk of white women's civic engagement, generally couched in Christian devotion and the older language of republican motherhood rather than the rights discourse of egalitarian feminism. In New Orleans, Baltimore, and St. Louis, the polyglot population could avail itself of competing newspapers, meet in ethnic lodges, host speakers in numerous meeting halls, and convene in the streets to celebrate national holidays. Even if southern public life only approximated the robustness of northern civil society, it nonetheless defied the claims of planters (and subsequent historians) that the sovereignty of the slaveholder effectually privatized the region's social relations.

Whereas scholars have typically recounted plantation struggles between slaveholders and slaves as aspects of slavery's social history, recent studies by Stephanie Camp and Anthony Kaye have recast those contests as fundamentally political and integrated into the broader public life of locality, state, and nation. Enslaved women and men remapped the terrain of bondage to elude white surveillance, to exchange information and resources, and to stretch social ties across plantations. Print materials and rumors stymied planters' efforts to monopolize news, which instead flowed along networks created by the "abroad" marriages of spouses living on different plantations, the mobility of men working as drovers, teamsters, and pilots, and the persistence of kin relations despite the family separations caused by sales. Plantation space proved further permeable as clergymen, salesmen, doctors, travelers, and local officials jeopardized the indivisible authority claimed by the master.

Especially important, as Edward Baptist has argued, was the "vernacular history" that enslaved men and women created in countless conversations transforming the personal experience of being sold into a collective understanding of slavery as institutionalized theft. If the slave system ultimately sought to reduce human beings to atomized units for sale, slaves' own practices of worship, healing, conflict resolution, and even recreation all served to produce solidarities with latent political content. The result was neither a generic "slave resistance," nor the formation of a harmonious "slave community," nor the attainment of "autonomy," but rather a set of contingent and shifting possibilities for limiting the boundless power that owners claimed for themselves. By injecting information into the circuits of communication that linked blacks and whites—an allegation of an overseer's abuse, for example—slaves generated fissures within the dominant society and managed to protect and sometimes expand whatever incremental gains had been won in the previous round of struggle. The South's localized, and largely informal, legal system routinely identified individual slaves as members of "the public" in prosecutions of abusive whites as "disturbers of the peace." This pattern of adjudication did not provide slaves with rights, nor even name them as the victims of the violence perpetrated against them, but as Laura Edwards has shown, created the possibility for slaves to channel the state's power for a modicum of protection or redress. Such mitigating victories were only possible because the plantation was in fact public space.

A remarkable "geopolitical literacy," to use Phillip Troutman's term, allowed enslaved men and women to intervene in the nation's broader public life. South Carolina planter James Henry Hammond was "astonished and shocked" in 1844 to learn that his slaves knew where presidential candidates James K. Polk and Henry Clay stood on slavery, and worse, "most of what the abolitionists are doing." Such knowledge allowed slaves to imagine distant allies, to envision the demise of their owners, and to map locations of freedom that included (at different moments) Mexico, the British West Indies, and Canada. Running away constituted the most frequent way in which enslaved men and women shaped the broader political landscape. The newspaper advertisements for their recapture created an extensive documentary record that abolitionists used to give the lie to slaveholder benevolence. The pursuit of escaped slaves raised crucial questions of state sovereignty and the degree to which property rights in slavery could be carried into "free" states; the Supreme Court's 1842 *Prigg v. Pennsylvania* decision sent northern states scrambling to pass personal liberty laws to protect suspected runaways, and left southern states clamoring for a new fugitive slave act, whose arrival in 1850 translated countless acts of slave resistance into one of the most divisive issues in electoral politics. Extraordinary acts of insurrection also had massive consequences in public life, none more so than the 1831 uprising in Southampton County, Virginia. Nat Turner's rebellion generated rumors of similar uprisings as far away as New Orleans, provoked retributive violence against innocent slaves in North Carolina, forced Virginia into an agonizing legislative debate about the future of human bondage in the state, and prompted Maryland to restrict the civil rights of free people of color. Slaves like Turner understood American politics, for it was no accident that he originally intended to launch his attack on the Fourth of July.

Even as political history has shifted on to broader terrain, scholars like Glenn Altschuler, Stuart Blumin, and Ronald Formisano have not ignored the parties that vied for voters' allegiances. Insofar as the Constitution did not institutionalize political parties in the structure of governance, groups like the Democrats and Whigs were voluntary associations that, like others, relied on print and ritual to organize public life. Parties infused American civic culture with a celebratory nationalism that resounded for voters and nonvoters alike. Electioneering rituals linked local communities to Americans elsewhere, especially as reports of boisterous barbeques ricocheted throughout an extensive network of partisan newspapers. Editors functioned as key party operatives, flattering readers with their presumptive equality at the ballot box, even when advocating candidates and policies undermining the democratic participation of immigrants, women, and people of color. The Democratic Party of Andrew Jackson and Martin Van Buren embraced the political equality of all white men, while at the same time erecting greater barriers to the participation of everyone else. In contrast, the Whig Party remained skeptical of all white men's equality—Protestants and property holders were surely more equal than immigrant, Catholic, and laboring men—but were more amenable to (though hardly advocates for) the participation of black men or white women with the correct class, education, and religious backgrounds. In an electoral system that counted only the votes of adult white men, the Whigs could hardly profess such elitism outright and soon learned to beat the Democrats at their own game of popular electioneering. If the Whigs tacitly preferred government by an elite that could discern the best interests of everyone else, the Democrats openly contended that what the majority of adult white men wanted was, by definition, the common good.

The right to vote was a coveted prize in American political life. Disfranchised groups pressed hard for formal citizenship rights, while entrenched powers guarded access to the ballot box. Nonetheless, recent scholarship by William Novak has downplayed these contests as the defining feature of Jacksonian-era political history. Citizenship rights (or lack thereof) organized only a portion of the political lives of most Americans, whose legal prerogatives and vulnerabilities were more likely to depend on such statuses as master/servant, husband/wife, and adult/minor. With the Fourteenth Amendment's universal birthright citizenship still several decades away, one's rights emerged from a patchwork of state and local standards and were made meaningful only in the context of associational, customary, and communal relationships. Civic identities derived from collective identifications with a denomination, heritage, neighborhood, or a generic American nationalism available to one and all. For the majority of adult Americans who could not vote (and even some who could), a church affiliation, lodge membership, or other kind of public "belonging" might shape political subjectivities as readily as party affiliation and formal citizenship. Persistent barriers to voting made civil society the crucial venue for those on the margins to claim membership in "We, the People." However, if the new political history of Jacksonian America has touted the democratic inclusiveness of multiplying voices claiming to speak as, for, and to "the People," it must still reckon with the tendencies toward exclusion, division, and subordination in so much of what was actually said, printed, and enacted in public spaces.

State, Empire, and the Transnational Turn

While one body of scholarship had situated politics in the informal realm of civil society, another has accentuated the role of government in Jacksonian America. In particular, the United States attained its continental proportions through the capacity of the nation-state to wage war, make treaties, transform land into private property, and assimilate conquered territories into the federal system of government. "Manifest Destiny" hardly conveys the state power facilitating geographical expansion, and this political slogan of the 1840s obscures the violence and dispossession accompanying its fulfillment. Some recent scholarship has recast the expanding nation as an empire, one whose ideological underpinnings and coercive state authority continue to structure America's encounter with the world. Although the equal political status of new states carved from conquered territories suggests an empire of unusual ambitions, an imperial framework nonetheless offers new perspectives on the militarism of the Jacksonian state, American settler incursions into Indian territories, and commercial and missionary ventures to far reaches of the globe. The result is a much more porous history of the "United States and the World" that highlights the transnational and oceanic flow of ideas, commodities, and peoples.

Scholarship on the American state has identified formidable governmental authority that could simultaneously sign treaties with foreign nations, issue corporate charters, and stipulate the size of loaves of bread in city markets. Here, "the state" refers not to the bureaucratic reach of Washington DC, but rather to the concurrent authority of local, state, and national administrative units. Government's regulatory capacity, power of coercion, and investment in commercial infrastructure undermine the mythology of a laissez-faire past. While Civil War–era expenditures would make the earlier operations of the national government appear insubstantial, federal outlays for harbor improvements, customs collections, military pensions, and postal service attest to a more robust central state than is often supposed. The Quartermasters Department, responsible for provisioning military personnel stationed across the continent, relied on a bureaucracy more sophisticated than any corporation of the era. As Brian

Balogh has argued, the Jacksonian state was "hidden in plain sight," especially on the nation's boundaries.

There was nothing hidden about the government's role in the expulsion of Indian nations from lands coveted by American settlers. The Indian Removal Act of 1830 authorized Andrew Jackson to offer lands west of the Mississippi River to native populations residing in the southeastern states. The policy presumed the willingness of Indian nations to sign treaties voluntarily, especially once they realized that the national government would neither respect native sovereignty within the borders of existing states nor protect Indian lands from encroachment by white settlers. The urgency of resettlement, according to Jackson, was that proximity to whites corrupted both Indian efforts to protect their cultural autonomy and to embrace "civilization"; Jackson cast removal as a benevolent undertaking to spare Indians an inevitable extinction. Such claims struck the Cherokee population in Georgia as ludicrous: they were in fact thriving, governed by a formal constitution, bound together through a written language and printing press, and prosperous as slaveholding cotton planters. Savvy leaders rallied northern philanthropists and marshaled the U.S. Supreme Court to their defense. Legal victories, however, offered little protection, and after a faction of the Cherokee government signed a removal treaty in 1835, the U.S. Army forcibly expelled the remaining Cherokees along the "Trail of Tears" in 1838. In these same years, U.S. forces suppressed Fox and Sac Indians attempting to reclaim lands in Illinois and launched a costly campaign against Seminoles resisting removal in Florida.

In some sense, American territorial growth owed less to a conscientious state policy than to a government constantly trailing behind its own aggressively mobile citizens. American settlers claimed land belonging to sovereign nations and then demanded the U.S. government protect their security through diplomacy or military force. In the Arkansas River Valley, Osage and Cherokee leaders called on the United States to restrain its lawless squatters. Mexican officials were unable to stem illegal immigration from the north, especially American slaveholders entering Texas in defiance of its emancipation law. Much of the story of American continental expansion speaks to the failure of the national government to police its borders or respect other nations' entreaties for greater vigilance. That nonstate actors—that is, settlers—were at the forefront of national geographic expansion situates the United States awkwardly in the history of modern empires, and the presumed grassroots nature of territorial growth sustains mythologies of American exceptionalism. However, one need not discount the bravery and fortitude of the "pioneers" to recognize their dependence on governmental action (and inaction), as well as that their ambitions came at substantial human cost to those who previously occupied western lands and to the enslaved men and women whose labor transformed the "untamed" terrain of the (then) Southwest into a landscape of cotton plantations and stately mansions. The Second Middle Passage that carried upward of one million slaves from the eastern seaboard to new territories further undermines older notions of the West as a site of democratic promise; settling the West necessarily looks different with slaves clearing the forests.

The framework of *borderlands* helps explains what earlier generations would have called the *frontier* between American settlers and the diverse occupants of the lands they coveted. Zones of commercial interaction, cultural affiliation, and state power did not share the same boundaries, and as a result American territorial expansion would have appeared halting to those on the ground in Los Angeles or Santa Fe. In tracing "how Mexico's Far North became the American Southwest," Andrés Reséndez recounts the experiences of those who "went from Spanish subjects, to Mexican citizens, to Texans, and wound up as Americans, in the short span of a lifetime." To explain Texan independence and subsequent statehood as functions of cross-cultural marriages, Indian diplomacy, speculative land schemes, and regional rivalries within the Mexican government introduces a high degree of contingency to the story of American national expansion.

The geopolitical history of North America requires attention to the imperial ambitions of Indian nations, especially a Comanche empire that controlled more of the continent than did the United States itself. Pekka Hämäläinen has reconstructed the "staggering geographical range, core-periphery hierarchies, vast hinterlands of extraction, systematic incorporation of foreign ethnicities, dynamic multiculturalism, and penetrating cultural influence" of a Comanchería that spanned the fictitious lines that Mexico, Texas, and the United States had drawn on maps. The Comanche had little need to negotiate territorial claims with United States and Mexico precisely because these states had minimal capacity to impede Comanche imperial goals. Indigenous rivalries were far more significant, and the 1840 "Great Peace" among the Comanche, Cheyenne, and several other native nations reconfigured the political order on the Great Plains. Ironically, one of the key beneficiaries was the United States: as Comanche raiders then intensified incursions into northern Mexico, they cleared a path for the U.S. Army. As Brian DeLay has documented, the invading American forces of 1846 found the region devastated and depopulated.

Historiographically speaking, the U.S.-Mexican War typically sets the United States on the path to disintegration: the fate of lands seized from Mexico undid the Second Party System and promoted the fatal antagonism between the sections. Only recently have scholars begun contending that the Mexican War recalibrates the timeline of an American empire a full half century before the Spanish-American War of 1898. The American victory depended not upon the mythologized citizen-soldier, but rather, as Paul Foos shows, upon enlisted Irish Catholic immigrants subject to coercive labor exploitation. Shelley Streeby observes that alienating military service scarcely comported with the sensational popular fiction that cast the war as a sexual conquest of a feminized Mexico and the proving ground of white supremacy. Soldiers' wartime disappointments, often the unfulfilled desire for wealth and masculine honor, fostered the many filibustering expeditions of private mercenary armies that followed. As Amy Greenberg notes, the United States "may not have achieved a proper empire in the antebellum era, but it was not for lack of trying." The American occupation of Mexico City in 1847—the "halls of Montezuma" in the Marines' Hymn—raised the possibility of annexing Mexico entirely, a question hinging on the assimilability of dark-skinned Catholics into a white Protestant nation. The expansionist Democratic Party was torn between its desire for territorial aggrandizement and its investment in racial exclusivity.

If the Mexican War marked a cultural encounter at the intersection of empire and race, it was not the first time that white Americans confronted a foreign "Other." John Kuo Wei Tchen has drawn attention to the exoticizing of New York's small Chinese population during the 1840s and 1850s, but even earlier the showman P. T. Barnum had exhibited the conjoined twins Chang and Eng Bunker. Born in Thailand (Siam), the brothers proved quick studies of American ways and transformed themselves from spectacles to North Carolina slaveholders. The Japanese teenager John Manjiro aroused similar curiosity: rescued at sea in 1843 and carried on a whaling ship to Massachusetts, Manjiro returned to Japan in time to translate the demands of Commodore Perry to the emperor. As Egyptian mummies toured the United States in the 1840s, leading American scientists debated whether Nile civilizations had been "black" or "white" and placed ancient history in the service of the American racial regime. American conflicts with North Africa had ceased in 1815, but Barbary captivity accounts like James Riley's *Authentic Narrative* educated generations of readers in the tropes of Orientalism. Perhaps the most prominent Muslim in the United States was Abd al-Rahman, an African-born Mississippi slave whose elite lineage and Arabic literacy facilitated his manumission, garnered him an introduction to President John Quincy Adams, and launched him on a journey to Liberia in 1828.

Rahman's voyage suggests the durability of Atlantic history beyond the abolition of the Atlantic slave trade in 1808 and the Latin American independence movements of the 1810s and 1820s. Efforts to exile former slaves to Liberia invested the U.S. government in colonizing the West African coast, and while approximately 10,000 black Americans pursued resettlement between 1820 and 1860, at least as many Africans were smuggled into the United States on illegal slaving voyages. Several New England merchants exploited Cuban connections to remain active in transatlantic slave trafficking long after the congressional ban. The 1839 capture of the *Amistad* off Long Island confronted Americans with the trade's continued vitality. European migration to the United States grew steadily in these same years, with substantial Irish immigration preceding the famine refugees of the late 1840s. Although recognized as crucial to urban politics, class formation, and new racial ideologies, Irish immigration remains understudied relative to its demographic scale. Intellectual currents across the Atlantic, however, are widely recognized, whether through émigré writers like Francis Lieber, American interest in Greek, Polish, and Hungarian liberation struggles, or the network of European correspondents who made American transcendentalists, abolitionists, and feminists more cosmopolitan than provincial. Historians are also following the flow of European capital into the American economy, in particular the transatlantic financing of plantation agriculture.

The Pacific Basin presented a new frontier for American economic and evangelical interests during the Jacksonian era. Fur traders explored the Alaskan coast and exchanged sealskins at Fort Ross, the Russian outpost on the California coast. Missionaries established settlements in Samoa in the 1820s and began publishing a Honolulu newspaper, *The Temperance Advocate and Seaman's Friend*, in 1843. New Bedford whaling vessels plied waters off the coast of Japan, excursions that inspired Herman Melville and fostered a scrimshaw renaissance. Commerce with China and the Indian subcontinent brought immense wealth to New England merchants, whose sizable involvement in the opium trade still remains shielded from public scrutiny. Decades of commercial and cultural exchange were steadily converting the Pacific's eastern shores into the American West well before the annexation of California and subsequent Gold Rush completed the transformation.

A hemispheric perspective on the Jacksonian era further accentuates the imperial ambitions of a United States whose Monroe Doctrine staked claim to the geopolitical center of the Americas. Support for Latin American independence helped enshrine national self-determination and representative democracy in the rhetoric of U.S. foreign policy, but slave emancipation in the former Spanish colonies and the British West Indies generated endless challenges for American diplomats. Alongside Brazil and Cuba, the United States spearheaded what Dale Tomich has called the "Second Slavery," the resurgence of an antiquated labor system within sophisticated regimes of production. Bound to fellow planters in the Caribbean basin, American slaveholders fashioned themselves both modern and cosmopolitan, and invoked Haiti and the "failures" of emancipation in the British West Indies to win political debates at home. By the 1840s, a cadre of "proslavery nationalists," to use Robert Bonner's term, envisioned a pan-American union of slaveholding states through the lenses of U.S. imperialism rather than proto-Confederate disunionism.

Slavery as a National Institution

American slaveholders had good reason to be confident, as they monopolized the presidency, judiciary, and major appointive offices of a nation-state aggressively acquiring new plantation lands. The political system protected their interests, both through a federal structure guaranteeing state sovereignty and a two-party system designed to promote interregional coalitions and minimize the divisiveness of slavery. A congressional gag rule on antislavery petitions contained abolitionist agitation, as did the censorship of southbound mail. Likewise, restrictive manumission laws, prohibitions on internal migration, and legal discrimination in northern states stood to prevent free people of color from confounding the boundary between white freedom and black slavery. These facts suggest that slavery was less a doomed regional labor system than a flourishing national institution infecting virtually all facets of American economics, politics, and culture. Some historians propose rethinking the era's fundamental geography: there was no North, no South, but instead a single slaveholding republic (to use the title of Don Fehrenbacher's book) organized on the principles and practices of a white-supremacist racial ideology. Such an interpretation need not minimize the rise of northern antislavery, ambivalence toward slavery in parts of the South, the divisiveness of slavery within Protestantism, or the differences between wage labor and slavery; nonetheless, placing slavery at the center of national, not regional, history offers a fresh vantage on older topics like the Market Revolution and the Second Party System.

Slavery's indispensability to the Jacksonian economy was less controversial 175 years ago than today. Slave-grown cotton was the nation's most valuable export, and one of the only goods capable of bringing specie into the vaults of the nation's proliferating banks. Cotton fed the Lowell mills, thereby marrying the industrial revolution to the advancing plantation frontier. The bales of raw cotton brought north and the bales of finished textiles returned south attested to national economic integration. New England entrepreneurs prospered making shoes, shirts, and shovels for slaves, while small-town merchants across the South drew on northern family ties to stock their inventories. When Charles Sumner decried the alliance of the "lords of the lash and the lords of the loom" in 1848, he might also have fingered the northern shippers, insurers, bankers, and dry goods wholesalers whose investment in the price of cotton was as great as any Mississippi planter's. Only a decade earlier, the Panic of 1837 had highlighted an interregional network of credit relations, as well as the prevalence of collateralized slaves vulnerable to sale in debt suits.

In the wake of the Missouri Compromise, political strategists like Martin Van Buren sought to relegate slavery to the margins of electoral competition, just as the 36°30' line would presumably preclude future congressional debate on slavery. Van Buren succeeded in assembling an improbable coalition of actual and aspiring southern slaveholders and northern workingmen, small farmers, and immigrants; insofar as the ensuing presidential contests foregrounded monetary policy and the personalities of the candidates themselves, party competition proved more unifying than divisive. However, slavery was never far from the surface. Slave-grown cotton was indispensible to the Whigs' "American System" and its vision of national integration through the synergies of commerce, manufacturing, and agriculture. Democrats sounded their support for slavery in paeans to the equality of all white men (relative to black men) and a "small" national government incapable of meddling in the affairs of the states (but potent in acquiring new plantation lands, capturing runaway slaves, and enforcing property rights in human beings). To be sure, Jonathan Earle has drawn attention to a small cohort of antislavery Democrats, none better known than

New York Congressman David Wilmot, whose proviso to a Mexican War funding bill reopened the question of slavery in the territories. Nonetheless, Democratic administrations worked assiduously to promote the interests of slavery, whether in seeking to lower tariffs, annex Texas, or enshrine "local control" as the mantra of American governance.

Slavery's hold on American life was so powerful because it organized a broader set of relationships and offered vivid metaphors for a range of social inequalities. Under the rubric of paternalism, as Stephanie McCurry argues, slaveholders located slavery and marriage within the same system of dependencies and obligations, which made the protection of slavery essential to white men of every class who hoped to remain masters of their own wives and children. Northern laborers decried workplace exploitation as "wage slavery," but their employers invoked actual slavery to recast the right to keep one's wages as the epitome of freedom itself. Tiya Miles exhibits the Cherokee use of slavery to claim "civilization" and defend their sovereignty, whereas in Daniel Mandell's account, intermarriage with former slaves left Narragansetts and Mohegans vulnerable to the misperception that Indians had disappeared from New England. Free people of color understood slavery as the basis of their continued oppression, especially as legal disfranchisement reduced them to a poverty that "proved" the folly of emancipation. This point coursed through David Walker's *Appeal to the Coloured Citizens of the World* (1829). Alexis de Tocqueville and his traveling companion Gustave Beaumont suggested that slavery's racial hierarchy provided one of the only certainties in an otherwise fluid society. Beaumont's novel *Marie* critiqued racism as an irrational form of majoritarian tyranny, while Tocqueville's chilling chapter in *Democracy in America*, "The Future Condition of the Three Races," predicted that slavery and white supremacy could neither be preserved nor eliminated but through an eventual race war.

The Jacksonian era witnessed what historians typically call the hardening of racial ideology, or the translation of some (but not all) physical features and facets of ancestry into categories of human difference deemed natural, unchanging, and determinative of the capacity for reason, morality, and ambition. Scholars see race not as a biological category, but rather a social fiction, albeit one with enormous power to configure opportunity and oppression in American society. Because two centuries of sex, manumission, and cross-cultural exchange had left "black" and "white" surprisingly mingled and potentially meaningless in a nation whose foundational document declared "all men are created equal," nineteenth-century jurists, doctors, scientists, and satirists had to work assiduously to make race "real." Race-making had particular urgency in the North once gradual emancipation policies removed slavery as a determinant of legal and social status. As Joanne Melish argues, New England states invented a past for themselves in which slavery had never existed and projected a future in which the descendents of slaves would always be marked as alien or erased altogether. Threatened by law and violence, free people of color lived in what Steven Hahn terms "maroon communities," or fugitive outposts within a fundamentally hostile society. But as white ethnologists measured skulls, theologians explicated the Biblical story of Ham, and printers marketed racist caricatures in phony dialect, African-American commentators like Hosea Easton located black identity in the shared historical experiences of the diaspora. Although the dominant white society had the power to enshrine its ideology of race in medical textbooks, legislation, and popular culture, these representations were always contested. Joshua Rothman reveals the instability of race through the many cases of blacks becoming whites (including some of the children of Thomas Jefferson and Sally Hemings), while Ariela Gross has catalogued the numerous judicial interventions required to categorize racially ambiguous individuals.

No discussion of slavery and race in the Jacksonian era can bypass recent studies of whiteness, or the historical process through which people of European ancestry constructed themselves as racially unmarked subjects whose possibilities in American society purportedly owed not to group membership but individual merit. Scholars like David Roediger recognize whiteness not as the absence of race, but as the donning of a racial cloak that opened doors in a society grounded on black slavery. Irish immigrants of the 1830s and 1840s had to become white, a status that depended less on skin tone than on performances of whiteness through affiliation with the Democratic Party, enthusiasm for minstrel shows, and antagonism toward the black men and women who occupied the same poor neighborhoods and competed for the same low-end jobs. Whiteness offers a crucial linkage between slavery and the transition to capitalism in the North: workers whose material prospects were declining with the advent of wage labor were reimbursed in "wages of whiteness," racial privileges that dulled the indignities of class oppression. Workers of European descent eagerly sought to differentiate themselves from actual slaves and, in the process, recalibrated the definition of American freedom downward from older notions of propertied republican independence to the simple status of not being a slave and not being black.

The Political Economy of Capitalism

Most historians refer to the economic transformation of Jacksonian America as the "Market Revolution," shorthand for a new commercial landscape of factories, banks, canals, and railroads that integrated producers and consumers in distant locales. After Charles Sellers published a book by that title in 1991, scholars debated whether economic development promoted or precluded democracy. For Sellers, capitalism was imposed from above by a cabal of bankers whom Andrew Jackson had to vanquish in defense of the egalitarian promises of the American Revolution. A contrasting liberal historiography made capitalism a source of political freedom in common people's pursuit of equality through innovation, enterprise, and consumerism. More recently, historians have moved from questions of capitalism's origins to those of capitalism's operations. A new body of scholarship neither laments the world that was lost, nor vindicates the market as a force of human liberation, but rather seeks to embed capitalism in the historically contingent rules and practices that governed its operation. Studies of political economy excavate the specific structural underpinnings of nineteenth-century capitalism: the state's role in establishing the infrastructure of commerce; the relations of class that determined who worked where and owned what; the cultural legitimation of self-interest; and the configuration of ecology and technology that placed the natural world in the service of profit.

The basic contours of nineteenth-century economic change are staggering, as John Larson makes clear. A new transportation network integrated city and countryside, hastening both urbanization and frontier settlement. The completion of the Erie Canal in 1825 transformed the Great Lakes region into New York City's hinterlands, and by the end of the 1840s, Chicago was already the gateway city to the trans-Mississippi West. New transportation technologies like steamboats made it possible to move manufactured goods and agricultural produce longer distances at greater speed for less cost, and encouraged mill owners and small farmers alike to produce for consumers in far-flung locales. The telegraph's acceleration of business information allowed entrepreneurs to meet changing market conditions with dexterity. Workshops, factories, farms, and plantations intensified production by standardizing goods, subdividing labor into discrete parts, and managing time with clocks and bells. Banks issued a vast quantity of paper money that served as a medium of exchange and as speculative capital to finance expansion. Older economic goals like household independence or a modest competency required a greater degree of market participation than ever before just to provide a son with some arable land or a wife with a respectable dress. Manufactured goods allowed a wider percentage of the population to claim a modicum of comfort and refinement, but behind every yard of cloth purchased at a crossroads store or an urban emporium were slaves picking cotton and mill girls toiling amid the whirl of machinery. Yet despite these inequalities, access to standardized consumer goods allowed more Americans to look and feel more equal than ever before. In this way, as Michael Zakim has wryly observed, the economic relations of capitalism became confused with the political possibilities of democracy.

Such outcomes were neither the inevitable products of the American character (as an older consensus history might argue), nor dictated by timeless interplay of supply and demand (as more recent economic history would contend), but rather the results of policy making, law, cultural production, and technological innovations. State legislatures invested corporations with limited liability and monopoly privileges, and poured funding into internal improvements. State law privileged improvement of natural resources over static usage, favoring the mill owner building a dam and not the small farmer whose access to water was thus impeded. More workers gained the ability to sell their time to the highest bidder and to quit jobs at will, but whereas capital could aggregate as a corporation, labor still lacked the right to act collectively. Striking workers were regularly prosecuted under state conspiracy laws, even as jurists proclaimed that workers and employers bargained freely as legal equals. A cadre of moralists, journalists, and political economists celebrated the workings of an impartial market whose outcomes were inherently fair and just. Cultural commentators invested individuals with an economic self-determination that cast success and failure as matters of personal choice and character. Meanwhile, technologies of management, finance, and surveillance proved as crucial as those of machinery and transportation in organizing capitalism: corporate bureaucracy, actuarial tables, and credit reporting created wide asymmetries of information among economic actors, while penitentiaries, almshouses, and asylums sought to rehabilitate inmates for market competition.

Whereas an earlier scholarship had connected party affiliation to class, ethnicity, and religiosity, most recent work (like John Ashworth's monumental study) stresses ideological differences over government's role in promoting economic development. China traders, cotton merchants, railroad magnates, and real estate speculators scarcely functioned as a unified political bloc, even as the Whig Party pursued a prodevelopmental agenda in which an energetic government could use tariffs, internal improvements, and banks to create a "harmony of interest" and promote values of thrift, sobriety, and self-control among the populace. Over the long term, economic development would foster broad-based opportunity; in the short term, it might require a bigger government privileging certain private interests, generating inequality, and acting contrary to the wishes of the voters. In contrast, the Democratic Party organized to protect the individual liberty of "the many" from the machinations of "the few" who would deploy state power to enrich themselves. Democrats believed that wealth (including land and slaves) should be widely diffused, but that the government should not pick the winners. It is an oversimplification to say that the Democrats were anticapitalist and the Whigs advocates of unfettered market relations. Democrats were not seeking to restrict economic development, but merely to put the national government out of the business of directing it. If Democrats could embrace grassroots economic development, Whigs worried about the social costs of rapid economic change—poverty, alcoholism, prostitution, gambling, and a hidden epidemic of masturbation—and advocated a strident agenda of social discipline. Neither party was liberal in the sense of believing that the market alone could serve as the glue of holding the American nation together.

The cultural history of capitalism reveals ambivalence, perhaps most vividly through the valorization of nonmarket relations in the ideologies of northern domesticity and southern paternalism. Christian moralists agonized over God and mammon, and sought to imbue the ethos of accumulation with commensurate obligations of service, a struggle recounted in Mark Noll's collection of essays. Efforts to reconcile self-interest and self-control stood at the center of a middle-class identity performed through religious devotion, membership in benevolent organizations, and a strict regime of bodily discipline. The preoccupation with private domestic space served as a rebuke to public spaces made ugly by relentless and unrestrained competition. Ambition and failure became problems for men on the make who never made it, as well as for the growing number of stultified white-collar workers exemplified by Melville's fictitious Bartleby. Clerks, counterfeiters, pawnbrokers, and confidence men were as representative of capitalism as the bankers, railroad barons, and tycoons who more immediately come to mind. The market beckoned to improvers, strivers, and schemers, but as Scott Sandage has shown, often produced losers.

The commodification of labor figures prominently in studies of political economy, but recent scholarship no longer privileges wages as the sine qua non of capitalism. Labor was available for purchase by the hour, day, season, year, and lifetime, and by placing waged and enslaved workers on the same continuum, historians are less inclined to see two antagonistic modes of production but instead a capitalism whose appetite for labor was nearly limitless. In producing staples for the global market, the slaveholding South erected an effective transportation infrastructure, pursued sophisticated methods of accounting to rationalize plantation agriculture, found new ways to extract labor from workers, and, as recovered in the scholarship of Walter Johnson, fostered a competitive male culture performed in the (slave) marketplace. In other words, the South had a Market Revolution. Those with capital maximized returns on their investments by buying slaves and plantations, not by building the factories whose absence would later convey the region's underdevelopment. At the same time, northern manufacturers relied on a range of legal privileges to impede the mobility of its "free" labor force, including vagrancy statutes, debt imprisonments, and wage forfeitures for early departures from a job. Northern workers escaped personal subordination to a master within an earlier craft economy, but now vended their labor in a marketplace that left them vulnerable to impersonal exploitation. Whereas a previous generation of labor historians had celebrated the efforts of skilled craftsmen to resist downward mobility and protect the prerogatives of artisan republicanism, recent work by Peter Way and Seth Rockman has focused on workers with even fewer possibilities for political mobilization. As a subfield, a markedly unromantic labor history invests less in processes of class formation, but more in slaves' membership in an American working class defined by its common commodification and material circumstances of poverty.

Why Jacksonian America?

A schematic essay of this length offers little prospect for addressing every dimension of recent historiography. The question remains, however, why the scholarly directions outlined here constitute *Jacksonian America*; put differently, why should Andrew Jackson retain a place of prominence in a synthesis of new histories that devote minimal discussion to the man himself? Certainly, the little that nonspecialists may remember about Jackson should nonetheless evoke issues of democratic participation, military power in territorial expansion, slaveholding as an avenue for white upward mobility, and the state's relationship with economic development. In this regard, Jackson bridges the four topics addressed here, linking the politics of public life, the transnational study of an imperial state, the centrality of slavery to the national experience, and the political economy of capitalism to one another with a modicum of coherence. Scholars and teachers alike might consider the analytical and pedagogical power of a phrase like "Jacksonian Democracy" when read critically: the term is not a misnomer that substitutes the experiences of the few for those of the many, but rather the description of a very particular society that predicated white male equality on the enforced inequality of virtually everyone else. In a *Jacksonian* democracy, an orphaned child of humble means could rise to be the president of a nation whose expanding boundaries, economic vitality, and promises of individual upward mobility could never be disentangled from slavery, Indian removal, imperial warfare, white racial identity, and capitalism. In this light, a *Jacksonian* America conveys the contingent relations of power that allowed some Americans to be freer than ever before precisely because others were not.

BIBLIOGRAPHY

Altschuler, Glenn C., and Stuart M. Blumin. *Rude Republic: Americans and Their Politics in the Nineteenth Century.* Princeton, NJ: Princeton University Press, 2000.

Ashworth, John. *Slavery, Capitalism, and Politics in the Antebellum Republic*, 2 vols. New York: Cambridge University Press, 1995–2008.

Balogh, Brian. *A Government Out of Sight: The Mystery of National Authority in Nineteenth-Century America.* New York: Cambridge University Press, 2009.

Baptist, Edward E. "'Stol' and Fetched Here': Enslaved Migration, Ex-slave Narratives, and Vernacular History." In Edward E. Baptist and Stephanie M. H. Camp, eds., *New Studies in the History of American Slavery*, 243–274. Athens: University of Georgia Press, 2006.

Bonner, Robert E. *Mastering America: Southern Slaveholders and the Crisis of American Nationhood.* New York: Cambridge University Press, 2009.

Boylan, Anne M. *The Origins of Women's Activism: New York and Boston, 1797–1840.* Chapel Hill: University of North Carolina Press, 2002.

Camp, Stephanie M. H. *Closer to Freedom: Enslaved Women and Everyday Resistance in the Plantation South.* Chapel Hill: University of North Carolina Press, 2004.

DeLay, Brian. *War of a Thousand Deserts: Indian Raids and the U.S.-Mexican War.* New Haven, CT: Yale University Press, 2008.

Earle, Jonathan H. *Jacksonian Antislavery and the Politics of Free Soil, 1824–1854.* Chapel Hill: University of North Carolina Press, 2004.

Edwards, Laura F. *The People and Their Peace: Legal Culture and the Transformation of Inequality in the Post-Revolutionary South.* Chapel Hill: University of North Carolina Press, 2009.

Fehrenbacher, Don E. *The Slaveholding Republic: An Account of the United States Government's Relations to Slavery.* New York: Oxford University Press, 2001.

Foos, Paul. *A Short, Offhand, Killing Affair: Soldiers and Social Conflict during the Mexican-American War*. Chapel Hill: University of North Carolina Press, 2002.

Formisano, Ronald P. *For the People: American Populist Movements from the Revolution to the 1850s*. Chapel Hill: University of North Carolina Press, 2008.

Ginzberg, Lori D. *Untidy Origins: A Story of Women's Rights in Antebellum New York*. Chapel Hill: University of North Carolina Press, 2005.

Greenberg, Amy S. *Manifest Manhood and the Antebellum American Empire*. New York: Cambridge University Press, 2005.

Greenberg, Joshua R. *Advocating the Man: Masculinity, Organized Labor, and the Household in New York, 1800–1840*. New York: Columbia University Press, 2009.

Gross, Ariela J. *What Blood Won't Tell: A History of Race on Trial in America*. Cambridge, MA: Harvard University Press, 2008.

Hahn, Steven. *The Political Worlds of Slavery and Freedom*. Cambridge, MA: Harvard University Press, 2009.

Hämäläinen, Pekka. *The Comanche Empire*. New Haven, CT: Yale University Press, 2008.

Henkin, David M. *City Reading: Written Words and Public Spaces in Antebellum New York*. New York: Columbia University Press, 1998.

Hershberger, Mary. "Mobilizing Women, Anticipating Abolition: The Struggle against Indian Removal in the 1830s." *Journal of American History* 86 (June 1999): 15–40.

Howe, Daniel Walker. *What Hath God Wrought: The Transformation of America, 1815–1848*. New York: Oxford University Press, 2007.

Isenberg, Nancy. *Sex and Citizenship in Antebellum America*. Chapel Hill: University of North Carolina Press, 1998.

Johnson, Walter. *Soul by Soul: Life inside the Antebellum Slave Market*. Cambridge, MA: Harvard University Press, 1999.

Jones, Martha S. *All Bound Up Together: The Woman Question in African American Public Culture, 1830–1900*. Chapel Hill: University of North Carolina Press, 2007.

Kaye, Anthony E. *Joining Places: Slave Neighborhoods in the Old South*. Chapel Hill: University of North Carolina Press, 2007.

Kelley, Mary. *Learning to Stand and Speak: Women, Education, and Public Life in America's Republic*. Chapel Hill: University of North Carolina Press, 2006.

Larson, John Lauritz. *The Market Revolution in America: Liberty, Ambition, and the Eclipse of the Common Good*. New York: Cambridge University Press, 2010.

Lockley, Timothy J. *Welfare and Charity in the Antebellum South*. Gainesville: University of Florida Press, 2007.

Mandell, Daniel R. *Tribe, Race, History: Native Americans in Southern New England, 1780–1880*. Baltimore: Johns Hopkins University Press, 2008.

McCarthy, Kathleen D. *American Creed: Philanthropy and the Rise of Civil Society*. Chicago: University of Chicago Press, 2003.

McCurry, Stephanie. *Masters of Small Worlds: Yeoman Households, Gender Relations, and the Political Culture of the Antebellum South Carolina Low Country*. New York: Oxford University Press, 1995.

Melish, Joanne Pope. *Disowning Slavery: Gradual Emancipation and "Race" in New England, 1780–1860*. Ithaca, NY: Cornell University Press, 1998.

Miles, Tiya. *Ties that Bind: The Story of an Afro-Cherokee Family in Slavery and Freedom.* Berkeley: University of California Press, 2005.

Noll, Mark A., ed. *God and Mammon: Protestants, Money, and the Market, 1790–1860.* New York: Oxford University Press, 2002.

Novak, William J. "The Legal Transformation of Citizenship in Nineteenth-Century America." In Meg Jacobs, William J. Novak, and Julian E. Zelizer, eds., *The Democratic Experiment: New Directions in American Political History*, 85–119. Princeton, NJ: Princeton University Press, 2003.

Rael, Patrick. *Black Identity and Black Protest in the Antebellum North.* Chapel Hill: University of North Carolina Press, 2002.

Reséndez, Andrés. *Changing National Identities at the Frontier: Texas and New Mexico, 1800–1850.* New York: Cambridge University Press, 2005.

Reynolds, David S. *Waking Giant: America in the Age of Jackson.* New York: Harper, 2008.

Rockman, Seth. *Scraping By: Wage Labor, Slavery, and Survival in Early Baltimore.* Baltimore: Johns Hopkins University Press, 2009.

Roediger, David R. *Wages of Whiteness: Race and the Making of the American Working Class.* New York: Verso, 1991.

Rothman, Joshua D. *Notorious in the Neighborhood: Sex and Families across the Color Line in Virginia, 1787–1861.* Chapel Hill: University of North Carolina Press, 2002.

Ryan, Mary P. *Civic Wars: Democracy and Public Life in the American City during the Nineteenth Century.* Berkeley: University of California Press, 1997.

Sandage, Scott A. *Born Losers: A History of Failure in America.* Cambridge, MA: Harvard University Press, 2005.

Sellers, Charles. *The Market Revolution: Jacksonian America, 1815–1846.* New York: Oxford University Press, 1991.

Streeby, Shelley. *American Sensations: Class, Empire, and the Production of Popular Culture.* Berkeley: University of California Press, 2002.

Tchen, John Kuo Wei. *New York before Chinatown: Orientalism and the Shaping of American Culture, 1776–1882.* Baltimore: Johns Hopkins University Press, 1999.

Tomich, Dale W. *Through the Prism of Slavery: Labor, Capital, and World Economy.* Lanham, MD: Rowman and Littlefield, 2004.

Troutman, Phillip. "Grapevine in the Slave Market: African American Geopolitical Literacy and the 1841 *Creole* Revolt." In Walter Johnson, ed., *The Chattel Principle: Internal Slave Trades in the Americas*, 203–233. New Haven, CT: Yale University Press, 2005.

Varon, Elizabeth R. *We Mean to Be Counted: White Women and Politics in Antebellum Virginia.* Chapel Hill: University of North Carolina Press, 1998.

Way, Peter. *Common Labour: Workers and the Digging of North American Canals, 1780–1860.* New York: Cambridge University Press, 1993.

Wells, Jonathan Daniel. *Origins of the Southern Middle Class, 1800–1861.* Chapel Hill: University of North Carolina Press, 2004.

White, Shane. *Stories of Freedom in Black New York.* Cambridge, MA: Harvard University Press, 2002.

Wilentz, Sean. *The Rise of American Democracy: Jefferson to Lincoln.* New York: W. W. Norton, 2005.

Zakim, Michael. *Ready-Made Democracy: A History of Men's Dress in the American Republic, 1760–1860.* Chicago: University of Chicago Press, 2003.

4

Slavery, the Civil War, and Reconstruction

ADAM ROTHMAN

The historian George Bancroft assured Abraham Lincoln in November 1861 that they had fallen upon times "which will be remembered as long as human events find a record." Historians have done their part in fulfilling Bancroft's prophesy, but they are contentious and fickle. Again and again, they have disagreed among themselves and revised their interpretations of the Civil War era in response to broader changes in social, political, and intellectual life, as well as research in new sources. If today most scholars agree with Lincoln that slavery was "somehow" the cause of the war, they argue over just how slavery did so, why the Confederacy lost and slavery ended, and what kind of freedom arose from the ruins. In each of these areas, historians debate the balance between "structure" and "agency," or in other words, between the historical forces that dictated people's choices and the choices people made that changed history. Striking this balance is complicated by the fact that historians cannot settle on *which* historical forces and *whose* choices should be placed on the scale.

Slavery and the Sectional Crisis

The historiography of American slavery has come a long way since the early twentieth century, when its leading historian, Ulrich B. Phillips, asserted that the southern plantation was "a school constantly training and controlling pupils who were in a backward state of civilization." Challenged first by pioneering scholars such as W.E.B. Du Bois and Carter G. Woodson, Phillips's essentially proslavery interpretation was not demolished until the 1940s and 1950s, when a wave of radical and liberal scholars rejected racism and the Jim Crow treatment of African Americans. Early classics included Melville J. Herskovits's *The Myth of the Negro Past* (1941), Herbert Aptheker's *American Negro Slave Revolts* (1943), Kenneth Stampp's *The Peculiar Institution* (1956), and Stanley Elkins's *Slavery* (1959). These scholars set a new agenda by taking black people's perspectives seriously and exposing the terror at the heart of slavery.

Since the first wave of post–World War II scholarship, the historiography of American slavery has continued to progress. Historians have recaptured the diversity of American slaveries across time and space, highlighting regional differences and changes from the early colonial era through the nineteenth century, a trend that culminated in Ira Berlin's *Generations of Captivity* (2003). Social historians have mined census records, slaveholders' papers, and the testimonies of former slaves to extract an understanding of life inside the "big house" and the slave quarters, as well as in the fields. Economic and labor historians have pored over planters' account books and developed sophisticated mathematical models to measure the profitability and productivity of slavery and to assess its effects on the southern economy as a whole. Religious historians have resurrected the fundamental importance of Protestant Christianity to masters and slaves in the nineteenth-century South.

Moreover, scholarship on North American slavery has become part of a broader trend concerning slavery in the Atlantic world and across the globe. Much of this work is comparative and transnational, including a rich literature on the Atlantic slave trade, which has recently been augmented by the online publication of a massive database of almost 35,000 transatlantic slaving voyages from Africa to the Americas from 1514 to 1866. It comes as a revelation to many students to learn that North America was just a minor destination for transatlantic slavers, and it is therefore also a puzzle to understand why more enslaved people lived in the United States in 1860 than anywhere else in the Americas. Just as the rise of North American slavery must now be viewed in the broader transatlantic context of the emergence of Atlantic capitalism, so too must its demise be placed in the context of a long, slow, and sometimes violent eradication of slavery in the Atlantic world beginning with the "Age of Revolution" in the late eighteenth century. Scholars have demolished the wishful thinking that American slavery would have slowly died out for purely economic reasons in the absence of concerted antislavery activity, showing that it remained a profitable and dynamic sector of the Atlantic economy. David Brion Davis's *Inhuman Bondage* (2006) offers one of the first attempts to synthesize this expanded history.

The recent debate at the center of modern U.S. slavery historiography was initiated by Eugene Genovese's seminal *Roll, Jordan, Roll* (1974). Genovese argued that the Old South was a "historically unique kind of paternalist society" with slavery at its core. Direct personal exploitation characterized masters' treatment of their slaves, but slave owners shrouded their brutality in an ideological veil of reciprocal obligations woven from Christian doctrine: they had a duty to take care of their slaves, and in return, their slaves had a duty to obey them. When slaves did not obey, moreover, their owners were obliged to punish them. In other words, slave owners' benevolence justified their violence. Proslavery ideologues insisted that their slaves were better off than poor workers in the northern states and Great Britain, who were forced to scrounge and starve in hard times. For Genovese, slave owners' moral commitment to slavery was the foundation of a distinctive worldview that explained secession and the creation of the Confederacy. It was also shaped by pressure from slaves themselves. Genovese argued that slaves accepted the paternalist bargain because they had no alternative, but at the same time they wrestled with cruel masters and struggled to carve out space for themselves within the system.

Genovese's interpretation has been fruitful. Taking paternalism as a touchstone, historians have traced its origins back to changes in southern society beginning in the late eighteenth century, including the rise of cotton, the closing of slave importation, intensifying antislavery pressure, and the spread of evangelical Christianity. Time and again, white southerners resorted to the Bible to defend slavery as a godly and Christian mission. Southern women's historians have illuminated the gender ideals and household dynamics that informed southern paternalism. Recent scholarship has demolished the idea that southern "ladies" were closet abolitionists, arguing instead that they derived all-important class advantages from slavery and endorsed the conceits of paternalism. When the crisis came, white planter women initially proved to be no less ardent secessionists and Confederate nationalists than their menfolk.

To be sure, historians have challenged Genovese's interpretation on a number of fronts. Some scholars reject Genovese's depiction of southern planters as resistant to moneygrubbing values. James Oakes's *The Ruling Race* (1982) argued that southern slave owners were more diverse, restless, profit driven, and racist than Genovese allowed. Genovese's planter elite did not represent the whole class. Walter Johnson and other recent historians of the internal slave trade contend that Genovese unduly minimized the significance of the buying and selling of slaves, which was crucial to the southern economy and the terrorizing of slaves and which undercuts the idea that planters saw their relationship to slaves as essentially "paternal." Planters' financial obligations to creditors and heirs (not to mention their own ambitions) routinely trumped the interests and desires of slaves themselves. If planters referred to their human property as childlike dependents or wards, they just as often described them as commodities: goods to be bought and sold like hogs or sacks of corn, used as collateral to secure a loan, or rented out for profit. And more powerful than slave owners' professions of benevolence were their deeply racist convictions about black minds and bodies that justified slavery.

From a different angle, historians of slave culture have argued that slaves saw through slave owners' delusions of benevolence, so that paternalism was never as suffocating ("hegemonic") as Genovese implied. On the one hand, slaves judged masters by deeds not words; the violence, robbery, and what the historian Nell Painter calls "soul murder" they endured was more than enough to render an indictment. On the other hand, while not neglecting the real power that slave owners wielded, these historians emphasize the autonomy, integrity, and vitality of slaves' own communities. Historians of slave culture seem to teeter on a high wire strung between the poles of slave owners' power and slaves' agency. Under the rubric of "agency," historians have examined slaves' networks of kinship, their egalitarian Afro-Christianity, and their ability to eke out subsistence from provision grounds, "overtime" work, and odd jobs on their own time. Moreover, historians have discovered a broad spectrum of resistance. Slaves shirked work, stole food, fought back against abuse, ran away, and plotted against overseers and owners. Sometimes slave owners spun rumors into conspiracies, but often something was afoot. Nat Turner's 1831 revolt in Southhampton County, Virginia, is well known; less familiar is the larger revolt among slaves in St. John the Baptist Parish above New Orleans in 1811. Walter Johnson has recently argued that that "agency" paradigm has outlived its usefulness, but no alternative paradigm seems poised to replace it.

A final challenge to Genovese's interpretation of the antebellum South comes from historians who contest the premise that the plantation milieu defined southern society. The white yeomanry did not leave as many records as their wealthier neighbors, nor have they been celebrated in novels and movies, so they were relegated to historical obscurity. But using the techniques of social history, scholars including Steven Hahn and Stephanie McCurry have brought them out of the shadows. Large planters comprised a small minority of slave owners (only 12 percent of slave owners owned twenty or more slaves in 1860), and a majority of white male southerners did not own slaves at all. Regions ecologically inhospitable to plantation agriculture, like southern Appalachia, harbored fewer big planters and had smaller black populations than in the South Carolina and Georgia lowcountry, the Black Belt, and the lower Mississippi Valley. A feisty lot, the white yeomanry treasured their independence and closely guarded their rights. White male suffrage gave them a vote and influence in politics, which the planter elite neglected at their peril. An influential historiography thus portrays the antebellum South as a "herrenvolk democracy" in which planters and yeomen colluded to maintain the privileges of white manhood while they fought over other matters. Of course, under the same criteria the antebellum North qualified as a herrenvolk democracy, as did the country as a whole. Scholars who emphasize the "wages of whiteness" have some difficulty explaining conflicts between white men—especially the one that split the Union in 1861.

The idea that slavery was the South's "peculiar institution" has obscured the myriad ways that it shaped the development of the entire country (Lincoln's point in his Second Inaugural when he referred to "American" and not "southern" slavery). Northern consumers ate sugar and rice, smoked tobacco, and wore clothing made from cotton grown by southern slaves, and the profits allowed slave owners to purchase goods produced by northern farmers and manufacturers. Runaway slaves who fled to northern states discovered that the fugitive slave clause of the Constitution required their return to their owners. There was no "free soil" for runaway slaves until they reached Canada, and even north of the U.S. border they remained vulnerable to kidnappers. As Don Fehrenbacher demonstrates in *The Slaveholding Republic* (2001), slave owners and their northern allies effectively used the power of the federal government when it served their interests and blocked the power of the federal government when it threatened their interests. The three-fifths clause, the antimajoritarian structure of the Senate, and the national party system provided slave owners with strong political and constitutional protection. Broad national commitments to limited government, state sovereignty, property rights, white supremacy, and the integrity of the Union provided ideological protection.

In retrospect it is too easy to view the abolition of slavery in the United States as an inevitable fulfillment of the American creed. In the 1830s it was difficult to imagine the end of slavery and almost impossible to predict how it would actually happen. Those who did were derided as "visionary" and "fanatic." Abolitionists faced a daunting challenge. Deeply entrenched interests and values, as well as American federalism, stood in the way of national action against slavery. Overcoming these obstacles would require a fundamental social and political transformation. That is what happened in the United States before the Civil War. The reasons for the rise of northern abolitionism, the subsequent emergence of a broad popular northern antislavery political coalition, and southern secession in response to Lincoln's election are complex, and the historiography has offered a range of views.

In 1858, New York's Republican Senator William Seward described the clash between freedom and slavery as an "irrepressible conflict." That memorable phrase has come to define a venerable school of thought on the origins of the war, most recently defended in Bruce Levine's *Half Slave and Half Free* (2005, originally published in 1992). In this view, economic, social, and cultural developments pushed the North and South apart and made political conflict between the sections inevitable. As the white southerners deepened their commitments to slavery and sought to extend it, the northern states gradually abolished slavery. The North became more commercial, industrial, and urban. Steeped in evangelical Christianity, northern reform movements aimed to improve self and society and cleanse the world of sin. Not all evangelical reformers were abolitionists, but recent historiography has emphasized that most abolitionists were evangelical reformers. Most northerners rejected the abolitionists' call for an immediate end to slavery, and northern society was deeply racist, yet white northerners increasingly viewed southern slavery as backward and oppressive. The popularity of Harriet Beecher Stowe's *Uncle Tom's Cabin* and other antislavery cultural icons signaled a shift in northern public opinion. As northern politics became more democratic, the Whig and Democratic parties could no longer contain disputes over slavery, which bubbled to the surface of politics in controversies over war with Mexico, organizing the western territories, filibusters in Cuba and Nicaragua, the slave trade, fugitive slaves, the Dred Scott case, and John Brown's raid at Harpers Ferry. Northern antislavery sentiment coalesced ideologically around opposition to the idea of a southern "Slave Power" and organized politically in the Republican Party. With Lincoln's election in 1860, sectional differences over slavery finally became irreconcilable.

Critics of the "irrepressible conflict" thesis argue that it exaggerates the differences between the North and the South. Abler politicians could have preserved the Union and allowed slavery to die from natural causes, argued historian James G. Randall in a bleak 1940 essay titled "The Blundering Generation." Recent political historians, including Michael Holt and William Gienapp, have advanced sophisticated versions of Randall's basic argument (shorn of its racism, it must be said), starting from the premise that the sectional crisis was rooted less in a clash of civilizations than in the breakdown of American political institutions caused by a perfect storm of controversies over the fate of republican liberty. Slavery had always been a volatile issue in American politics. Why did it become a fatal one in the 1850s? These scholars emphasize the similarities between white northerners and southerners, the impact of ethnocultural and economic issues other than slavery on the collapse of the second party system, the mutual miscalculations that deepened the crisis, and the crookedness of the road to disunion. Political historians are far from monolithic, however. Some focus on individual leadership and personality; others emphasize institutional dynamics such as constitutional structure, electoral competition, and patronage. David Potter's classic *The Impending Crisis, 1848–1861* (1976) remains a valuable guide through the labyrinth of national politics, while Sean Wilentz's more recent *The Rise of American Democracy* (2005) offers a provocative synthesis of current scholarship. In Wilentz's view, the crisis of the 1850s represented a clash between rival versions of American democracy, "the free-labor democracy of the North and the slaveholders' democracy of the South," that had grown up alongside each other since the 1780s, but, finally, could no longer coexist under one national roof.

The tension between structure and agency permeates this historiography, and as in the debate among historians of slave culture, it is not likely to be decided soon. On each side, however, innovative new work continues to energize the debate. Julie Roy Jeffrey and Michael Pierson have shown how changes in northern middle-class family structure and ideals enabled northern women's antislavery activism and shaped abolitionist visions of slavery's sexual disorder. Taking a cue from Benedict Anderson's view of nations as "imagined communities," historians of northern and southern nationalism have traced the production of competing national identities through oratory and print. A number of historians have identified important contributions of people of African descent to the northern antislavery movement, particularly as eyewitnesses to slavery's horrors and critics of colonization (the removal of the black population from the United States). Political and cultural historians have rediscovered the significance of the Mexican War, both as a crucial moment for U.S. continental expansion and the western spark of the political crisis over slavery. One "war of northern aggression" led to another. Understanding the Civil War era in terms of the contradictions within Jefferson's "empire of liberty" offers the possibility of integrating multiple grand narratives of nineteenth-century American history: national state formation, western expansion, and the struggle over slavery.

As the U.S.-Mexican War reveals, the dynamics that led to the Civil War were not merely sectional and national; they had transnational and even global dimensions. Scholars looking toward the Atlantic world are embedding the U.S. crisis within the broader political and economic contexts. Accelerating European immigration in the 1840s and 1850s helped to topple the second party system; Lincoln's Republican Party emerged from the rubble. Proslavery and antislavery thinkers in the United States paid close attention to the British antislavery crusade and drew opposite lessons from Caribbean emancipation. Proslavery designs on Cuba and Nicaragua and schemes for resuming African slave importation inflamed American politics in the 1850s. Sven Beckert and Brian Schoen have recently emphasized the importance of the transatlantic cotton economy to southern secessionists' dreams of independence, and Beckert has argued that the economic disruption caused by the Civil War contributed to a surge in cotton production elsewhere in the world. Historians have only begun to explore the many ways that the transnational movement of people, goods, and ideas in the nineteenth century shaped the causes and effects of the U.S. Civil War. Spurred by renewed interest in globalizing U.S. history, more scholarship is on the horizon.

The Civil War and Emancipation

"The real war will never get in books," predicted Walt Whitman. Unlike Bancroft, the poet's nighttime stalking of hospital wards left him convinced that the "seething hell" and "interior history" of the Civil War could not and should not be fully told. Yet the war continues to fascinate scholars and buffs for compelling reasons. It was a searing drama in human terms and a pivotal moment for the nation. The drumbeats echoed around the world. The war left behind a bottomless archive of public records, private reflections, art, and literature. There is something for everyone. Just when it seems there is nothing more to learn, historians uncover new sources, ask original questions, and energize fresh debates about the conduct of the war, the relationship between war and society, and the balance of structure and agency.

A basic question animating much scholarship is straightforward: Why did the Union win? After the war, Lost Cause partisans insisted that the mighty North merely bludgeoned the Confederacy to death. Most modern historians agree that the Union enjoyed important advantages. The Union army and navy drew from a larger population of able-bodied men (especially considering that one-third of the Confederate population was enslaved). It possessed the lion's share of industrial resources needed to wage one of the world's first mechanized wars, while the Union's naval superiority and diplomatic talent made it difficult for the Confederacy to break the blockade and secure matériel from Europe. Recent scholarship adds that the administrative capacity of the federal government meshed with the associational energy of northern civil society to generate a powerful war machine capable of containing internal dissent while grinding down Confederate resistance. In retrospect, the balance sheet makes one wonder why so many secessionists expected to win their independence so easily. South Carolina's senator James Chesnut must have regretted his premature pledge to "drink all the blood shed in the war."

Running parallel to arguments about northern power are those blaming southern weaknesses. Older scholarship argued that however efficient and productive slavery might have been as a system of agricultural labor, it impeded industrial development and left the South poorly positioned to defend itself. Newer scholarship has been more impressed by Confederate industrial mobilization; ironically, the Confederacy suffered more from shortages of food than of factories. Other autopsies of the Confederacy conclude that the fledgling nation died of internal bleeding caused by political commitments to state rights and local autonomy or by class conflict exacerbated by the pressures of war. Armstead L. Robinson's *Bitter Fruits of Bondage* (2005) recently offered the latter diagnosis. Focusing on the often-neglected theater of the lower Mississippi Valley, Robinson argued that class conflict rooted in the social structure of slavery undermined the Confederate war effort. He found evidence of stubborn resistance among slave owners to Confederate efforts to impress their slaves into military labor, as well as intensifying disaffection among ordinary Confederate soldiers who resented fighting a "rich man's war." Such disaffection resulted in pivotal moments of failure, as at Missionary Ridge, when Johnny Reb's morale broke in the heat of battle. Several historians of the southern home front have likewise suggested that southern white women, especially those from non-slave-owning households, eroded Confederate morale through their pressure on fathers, husbands, and sons to return from the battlefield and take care of their suffering families. Stephanie McCurry's *Confederate Reckoning* (2010) shows how the war opened the door for poor women to enter the political arena, claiming, as soldiers' wives, a right to financial assistance from Confederate authorities. In *Mothers of Invention* (1996), Drew Gilpin Faust argues that even elite women grew unwilling to sacrifice their own interests for the good of the Confederacy. "Give up now while you have life," Octavia Stephens pleaded with her husband in March 1862.

But historians from a range of perspectives dispute the idea that structural dynamics guaranteed Union victory. Rather, they argue that the outcome of the war was always in doubt. As James McPherson, the most prominent Civil War scholar of the past generation, emphatically contends, "*There was nothing inevitable about Northern victory in the Civil War*" (italics in the original!). The Confederacy had its own advantages, including local knowledge, interior lines, and a martial culture, while the Union also suffered from political infighting, class conflict, and desertion. Most military historians emphasize the contingency of the battlefield, where strategy and tactics meet skill, character, and luck. General George B. McClellan should have hammered General Robert E. Lee at Antietam, but he frittered away a golden opportunity. In contrast, Gettysburg could easily have ended in victory for Lee, which might have dramatically altered the outcome of the war. And if General William T. Sherman had not captured Atlanta in September 1864, Lincoln might have lost the election to McClellan and the war ended with a negotiated peace. The best battle histories, such as McPherson's *Crossroads of Freedom: Antietam 1862* (2002) and George Rable's *Fredericksburg! Fredericksburg!* (2002), can be brilliant examples of historians' art and should not be dismissed as passé. They mesh technical details of warfare with broader social and political contexts.

On a deeper level, military historians debate whether or not the Civil War was "modern." The war pioneered the military use of new technologies of communication, transportation, and weaponry. Lincoln, for example, spent many hours at the telegraph office. Some historians and political scientists view the Union's strategy in the late stages of the war as a precursor to the "total war" of the twentieth century; the entrenchments outside Petersburg in 1864–1865 ominously prefigure World War I. Still, it was a long way from Savannah to the firebombing of Dresden. Instead of total war, Mark Grimsley argues in *The Hard Hand of War* (1995), the Union abandoned a conciliatory strategy toward the Confederacy in favor of a "hard war" against Confederate civilian resources and morale. The Emancipation Proclamation, above all, signified the Union's intention to take the gloves off. Grimsley argues that the Union's hard-war policy stemmed in part from the Union armies' logistical need to live off the land, and that even at its hardest, as in Sherman's March to the Sea, the Union could have done far worse. Recent scholarship on the Civil War as a religious experience also raises doubts about the war's modernity. The deep and widespread providentialism of both northerners and southerners—the idea that God's will directed the war—cannot easily be reconciled with an emphasis on the war's modern technology and strategy.

It is widely acknowledged that military historians are losing the battle for Civil War historiography within the academy. The front has shifted to the terrain of social and cultural historians, who are more interested in what the war meant for soldiers, women, and slaves than in how particular battles were fought or why the war ended in Union victory at Appomattox. Yet at the same time, the best social and cultural histories offer new perspectives on the conduct and outcome of the war. Drawing from thousands of soldiers' letters, Chandra Manning's *What This Cruel War Was Over* (2007) demonstrates that slavery lay at the heart of both Union and

Confederate soldiers' own understanding of what they were fighting for, although in opposite ways. Everything Confederates cherished depended on preserving slavery, but once the pressures of war compelled the Confederate government to consider arming black soldiers, they had nothing left to fight for. An intensifying desire to crush the rebellion turned many white Union soldiers against slavery, which they recognized as a pillar of Confederate power. Black Union soldiers did not need a war to turn against slavery; they just needed someone to hand them a gun and let them fight. As one black Louisianian told a Union officer, "We not only knows *how* to shoot, but *who* to shoot."

Military historians who emphasize contingency and social historians who emphasize the experience of ordinary soldiers and civilians have more in common than they realize. They march together under the flag of agency, but they attribute agency to different groups of people. For military historians, agency resides with strategists, generals, officers, and sometimes the rank and file who stood firm or wilted. For social historians, agency resides not only with rank-and-file soldiers, but also with the women who ran households in the absence of their menfolk, or enslaved men and women who fled to Union lines. These clashing perspectives inform the debate over the process of wartime emancipation. Here is the puzzle. At the beginning of the war, Lincoln and Congress pledged to uphold slavery wherever it existed. Four years later, the Union ratified the Thirteenth Amendment and abolished slavery in the United States. How did this all-important change happen? Who freed the slaves?

Considered from a structural perspective, the answer lies deep within tectonic shifts of world history. The rise of industrial capitalism strengthened a bourgeois faith in progress. New moral sensibilities undermined slavery's legitimacy. New forms of state power emerged with the capacity to overthrow ancient evils. Only such a broad view can explain why slavery was abolished everywhere in the Americas across the long nineteenth century, from Vermont in 1777 to Brazil in 1888. Moreover, recognizing the broad sweep of emancipation has helped historians to recognize antislavery connections throughout the Atlantic world, the impact that earlier episodes of emancipation had on later ones, and the similarities and differences in the dynamics of emancipation in various national and imperial settings. Still, tectonic shifts of industrial capitalism, humanitarianism, and imperialism cannot fully explain the local eruptions that shook the United States or anywhere else, let alone the astonishingly sudden and unexpected collapse of southern slavery in the 1860s. Abstract forces did not free the slaves.

Lincoln's reputation as the Great Emancipator suggests the opposite interpretive extreme. Coined during the war and popularized after his assassination, the epitaph remains the dominant public image of Lincoln. Some recent Lincoln biographers lend scholarly credence to this classic Great Man thesis by portraying the president as a latent abolitionist and political maestro who maneuvered behind the scenes to nudge the timid Union toward emancipation. Constitutional scruples and geopolitical calculations initially held Lincoln in check, but stubborn Confederate resistance allowed him to attack slavery by increments under the banner of "military necessity." Lincoln humbly denied his own agency in 1864, writing to a newspaper editor in Kentucky, "I claim not to have controlled events, but confess plainly that events have controlled me." Like many other Americans of his time, Lincoln attributed the events compelling emancipation solely to God's will. Adoring biographers view Lincoln's public profession of humility as further evidence of his calculating genius.

More critical biographers view Lincoln as a reluctant, even racist emancipator. He eschewed black equality in his debates with Stephen Douglas in 1858. His preferred method of emancipation, exemplified by the abolition of slavery in the nation's capital in 1862, included compensating slave owners for the loss of their human property and subsidizing the emigration of freed people out of the country. He finally abandoned "colonization" only because he needed black men to fight for the Union. It did not take political genius to recognize that he could not ask black men to fight for their country and then leave it once the war was won. Yet one of Lincoln's fiercest abolitionist critics, Frederick Douglass, offered a generous assessment of the slain president in a speech dedicating the Freedmen's Monument to Lincoln in Washington, DC, in 1876. Lincoln was the white man's president, Douglass admitted, but he loved his country and hated slavery, and though driven by necessity, he "delivered us from bondage." Freed people honored Lincoln, but they did not think he was solely responsible for their emancipation. Deeply religious, they believed their freedom came from the hand of God. Eric Foner's *The Fiery Trial* (2010) offers the most balanced assessment of Lincoln's pivotal but complex role in ending slavery.

A complex, secular view of wartime emancipation has emerged from recent scholarship, even though nobody has fully synthesized it yet in a single narrative integrating slaves, soldiers, civilians, politicians, and the public. As the historians in the Freedmen and Southern Society Project have demonstrated, such a narrative would begin with the thousands of slaves who fled to Union lines from the very beginning of the war, striking a double blow against the Confederacy by shifting their labor to its enemies. It would then turn to the Union soldiers and officers who refused to return runaway slaves to their owners, and who wrote letters to their families, friends, local newspaper editors, and politicians bearing witness to the horror of slavery and its importance to the rebellion. It would follow the progress of white and black abolitionists of both sexes as they tried to abolitionize the northern public and lobby political and military leaders to strike against bondage and to allow black men to fight. It would trace the intricate political wrangling within the Union army, the Republican Party, Congress, and the Lincoln administration that resulted in concrete changes to military strategy, tactics, and rules from General Benjamin

Butler's declaration of runaway slaves as "contraband" to the first Confiscation Act to the Emancipation Proclamation to the provision of equal pay for black soldiers.

The second half of the story would then follow the military progress of the Union army after the proclamation as it penetrated deeper into the Confederacy, liberating enslaved people in its swath but also exposing them to new dangers and difficulties. Behind the lines, black military recruitment corroded slavery in the Union slave states and in Union-controlled Confederate territory where the Emancipation Proclamation did not apply. As slavery crumbled on the ground, it was outlawed in new southern and border state constitutions, beginning with Arkansas in March 1864. Later that year Lincoln's reelection and the Republicans' landslide victory in Congress sustained the antislavery momentum of the Union war effort. Michael Vorenberg's meticulous account of the political twists and turns leading to ratification of the Thirteenth Amendment by the end of 1865 emphasizes the historical contingency of the democratic process and the distinctive Americanism of abolishing slavery through constitutional amendment. It is a paradox of legal history that the first time the word "slavery" appears in the U.S. Constitution is in the amendment abolishing it. The terse constitutional language offered few clues as to the status of the people it liberated. They would no longer be slaves, but would they be citizens?

On Juneteenth, many African-American communities throughout the United States commemorate the end of slavery. The official date of the holiday has been fixed at June 19, the anniversary of General Gordon Granger's arrival in Galveston in 1865 with news of freedom for the town's slaves, but the ambiguity of "Juneteenth" offers its own history lesson. Freedom came at different times in different ways for different people, because emancipation was not merely a legal enactment. It was a dynamic historical process that unfolded in secular and sacred time.

Reconstruction and Freedom

Did the Civil War lead to a "new birth of freedom" as Lincoln put it in his Gettysburg Address? The historiography of Reconstruction revolves around this question. At first glance, the answer is clear. Defeated Confederates returned to a different Union. The supremacy of the national government over the states had been confirmed. The federal government was bigger and the Republican Party stronger than before. Slavery had been overthrown and slave owners' political power devastated. Some of the most impressive recent work on emancipation has emphasized the remarkable transformation in the status and condition of freed people. Former slaves seized the opportunity to reunite families torn apart by slavery. They married, built schools and churches, bargained for new terms of labor, and organized politically. As Reconstruction proceeded, the Fourteenth and Fifteenth Amendments to the U.S. Constitution recognized former slaves as citizens and prohibited the states from depriving black men (but not women) of the right to vote. The whole relationship between the American people and their government—indeed the very definition of who the "people" were—passed through a revolution.

Or did it? Within a decade of the passage of the Fourteenth and Fifteenth Amendments, Reconstruction was in shambles. The Republicans failed to fashion a stable, strong coalition of freedmen and white Unionists in the South. Using paramilitary terrorism, white Democrats regained political power in the southern states. Former slaves' dreams of landed independence were frustrated, and many slipped into the limited freedom of wage labor, sharecropping, and tenancy, or the near slavery of debt peonage and convict labor. The Supreme Court began to whittle away at the constitutional guarantees of black citizenship in a series of decisions that would culminate at the end of the century in *Plessy v. Ferguson*. The federal government shrank down, and federalism reasserted itself. In his magisterial 1988 synthesis of modern revisionist scholarship, Eric Foner described Reconstruction as "America's unfinished revolution." While acknowledging the real progress that took place, many historians today regret that Reconstruction did not do more to secure real freedom and equality for African Americans. The challenge is explaining why.

Like W.E.B. Du Bois, who began his pioneering *Black Reconstruction in America . . . 1860–1880* (2007, originally published in 1935) with a chapter titled "The Black Worker," Foner placed freed people at the center of the story, and much recent scholarship has followed his lead. Using records from government institutions like the Freedmen's Bureau, the Southern Claims Commission, and the pension office, historians have tried to recover the voices of freed people as they wrestled with former owners, federal officials, and each other over the meaning of free labor. Former slaves believed that justice and freedom depended on their owning land, the proverbial "forty acres and a mule." Generations of unrequited toil gave them a right to the land, they argued, and landownership would ensure their self-sufficiency and independence. Some northern allies endorsed these claims, but others believed that the former slaves deserved nothing more than freedom of contract so that they could earn market wages for their work. Encouraging wage labor would restore plantation agriculture and give former slaves a powerful incentive to work, while granting former slaves their own land would cripple the plantation system and bestow special favors on the freedmen that white workers would envy. Like many white northerners, ex-masters feared that the freed people would become idle and dependent if left to their own devices, but they had little faith in northern instruments like contracts and wages. They refused to believe that freed people would work at all without the threat of the whip. The Black Codes enacted by Confederate-dominated southern state legislatures in 1865–1866 provide a chilling view of former Confederates' narrow idea of freedom. The codes included harsh laws against vagrancy and schemes for the apprenticeship of freed children that looked a lot like the restoration of slavery in disguise.

Recent scholarship on women and gender in the postwar South has added a new dimension to the conflicts over labor. It is no secret that the widespread withdrawal of freedwomen from plantation labor contributed to the postwar transformation of southern agriculture and was essential to freed people's idea of freedom. But some historians argue that freedwomen were emancipated into a patriarchal system of labor and citizenship that limited their freedom in new ways and distinguished their experience of emancipation from that of freedmen. Low wages and legal handicaps put freedwomen at a disadvantage; even so, their labor inside and outside their own households aided their families and communities. In *Out of the House of Bondage* (2008), Thavolia Glymph exposes the fraught bargaining that took place between former mistresses and former slave women as both adjusted to the new dynamics of wage labor in domestic service. In the public sphere, freedwomen did not have the opportunity to serve in the Union Army or vote in elections, but they were mainstays of their church congregations and self-help societies. Freedwomen often appeared in courts and Freedmen's Bureau offices to protest against abuse and plead for their interests. They, too, left their mark on Reconstruction.

Ranging widely across the South, Steven Hahn's *A Nation under Our Feet* (2003) offers the most comprehensive analysis of black southerners' formal and informal political activity in the second half of the nineteenth century. Challenging what he calls the "liberal integrationist" view of black politics, Hahn argues that black southerners organized politically around a shared vision of communal self-defense and autonomy. That vision emerged from the experience of enslavement, wartime military service, membership in local Union League councils, participation in the Republican Party and local government, and formation of militias to fend off Klan and White League paramilitary terrorism. Hahn rejects the conventional view that Reconstruction ended with the contested presidential election of 1876; instead he traces organized black political activity into the 1890s. By building coalitions ("fusion") with dissident white southerners and cultivating federal patronage, they maintained a presence at the polls. And as white Democrats bulldozed black southerners out of the political arena, black southerners contemplated emigration, created autonomous black towns, and redoubled their efforts to acquire and hold onto land.

Strangely, there is no counterpart to Hahn's interpretation of black politics that provides a full and current reckoning of white southerners' political struggles from the defeat of the Confederacy onward. Drawing more from the techniques of cultural studies than from traditional political history, recent scholars such as Laura Edwards and Steve Kantrowitz have argued that elite white supremacists' rhetoric of white manhood secured the allegiance of ordinary white men and women in a racist Democratic coalition that toppled Reconstruction and kept a lid on dissent. Several examples of this approach can be found in *Jumpin' Jim Crow* (Dailey, Gilmore, and Simon 2000), a collection of essays that show how racism permeated everyday life and swept across political institutions. The volume's editors contend that white supremacy is the "central theme" of southern history, and they insist that the history of white supremacy has been more varied, contested, and complicated than historians have previously allowed. In their view, Jim Crow was a "dance in which the wary partners matched their steps, bent, and whirled in an unending series of deadly serious improvisations." The metaphor is not apt. While it is true that "Jim Crow" was originally a dance (invented by Thomas Dartmouth Rice, a pioneer of northern blackface minstrelsy, in the late 1820s), the practices it eventually came to signify were something different altogether. An oppressive system characterized by fraud and murder on one side and desperate attempts at self-defense on the other was no longer a dance.

In today's "age of terror," the post–Civil War South offers Americans a lesson in their own home-grown history of terrorism. Scholars have long recognized that former Confederates mounted terrorist campaigns against freed people and the Reconstruction governments that protected them. Racist violence in Memphis and New Orleans in 1866 helped to persuade Congress to take the reins of Reconstruction from President Andrew Johnson and the former Confederate states. Five years later, Klan violence provoked President Ulysses S. Grant to protect black and white Republicans in the South through a renewed assertion of federal power. By the mid-1870s, local White Leagues provided paramilitary firepower for the Democratic Party across the South, and political setbacks at the national level eroded southern Republicans' ability to stand the storm. James Hogue's *Uncivil War* (2006) explores the militarization of politics in New Orleans during Reconstruction. Turning Clausewitz's famous dictum on its head, Hogue suggests that Reconstruction politics should be seen as "war by other means." Nor did this violence conclude with the Democratic takeover of the last southern state governments in 1877. After state militias brutally crushed a sugar workers' strike in Thibodaux, Louisiana, in 1887, one woman mistakenly predicted, "I think this will settle the question of who is to rule[,] the nigger or the white man?"

While the racist backlash of southern whites against black freedom and enfranchisement limited Reconstruction's achievements, the efficacy of terrorism raises questions about the durability and will of the Republican coalition. Southern Republicans suffered from conflicts over leadership, patronage, and policy. The party could not expand support among southern whites while retaining its mass base among freed people. The antagonisms of the Civil War infused postwar political affiliation, as former Confederates shunned the Republican Party. They condemned freed people as dupes and harassed southern white Republicans as "scalawags." White southerners with Unionist backgrounds were more likely to support the Republican Party, but their interests were different from the freedmen and often hostile to them. When white Unionists formed a "free state" government for Louisiana in 1864, for example, they refused to extend the suffrage to New Orleans's wealthy and educated men of color. Throughout the South, former Whigs in the Republican Party threw money at railroads but balked at funding schools for freed people. Although bribery and favoritism plagued Republican state governments, corruption was not unique to them and did not disappear when the Democrats took control.

Other historians look to changes in northern society and politics—especially the postwar acceleration of industrial capitalism—to understand the Republicans' retreat from Reconstruction. Issues that were not directly related to the freedmen had a powerful impact on their fate. Heather Cox Richardson's *The Death of Reconstruction* (2001) argues that as class conflict intensified in the centers of American industry, northern Republicans lost faith in former slaves' ability to live up to the ideal of free labor, and so they rejected government intervention on their behalf. In *The Monied Metropolis* (2001), Sven Beckert finds that the New York bourgeoisie grew disenchanted with democracy in its own backyard. They worried that democracy empowered the immigrant working class, fed corruption, and led to high taxes. Liberal reformers in the North sympathized with white Democrats' critique of corruption in southern state governments under Republican rule and proved eager to have the "best men" govern rather than the masses. Within a decade of the Civil War, the Republicans splintered while the Democrats regained their footing. With the intensification of the Sioux wars and the railroad strikes of 1877, new challenges of western expansion and industrial conflict eclipsed those of southern Reconstruction.

Yet memories of the Civil War era resonated long after the election of Rutherford B. Hayes in 1876. In the wake of Reconstruction, Civil War veterans' reunions honored the common valor of white Union and Confederate soldiers; they shut out black soldiers and papered over their differences concerning slavery. At the same time, white southerners celebrated Confederate Memorial Day, tended Confederate graves, and erected statues of defiant Confederate soldiers at every town and crossroads. They told stories of selfless black mammies and faithful slaves who hid their masters' silver when the Yankees came. Freed people told different stories—of loved ones being whipped or sold down the river, of spying for the Union, of persecution by the Ku Kluxers. Mary Francis Berry's 2005 biography of Callie House, a black woman from Tennessee who founded the National Ex-Slave Mutual Relief, Bounty, and Pension Association in 1894, reveals that many former slaves and their descendants also harbored memories of stolen labor and broken promises, and clung to the hope of compensation. When the Federal Writers' Project interviewed former slaves in the 1930s, their recollections of those olden days could still be intense and raw.

We are more distant from the Civil War era today, but it continues to resonate in American collective memory. Real or not, its history is not just found in books. It is everywhere—invoked in political debates, enshrined in national parks and monuments, mounted in museums, imagined in novels, acted on stage and screen, reenacted on battlefields and in video games, celebrated on holidays, passed on through genealogy, and studied in schools. In this environment, historians have no monopoly on understanding or arguing about the past, but as long as we continue to ask new questions and question old answers, the historiography of slavery, the Civil War, and Reconstruction will remain fascinating and controversial because it unearths the struggles at the root of American national identity.

BIBLIOGRAPHY

Slavery

Aptheker, Herbert. *American Negro Slave Revolts.* New York: Columbia University Press, 1943.

Baptist, Edward E. *Creating an Old South: Middle Florida's Plantation Frontier before the Civil War.* Chapel Hill: University of North Carolina Press, 2002.

Berlin, Ira. *Generations of Captivity: A History of African-American Slaves.* Cambridge, MA: Belknap/Harvard University Press, 2003.

Davis, David Brion. *Inhuman Bondage: The Rise and Fall of Slavery in the New World.* New York: Oxford University Press, 2006.

Deyle, Steven. *Carry Me Back: The Domestic Slave Trade in American Life.* New York: Oxford University Press, 2005.

Elkins, Stanley M. *Slavery; A Problem in American Institutional and Intellectual Life.* Chicago: University of Chicago Press, 1959.

Genovese, Eugene. *Roll, Jordan, Roll: The World the Slaves Made.* New York: Vintage Books, 1974.

Herskovits, Melville J. *The Myth of the Negro Past.* New York: Harper, 1941.

Fogel, Robert. *Without Consent or Contract: The Rise and Fall of American Slavery.* New York: W. W. Norton, 1989.

Follett, Richard. *The Sugar Masters: Planters and Slaves in Louisiana's Cane World, 1820–1860.* Baton Rouge: Louisiana State University Press, 2005.

Ford, Lacy, Jr. *Deliver Us from Evil: The Slavery Question in the Old South.* New York: Oxford University Press, 2009.

Fox-Genovese, Elizabeth. *Within the Plantation Household: Black and White Women of the Old South.* Chapel Hill: University of North Carolina Press, 1988.

Hahn, Steven. *The Roots of Southern Populism: Yeoman Farmers and the Transformation of the Georgia Upcountry.* New York: Oxford University Press, 1983.

Johnson, Walter. "On Agency." *Journal of Social History* 37, 1 (Autumn 2003): 113–124.

———. *Soul by Soul: Life inside the Antebellum Slave Market.* Cambridge, MA: Harvard University Press, 1999.

Kaye, Anthony E. *Joining Places: Slave Neighborhoods in the Old South.* Chapel Hill: University of North Carolina Press, 2007.

Kolchin, Peter. *American Slavery, 1619–1877.* New York: Hill and Wang, 1993.

McCurry, Stephanie. *Masters of Small Worlds: Yeoman Households, Gender Relations, and the Political Culture of the Antebellum South Carolina Low Country.* New York: Oxford University Press, 1995.

Oakes, James. *The Ruling Race: A History of American Slaveholders.* New York: Knopf, 1982.

Painter, Nell. *Southern History across the Color Line.* Chapel Hill: University of North Carolina Press, 2002.

Phillips, Ulrich Bonnell. *American Negro Slavery: A Survey of the Supply, Employment and Control of Negro Labor as Determined by the Plantation Regime.* New York: D. Appleton, 1918.

Stampp, Kenneth M. *The Peculiar Institution: Slavery in the Ante-Bellum South.* New York: Knopf, 1956.

Voyages: The Transatlantic Slave Trade Database. http://www.slavevoyages.com/tast/index.faces.

White, Deborah G. *Ar'n't I a woman? Female Slaves in the Plantation South.* New York: W. W. Norton, 1985.

The Sectional Crisis

Anderson, Benedict. *Imagined Communities: Reflections on the Origin and Spread of Nationalism.* New York: Verso, 1991.

Beckert, Sven. "Emancipation and Empire: Reconstructing the World Wide Web of Cotton Production in the Age of the American Civil War." *American Historical Review* 109 (December 2004): 1405–1438.

Dew, Charles B. *Apostles of Disunion: Southern Secession Commissioners and the Causes of the Civil War.* Charlottesville: University Press of Virginia, 2001.

Fehrenbacher, Don Edward. *The Dred Scott Case, Its Significance in American Law and Politics.* New York: Oxford University Press, 1978.

———. *The Slaveholding Republic: An Account of the United States Government's Relations to Slavery.* Completed and edited by Ward M. McAfee. New York: Oxford University Press, 2001.

Foner, Eric. *Free Soil, Free Labor, Free Men: The Ideology of the Republican Party before the Civil War.* New York: Oxford University Press, 1970.

Ford, Lacy, Jr. *Origins of Southern Radicalism: The South Carolina Upcountry, 1800–1860.* New York: Oxford University Press, 1988.

Freehling, William. *The Road to Disunion*, 2 vols. New York: Oxford University Press, 1990–2007.

Gienapp, William E. *The Origins of the Republican Party, 1852–1856.* New York: Oxford University Press, 1987.

Holt, Michael F. *The Fate of Their Country: Politicians, Slavery Extension, and the Coming of the Civil War.* New York: Hill and Wang, 2004.

———. *The Political Crisis of the 1850s.* New York: Wiley, 1978.

Jeffrey, Julie Roy. *The Great Silent Army of Abolitionism: Ordinary Women in the Antislavery Movement.* Chapel Hill: University of North Carolina Press, 1998.

Levine, Bruce. *Half Slave and Half Free: The Roots of the Civil War*, rev. ed. New York: Hill and Wang, 2005.

Morrison, Michael A. *Slavery and the American West: The Eclipse of Manifest Destiny and the Coming of the Civil War.* Chapel Hill: University of North Carolina Press, 1997.

Pierson, Michael D. *Free Hearts and Free Homes: Gender and American Antislavery Politics.* Chapel Hill: University of North Carolina Press, 2003.

Potter, David M. *The Impending Crisis, 1848–1861.* Completed and edited by Don E. Fehrenbacher. New York: Harper and Row, 1976.

Randall, James G. "The Blundering Generation." *Mississippi Valley Historical Review* 27, 1 (June 1940): 3–28.

Roediger, David. *The Wages of Whiteness: Race and the Making of the American Working Class.* New York: Verso, 1991.

Rugemer, Edward. *The Problem of Emancipation: The Caribbean Roots of the American Civil War.* Baton Rouge: Louisiana State University Press, 2008.

Schoen, Brian. *The Fragile Fabric of Union: Cotton Federal Politics, and the Global Origins of the Civil War.* Baltimore: Johns Hopkins University Press, 2009.

Sinha, Manisha. *The Counterrevolution of Slavery: Politics and Ideology in Antebellum South Carolina.* Chapel Hill: University of North Carolina Press, 2000.

Stauffer, John. *The Black Hearts of Men: Radical Abolitionists and the Transformation of Race.* Cambridge, MA: Harvard University Press, 2002.

Wilentz, Sean. *The Rise of American Democracy: Jefferson to Lincoln.* New York: W. W. Norton, 2005.

Civil War

Berlin, Ira, Barbara J. Fields, Steven F. Miller, Joseph P. Reidy, and Leslie S. Rowland. *Slaves No More: Three Essays on Emancipation and the Civil War.* New York: Cambridge University Press, 1992.

Bernstein, Iver. *The New York City Draft Riots: Their Significance for American Society and Politics in the Age of the Civil War.* New York: Oxford University Press, 1990.

Blight, David W. *Frederick Douglass' Civil War: Keeping Faith in Jubilee.* Baton Rouge: Louisiana State University Press, 1989.

Clinton, Catherine, and Nina Silber, eds. *Divided Houses: Gender and the Civil War.* New York: Oxford University Press, 1992.

Donald, David Herbert. *Lincoln.* New York: Simon and Schuster, 1995.

Faust, Drew Gilpin. *Mothers of Invention: Women of the Slaveholding South in the American Civil War.* Chapel Hill: University of North Carolina Press, 1996.

———. *This Republic of Suffering: Death and the American Civil War.* New York: Knopf, 2008.

Foner, Eric. *The Fiery Trial: Abraham Lincoln and American Slavery.* New York: W. W. Norton, 2010.

———, ed. *Our Lincoln: New Perspectives on Lincoln and his World.* New York: W. W. Norton, 2008.

Gallagher, Gary W. *The Confederate War.* Cambridge, MA: Harvard University Press, 1997.

Grimsley, Mark. *The Hard Hand of War: Union Military Policy toward Southern Civilians, 1861–1865.* New York: Cambridge University Press, 1995.

Goodwin, Doris Kearns. *Team of Rivals: The Political Genius of Abraham Lincoln.* New York: Simon and Schuster, 2005.

Manning, Chandra. *What This Cruel War Was Over: Soldiers, Slavery, and the Civil War.* New York: Knopf, 2007.

McCurry, Stephanie. *Confederate Reckoning: Power and Politics in the Civil War South.* Cambridge, MA: Harvard University Press, 2010.

McPherson, James M. *Battle Cry of Freedom: The Civil War Era.* New York: Oxford University Press, 1988.

———. *Crossroads of Freedom: Antietam 1862.* New York: Oxford University Press, 2002.

———. *Drawn with the Sword: Reflections on the American Civil War.* New York: Oxford University Press, 1996.

Neely, Mark E., Jr. *The Civil War and the Limits of Destruction.* Cambridge, MA: Harvard University Press, 2007.

Oakes, James. *The Radical and the Republican: Frederick Douglass, Abraham Lincoln, and the Triumph of Antislavery Politics.* New York: W. W. Norton, 2007.

Paludan, Phillip Shaw. *A People's Contest: The Union and Civil War, 1861–1865.* New York: Harper and Row, 1988.

Rable, George C. *Civil Wars: Women and the Crisis of Southern Nationalism.* Urbana: University of Illinois Press, 1989.

———. *Fredericksburg! Fredericksburg!* Chapel Hill: University of North Carolina Press, 2002.

Robinson, Armstead L. *Bitter Fruits of Bondage: The Demise of Slavery and the Collapse of the Confederacy, 1861–1865.* Charlottesville: University of Virginia Press, 2005.

Siddali, Silvana R. *From Property to Person: Slavery and the Confiscation Acts, 1861–1862.* Baton Rouge: Louisiana State University Press, 2005.

Vorenberg, Michael. *Final Freedom: The Civil War, the Abolition of Slavery, and the Thirteenth Amendment.* New York: Cambridge University Press, 2001.

Wills, Garry. *Lincoln at Gettysburg: The Words that Remade America.* New York: Simon and Schuster, 1992.

Reconstruction

Beckert, Sven. *The Monied Metropolis: New York City and the Consolidation of the American Bourgeoisie, 1850–1896.* New York: Cambridge University Press, 2001.

Brown, Thomas J., ed. *Reconstructions: New Perspectives on the Postbellum United States.* New York: Oxford University Press, 2006.

Dailey, Jane, Glenda Elizabeth Gilmore, and Bryant Simon. *Jumpin' Jim Crow: Southern Politics from Civil War to Civil Rights.* Princeton, NJ: Princeton University Press, 2000.

Du Bois, W.E.B. *Black Reconstruction in America: An Essay toward a History of the Part Which Black Folk Played in the Attempt to Reconstruct Democracy in America, 1860–1880.* With an introduction by David Levering Lewis. New York: Oxford University Press, 2007.

Edwards, Laura F. *Gendered Strife and Confusion: The Political Culture of Reconstruction.* Urbana: University of Illinois Press, 1997.

Foner, Eric. *Nothing but Freedom: Emancipation and Its Legacy.* Baton Rouge: Louisiana State University Press, 1983.

———. *Reconstruction: America's Unfinished Revolution, 1863–1877.* New York: Harper and Row, 1988.

Glymph, Thavolia. *Out of the House of Bondage: The Transformation of the Plantation Household.* New York: Cambridge University Press, 2008.

Hahn, Steven. *A Nation under Our Feet: Black Political Struggles in the Rural South, from Slavery to the Great Migration.* Cambridge, MA: Belknap/Harvard University Press, 2003.

Hogue, James K. *Uncivil War: Five New Orleans Street Battles and the Rise and Fall of Radical Reconstruction.* Baton Rouge: Louisiana State University Press, 2006.

Kantrowitz, Stephen David. *Ben Tillman and the Reconstruction of White Supremacy.* Chapel Hill: University of North Carolina Press, 2000.

Penningroth, Dylan. *The Claims of Kinfolk: African American Property and Community in the Nineteenth-Century South.* Chapel Hill: University of North Carolina Press, 2003.

Perman, Michael. *The Road to Redemption: Southern Politics, 1869–1879.* Chapel Hill: University of North Carolina Press, 1984.

O'Donovan. Susan Eva. *Becoming Free in the Cotton South.* Cambridge, MA: Harvard University Press, 2007.

Richardson, Heather Cox. *The Death of Reconstruction: Race, Labor, and Politics in the Post–Civil War North, 1865–1901.* Cambridge, MA: Harvard University Press, 2001.

Scott, Rebecca J. *Degrees of Freedom: Louisiana and Cuba after Slavery.* Cambridge, MA: Belknap/Harvard University Press, 2005.

Scully, Pamela, and Diana Paton, eds. *Gender and Slave Emancipation in the Atlantic World.* Durham, NC: Duke University Press, 2005.

Stanley, Amy Dru. *From Bondage to Contract: Wage Labor, Marriage, and the Market in the Age of Slave Emancipation.* New York: Cambridge University Press, 1998.

The Civil War Era in American Memory

Berry, Mary Frances. *My Face Is Black Is True: Callie House and the Struggle for Ex-Slave Reparations.* New York: Knopf, 2005.

Blight, David W. *Race and Reunion: The Civil War in American Memory.* Cambridge, MA: Belknap/Harvard University Press, 2001.

Born in Slavery: Slave Narratives from the Federal Writers' Project, 1936–1938, American Memory, Library of Congress, http://memory.loc.gov/ammem/snhtml/snhome.html.

Foster, Gaines M. *Ghosts of the Confederacy: Defeat, the Lost Cause, and the Emergence of the New South, 1865 to 1913.* New York: Oxford University Press, 1987.

Horwitz, Tony. *Confederates in the Attic: Dispatches from America's Unfinished Civil War.* New York: Pantheon Books, 1998.

Morrison, Toni. *Beloved.* New York: Knopf, 1987.

Savage, Kirk. *Standing Soldiers, Kneeling Slaves: Race, War, and Monument in Nineteenth-Century America.* Princeton, NJ: Princeton University Press, 1997.

5

The Possibilities of Politics: Democracy in America, 1877 to 1917

ROBERT D. JOHNSTON

Each major era in American history possesses a strong and distinctive claim as a—perhaps the—foundation of our current age. The late eighteenth century, for instance, provided the basic constitutional structure of the American republic; the mid-nineteenth century seeded later-day racial struggles. Yet scholars of the period from 1877 to 1917 may be the most insistent in their claims that these decades, more than any others, gave rise to modern America.

These claims contain genuine legitimacy, since the late nineteenth and early twentieth centuries witnessed the origins or consolidation of a host of features of our own time, including the following:

- The rise of corporations, along with a grudging acceptance of unions
- The rapid growth and transformation of urban areas into genuine metropolises, decisively changing the balance between city and countryside
- Major technological changes in areas ranging from the telephone to the assembly line
- A mass immigration that brought millions of Europeans and Asians to these shores, followed in turn by a sharp reaction against immigration
- The development of a vigorous consumer culture that helped constitute a new lifestyle for many staid members of the middle class, but which also contained special appeals for workers and youth

- The incorporation of the postfrontier West and post-Reconstruction South into a truly continental nation, followed by the rise of the United States to world power by means of empire building and participation in global military conflict

Informing all these developments, and arguably for contemporary historians the most fundamental issue among them, was the conflict over the meanings and practices of democracy. I propose no formal definition of "democracy," but rather suggest a loose and flexible mix of popular rule, political participation, equality in matters public and private, civic tolerance, robust grassroots activism, and social justice, along with peace, love, and understanding—the last three themes being values that many of the period's reformers in fact cared about deeply. New and innovative work has, of course, not created any consensus about democracy in America during these years. Indeed, one of the most exciting qualities of the scholarship is how historians, in many cases building on century-old disputes, vigorously disagree over the period's democratic qualities. One influential group has contended that the era's "rebirth of a nation" witnessed not only a constriction of democracy in the realm of formal politics but also continuous setbacks for workers, women, blacks and other minorities, and immigrants—not to mention the victims of American might overseas. Other historians, while not denying the period's serious obstacles to egalitarianism, have in contrast emphasized the era's often remarkable democratic aspirations—and achievements.

Both sides of the dispute over democracy are able to marshal powerful interpretations. Indeed, it is clear that both sides need each other, for we cannot fully understand popular struggles without concomitantly coming to grips with oppression, exploitation, and inequality. That said, a broad exploration of the scholarship of the period from 1877 to 1917 continues to reveal the remarkable possibilities—indeed, the distinctive democratic vistas—of this intensely public age.

The Politics of Historical Synthesis

The problem of democracy serves as a centerpiece for the most influential scholarly overviews of these years. Intriguingly, the synthesis that most fully casts its shadow over considerations of the period dates from more than a half century ago. One of the classics of American historiography, Richard Hofstadter's *The Age of Reform: From Bryan to FDR* (1955) formulated critiques of Populism, Progressivism, and the New Deal that flowed from the disenchantment of many New York intellectuals with American society during the age of McCarthyism and suburban conformity. Hofstadter's deft and elegant treatment was complex in ways that few of his critics have credited. Yet his main goal was to shine light on the antidemocratic qualities of late-nineteenth- and early-twentieth-century reform. Populists, Hofstadter claimed, were self-deluded agrarians who bought into the myth of rural virtue, denied their own self-interest, and indulged in conspiracy thinking and antisemitism. Progressives, while not as benighted as their country cousins, were seized with anxiety about their declining middle-class status and fearful of the rising tide of immigrants and working-class power.

Ever since the publication of *The Age of Reform*, scholars of the period have been wrestling with Hofstadter's interpretations. For about two decades after its publication in 1967, Robert Wiebe's *The Search for Order, 1877–1920* became perhaps the dominant interpretation of the period. Maintaining Hofstadter's focus on the middle class, Wiebe claimed that a new set of professional white-collar workers used bureaucratic techniques to bring together and modernize America's isolated small-town and rural "island communities." Along with similar accounts that came to be known as the "organizational synthesis," Wiebe left little room for genuine democracy. Reformers, ranging from the Knights of Labor to Theodore Roosevelt, may have been humane in their motivations, but they were either ineffective or—whether intentionally or not—helped imprison Americans in a kind of gentle, efficient version of Max Weber's modern bureaucratic iron cage.

By the 1970s and 1980s, the twin legacies of Hofstadter and Wiebe seemed to have killed off the old progressive interpretation of the period, most fully embodied in Charles and Mary Beard's immensely popular *The Rise of American Civilization* (first published in 1927). The Beards saw American history through the prism of the democratic masses ("The People") constantly struggling against monied elites ("The Interests"). Liberals such as Hofstadter and Wiebe debunked the democratic motives and achievements of the decades after Reconstruction, while New Left–inspired scholars such as Gabriel Kolko, James Weinstein, and Jeffrey Lustig contended that the reform movements of the period were little more than fig leaves that effectively served the corporate capitalist juggernaut. The historiographical landscape before 1990 then, with only few exceptions, left little opening for any robust sense of democratic possibilities from 1877 to 1917.

Yet democracy, ever irrepressible, would return. The work that both reflected and forged a new opening for mass movements and democratic aspirations was Nell Irvin Painter's *Standing at Armageddon: The United States, 1877–1919* (1987). To be sure, Painter emphasized the rapacity of northern capitalists along with the murderous terrorism of southern white elites, and she placed poverty, inequality, and misery firmly in the foreground. Nonetheless, she sought most of all to show the successes of the democratic responses to inequality and oppression from farmers, workers, and the middle class. The Knights of Labor, Populists, civil rights activists such as Ida B. Wells-Barnett and W.E.B. Du Bois, and social welfare advocates such as Jane Addams served as Painter's admittedly imperfect heroes. Indeed, in rethinking and revising this period, Painter presented a model for doing bottom-up history while still paying full attention to mainstream politics.

Painter made a progressive interpretation of the period newly respectable. Of course, this emphasis on democracy has not convinced all scholars. The most sweeping recent interpretation of the age is Jackson Lears's *Rebirth of a Nation: The Making of Modern America, 1877–1920* (2009). Lears despairs of the many ways in which pursuits of personal and national revitalization, often rooted in a masculinist evangelical Protestantism, led ultimately to the tightening grip of corporate and managerial elites, violent racism, and an imperialism that violated democratic ideals. Lears does not entirely discount democratic activism. The main difference between the two historians is, though, that the limited triumphs of Painter's rebels turn, in *Rebirth of a Nation*, into sustained defeats.

Though the major voices interpreting the era have written across the entire period from 1877 to 1917 (and, at times, beyond), there is also significant intellectual ferment in syntheses that explore, separately, either the Gilded Age or the Progressive Era. As for the earlier period, important overviews from the Reagan years saw the era as ruled by "bars of gold," in the words of Sean Cashman's *America in the Gilded Age*, or bound intimately to the "incorporation of America," the title of Alan Trachtenberg's 1982 exploration of the connection between politics and culture.

A fundamental challenge to these scholars' emphasis on the rule of capital, however, has recently arisen from historians who, while caring deeply about class and mainstream politics, are equally concerned with issues of gender and race. Heather Cox Richardson's *West from Appomattox* returns to Hofstadter and Wiebe's focus on the middle class, arguing that between 1865 and 1901 middling folks turned from Lincoln's generous egalitarianism to an exclusive and repressive individualism that, ironically, used a newly enlarged government to lock out workers and minorities. More influential has been Rebecca Edwards's *New Spirits: America in the Gilded Age*. Like Richardson, Edwards is ever mindful of the limits to democracy as Americans embraced consumerism and empire. Yet through an exploration of areas ranging from science to sex, courtship to the cooperative commonwealth, Edwards uncovers a Whitmanesque exuberance in both the formal dissent and the personal dreams of ordinary Americans.

One of the most important elements of Edwards's book is a powerful challenge to the chronological labeling and conceptualization of the late nineteenth century. For Edwards, concern about chronology involves interpretive conflict relating directly to how we envision the nature of democracy during the period. Though "Gilded Age" was a term coined by Mark Twain and Charles Dudley Warner in their 1873 novel of the same name, contemporary Americans did not actually use the phrase to describe their times; that practice came nearly half a century later. Since then, the negative connotations of the term have become so prevalent that political commentators in our own time speak routinely of the coming of a "new Gilded Age." As Jack Beatty entitles a recent popular history, the Gilded Age was "an age of betrayal" representing the "triumph of money." According to Edwards, however, the conventional focus on robber barons, inequality, and political corruption obscures vigorous movements for political reform, along with genuine government achievements in an age of supposed laissez-faire (such as the 1883 Pendleton Act that created a federal merit-based civil service and the 1887 establishment of the Interstate Commerce Commission to regulate railroads). Rather than a "Gilded Age," Edwards asks us to consider a "long Progressive Era" ranging from 1865 to World War I—and perhaps even including the New Deal.

As for "the Progressive Era," perhaps the most remarkable feature about that label is its survival. In the 1960s and 1970s, several scholars—most notably Peter Filene—issued manifestos for its elimination, largely because of the incoherence of any unified notion of progressivism and progressive reform. Today, however, such debunking has largely gone underground, as incoherence has transformed into a celebrated multiplicity. The one major exception is James Connolly's provocative argument in *The Triumph of Ethnic Progressivism.* Connolly views "progressivism" not as a coherent movement or ideology, but rather as an infinitely elastic linguistic usage that interest groups from across the political spectrum could lay claim to, sometimes cynically, and sometimes with the goal of empowering groups previously excluded from the political universe.

In an extremely influential article-length historiographical intervention in 1982, Daniel Rodgers pioneered the new emphasis on plural progressivisms by pointing to three distinct ideological strains of the reform impulse: antimonopoly, social cohesion, and efficiency. A quarter century later, Maureen Flanagan produced an important survey that has at its heart the pluralization of "progressivisms." In Flanagan's *America Reformed*, social justice reformers (largely women), working alongside other progressives concentrating on economic, political, or foreign policy reforms, "challenge[d] one another as much as they challenged the existing institutions." Flanagan gives as much voice to opponents of child labor as to Theodore Roosevelt, as much to suffragists as to Woodrow Wilson. And she largely vindicates the altruism of the Progressives: those who fought political corruption did not necessarily have a distaste for working-class involvement in urban politics, and those who fought to regulate commercialized sex and leisure were not simply imposing their middle-class morality on the poor immigrant masses. Social responsibility, according to Flanagan, won out over individualism during the Progressive Era, and plural progressivisms were signs of, as well as a triumph for, democracy.

Not all scholars have gone along with the new trend toward multiple progressivisms. Michael McGerr has become the most significant of those who work out of the unitary tradition. In *A Fierce Discontent: The Rise and Fall of the Progressive Movement in America, 1870–1920*, McGerr aims squarely at the era's old historiographical target: the middle class. McGerr's middle class is much like Hofstadter's: squeezed between a rapacious elite and a troublesome proletariat, it responded with a set of supposedly utopian reforms that, in the end, served to preserve middle-class culture in a narrow, exclusivist, self-interested way. Middle-class economic reform tended to be shallow and ineffectual, more aimed at class harmony than equality or justice. Through the prohibition of alcohol and the regulation of the leisure of the lower classes, middle-class Progressives above all sought a solution to a crisis in their own ideology of gender. Moreover, Progressives were the chief culprits in the rise of segregation, viewing the separation of the races as a modern and scientific way to keep blacks and whites from killing each other. Ultimately, McGerr's Progressives so betrayed democracy that we must even hold them responsible for the deep cynicism that has animated American politics over the entire course of the last century.

Other scholars with a unitary vision of Progressivism have, however, seen in that reform movement a much more robust set of democratic accomplishments. In Alan Dawley's *Struggles for Justice: Social Responsibility and the Liberal State*, the Progressives represent a democratic coalition: middle-class activists seeking to cast off their class's affinity for laissez-faire and exclusion, and insurgent workers fighting to remake the political world through unions and socialism. Walter Nugent also uses his *Progressivism: A Very Short Introduction* to create a direct connection between late-nineteenth-century Populist radicals and the Progressives, who—especially through the vigorous reform efforts of Theodore Roosevelt—both sought and achieved significant democratization of the corporate economy and hierarchical political system.

The State: Governance and the Realm of Politics

The Beards' progressive interpretation of the period from 1877 to 1917 is thus alive and kicking, even if reenvisioned for our own moment, when scholars are much more likely to highlight the analytical categories of race and gender. Historians can therefore in good conscience continue to make a compelling case that democracy, no matter how imperfect, flourished during this period. In fact, they can even go beyond that insight to contend that the Progressive Era may well have witnessed some of the most powerful democratic experiments of any age in American history.

Democracy extends well beyond a society's type of government, but the state remains a natural place to begin an exploration. The conventional account of this period's governance contends that a barely functioning and deeply corrupt late-nineteenth-century government was superseded by a newly vigorous and activist democratic state. At all levels, this state took on, for the first time, responsibility for the general welfare while expanding popular political participation. Recent scholars, however, have hopelessly complicated the story.

The most forthright revision to the standard narrative addresses the qualities of the nineteenth-century state. Building on his work exploring the period before 1877, William Novak has forcefully argued against the "myth of the 'weak' American state." Instead of comparing an authoritative European-style national bureaucracy to a supposedly powerless American government, we need to consider the many diverse forms of state capacity that became effectively embedded in a highly localist and federal system.

For example, the pioneering scholar of the late-nineteenth-century state, political scientist Stephen Skowronek, demonstrated in *Building a New American State: The Expansion of National Administrative Capacities, 1877–1920* that the United States during the Gilded Age had a relatively weak, but still vigorously functioning, "state of courts and parties." This contention, reaffirmed by the scholarship of Morton Keller, holds that the judiciary, along with the Democrats and Republicans, did effectively govern—even in the absence of the national bureaucracy that would be born during the Progressive Era. Richard L. McCormick put together an even stronger case for the coherence and strength of the nineteenth-century "party period" in American politics. In his influential synthesis, McCormick explored the ways in which party dominance linked voters and political elites through a set of redistributive practices that provided leaders of the Democrats and Republicans the opportunity to hand out patronage to a highly mobilized electorate. Progressive reformers would, for good reasons, see in such political patterns systematic corruption, and the reformers' attack on the power of parties would help bring into existence a new administrative state that adjudicated between modern special interest groups. But in a relatively nonideological age, the party system served the democratic requirements of the mass of white, male voters.

Historian Brian Balogh, in *A Government Out of Sight: The Mystery of National Authority in Nineteenth-Century America*, perhaps extends this line of thinking the furthest. As does Novak, Balogh argues hard for the surprising strength of the state during most of the 1800s. He derives much of his thinking from a vast body of works in "American Political Development" (APD), arguably the most important strain of scholarship in American political history over the last quarter century. APD scholars are, generally, historically minded political scientists who tend to emphasize political institutions in their explorations of the relationship between state and society. Besides Skowronek, the most important APD scholar for this period has been Theda Skocpol, who in *Protecting Soldiers and Mothers: The Political Origins of Social Policy in America* contended that the United States actually developed a "precocious" system of social provision in the late nineteenth century, particularly through pensions for northern Civil War veterans. Women activists and other professional reformers then continued advocacy for the weak, aged, and dependent during the Progressive Era, creating the foundation for a "maternalist" welfare state for women and children. Institutional political dynamics, however, prevented the extension of welfare policies to the citizenry generally, finally causing the United States to fall behind Europe in the granting of state social welfare benefits.

APD scholars disagree vigorously about which institutions were most important in the American state-building process, as well as about the limits to the development of a powerful state. Yet almost all point to the general expansion—and, provisionally, to the significant democratization—of government. The historian Robert Harrison, for example, sees partisan dynamics in Congress as the chief locus of national reform. Harrison shows how a coalition of southern Democrats and insurgent Republicans loosened the grips of conservative party elites, passing measures that strengthened regulation of railroads, food, and drugs; created a postal savings bank; lowered the tariff; and, most controversially, offered some limited protection to workers. The political scientist Scott James points to the outsized role of the electoral college in leading the Democrats to become the primary progressive party as they moved toward policies of statist economic regulation. Consciously placing the birthplace of the modern American state in the Progressive Era (and not the New Deal), the political scientist Daniel Carpenter highlights the bureaucratic autonomy won by certain federal agencies, especially the Department of Agriculture and Post Office, which used their connections with popular constituencies to build their institutional reputations and, therefore, power. The historian and economist David Moss focuses on the energetic advocacy of the American Association of Labor Legislation, which, although largely unsuccessful during the early twentieth century because of "degenerative competition" between states, paved the way for the country's later embrace of Social Security. Finally, the sociologist Elisabeth Clemens has forcefully moved the APD literature into a full exploration of popular political movements, demonstrating how women, farmers, and workers were able to mobilize as interest groups during the early twentieth century in states such as California, Washington, and Wisconsin, helping to give considerable power to mass-based private organizations.

To be sure, the work of these scholars by no means allows for the simplistic celebration of the triumph of democracy and social welfare; in many ways, their investigations sharply reveal the limits to popular rule during the Progressive Era. Nevertheless, the collective work of APD does cast doubt on the interpretation of scholars, such as Morton Keller in *America's Three Regimes: A New Political History*, that substantive change in the political system waited until the advent of the New Deal.

Moving from governance to the political process, the debate becomes considerably messier, with critics alleging that in this realm democracy has an even weaker claim to precedence. Indeed, most historians who have examined the political rules of the game for the Gilded Age and Progressive Era have highlighted, as has Michael McGerr, the age's "decline of popular politics," contending that this was when "America stopped voting" (the title of a book by Mark Kornbluh). The reasons for electoral decline are varied, ranging from reformers' attacks on a culture of male partisan spectacle that mobilized record numbers of voters, to restrictive institutional changes such as voter registration, the secret ballot (effectively disfranchising the illiterate), and candidate-centered (as opposed to mass party-centered) elections. The most influential treatment of the subject, Alexander Keyssar's *The Right to Vote: The Contested History of Democracy in the United States*, contends that an overt repudiation of democracy among the middle class and elite led to the intimidation and legal disfranchisement of lower-class voters across the country—not just blacks in the South, but the poor and immigrants in the North as well.

While the rapid early twentieth-century decline in voting is undeniable, we should not necessarily see this electoral demobilization as a sure sign of the thinness or collapse of democracy. Glenn Altschuler and Stuart Blumin have thrown down this interpretive gauntlet most forcefully in *Rude Republic: Americans and Their Politics in the Nineteenth Century*, demanding that scholars "refrain from using the nineteenth century as a club with which to beat subsequent generations of declining voter turnout." They contend that the high number of voters during the Gilded Age indicated only the most shallow of popular commitments to politics, which governing elites were able to manipulate for a time but which ultimately led to popular cynicism and an accurate recognition of mass powerlessness over policy making. Mark Summers confirms this insight in *Party Games: Getting, Keeping, and Using Power in Gilded Age Politics*, showing the myriad ways in which voters, in spite of the high level of mobilization of labor and agrarian dissent, were presented with tightly circumscribed electoral choices that flowed from the jealously guarded prerogatives of a narrow political elite.

The upshot here is complex. Overall, recent scholarship, while by no means speaking with one voice, depicts Gilded Age politics as simultaneously less romantic and more effective than did previous portraits. Progressive Era governance, in turn, now resists any simple tale of reformers using their power either to do purely good or to oppress the masses.

Political Economy and Class

When ordinary voters and governing elites cast their ballots and formulated policy from 1877 to 1917, one of the most fundamental issues that they confronted was a dramatically changing political economy—along with associated transformations in class relations. Here, too, scholars energetically debate the fate of democracy. The traditional and dominant interpretation, recently reinvigorated, sees the power of elites renewed and strengthened through the political and economic changes that produced the triumph of corporate capitalism. A different kind of analysis, however, sees capitalism as varied and essentially contested throughout the Gilded Age and Progressive Era, leading to a relatively democratic landscape of class that produced surprisingly powerful political consequences.

The prevailing historiographical tradition, which stresses the triumph of corporations, comes in both Marxist and more capitalist-friendly varieties. As for the latter, Alfred Chandler's landmark *The Visible Hand* (1977) focused on the rise of managerial hierarchies that allowed huge capital-intensive industries, such as railroads, to use dramatic new technological developments to monopolize markets. The economic historian Naomi Lamoreaux's *The Great Merger Movement in American Business, 1895–1904*, confirmed the ascendancy of corporations. In turn, the Marxist Martin Sklar produced a work just as ambitious and, within certain circles, as influential as Chandler's. Sklar (unlike Chandler) duly noted the power of small property, but his title alone exposed the hegemon: *The Corporate Reconstruction of American Capitalism, 1890–1916*. Massive, and relatively sympathetic, trade press biographies of John D. Rockefeller by Ron Chernow and of Andrew Carnegie by David Nasaw have also underscored the centrality of corporate titans to the American economy.

With the huge and hierarchical corporation as the period's featured economic protagonist, it should come as no surprise that scholars have typically depicted a polarized class structure. Labor historians, continuing to draw on the foundational work of David Montgomery, Herbert Gutman, Melvyn Dubofsky, and Leon Fink, have insisted that the period witnessed the rise of a multifaceted and highly visible American working class. Meanwhile, some of the most creative work in the history of class now comes from those studying the elite; scholars such as Sklar and James Livingston (*Origins of the Federal Reserve System*) see their work as revealing the birth of a self-conscious corporate ruling class. A landmark in this scholarship is Sven Beckert's *The Monied Metropolis: New York City and the Consolidation of the American Bourgeoisie, 1850–1896*. Blending cultural, economic, and political analyses of Manhattan capitalists, Beckert compellingly argues that the European term "bourgeoisie"—denoting not a "middle class," but a genuine ruling elite—needs be placed at the forefront of American discussions of class and power.

These interpretations hold considerable power. Alternative recent analyses have, however, significantly complicated the master narrative of class and political economy. Philip Scranton has productively pursued a non-Chandlerian model that emphasizes not the hegemony of corporations but the continued survival, in a wide variety of industries, of proprietary enterprises. My own *The Radical Middle Class: Populist Democracy and the Question of Capitalism in Progressive Era Portland, Oregon*, has shown how, in Portland but also in cities ranging from Atlanta to Los Angeles to New York, small business owners controlled large swaths of the economy even in this supposed age of "corporate capitalism." Indeed, it is questionable whether we should even call these members of the petite bourgeoisie and frequent advocates of a moral economy "capitalists." Andrew Wender Cohen, in *The Racketeer's Progress*, has provided a similar analysis for Chicago, demonstrating how an alliance of unionized craftsmen and owners of small enterprise used politics—and plenty of violence—to resist the economic and political power of corporations. Beyond challenging the reigning corporate model of political economy, this work collectively also asks us to rethink our ordinary conception of a "middle class," moving away from Hofstadter and Wiebe's relatively unified set of comfortable professionals to a much more mixed and variegated set of middling folks, ranging from unionized carpenters to self-employed printers to social workers, lawyers, and doctors.

The fluid, contingent, and often unexpected patterns of class and political economy that we can now see in the Gilded Age and Progressive Era directly influenced the period's democratic politics. Victoria Hattam's *Labor Visions and State Power* explores how a vision of a small producers' republican political economy united workers, artisans, and small business owners throughout the nineteenth century, ultimately generating the utopian politics of the Knights of Labor. Richard Schneirov, in *Labor and Urban Politics*, contends that as workers embraced a distinct class identity during the Progressive Era, they simultaneously reached out to make political alliances with their antagonists in the middle and upper classes. In so doing they initiated significant government activism that laid the basic foundations of modern liberalism. Martin Sklar also views cross-class alliances as key to the antitrust impulse that stood at the heart of Progressive Era politics, since liberals, progressives, and even socialists had to win over the petite bourgeoisie and the working class if they were to achieve their desired political and economic solutions. And at the local level, my book on Portland underscores how a powerful alliance of working class and lower middle class inspired an anticorporate flowering of populist direct democracy.

To be sure, some scholars, such as Robert Wiebe in *Self-Rule: A Cultural History of American Democracy* and Shelton Stromquist in *Reinventing "The People": The Progressive Movement, the Class Problem, and the Origins of Modern Liberalism*, continue to argue for a class polarization that politicians and reformers could not—indeed did not wish—to bridge. Here the middle class sought above all to keep the working class down. Yet even for an age that witnessed the most intense labor violence and radicalism in American history, the more nuanced accounts of the relationship between the middle class and the working class provide significant evidence that the era's distinctive democratic experiments had a substantive social foundation.

Race, Empire, and Environment

If the realms of politics and political economy provide various openings for uncovering democratic possibilities during the late nineteenth and early twentieth centuries, the issues of race and empire seem to quite definitively close down those democratic moments. This was the era, after all, when hierarchical ideas about "race" reached their height of cultural and scientific respectability; when the egalitarian dreams of Reconstruction gave way to systematic terror, murder, and disfranchisement of African Americans; when race-based immigration exclusion became systematically entrenched in American law; when the attempted ethnic cleansing of

Indians reached its far-beyond-symbolic climax at the 1890 massacre at Wounded Knee; and when the American empire began an aggressive overseas tour that shows few signs of an exit strategy.

The scholarship proclaiming the many deaths of democracy as white Americans embraced lynching and conquest between 1877 and 1917 has, over the last twenty years, grown relentlessly. The political scientist Rogers Smith, in his magisterial examination of American citizenship law, *Civic Ideals*, has provided the most powerful overview of the "ascriptive inegalitarianism" that came to dominate these years. Much of the labor on behalf of racial inequality was cultural. In *Race and Reunion: The Civil War in American Memory*, David Blight brilliantly reveals how, during the half century after Appomattox, the idea of reconciliation between North and South overwhelmed (although did not eliminate) ideals of emancipation and racial justice. Gail Bederman's *Manliness and Civilization*, in turn, showcases the fusing of concerns about masculinity with racialized anxiety over the decline of civilization to produce a toxic brew of white supremacist dreams and nightmares. Such principles of racial hierarchy were, of course, extremely deadly, as a burgeoning literature on lynching led by historians such as Fitzhugh Brundage, Grace Hale, and Amy Louise Wood tragically attests.

The scholarly terrain of race relations has, however, dramatically shifted in recent years throughout the discipline, away from an exclusive black/white polarity to the contested ground of many races. Here, too, the narrative of exclusion and oppression predominates. For example, Frederick Hoxie's *A Final Promise: The Campaign to Assimilate the Indians, 1880–1920* examines how white attitudes and official government policy changed from a flawed promise of ultimate citizenship to a colonialist exclusion from the polity. Hoxie points out how such a hardening of Indian policy both drew inspiration from and served as a model for the segregation of other races. More recently, in *The Plains Sioux and U.S. Colonialism from Lewis and Clark to Wounded Knee*, Jeffrey Ostler has forcefully argued that scholars should not be afraid to employ the concepts of conquest and colonialism in order to explain systematic violence toward Indians.

Moving to the southwestern borderlands, Linda Gordon explores the intimate, complex nature of the period's racial ideology in *The Great Arizona Orphan Abduction*. Using a single episode—the Anglo kidnapping of Irish immigrant orphans who were sent from New York to Arizona for adoption by Mexican immigrant families—Gordon joins many other scholars in emphasizing the oppressive conceptions of whiteness that pervaded the era. Erika Lee, in turn, links the theories and politics of racial domination to the growth of state apparatuses of exclusion in *At America's Gate: Chinese Immigration during the Exclusion Era, 1882–1943*. And in an important recent blending of many different histories of "race" in American history, Peggy Pascoe, in *What Comes Naturally: Miscegenation Law and the Making of Race in America* also documents the pernicious but muscular effects of race on state building. Highlighting the pedestrian subject of marriage licensing as well as the more rarified landscape of legal judgments, Pascoe shows the project of white supremacy extending well beyond the South to include various schemes for the racial classification of "Mongolians," Mexicans, and other threats to white purity.

Amid all the era's murderous, and very modern, oppressions of nonwhites—often performed with the blessing, or at least silent complicity, of self-proclaimed Progressives—it is difficult indeed to recover much evidence of racial egalitarianism. Yet, as a number of scholars have recently pointed out, it is far from impossible. The most promising way to bring democracy back in has been the refocusing of scholarship to restore the agency of nonwhites, particularly of African Americans. Such revisioning considerably complicates the past, in a way that reveals significant democratic possibilities after all.

The most visible African-American resistance came from figures whom even textbooks now place on center stage. Significant biographies of prominent activists, such as those of W.E.B. Du Bois (by David Levering Lewis) and Ida B. Wells (by Paula Giddings), are masterpieces of historical reconstruction and reinterpretation, while Robert Norrell, in the most challenging revision, seeks to rehabilitate the reputation of Booker T. Washington. An even more significant reconsideration of the period has come from historians who have dug deep to uncover the activism of ordinary blacks, especially women. Stephanie Shaw, Evelyn Higginbotham, and Glenda Gilmore see female middle-class activism in matters ranging from education to religion to public health as a distinct strand of democratic women's politics that, because of the disfranchisement of southern black men, moved to the forefront of black civic action. Gilmore's *Gender and Jim Crow: Women and the Politics of White Supremacy in North Carolina, 1896–1920* has been particularly influential as a reinterpretation that places previously overlooked African-American middle-class women's politics at the center of New South Progressivism. Tera Hunter offers a similar extension of the "political" in her study of black domestic workers. Her protagonists, though, are working-class women who frequently quit their jobs, established communal organizations, and fought for their right to leisure in order to gain autonomy amid recurrent racial violence.

The focus on ordinary people's lives and politics has its broadest reach in two revisionist works of southern history. Edward Ayers's *The Promise of the New South* does not focus on ordinary African Americans, but they play crucial roles in a synthetic narrative that foregrounds significant possibilities amid severe constraints. Most powerful in its challenge to traditional orthodoxy is Steven Hahn's *A Nation under Their Feet: Black Political Struggles in the Rural South from Slavery to the Great Migration*. Hahn contends that ordinary blacks formulated a genuine "politics" under slavery. During and after the Civil War, rural African Americans used this nonelectoral political tradition to protect their communities, establish economic autonomy, and fight for formal civil and civic rights. Consistently betrayed by the limited interracial alliances available, such as with Virginia's Readjusters and the Populists, rural blacks, according to Hahn, became increasingly involved with separatist politics, including emigrationism.

The most daring argument for the relative democratic possibilities of race during this era, however, comes not from a bottom-up approach, but instead from an analysis of the political theory of intellectuals and major political figures. Gary Gerstle's *American Crucible: Race and Nation in the Twentieth Century* clearly recognizes that American nationalism could inspire violent exclusion of nonwhites and immigrants, but he maintains that Americanism could just as powerfully inspire dreams of racial inclusion. He places the origins of democratic racial ideals firmly in the Progressive Era, exemplified above all by Theodore Roosevelt. According to Gerstle, we should not absolve T.R. for his racist actions toward African Americans, such as his refusal to seat black and mixed-race delegations from the southern states at the 1912 Progressive Party convention. Moreover, Roosevelt firmly believed in a hierarchy of races, with whites at the top, Japanese in the middle, and blacks at the bottom; he also feared that a low birthrate was leading to race suicide among whites.

All that said (and that is a lot), Gerstle contends that historians also need to recognize the progressive elements in T.R.'s thinking about race. Roosevelt refused to countenance racial purity, instead celebrating hybridity and race mixing and reveling in the mongrelization that produced true upstanding Americans. He disavowed anti-Catholicism and antisemitism and even "passionately defended the political rights and aspirations of [those] African Americans and Asians" whom he believed to be his intellectual and moral equals. For all the deficiencies in the thoughts and sentiments of the great Bull Moose, Gerstle grandly states that "the American creed of a Gunnar Myrdal and the integrationist dream of a Martin Luther King Jr. sprang from the same taproot of civic nationalism that Theodore Roosevelt espoused in the early years of this century."

If it is possible to rescue democracy even from the tortuous history of race during the late nineteenth and early twentieth centuries, there remains one major area of American life where scholars find it nearly impossible to claim any redeeming democratic qualities. Despite the best efforts of many vigorous anti-imperialists, the United States moved decisively toward formal and informal empire. In fact, much of the best new history of American expansion closely links the domestic politics of race to the post-1898 acquisition of colonies and global cultural and economic influence.

Matthew Jacobson's *Barbarian Virtues: The United States Encounters Foreign Peoples at Home and Abroad, 1876–1917* makes the most compelling case for such a connection. Jacobson fuses the history of immigration and imperialism, contending that they were two sides of the same economic coin as the United States sought to meet its hunger for new sources of labor and markets. Racial hierarchy at home, fueled by a Rooseveltian quest for rough, manly, and muscular experience, produced a violent imperial order abroad, especially in places like the Philippines and the Caribbean. Such a perspective does not go uncontested; Eric Love, in *Race over Empire*, boldly goes against the grain in arguing that advocates of imperialism did all they could to avoid entanglements with uncivilized nonwhites, and that therefore racism actually limited the extension of empire. Paul Kramer, however, returns to the more common recent analysis, while also underlining the transnational and reciprocal cultural, commercial, and political relations between the United States and the Philippines in *The Blood of Government.* According to Kramer, race was central to the near-exterminationist prosecution of the initial war against the Filipinos starting in 1898, as well as to the twists and turns of American colonial administration of the archipelago in ensuing decades. Kramer's most important innovation is to reveal how empire in turn rebounded to influence "race," as American-Filipino interactions mutually constituted each country's ideas of difference and hierarchy.

Overseas empire followed straight on from the aggressive white settlement of the continent; the conquest of the Philippines occurred a mere eight years after Wounded Knee. Beyond the issue of race, an increasingly common way of evaluating domestic expansionism has linked settler colonialism with rapacious environmental despoliation. Patricia Limerick remains the most vocal proponent of this analysis in her classic work of "New Western History," *The Legacy of Conquest.* Yet as Aaron Sachs has argued in *The Humboldt Current: Nineteenth-Century Exploration and the Roots of American Environmentalism*, many of the most important members of the nation's corps of explorers were not only surprisingly democratic in their approach to native cultures, they frequently sought connection more than conquest in their relationship to the earth itself. To be sure, there were plenty of currents within the burgeoning conservation and environmental movements that were antidemocratic. Karl Jacoby, for example, has shown in *Crimes against Nature* how the conservationists who set up grand parks in the Adirondacks, Yellowstone, and the Grand Canyon did so in large part by waging a kind of class warfare against Indians and working-class white poachers and squatters. We must not ignore this new "hidden history" of environmentalism. Yet recent biographies of John Muir (by Donald Worster) and Theodore Roosevelt (by Douglas Brinkley) demonstrate the power of a distinctively American environmentalism that did tap into genuinely democratic—and, as Sachs would ask us to consider, at times even anti-imperialist—ideals.

Women and the Gender of Politics

By no means has all recent innovative scholarship on empire focused on race; other scholars, following lengthy traditions, continue to emphasize economics, national interest, and culture. Historians have also begun to place women, and issues relating to gender more broadly, at the heart of their explorations of empire. Kristin Hoganson is the chief exemplar of this trend. The thesis of her first book, *Fighting for American Manhood*, is summed up well in her subtitle: *How Gender Politics Provoked the Spanish-American and Philippine-American Wars*, while her second, *Consumers' Imperium*, reveals how the quest of cosmopolitan middle-class women for foreign food, fashion, and fiction helped fuel an international political economy of consumption that proved vital to consolidating the American empire.

Indeed, the influence of women's history upon the rethinking of the period from 1877 to 1917, and especially the Progressive Era, has been immense. To be sure, not all women's historians view the era as a time of flowering democracy and rising sexual equality. Despite the triumph of woman suffrage and the proliferation of women's political activism, in some significant ways public roles for women narrowed. The era's focus on "race suicide" was by no means solely about race. As Laura Lovett contends in *Conceiving the Future: Pronatalism, Reproduction, and the Family in the United States, 1890–1938*, activists as different as Mary Lease and Theodore Roosevelt employed a nostalgic agrarianism rooted in an ideal of sturdy farm families. Such traditionalist ideology inspired a pronatalism that, at its most expansive, increasingly sought to restrict women to eugenic reproduction. In *Delinquent Daughters*, Mary Odem shows how the state—at the behest of both middle-class reformers and working-class fathers and mothers—significantly increased its power during the Progressive Era in order to more coercively regulate adolescent female sexuality. And carrying forward the impulse within women's history to explore the full range of gender relations, Nancy Cott notes, in *Public Vows: A History of Marriage and the Nation*, the ways in which official government regulation (and often persecution) of nonnormative marriage practices involving freed blacks, Indians, Mormons, and immigrants led to an overall assault on noncomformists who might seek to practice alternative forms of wedlock—and thus destabilize state-sanctioned patriarchal monogamy.

Despite this focus on supervision, regulation, and surveillance, other currents in women's history have served to reinforce scholarly efforts to redemocratize the period from 1877 to 1917. We can start with the most visible: the victory of woman suffrage after a campaign of more than seven decades. Ever since Aileen Kraditor's *The Ideas of the Woman Suffrage Movement*, scholars have been attentive to the hostility of many suffragists toward blacks, immigrants, and workers; Lori Ginzberg's biography of a radical, but undeniably racist and elitist, Elizabeth Cady Stanton is the latest work in this tradition. That said, there is no denying that the Nineteenth Amendment represented the culmination of one of the great democratizing movements in American history. Alas, as Jean Baker correctly notes, woman suffrage has been relatively marginalized in recent studies of the period, submerged beneath others forms of female activism such as women's clubs and child welfare crusades. Works by Ellen DuBois, Gayle Gullett, Suzanne Marilley, Rebecca Mead, and Rosalyn Terborg-Penn, though, portend a new renaissance of interest in the subject.

The proliferation of women's political activism beyond suffrage has, however, definitely been the primary focus of scholarly concern over the last two decades. In *Angels in the Machinery*, Rebecca Edwards has uncovered women's active involvement in party politics—especially during the Gilded Age, and especially in third parties such as the Prohibitionists and Populists. Lisa Materson has extended the focus on electoral politics in a fine study of black women in Illinois. In contrast, and exploring matters largely outside mainstream politics, Nancy Cott in *The Grounding of Modern Feminism* has uncovered the energy behind the birth of "feminism" as women sought social, political, economic, and sexual independence. Sharing some of Cott's characters, Christine Stansell in *American Moderns* marvelously recreates the radical writing, talking, and loving that grew out of Greenwich Village as feminist women, along with their male partners, sought to reconstruct modern gender relations.

Above all, historians have focused on the settlement-house residents and social workers who created a "female dominion in American reform," as Robyn Muncy titled a pioneering book. The first volume of Kathryn Kish Sklar's biography of Florence Kelley reveals the centrality of women to labor regulation and the rise of social welfare politics. Kelley's close friend and political comrade Jane Addams has also received considerable recent attention as arguably the most important Progressive after Theodore Roosevelt and Woodrow Wilson. Recent biographies of the first half of Addams's life by Victoria Brown and Louise Knight underscore different parts of Addams's personal and familial evolution, but both see in Addams a fundamental commitment to peace, justice, and an ethic of genuine democratic mutuality—an analytical and political path also trod by the political theorist Jean Elshtain's *Jane Addams and the Dream of American Democracy*. Much of the action in these books takes place in Chicago—the focus as well of Ellen Fitzpatrick's *Endless Crusade*, a study of the first generation of reformist women social scientists. The culmination of such scholarship is Maureen Flanagan's *Seeing with Their Hearts*, which contends that women were, because of their humanitarianism and concern for social justice, the Second City's true Progressives.

Varieties of Democratic Experience

Elshtain notes that Jane Addams possessed "a vision of generosity and hopefulness that made the American democracy more decent and more welcoming today than it otherwise would be." Yet Addams is merely the most visible embodiment of the period's democratizing impulses. She helps us see that even after accounting for all the hierarchy and elitism, racism and violence, regulation and restriction, it is the complex and imperfect—but still grand and occasionally even noble—movements toward democracy that give the years from 1877 to 1917 their distinctiveness and most important meaning.

Each of the era's many political movements, from the Knights of Labor to the IWW, has a complex historiography. Arguably the richest current scholarly literature deals with the Populists. Until recently, debate about the Populists swirled around two poles: Hofstadter's hypocritical and conspiracy-minded reformists in *Age of Reform* and Lawrence Goodwyn's cooperative democratic radicals in *Democratic Promise.* Recently, however, Charles Postel, in the most innovative treatment of the group in decades, has complicated the discussion. Postel argues that the Populists were not nostalgic agrarians but, instead, fundamentally *modern* reformers. From the city as well as the countryside, they embraced science and technology as well as large-scale forms of economic organization in order to create a viable alternative to corporate capitalism. Postel's Populists are much more feminist and free-thinking than those of other scholars, but they are even more racist; one of the highest forms of modernity that they embraced was segregation. Here Postel steps decisively into a long controversy about the Populists and race. Older works, beginning with C. Vann Woodward's magnificent *Tom Watson: Agrarian Rebel*, provide evidence of incomplete—but still heroic—movements toward racial egalitarianism on the part of white Populists. More recently, Ben Johnson's portrait of the white Populist rebel T. A. Bland shows how Bland became an egalitarian Indian reformer in both word and deed—and how his commitment to racial equality flowed directly from his Populist beliefs about the virtues of small property ownership.

The legacy of the Populists has also received considerable exploration in recent years. Whereas scholars used to be quite cautious about letting "populism" survive the 1880s and 1890s, it is now common custom to acknowledge a "small-*p*" populism with ancestral links to the farmers' revolt. Michael Kazin has pioneered here, both with *The Populist Persuasion* (which depicts his protagonists as largely democratic until the uncoupling of economic and cultural populism after the 1930s) and his generous and illuminating biography of William Jennings Bryan as a godly politician deeply connected to the masses. In *Goldbugs and Greenbacks*, Gretchen Ritter inserts the financial concerns of the People's Party into a long-standing, and surprisingly successful, antimonopoly tradition. Such populism failed not because of a deficit of economic wisdom but because of the strength of specific political forces at particular times. And despite the greenbackers' lack of short-term success, they bequeathed a powerful legacy to future Americans, who continued to wrestle with the power of banks and the problems of money. Steven Kantrowitz, in contrast, provides a more troubling portrait of the populist legacy in his biography of South Carolina governor and senator Pitchfork Ben Tillman. Although Tillman was a determined enemy of the People's Party, he effectively (and violently) harnessed Jeffersonian agrarian ideology on behalf of a vicious campaign of white supremacy well into the twentieth century. Most broadly, Christopher Lasch's tour de force, *The True and Only Heaven: Progress and Its Critics*, traces the populist legacy both backward (to Jonathan Edwards) and forward (to Martin Luther King, Jr.) to rediscover—and advocate for—an anticapitalist small-propertied populism with a genuine sense of humility and cultural and environmental limits—as well as a more democratic philosophy than its ideological counterparts on either the left or the right.

Lasch's exploration of populism is just one of many fine intellectual histories of the period that speak powerfully to the issue of democracy. Here the cast of characters is surprisingly uniform, as a wide range of scholars take on the task of reinterpreting, among others, Henry George and Simon Patten, Charles Horton Cooley and Herbert Croly, and (most of all) William James and John Dewey. Some historians have launched serious critiques of such figures; Nancy Cohen and Jeffrey Sklansky, in particular, have perceived the new social scientific liberalism of the late nineteenth and early twentieth century as an ambivalent accommodation to, if not an outright ideological covering for, class inequality and corporate capitalism.

In contrast, the philosophical opponents of laissez-faire who moved American social thought decisively away from its previous roots in individualism have received a thoroughgoing rehabilitation in studies from authors such as Mary Furner, James Livingston, and John Recchiuti. In *Uncertain Victory* (1986), James Kloppenberg began an important internationalizing of the era's intellectual history by placing American pragmatists and Progressives within a transatlantic context of social democracy and a democratic "via media" between capitalism and socialism. Daniel Rodgers, in his acclaimed *Atlantic Crossings*, extended this globalization by exploring how the good that American Progressives thought and did derived from their willingness to borrow concepts of "social politics" and planning from Europe. From a more determinedly American angle, Robert Westbrook properly insisted on positioning John Dewey's committment to radical democracy on the left wing of a Progressivism that, in other guises, was frequently managerial and disempowering. And Louis Menand's *The Metaphysical Club* vindicated the deeply moral ways in which pragmatism loosened the grip of determinism and abstraction on American political and intellectual life, serving as a midwife for modern American conceptions of tolerance, pluralism, and democracy.

As many of these works suggest, the line between intellectual life and mass movements was surprisingly thin during the Gilded Age and Progressive Era—indeed, such fluidity between ordinary politics and academic life was itself one of the hallmarks of the democratic nature of the political culture of the age. Only recently, though, have scholars truly reckoned with the depth, and often radicalism, of the period's self-conscious democratic thought and activism. Leon Fink has championed the ways in which early twentieth-century intellectuals (unlike so many of their latter-day counterparts), often embraced the democratic intelligence and political participation of the masses. Kevin Mattson reinforces this insight in *Creating a Democratic Public*, which argues that what distinguished many Progressives was the serious care they took in nurturing the process and craft of democracy. Progressive figures such as Charles Zueblin, Frederic Howe, and especially Mary Parker Follett both theorized and created places, such as adult education courses, people's institutes, and neighborhood social centers, where citizens could come together and deliberate on the most important political issues of the day. The method of democracy is also the subject of Laura Westhoff's book on the attempt by Chicago Progressives to perfect a "democratic social knowledge"—a set of practices and ideas that emphasized inclusivity, deliberation, close interaction with "others," and sympathetic respect and understanding. And biographers such as Nick Salvatore and Nancy Unger have lucidly described the complex embodiment of such deep democratic convictions in individuals ranging from Eugene Debs to Fighting Bob LaFollette.

Nor was democracy merely a set of ideas; such practices were deeply embedded in the political lives of ordinary citizens. In one of the most impressive studies of raucuous early twentieth-century grassroots citizen participation, *Distilling Democracy*, Jonathan Zimmerman demonstrates how the Women's Christian Temperance Union's Scientific Temperance Instruction was able to inspire, through the medium of the seemingly prosaic issue of appropriate alcohol education, an energetic profusion of debates among an engaged citizenry. Advocates of grassroots democracy devised many institutional forms to nurture its full flowering; arguably the most successful in the long run were the initiative, referendum, and recall. I have argued in *The Radical Middle Class* that in their birthplace of Portland, Oregon, these devices of direct democracy flowed out of a lower-middle-class program to bring full economic and political equality to workers as well as middling folk, women as well as men.

Such daring democratic dreams were startlingly successful, especially during the Progressive Era, although it should come as no surprise that radical democracy did not triumph fully, or for long. Nevertheless, the robust nature of democratic activism within mainstream politics between 1877 and 1917 can still astound even the cynical. Indeed, in many ways it is the most materialist of scholars who have demonstrated the greatest power of democratic ideals during this period. The political scientist Richard Bensel, for example, roots the foundational political patterns of late-nineteenth-century politics in a bitter sectional divide between the capital-intensive Northeast and Midwest and the exploited agrarian South and West. Yet Bensel raises a larger comparative issue, noting how the partisan system of political economy in place during the Gilded Age to manage monetary, tariff, and market policy ultimately produced a critically important rarity in global history—a nation that industrialized under a democratic regime. The political scientist Elizabeth Sanders, in one of the most influential books of recent years, extends this sectional analysis into the Progressive Era. Whereas the procapitalist Republicans win most of the battles in Bensel's book, in Sanders's *Roots of Reform: Farmers, Workers, and the American State, 1877–1917* the Democrats become the party that transformed American political economy and gave birth to the American regulatory state. The agrarians who controlled the Democratic Party were most responsible for formulating, and passing, classic Progressive legislation in areas ranging from banking to antitrust, from education to railroads. Their vision for such legislation was intensely democratic; agrarians sought to ensure that the people, through their representatives in Congress, would keep tight control over administrative agencies, preventing the growth of an unaccountable bureaucracy. That the twentieth-century welfare state largely became the plaything of experts more accountable to corporations than to the populace resulted not from a flawed initial vision, but from the political compromises necessary to pass legislation.

Two more political scientists, celebrating a pair of classic Progressive protagonists, round out the case for the strength of the era's democracy. Gerald Berk argues that we have significantly misconceived the supposed triumph of corporate capitalism during the first decades of the twentieth century. "Regulated competition," a theory introduced by Louis Brandeis into national political discourse during the classic presidential campaign of 1912, represented a middle ground between advocates of competitive free markets and regulated corporations that represented a powerful template for a genuinely democratic political economy. Sidney Milkis, in turn, focuses on one of Brandeis's primary nemeses, Theodore Roosevelt. Milkis contends that during his 1912 run for president with the Progressive Party, T.R. articulated an impressively democratic vision that went on to inform national politics all the way up through the age of Obama. Roosevelt rallied his troops to create a government strong enough to put into place a genuine social welfare state, and he envisioned a set of political institutions that would place the power of this new state directly in the hands of the people.

The Legacy of the "Long Progressive Era"

World War I and its violent aftermath have often been seen as the end to the age of reform, and for good reason. Left-wing Progressives such as John Dewey, W.E.B. Du Bois, and the socialist William English Walling threw their support behind a war that they hoped would revitalize democracy at home and abroad. Yet their dreams were dashed amid murderous trench warfare in Europe; the government's assault on civil liberties, immigrants, and unions; Woodrow Wilson's concessions at Versailles to imperialism and traditional diplomacy; and savage postwar race riots and labor strife. Yet despite such bitter betrayals of democracy, democratic crosscurrents continued through and after the war, including both expansion of the state and resistance to it, both a hopeful internationalism and an isolationism suspicious of corporate interests and the dangers of nationalism.

Whatever conclusions we might reach about the effects of the Great War on American democracy, the long-term legacies of the period from 1877 to 1917 clearly included the introduction of many democratizing currents into twentieth-century life. The contours of current American politics owe much to the social transformations, institutional changes, activist movements, and mainstream political activities of millions of ordinary Americans during what may well now indeed look like a very "long Progressive Era."

To be sure, much of progressivism was exclusionary. Yet we can now recognize not a singular political persuasion, but rather a truly plural set of progressivisms, with workers, African Americans, women, and even Native Americans—along with a diverse and contentious set of middling folk—taking up the languages and ideas of what was once conceived of as an almost entirely white, male, middle-class movement. As for the dreams of democracy from the period: despite the frequent blindness of those who embodied them, they remain bold, diverse, and daring. It is for this reason that democratic political theorists such as Michael Sandel and Robert Putnam have looked so longingly at the active citizenship of the Progressive Era, seeking ways to rekindle the democratic impulses of a century ago. It is also why literary scholar and self-conscious latter-day progressive Cecelia Tichi has written a politically charged paean, *Civic Passions*, to a heroic set of *Seven Who Launched Progressive America*: Alice Hamilton, John Commons, Julia Lathrop, Florence Kelley, Louis Brandeis, Walter Rauschenbusch, and Ida B. Wells-Barnett. In our current neoliberal age, where communal bonds continue to fray and "The People" seem to be drifting further away from genuine control over their destinies, we could do much worse than continue to learn from—and even be inspired by—these dreams, these heroes, and these histories.

BIBLIOGRAPHY

Altschuler, Glenn C., and Stuart M. Blumin. *Rude Republic: Americans and Their Politics in the Nineteenth Century.* Princeton, NJ: Princeton University Press, 2000.

Ayers, Edward L. *The Promise of the New South: Life after Reconstruction.* New York: Oxford University Press, 1992.

Baker, Jean H. "Getting Right with Women's Suffrage." *Journal of Gilded Age and Progressive Era* 5 (January 2006): 7–18.

———. *Sisters: The Lives of America's Suffragists.* New York: Hill and Wang, 2005.

Balogh, Brian. *A Government Out of Sight: The Mystery of National Authority in Nineteenth-Century America.* New York: Cambridge University Press, 2009.

Beatty, Jack. *Age of Betrayal: The Triumph of Money in America, 1865–1900.* New York: Knopf, 2007.

Beard, Charles A., and Mary R. Beard. *The Rise of American Civilization.* New York: Macmillan, 1927.

Beckert, Sven. *The Monied Metropolis: New York City and the Consolidation of the American Bourgeoisie, 1850–1896.* New York: Cambridge University Press, 2001.

Bederman, Gail. *Manliness and Civilization: A Cultural History of Gender and Race in the United States, 1880–1917.* Chicago: University of Chicago Press, 1995.

Bensel, Richard Franklin. *The Political Economy of American Industrialization.* New York: Cambridge University Press, 2000.

Berk, Gerald. *Louis D. Brandeis and the Making of Regulated Competition.* New York: Cambridge University Press, 2009.

Blight, David W. *Race and Reunion: The Civil War in American Memory.* Cambridge, MA: Harvard University Press, 2001.

Brinkley, Douglas. *The Wilderness Warrior: Theodore Roosevelt and the Crusade for America.* New York: Harper, 2009.

Brown, Victoria Bissell. *The Education of Jane Addams.* Philadelphia: University of Pennsylvania Press, 2004.

Brundage, W. Fitzhugh. *Lynching in the New South: Georgia and Virginia, 1880–1930.* Urbana: University of Illinois Press, 1993.

Carpenter, Daniel. *The Forging of Bureaucratic Autonomy: Reputations, Networks, and Policy Innovation in Executive Agencies, 1862–1928.* Princeton, NJ: Princeton University Press, 2001.

Cashman, Sean Dennis. *America in the Gilded Age: From the Death of Lincoln to the Rise of Theodore Roosevelt.* New York: New York University Press, 1984.

Chandler, Alfred D., Jr. *The Visible Hand: The Managerial Revolution in American Business.* Cambridge, MA: Harvard University Press, 1977.

Chernow, Ron. *Titan: The Life of John D. Rockefeller, Sr.* New York: Random House, 1998.

Clemens, Elisabeth S. *The People's Lobby: Organizational Innovation and the Rise of Interest Group Politics in the United States, 1890–1925.* Chicago: University of Chicago Press, 1997.

Cohen, Andrew Wender. *The Racketeer's Progress: Chicago and the Struggle for the Modern American Economy, 1900–1940.* New York: Cambridge University Press, 2004.

Cohen, Nancy. *The Reconstruction of American Liberalism, 1865–1914.* Chapel Hill: University of North Carolina Press, 2002.

Connolly, James J. *The Triumph of Ethnic Progressivism: Urban Political Culture in Boston, 1900–25.* Cambridge, MA: Harvard University Press, 1998.

Cott, Nancy F. *The Grounding of Modern Feminism.* New Haven, CT: Yale University Press, 1987.

———. *Public Vows: A History of Marriage and the Nation.* Cambridge, MA: Harvard University Press, 2000.

Dawley, Alan. *Struggles for Justice: Social Responsibility and the Liberal State.* Cambridge, MA: Harvard University Press, 1991.

Dubofsky, Melvyn. *We Shall Be All: A History of the Industrial Workers of the World.* Chicago: Quadrangle, 1969.

DuBois, Ellen Carol. *Harriot Stanton Blatch and the Winning of Woman Suffrage.* New Haven, CT: Yale University Press, 1997.

Edwards, Rebecca. *Angels in the Machinery: Gender in American Party Politics from the Civil War to the Progressive Era.* New York: Oxford University Press, 1997.

———. *New Spirits: America in the Gilded Age, 1865–1905.* New York: Oxford University Press, 2006.

———. "Politics, Social Movements, and the Periodization of U.S. History," part of forum on "Should We Abolish the 'Gilded Age'?" *Journal of the Gilded Age and Progressive Era* 8 (October 2009).

Elshtain, Jean Bethke. *Jane Addams and the Dream of American Democracy: A Life*. New York: Basic Books, 2002.

Filene, Peter. "An Obituary for the 'Progressive Movement.'" *American Quarterly* 22 (Spring 1970): 20–34.

Fink, Leon. *Progressive Intellectuals and the Dilemmas of Democratic Commitment*. Cambridge, MA: Harvard University Press, 1997.

———. *Workingmen's Democracy: The Knights of Labor and American Politics*. Urbana: University of Illinois Press, 1983.

Fitzpatrick, Ellen. *Endless Crusade: Women Social Scientists and Progressive Reform*. New York: Oxford University Press, 1990.

Flanagan, Maureen. *America Reformed: Progressives and Progressivisms, 1890s–1920s*. New York: Oxford University Press, 2007.

———. *Seeing with Their Hearts: Chicago Women and the Vision of the Good City, 1871–1933*. Princeton, NJ: Princeton University Press, 2002.

Furner, Mary O. "Knowing Capitalism: Public Investigation of the Labor Question in the Long Progressive Era." In Mary O. Furner and Barry Supple, eds., *The State and Economic Knowledge: The American and British Experience*, 241–286. New York: Cambridge University Press, 1990.

Gerstle, Gary. *American Crucible: Race and Nation in the Twentieth Century* Princeton, NJ: Princeton University Press, 2001.

Giddings, Paula J. *Ida: A Sword Among Lions: Ida B. Wells and the Campaign against Lynching*. New York: Amistad, 2008.

Gilmore, Glenda E. *Gender and Jim Crow: Gender and the Politics of White Supremacy in North Carolina, 1896–1920*. Chapel Hill: University of North Carolina Press, 1996.

Ginzberg, Lori D. *Elizabeth Cady Stanton: An American Life*. New York: Hill and Wang, 2009.

Goodwyn, Lawrence. *Democratic Promise: The Populist Moment in America*. New York: Oxford University Press, 1976.

Gordon, Linda. *The Great Arizona Orphan Abduction*. Cambridge, MA: Harvard University Press, 1999.

Graham, Sara Hunter. *Woman Suffrage and the New Democracy*. New Haven, CT: Yale University Press, 1996.

Gullett, Gayle. *Becoming Citizens: The Emergence and Development of the California Women's Movement, 1880–1911*. Urbana: University of Illinois Press, 2000.

Gutman, Herbert. *Work, Culture, and Society in Industrializing America: Essays in American Working-Class and Social History*. New York: Knopf, 1976.

Hale, Grace Elizabeth. *Making Whiteness: The Culture of Segregation in the South, 1890–1940*. New York: Pantheon, 1998.

Hahn, Steven. *A Nation under Our Feet: Black Political Struggles in the Rural South from Slavery to the Great Migration*. Cambridge, MA: Harvard University Press, 2003.

Harrison, Robert. *Congress, Progressive Reform, and the New American State*. New York: Cambridge University Press. 2004.

Hattam, Victoria C. *Labor Visions and State Power: The Origins of Business Unionism in the United States*. Princeton, NJ: Princeton University Press, 1993.

Hertzberg, Hazel W. *The Search for an American Indian Identity: Modern Pan-Indian Movements*. Syracuse, NY: Syracuse University Press, 1971.

Higginbotham, Evelyn Brooks. *Righteous Discontent: The Women's Movement in the Black Baptist Church, 1880–1920*. Cambridge, MA: Harvard University Press, 1993.

Hofstadter, Richard. *The Age of Reform: From Bryan to F.D.R.* New York: Knopf, 1955.

Hoganson, Kristin L. *Consumers' Imperium: The Global Production of American Domesticity, 1865–1920*. Chapel Hill: University of North Carolina Press, 2007.

———. *Fighting for American Manhood: How Gender Politics Provoked the Spanish-American and Philippine-American Wars*. New Haven, CT: Yale University Press, 1998.

Hoxie, Frederick E. *A Final Promise: The Campaign to Assimilate the Indians, 1880–1920*. Lincoln: University of Nebraska Press, 1984.

Hunter, Tera W. *To 'Joy My Freedom: Southern Black Women's Lives and Labors after the Civil War*. Cambridge, MA: Harvard University Press, 1997.

Jacoby, Karl. *Crimes against Nature: Squatters, Poachers, Thieves, and the Hidden History of American Conservation*. Berkeley: University of California Press, 2001.

Jacobson, Matthew Frye. *Barbarian Virtues: The United States Encounters Foreign Peoples at Home and Abroad, 1876–1917*. New York: Hill and Wang, 2000.

James, Scott C. *Presidents, Parties, and the State: A Party System Perspective on Democratic Regulatory Choice, 1884–1936*. New York: Cambridge University Press, 2000.

Johnson, Benjamin Heber. "Red Populism? T. A. Bland, Agrarian Radicalism, and the Debate over the Dawes Act." In Catherine McNicol Stock and Robert D. Johnston, eds., *The Countryside in the Age of the Modern State: Essays in Twentieth-Century Rural Political History*, 15–37. Cornell University Press, 2001.

Johnston, Robert D. *The Radical Middle Class: Populist Democracy and the Question of Capitalism in Progressive Era Portland, Oregon*. Princeton, NJ: Princeton University Press, 2003.

———. "Re-Democratizing the Progressive Era: The Politics of Progressive Era Political Historiography." *Journal of the Gilded Age and Progressive Era* 1 (Jan. 2002): 68–92.

Kantrowitz, Stephen. *Ben Tillman and the Reconstruction of White Supremacy*. Chapel Hill: University of North Carolina Press, 2000.

Kazin, Michael. *A Godly Hero: The Life of William Jennings Bryan*. New York: Knopf, 2006.

———. *The Populist Persuasion: An American History*. New York: Basic Books, 1995.

Keller, Morton. *Affairs of State: Public Life in Late Nineteenth Century America*. Cambridge, MA: Harvard University Press, 1977.

———. *America's Three Regimes: A New Political History*. New York: Oxford University Press, 2007.

Keyssar, Alexander. *The Right to Vote: The Contested History of Democracy in the United States*. New York: Basic Books, 2009 [2000].

Kloppenberg, James T. *Uncertain Victory: Social Democracy and Progressivism in European and American Thought, 1870–1920*. New York: Oxford University Press, 1986.

Kolko, Gabriel. *The Triumph of Conservatism: A Reinterpretation of American History, 1900–1916*. New York: Free Press, 1963.

Kornbluh, Mark Lawrence. *Why America Stopped Voting: The Decline of Participatory Democracy and the Emergence of Modern American Politics*. New York: New York University Press, 2000.

Kraditor, Aileen. *The Ideas of the Woman Suffrage Movement, 1890–1920*. New York: Columbia University Press, 1965.

Kramer, Paul A. *The Blood of Government: Race, Empire, the United States, and the Philippines*. Chapel Hill: University of North Carolina Press, 2006.

Knight, Louise. *Citizen: Jane Addams and the Struggle for Democracy*. Chicago: University of Chicago Press, 2005.

Lamoreaux, Naomi. *The Great Merger Movement in American Business, 1895–1904*. New York: Cambridge University Press, 1985.

Lasch, Christopher. *The True and Only Heaven: Progress and Its Critics*. New York: W. W. Norton, 1991.

Lears, Jackson. *Rebirth of a Nation: The Making of Modern America, 1877–1920*. New York: Harper, 2009.

Lee, Erika. *At America's Gates: Chinese Immigration during the Exclusion Era, 1882–1943*. Chapel Hill: University of North Carolina Press, 2003.

Lewis, David Levering. *W.E.B. Du Bois: Biography of a Race, 1868–1919*. New York: Holt, 1993.

Limerick, Patricia Nelson. *The Legacy of Conquest: The Unbroken Past of the American West*. New York: W. W. Norton, 1987.

Livingston, James. *Origins of the Federal Reserve System: Money, Class, and Corporate Capitalism, 1890–1913*. Ithaca, NY: Cornell University Press, 1986.

———. *Pragmatism and the Political Economy of Cultural Revolution, 1850–1940*. Chapel Hill: University of North Carolina Press, 1994.

Love, Eric T. L. *Race over Empire: Racism and U.S. Imperialism, 1865–1900*. Chapel Hill: University of North Carolina Press, 2004.

Lovett, Laura L. *Conceiving the Future: Pronatalism, Reproduction, and the Family in the United States, 1890–1938*. Chapel Hill: University of North Carolina Press, 2007.

Lustig, R. Jeffrey. *Corporate Liberalism: The Origins of Modern American Political Theory, 1880–1920*. Berkeley: University of California Press, 1982.

Marilley, Suzanne M. *Woman Suffrage and the Origins of Liberal Feminism in the United States, 1820–1920*. Cambridge, MA: Harvard University Press, 1996.

Materson, Lisa G. *Freedom of Her Race: Black Women and Electoral Politics in Illinois, 1877–1932*. Chapel Hill: University of North Carolina Press, 2009.

Mattson, Kevin. *Creating a Democratic Public: The Struggle for Urban Participatory Democracy during the Progressive Era*. University Park: Pennsylvania State University Press, 1998.

McCormick, Richard L. *The Party Period and Public Policy: American Politics from the Age of Jackson to the Progressive Era*. New York: Oxford University Press, 1986.

McGerr, Michael E. *The Decline of Popular Politics: The American North, 1865–1928*. New York: Oxford University Press, 1986.

———. *A Fierce Discontent: The Rise and Fall of the Progressive Movement in America, 1870–1920*. New York: Free Press, 2003.

Mead, Rebecca J. *How the Vote Was Won: Woman Suffrage in the Western United States, 1868–1914*. New York: New York University Press, 2004.

Menand, Louis. *The Metaphysical Club.* New York: Farrar, Straus and Giroux, 2001.

Milkis, Sidney M. *Theodore Roosevelt, the Progressive Party, and the Transformation of American Democracy.* Lawrence: University Press of Kansas, 2009.

Montgomery, David. *The Fall of the House of Labor: The Workplace, State, and American Labor Activism, 1865–1925.* New York: Cambridge University Press, 1987.

Moss, David A. *Socializing Security: Progressive-Era Economists and the Origins of American Social Policy.* Cambridge, MA: Harvard University Press, 1995.

Muncy, Robyn. *Creating a Female Dominion in American Reform, 1890–1935.* New York: Oxford University Press, 1991.

Nasaw, David. *Andrew Carnegie.* New York: Penguin, 2006.

Norrell, Robert J. *Up from History: The Life of Booker T. Washington.* Cambridge, MA: Harvard University Press, 2009.

Novak, William J. "The Myth of the 'Weak' American State." *American Historical Review* 113 (June 2008): 752–772.

Nugent, Walter T. K. *Progressivism: A Very Short Introduction.* New York: Oxford University Press, 2010.

Odem, Mary E. *Delinquent Daughters: Protecting and Policing Adolescent Female Sexuality in the United States, 1885–1920.* Chapel Hill: University of North Carolina Press, 1995.

Ostler, Jeffrey. *The Plains Sioux and U.S. Colonialism from Lewis and Clark to Wounded Knee.* New York: Cambridge University Press, 2004.

Painter, Nell Irvin. *Standing at Armageddon: The United States, 1877–1919*, 2nd ed. New York: W. W. Norton, 2008 [1987].

Pascoe, Peggy. *What Comes Naturally: Miscegenation Law and the Making of Race in America.* New York: Oxford University Press, 2009.

Postel, Charles. *The Populist Vision.* New York: Oxford University Press, 2007.

Putnam, Robert D. *Bowling Alone: The Collapse and Revival of American Community.* New York: Simon and Schuster, 2000.

Rauchway, Eric. *Murdering McKinley: The Making of Theodore Roosevelt's America.* New York: Hill and Wang, 2003.

Recchiuti, John Louis. *Civic Engagement: Social Science and Progressive-Era Reform in New York City.* Philadelphia: University of Pennsylvania Press, 2007.

Richardson, Heather Cox. *West from Appomattox: The Reconstruction of America after the Civil War.* New Haven, CT: Yale University Press, 2007.

Ritter, Gretchen. *Goldbugs and Greenbacks: The Antimonopoly Tradition and the Politics of Finance, 1865–1896.* New York: Cambridge University Press, 1997.

Rodgers, Daniel T. *Atlantic Crossings: Social Politics in a Progressive Age.* Cambridge, MA: Harvard University Press, 1998.

———. "In Search of Progressivism." *Reviews in American History* 10 (December 1982): 113–132.

Sachs, Aaron. *The Humboldt Current: Nineteenth-Century Exploration and the Roots of American Environmentalism.* New York: Viking, 2006.

Salvatore, Nick. *Eugene V. Debs: Citizen and Socialist.* Urbana: University of Illinois Press, 1982.

Sandel, Michael J. *Democracy's Discontent: America in Search of a Public Philosophy.* Cambridge, MA: Harvard University Press, 1996.

Sanders, Elizabeth. *Roots of Reform: Farmers, Workers, and the American State, 1877–1917.* Chicago: University of Chicago Press, 1999.

Schneirov, Richard. *Labor and Urban Politics: Class Conflict and the Origins of Modern Liberalism in Chicago, 1864–1897.* Urbana: University of Illinois Press, 1998.

Scranton, Philip. *Figured Tapestry: Production, Markets and Power in Philadelphia Textiles, 1855–1941.* New York: Cambridge University Press, 1989.

Shaw, Stephanie J. *What a Woman Ought to Be and to Do: Black Professional Women Workers during the Jim Crow Era.* Chicago: University of Chicago Press, 1996.

Sklansky, Jeffrey. *The Soul's Economy: Market Society and Selfhood in American Thought, 1820–1920.* Chapel Hill: University of North Carolina Press, 2002.

Sklar, Kathryn Kish. *Florence Kelley and the Nation's Work: The Rise of Women's Political Culture, 1830–1930.* New Haven, CT: Yale University Press, 1995.

Sklar, Martin J. *The Corporate Reconstruction of American Capitalism, 1890–1916: The Market, the Law, and Politics.* New York: Cambridge University Press, 1988.

Skocpol, Theda. *Protecting Soldiers and Mothers: The Political Origins of Social Policy in the United States.* Cambridge, MA: Harvard University Press, 1992.

Skowronek, Stephen. *Building a New American State: The Expansion of National Administrative Capacities, 1877–1920.* New York: Cambridge University Press, 1982.

Smith, Rogers M. *Civic Ideals: Conflicting Visions of Citizenship in U.S. History.* New Haven, CT: Yale University Press, 1997.

Stansell, Christine. *American Moderns: Bohemian New York and the Creation of a New Century.* New York: Metropolitan Books, 2000.

Stromquist, Shelton. *Re-inventing "The People": The Progressive Movement, the Class Problem, and the Origins of Modern Liberalism.* Urbana: University of Illinois Press, 2006.

Summers, Mark Wahlgren. *Party Games: Getting, Keeping, and Using Power in Gilded Age Politics.* Chapel Hill: University of North Carolina Press, 2004.

Terborg-Penn, Rosalyn. *African American Women in the Struggle for the Vote, 1850–1920.* Bloomington: University of Indiana Press, 1998.

Tichi, Cecelia. *Civic Passions: Seven Who Launched Progressive America.* Chapel Hill: University of North Carolina Press, 2009.

Trachtenberg, Alan. *The Incorporation of America: Culture and Society in the Gilded Age.* New York: Hill and Wang, 2007 [1982].

Unger, Nancy C. *Fighting Bob La Follette: The Righteous Reformer.* Chapel Hill: University of North Carolina Press, 2000.

Weinstein, James. *The Corporate Ideal in the Liberal State, 1900–1918.* Boston: Beacon, 1968.

Westbrook, Robert. *John Dewey and American Democracy.* Ithaca, NY: Cornell University Press, 1991.

Westhoff, Laura M. *A Fatal Drifting Apart: Democratic Social Knowledge and Chicago Reform.* Columbus: Ohio State University Press, 2007.

Wiebe, Robert H. *The Search for Order, 1877–1920.* New York: Hill and Wang, 1967.

———. *Self-Rule: A Cultural History of Democracy.* Chicago: University of Chicago Press, 1995.

Wood, Amy Louise. *Lynching and Spectacle: Witnessing Racial Violence in America, 1890–1940*. Chapel Hill: University of North Carolina Press, 2009.

Woodward, C. Vann. *Origins of the New South, 1877–1913*. Baton Rouge: Louisiana University Press, 1951.

———. *Tom Watson: Agrarian Rebel*. New York: Oxford University Press, 1938.

Worster, Donald. *A Passion for Nature: The Life of John Muir*. New York: Oxford University Press, 2008.

Zimmerman, Jonathan. *Distilling Democracy: Alcohol Education in America's Public Schools, 1880–1925*. Lawrence: University Press of Kansas, 1999.

6

The Interwar Years

LISA McGIRR

In *The Age of Extremes*, the British historian Eric Hobsbawm labeled the years from World War I to World War II the "era of catastrophe." He pointed above all to the unprecedented human devastation wrought in a span of less than thirty years: Two global conflagrations bookended the near collapse of world capitalism and the rise of new authoritarian regimes. For one belligerent, however, this age of "catastrophe" brought triumph as well as tragedy. By the end of World War I, the United States was the world's largest economy and most powerful state. In the decades that followed, Americans grappled with the rigors and rewards of this new role—vast economic growth sparked revolutions in consumption, leisure, and work but also demanded a newly active state that redrew the bounds of citizenship and struggled to find its place as a world leader. The collapse of the pillars of the world economy in 1929 brought a more inclusive, democratic capitalism in the United States in sharp contrast to the authoritarianism that prevailed in much of Europe. During World War II, ideas about the state's relationship to citizens advanced during the New Deal gained firmer footing and became the foundation of the social order during America's "Golden Years." The interwar years arguably gave birth to the ideas, institutions, and politics of the modern United States.

Early accounts, such as Frederick Lewis Allen's popular portrait, *Only Yesterday*, emphasized the sharp break between the prosperous but culturally turbulent 1920s and the decade of economic struggle and political reform that followed. Professional historians, too, emphasized the contrast between the irresponsible era of so-called freewheeling capitalism and the new path of modern liberalism that America embarked on with the New Deal "revolution." Since then, however, historians have looked beyond stark morality tales to understand how the 1920s set the stage for what followed. Historical interpretations now lean to a view of the 1920s not so much as an anomalous period sandwiched between two eras of reform but as a decade that helped lay the groundwork for the expansion of state authority during the New Deal.

Above all, historians have discovered that the interwar period as a whole was marked by increases in federal authority. The relationship between the state and its citizens was redefined first in wartime, then through the far-reaching experiment of national Prohibition, and most consequentially, through the New Deal and World War II. Out of this period, a distinctly American warfare/welfare state emerged, a product of the unprecedented demands of global crisis but also America's deep antistatist traditions. The state that emerged from World War II as the world's first superpower was limited and shaped, scholars emphasize, by the distrust of central authority, substantial political and constitutional arrangements impeding change, and a meager (by European standards) administrative state. Just as scholars have found more statism in the "conservative" 1920s, they have tempered their accounts of the New Deal "revolution" to take into account the limits of reform.

Given the importance of the transformations of the state during these years, many historians, not surprisingly, have focused on national policy and politics. Yet textured social and cultural histories, like those that have so enriched our interpretations of earlier periods of U.S. history, are now plentiful. Investigations by a generation of historians have now enhanced our understanding of the experiences of distinctive communities in the interwar years. Important themes that would preoccupy Americans after World War II, from sexual freedom and consumption to civil rights, are being traced back through these decades with many exciting discoveries.

The World the War Made

Despite its brevity, America's intervention in World War I had profound international and domestic consequences. Ellis Hawley, William Leuchtenburg, Lynn Dumenil, and David Kennedy have painted in broad strokes the "Great War's" impact on the American economy, state, and culture. The war, they all agree, positioned the United States as the world's leading capitalist economy. While the decade opened with a recession, national income increased by more than 40 percent from 1922 to 1929. The war, as scholars note, expanded state authority in multiple ways. Wartime planning boards instituted wage and price controls, consumer rationing, and economic planning. Private authorities, however, quickly regained authority upon conversion to peacetime, leading William Leuchtenburg, in *The Perils of Prosperity*, to conclude that business emerged if anything more dominant. Other scholars, however, such as Ellis Hawley, argue that the trend toward central, managerial planning evident in wartime marched forward inside the nation's giant corporations as well as in state agencies charged with serving the economy. An "organizational revolution," according to Hawley and other scholars of the "organizational synthesis," defined the process of historical change in the late nineteenth and twentieth centuries, stretching across the Progressive period, wartime, and into the 1920s as power shifted to bureaucracies and organized interest groups. Managerial elites pursued progressive goals of "social efficiency" and a more ordered economy, stressing, however, that these goals were to be achieved through voluntary arrangements not public authority. Herbert Hoover's "associationalism" and the growth of trade associations served as important examples of business-government cooperation that belied the laissez-faire rhetoric of the period and linked scientific expertise, efficiency, and planning to bring "order" to capitalism. Beneath the clash of federal agents and radical groups, Ellis Hawley and others saw an arguably more significant economic centralization that began earlier and would only accelerate in later years.

Other scholars, more concerned with political culture than with managerial organization, have emphasized social and political conflict and the drive for conformity that, they argue, shaped these years. The war brought with it a new heavy-handed repression by the state, with antiwar dissenters the prime target. Earlier scholars including John Higham, William Leuchtenburg, and William Preston emphasized the tragic consequences of wartime drives for conformity for personal freedoms and liberties. Recently, Christopher Capozzola has added a new dimension to these discussions. He argued that the war was a turning point when state coercion superseded voluntaristic vigilantism. In a similar vein Jennifer Fronc, looking at New York, argued that the war fostered a new intersection of the state with private antivice citizen organizations. The army worked closely with already established private groups to control prostitution and repress "vice." According to these latest studies, the activism and reach of social control efforts during World War I contributed to expanded state authority. The antiradical drives that continued after the war—the "Red Scare"—were driven, however, not only by exaggerated fears of internal enemies first generated in the frenzy of wartime repression, but also by actual deeds of revolutionary violence by a small faction of the American left. Beverly Gage's evocative description of the September 1920 Wall Street bombing in which thirty-eight people were killed and hundreds injured marked this moment as "America's first age of terror," a bitter new chapter in the long history of violence in America's class relations.

Wartime drives for conformity and the postwar Red Scare consolidated the state's investigative bureaucracy. Importantly, however, heavy-handed repressive crusades also launched campaigns to defend civil and personal liberty. Ernest Freeberg sees the clemency movement to free Eugene Debs from prison, for example, as an anticipation of important strains of modern liberalism. The war was a major episode of nationalism, conformity, and state coercion that in its extremism gave rise to new ideas and new organizations concerned with civil and personal liberties.

Few scholars dispute that the exigencies of the war marginalized the public debates that had animated the Progressive period: questions of equity, concentration of private economic power, and the nature of participation in a democratic polity. Wartime missionary zeal contributed to the achievement of a few signal Progressive goals such as woman suffrage and national Prohibition, but most historians, echoing contemporary social critics such as Randolphe Bourne, have stressed the devastating consequences of the war for the larger goals of progressivism and, all the more so, for dissent and critical debate from figures on the radical left.

What happened, then, to progressivism in the war's wake? Early accounts such as William Leuchtenburg's influential synthesis labeled 1920s progressivism "tired" and emphasized a deep retreat into the private and away from reformist impulse of the prewar years. Other historians, however, challenged this view. Arthur Link, in an influential article written around the same time as *The Perils of Prosperity*, called on scholars to investigate continuities between the earlier Progressive movement and reform in the 1920s. He emphasized the continued strength of progressivism on the state and local level, despite the conservative national Republican administrations. Recent scholars concur: Alan Dawley has charted the "leaner and meaner" progressivism of the 1920s, more self-consciously left-wing and internationalist. "Progressivism," he contends, "trekked through the political desert of the Coolidge years," helping to prepare the ground for New Deal reform. Daniel Rodgers, while pointing to the devastating consequences of the war for "reform brokers," also saw continuity in the transatlantic Progressive vision that stretched from the 1890s through the New Deal. Reform brokers' municipal ownership campaigns in the late nineteenth century, cooperative experiments of the 1920s, and New Deal social security and unemployment programs borrowed heavily from European ideas. Cosmopolitan reformers contributed to a distinctive "anti-exceptionalist" moment, seeking to abandon the parochial blinders of an earlier more provincial America. Transnational borrowings, moreover, moved in both directions. Even though Republican administrations retreated into isolationism and a "return to normalcy," "Wilsonian internationalism" strongly influenced the ideas and aspirations of reformers abroad. In Erez Manela's telling, nationalist reformers from Egypt to India drew on Wilson's discourse of self-determination in building their own anticolonial movements for independence.

Artists and writers in the United States rejected provincial political culture as well. They found inspiration abroad, rejecting what they saw as the moralistic and commercially oriented middle-brow American culture just as such elements of American culture as the blues and jazz found audiences in Europe. Drawing on European modernism, artists and writers forged a "modernist" sensibility. Synthetic cultural treatments of the period, such as Stanley Coben's *Rebellion against Victorianism*, as well as works by Ann

Douglas and Christine Stansell on New York and Brooke Blower's book on American sojourners in Paris, chart this emerging ethos. Stansell focuses on a group of New York "bohemians" and the blossoming of ideas of sexual radicalism and individual freedom in the 1910s. Important developments within the culture of the 1920s (from the popularization of Freud to scientific relativism, secularism, and the "new womanhood") had roots in the prewar years. These cultural currents were welcome antidotes to the values of Anglo-Saxon Protestantism. While this was a liberating development for some segments of the population, it produced tremendous uncertainty for others. For every flapper or urban bohemian enchanted with these changes there were many religious white Protestant men and women worried that the dominance of a set of beliefs undergirding their way of life was under challenge, as George Marsden's work on religious fundamentalism reminds us.

The sense of living in "modern times" in the interwar years was undergirded by changes in the economy, especially the emergence of a new Fordist model of capitalism, and the arrival of mass consumption and mass culture. The availability of new products, new debt structures, and an increasingly sophisticated national advertising industry fueled the new mass-consumption society. Louis Hyman's innovative work charts the new debt practices that shaped the emergence of the modern credit system in the wake of World War I. Earlier, Roland Marchand and Jackson Lears investigated the role of advertisers and advertisements in soothing the adjustment process to a new world of plentiful goods. In other words, advertisers served therapeutic as well as economic functions. These new experts, Marchand emphasizes, geared their ads to a "class market" of affluent consumers. Advertisers were attuned to the fact that most Americans' incomes precluded full participation in the world of mass consumption. While earlier studies assumed widespread prosperity, Marchand's work reminds us of the unevenness of the prosperity of the 1920s. Frank Stricker tells us that despite economic growth and rising per capita income, layoffs and periodic unemployment undermined security for working-class men and women.

We now have a deepening understanding of these working-class men and women thanks to the work of a generation of social historians. While few would disagree with Irving Bernstein that these were "lean years" for organized labor, recent historians have uncovered rich veins of working-class experience in this period of relative labor quiescence by turning to the realm of community, culture, and consumption. George Sanchez's *Becoming Mexican American*, for example, investigates the aspirations and adaptive strategies of Mexican American workers in Los Angeles who labored in service and unskilled industry. Focusing on community and ethnic identity, he contends that Americanization efforts by private organizations and employers met resistance because of Mexican Americans' deep allegiances and ties to Mexico. Mexican identity and culture was continually reinforced through immigration and return migration. Persistent and widespread racial discrimination also bred ambivalence about Americanization.

Becky Nicolaides's *My Blue Heaven* investigates white working-class men and women in Los Angeles. She charts how the social, community, and economic setting of these workers influenced their political beliefs and their economic strategies. Homeownership, for example, was a key strategy to achieve security. Its importance to workers' identities shifted the center of gravity in their lives away from the workplace and contributed to the nationally significant emergence of post–World War II political conservatism.

Lizabeth Cohen has identified the rise of a somewhat different set of political loyalties in her study of Chicago workers. She traces the rise of industrial unionism and the New Deal among the Windy City's ethnic industrial workers to significant changes in the popular attitudes of ordinary workers in the 1920s. Mass culture and mass consumption did not make ethnic workers more "middle class," but it did contribute to shared national, ethnic, and working-class identities. The failure of ethnic institutions and welfare capitalism during the Great Depression in turn opened doors for shifting loyalties to the Democratic Party and industrial unionism. In a somewhat different vein, Dana Frank's study of Seattle workers also points to the political meanings of consumption and its use by workers in that locale as a labor organizing strategy. These investigations suggest that what was once thought to be antithetical to working-class consciousness was in fact a building block for labor organizing and even for a new form of mass unionism, and thus a crucial site of investigation for historians.

Mass consumption and mass culture have been a powerful new frame of reference not only for historians' studies of ethnic white workers, but also as a lens to study flourishing black urban life. In the wake of the migration of African Americans to the North so artfully detailed by James Grossman, African Americans in the 1920s enjoyed new cultural, community, and political mobilization. Davarian Baldwin's *Chicago's New Negroes* investigates the tensions between newcomers and older residents in Chicago and argues that the new mass-consumption marketplace enabled the black masses and intellectuals to forge new ideas and cultural creations. Recent scholars have also enriched our understanding of the Harlem Renaissance. Earlier investigations by Nathan Huggins and David Levering Lewis have now been supplemented by the work of scholars such as A. B. Christa Schwarz, Geneviève Fabre, and Michel Feith, who are struck by its sexual boundary crossing and international dimensions. Claudrena Harold, in addition, has deepened our knowledge of the vast mobilizations of African Americans led by Marcus Garvey. She persuasively argues that urban centers not just in the North but also in New South cities, like New Orleans, were strongholds for Garvey's variant of black nationalism. The civil rights movement, moreover, commonly centered decades later, has also been pushed back into the 1920s. Mark Schneider, Alfred Brophy, and Glenda Gilmore identify the years immediately following World War I as a time of heightened black militancy driven in part by racial violence and virulent discrimination. These historians locate the ancestors of the later civil rights movement in the relatively unsung tales of the interwar period.

If the interwar period brought new visibility and cultural assertiveness to African Americans, it also propelled social, cultural, and political change for women. Nancy Cott, Kimberly Jensen, and Maurine Greenwald, among others, have charted the distinctive meaning of this moment for women and for gender roles more broadly, at work, in politics, and in the realm of ideas. Greenwald and Jensen investigate women within wartime mobilization, in the military and industry, respectively. Jensen homes in on specific groups of women such as nurses and physicians in the military, while Greenwald investigates women workers within three industries. Both point to the limited gains women made during World War I and the persistence of a gendered understanding of citizenship. Greenwald concludes that while World War I accelerated trends already under way, with proportions of women in the labor force increasing and women moving into different types of jobs, most of these jobs were still within the realm of traditional female work. Cott looks more closely at changes in the wake of the war. With the achievement of female suffrage, older ideas of female decorum were superseded by new images of womanhood and new opportunities in education and work. With the vote in hand, women continued to be active in business organizations, women's clubs, and international peace mobilizations. Women in the 1920s, moreover, sought to bring ideas of modernity and scientific competence to their traditional roles of housework and child rearing. More recent work by Nikki Brown, Lisa Materson, and Victoria Wolcott broaden the analysis by focusing on the experiences and activism of African-American women, reminding us of their important contributions to community formation and gender, racial, and electoral politics in the interwar years. And chapters on the interwar years in broader synthetic surveys by Judy Yung and Vicki Ruiz complicate efforts to speak of a "unified" women's experience by pointing to the distinctive histories of Chinese and Mexican women.

The social and cultural histories of distinctive communities suggest that this was a moment of deepening pluralism and cultural experimentation. This interpretation is, however, only partial. At least one scholar has labeled these years the "tribal twenties," pointing to the prevailing nativism, ideas of scientific racism, and immigration restriction. The period was one of tension and paradox. Ever since Robert and Helen Lynd's classic sociological study of Middletown, historians have sought to understand these tensions. The Lynds argued that the rapid modernization dating to the late nineteenth century increased social stratification, weakened community solidarity, and fractured a "value consensus" that had marked earlier years. Later historians have sought to identify the fault lines of this fractured consensus. Richard Hofstadter and William Leuchtenburg, among others, have placed the fault line along a primarily urban-rural divide. Recent scholarship has complicated this view. Lynn Dumenil, for example, identifies the pattern of conflict not so much as an urban-rural divide but as a struggle between white, Protestant, and religious (both urban and rural) men and women and increasingly secular and pluralist sensibilities forged by a new middle class, immigrants, and Catholics. As Kenneth Jackson notes, after all, the Klan flourished in urban as well as in rural areas. And David Kyvig and John Timberlake suggest that the crusade to dry up America drew support not only in purportedly antimodern rural communities, but among many urban, middle-class Progressives as well.

Nativist impulses, so well charted by John Higham's classic study *Strangers in the Land*, contributed to the push for immigration restriction and culminated in the Johnson-Reed Act of 1924. Mae Ngai and Matthew Jacobson have added to our understanding of the significance of this important legislation. Jacobson sees it as an important turning point on the path to a more unified and consolidated vision of the "white race" that took hold between the 1920s and 1940s. This new idea of a consolidated "whiteness" superseded an earlier emphasis on a hierarchy of distinctive white European races. Cultural products (movies such as *The Jazz Singer*) as well as legislation, according to Jacobson, contributed to "whitening" "probationary" white groups such as Jews and Eastern and Southern Europeans.

Mai Ngai reinterprets Johnson-Reed from a different angle. In *Impossible Subjects*, she investigates new understandings of race and citizenship encoded in the national quota system. She agrees with Jacobson that the law both affirmed a hierarchy among Europeans and unified them as one "white" race, marginalizing immigrants from outside Europe. But Ngai emphasizes something else about this moment: The law not only marked the culmination of a long history of Asian exclusion by barring all East and South Asians from immigration or becoming citizens, but also created a new, racialized category of "illegal aliens." Both these studies point to the heightened racial thinking of this era. Gary Gerstle also characterized this as a period when "racial nationalism" dominated over the strands of "civic nationalism" in a sweeping study of competing ideas of American nationhood in the twentieth century.

No organization contributed to the visibility of ideas of racial nationalism during these years more than the Ku Klux Klan. Generations of historians have sought to explain the second Klan's vast influence, with a membership of between three and five million at its peak. Earlier scholars emphasized the Klan's right-wing extremism and portrayed its adherents as marginal men and women. More recent scholarship has provided a starkly different portrait. Leonard Moore, Kathleen Blee, and Nancy MacLean, among others, have emphasized the Klan's appeal to a broad population of white, Protestant men and women throughout the Midwest, West and South. Leonard Moore's *Citizen Klansman* provides a revealing investigation of the Klan's success in the stronghold state of Indiana, where it took the form of a civic association, not terribly unlike other fraternal orders such as the Elks or the Odd Fellows. Kathleen Blee, also looking at Indiana, concurs in her study of the women of the Ku Klux Klan. White Protestant women viewed the women's Klan as a kind of respectable "social club," albeit one whose purpose was to uphold 100 percent Americans against Catholics, African Americans, and immigrants. Klan adherents' innocuous self-definitions, however, belied the real damage done by their boycotts and whispering campaigns against Catholic and Jewish businesses, as well as Protestants deemed guilty of "illicit" behavior. In contrast to Indiana's relatively peaceful Klan, Nancy MacLean finds the Klan in Atlanta just as "normal" but much more violent. Violence and terror, she argues, were central to the Klan's brand of "reactionary populism." The southern order engaged in violence to a greater degree because local power structures made it possible. By looking at the Klan at the grass roots, these historians have provided a nuanced portrait of who joined the organization in different regions of the country and why. We still need, however, a better understanding of the reasons for the Klan's meteoric rise and fall. If the Klan drew so heavily from broadly shared white Protestant ideas of white supremacy, why was it so short-lived and so vulnerable to attacks by other social groups?

One of the interesting findings of recent scholarship on the Klan is the intersection between militant temperance sentiments and the hooded order. Blee contends that temperance activism was one route into the Klan, and Moore agrees that crusades to dry up local new towns were important to Klan recruitment efforts. The Athens Klan that MacLean charts also got its start in a campaign to dry up the city. By organizing drives to "clean up" communities and put bootleggers out of business, the Klan became a popular means of acting on militant temperance sentiments.

Prohibition not only contributed to shaping Klan drives for "law and order," but was, indeed, the most important issue driving public debate during these years. Ratified in January 1919, the Eighteenth Amendment, which outlawed the sale, manufacture, transportation, import, and export of intoxicating beverages, went into effect in January 1920 and was rescinded fourteen years later. The United States' "dry" experiment, with its fascinating stories of bootleggers, moonshine, and bathtub gin, continues to appeal to popular audiences, demonstrated most recently by Ken Burns's scheduled television documentary and the accompanying narrative history by journalist Dan Okrent. Yet, while we have a vast body of scholarly work on the close to one hundred year long temperance movement, there are fewer works of scholarship on national Prohibition itself. This is unfortunate, because as Robert Post in an important article on the Taft Supreme Court reminds us, this social experiment wrought the single greatest expansion of federal authority since Reconstruction. It caused a major crisis in the theory and practices of American federalism. Justices on the Court were forced to revise their judicial philosophies on the assumption that the administrative state was an unalterable reality. Still, recent work has debunked the outdated psychological and clinical portrait by Andrew Sinclair of Prohibition as a rural virus. Scholars have charted the movement's ties to urban progressive reformers. Michael Lerner's case study of the dry years in New York, for example, arguably one of the the wettest cities of the nation, reveals a far more complex struggle within urban polities. He points to the support for Prohibition among many middle-class reformers and emphasizes the opposition of working-class ethnic New Yorkers, who were the special targets of urban reform and law enforcement efforts to stop the flow of bootleg liquor. George Chauncey, Chad Heap, and Kevin Mumford have charted how Prohibition contributed to the flourishing of "illicit" urban subcultures, such as gay life and new interracial zones of socializing that challenged the agenda of "moral purity" forces. David Burner and Kristi Andersen have traced the divisions over Prohibition within the Democratic Party. Burner argues that prohibition contributed to the split between the Democratic Party's rural, dry, and Protestant wing and its urban Catholic "wet" wing. The party's two wings fought bloody battles over nativism, the Klan, and Prohibition at its 1924 convention. And by 1928, the party's urban wet wing demonstrated its newfound strength when Al Smith won the presidential nomination.

Kristi Andersen identifies this moment as crucial to the increased allegiance of immigrant ethnic voters to the Democratic Party after 1928, an alignment that would solidify during the New Deal. Hoover trumped Smith in a landslide vote with strong support among the "dry forces" (including luminous Progressive leaders such as Jane Addams). But the passage of the Jones Act in 1929, which made first offenses a felony, galvanized opposition to prohibition. David Kyvig and Kenneth Rose have charted deepening opposition to the amendment, investigating the critical role of an influential group of men and women in the Association Against the Prohibition Amendment (AAPA) and the Women's Organization for National Prohibition Reform. Opposition, however, extended well beyond the elite ranks of the AAPA. My own forthcoming work traces these wider currents of opposition and the broad implications of how Prohibition was enforced in distinct regions and among different social classes. I argue that the amendment was central to reshaping politics and political culture in these years. While many historians, moreover, have argued that Prohibition contributed to deepening antistatist sensibilities and a distrust of state power, I argue that it did at least as much to encourage the opposite: Ironically, a decade of debate over the merits of Prohibition in public and private discourse helped to legitimize state regulation. The debate challenged not so much the government's right to regulate as what the parameters of regulation should be.

The economic crisis of the Great Depression sealed the fate of this radical experiment, already weakened by a decade of federal failure to enforce the law. Policy makers grew increasingly receptive to wet arguments that legalizing the liquor industry would generate employment and tax revenue. One of Roosevelt's first acts in office was to sign the Beer and Wine Revenue Act, anticipating the repeal of national Prohibition and effectively ending the social experiment. The experience of national Prohibition had highlighted for a broad segment of the public the real danger posed to personal liberty by the linkage of "morality" and politics. During the New Deal, state regulation focused on economic life, steering clear of the regulation of public "moral" behavior that had convulsed the legal and political system during the 1920s.

The Great Depression

The Great Depression, according to Eric Hobsbawm, was "the largest global earthquake ever to be measured on the economic historians' Richter scale." The United States was its epicenter. Nobody knew if or when the capitalist economy would recover. The popular notion that the stock market crash in and of itself caused the Great Depression has been widely discredited by economic historians. Yet scholars vary widely in their emphasis on other causal factors. Keynsian explanations, favored by those like Arthur Schlesinger and John Kenneth Galbraith, place blame on the imbalances in the U.S. domestic economy in the 1920s. The deep agricultural depression during the decade contributed to a vast imbalance between the rural and industrial economies. Not only was prosperity uneven, but rising income inequality also meant that mass demand could not keep pace with rising productivity. By the decade's end, businesses had amassed a staggering surplus of unsold inventory. That so many consumer goods were purchased on installment plans, moreover, meant that business was balanced on a shaky foundation of consumer debt. Easy credit in housing and other sectors had also contributed to a speculative bubble. The credit-fueled speculative frenzy came to a crashing halt with the stock market's fall. In the wake of the crash in October 1929, undercapitalized banks struggled to keep afloat. The causes of the Great Depression for Keynsians were thus rooted in underconsumption, income inequality, and insufficient regulation of the free market, especially the banking sector. It was a crisis, these historians argue, of "the old order" of laissez-faire capitalism.

Other economists and historians have offered different perspectives. While not ignoring national economic problems, they emphasize the imbalances in the international economy to explain the worldwide scope and depth of the crisis. The punitive reparations policies after World War I, according to Charles Kindelsberger, Eric Hobsbawm, and David Kennedy, among others, made a stable world economy impossible. Debt repayment had only taken place with massive American loans during the 1920s. When American lending declined between 1927 and 1933, international lending dropped by 90 percent, and the postwar order in Europe effectively collapsed. The United States, while undeniably the powerhouse for world capitalism, failed to act as a global stabilizer in its role as the leading creditor nation. Each state, instead, attempted to protect its economy from outside threats. The Great Depression in America, according to this more global view, was both a cause and a consequence of a larger international crisis.

While scholars have pointed to a multiplicity of causal factors in the national and international economy to explain the Great Depression, some influential economists have contributed narrower, technical explanations.

Monetarists Anna Schwartz and Milton Friedman, and Peter Temin, for example, blame the feckless policies of the Federal Reserve that supplied loose credit and then unwisely restricted the money supply at a moment of contraction. This decision, in turn, exacerbated a deflationary spiral and contributed to the collapse of the economy. The unprecedented scope of the crisis was due to inept policy elites, whose actions distorted the cyclical workings of the free market and unwittingly made the Depression "great." While the monetarist theory is appealingly simple, most scholars continue to argue that broader domestic and international imbalances of the economy that arose in the wake of World War I were the essential ingredients of the global worldwide crisis.

To these explanations, Michael Bernstein's *The Great Depression: Delayed Recovery and Economic Change* has contributed another layer of interpretation by asking why recovery efforts came to naught until World War II. What made the Great Depression great, Bernstein argues was a "secular shift" in the United States economy that coincided with a cyclical downturn. The nation's economic growth was increasingly driven by industries in their infancy—from petrochemicals and processed food to plastics and glass. These dynamic sectors, just taking off at a moment of cyclical downturn, were too small and vulnerable to drive a robust recovery. New Deal policies exacerbated this problem because they understandably but unwisely focused on reviving the older engines of industrial growth. As a result, only the unprecedented production demands of World War II inspired a full economic recovery. While it failed to end the Depression, however, the New Deal did continue and consolidate the long-term emergence of the federal government as a key actor in the nation's social and economic life.

The New Deal

The New Deal is still seen as a landmark in the emergence of the modern political economy of the United States. It cemented federal responsibility for economic regulation, provided a federal safety net for citizens, and forged public policies that significantly enhanced the rights of ordinary workers. Not surprisingly, historians (as well as sociologists and political scientists) ever since have sought to understand the origins, character, and social forces behind this burst of policy innovation. The literature is far too vast to be summarized here. Instead, this chapter seeks to sketch the broadest analytical contours of historical interpretation.

Presidential syntheses dominated early accounts of the New Deal with Franklin D. Roosevelt towering front and center in grand synthetic narratives by Arthur Schlesinger, Frank Freidel, William Leuchtenburg, and others. These scholars wrote with the battles over New Deal reform fresh in mind, and from a largely sympathetic liberal perspective, though many had hoped for more far-reaching reform. Roosevelt's confident charismatic personality, his experimentalism, liberal adaptability, and leadership skills, according to these historians, were at the heart of the successful passage of many policy initiatives. Out of the Depression crisis, Roosevelt navigated treacherous political waters with aplomb, distanced himself from his patrician roots, championed the "people" as against the "interests," and in the process consolidated a new Democratic coalition. While these scholars acknowledged Roosevelt's lack of a consistently modern liberal vision (demonstrated by his concern with balanced budgets), they emphasized the deep roots of his progressive reform ethos, apparent during his term as governor of New York, and his call for a more expansive and active administrative state that strongly contrasted with the conservatism of his predecessor, Herbert Hoover. With Franklin D. Roosevelt at the helm, the New Deal reformed capitalism in a more equitable vein, leaving behind the laissez-faire nostrums of the Republican "old order." This interpretative line continues to find voice in the venerable popular presidential biographies churned out for a general audience, most recently H. W. Brands's provocatively titled *Traitor to His Class: The Privileged Life and Radical Presidency of Franklin Delano Roosevelt.*

Another influential interpretation of the New Deal stresses the antecedents of its policies in developments already under way in the "period of prosperity." Herbert Hoover looms large in these revisionist accounts. Ellis Hawley, Joan Hoff Wilson, and most recently David Kennedy all emphasize Hoover's "progressive" philosophy of government. In contrast to earlier laissez-faire Republicans, Hoover sought to utilize the state to provide knowledge and expertise to business to drive economic growth. While he refused to embrace a public authority to regulate business directly, he hoped to manage social change through informed, albeit limited, state activism as a sponsor for industrial associations. He championed the use of social scientific expertise, knowledge, and information in order to sustain a sound economy. Hoover drew from a broad font of progressive ideas but remained firm in his commitment to what he called "American Individualism." After the stock market crash, he sought to utilize the existing instruments of the state in cooperation with business to alleviate the crisis. Indeed, these scholars point out, Franklin D. Roosevelt's legislative efforts of the first one hundred days drew on many ideas first formulated by the Hoover administration.

Other scholars have deemphasized Hoover in favor of broader private organizational strategies in the post–World War I period that similarly informed New Deal policies. Colin Gordon, for example, argues that the New Deal was the culmination of strategies of economic organization and regulation promoted by capitalists with a thirst for order first tasted under the wartime production regime. These capitalist reformers pursued a shaky framework of private regulation during the 1920s: They organized in trade associations and sought to manage labor relations through welfare capitalist schemes and a less adversarial "new unionism." These private efforts foundered, however, due to shortsightedness, disorganization, and competition. The variety of experiments undertaken in the 1920s, including a "pastiche of labor-management accords," were given institutional and legal substance during the New Deal. In a somewhat different vein, Lizabeth Cohen also points to the debt the New Deal (and successful efforts to organize industrial workers in the 1930s) owed to shifts in cultural attitudes among workers under way since the 1920s. Workplace entitlements like welfare capitalism, mass consumption, and mass culture altered workers' expectations and experiences. When the Great Depression brought ethnic institutions and welfare capitalist schemes to their knees, workers turned their allegiances to the Democratic Party and the new industrial unions.

If the New Deal owed a debt to developments already under way in the 1920s, that raises the question of whether New Deal reform was radical or conservative. Was there, moreover, any ideological vision behind New Deal policy? And who among all these actors old and fresh "made the New Deal"? Such questions have animated investigations of the New Deal for several decades. Liberal champions, like Arthur Schlesinger, originally cast the New Deal as a struggle of "the people against the interests" and emphasized the social revolution that the New Deal accomplished. Later historians, still sympathetic to the New Deal project, felt compelled to take a more nuanced view. Anthony Badger and William Leuchtenburg, for example, highlight the many somewhat contradictory programs that constituted the New Deal's legislative response to relief, reform, and recovery. Leuchtenburg emphasizes the pluralism at the New Deal's heart: its ideological core was its willingness to experiment. More recently, David Kennedy has found a unifying principle for New Dealers that he labels "security." By providing protection to business groups as well as ordinary Americans against the vagaries of free-market capitalism, the New Deal sought to reduce risk and provide a minimal safety net by making the state the lender, spender, and employer of last resort. Kennedy emphasizes, however, that the New Deal was built along distinctly American lines, falling far short of a European-style welfare state, thereby leaving many citizens at the mercy of the market.

Given this marked contrast with European states, many scholars have explored why the New Deal took the shape it did, with programs that were often flawed and cobbled together. Even the New Deal's signature triumph, Social Security, as Mark Leff has reminded us, was financed, after all, with regressive payroll taxes and excluded domestic and agricultural workers from benefits, a signature departure from other models of universal insurance. In the late 1960s, New Left scholars cast an even more critical eye toward the New Deal, pointing to its failure to resolve issues of poverty and discrimination. They argued that the New Deal was, in fact, conservative in its achievements. According to Barton Bernstein, Howard Zinn, and others, Franklin D. Roosevelt succeeded in rescuing capitalism and co-opting demands for more radical social change from below. Writing at a time when the New Left was struggling to break the hold of a seemingly hegemonic corporate liberal order, these authors held the New Deal responsible for its creation.

Faced with the decline of even moderate liberalism in the 1970s and 1980s, another group of scholars has sought to understand the collapse of what they see as a relatively stable "New Deal order" by investigating the distinctive social forces that made the New Deal possible. They emphasize the often contradictory elements that joined to create the New Deal "breakthrough." Steve Fraser and Thomas Ferguson argue that the New Deal forged a new "historic bloc" of organized labor, the state, and a powerful segment of capital. This coalition, which found its home in the Democratic Party, shaped and constrained the more radical impulses of reformers. For Ferguson, an alliance of multinational and capital-intensive industries along with organized labor interests enabled the later New Deal. Steve Fraser emphasizes, in contrast, the importance of progressive capitalists like Peter Filene and union leaders like Sidney Hillman who promoted mass consumption and favored a new alliance between business, labor, and the state to promote a high standard of living and economic growth. Although different in their emphases, both Fraser and Ferguson agree on the centrality of managerial elites in shaping the New Deal. Its success as a political movement was best explained not as a radical flowering of ideas from below but as a top-down achievement orchestrated from above. Social contradictions at the New Deal's heart, these scholars emphasize, explain both the limits of the New Deal's achievements and its later fragmentation.

Other political scientists, sociologists, and historians, however, have explained the limits of the New Deal by emphasizing the constraining political environment of the 1930s. Barry Karl has pointed to the deep traditions of antistatism, a federal system with a sometimes crippling separation of powers, and powerful brakes on major policy shifts and the pursuit of a coordinated national program. James Patterson has emphasized the limiting effect of the conservative southern Democrats and their strong ideological opposition to an overt system of government welfare. While central to the Roosevelt coalition, southern Democrats chafed against the urban-liberal tilt within the party and fought energetically with the proponents of more radical reform Their opposition, according to Patterson, played a key role in shaping the clumsy, partial welfare system that emerged. Charles Trout, Bruce Stave, and others have also noted the extent to which the New Deal strengthened urban political machines by giving them control of new federal programs rather than centralizing power in Washington.

All these constraints speak to the importance of the nature of American governmental and political institutions in shaping the New Deal's limited accomplishments. Indeed, a group of sociologists and political scientists have argued that the character of the American state itself is critical to understanding the failings of the New Deal. Kenneth Finegold, Theda Skocpol, and Margaret Weir, among others, have sought to "bring the state back in" to understand these limits. Prior administrative state capacity as well as political-constitutional forms such as winner-take-all elections are both critical factors that influenced the shape of the New Deal. Looking at the National Recovery Administration, for example, Skocpol argues that the absence of prior sufficient state capacity contributed to the agency's poor enforcement record. The federal bureaucracy was simply too small and inexperienced to successfully undertake large-scale reform of this scope. In the absence of governmental institutions capable of overseeing an industrial economy, the control of code boards defaulted to the very businessmen they were created to regulate.

State-centered explanations emphasize the structural and institutional environment in which reformers acted. Some historians have, however, sought to study more closely the ideas embraced by reformers themselves. While acknowledging that external constraints shaped reformers' ideas about political economy, Alan Brinkley, for example, focuses on a group of academics and policy makers who might be considered the architects of the New Deal. In so doing, he charts an important evolution within liberalism itself. In the late New Deal and the opening years of World War II, policy makers jettisoned earlier ambitious goals of economic planning and institutional regulation in favor of the limited goals of creating a healthy economic environment for capitalist institutions to operate. Once concerned with addressing the concentration of private economic power, rooted in antimonopoly thought, this group of chastened liberals instead promoted consumption and fiscal policy to promote broad economic growth. Consumption, not investment, they now argued, drove modern industrial economies. Therefore, public spending and the resulting increased mass purchasing power were the means to stimulate the economy. The outbreak of war in Europe and the goal of ensuring war production completed the narrowing of liberal ambition. By the end of the war, a new liberal consensus had emerged centered on economic growth, mass consumption, and individual rights.

Brinkley has since been joined by other scholars investigating the centrality of ideas about consumption to New Deal reformers. "Consumer politics," Meg Jacobs argues, was the common ground for the construction of new organizations, new coalitions, and ultimately new state institutions. The Wagner Act was a means to guarantee the right to organize and bargain collectively, but it won support because it empowered labor to increase its purchasing power. Landon Storrs investigates the domestic champions of consumer purchasing power, which she located in women activists and such organizations as the National Consumer's League, which sought to use consumption as a strategy to improve labor standards.

The problem of underconsumption, historians have told us, shaped New Dealers' understanding of the causes of the Great Depression. Nowhere, arguably, was this problem graver than in the agricultural sector. Programs such as the Agricultural Adjustment Act, regional planning experiments like the Tennessee Valley Authority, and other power distribution projects sought to rectify the imbalance between rural and urban areas and increase farm purchasing power. While a number of studies have investigated the rural programs of the New Deal, much more attention has gone toward exploring efforts to empower workers and secure recovery in the industrial sector. In a groundbreaking study, Sarah Phillips interrogates the web of New Deal environmental policies and argues that conservation was at the heart of New Dealers' rising liberalism. Rural policy, whether through the government financed construction of hydroelectric dams, irrigation, the closing of the public domain, purchase of marginal farmland, technical assistance to end soil erosion, or rural electrification, added to earlier conservationist ideas a new set of concerns about social justice and redistribution. Her narrative charts the limits of this vision, the obstacles it encountered, and its demise during World War II when it conflicted with the demands of industrial output. Yet New Deal environmental policy had lasting legacies. It shaped the evolution of the modern state, planted the seeds for the emergent Sun Belt, and laid the roots for the modern environmental movement (according to Neil Maher's recent work).

Another recent study has emphasized a different New Deal policy area that had a long-range impact on economic development: public works. High levels of spending and unprecedented construction activity, Jason Smith argues, fueled a "public works revolution"—a transformation that laid the foundations of future prosperity, altered the nation's political landscape, and legitimized the Keynesian management of the economy, both intellectually and physically. The state, Smith suggests, used public works—schools, courthouses, post offices, roads, and other improvements—to significantly spur economic development. Public works funding, he emphasizes, also played a key role in building and solidifying the Democratic Party at federal, state, and local levels of government. It was effective both economically and politically.

To the continuing debate seeking to explain the New Deal's achievements and its limits, a generation of scholars attuned to questions of gender has added a new layer of interpretation. Alice Kessler-Harris, Gwendolyn Mink, Suzanne Mettler, and Linda Gordon have pointed out how much of the discourse of social provision was gendered. A "gendered imagination," in Kessler-Harris's words, shaped social policies such as social security and unemployment insurance. The two-tiered welfare state that emerged treated men and women unequally: White men benefited from the national standardized social entitlement programs such as old age insurance on the basis of economic citizenship, but supplemental welfare programs intended for mothers and children were administered by the states, which set their own eligibility requirements. That these programs did so was due not only to men's gendered visions, but also to the aspirations of women reformers themselves, as Linda Gordon emphasized. The New Deal, then, may not have done a good deal to advance feminist goals, but it did support an active female network in government agencies, as Gordon, Kristin Downey, and Susan Ware have reminded us. Many of these activists rooted in female reform networks advocated for special protections for women, rather than more abstract equal rights.

If a recent generation of scholars has focused attention on the gendered aspects of New Deal social policy, another group of scholars has called our attention to its racial aspects. Mary Poole and Ira Katznelson, for example, have investigated the way racism and segregation influenced legislation. To accommodate southern Democrats in Congress, federal policies and programs were designed to protect white interests and advantages. Government interventions, such as social security and minimum wages, excluded agricultural and domestic workers, central occupations for African Americans. While ostensibly color-blind, New Deal legislation (and its decentralized administration that enabled regional and local discrimination) produced a massive preferential resource distribution to whites. Building on the influential work of Kenneth Jackson and Tom Sugrue, which charts the intersection between federal New Deal policy and postwar residential segregation, David Roediger has recently argued that New Deal housing policy helped to forge an "exclusion-based white nationalism." If the New Deal institutionalized new patterns of discrimination and inequality, however, it also opened up spaces for African Americans in their struggle for equal rights. Harvard Sitkoff, indeed, has argued that it was during the New Deal that civil rights emerged as a national issue, an account supported by a host of subsequent studies on African Americans during the Depression and New Deal. Recent scholarship pointed out that where the 1930s did sow new spaces for black political struggle, it also witnessed a fragmentation of racial solidarity in the black community. Karen Ferguson's investigation of the black elite response to the New Deal argues that many black reformers were willing to trade representation in New Deal program bureaucracies for the right to challenge the more discriminatory aspects of many of the programs.

In contrast, Patricia Sullivan, Robin Kelly, and Glenda Gilmore, among others, paid more attention to those within the African-American community who challenged the paradigms of southern discrimination and worked to link racial and economic justice. The Depression crisis created political space for new movements as diverse as the Communist Party and the Southern Conference for Human Welfare. African Americans used these new institutional spaces, however fragile, to challenge the southern power structure. These studies emphasize the agency of African Americans in mobilizing for social change and the realities of repression and obstacles they faced.

Given the centrality of national politics to so many developments in the 1930s, it should not surprise us that so many of the studies discussed here focus on New Deal policy. During these "turbulent years," however, ordinary workers managed a partial reconfiguration of power relations with an upsurge of labor militancy. A generation of historians has investigated their dynamic struggles at the grassroots and national levels. Nelson Lichtenstein and Robert Zieger, among others, emphasize the remarkable accomplishments that were made in the 1930s with the rise of industrial unionism (even if later structural developments and mistakes contributed to labor's increased impotence). Others, including Elizabeth Faue and Staughton Lynd, see the early 1930s as a "heroic spring" of organized labor and lament the rise of bureaucratic organization in the later part of the decade. National structures, Faue emphasizes, marginalized women who had been central to an earlier community-based model of organizing. Lynd argues that "conservative" national leaders undercut a more radical, democratic unionism. These scholars locate labor's much later demise in its failure to heed this "community-based vision" of the 1930s. They may, however, romanticize worker militancy, for, as Robert Zieger and Lizabeth Cohen remind us, pragmatic gains and, in Cohen's words, a vision of a "moral capitalism" appealed to the bulk of ordinary rank-and-file industrial workers over more radical ideologies.

All scholars acknowledge the Communist Party's important role in the labor upsurge of the 1930s. While Communists were small in number, they were influential as organizers. As Lizabeth Cohen, Robin Kelly, Ronald Schatz, Mary Triece, and Robert Zieger, among others, have argued, their presence contributed to progressive racial and gender egalitarianism. At the same time, Zieger reminds us that the party's fealty to Moscow damaged the Popular Front, and, as Eric Arnesen contends, left a legacy of betrayal for African Americans. Robin Kelly seeks to sidestep the question of "Moscow machinations" in his history of the Alabama party. African-American members in Alabama forged a unique working-class radicalism that drew on the culture of the black masses and rural traditions of resistance. Glenda Gilmore's grand narrative on the radical roots of civil rights similarly investigates the Communist Party as a critical force in an international freedom struggle that linked both race and class. Black radicals with an internationalist vision challenged white supremacy and economic injustice well before *Brown v. Board of Education.*

To these discussions of 1930s radicalism, Michael Denning's magisterial work on the Popular Front reminds us that the Communist Party was but one agent in a broad social movement. The "Age of the CIO" created a left-wing alliance that flourished within a much larger bloc of the New Deal coalition. The organized left linked blue-collar workers to a new class of mass-culture workers whose aims were cultural as well as economic. The resulting "laboring of American culture," Denning persuasively argues, outlived the demise of the Popular Front as a political movement and indelibly shaped American culture in the postwar years.

Many scholars have charted the flourishing radicalism of the period, but others, such as Alan Brinkley, remind us that dissidence took on more populist dimensions among lower-middle-class men and women attracted to demagogues such as Huey Long and Father Coughlin. Social historians, such as James Gregory, additionally, have enriched our understanding of the experiences of rural migrants in distinct settings from Oklahoma to California. Still others, including Joel Carpenter and Susan Currell have investigated shifts in popular culture and religion. Most recently, Gabrielle Esperdy, Linda Gordon, and Colleen McDannell have contributed to a deeper understanding of the people and innovative movements in art, architecture, and photography during the Depression years. Even here, the significance of New Deal public policy innovations in shaping cultural mobilizations is in full evidence. For scholars who are interested in the intersection between society, politics, culture, and class, the interwar period offers rich avenues for further research.

This partial and selective investigation of a vast body of scholarship highlights the large cast of characters central to any full historical understanding of the United States during the interwar period. While historians have not lost sight of the significance of institutions, national politics, and policy makers as central sites of historical investigation (particularly for the New Deal period), we have come to better appreciate the importance of such diverse groups as consumers, radicals, ordinary workers, female reformers, and African Americans, among many others, in the making of the modern United States during its years of "tragedy and triumph."

BIBLIOGRAPHY

Allen, Frederick Lewis. *Only Yesterday: An Informal History of the Nineteen Twenties*. New York: Harper, 1931.

Andersen, Kristi. *The Creation of a Democratic Majority, 1928–1936*. Chicago: University of Chicago Press, 1979.

Arnesen, Eric. "No 'Graver Danger': Black Anticommunism, the Communist Party, and the Race Question." *Labor: Studies in Working-Class History of the Americas* (Winter 2006).

Badger, Anthony J. *FDR: The First Hundred Days*. New York: Hill and Wang, 2008.

———. *The New Deal: The Depression Years, 1933–40*. New York: Hill and Wang, 1989.

Baldwin, Davarian. *Chicago's New Negroes: Modernity, the Great Migration and Black Urban Life*. Chapel Hill: University of North Carolina Press, 2007.

Bernstein, Barton J. "The New Deal: The Conservative Achievements of Liberal Reform." In Barton J. Bernstein, ed., *Towards a New Past: Dissenting Essays in American History*, 163–288. New York: Pantheon, 1968.

Bernstein, Irving. *The Lean Years: A History of the American Worker, 1920–1933*. Boston: Houghton Mifflin, 1960.

———. *Turbulent Years: A History of the American Worker, 1933–1941*. Boston: Houghton Mifflin, 1969.

Bernstein, Michael. *The Great Depression: Delayed Recovery and Economic Change in America, 1929–1939*. New York: Cambridge University Press, 1989.

Blee, Kathleen M. *Women of the Klan: Racism and Gender in the 1920s*. Berkeley: University of California Press, 1991.

Blower, Brooke. *Becoming Americans in Paris: Transatlantic Politics and Culture between the World Wars*. New York: Oxford University Press, 2010.

Brands., H. W. *Traitor to His Class: The Privileged Life and Radical Presidency of Franklin Delano Roosevelt*. New York: Doubleday, 2008.

Brinkley, Alan. *The End of Reform: New Deal Liberalism in Recession and War*. New York: Knopf, 1995.

———. *Voices of Protest: Huey Long, Father Coughlin and the Great Depression.* New York: Knopf, 1982.

Brophy, Alfred. *Reconstructing the Dreamland: The Tulsa Riot of 1921: Race, Reparations, and Reconciliation.* New York: Oxford University Press, 2002.

Chauncey, George. *Gay New York: Gender, Urban Culture, and the Making of the Gay Male World, 1890–1940.* New York: Basic Books, 1994.

Brown, Nikki. *Private Politics and Public Voices: Black Women's Activism from World War I to the New Deal.* Bloomington: Indiana University Press, 2006.

Burner, David. *Herbert Hoover: A Public Life.* New York: Knopf, 1979.

———. *The Politics of Provincialism: The Democratic Party in Transition, 1918–1932.* New York: Knopf, 1967.

Capozzola, Christopher. *Uncle Sam Wants You: World War I and the Making of the Modern American Citizen.* New York: Oxford University Press, 2008.

Carpenter, Joel. *Revive Us Again: The Reawakening of American Fundamentalism.* New York: Oxford University Press, 1997.

Coben, Stanley. *Rebellion Against Victorianism: The Impetus for Cultural Change in the 1920s.* New York: Oxford University Press, 1991.

Cohen, Lizabeth. *Making a New Deal: Industrial Workers in Chicago, 1919–1939.* New York: Cambridge University Press, 1990.

Cott, Nancy. *The Grounding of Modern Feminism.* New Haven, CT: Yale University Press, 1987.

Currell, Susan. *The March of Spare Time: The Problem and Promise of Leisure in the Great Depression.* Philadelphia: University of Pennsylvania Press, 2005.

Cushman, Barry. *Rethinking the New Deal Court: The Structure of a Constitutional Revolution.* New York: Oxford University Press, 1998.

Dawley, Alan. *Changing the World: American Progressives in War and Revolution.* Princeton, NJ: Princeton University Press, 2003.

Denning, Michael. *The Cultural Front: The Laboring of American Culture.* New York: Verso, 1997.

Downey, Kirstin. *The Woman behind the New Deal: The Life of Frances Perkins, FDR's Secretary of Labor and His Moral Conscience.* New York: Nan A. Talese/Doubleday, 2009.

Douglas, Ann. *Terrible Honesty: Mongrel Manhattan in the 1920s.* New York: Farrar, Straus and Giroux, 1995.

Dumenil, Lynn. *The Modern Temper: American Culture and Society in the 1920s.* New York: Hill and Wang, 1995.

Esperdy, Gabrielle. *Modernizing Main Street: Architecture and Consumer Culture in the New Deal.* Chicago: University of Chicago Press, 2008.

Fabre, Geneviève, and Michel Feith, eds. *Temples for Tomorrow: Looking Back at the Harlem Renaissance.* Bloomington: Indiana University Press, 2001.

Fass, Paula. *The Damned and the Beautiful: American Youth in the 1920s.* New York: Oxford University, Press, 1977.

Faue, Elizabeth. *Community of Suffering and Struggle: Women, Men, and the Labor Movement in Minneapolis, 1915–1945.* Chapel Hill: University of North Carolina Press, 1991.

Ferguson, Karen. *Black Politics in New Deal Atlanta.* Chapel Hill: University of North Carolina Press, 2002.

Finegold, Kenneth, and Theda Skocpol. *State and Party in America's New Deal.* Madison: University of Wisconsin Press, 1995.

Frank, Dana. *Purchasing Power: Consumer Organizing, Gender, and the Seattle Labor Movement, 1919–1929.* New York: Cambridge University Press, 1994.

Fraser, Steve. *Labor Will Rule: Sidney Hillman and the Rise of American Labor.* New York: Free Press, 1991.

Fraser, Steve, and Gary Gerstle, eds. *The Rise and Fall of the New Deal Order, 1930–1980.* Princeton, NJ: Princeton University Press, 1989.

Freeberg, Ernest. *Democracy's Prisoner: Eugene V. Debs, the Great War, and the Right to Dissent.* Cambridge, MA: Harvard University Press, 2008.

Freidel, Frank. *Franklin D. Roosevelt*, vols. 1–4. Boston: Little, Brown, 1952, 1954, 1956, 1973.

———. *Franklin D. Roosevelt: A Rendezvous with Destiny.* Boston: Little, Brown, 1990.

Friedman, Milton, Anna Jacobson Schwartz, and the National Bureau of Economic Research. *The Great Contraction.* Princeton, NJ: Princeton University Press, 1965.

Fronc, Jennifer. *New York Undercover: Private Surveillance in the Progressive Era.* Chicago: University of Chicago Press, 2009.

Gage, Beverly. *The Day Wall Street Exploded: A Story of America in Its First Age of Terror.* New York: Oxford University Press, 2009.

Galbraith, John Kenneth. *The Great Crash, 1929.* Boston: Houghton Mifflin, 1955.

Gerstle, Gary. *American Crucible: Race and Nation in the Twentieth Century.* Princeton, NJ: Princeton University Press, 2001.

Gilmore, Glenda. *Defying Dixie: The Radical Roots of Civil Rights, 1919–1950.* New York: W. W. Norton, 2008.

Gordon, Colin. *New Deals: Business, Labor, and Politics in America, 1920–1935.* New York: Cambridge University Press, 1994.

Gordon, Linda. *Dorothea Lange: A Life beyond Limits.* London: W. W. Norton, 2010.

———. *Pitied but Not Entitled: Single Mothers and the History of Welfare, 1890–1935.* New York: Free Press, 1994.

Grant, Colin. *Negro with a Hat: The Rise and Fall of Marcus Garvey.* New York: Oxford University Press, 2008.

Greenberg, Cheryl Lynn. *"Or Does It Explode?": Black Harlem in the Great Depression.* New York: Oxford University Press, 1991.

Greenwald, Maurine. *Women, War, and Work: The Impact of World War I on Women Workers in the United States.* Westport, CT: Greenwood, 1980.

Gregory, James. *American Exodus: The Dust Bowl Migration and Okie Culture in California.* New York: Oxford University Press, 1989.

Grossman, James. *Land of Hope: Chicago, Black Southerners, and the Great Migration.* Chicago: University of Chicago Press, 1989.

Harold, Claudrena N. *The Rise and Fall of the Garvey Movement in the Urban South.* New York: Routledge, 2007.

Hawley, Ellis W. *The Great War and the Search for a Modern Order: A History of the American People and Their Institutions, 1917–1933.* New York: St. Martin's, 1979.

———. *The New Deal and the Problem of Monopoly: A Study in Economic Ambivalence.* Princeton, NJ: Princeton University Press, 1966.

Heap, Chad. *Slumming: Sexual and Racial Encounters in American Nightlife 1885–1940.* Chicago: University of Chicago Press, 2009.

Higham, John. *Strangers in the Land: Patterns of American Nativism, 1860–1925.* New Brunswick, NJ: Rutgers University Press, 1955, 2002.

Hobsbawm, Eric. *The Age of Extremes: The Short Twentieth-Century, 1914–1991*. New York: Vintage, 1994.

Hofstadter, Richard. *The Age of Reform: From Bryan to F.D.R.* New York: Knopf, 1955.

Huggins, Nathan. *Harlem Renaissance*. New York: Oxford University Press, 1971.

Hyman, Louis. *Debtor Nation: The History of America in Red Ink*. Princeton, NJ: Princeton University Press, 2011.

Jackson, Kenneth. *Crabgrass Frontier: The Suburbanization of the United States*. New York: Oxford University Press, 1985.

———. *The Ku Klux Klan in the City*. New York: Oxford University Press, 1967.

Jacobs, Meg. *Pocketbook Politics: Economic Citizenship in Twentieth-Century America*. Princeton, NJ: Princeton University Press, 2005.

Jacobson, Matthew Frye. *Whiteness of a Different Color: European Immigrants and the Alchemy of Race*. Cambridge, MA: Harvard University Press, 1998.

Jensen, Kimberly. *Mobilizing Minerva: American Women in the First World War*. Urbana: University of Illinois Press, 2008.

Karl, Barry D. *The Uneasy State: The United States from 1915 to 1945*. Chicago: University of Chicago Press, 1983.

Katznelson, Ira. *When Affirmative Action Was White: An Untold Story of Racial Inequality in Twentieth-Century America*. New York: W. W. Norton, 2005.

Kelly, Robin. *Hammer and Hoe: Alabama Communists during the Great Depression*. Chapel Hill: University of North Carolina Press, 1990.

Kennedy, David M. *Freedom from Fear: The American People in Depression and War, 1929–1945*. New York: Oxford University Press, 1999.

———. *Over Here: The First World War and American Society*. New York: Oxford University Press, 1980.

Kessler-Harris, Alice. *In Pursuit of Equity: Women, Men, and the Quest for Economic Citizenship in 20th Century America*. New York: Oxford University Press, 2001.

Kindlesberger, Charles. *The World in Depression, 1929–1939*. Berkeley: University of California Press, 1986 [1973].

Kyvig, David E. *Repealing National Prohibition*, 2nd ed. Kent, OH: Kent State University Press, 2000.

Ladd-Taylor, Molly. *Mother-Work: Women, Child Welfare, and the State, 1890–1930*. Urbana: University of Illinois Press, 1994.

Lay, Shawn, ed. *The Invisible Empire in the West: Toward New Historical Appraisal of the Ku Klux Klan in the 1920s*. Urbana: University of Illinois Press, 1992.

Lears, T. J. Jackson. *Fables of Abundance: A Cultural History of Advertising in America*. New York: Basic Books, 1994.

Leff, Mark. *The Limits of Symbolic Reform: The New Deal and Taxation, 1933–1939*. New York: Cambridge University Press, 1984.

Lenthall, Bruce. *Radio's America: The Great Depression and the Rise of Modern Mass Culture*. Chicago: University of Chicago Press, 2007.

Lerner Michael A. *Dry Manhattan: Prohibition in New York City*. Cambridge, MA: Harvard University Press, 2007.

Leuchtenburg, William E. *The FDR Years: On Roosevelt and His Legacy*. New York: Columbia University Press, 1995.

———. *Franklin D. Roosevelt and the New Deal, 1932–1940*. New York: Harper and Row, 1963.

———. *The Perils of Prosperity, 1914–1932*. Chicago: University of Chicago Press, 1958.

Lewis, David Levering. *When Harlem Was in Vogue*. New York: Oxford University Press, 1981; Penguin, 1997.

Lichtenstein, Nelson. *State of the Union: A Century of American Labor*. Princeton, NJ: Princeton University Press, 2002.

Link, Arthur. "Whatever Happened to the Progressive Movement in the 1920s?" *American Historical Review* 64 (July 1959): 833–851.

Lynd, Robert S., and Helen Merrell Lynd. *Middletown: A Study in American Culture*. New York: Harcourt, Brace, 1959 [1929].

Lynd, Staughton. *"We Are All Leaders": The Alternative Unionism of the Early 1930s*. Urbana: University of Illinois Press, 1996.

MacLean, Nancy. *Behind the Mask of Chivalry: The Making of the Second Ku Klux Klan*. New York: Oxford University Press, 1994.

Maher, Neil. *Nature's New Deal: The Civilian Conservation Corps and the Roots of the American Environmental Movement*. New York: Oxford University Press, 2007.

Manela, Erez. *The Wilsonian Moment: Self-Determination and the International Origins of Anticolonial Nationalism*. New York: Oxford University Press, 2007.

Marchand, Roland. *Advertising the American Dream: Making Way for Modernity, 1920–1940*. Berkeley: University of California Press, 1985.

Marsden, George. *Fundamentalism and American Culture*. New York: Oxford University Press, 2006.

Materson, Lisa. *For the Freedom of Her Race: Black Women and Electoral Politics in Illinois, 1877–1932*. Chapel Hill: University of North Carolina Press, 2009.

McDannell, Colleen. *Picturing Faith: Photography and the Great Depression*. New Haven, CT: Yale University Press, 2004.

Mettler, Suzanne. *Dividing Citizens: Gender and Federalism in New Deal Public Policy*. Ithaca, NY: Cornell University Press, 1998.

Mink, Gwendolyn. *The Wages of Motherhood: Inequality in the Welfare State, 1917–1942*. Ithaca, NY: Cornell University Press, 1995.

Moore, Leonard J. *Citizen Klansmen: The Ku Klux Klan in Indiana, 1921–1928*. Chapel Hill: University of North Carolina Press, 1991.

Mumford, Kevin. *Interzones: Black/White Sex Districts in Chicago and New York in the Early Twentieth Century*. New York: Columbia University Press, 1997.

Ngai, Mae. *Impossible Subjects: Illegal Aliens and the Making of Modern America*. Princeton, NJ: Princeton University Press, 2004.

Nicolaides, Becky. *My Blue Heaven: Life and Politics in the Working-Class Suburbs of Los Angeles, 1920–1965*. Chicago: University of Chicago Press, 2002.

Orent, Daniel. *Last Call: The Rise and Fall of Prohibition*. Scribner: New York, 2010.

Patterson, James T. *Congressional Conservatism and the New Deal: The Growth of the Conservative Coalition in Congress, 1933–1939*. Lexington: University of Kentucky Press, 1967.

———. *The New Deal and the States: Federalism in Transition*. Princeton, NJ: Princeton University Press, 1969.

Phillips, Sarah. *This Land, This Nation: Conservation, Rural America, and the New Deal*. New York: Cambridge University Press, 2007.

Poole, Mary. *The Segregated Origins of Social Security: African Americans and the Welfare State.* Chapel Hill: University of North Carolina Press, 2006.

Post, Robert. "Federalism, Positive Law, and the Emergence of the Admnistrative State: Prohibition in the Taft Court Era." *William and Mary Law Review* 48 (October 2006): 181.

Preston, William. *Aliens and Dissenters: Federal Supression of Radicals, 1903–1933.* Cambridge, MA: Harvard University Press, 1963.

Ritchie, Donald A. *Electing FDR: The New Deal Campaign of 1932.* Lawrence: University Press of Kansas, 2007.

Rodgers, Daniel. *Atlantic Crossings: Social Politics in a Progressive Age.* Cambridge, MA: Belknap/Harvard University Press, 1998.

Roediger, David. *Working toward Whiteness: How America's Immigrants Became White: The Strange Journey from Ellis Island to the Suburbs.* New York: Basic Books, 2005.

Rose, Kenneth D. *American Women and the Repeal of Prohibition.* New York: New York University Press, 1996.

Ruiz, Vicki. *From Out of the Shadows: Mexican Women in Twentieth-Century America.* New York: Oxford University Press, 1998.

Sanchez, George. *Becoming Mexican American: Ethnicity, Culture, and Identity in Chicano Los Angeles, 1900–1945.* New York: Oxford University Press, 1993.

Schlesinger, Arthur M. *The Age of Roosevelt*, 3 vols. Boston: Houghton Mifflin, 1957–1960.

Schneider, Mark. *"We Return Fighting": The Civil Rights Movement in the Jazz Age.* Boston: Northeastern University Press, 2002.

Schatz, Ronald. *The Electrical Workers: A History of Labor at General Electric and Westinghouse: 1923–1960.* Urbana: University of Illinois Press, 1983

Schwarz, A. B. Christa. *Gay Voices of the Harlem Renaissance.* Bloomington: Indiana University Press, 2003.

Sinclair, Andrew. *Era of Excess: A Social History of the Prohibition Movement.* New York: Harper and Row, 1964.

Sitkoff, Harvard. *A New Deal for Blacks: The Emergence of Civil Rights as a National Issue*, vol. 1: *The Depression Decade.* New York: Oxford University Press, 2009 [1979].

Smith, Jason Scott. *Building New Deal Liberalism: The Political Economy of Public Works, 1933–1956.* New York: Cambridge University Press, 2006.

Stansell, Christine. *American Moderns: Bohemian New York and the Creation of a New Century.* New York: Metropolitan Books, 2000.

Stave, Bruce. *The New Deal and the Last Hurrah: Pittsburgh Machine Politics.* Pittsburgh: University of Pittsburgh Press, 1970.

Storrs, Landon R.Y. *Civilizing Capitalism: The National Consumer's League, Women's Activism, and Labor Standards in the New Deal Era.* Chapel Hill: University of North Carolina Press, 2000.

Stricker, Frank. "Affluence for Whom? Another Look at Prosperity and the Working Classes in the 1920s." *Labor History* 24 (Winter 1983): 5–33.

Sugrue, Thomas Joseph. *The Origins of the Urban Crisis: Race, Industrial Declie and Housing in Detroit, 1940–1960.* Princeton, NJ: Princeton University Press, 1992.

Sullivan, Patricia. *Days of Hope: Race and Democracy in the New Deal Era.* Chapel Hill: University of North Carolina Press, 1996.

Temin, Peter. *Did Monetary Forces Cause the Great Depression?* New York: W. W. Norton, 1976.

———. *Lessons from the Great Depression.* Cambridge, MA: MIT Press, 1989.

Timberlake, John. *Prohibition and the Progressive Movement, 1900–1920.* Cambridge, MA: Harvard University Press, 1963.

Triece, Mary E. *On the Picket Line: Strategies of Working-Class Women during the Depression.* Urbana: University of Illinois Press, 2007.

Trout, Charles. *Boston, the Great Depression, and the New Deal.* New York: Oxford University Press, 1977.

Ware, Susan. *Beyond Suffrage, Women in the New Deal.* Cambridge, MA: Harvard University Press, 1981.

———. *Partner and I: Molly Dewson, Feminism, and New Deal Politics.* New Haven, CT: Yale University Press, 1987.

Weir, Margaret, Ann Shola Orloff, and Theda Skocpol, eds. *The Politics of Social Policy in the United States.* Princeton, NJ: Princeton University Press, 1988.

Weiss, Nancy. *Farewell to the Party of Lincoln: Black Politics in the Age of FDR.* Princeton, NJ: Princeton University Press, 1983.

Wilson, Joan Hoff. *Herbert Hoover: Forgotten Progressive.* Boston: Little, Brown, 1975.

Wolcott, Victoria. *Remaking Respectability: African American Women in Interwar Detroit.* Chapel Hill: University of North Carolina Press, 2001.

Yung, Judy. *Unbound Feet: A Social History of Chinese Women in San Francisco.* San Francisco: University of California Press. 1995.

Zieger, Robert H. *The CIO, 1935–1955.* Chapel Hill: University of North Carolina Press, 1995.

Zinn, Howard, ed. *New Deal Thought.* Indianapolis: Bobbs-Merrill, 1966.

7
The Uncertain Future of American Politics, 1940 to 1973

MEG JACOBS

For many years, conventional wisdom held that a stable New Deal Democratic coalition and a liberal consensus defined postwar American politics until the 1970s. Beginning with Arthur Schlesinger, Jr.'s *The Vital Center* (1949), most journalists and scholars believed Americans broadly shared an ideology of New Deal liberalism. Focused on the cold war split between Soviet communism and American democracy, contemporaries saw domestic politics through the prism of consensus. American political culture, according to this view, centered on a commitment to individualism, private property, and representative government, which now tilted in a liberal direction. "During most of my political consciousness," Schlesinger wrote, "this has been a New Deal country. I expect that it will continue to be a New Deal country." If Americans had more work to do to improve civil rights and social welfare, a strong Democratic Party would shepherd the country through those changes. So, too, would the Democrats lead and prevail in fighting the cold war. In 1952, Democrat John F. Kennedy's defeat of Henry Cabot Lodge for U.S. senator from Massachusetts seemed more portentous as a sign of the triumph of cold war liberalism than Dwight D. Eisenhower's Republican presidential victory.

The dominance of New Deal liberalism rested on several assumptions. First was the idea of a broker state in which the federal government managed the interests of organized groups. Economist John Kenneth Galbraith, in *American Capitalism* (1952), referred to these organized interest groups as countervailing powers, and he saw the government's job largely as a referee in this organized competition. Rather than pitched warfare, for example, unions and management would resolve their differences at the bargaining table instead of on the picket line. The second pillar of New Deal liberalism was a shared commitment to liberal values, including anticommunism, cultural pluralism, and even incremental racial progress. Finally, the phenomenal economic growth of the period sustained this political order.

Whereas public intellectuals like Schlesinger championed the New Deal order, praising its social accord and stability, beginning in the 1960s a younger generation of New Left scholars criticized its tepid nature, pointing to the limits of New Deal reform. Harvard Sitkoff wrote powerfully of the origins of civil rights struggle in the Depression years, with an eye to what the New Deal failed to achieve for the poorest, most disenfranchised members of society. As much as the New Deal state could champion liberal progress, there were fundamental limits to the redistribution of wealth and power, as Nelson Lichtenstein and other labor historians made clear in their New Left accounts published in the 1970s and 1980s. But the critics did not challenge the idea of the dominance of New Deal liberalism from the 1930s through the 1970s.

Yet, from the point of view of 2011, and of the scholarship of the last twenty years, the idea of a New Deal consensus seems untenable. The past generation of historiography has raised profound questions about the consensual nature of politics during these postwar decades and the character of the New Deal liberal political culture that defined the period. The scale of the intervention brought about by the New Deal was much more extensive than earlier historians had suggested. The New Deal was not simply a pragmatic program to save capitalism but a bold institutional experiment that changed basic elements of political culture and political economy. Because its impact was so great, the New Deal triggered an immediate reaction from opponents who, from the 1930s on, mobilized to limit, delegitimize, and dismantle its program and legacies. As a result, it is unclear whether a coherent postwar New Deal "order" ever actually existed. In some ways, the New Deal state was more expansive and enduring, yet in others it became subject to challenge much earlier than previous scholars realized. Thus the postwar years were both more liberal and more conservative than we previously thought. This chapter looks at key developments in the historiography, which have opened up a new understanding of the postwar years and have helped reveal the roots of post-1970s politics—the so-called Reagan era—in this earlier period of American history.

Three trends help explain this shift in the historical literature. First, scholars have a new understanding of the role of the state in twentieth-century politics. In the 1960s and 1970s, New Left scholars had largely eschewed political history, looking to the social and the cultural as important sites for historical investigation. But in the 1980s, political scientists and historical sociologists such as Steven Skowronek and Theda Skocpol suggested that the American state functioned as more than just a neutral broker of interests. Instead, American political institutions were in and of themselves worthy of investigation. Through detailed studies, they showed how bureaucracies, federalism, and the separation of powers worked to enhance as well as limit the power of the modern state. In the 1990s, scholars such as Ira Katznelson and Julian Zelizer returned to the study of the state and helped to reinvigorate the field of American political history. They discovered new explanations for why postwar political institutions were both more enduring and more constrained than previously thought.

Second, since the era of Ronald Reagan, historians have looked for the historical roots of the rise of the right before the 1970s. These recent investigations into conservatism suggest that New Deal liberalism never went uncontested. In some of the earliest accounts of the right, Richard Hofstadter and Daniel Bell saw conservatives as outliers, part of a radical fringe standing outside mainstream culture. But more recently, scholars have treated conservatism as less of an aberration, motivated not by psychological concerns, but rather by serious convictions. As scholars of conservatism such as Leo Ribuffo and Lisa McGirr have shown, Americans divided over the question of how much government was good for the country. In part, conservatism became such a powerful political force in the 1980s and 1990s because it had been building strength for several decades.

Third, in the wake of the deindustrialization and globalization that transformed the economy in the 1970s, scholars have returned to a focus on political economy and regional development. Rather than seeing the period from 1945 to 1973 as a golden age of American capitalism, scholars now appreciate the ways in which economic growth masked structural changes in the economy. An entire deregulated, nonunionized, and nonmanufacturing political economy, primarily in the Sun Belt South and West, existed alongside of, and often in competition with, the Detroit-centered, heavy manufacturing, unionized economy of the North. As Nelson Lichtenstein has recently shown, Wal-Mart became the template for American capitalism toward the end of the twentieth century. But the roots of this low-wage, decentralized service economy lay in the postwar years, posing a challenge to the New Deal political economy.

For too long, the cold war blinded historians to the deep divides that existed within American politics, culture, and society in these years. Indeed, his ideological commitment to the cold war led Schlesinger to minimize differences on the American political scene. One of his contemporaries, the political journalist Samuel Lubell, however, painted a very different picture in *The Future of American Politics* (1952). Interested in the daily experience of Americans, Lubell went around ringing doorbells and conducting interviews. He discovered ambivalence, anxieties, and tensions. Americans disagreed on foreign policy, worried about their economic future, and held onto their prejudices. Whereas Schlesinger saw a vital center, Lubell wrote of the "dead center of stalemate." The Democrats would remain the dominant party, Lubell predicted, but the postwar era would witness electoral instability, as Americans routinely rethought their political allegiances. In addition to this instability, Lubell already saw signs of significant splits within the Democratic Party, which made the New Deal coalition all the more unstable. After interviewing thousands of voters, Lubell saw only mixed evidence for an ascendant New Deal liberalism. "This conflict over the proper limits of government has intensified until it has become the sharpest single divider in the country," Lubell wrote. He might have done well to call his book "The Uncertain Future of American Politics."

This chapter reexamines the postwar period to look for the cracks and strains in the New Deal order. To explain what they saw as the eventual collapse of a cold war consensus and the unraveling of the New Deal coalition, historians had traditionally pointed to the backlash against the 1960s civil rights movement and Great Society liberalism, the fight over the Vietnam War, and the stagflation of the 1970s. But that literature concealed the deep divisions and tensions that shaped this entire period as well as the fragility of the New Deal coalition. As scholars now appreciate, from the economy to race to regional differences, fundamental fissures within and challenges to the New Deal order existed throughout the postwar period. The late 1960s and early 1970s must thus be seen as the culmination of a three-decade struggle and the untangling of a tenuous political coalition rather than the sudden implosion of liberalism around Vietnam and race in the 1960s. This approach gives us a different understanding of the three critical decades that followed the presidency of Franklin D. Roosevelt.

In three key areas, historians now offer a more complex picture of the so-called postwar New Deal order. First, the period of post–World War II reconversion, which lasted through the early 1950s, witnessed intense partisanship and fighting over the extension of New Deal liberalism at home and abroad. Acceptance of the New Deal did not define the period from the 1940s onward as the consensus school and New Left scholars once thought. Rather, recent literature on the wartime state, organized labor, and the cold war makes clear that the period of reconversion proved an important moment of debate over the future of New Deal liberalism. Second, as early as the 1950s, the questions of civil rights and of how the South would align politically came to the fore. As Republicans sought to disrupt the Democratic coalition, the South, especially the Sun Belt suburbs, seemed the most likely region to join the GOP. Third, in the 1960s and 1970s, an antigovernment deregulatory agenda drew support from both the Sun Belt service economy and the conservative mobilization that was taking place in think tanks and at the grass roots. By the end of the period, the fractures within New Deal liberalism had become stronger than the glue that held it together.

Had Enough?

In 1946, congressional Republicans ran on a simple platform: Had Enough? After more than a decade out of power, they were asking voters to consider whether "the Roosevelt Revolution" should come to an end. Since the 1990s, New Deal scholarship has captured the transformative nature of reform in the 1930s, especially in popular attitudes about the positive role of government. By creating new labor rights, providing benefits to out-of-work Americans and pensions to the elderly, and bringing rural electrification to the South, the New Deal had stitched together a political coalition of urban workers, organized labor, northern blacks, white ethnic groups, Catholics, Jews, liberals, intellectuals, progressive Republicans, middle-class families worried about unemployment and old age, and southern whites. The impact on the political culture was powerful, as social histories of the New Deal by scholars such as Lizabeth Cohen, Gary Gerstle, Elizabeth Faue, and Robin Kelley make clear. For example, paying a black tenant sharecropper federal relief disrupted traditional social relations and raised expectations of what ordinary citizens, including the least powerful members of society, could hope for from the federal government. "The gover'ment is the best boss I ever had," said a black WPA worker in North Carolina.

Like most revolutions, this one was inherently unstable and plagued by factions, and triggered its own counterrevolution. Roosevelt was masterful, his 1936 reelection overwhelming. But studies of the New Deal state stress its limitations as politicians had to navigate complicated political waters and work within what was both politically acceptable and institutionally possible. As Ira Katznelson and Robert Lieberman have shown, the Democratic Party was split between its southern white conservative members who opposed labor and civil rights and its northern urban counterparts who favored them. To get his bills passed, Roosevelt had to strike compromises with powerful southern committee chairmen, who dominated Capitol Hill, agreeing to local administration of many programs so as not to disrupt regional race relations. In the 1938 congressional elections, Roosevelt unsuccessfully tried to purge eight conservative Democrats by campaigning against them in the primary. From that point on Republicans, who regained some of their power in Congress, began an alliance with southern Democrats to limit the New Deal on issues involving race relations and unionization.

Mobilization for World War II led to another dramatic expansion of the federal government. Rather than seeing the war as spelling the end of reform, political historians have discovered how the mobilization effort created opportunities for the development of greater state capacity and an even more robust rights-consciousness. As Nelson Lichtenstein and Steve Fraser have shown, labor used its wartime strength to claim new rights and increase its numbers. By the end of the war, almost 15 million unionized workers (30 percent of the nonagricultural workforce) stood poised to use their organizational might and the power of the wartime state to preserve their wage gains and shop-floor rights. African Americans, too, sought to use the wartime state to fight racial inequality as part of what scholars such as Jacquelyn Dowd Hall and Thomas Sugrue see as an important moment in the "long civil rights era." Activists pushed for the creation of the Fair Employment Practices Commission set up by Roosevelt and were willing to mobilize at the grass roots to press their cause. As my own work shows, consumers also became politically involved in enforcing wartime regulations such as price controls as a way of keeping inflation under control and preserving their purchasing power. In this era, according to new histories of the left-liberal alliances by Michael Denning and Douglas Rossinow, activists looked to the state to promote liberal causes from economic redistribution to civil rights to interracial solidarity.

As much as the wartime state conferred rights, it also could reinforce patterns of discrimination. As part of the New Deal, the Federal Housing Authority had created a system of federally guaranteed, long-term home mortgages, which made homeownership a possibility for ordinary Americans. After the war, the GI Bill gave government loans to millions of returning veterans for down payments, which further facilitated buying homes. Yet, as recent scholarship on the wartime state demonstrates, government programs like low-interest mortgages, school tuition, and business loans for veterans compounded racial inequality when the federal government delegated implementation to states and localities. At the state level, as Ira Katznelson and Kathleen Frydl show, African Americans faced unequal treatment and discrimination, and as a result, government programs entrenched racial divides and widened the economic gap between the races. Margot Canaday argues that the same also happened between homosexual and heterosexual citizens. Neither African Americans nor homosexuals could take as much advantage of the GI bill as heterosexual white men, who came to see these government programs as an exclusive privilege rather than a universal benefit of citizenship. The absence of universalistic welfare benefits had the effect of inscribing gender differences into public policy, a pattern illuminated in the scholarship of Alice Kessler-Harris, Linda Gordon, and Eileen Boris.

If state capacity and existing racial and gender attitudes constrained the New Deal–wartime state, still the Roosevelt-era public policies proved enduring and far-reaching. In his widely praised narrative history of the Roosevelt presidency, *Freedom from Fear* (1999), David Kennedy has shown that both the New Deal and the mobilization for World War II changed American attitudes about government, creating a belief that the national state had a fundamental obligation to provide for the basic economic well-being of its citizens. The creation of a new sense of entitlement set in motion new expectations about government obligations, even if many were not fulfilled. "Citizens witnessed the national government working on their behalf," as political scientist Suzanne Mettler writes about the New Deal–World War II generation. My own work argues that this vision of government-backed security required leadership at the top and also political mobilization at the grass roots among the beneficiaries of government's growth. This liberal political culture and the expansion of the state, in turn, set in motion contestation in the postwar period.

The end of the war set up a confrontation between liberals who wanted to preserve and expand the New Deal and conservatives who were hoping to restrain and roll back the expansion of government. By 1945, New Deal opponents, especially businessmen, were in a strong position to fight against what they saw as an intrusive government. Contributing to the war effort not only was lucrative, particularly for the largest corporations, but also enabled businessmen to rehabilitate their public image, severely tarnished by the Depression, and to claim they had successfully defended the nation as their factories became, in Roosevelt's words, the "arsenal of democracy." With the help of their Republican allies in Congress, they lobbied to remove price controls, roll back the power of organized labor, and reduce federal regulations governing workplace conditions. Instead of government-guaranteed full employment, businessmen promised postwar prosperity through free enterprise, as Elizabeth Fones-Wolf and Howell John Harris have shown. Recent studies by Alan Brinkley and Robert Collins reveal how businessmen and policy makers accepted Keynesian tools of fiscal management as an alternative to more heavy-handed forms of state intervention.

The opponents of the New Deal scored a decisive victory in the elections of 1946. Labor histories of reconversion by scholars such as Robert Zieger, George Lipsitz, Rick Halpern, and Joshua Freeman capture the disruptive nature of the strike waves in auto, steel, coal, meatpacking, and countless other industries. Amid this unrest, the 1946 slogan "Had enough? Vote Republican" gained traction.

The other election issue was anticommunism, which Republicans invoked against the party that had led the nation to victory in World War II. In November, Republicans scored a decisive victory, winning majorities in both houses (245 to 188 in the House and 51 to 45 in the Senate) and controlling Congress for the first time since 1930. A new generation of conservative young Republicans such as Richard Nixon of California, John Bricker of Ohio, and Joseph McCarthy of Wisconsin came to power. Greg Mitchell and Steve Gillon reveal the challenge of anticommunism for liberal politics in this early cold war moment. Conservatives had attacked the New Deal as communistic in the 1930s, and in the context of the cold war, their arguments found a wider audience. They feared communist subversion at home and opposed any extension of the state as a form of socialism. Once in office, these young conservatives allied with more traditional Republicans like Senator Robert Taft and southern Democrats.

Their victory would shape the contours of American political economy for the postwar period. The most significant accomplishment was the Taft-Hartley Act, passed in 1947, which as Christopher Tomlins and Kevin Boyle demonstrate, imposed serious limitations on organized labor. The act gave the president the authority to order a cooling-off period before workers went on strike, prohibited the closed shop, and enabled states to pass "right-to-work" laws, all of which made union organizing more difficult. It also banned supervisors from joining unions, which meant that millions of white-collar and managerial jobs would fall outside the union orbit. Finally, the act required labor leaders to sign noncommunist affidavits for union certification, a provision that had the effect of purging many officials from union ranks. The measure, which its liberal opponents dubbed the "slave labor law," passed over President Harry S Truman's veto. Labor historians of the South such as Barbara Griffith and Michael Honey show how racial divides between black and white workers also contributed to the failure to extend the union movement beyond the North and Midwest. As a result of legislative constraints and racial tensions, the South would remain a nonunionized haven for low-wage employers.

Just as important as the challenges from the GOP, Truman's liberal internationalism exposed the cracks within the New Deal order. Recent evaluations of the Truman years by Alonzo Hamby, Steve Fraser, and Nelson Lichtenstein reveal the difficulty he had in holding together a liberal coalition. In 1948, Truman faced opposition from his left and right. Former Secretary of State Henry Wallace, who had resigned from the administration in opposition to Truman's cold war policy of containment, argued that it would engender greater hostilities with the Soviet Union and require cutting social spending in favor of military spending. Wallace ran as the candidate of the Progressive Party. To undercut Wallace's appeal among liberals, Truman vowed to repeal Taft-Hartley. He also campaigned hard for the protection and extension of such key welfare measures as Social Security, the minimum wage, and health care. To hold blacks in the North, whose votes were critical to winning in large cities, Truman supported the inclusion of a civil rights plank in the Democratic Party platform. Truman called for a permanent Fair Employment Practices Commission, a federal antilynching bill, and the abolition of the poll tax in the South that, along with more aggressive forms of intimidation, had long disenfranchised blacks.

These moves to the left, especially on civil rights, triggered a defense of white supremacy predicated on legally enforced segregation, a largely agricultural economy, and a single-party Solid South. They inspired Strom Thurmond to run for president on the segregationist Dixiecrat ticket. The usual story of massive resistance begins with the 1954 Supreme Court ruling of *Brown v. Board of Education*. But recent political histories of local southern communities by scholars such as Kari Frederickson and Bryant Simon stress the complicated and deep-seated racial attitudes of the white working class that preceded the Brown decision. Thurmond's successful appeal to segregationist white Southern voters made sense, as these works show, only after the failure of a class-based New Deal agenda and the emergence of black activism in the 1940s. After the Supreme Court declared the all-white primary unconstitutional during World War II, a million African-American southerners registered to vote.

Although Truman squeaked out an unexpected victory in 1948 and Congress returned to Democratic hands, the conservative coalition was growing in strength. The cold war enhanced their political power. The recent scholarship on the cold war by historians such as Melvyn Leffler, Michael Hogan, and Michael Schaller demonstrates how powerful the fears of communists were in these early cold war years. Announcing the Truman Doctrine in 1947, the administration committed the United States to defending non-Communist governments around the world against Soviet aggression. Truman established permanent intelligence and defense institutions, and through the Marshall Plan, the United States sent economic aid to rebuild the democracies of Western Europe as a bulwark against communism. Still, conservatives attacked Truman for not doing enough. In contrast to bipartisan consensus, historians now emphasize the fractious and political nature of foreign policy in this period. The work of Julian Zelizer, Fred Logevall, and Campbell Craig shows that politicians used foreign policy for partisan advantages, at times even exacerbating cold war tensions.

The conservative attack on Democrats came to the fore in the age of McCarthyism. After China fell to communism and the Soviets detonated their first atomic bomb in 1949, Democrats became even more vulnerable to Republican charges of weakness on defense. The stalemate of the Korean War also undermined support for Democrats. By this time, the Republican right, under the leadership of Senator Joseph McCarthy, had launched a successful anticommunist campaign that reinforced the partisan attacks on the Democrats. New literature on the Red Scare, including works by Ellen Schrecker, Steve Whitfield, and Steve Rosswurm, captures how wide-ranging anticommunist attacks were, playing out in arenas from Congress to college campuses to union halls to Hollywood. If an older generation of scholars saw Truman's vigorous pursuit of domestic communism as limited and necessary, the recent trend demonstrates how the administration in effect sanctioned the more extreme efforts to root out subversives. By giving legitimacy to the actions of his political opponents, Truman was unable to thwart attacks on the Fair Deal as communistic, and in the end he saw none of his reforms enacted by Congress.

As the Fair Deal died a political death, organized labor sought to protect the interests of its members. Whereas old studies of labor saw its leaders as complicit in a liberal compromise, new literature shows the political and institutional challenges of constructing a public welfare state. Only when it became clear that labor could not secure public benefits did it become more accepting of private benefits offered at the bargaining table by employers. In their 1948 negotiations, union leaders accepted cost-of-living agreements in their annual contracts. Instead of holding out hope that the government could moderate inflation, labor accepted the offer from their employers to adjust wages upward to keep pace with inflation. When the United Autoworkers signed a five-year agreement with General Motors in 1950, with built-in cost-of-living adjustments, contemporaries hailed it as the Treaty of Detroit. As Nelson Lichtenstein writes, "The Treaty of Detroit proved a milestone from which there was no turning back." Indeed, in the same year, Robert Taft won reelection as senator in the heavily industrial state of Ohio, positioning him for a serious run for the Republican presidential nomination in 1952.

The labor accord benefited well-organized union workers but left out the unorganized. As James Patterson has written, "Well-established interest groups ultimately agreed to accommodate each other while giving lip service at best to the needs of the unorganized." The number of white-collar workers, who received a salary, would soon exceed the number of blue-collar workers who bargained for inflation-adjusted wages. "Inflation has become the breaking point of the Roosevelt coalition," observed Samuel Lubell, exacerbating tensions between different interests. As the journalist put it, "No new economic gains could be promised any group of Democrats without threatening the gains of other Democrats." As part of this private welfare state, workers also received benefits, including health care, life insurance, paid vacations, and old-age pensions. These advances for organized workers created rifts between union and nonunion workers, the skilled and unskilled, full-time and part-time employees, male and female, manufacturing and service workers, and whites and blacks. New work on the private welfare state, including studies by Jennifer Klein, Jacob Hacker, and Colin Gordon, makes it clear that the institutionalization of private benefits sapped support for further advances in public welfare.

Political rifts among the working classes were exacerbated at the local level, especially between the races. Traditionally, scholars have seen the phenomenal growth of the postwar years as forestalling conflict. But even in Detroit, the home to automobile manufacturing, there was still competition over jobs, housing, and public amenities. Both white and black workers came out of the war with what James Patterson calls grand expectations. But those expectations could fuel tensions, as individuals and groups pursued their own interests. In the 1940s, Detroit had grown quickly, with manufacturing jobs increasing by 40 percent, and the city's employers paid its blue-collar war workers the highest wages in the country. The percentage of African Americans in Detroit went from 10 percent in 1940 to 25 percent by 1960. Along with this growth in minority population came an expansion of regulations to ensure equality of opportunity in hiring. Although President Truman failed to get a federal FEPC bill passed, states and counties passed their own laws, with the result that nondiscrimination fair employment rules covered 25 percent of the total population by 1952.

As Thomas Sugrue argues in *The Origins of the Urban Crisis*, at the local level competition over resources triggered an urban antiliberalism, even among Democratic voters. Sugrue, as well as scholars such as Jonathan Rieder and Robert Self, show how white working-class Americans defined their security and sense of entitlement in conservative and individualistic terms, specifically as the right to a private home often in a racially segregated urban neighborhood or suburb and a good job. The New Deal had created a new kind of rights-based liberalism for whites predicated on black exclusion. In Detroit, those political sentiments translated into the defeat of a Democratic liberal candidate for mayor in 1949 at the hands of a conservative who made good on his promise to dismantle public housing, largely intended for African Americans. As Sugrue explains, "White Detroiters expected the state to protect the privileges associated with property ownership and race." Above all, those who had taken to the streets in the 1930s now wanted to preserve what they had achieved. "The inner dynamics of the Roosevelt coalition have shifted from those of *getting* to those of *keeping*," Lubell noted.

From the beginning, it was clear that different parts of the New Deal Democratic Party sat in uncomfortable tension with each other. As each group developed political muscle, the friction only increased. Moreover, voters were not blindly committed to the Democratic Party, and a shift in economic or diplomatic circumstances could undermine their loyalty. In 1952, the Republican Dwight Eisenhower won a decisive victory, including winning four southern states, and Republicans retook Congress. They were not strong enough to roll back New Deal programs like Social Security and minimum wages, nor did Eisenhower, a Republican moderate, advocate such steps, and provisions actually became more generous over time. Still, as recent studies of the period show, Eisenhower's fiscal conservatism revealed continued resistance to an activist liberal government. Thus, by the early 1950s, challenges to the New Deal order were already strongly in evidence.

The South and the Suburbs

Traditionally, scholars have written about the South as exceptional, a backward region shaped by the legacy of slavery and white backlash to the civil rights revolution. In those narratives, the central cast of characters included liberal northerners and heroic southern blacks, both of whom were willing to risk their lives and livelihoods to break down the barriers of segregation that had ruled the region since the end of the Civil War. Recent scholarship has shifted the discussion away from southern exceptionalism and instead sees a more complex array of political, economic, and social forces at work. Moving beyond a story of reactionary racism, these studies explore the impact of the growth of the military-industrial complex, economic development, and suburbanization to better understand the region.

The result has been to show that the South not only reflected larger national trends, but even established the template. If Roosevelt's New Deal coalition had its roots among the urban masses, what would become Ronald Reagan's conservative coalition grew up outside the cities. In the Sun Belt suburbs and rural areas, it was not only the issue of civil rights and race that motivated voters to leave the Democratic Party. Just as significant, if not more so, demographic and economic changes challenged the New Deal order and led to a Republican resurgence.

As part of the return to political history, recent scholarship has explored the role of public spending as an important influence on the economy and regional development. Jordan Schwarz, Jason Scott Smith, and most importantly, Bruce Schulman demonstrate the role of government funding in the economic expansion of the Sun Belt beginning with the New Deal. During World War II, fifteen million Americans, one-third of the workforce, moved into new jobs in war production centers, many of them located in the South and Southwest. Besides Detroit, the other major center of defense production was California, as studies by Marilynn Johnson, Roger Lotchin, and Gerald Nash demonstrate. Overnight, Los Angeles, with its factories, refineries, military bases, and ports, became a major manufacturing center. Between 1940 and 1945, California received almost $20 billion from the federal government for defense contracts; half of the area's income came from federal spending. After the war, federal highway construction and military spending spurred continued growth in the Sun Belt. For the two decades following World War II, as Schulman has shown, defense spending accounted for one-third of the area's jobs. Many of these jobs were in high-tech industry, which reinforced the racial divide between white middle-class professionals and poor African Americans.

In addition to federal spending, the political economy of the South attracted capital to the region. In their work on manufacturing centers, Thomas Sugrue, Jefferson Cowie, and Tami Friedman examine the deindustrialization of the North and capital flight to the South. Between 1948 and 1967, Detroit lost approximately 130,000 manufacturing jobs. In the same period, the Sun Belt was expanding at a rate twice that of the Rust Belt in the Northeast and Midwest. In response to the strength of unions in the North, many firms decided to relocate to the South in search of cheaper, nonunionized labor and low taxes.

The shift to metropolitan suburban living within the Sun Belt typified the patterns of growth elsewhere. Suburbanization, which began in 1920s, accelerated after World War II. By 1950, the suburbs were growing at a rate ten times faster than the cities. The application of mass-production techniques to building homes made mass ownership a real possibility. Ten percent of the construction firms built 70 percent of postwar homes, enabling speed, efficiency, and low cost. At the peak of production, the Levitt Brothers, famous for their creation of Levittown as one of the first planned suburbs built entirely from prefabricated housing, put up thirty homes a day. Between 1945 and 1955, builders erected fifteen million new housing units. These were modern suburban homes with indoor plumbing, central heating, appliances, and telephones, and, by 1960, most had televisions.

Government policies, which favored private homeownership over renting and public housing, made this growth possible. Favorable tax deductions made it cheaper to pay for a mortgage than to pay rent. The Federal Highway Act of 1956 also furthered this demographic trend. As Kenneth Jackson has explained, suburbanization resulted not just from geography, technology, and culture, but also from specific government policies, which taxpayers subsidized. Other government policies, including the exemption of the transportation of food from regulated trucking rates, facilitated suburban living. As Shane Hamilton has shown, Americans ate well and cheaply in the postwar years because agribusiness and factory farmers employed the labor of nonunionized long-haul rural truck drivers to deliver cheap food to America's suburban supermarkets.

In the 1950s, public intellectuals offered unflattering portraits of postwar suburban culture, seeing it as stultifying, suffocating, and isolating. According to critics such as Vance Packard, David Riesman, and William Whyte, as Americans moved away from urban centers, they traded the richness of strong ethnic, family, and community bonds for middle-class conformity. Influenced by the work of sociologists and behavioral psychologists, earlier studies of suburban culture focused on psychological interpretations rooted in notions of status anxiety. Betty Friedan offered the most scathing portrait of domesticity for suburban women in her 1963 *The Feminine Mystique.* Indeed, some of the early social and women's histories of the postwar years saw this period as one of conservatism and constraints, wedged between the opportunities of the war years and the activism of the 1960s. In her work on suburban culture, Elaine Tyler May explained how Americans embraced suburban living and nuclear families as an antidote to the stress and anxiety of the cold war.

More recently, however, scholars have emphasized the diversity of experiences, especially for women. The work of Joanne Meyerowitz, Jacqueline Jones, Cynthia Harrison, and Sara Evans suggests that women, especially working-class women, were more active politically than previous portraits suggested. In her study of "the other women's movement," Dorothy Sue Cobble shows how even if female union activists did not challenge the sex segregation of employment, they continued the activism of war years for workplace rights.

Even the cold war itself could spawn liberal reform. From the Fair Deal to labor policy to civil rights, scholars had traditionally painted the cold war years as a moment of conservatism in domestic politics. Amid the Red Scare, many liberal campaigns became suspect as communist inspired. But the recent civil rights literature offers a different view. Even as the cold war made redistributive programs less accessible, the international struggle for democracy lent legitimacy and momentum to civil rights struggles. Mary Dudziak, Penny Von Eschen, and Thomas Borstelmann explore how American commitment to anticolonialism abroad created political space for civil rights reform at home. Historians such as Charles Payne and John Dittmer are rewriting the master narrative of civil rights by focusing on local movements.

If some have rediscovered political activism on the left, other recent studies see the emergence of a new conservatism on the right, especially in the South with the growth of a new suburban middle class. To be sure, a nationwide political realignment depended in part on how white southerners responded to the Democratic Party's commitment to civil rights, a reaction that would become even more pronounced after the *Brown v. Board* decision. But just as important to the decline of the Democratic Party in the South, as Earl Black and Merle Black write, were shifting demographics within the region, specifically the growth of a new professional urban middle class, Republican in political sympathies. Between 1940 and 1948, the number of southerners who voted for the Republican presidential candidate increased by 50 percent, with gains coming in the most urbanized states. "It is this new middle class," wrote Samuel Lubell, "the branch plant managers and their college-trained supervisors, merchants, doctors and lawyers, newspaper publishers, and realtors, all seemingly so conservative, who are the real political rebels in the South today."

This demographic shift to the Sun Belt suburbs represented what Lubell identified as early as 1952 as the beginnings of a "conservative revolution" in the South. In 1950, the defeat of Senators Frank Graham (D, North Carolina) and Claude Pepper (D, Florida), two liberal New Dealers, by conservative foes signaled the change. These two lost support not only among poor whites, but also among the rapidly expanding middle classes in the cities and in the suburbs, among whom racial integration could be presented as an attack on their rights as homeowners, taxpayers, and school parents. As Kevin Kruse and Joseph Crespino show, even in the Deep South racial appeals were steeped in an ideology of middle-class privilege and individual entitlement as much as in outright racial hatred. This new work on the Sun Belt suburbs explores the mixture of racial moderation, economic entitlement, and commitment to law and order that made these regions tilt rightward, laying the basis for the death of the solid Democratic South and the emergence of the GOP in the region.

Rightward Bound

Between the landslide elections of Democrat Lyndon Johnson in 1964 and Republican Richard Nixon in 1972, changes in liberalism and conservatism both accelerated, building on trends from the earlier period. Traditionally, scholars have counterpoised a radical sixties with a conservative seventies. In fact, as the essays in Bruce Schulman and Julian Zelizer's *Rightward Bound* argue, the two periods reflect much more continuity, with liberal and conservative impulses present in both. The forces pushing in a rightward direction had deeper roots than simply a reaction against the liberal advances of the 1960s; at the same time, liberalism had enduring accomplishments.

One of the greatest liberal achievements of modern state building came with the creation of Medicare, a program for health insurance for the elderly. In the absence of a system of public health care, Americans depended on private insurance obtained through their jobs. As a result, half of the population over 65 did not have health insurance. As life expectancy increased and medical expenses grew, the nation faced a serious health care problem. Under President Johnson's leadership, Congress designed a program to allocate Social Security taxes for the public provision of elderly health care. Like Medicare, which benefited a large portion of the population, including white middle-class Americans, the Elementary and Secondary Education Act won support once congressmen realized that their districts would receive tangible benefits. Histories of the decade have traditionally been consumed with issues of civil rights and the war in Vietnam. Scholars of the state such as Julian Zelizer and Gareth Davies have only recently begun to explore this moment of governmental expansion.

Other aspects of Johnson's Great Society generated more opposition. Unlike Medicare, Johnson's War on Poverty became associated with welfare for the undeserving poor. Recent work by Michael Katz, Alice O'Connor, Jennifer Mittelstadt, and Felicia Kornbluh explores the political and policy limitations for this kind of liberal reform. Building on new notions of community participation, many programs circumvented the Department of Health, Education, and Welfare to dispense welfare and instead recruited neighborhood networks to deliver legal services, secure welfare payments, fight evictions, and obtain medical services. Many of the programs came into conflict with local political establishments, who found equally problematic how civil rights activists sought to use community action programs to mobilize the poor, march on city hall, and file lawsuits against the city.

If poverty programs ran into political trouble, civil rights reform fared better and had more staying power. Hugh Davis Graham and John Skrentny have stressed the importance of legislative and judicial change in Washington in destroying the legal edifice of white supremacy in the South and creating a new legal framework for a rights-based liberalism. The notion of legally enforceable rights through new government agencies like the Equal Employment Opportunity Commission set an important precedent for powerful new forms of identity politics, social movements, and political activism. Paul Frymer has documented the emergence of a legal apparatus, which African Americans used to challenge unions on questions of civil rights and discrimination. As Nancy MacLean demonstrates, the civil rights movement, with its focus on the vote and public accommodations, gave way to a new rights-based mobilization as different classes of citizens made demands for compensation and regulatory protection based on special claims rooted in race, sex, ethnicity, religion, language, age, physical handicap, or sexual orientation.

Yet, at the same time, recent work on civil rights in the North reveals the limits of reform for African Americans. The legal scholar Risa Goluboff argues that the civil rights movement, with its demands for equal access to public accommodations and the vote, precluded a more expansive vision of reform that embraced economic distribution and structural poverty. Those limitations became evident in the North when deindustrialization led to the disappearance of jobs and competition over scarce resources just as blacks were migrating by the millions. Recent scholarship makes clear that the problems of the inner-city ghettos transcended the demand for voting rights. Martha Biondi, Matthew Countryman, and Thomas Sugrue explore the complicated story of white flight, municipal politics, and other patterns of structural and racial discrimination, which led to the creation of what some saw as a permanent underclass. Instead of voting rights, in the North, the struggle was over far more intractable issues such as poor housing, police brutality, and urban decay.

The latest work on activism of the 1960s places it in an international context. What had started as a movement in support of civil rights and for free speech on college campuses erupted into an antiwar movement of the young with global dimensions. That phenomenon occurred in many western industrialized democracies, as new work by scholars such as Jeremi Suri, Martin Klimke, and Jeremy Varon on the global student movement demonstrates. The baby boom of the postwar years, along with economic growth, resulted in a generation increasingly critical of the affluence in which they grew up.

At exactly the same moment, the New Right was also sprouting a grassroots network of conservative organizations. These emerged not simply in reaction to the social upheaval and liberal reforms of the 1960s, but dated back to the 1950s when conservative intellectuals founded new outlets for their anticommunist ideas, including journals like William Buckley's *National Review*. In her work on southern California, Lisa McGirr writes about the grassroots origins of what became the American New Right, a movement that emphasized the evils of communism as well as the dangers of liberal permissiveness and social welfare. By the 1960s, the Young Americans for Freedom had a presence on some college campuses to rival the New Left. In his work on conservatism and Phyllis Schlafly, Donald Critchlow lays out the antifeminist aspects of this new rightward trend.

The appeal of the New Right was so far-reaching, recent scholars argue, precisely because it was grounded in neoliberal, market-based language. In 1968, Richard Nixon employed what Republican strategist Kevin Phillips dubbed the southern strategy, by which Nixon promised to ease pressure on integration as a way of attracting the South into the GOP fold. But, as Matthew Lassiter argues, Nixon won not by making outwardly racist appeals to white southerners but instead by appealing to a sense of colorblind middle-class entitlement rooted in a culture of work and reward. He was particularly successful in winning support among white middle-class Protestants, especially in higher-income suburbs that had already been trending Republican. In appealing to these voters, as well as to their suburban counterparts outside the South, as Robert Self argues in his study of Oakland, California, Nixon played to their identities as homeowners, taxpayers, and school parents, or as he put it, those who worked, paid taxes, and did not demonstrate, picket, or protest loudly—what he called the Silent Majority.

These color-blind appeals provided a new rhetoric for even the most racially charged campaigns. Segregationists like Alabama Governor George Wallace, who ran as the American Independent candidate for president in 1968, traded traditional arguments rooted in states' rights and white supremacy for a populist rhetoric that exalted the little man, both the small business proprietor and the blue-collar worker. As Dan Carter and Michael Kazin have shown, Wallace successfully appealed to working-class voters outside the South, winning 34 percent of the primary vote in Wisconsin, 43 percent in Indiana, and 43 percent in Maryland. In a new book on the working class in the 1970s, Jefferson Cowie demonstrates how Nixon employed a deliberate strategy to attract lower-middle-class ethnics and blue-collar workers in the North who were disillusioned with the Democratic Party in 1972. Democratic candidate George McGovern won only 18 percent of the Southern vote and 38 percent of the urban Catholic vote.

In the 1960s and 1970s, the rapid expansion of a Sun Belt service-oriented political economy would push American politics in a rightward direction. General Motors, with its hundreds of thousands of unionized workers, factory assembly lines, and modern corporate organization, offered one model of postwar political economy. But recent studies of political economy have explored how the rapidly expanding suburban malls, supermarkets, fast-food restaurants, and discount stores followed a different path. In 1962, Wal-Mart, which, as Nelson Lichtenstein argues, would become a template for an anti–New Deal political economy, opened its first store in rural Arkansas. Reliance on low-wage, part time, non-union workers was a crucial ingredient to its success. Similarly, as Eric Schlosser has shown, McDonald's built its success on the shoulders of cheap, teenage, nonunionized labor. In 1972, the fast-food industry lobbied successfully for what became known as the McDonald's bill to allow employers to pay teenagers 20 percent less than the minimum wage. Lizabeth Cohen makes the point that the shopping malls, too, relied on workers who, as a part-time, female nonunion labor force, fell outside many labor regulations.

These new industries provided fertile ground for an antiregulatory counterattack on the New Deal state. From the 1930s on, as Kimberly Phillips-Fein and Elizabeth Shermer have shown, business organizations mounted a collective assault on unions, regulation, and government spending while defending profits and large corporations as social goods. Their efforts bore fruit in the "right-to-work" campaigns launched by conservative politicians throughout the Sun Belt where labor was more local, decentralized, nonindustrial, and service oriented. In Phoenix, Arizona, Barry Goldwater got his start as a spokesman for the antiunion right. He won his first campaign as senator in 1952 and built a reputation by attacking organized labor, especially after the AFL-CIO merger in 1955.

In addition to these political campaigns, leading American businessmen helped to proselytize the free-market arguments put forward by economists like Frederick Hayek and Milton Friedman. In the 1960s and 1970s, corporate executives founded organizations, foundations, and think tanks to advance a probusiness agenda. In the same year that Sam Walton opened his first store, free-market economist Milton Friedman published *Capitalism and Freedom*, which would serve as a foundational treatise for market-oriented policies. The connection was not just incidental, as Bethany Moreton argues. As Wal-Mart expanded, it recruited managers from the region's Christian colleges, many of which had established business courses with donations from Sun Belt industries. These colleges then educated the next generation of college students about free-market ideas.

Just as the so-called liberal era was not as united and consensual as historians once thought, neither was the conservative period that followed. This fact became clear right from the start of what Sean Wilentz calls the "Age of Reagan." Beginning with the presidency of Richard Nixon, conservatives found it hard to shift the country to the right. It was easier to run as a conservative than to govern as one. New work on the 1970s demonstrates the competing pressures Nixon faced between liberalism and conservatism. As Nixon understood, New Deal programs such as Social Security and Medicare retained their popularity and proved hard to scale back. In a time of economic troubles, Americans still looked for government's help. As the country began to experience stagflation, Nixon imposed wage and price controls to tame inflation while increasing government spending to stimulate the economy. He also agreed to tie increases in Social Security to the rate of inflation, which institutionalized enormous amounts of future government spending.

In addition to expanding these liberal programs, Nixon also supported new kinds of government social regulation, including the creation of the Environmental Protection Agency. By the end of the 1970s, New Deal–style price controls and Keynesian tools of fiscal management became vulnerable in the wake of the decade's economic troubles and the collapse of the international political economy. But recent studies, including work by Joan Hoff and Judith Stein, map out the ways in which Nixon put in place a vast expansion of government regulations. In foreign policy, too, Nixon came under pressure to moderate his approach, initiating a program of détente with the Soviet Union, including the signing of a Strategic Arms Limitation Treaty, and softening relations with China.

The legacies of détente and the expansion and further entrenchment of liberal programs under Nixon and his successor Gerald Ford would impel Ronald Reagan to challenge Ford from the right in the 1976 Republican primary. A political mobilization of conservatives in the 1970s and 1980s would enable the next generation to try even harder to push the country to the right.

As recent scholarship has amply demonstrated, these challenges to liberalism were not simply a product of post-1960s America. Indeed, the divisions and the basic lines of political battle had been evident almost from the moment the New Deal was born. The New Deal coalition and its policy agenda were always more contested than we remember. That contestation resulted in part from the far-reaching agenda and institutional strength of liberal reforms, which, in many ways, expanded and grew in the decades following F.D.R. As much as the New Deal order defined the postwar period, so, too, did the tensions between liberalism and conservatism that existed within it.

BIBLIOGRAPHY

Biondi, Martha. *To Stand and Fight: The Struggle for Civil Rights in Postwar New York City*. Cambridge, MA: Harvard University Press, 2003.

Black, Earl, and Merle Black. *The Rise of Southern Republicans*. Cambridge, MA: Harvard University Press, 2002.

Boris, Eileen. *Home to Work: Motherhood and the Politics of Industrial Homework in the United States*. New York: Cambridge University Press, 1994.

Borstelmann, Thomas. *The Cold War and the Color Line: American Race Relations in the Global Arena*. Cambridge, MA: Harvard University Press, 2001.

Boyle, Kevin. *The UAW and the Heyday of American Liberalism, 1945–1968*. Ithaca, NY: Cornell University Press, 1995.

Brinkley, Alan. *The End of Reform: New Deal Liberalism in Recession and War*. New York: Knopf, 1995.

Canaday, Margot. *The Straight State: Sexuality and Citizenship in Twentieth-Century America*. Princeton, NJ: Princeton University Press, 2009.

Carter, Dan T. *The Politics of Rage: George Wallace, the Origins of New Conservatism, and the Transformation of American Politics*. New York: Simon and Schuster, 1995.

Cobble, Dorothy Sue. *The Other Women's Movement: Workplace Justice and Social Rights in Modern America*. Princeton, NJ: Princeton University Press, 2004.

Cohen, Lizabeth. *A Consumer's Republic: The Politics of Mass Consumption in Postwar America*. New York: Knopf, 2003.

———. *Making a New Deal: Industrial Workers in Chicago, 1919–1939*. New York: Cambridge University Press, 1990.

Collins, Robert M. *More: The Politics of Economic Growth in Postwar America*. New York: Oxford University Press, 2000.

Countryman, Matthew J. *Up South: Civil Rights and Black Power in Philadelphia*. Philadelphia: University of Pennsylvania Press, 2005.

Cowie, Jefferson R. *Capital Moves: RCA's Seventy-Year Quest for Cheap Labor*. New York: New Press, 1999.

———. *Stayin' Alive: The 1970s and the Last Days of the Working Class*. New York: New Press, 2010.

Crespino, Joseph. *In Search of Another Country: Mississippi and the Conservative Counterrevolution*. Princeton, NJ: Princeton University Press, 2007.

Critchlow, Donald. *Phyllis Schlafly and American Conservatism: A Woman's Crusade*. Princeton, NJ: Princeton University Press, 2005.

Davies, Gareth. *From Opportunity to Entitlement: The Transformation and Decline of Great Society Liberalism*. Lawrence: University Press of Kansas, 1996.

———. *See Government Grow: Education Politics from Johnson to Reagan*. Lawrence: University Press of Kansas, 2007.

Denning, Michael. *The Cultural Front*. New York: Verso, 1997.

Dittmer, John. *Local People: The Struggle for Civil Rights in Mississippi*. Urbana: University of Illinois Press, 1994.

Dudziak, Mary L. *Cold War Civil Rights: Race and the Image of American Democracy*. Princeton, NJ: Princeton University Press, 2000.

Edsall, Thomas Byrnes, and Mary D. Edsall. *Chain Reaction: The Impact of Race, Rights, and Taxes on American Politics*. New York: W. W. Norton, 1991.

Evans, Sara M. *Tidal Wave: How Women Changed America at Century's End*. New York: Free Press, 2003.

Faue, Elizabeth. *Community of Suffering and Struggle: Women, Men, and the Labor Movement in Minneapolis, 1915–1945.* Chapel Hill: University of North Carolina Press, 1991.

Fones-Wolf, Elizabeth A. *Selling Free Enterprise: The Business Assault on Labor and Liberalism, 1945–60.* Urbana: University of Illinois Press, 1994.

Fraser, Steve. *Labor Will Rule: Sidney Hillman and the Rise of American Labor.* New York: Free Press, 1991.

Fraser, Steve, and Gary Gerstle. *The Rise and Fall of the New Deal Order, 1930–1980.* Princeton, NJ: Princeton University Press, 1989.

Frederickson, Kari A. *The Dixiecrat Movement and the Origins of Massive Resistance: Race, Politics, and Political Culture in the Deep South, 1932–1955.* New Brunswick, NJ: Rutgers University Press, 1996.

Freeman, Joshua B. *In Transit: The Transport Workers Union in New York City, 1933–1966.* New York: Oxford University Press, 1989.

Friedan, Betty. *The Feminine Mystique.* New York: W. W. Norton, 1963.

Friedman, Milton. *Capitalism and Freedom.* Chicago: University of Chicago Press, 1962.

Friedman, Tami J. "Exploiting the North-South Differential: Corporate Power, Southern Politics, and the Decline of Organized Labor after World War II." *Journal of American History* 95 (September 2008): 323–348.

Frydl, Kathleen. *The G.I. Bill.* New York: Cambridge University Press, 2009.

Frymer, Paul. *Black and Blue: African Americans, the Labor Movement, and the Decline of the Democratic Party.* Princeton, NJ: Princeton University Press, 2007.

Galbraith, John Kenneth. *American Capitalism.* New York: Houghton Mifflin, 1952.

Gerstle, Gary. *Working Class Americanism: The Politics of Labor in a Textile City, 1914–1960.* New York: Cambridge University Press, 1989.

Gillon, Steven M. *Politics and Vision: The ADA and American Liberalism, 1947–1985.* New York: Oxford University Press, 1987.

Goldberg, Chad Alan. *Citizens and Paupers: Relief, Rights, and Race from the Freedman's Bureau to Workfare.* Chicago: University of Chicago Press, 2007.

Goluboff, Risa L. *The Lost Promise of Civil Rights.* Cambridge, MA: Harvard University Press, 2007.

Gordon, Colin. *Dead on Arrival: The Politics of Health Care in Twentieth-Century America.* Princeton, NJ: Princeton University Press, 2003.

Gordon, Linda. *Pitied but Not Entitled: Single Mothers and the History of Welfare.* New York: Free Press, 1994.

Graham, Hugh Davis. *Collision Course: The Strange Convergence of Affirmative Action and Immigration Policy in America.* New York: Oxford University Press, 2002.

Griffith, Barbara S. *The Crisis of American Labor: Operation Dixie and the Defeat of the CIO.* Philadelphia: Temple University Press, 1988.

Hacker, Jacob S. *The Divided Welfare State: The Battle over Public and Private Benefits in the United States.* New York: Cambridge University Press, 2003.

Hall, Jacquelyn Dowd. "The Long Civil Rights Movement and the Political Uses of the Past." *Journal of American History* 91 (March 2005): 1233–1263.

Hamby, Alonzo. *Man of the People: A Life of Harry S. Truman.* New York: Oxford University Press, 1995.

Hamilton, Shane. *Trucking Country: The Road to America's Wal-Mart Economy.* Princeton, NJ: Princeton University Press, 2008.

Harris, Howell John. *The Right to Manage: Industrial Relations Policies of American Business in the 1940s*. Madison: University of Wisconsin Press, 1982.

Harrison, Cynthia. *On Account of Sex: The Politics of Women's Issues, 1945–1968*. Berkeley: University of California Press, 1988.

Hoff, Joan. *Nixon Reconsidered*. New York: Basic Books, 1994.

Hofstadter, Richard. *The American Political Tradition and the Men Who Made It*. New York: Knopf, 1948.

Hogan, Michael J. *A Cross of Iron: Harry S. Truman and the Origins of the National Security State, 1945–1954*. New York: Cambridge University Press, 1998.

———. *The Marshall Plan: America, Britain, and the Reconstruction of Western Europe, 1947–1952*. New York: Cambridge University Press, 1987.

Honey, Michael. *Southern Labor and Black Civil Rights: Organizing Memphis Workers*. Chicago: University of Illinois Press, 1993.

Jackson, Kenneth T. *Crabgrass Frontier: The Suburbanization of the United States*. New York: Oxford University Press, 1987.

Jacobs, Meg. "How about Some Meat? The Office of Price Administration, Consumption Politics, and State Building from the Bottom Up." *Journal of American History* 84 (December 1997): 910–941.

———. *Pocketbook Politics: Economic Citizenship in Twentieth-Century America*. Princeton, NJ: Princeton University Press, 2005.

Jones, Jacqueline. *Labor of Love, Labor of Sorrow: Black Women, Work, and the Family, from Slavery to the Present*. New York: Basic Books, 1985.

Katz, Michael B. *The Undeserving Poor: From the War on Poverty to the War on Welfare*. New York: Pantheon, 1989.

Katznelson, Ira. *When Affirmative Action Was White: An Untold History of Race and Inequality in Twentieth Century America*. New York: W. W. Norton, 2005.

Kazin, Michael. *The Populist Persuasion: An American History*. New York: Basic Books, 1995.

Kelley, Robin D. G. *Hammer and Hoe: Alabama Communists during the Great Depression*. Chapel Hill: University of North Carolina Press, 1990.

Kennedy, David M. *Freedom from Fear: The American People in Depression and War, 1929–1945*. New York: Oxford University Press, 1999.

Kessler-Harris, Alice. *In Pursuit of Equity: Women, Men, and the Quest for Economic Citizenship in 20th-Century America*. New York: Oxford University Press, 2001.

Klein, Jennifer. *For All These Rights: Business, Labor, and the Shaping of America's Public-Private Welfare State*. Princeton, NJ: Princeton University Press, 2003.

Klimke, Martin. *The Other Alliance: Student Protest in West Germany and the United States in the Global Sixties*. Princeton, NJ: Princeton University Press, 2009.

Kornbluh, Felicia. *The Battle for Welfare Rights: Politics and Poverty in Modern America*. Philadelphia: University of Pennsylvania Press, 2007.

Kruse, Kevin M. *White Flight: Atlanta and the Making of Modern Conservatism*. Princeton, NJ: Princeton University Press, 2005.

Lassiter, Matthew D. *Silent Majority: Suburban Politics in the Sunbelt South*. Princeton, NJ: Princeton University Press, 2005.

Leffler, Melvyn P. *Preponderance of Power: National Security, the Truman Administration, and the Cold War*. Palo Alto, CA: Stanford University Press, 1992.

Lichtenstein, Nelson. *The Most Dangerous Man in Detroit: Walter Reuther and the Fate of American Labor.* New York: Basic Books, 1995.

———. *The Retail Revolution: How Wal-Mart Created a Brave New World of Business.* New York: Metropolitan, 2009.

———. *State of the Union: A Century of American Labor.* Princeton, NJ: Princeton University Press, 2002.

Lieberman, Robert C. *Shifting the Color Line: Race and the American Welfare State.* Cambridge, MA: Harvard University Press, 1998.

Lipsitz, George. *Rainbow at Midnight: Labor and Culture in the 1940s.* Urbana-Champaign: University of Illinois Press, 1994.

———. *Time Passages: Collective Memory and American Popular Culture.* Minneapolis: University of Minnesota Press, 1990.

Logevall, Fredrik. *Choosing War: The Lost Chance for Peace and the Escalation of War in Vietnam.* Berkeley: University of California Press, 1999.

Logevall, Fredrik, and Campbell Craig. *America's Cold War: The Politics of Insecurity.* Cambridge, MA: Belknap/Harvard University Press, 2009.

Lotchin, Roger W. *The Bad City in the Good War: San Francisco, Los Angeles, Oakland, and San Diego.* Bloomington: Indiana University Press, 2003.

Lubell, Samuel. *The Future of American Politics*, 2nd ed. New York: Doubleday, 1956.

MacLean, Nancy. *Freedom Is Not Enough: The Opening of the American Workplace.* Cambridge, MA: Harvard University Press, 2006.

Matusow, Allen J. *Nixon's Economy: Booms, Busts, Dollars, and Votes.* Lawrence: University Press of Kansas, 1998.

McGirr, Lisa. *Suburban Warriors: The Origins of the New American Right.* Princeton, NJ: Princeton University Press, 2001.

Mettler, Suzanne. *Soldiers to Citizens: The G.I. Bill and the Making of the Greatest Generation.* New York: Oxford University Press, 2005.

Meyerowitz, Joanne. *Not June Cleaver: Women and Gender in Postwar America, 1945–1960.* Philadelphia: Temple University Press, 1994.

Mitchell, Greg. *Tricky Dick and the Pink Lady: Richard Nixon vs. Helen Gahagan Douglas—Sexual Politics and the Red Scare, 1950.* New York: Random House, 1998.

Mittelstadt, Jennifer. *From Welfare to Workfare: The Unintended Consequences of Liberal Reform, 1945–1965.* Chapel Hill: University of North Carolina Press, 2005.

Moreton, Bethany. *To Serve God and Wal-Mart: The Making of Christian Free Enterprise.* Cambridge, MA: Harvard University Press, 2009.

Nash, Gerald D. *The American West Transformed: The Impact of the Second World War.* Bloomington: Indiana University Press, 1985.

O'Connor, Alice. *Poverty Knowledge: Social Science, Social Policy, and the Poor in Twentieth-Century U.S. History.* Princeton, NJ: Princeton University Press, 2001.

Packard, Vance. *The Status Seekers.* New York: D. McKay, 1959.

Patterson, James T. *Grand Expectations: The United States, 1945–1974.* New York: Oxford University Press, 1996.

Payne, Charles M. *I've Got the Light of Freedom: The Organizing Tradition and the Mississippi Freedom Struggle.* Berkeley: University of California Press, 1995.

Perlstein, Rick. *Before the Storm: Barry Goldwater and the Unmaking of the American Consensus.* New York: Hill and Wang, 2001.

Phillips-Fein, Kimberly. *Invisible Hands: The Making of the Conservative Movement from the New Deal to Reagan.* New York: W. W. Norton, 2009.

Rieder, Jonathan. *Canarsie: The Jews and Italians of Brooklyn against Liberalism.* Cambridge, MA: Harvard University Press, 1985.

Riesman, David. *The Lonely Crowd: A Study of the Changing American Character.* New Haven, CT: Yale University Press, 1950.

Rossinow, Douglas. *Visions of Progress: The Left-Liberal Tradition in America.* Philadelphia: University of Pennsylvania Press, 2008.

Rosswurm, Steve. *The FBI and the Catholic Church, 1935–1962.* Amherst: University of Massachusetts Press, 2009.

Schaller, Michael. *Altered States: The United States and Japan since the Occupation.* New York: Oxford University Press, 1997.

Schlesinger, Arthur M., Jr. *The Vital Center: The Politics of Freedom.* Boston: Houghton Mifflin, 1949.

Schlosser, Eric. *Fast Food Nation: The Dark Side of the All American Meal.* Boston: Houghton Mifflin, 2001.

Schrecker, Ellen. *Many Are the Crimes: McCarthyism in America.* New York: Little, Brown, 1998.

Schulman, Bruce J. *From Cotton Belt to Sunbelt: Federal Policy, Economic Development, and the Transformation of the South, 1938–1980.* New York: Oxford University Press, 1991.

———. *Lyndon Johnson and American Liberalism: A Brief History with Documents.* Boston: Bedford, 2006.

Schulman, Bruce J., and Julian E. Zelizer. *Rightward Bound: Making America Conservative in the 1970s.* Cambridge, MA: Harvard University Press, 2008.

Schwarz, Jordan A. *The New Dealers: Power Politics in the Age of Roosevelt.* New York: Knopf, 1993.

Self, Robert O. *American Babylon: Race and the Struggle for Postwar Oakland.* Princeton, NJ: Princeton University Press, 2003.

Shermer, Elizabeth. "Origins of the Conservative Ascendancy: Barry Goldwater's Early Senate Career and the De-legitimization of Organized Labor." *Journal of American History* 95 (December 2008): 678–709.

Simon, Bryant. *A Fabric of Defeat: The Politics of South Carolina Millhands, 1910–48.* Chapel Hill: University of North Carolina Press, 1998.

Skrentny, John D. *The Minority Rights Revolution.* Cambridge, MA: Belknap/Harvard University Press, 2002.

Smith, Jason Scott. *Building New Deal Liberalism: The Political Economy of Public Works, 1933–1956.* New York: Cambridge University Press, 2006.

Stein, Judith. *Running Steel, Running America: Race, Economic Policy, and the Decline of Liberalism.* Chapel Hill: University of North Carolina Press, 1998.

Sugrue, Thomas J. *The Origins of the Urban Crisis: Race and Inequality in Postwar Detroit.* Princeton, NJ: Princeton University Press, 1996.

———. *Sweet Land of Liberty: The Forgotten Struggle for Civil Rights in the North.* New York: Random House, 2008.

Suri, Jeremi. *Power and Protest: Global Revolution and the Rise of Détente.* Cambridge, MA: Harvard University Press, 2003.

Tomlins, Christopher L. *The State and the Unions: Labor Relations, Law, and the Organized Labor Movement in America, 1880–1960.* New York: Cambridge University Press, 1985.

Varon, Jeremy. *Bringing the War Home: The Weather Underground, the Red Army Faction, and Revolutionary Violence in the Sixties and Seventies*. Berkeley: University of California Press, 2004.

Von Eschen, Penny. *Race against Empire: Black Americans and Anticolonialism, 1937–1957*. Ithaca, NY: Cornell University Press, 1997.

Whitfield, Stephen J. *The Culture of the Cold War*. Baltimore: Johns Hopkins University Press, 1991.

Whyte, William Hollingsworth. *The Organization Man*. New York: Simon and Schuster, 1956.

Wilentz, Sean. *The Age of Reagan: A History, 1974–2008*. New York: Harper, 2008.

Zelizer, Julian E. *Arsenal of Democracy: The Politics of National Security—From World War II to the War on Terror*. New York: Basic Books, 2010.

———. *On Capitol Hill: The Struggle to Reform Congress and Its Consequences, 1948–2000*. New York: Cambridge University Press, 2004.

———. "Political History and Political Science: Together Again?" *Journal of Policy History* 16 (2004): 126–136.

———. *Taxing America: Wilbur D. Mills, Congress, and the State, 1945–1975*. New York: Cambridge University Press, 1998.

Zieger, Robert. *The CIO, 1935–1955*. Chapel Hill: University of North Carolina Press, 1995.

8

1973 to the Present

KIM PHILLIPS-FEIN

In the introduction to his book *The Age of Empire*, the historian Eric Hobsbawm writes of the "twilight zone between memory and history," where the past ceases to simply exist in the past and instead becomes interwoven with the events of one's own life. The beginning and end of a war, the dip and rise of the stock market, the invention of a new technological marvel, or the election of a president—these are not part of some general historical past, made remote by the distance of time, but instead are inextricably linked to our personal memories and the timeline of our own lives. Such recent history—history that has not yet come to seem like "real" history—has inevitable pitfalls for those who seek to write about it, and perhaps for this reason, the historical scholarship on the years from 1973 onward is still limited, fragmentary, and politically conflicted. Some scholars see this as a period of decline and frustration, marking the onset of a reduced vision of the common good and the rise of pronounced economic inequality, while others have argued that the period is one of America triumphing over international communism abroad and economic stagnation at home. The immediacy of the era makes such disparate judgments predictable. After all, it is only recently that it has even started to seem a distinct period, instead of being grouped into the broader category of post–World War II America (as was the case in the previous edition of this book). And the question still remains—when the era that began in 1973 ended—or if it has.

But despite the problems of writing such contemporary history, these years contain many fascinating questions and problems for historians. For no matter how we make sense of the changes, there is no doubt that they were profound. In 1973, the American economy was reaching the end of its long postwar expansion. The energy shocks of that year and the accompanying inflation were the first suggestion that a new period of greater economic instability might be on the horizon. The faith in government activism as a way of solving social problems that had existed throughout much of the postwar period had not yet started to dim, as suggested by the creation of the Environmental Protection Agency and the Occupational Safety and Health Administration under Republican president Richard Nixon. The cold war still defined American politics; the Vietnam War had not yet ended. The feminist and gay rights movements were only a few years old, and the legal and constitutional victories of the civil rights movement still recent events. Self-conscious conservatism, despite gaining in strength during the postwar years, remained marginal in national politics. The central assumptions about American society and politics that had emerged during and immediately after the New Deal and World War II—the belief in mass consumption as a way of improving not only one's personal well-being but the society as a whole, the confidence in upward mobility, the sense of the importance and legitimacy of institutions such as labor unions and political parties, the relative ambivalence toward an untrammeled free market—remained largely intact.

By the early twenty-first century, the cold war was over; conservatives, despite tensions within their movement, had become one of the dominant political forces in American life; politicians from both political parties celebrated the free market as the solution to virtually all social and economic problems; the traditional models of the family had been upended; and the struggle for civil rights for women, gay and lesbian people, and African Americans had taken on dimensions that were hard to imagine in the early 1970s, even as thinking about race, gender, sexuality, and political activism itself had been transformed.

How should we understand this complicated period, one that remains so near to us as to be hard to see clearly? Much of the scholarship has approached it through the lens of an implicit contrast with the earlier postwar years. The post-1973 years have been viewed as a time of economic uncertainty and widening inequality as compared to steady growth; as an epoch of ambivalence, skepticism, and even hostility toward politics, in contrast to the idealism and optimism of the 1940s, 1950s and 1960s; and perhaps most of all, as an age of conservatism that rejected the liberalism of the postwar years. The major efforts to write about the entire post-1973 period as a whole have generally sought to explain the rightward shift of American politics, exploring questions related to the rise of a new conservatism and the breakdown of the liberal order associated with the New Deal. Sean Wilentz, for example, has described the last third of the twentieth century as an "era of conservatism" and the "Age of Reagan," a time when the common wisdom about what Americans might expect from their government underwent a fundamental transformation. Emphasizing the economic history of the period, Godfrey Hodgson has argued that the period should be seen as one of "disappointment and denial," a time of rapidly widening economic and social inequality accompanied by a frenetic celebration of the idea of the free market. Not all assessments are so bleak: James Patterson, by contrast, has emphasized the technological innovations of the era, such as the rise of the personal computer and the Internet, and argued that during these years America became a society more tolerant of racial, religious, and sexual difference than it had been during the years of the great postwar boom. Although these accounts—and a few others—seek to explore the entire period from 1973 onward, more common are studies that break the era into decade-long units, sometimes with a few years added on the beginning or end in order to evade the arbitrary nature of such chronologies. For example, Bruce Schulman has suggested that the seventies were a time of the rise of a new interest in the private sphere in American culture, one that spanned the left and right alike, while Gil Troy has interpreted the eighties as years when conservative political and economic ideas were reconciled with the cultural liberalism of the sixties.

Perhaps what is most striking about the historiography of post-1973 America is how intensely concerned much of it is with politics, even though in some ways American society itself became far more ambivalent about politics over these years. This is true even for work that is not explicitly on political history; much of the new scholarship about social life, culture, gender and sexuality, family, the economy, and technology takes as its underlying theme the political transformations of the late twentieth century. Why did the conservative movement, which once seemed so marginal, come to be so powerful, and how did its ideas about the market come to be so widely accepted? Did these years witness the resounding defeat of American liberalism and the rise of a new conservative framework? Or did the basic structures and institutions of liberalism remain intact, with the conservative onslaught ultimately unable to change much? Some historians—such as Nick Salvatore and Jefferson Cowie—are sufficiently impressed with the power of the conservative revival that they have argued that the entire postwar liberal era from 1945 to 1973 was no more than a "long exception," a detour away from the laissez-faire individualism that seems to define American history in both the nineteenth and early twenty-first centuries. In fact, they suggest that the strength of conservatism indicates the relative weakness throughout the twentieth century of liberalism; in a way, the transformations of American society since the early 1970s serve to show us how limited and weak the liberal era itself was even at its height. Other scholars—for example, Julian Zelizer and Meg Jacobs—suggest that despite the many changes brought about by an era of conservative rule, the transformations of the state that took place in the 1930s and 1940s created a regulatory welfare state far more durable than suggested by the rhetoric of a Reagan "revolution."

Another major theme in the historiography concerns the fate of the social movements of the 1960s and early 1970s—for civil rights, feminism, and gay and lesbian rights—in the late 1970s and afterward. Did the electoral success of the conservative movement mean their defeat or failure? How to think about the tension between the apparently greater tolerance of American society in the early twenty-first century—symbolized by the election of the country's first African-American president, which would have been difficult to imagine in the postwar era—and its increased economic inequality? What is the relationship between the development of sexual and racial liberalism and the rise of conservative politics? Finally, the period was also one of far-reaching economic transformations, as the United States lost much of its industrial base and instead became far more oriented toward a service and finance economy, while also becoming more deeply oriented toward a global economic order, and yet the ways that these economic changes were perceived and experienced depended deeply on political ideas.

The 1970s

Almost since they ended, the 1970s have been seen as a time stranded between the Great Society and the Age of Reagan, the half-life of the 1960s and the preview to the 1980s, defined more by what came before and after than by anything particular about the period itself. Contemporaries viewed the 1970s as a period of defeat, alienation, and disaffection brought about by the failure to realize the utopian imaginings of the 1960s as well as by the political scandals of the early part of the decade, most importantly Watergate. As Christopher Lasch put it in his 1979 best seller, *The Culture of Narcissism: American Life in an Age of Diminished Expectations*, it was a time of withdrawal from public life: "After the political turmoil of the sixties, Americans have retreated to purely personal preoccupations." The revelations of the Watergate scandal diminished faith in political institutions overall. In a 1974 essay in the magazine *Dissent*, Michael Harrington described a "collective sadness" that was gripping the country: people "can't believe in either their God or their country in the way that they used to; people just don't know what to believe in at all." The earlier histories of the decade echoed this vision, depicting the 1970s in terms of a retreat from politics and a new engagement with the private sphere on left and right alike. Peter Carroll gave his 1982 history of the decade a title that reflected the widespread sense of the absurdity of writing about the 1970s at all: it was a time when "it seemed like nothing happened." Bruce Schulman wrote that the predominant mood of the period was one of "contempt for authority," a widespread sense that "the powers that be had rotted to the core." Americans turned away from collective efforts to transform or improve society, instead embarking on fantastic voyages of self-exploration and carving out niches of communal identification outside a national public culture. They became born-again Christians and joined New Age spiritual groups; some became obsessed with eating and exercise regimens; while others immersed themselves in a decadent nightlife culture. And in sharp contrast to the moral seriousness of civil rights, the War on Poverty, and the antiwar movement, the reigning cultural attitude became one of ironic distance, as people mocked the fads that were sweeping the country (disco, or bell-bottoms, or Pet Rocks) even when they were at their most popular.

Recent years have seen an intense scholarly reengagement with the 1970s, one that revises this earlier view substantially. Instead of being a "lost decade" and a time of declining political engagement, historians now argue that the period actually contains within itself both the fruition of the radical changes of the 1960s and the onset of the conservative reaction that would come to power at the end of the decade. Far from a trivial interregnum between the age of Lyndon Johnson and that of Ronald Reagan, the 1970s were the moment when the critical political and economic features of contemporary America came into existence: the rise of feminism and gay rights, the onset of deindustrialization and the growing importance of the service and financial sectors, and perhaps most of all, the emergence of conservatism as a mainstream political force. As scholars such as Laura Kalman have argued, it was a time of intense political controversy rather than disillusionment with politics. During the 1970s, American society was in flux and transformation, the breakdown of the New Deal order reshaping expectations and possibilities. This was the moment before the definitive ascendance of the right, yet it was when it became clear that the country had changed in ways that made the rise of conservatism possible. At the same time, the 1970s were not simply a time of conservative victory. Scholars such as Julian Zelizer and Bruce Schulman have made the case that even as the right gained strength, the obstacles that it had to confront revealed the profound changes that liberalism and the social movements of the 1960s had brought about in American institutions and culture. And beyond this, the rebellions of the decade, the explosive outbursts of protest on both the left and the right, and the prevailing cultural mood of skepticism and uncertainty about established power and authority make the 1970s difficult to see simply as a precursor to the conservative shift; the old patterns might have been in decline, but the future remained uncertain and open. This sense of indeterminacy is part of why the word "crisis" appears so often in accounts of the era, from the "fiscal crisis" of New York to the "energy crisis" affecting the country as a whole. The old order was collapsing, and it was not yet clear what would emerge to take its place.

What was the cause of this upheaval and uncertainty? The overwhelming political reality of the 1970s was the end of the economic growth that had defined the postwar period, as the country was rocked by energy shortages, rising unemployment, and inflation. Economic growth slowed sharply in the early 1970s, with real gross national product falling by more than 2 percent in 1974 and nearly 3 percent in 1975, while inflation mounted (retail prices increased by 11 percent in 1974) along with unemployment, which reached a postwar high of 8.5 percent in 1975. Like the Great Depression forty years earlier, the economic problems of the 1970s inspired political unrest. Even though the economic troubles of the 1970s were not as severe as those of the 1930s, their resolution seemed to be beyond the ken of the Keynesian economists who still dominated policy making. When both inflation and unemployment began to rise following the decade's first energy shortage in 1973 (itself the result of a boycott of the Organization of Petroleum Exporting Countries in retaliation for the West's support for Israel during the Yom Kippur War), these Keynesians were puzzled and confused about the phenomenon that would be dubbed "stagflation." They found themselves stymied when seeking to apply the economic tools they had used earlier in the postwar period. Countercyclical fiscal policy might help with unemployment, but it would only stimulate prices; the Nixon administration attempted an ambitious program of price controls, which failed miserably. The result was an intellectual and political vacuum. Although there were some proposals from the left for broader economic planning or for finding ways to empower consumers and keep corporations from maintaining artificially high prices, conservative solutions to the economic problems of the day that emphasized rolling back state programs and expanding the reach of the free market ultimately were able to win greater support in Washington. Part of the difficulty was that the economic slowdown of the 1970s (as Charles Maier has written) was no simple business cycle recession—it was in fact the beginning of a broader structural shift in employment and investment, a movement away from manufacturing and into services, and in particular the rise of the financial sector and the decline of manufacturing.

Historians are beginning to revisit the politics of this period of economic anxiety, looking at how the recession destabilized intellectual and political support for the liberal economic order, throwing open a fierce debate about the right way to address the reality of dramatically slowed economic growth. Meg Jacobs, for example, has examined the ways in which the conservatives in power in the Nixon administration took advantage of the energy crisis of the early part of the decade to press for their antigovernment agenda. Greta Krippner has suggested that the shift toward financial deregulation began as the country sought to respond to inflation and the economic slowdown, and that this helped contribute to the growing importance of the financial sector in the overall economy. And Judith Stein has written about the politics of deindustrialization—the intense political fights that wracked the country over who would bear the brunt of economic restructuring. Although in some ways the core ideas and institutions that had supported New Deal liberalism had been hollowed out earlier in the postwar years, as labor unions were weakened by antiunion activity and capital flight, the economic difficulties of the 1970s created the perfect atmosphere for a wholehearted attack on that faith and the rise of a new economic ideology focused on the idea of the free market.

Labor historians have been drawn to the 1970s as well, because the decade seems the critical turning point for the history of the union movement in the second half of the twentieth century. The early years of the decade saw the largest strike wave since World War II. A national debate about the plight of blue-collar workers (the "blue-collar blues") began after the 1972 strike of young, countercultural workers at a General Motors factory in Lordstown, Ohio, which was notable for its focus on the draconian working conditions at the plant instead of on salary or benefits. There were certain high-profile organizing campaigns during the decade, such as that at J. P. Stevens, the North Carolina textile company, which turned into a national boycott and became the subject of a Hollywood movie (*Norma Rae*). Joseph McCartin has written about the wave of organizing among public-sector workers in the 1960s and 1970s, one of the few areas where the labor movement grew over the postwar period. Dorothy Sue Cobble has shown the ways in which women workers helped to reshape the labor movement, suggesting that the influx of women into the workforce (particularly into "pink-collar" jobs) transformed the American working class and arguing that labor feminism comprises an alternate way of understanding the women's movement. Yet what is most remarkable about the 1970s is that despite the radicalism and militancy evident in the decade, the overall shift in American politics—and even in the working class—was still to the right. Jefferson Cowie has argued that during the 1970s the very idea of the working class started to cease to have political salience, as it was slowly being replaced by a vision of individual entrepreneurs. The markers of class became cultural rather than economic or political; Richard Nixon pioneered the strategy of appealing to white male workers through a language of authenticity, even though he was not particularly sympathetic to their economic needs or interests. The mystery of the decade is that class became at once more and less important—even as American society became increasingly stratified by wealth and income, the language of class disappeared from American politics.

The complexity that scholars have discerned in the world of labor and class politics—the way in which American labor seemed at once radical and quiescent—is evident as well in the literature dealing with the left and the fate of the social movements of the 1960s. This body of work has substantially changed in recent years. Many older interpretations (often advanced by people who had actually participated in the various movements) argued that the civil rights movement and the New Left entered into a tragic decline in the 1970s, as civil rights turned toward black power and the optimistic idealism of Students for a Democratic Society gave way to the rage of the Weather Underground. Recent scholarship on social movements in the 1970s, however, emphasizes their continued vibrancy and importance throughout the decade. Scholars such as Jacquelyn Hall have advanced the idea of a "long civil rights movement" that goes back to the 1940s and extends through the 1970s and beyond, offering a new framework for the entire period that foregrounds economic issues in the struggle for racial equality. Scholars of the black power movement (including Peniel Joseph and Robert Self) have argued that it reflected a long-standing tradition in black politics that was focused on urban poverty, de facto segregation, and economic discrimination rather than on the southern legal regime of Jim Crow. Black power did not emerge solely out of the frustrations and limitations of the civil rights movement, and what is more, it was not primarily nihilistic or violent, as earlier work implied, but rather its militant vision gave rise to a legacy of welfare rights organizing and black electoral politics in places such as Oakland, California. In another take on the legacy of the civil rights movement, John Skrentny has described the ways that other minority groups (women, disabled people, Latinos, and Asian Americans) sought to use the legal reforms that it had created to bring about a "minority rights revolution," in which the definition of who a minority might be was expanded and changed to afford a larger number of people access to the victories that the civil rights movement had won.

Work on the history of the New Left and of radicalism is also moving away from a narrative of declension. Jeremy Varon's study of the Weather Underground in the United States and the Red Army Faction in West Germany suggests that the turn toward radical violence at the end of the 1960s should be understood in terms of the genuine dilemmas confronting the antiwar movement at this time, rather than simply as a morality story about the dangers of extremism. Meanwhile, the feminist and gay rights movements—which were both descended from the civil rights movement and the New Left—flourished only in the 1970s, making it harder still to see the decade as one of decline. Alice Echols has looked at the evolution of internal feminist movement politics during the 1970s, focusing on the tensions between radical egalitarian feminism and cultural feminism, while Nancy MacLean has told the story of how women and African Americans used the Civil Rights Act to legally challenge workplace discrimination in the 1970s and afterward. David Eisenbach has described the ways that the early gay rights movement shifted from the moderate politics of the Mattachine Society and the homophile movement of the 1960s to a more intensely radical agenda in the aftermath of the Stonewall riots of 1969, while Robert Self has considered the emergence in the 1970s of sexual liberalism alongside a law-and-order politics in Los Angeles that permitted the policing of public sex shops in order to preserve property values, even as it proclaimed the freedom of "private" sexual activity—suggesting the significance of the context of economic decline and the rise of conservatism for the development of gay rights. Common to all these works is a desire to see the openly provocative and confrontational political style of the left in the early 1970s as arising out of complex tensions and political disagreements. It reflected serious debates about how to keep building on the political victories of the 1960s, and should not be reduced to a mere politics of desperation.

But in some ways the most important scholarship on the 1970s has dealt with the decade as the critical turning point in the fortunes of the American right—the moment when conservatism emerged onto the national political scene. The decade, after all, began with Richard Nixon in the White House and ended with Ronald Reagan winning the presidency. What accounts for the rise of conservatism in American politics? The older narratives of the rise of the right (such as those put forward by Dan Carter and Thomas Byrne Edsall) told the story as one of top-down manipulation by political elites around the Republican Party. The argument was that starting with Nixon's campaign in 1968 (inspired in part by the surprising popularity of former segregationist George Wallace in his third-party presidential bid that year), Republicans sought to play on racism and the mounting "white backlash" against the civil rights movement to garner support for conservative political candidates. Nixon helped to invent a new faux-populist conservative politics organized around ideas of fighting crime and moral corruption and defending "law and order," seeking to appeal to the southern Democrats who had grown alienated from the national party because of the civil rights movement in what became known as his southern strategy. Scholars then began to tell the social history of these white working-class conservatives, showing the underlying reasons that they were receptive to appeals that focused on race. The work of Ronald Formisano and Jonathan Rieder on "reactionary populism" (as Formisano called it) in Boston and Brooklyn depicted white working-class people struggling to maintain control over their homes, their neighborhoods, and their community institutions in an era of economic decline. These historians suggested that the "Reagan Democrats" were motivated by their own local histories, rather than simply being manipulated by canny political operatives working from above.

Newer scholarship on the right in the 1970s has broadened the focus still further to consider the rise of a self-conscious conservative movement during the decade. This research has suggested that middle- and upper-middle-class suburbanites—rather than the working-class urbanites focused on by earlier scholars—were the key political actors in the conservative mobilization. Lisa McGirr, for example, chronicles the rise of a conservative subculture and politics among well-to-do professionals in Orange County, California, showing the ways in which conservative evangelical churches expanded in the early 1970s as part of a broader network of movement institutions. Matthew Lassiter and Kevin Kruse are among the foremost practitioners of the "new suburban history," which has looked at the creation of the suburbs as a physical space that nurtured a worldview that was consonant with a politics which, while not necessarily conservative, was critical of the old New Deal liberalism. Their story of the rise of the right is not one of the open racism of the Jim Crow South coming to dominate national politics through coded appeals. Rather, they argue that the political economy of Keynesian liberalism itself helped to create a population of middle-class homeowning suburbanites in the Sun Belt and around the country, who pursued a vision of individual choice and meritocracy that legitimated existing spatial and economic arrangements and fostered opposition to state policies that might redress inequality. But they did so through a language of "color blindness" and market choice, rather than by espousing open racism. In this account, the support that liberalism offered to suburbia ultimately helped to foster a political culture that would prove more receptive to free-market arguments.

Meanwhile, Shane Hamilton has described the rise of a populist conservatism that was not focused on race but rather on economic deregulation among long-haul truckers, who found in the rhetoric of the market a way to preserve their sense of masculine independence in an era of rising economic instability. The work of Bethany Moreton on the history of Wal-Mart has depicted the rise of "Christian free enterprise" as a political project with roots in the culture of the Ozark Mountains that became resonant with political and cultural issues facing the country as a whole in the age of deindustrialization. Historians such as Donald Critchlow and Marjorie Spruill have looked at the central role of antifeminism in the rise of the conservative movement, especially around the resistance to the Equal Rights Amendment, suggesting that the rise of feminist politics also spurred the creation of an alternative network of women's politics, one devoted to embracing the rhetoric of sexual difference. And Daniel Williams and Darren Dochuk have described the ways that the politicization of evangelical churches (whose congregations were gaining in strength over the decade) contributed to the force of the conservative reaction.

In all these ways, the newer scholarship on the rightward shift in American politics has sought to treat it in terms of broad social and economic changes at the grass roots that made the nation more receptive to the conservative agenda, instead of describing it primarily in terms of the political strategies adopted by Republican Party organizers. All these scholars trace the lineage of the conservative shift deep in the postwar years, although they see it coming to fruition in the 1970s, when conservatives were able to seize on the weaknesses in liberalism that were exposed as the economy slowed and as conflicts erupted about race and sexuality. The growing conservative reaction on cultural issues did not exactly turn back the clock in terms of people's lives: women kept moving into the workplace, sexuality would not be again confined to marriage, and the formerly subterranean world of gay and lesbian life continued to move out into the open. But the hostility that these changes provoked did make it harder for the political movements that defended such choices to keep gaining in momentum. And the movement was able to achieve a common language for criticizing the state that could link business conservatives to religious traditionalists, in part through a shared vision around the free market.

While it might seem focused on the social and political history of the grass roots, this new scholarship has also transformed the understanding of presidential politics during the decade. Even though more and more of the Nixon tapes have been made public, so that it is now possible to have a fuller view of the extralegal activities of the Nixon administration, many historians now see Nixon primarily as a major transitional figure in the rise of conservative politics, whose political popularity is at least as notable as his crimes in the White House. Rick Perlstein has described America in the early 1970s as "Nixonland," divided between those who supported the radical challenges of the day and those who agreed with the president about the need to use any possible means to counter the threats of leftism.

Meanwhile, scholars such as Bruce Schulman, W. Carl Biven, and Daniel Horowitz have treated Jimmy Carter in terms of the conservative shift as well, seeing his ambivalent relationship to New Deal ideals of governance as a precursor to supply-side economics. His famous "crisis of confidence" speech of 1979—which came while the nation faced yet another energy shortage—argued that the government could not take responsibility for the problems facing the American public: the real culprit lay in the country's culture of mass consumption. Although the speech was pilloried at the time for what many saw as an abdication of leadership, it suggested a deepening skepticism about the power of government to shape social life—a sense of the limits of the state, in contrast to the optimism and confidence of postwar liberalism. According to these accounts, Carter built upon certain long-standing ambivalences within postwar liberalism toward organized labor and the welfare state—in the end helping to shift the dynamic around liberalism away from the more progressive tendencies that it had inherited during the New Deal and after.

Finally, historians have started to write in depth about the cultural changes that swept 1970s America and the apocalyptic sense of imminent decline that characterized the decade. What is most interesting about this body of scholarship is the way in which it addresses the significance of the context of recession and anxiety about American power internationally for the trajectory of the feminist and antiwar movements. Natasha Zaretsky has looked at the ways in which fears about changing family structures and gender roles were connected to larger anxieties about American decline in the wake of defeat in Vietnam, the energy crisis, and economic recession, so that the Republican victory in 1980 became at once a struggle over family, the meaning of home, and the nature of the national community. Michael Allen has explored the rise of the cause of the "prisoners of war" in Vietnam—those soldiers who were missing but not proclaimed dead—as a way of understanding how Americans grappled with military loss in the wake of the antiwar movement. William Graebner has tried to understand the tremendous interest in the figure of Patricia Hearst, the heiress kidnapped by a radical cult group (the Symbionese Liberation Army) who came to declare her allegiance to its revolutionary ideals and to participate in bank robberies with the organization. This mood of cultural tumult may have helped to fuel the dramatic expansion of evangelical and fundamentalist Christian churches during the decade, as described by historians Paul Boyer and William Martin. At the same time, the 1970s were a time of tremendous artistic creativity, especially in some of the places that were hit the hardest by the recession and by disinvestment in urban areas such as New York City, chronicled by Jeff Chang in his history of hip-hop music and culture.

The developing historical literature on the 1970s depicts a country in the midst of profound and unsettling transformations, in which old hierarchies of race and sex were being challenged and overturned even as the economic confidence and easy sense of international superiority that had characterized the postwar years were no longer available. It was a time when free-market ideas were on the rise, but still not widely accepted; a time when working-class people might participate in strikes but also flock to churches preaching deeply conservative principles; and a time when radical movements remained strong but were increasingly met by a newly powerful right. By the end of the decade, there was a new openness at both the top and the bottom of American society to political choices that would weaken the welfare state, deregulate parts of the economy, and turn to market solutions rather than state intervention to solve the economic problems of the day. Yet this openness did not by any means reflect a complete consolidation around these ideas. The result was that at the start of the 1980s, with Ronald Reagan—himself a true movement conservative—in the White House, the tide of economic conservatism rose, even as the country was in the throes of transition from one kind of economy to another, and even though Americans were still divided about the right way to resolve the many problems the country confronted.

The 1980s

The scholarship on the 1980s is much more limited than on the 1970s. Many of the works that exist are synthetic accounts of the period, even though the archival and monographic work upon which definitive accounts of the era could rest has not yet been done. The central issues in the historiography concern the conservative movement in power and the entrenchment in the federal government of a new way of seeing the relationship between the market and the state. Was the conservative movement that Ronald Reagan represented—the push for smaller government, more market deregulation, and traditional social values—successful in achieving its aims and agenda during the 1980s? To what extent were the changes that came about in American politics and culture the result of the activism of the conservative movement, and to what extent did they emerge for other reasons? What resistance and obstacles did the conservative push face? More deeply, how should we think about the changes in American culture and politics over the 1980s—years when the values of profit making and of the free market began to be extolled by the country's political and economic leaders as the highest moral principles? How did the tensions of the 1970s become resolved in the 1980s around a new conservatism and faith in the free market—if in fact they did?

A great many of the histories of the 1980s have focused closely on Ronald Reagan, a confounding figure for scholars who have been troubled by the contrast between Reagan's perpetually cheerful and sunny demeanor and the various problems of the 1980s—among them inequality, AIDS, homelessness, urban poverty, the collapse of the nation's savings and loan industry, and the Iran-Contra scandal. Early work on Reagan—such as that by Michael Rogin and Robert Dallek—sought to explain why he exercised such appeal for the American public, arguing that Reagan represented a fantasy of restoration of wholeness and purity, a dream of transcending the splits opened up by the radicalism of the 1960s and 1970s. In the early 1990s, Michael Schaller wrote a narrative of the 1980s that emphasized political corruption in the Reagan administration, the creation of a culture that celebrated greed and material acquisition, and the cultivation of an atmosphere of ignoring obvious social problems in the hopes that they would simply disappear—an attitude that "saying something made it so."

Several more-recent works (by Gil Troy, Robert Collins, and John Ehrman) have revised this vision of the decade and taken a guardedly favorable stance toward Reagan, arguing that the economy made improvements in the decade and giving Reagan credit for ending the cold war. These new accounts seem to be framed by the political debates over the Reagan years. Was Reagan driven by ideology at the expense of reality, or was he a conscientious and pragmatic politician? Were the economic reforms that he embarked upon—cutting individual tax rates sharply across the board, breaking the air traffic controllers' strike—good or bad for the American economy? Did they encourage risk, innovation, and technological development, or did they lead to ever-expanding inequality and the abandonment of the urban poor? Was Reagan reasonable, sensible, and astute in his approach to foreign affairs, carefully developing a relationship with Mikhail Gorbachev to the horror of those to his right, guiding the United States to victory in the cold war? Or did he pursue an illegal and dangerous policy of financing counterrevolutionary dictatorships in Latin America and elsewhere, seeking to avoid congressional authority through maneuvers that ultimately resulted in trading arms to Iran in return for the release of hostages and funneling the money to the Nicaraguan contras?

Yet some new analytic approaches are starting to emerge, putting the Reagan years in perspective by looking at the evolution of conservatism since the 1980s. Meg Jacobs and Julian Zelizer, for example, challenge the idea that conservatism was easily able to dominate American politics in the 1980s. They have instead emphasized the many limits that the Reagan administration encountered, arguing that the conservative movement in power was confronted by a paradox: it was a movement dedicated to antigovernment ideals that was nonetheless expected to govern. They suggest that out of this tension the conservative movement evolved new tactics for undermining the state from within, by appointing ideologically sympathetic judges, allowing regulatory agencies to be run by people who were philosophically opposed to regulation, and expanding the power of the executive branch. But the very need to develop such strategies indicated the extent to which the movement had difficulties winning the truly broad support that it would have needed to enact the full sweep of its agenda, as well as the continued resistance it had to confront in the shape of a state that included many programs (such as Social Security) that remained deeply popular. Although voters would elect Republican politicians and conservative Democrats, it remained unclear how deeply most people—even those who voted for Reagan—really saw themselves as part of a conservative political project. This made it hard for Reagan to accomplish the full agenda that he proposed when coming into office, and which the leaders of the conservative movement still dreamed of seeing realized. Another interpretation of the decade has focused on the limited ability of conservatives to reshape American culture. Robert Collins argues that there was a divide between the politics and the culture of the country during the 1980s; even though politics became more dominated by conservative views, the cultural life of the nation became more "secular, postmodern, multicultural and therapeutic."

Historians have written about the intellectual sources and the economic impact of supply-side economics—the idea that tax cuts and stimulus to the investment, or "supply," side of the economy, rather than to demand or consumption, would fuel economic growth. But less has been written about the interaction between Reagan's policies and the economic transformation of the country. Reagan's economic policies were implemented as the economy underwent a shift from industry and manufacturing toward "services," a category that could include everything from finance to computers, health care, and retail sales. Two million industrial jobs were lost over the course of the decade; employment in the steel industry dropped by half. American-made products were being replaced by goods made in countries around the world—often by American-owned companies, which were seeking out labor costs lower than in the United States. The closure of manufacturing plants was speeded by the decision of the Federal Reserve to raise interest rates sharply in order to curb the inflation of the 1970s. This brought unemployment rates to 9.7 percent and threw the country into a recession. Across the Midwest, factories closed their doors, and jobs that had once supported a middle class disappeared. Once the economy began to recover from the 1981–1982 recession, the jobs that it added were likely to be in sales and services—ones that had a much greater variation in compensation pay than the old industrial jobs, with some very well-paid jobs for professionals alongside many jobs that hardly paid a living wage. At the same time, the stock market began to go up, driven in part by Reagan's first moves to deregulate the financial industry. Leveraged buyouts—in which private investors used debt financing to buy up all the stock of public companies, then closed divisions and laid off workers in order to make the companies profitable—helped inspire new norms in the business world. Taking a confrontational stance toward workers and unions became the general practice. The celebration of the private sector and of free enterprise in the Reagan administration and in public life helped legitimate ever-higher salaries for the chief executive officers of major corporations. When economic growth returned in the 1980s, the benefits were much more skewed toward the upper end of the income spectrum than had been the case for most of the postwar period.

The changes in the American economy that drove the dispersion of wages and salaries were certainly not all brought about by the conservative movement; they reflected structural transformations in the economy. But the conservative ascendancy provided an ideological lens through which these changes could be viewed and understood, and as such shaped the political response to them. Nor are politics and economy entirely separate; the conservative critique of unions and the state helped to create and justify a more unequal economy. Jefferson Cowie has written about deindustrialization and the ways in which the flight of American manufacturing companies across the border to Mexico emerged out of the effort to evade labor unions and class-conscious workers, with companies leaving the United States as a last resort after first moving to the American South. Steve Fraser's work on Wall Street in American culture has dissected the changing image of the stock market, and Michael Katz has written about the persistence of urban poverty during the decade. Marisa Chappell's work on the evolution of ideas about welfare between the 1960s and the 1990s argues that the debate over welfare took place in the larger context of the decline of the "family wage" system, according to which a male breadwinner should be the primary economic support for a dependent wife and children, as more and more mothers entered the workforce.

Although the standard narrative sees the triumph of conservatism as the central problematic for the history of the decade, new scholarship on the 1980s is examining the persistence of liberalism in the decade and even the continued vitality of more radical challenges to the new conservative order. Over the course of the decade the dominance of conservative politics continued to be challenged by social movements that grew out of the activism of earlier generations: the antinuclear movement that was the descendent of the antiwar movement of the 1960s; the organizing against American intervention in Central America, which kept the Iran-Contra scandal in the headlines; the many developments within the world of feminist politics; the evolution of the gay rights movement, which popularized new direct-action techniques in order to raise awareness about AIDS, the new illness that claimed nearly 50,000 lives by the end of Reagan's second term. Jennifer Brier's work on AIDS, for example, suggests that progressive activists sought out new strategies for advancing their efforts in the context of the diminished power of the state. Even the large strikes of the era—while mostly losses for labor—indicated the desperate attempts on the part of unions and organized workers to retain the benefits they had once possessed. In contrast to later years, when the era of union power would seem increasingly distant, there remained throughout the 1980s an awareness of the potential strength of organized labor, even as it was publicly defeated. In short, although they existed in an increasingly hostile climate, the social movements of earlier generations continued to mobilize during the Reagan years, and their complex legacies and struggles need to be examined in any full understanding of the politics of the decade.

What is more, even though in later years conservatives would celebrate Reagan, during the 1980s many people on the right were frustrated by the seeming triumph in American life of a kind of libertarian ethos—a rhetoric of consumer choice trumping absolute morality that Gil Troy describes as a fusion of the politics of the 1960s with the materialism of the 1980s.

By the end of the decade, some antiabortion activists had taken to adopting direct-action techniques themselves, blocking access to abortion clinics and even taking violent action against doctors who performed abortions. Within the business community, too, there was disagreement about the impact of Reagan's policies on the economy. Future scholarship will surely address the mounting tensions within the conservative movement itself over the course of the Reagan years.

Yet despite the extent to which political life was still shaped by the veterans of the 1960s mobilizations, there was another sense in which the world of politics was growing thinner during the decade. Daniel Rodgers has argued that the 1980s—despite Reagan's reputation for being an intellectual lightweight—was a decade when people were possessed by political ideas. The ideas they were drawn to, however, were increasingly ones that rejected any attempts to analyze society in terms of historical institutions or relationships of power. The vision of the economy as a perfect marketplace composed of free and equal individuals, modeled with ever-increasing mathematical complexity, began to replace older models that had viewed market imperfections as the norm. Ideas about gender and race as performance started to edge out older "essentialist" visions of historical identity that formed the basis for community or political organization. In some ways, over the course of the 1980s, it became increasingly difficult to think clearly about power at all, or to speak about it in public life. The old era of political ideologies seemed to have been replaced by a new sense of social atomism, a world in which people were connected by little except their own free choices. The idea popularized by Francis Fukuyama in the wake of the collapse of the Soviet Union that liberal democracies had emerged at the "end of history"—that in the future there would be no true innovations in political institutions, but simply a steady increase in wealth and prosperity and the addition of new nations to the ranks of the liberal democracies—summed up this sense that the world had been somehow released from history, that society no longer exerted a necessary force on the individual. The impact of these new ideas about society is hard to measure, and yet they capture something about the way that experience of political life was changing during the 1980s.

Much remains to be written about the history of the 1980s. While there are many volumes on Reagan and on Washington politics during the decade, there have not yet been many social histories of life during these years. Few local studies examine particular communities to see how they were affected and transformed by the new ethos, and few works study the political and cultural implications of the rise of the service economy. The literature is in some ways so defined by the political questions about conservatism in power that relatively little attention has been paid so far to the transformations that were not directly affected by electoral shifts and trends—for example, the rise of new populations of immigrants from Latin American, Asian, and African countries, or the evolution of sexual and familial norms. Few scholarly studies have as yet looked at the remarkable growth of the prison population in the 1980s in historical perspective, although sociologists and others have done work on the impact of such trends, especially for black Americans. Despite the limits of the historiography, however, a framework for thinking about the decade is slowly beginning to emerge: The Reagan administration, although able to transform tax politics and begin the rollback of regulations, did not completely change American politics. It encountered substantial opposition in meeting its policy goals and continued to be to the right of the mainstream American public, even as it frustrated the hopes of conservatives who wanted it to go farther faster. Nonetheless, perhaps because it was taking place alongside a broader set of changes in American political economy, the ideology of the free market seemed to take root at a much deeper level. Although the institutions of American liberalism endured, and although parts of the left that had come about in the 1960s continued to exist, much of American society came to adopt and celebrate an entrepreneurial style of economic engagement as the new common sense, while in Washington, both political parties seemed to share an agenda of economic deregulation and opposition to the expansion of a welfare state.

For much of the twentieth century, the ideals of the New Deal years and the impact of the Great Depression had seemed to shape American politics. By the end of the 1980s, the earlier mode of thinking about economic life seemed less and less relevant. In some ways, the victories of the civil rights movement and the feminist and gay and lesbian movements proved more lasting and harder to undo than the political economy of New Deal liberalism. The civil rights movement may not have continued to move forward, but it was not undone, and women continued to move into the workforce, although with little of the social support that might have made the workplace more open to family life. But even here, over the course of the 1980s there was a diminishing sense of the possibilities of politics, a sense that individuals were on their own when it came to determining their fates.

The fall of the Soviet Union in 1989 and the end of communism in Eastern Europe were perceived through the lens of these political and ideological developments. Even though most scholars believe that the reasons for the dissolution of the Communist regimes have more to do with the internal dynamics of Soviet politics than the policies of the Reagan administration, the end of communism seemed to affirm the broadest principles of Reaganism: that individuals and markets, not states, were the dynamic actors in history, and that the attempts of people to act collectively to consciously shape and transform the world were likely to be futile.

Since 1990

While much has been written about America in the twenty years following Reagan's presidency, most of it has not really been history. There are journalistic accounts, works of reportage, sociological studies, memoirs—the raw material of historical inquiry—but not many true works of scholarship based on original research in archives. However, the syntheses that seek to cover the entire post-1973 period outline some of the major historical problems that scholars will seek to address as they turn their attention to this most recent period of all.

The debates over the extent and reach of the Reagan revolution and the victories of the conservative movement have remained at the center of scholarship on the 1990s and the 2000s. Some historians (such as Sean Wilentz) suggest that the paradigm for government established during the Reagan years continued to shape the Democratic administration of William Jefferson Clinton. According to this argument, just as the election of Republican president Dwight D. Eisenhower in 1952 did not signal the end of the New Deal era but in some ways marked its consolidation, since a president from the rival party could not break with the framework established by his predecessors, the election of Clinton did not mean the dawn of a new political age but rather the enshrinement of the old one. By the early 1990s, the Democratic Party had abandoned the basic principles of New Deal liberalism. Clinton was closely associated with the Democratic Leadership Council, an organization of younger leaders within the party who thought that the only road back to political victory lay in making clear that the Democrats were no longer the party of state intervention. They believed that Democrats could continue to count on the electoral support of labor unions and African Americans, even as they distanced the party from these constituencies and declared (as Clinton put it) that "the era of big government is over." At the same time, the conservative movement was able to gain substantial momentum during the 1990s, consistently attacking Clinton from the right and even ultimately bringing about his impeachment over his affair with a White House intern. The effect was a strange kind of politics—the activist conservatives attacked a chimerical left that they insisted was embodied by Clinton, even as Clinton himself pursued free trade and deregulation, promising (as when he ended the program of cash entitlements for very poor women and their children) to "end welfare as we know it."

Historians have also debated the nature and effect of the economic changes of the period, especially the legacy of the deregulation of the economy. Many popular histories of the 1990s and afterward have emphasized the idea of globalization—the vision of the United States as part of a newly international economic order, in which the American economy must compete against other developing economies with lower wages and standards of living. To many observers, the global community, connected by airplanes and telecommunications technologies, seemed to be rendering irrelevant the nation-state. At the same time, the Internet captured the cultural imagination as a realm where the individual could move speedily from one site to the next, creating his or her own identity and communicating with lightning speed. Scholars have sought to contextualize these images of technology and globalization, suggesting that the rise of international competition and capital mobility, the idea of a new "frontier" in cyberspace to be explored and mined for new sources of wealth (which echoes the old thesis of Frederick Jackson Turner about the importance throughout American history of the idea of an unexplored frontier) did not end economic inequality. Historian Fred Turner has argued that the promoters of the Internet and of Silicon Valley borrow heavily from the utopian dreams of the 1960s counterculture, while Leon Fink's detailed history of the struggle of Guatemalan immigrants in North Carolina to organize a union at the poultry plant where they work offers a vision of globalization from below, in which the Mayan traditions of the workers provide a reservoir from which to build a political vision. Nelson Lichtenstein's work on the central role of computers in tracking inventories at Wal-Mart shows a way in which the use of information technology helps to underwrite low wages in the United States and around the world.

The second half of the 1990s did see several years of strong economic expansion in which even the wages of the poorest people began to rise slightly (the only time in the entire period since the mid-1970s when this was the case). The stock market began a remarkable rise during this period, and many observers predicted (as they had in the 1920s) that in the new era of computer technology and the globalization of the economy there would be no limit to its gains. At the same time, though, the increases in wealth in this new economic order were concentrated at the top—the very rich and the well-off did much better than working-class, middle-class, or poor people. Even at its peak, the boom of the 1990s favored some people more than others, and some economic writers (such as Paul Krugman) have argued that the period ushered in a "new Gilded Age." Organized labor continued to decline during the 1990s; in 2009 it represented only 7.2 percent of the private-sector workforce, about the same proportion as before the New Deal (when public-sector workers are included, unions represent a little more than 12 percent of the total labor force). Twice, the stock market boom was revealed to be a bubble, bursting early in 2000 and again in 2008, when economic growth came to an abrupt halt.

Looking back over the entire history of the United States since the 1970s, it seems as though we are still living within a moment that began then. We are, in some ways, still grappling with the end of the postwar economic expansion, the decline of manufacturing, and the rise of a much less egalitarian and much more unstable economy. Conservatism has faced many setbacks, but there has been no subsequent political transformation that has superseded it entirely. And yet it seems likely that future historians will broaden their vision of the period to move away from the intense focus on conservatism, even to question its dominance. There are many other issues that historians of the future will need to explore when they write about the 1990s and 2000s—the complicated nature of race relations over a period that saw the election of the first African-American president of the United States; the rise of a massive prison system; the debates over immigration; the impact of the "culture wars" of the 1990s; the origins of anti-American sentiment and its expression in violence and terrorism; the ways that fear of this violence shaped American politics in the early twenty-first century; the changing definitions of marriage, sexuality and family life; the attempts of the United States to maintain its dominant military presence; the slowly growing awareness of environmental depredation; the lasting legacy of economic deregulation and financial crisis. This historical work has not yet been done, and as it is, it will also cast light backward on to the 1970s and before—on the era of the breakdown of the postwar liberal world-view and economy, and the ways in which the American people sought to struggle with—or to evade—their new political and economic realities.

BIBLIOGRAPHY

Allen, Michael. *Until the Last Man Comes Home: POWs, MIAs, and the Unending Vietnam War.* Chapel Hill: University of North Carolina Press, 2009.

Berkowitz, Edward. *Something Happened: A Political and Cultural Overview of the Seventies.* New York: Columbia University Press, 2006.

Biven, W. Carl. *Jimmy Carter's Economy: Policy in the Age of Limits.* Chapel Hill: University of North Carolina Press, 2002.

Boyer, Paul. "The Evangelical Resurgence in 1970s American Protestantism." In Bruce Schulman and Julian E. Zelizer, eds., *Rightward Bound: Making America Conservative in the 1970s*, 29–51. Cambridge, MA: Harvard University Press, 2008.

Brier, Jennifer. *Infectious Ideas: U.S. Political Responses to the AIDS Crisis.* Chapel Hill: University of North Carolina Press, 2009.

Carroll, Peter. *It Seemed Like Nothing Happened: The Tragedy and Promise of America in the 1970s.* New York: Holt, Rinehart, and Winston, 1982.

Carter, Dan. *From George Wallace to Newt Gingrich: Race in the Conservative Counterrevolution, 1963–1994.* Baton Rouge: Louisiana State University Press, 1996.

Chang, Jeff. *Can't Stop Won't Stop: A History of the Hip-Hop Generation.* New York: St. Martin's Press, 2005.

Chappell, Marisa. *The War on Welfare: Family, Poverty, and Politics in Modern America.* Philadelphia: University of Pennsylvania Press, 2010.

Cobble, Dorothy Sue. *The Other Women's Movement: Workplace Justice and Social Rights in Modern America.* Princeton, NJ: Princeton University Press, 2004.

Collins, Robert. *Transforming America: Politics and Culture in the Reagan Years.* New York: Columbia University Press, 2007.

Cowie, Jefferson. *Stayin' Alive: The 1970s and the Last Days of the Working Class.* New York: New Press, 2010.

———. "'Vigorously Left, Right and Center': The Crosscurrents of Working-Class America in the 1970s." In Beth Bailey and David Farber, eds., *America in the Seventies.* Lawrence: University Press of Kansas, 2004.

Cowie, Jefferson, and Nick Salvatore. "The Long Exception: Rethinking the Place of the New Deal in American History." *International Labor and Working-Class History* 74 (Fall 2008): 3–32.

Critchlow, Donald. *Phyllis Schlafly and Grassroots Conservatism: A Woman's Crusade.* Princeton, NJ: Princeton University Press, 2005.

Dallek, Robert. *Ronald Reagan: The Politics of Symbolism*. Cambridge, MA: Harvard University Press, 1984.

Dochuk, Darren. *From Bible Belt to Sunbelt: Plain-Folk Religion, Grassroots Politics, and the Rise of Evangelical Conservatism*. New York: W. W. Norton, 2010.

Echols, Alice. *Daring to Be Bad: Radical Feminism in America, 1967–1975*. Minneapolis: University of Minnesota Press, 1989.

Edsall, Thomas Byrne. *The New Politics of Inequality*. New York: W. W. Norton, 1984.

Ehrman, John. *The Eighties: America in the Age of Reagan*. New Haven, CT: Yale University Press, 2005.

Ehrman, John, and Michael Flamm. *Debating the Reagan Presidency*. Lanham, MD: Rowman and Littlefield, 2009.

Eisenbach, David. *Gay Power: An American Revolution*. New York: Carroll and Graf, 2006.

Ferguson, Niall, Charles Maier, Erez Manela and Daniel Sargent, eds. *The Shock of the Global: The 1970s in Perspective*. Cambridge, MA: Harvard University Press, 2010.

Fink, Gary, and Hugh Carter Graham, eds. *The Carter Presidency: Policy Choices in the Post–New Deal Era*. Lawrence: University Press of Kansas, 1998.

Fink, Leon. *The Maya of Morgantown: Work and Community in the Nuevo New South*. Chapel Hill: University of North Carolina Press, 2003.

Formisano, Ronald. *Boston against Busing: Race, Class, and Ethnicity in the 1960s and 1970s*. Chapel Hill: University of North Carolina Press, 1991.

Fraser, Steve. *Wall Street: America's Dream Palace*. New Haven, CT: Yale University Press, 2008.

Fukuyama, Francis. *The End of History and the Last Man*. New York: Free Press, 1992.

Graebner, William. *Patty's Got a Gun: Patricia Hearst in 1970s America*. Chicago: University of Chicago Press, 2008.

Hall, Jacquelyn. "The Long Civil Rights Movement and the Political Uses of the Past." *Journal of American History* 91 (March 2005): 1233–1263.

Hamilton, Shane. *Trucking Country: The Road to America's Wal-Mart Economy*. Princeton, NJ: Princeton University Press, 2008.

Harrington, Michael. "A Collective Sadness." *Dissent* 21 (September 1974): 486–491.

Hobsbawm, Eric. *The Age of Extremes: A History of the World, 1914–1991*. New York: Vintage Trade Paperbacks, 1996.

Hodgson, Godfrey. *More Equal Than Others: America from Nixon to the New Century*. Princeton, NJ: Princeton University Press, 2006.

Horowitz, Daniel. *Jimmy Carter and the Energy Crisis of the 1970s: The "Crisis of Confidence" Speech of July 15, 1979: A Brief History with Documents*. Boston: Bedford/St. Martin's, 2005.

Jacobs, Meg. "The Conservative Struggle and the Energy Crisis." In Schulman and Zelizer, eds., *Rightward Bound*, 193–210.

Jacobs, Meg, and Julian Zelizer. *Conservatives in Power: The Reagan Years, 1981–1989*. Cambridge, MA: Bedford/St. Martin's, 2010.

Joseph, Peniel. *Waiting 'til the Midnight Hour: A Narrative History of Black Power in America*. New York: Henry Holt, 2008.

Kalman, Laura. *Right Star Rising: A New Politics, 1974–1980*. New York: W. W. Norton, 2010.

Katz, Michael. *The Price of Citizenship: Redefining the American Welfare State.* Philadelphia: University of Pennsylvania Press, 2008.

Kruse, Kevin. *White Flight: Atlanta and the Making of Modern Conservatism.* Princeton, NJ: Princeton University Press, 2005.

Krippner, Greta. *Capitalism in Crisis: The Political Origins of the Rise of Finance in the United States Economy.* Cambridge, MA: Harvard University Press, 2010.

Lasch, Christopher. *The Culture of Narcissism: American Life in an Age of Diminishing Expectations.* New York: W. W. Norton, 1979.

Lassiter, Matthew. *The Silent Majority: Suburban Politics in the Sunbelt South.* Princeton, NJ: Princeton University Press, 2006.

Lichtenstein, Nelson. *The Retail Revolution: How Wal-Mart Created a Brave New World of Business.* New York: Metropolitan Books, 2009.

———. *State of the Union: A Century of American Labor.* Princeton, NJ: Princeton University Press, 2003.

Lowenstein, Roger. *Origins of the Crash: The Great Bubble and Its Undoing.* New York: Penguin, 2004.

MacLean, Nancy. *Freedom Is Not Enough: The Opening of the American Workplace.* Cambridge, MA: Harvard University Press, 2006.

Martin, William. *With God on Our Side: The Rise of the Religious Right in America.* New York: Broadway Books, 1996.

McCartin, Joseph. "'A Wagner Act for Public Workers': Labor's Deferred Dream and the Rise of Conservatism, 1970–1976." *Journal of American History*, 95 (2008): 123–148.

McGirr, Lisa. *Suburban Warriors: The Origins of the New American Right.* Princeton, NJ: Princeton University Press, 2001.

Moreton, Bethany. *To Serve God and Wal-Mart: The Making of Christian Free Enterprise.* Cambridge, MA: Harvard University Press, 2009.

Patterson, James. *Restless Giant: The United States from Watergate to Bush v. Gore.* New York: Oxford, 2007.

Perlstein, Rick. *Nixonland: The Rise of a President and the Fracturing of America.* New York: Scribner, 2008.

Phillips-Fein, Kim. *Invisible Hands: The Making of the Conservative Movement from the New Deal to Reagan.* New York: W. W. Norton, 2009.

Rieder, Jonathan. *Canarsie: The Jews and Italians of Brooklyn against Liberalism.* Cambridge, MA: Harvard University Press, 1985.

Rodgers, Daniel. *Age of Fracture.* Cambridge, MA: Harvard University Press, 2011.

Rogin, Michael. *Ronald Reagan: The Movie.* Berkeley: University of California Press, 1988.

Schulman, Bruce. *The Seventies: The Great Shift in American Society, Politics and Culture.* New York: Da Capo Press, 2002.

Schulman, Bruce, and Julian Zelizer, eds. *Rightward Bound: Making America Conservative in the 1970s.* Cambridge, MA: Harvard University Press, 2008.

Self, Robert. *American Babylon: Race and the Struggle for Postwar Oakland.* Princeton, NJ: Princeton University Press, 2003.

———. "Sex and the City: The Politics of Sexual Liberalism in Los Angeles, 1960–1984." *Gender and History* 20 (August 2008): 288–311.

Schaller, Michael. *Reckoning with Reagan: America and Its President in the 1980s.* New York: Oxford University Press, 1992.

———. *Right Turn: American Life in the Reagan-Bush Era, 1980–1992.* New York: Oxford University Press, 2007.

Skrentny, John. *The Minority Rights Revolution*. Cambridge, MA: Harvard University Press, 2002.

Stein, Judith. *Pivotal Decade: How the United States Traded Factories for Finance in the Seventies*. New Haven, CT: Yale University Press, 2010.

———. *Running Steel, Running America: Race, Economic Policy, and the Decline of Liberalism*. Chapel Hill: University of North Carolina Press, 1998.

Spruill, Marjorie. "Gender and America's Right Turn." In Schulman and Zelizer, eds., *Rightward Bound*, 71–90.

Teles, Steven. *The Rise of the Conservative Legal Movement: The Battle for Control of the Law*. Princeton, NJ: Princeton University Press, 2008.

Troy, Gil. *Morning in America: How Ronald Reagan Invented the 1980s*. Princeton, NJ: Princeton University Press, 2005.

Turner, Fred. *From Counterculture to Cyberculture: Stewart Brand, the Whole Earth Network, and the Rise of Digital Utopianism*. Chicago: University of Chicago Press, 2006.

Turner, James Morton. "'The Specter of Environmentalism:' Wilderness, Environmental Politics, and the Evolution of the New Right." *Journal of American History* 96 (June 2009): 123–149.

Varon, Jeremy. *Bringing the War Home: The Weather Underground, the Red Army Faction, and the Revolutionary Violence of the Sixties and Seventies*. Berkeley: University of California Press, 2004.

Wilentz, Sean. *The Age of Reagan, 1974–2009*. New York: HarperCollins, 2009.

Williams, Daniel. *God's Own Party: The Making of the Christian Right*. New York: Oxford University Press, 2010.

Zaretsky, Natasha. *No Direction Home: The American Family and the Fear of National Decline*. Chapel Hill: University of North Carolina Press, 2007.

II

MAJOR THEMES IN THE AMERICAN EXPERIENCE

9

The United States in the World

EREZ MANELA

In the past decade or so, the study of the history of the United States in the world has undergone radical, perhaps unprecedented transformations. The broad shifts in the scope and nature of the field reflect a sea change in how a new generation of historians who study U.S. interactions with the wider world sees their field, and how the discipline of history as a whole views it.

The most immediate piece of evidence for this assertion is the chapter title at the top of this page. In the previous edition of this volume, published in 1997, the closing chapter, authored by the distinguished Cornell University historian Walter LaFeber, was titled "Liberty and Power: U.S. Diplomatic History, 1750–1945." But if not so long ago it was still common for history departments across the country to hire historians of "American diplomacy" or "U.S. foreign relations," these days young historians in the field compete for positions in the history of "the United States in the World," "the United States *and* the World," or simply "U.S./World." The speed with which these new designations have taken hold reflects the sense of many historians in the field that the older ones are insufficiently capacious to capture the breadth of their common intellectual project. But the rapid evolution of the field has also left historians both within and outside the field unsure about its precise contours and content. In recent years the halls of professional conferences and the pages of scholarly journals have seen numerous debates, often quite heated, around this question. This essay, therefore, endeavors to trace the shape of a field that is in an extraordinarily dynamic state of flux, capturing its diversity while also lending it a measure of coherence.

A Resurgent Field

A striking aspect of recent developments in the historiography of the United States in the world is its return to a place of prominence within the broad landscape of the American historical profession. From the interwar era through the 1950s, the study of American diplomacy was central to the historical profession in the United States, and its most eminent practitioners—historians such as Samuel Flagg Bemis and Dexter Perkins—were recognized leaders in the discipline who served as presidents of the American Historical Association. But with the rise of new approaches to the study of American history, first social history in the 1960s and 1970s and then cultural history in the 1980s and 1990s, diplomatic as well as political historians saw themselves increasingly marginalized. Thus, Charles S. Maier's rebuke in a 1980 historiographical essay that American diplomatic history "cannot, alas, be counted among the pioneering fields of the discipline during the 1970s" launched a wave of agonizing introspection, self-criticism, and self-defense that played out within the pages of *Diplomatic History*, the journal of record of the Society for Historians of American Foreign Relations (SHAFR), as well as elsewhere.

These days, however, the fog of self-doubt has been replaced among historians of U.S. relations with the world with a creative frenzy that is redefining the field through the relentless expansion of its spatial, thematic, and methodological boundaries. This newfound confidence was on display in a state-of-the-field roundtable published in the March 2009 issue of *The Journal of American History*. In the lead essay, Thomas W. Zeiler wasted no time in turning the page on Maier's critique, announcing at the outset that "an era of innovation among historians of American foreign relations is upon us." The four respondents to Zeiler's essay presented a variety of viewpoints, some taking issue with his triumphalist tone. But the very fact of the roundtable's publication in such a prominent venue signaled the renewed interest in this field within the American historical profession at large and the growing appreciation for its contributions and perspectives. Two factors help explain this reemergence: first, the dramatic changes in the discipline as a whole over the course of the last decade or so, and second, the deep and multifarious transformation of the U.S./world-field itself.

The great transformation of American history in the 1980s and the 1990s was centered on the "cultural turn," which saw the rise of cultural history from the margins of the profession to its commanding heights. The cultural turn profoundly revolutionized the writing of history, introducing new actors, sources, themes, interpretive lenses, and methodologies. Over the last decade or so, however, the cultural turn has come to an end. This does not mean that cultural history has ceased to be a central part of the discipline, quite the contrary. Rather, its centrality has become a given, universally accepted and no longer eliciting the surprise, indignation, or passionate debate that it once did. Cultural history remains important, but that is hardly news anymore. Instead, if there is one overarching trend that charts the most exciting recent changes in the American historical profession across its various fields it is the increasing dissatisfaction with the national and regional enclosures that have long defined historical fields and the growing willingness of scholars of all stripes to push against and transcend these boundaries. This shift has become known as the "transnational turn."

One implication of the transnational turn is that American historians as a whole have increasingly been seeking to transcend the nation in their topical interests and analytical frames. In place of a traditional American history whose narrative—even on topics, such as immigration or the American West, where a transnational framing would seem natural—stopped at the water's edge, American historians are now more willing, indeed eager, to frame their investigations in ways that go beyond the borders of the nation. A few intrepid historians, such as Thomas Bender in *Nation among Nations* (2006) and Ian Tyrrell in *Transnational Nation* (2007) have recently even attempted to recast the entire narrative of U.S. history in a global context. Granted, these pioneering efforts at constructing transnational narratives of U.S. history are not robust enough to displace the traditional storyline just yet. Indeed, the tension inherent in any effort to recast a *national* history within a *trans*national frame suggests that it may be a while before they are. Nevertheless, the influence of the transnational turn is now clearly pervasive in the field as a whole.

For our current purposes, the most interesting result of the transnational turn in the writing of history is that historians who have long focused on the interactions of Americans with other countries, peoples, and regions now find themselves working at the cutting edge of the profession. But they themselves have also changed radically in the intervening decades. They have brought new perspectives and methodologies to bear on the perennial questions of the history of American foreign relations, such as the sources of U.S. foreign policy, the character and uses of U.S. power, the role of American ideas and perceptions in shaping relations with other peoples, and the U.S. role in the history of the cold war. They have also, in addition, opened entirely new vistas on the history of the United States in the world, tackling questions that had received relatively little attention in previous eras. Among these are the active roles of non-Western peoples in shaping U.S. actions in the international arena; the significance of nonstate actors such as international organizations, NGOs, multinational corporations, transnational activists, and others; and the integration of whole new areas of human endeavor, such as family planning, food production, disease control, and human relations with the natural environment into the historiography of the United States in the world. This essay will attempt to outline the emerging contours of these developments.

The Cultural Turn: Race, Gender, Culture, and Foreign Relations

In the previous edition of this volume, Walter LaFeber wrote that the great debate that defined the historiography of U.S. foreign relations in the postwar decades, beginning in the 1950s and lasting well in the 1970s, was the one between the "realists" and the "revisionists." In this debate, both sides critiqued U.S. foreign policies, but they did so from opposite perspectives. The realist critique, most famously articulated by George F. Kennan in his *American Diplomacy* (1950) and further elaborated in the work of such scholars as Norman Graebner and Lloyd Ambrosius, viewed U.S. policies as excessively naive and idealistic and recommended a more hardheaded approach to foreign affairs, one based squarely on considerations of national interest and an understanding of great power politics. The revisionist critique, launched in William Appleman Williams's *The Tragedy of American Diplomacy* (1959) and further developed in the work of "Wisconsin School" historians such as Thomas J. McCormick and LaFeber himself, turned the realists' argument on its head, criticizing U.S. policy makers for their cynical pursuit of narrow interest, particularly, in their view, the economic interest in finding new markets for surplus U.S. goods and capital.

But the revisionists' most important impact on the field was arguably not the specific nature of their critique but rather their framing of the history of U.S. foreign relations and the methods they used to study it. Earlier scholars of the history of U.S. diplomacy, from Bemis and Perkins to Ernest R. May, had invariably framed their work within the context of international politics, placing their understanding of U.S. policy options and decisions within the context of similar deliberations in the chancelleries of the other major powers—British, French, German, Russian, and occasionally (as in the work of John K. Fairbank on U.S.-China relations) of non-European powers. Williams and his students, however, turned their gaze inward, framing their study of U.S. foreign policies not primarily in the context of international politics but rather within the confines of the domestic U.S. sphere. Broadly speaking, their focus was on the domestic forces and interests—ideological, economic, and political—that shaped U.S. actions in the world. While this shift opened up important new directions in the field, it also meant that historians of U.S. foreign relations turned increasingly inward, limiting themselves to research in U.S. archives and focusing on the ideas and actions of Americans to explain U.S. policy.

Williams and his early students focused on *economic* ideas and interests as the primary drivers of policy, and that focus occupied much of the new work in the field in the 1960s and into the 1970s. Among the most influential of these works was LaFeber's *The New Empire* (1963). Applying to the period from 1860 to 1898 Williams' notion that the pursuit of "open door imperialism" could serve as the key to understanding U.S. foreign policy, LaFeber explained post–Civil War expansionism as the result of a desperate search for new markets following the crises of overproduction that attended American industrialization in those decades. Another Williams student, Thomas McCormick, made a similar argument about U.S. expansion in East Asia in the 1890s in his *China Market* (1967). Such arguments about the centrality of economic interests grew more elaborate over time, evolving in the 1970s and 1980s into what became known as the "corporatist synthesis," developed by Michael J. Hogan and others. Hogan's *Informal Entente* (1977), which focused on the interwar years, argued that U.S. officials and business leaders collaborated closely with each other and with their counterparts in major European countries to organize transatlantic cooperative mechanisms that would eliminate the wasteful competition of the laissez-faire system and help solve problems of recovery, debts, reparations, and budgets.

By the 1980s, however, the interpretive emphasis in the field was moving away from economics and toward approaches that reflected the discipline-wide turn toward cultural history, highlighting the role of discourses of race and gender, and (more recently) religion. An important transitional text in this context was Emily S. Rosenberg, *Spreading the American Dream* (1982), which showed the connections between the economic and the cultural aspects of U.S. expansion from 1890 to 1945, arguing that they were intimately tied together in the American ideology of "liberal developmentalism." This notion presaged the now burgeoning literature on the role of ideas in U.S. relations with other peoples. A seminal text that influenced much subsequent work in this vein focusing on ideology and race as major factors in foreign relations was Michael H. Hunt, *Ideology and U.S. Foreign Policy* (1987). Encompassing the entire history of U.S. foreign relations, Hunt argued that it rested on three main ideological pillars: an abiding faith in U.S. national greatness, or Manifest Destiny; a racist conception of nonwhite peoples; and a fear of social (as distinct from political) revolution, rooted in the American rejection of the radicalism of the French Revolution.

In recent years, numerous scholars have probed the influence of race on the history of U.S. foreign relations. Among the pioneers were Reginald Horsman, *Race and Manifest Destiny* (1981), and Alexander DeConde, *Ethnicity, Race, and American Foreign Policy* (1992), which showed how racial identification, especially Anglo-American identity, have shaped U.S. foreign policies and expansion throughout its history. More recently, Joseph M. Henning, *Outposts of Civilization* (2000), explained how conceptions of race and religion have shaped relations between the United States and Japan from the outset. Mary Renda, *Taking Haiti* (2001) showed how U.S. racial views, particularly those of U.S. Marines from the Jim Crow South, shaped the U.S. invasion and nearly two decades of military rule in Haiti, from 1916 to 1934. Paul A. Kramer, *The Blood of Government* (2006), explored how U.S. and Filipino elites joined to construct hierarchies of race and civilization that underpinned U.S. colonial rule over the islands. These last two works are among the outpouring of excellent new scholarship on

U.S. colonial rule, not only in Haiti and the Philippines but also in Puerto Rico and elsewhere.

Attention to questions of race and the ways in which it shapes politics and policy has also enriched our understanding of the history of the United States in the world during the postwar era, giving rise to a rich vein of scholarly work on "cold war civil rights" literature, after the title of Mary L. Dudziak's pioneering 2000 book. This work has illuminated important connections and cross influences between U.S. postwar foreign policy, particularly toward the developing world, and the domestic struggle over African-American civil rights. Works such as Dudziak's and Thomas Borstelmann's *The Cold War and the Color Line* (2001) showed how, after 1945, U.S. officials in the White House and the State Department viewed the practices of segregation and racial discrimination in the United States as a liability for America's image abroad, serving as it did as a recurring theme in Soviet propaganda at a time when American elites saw themselves as fighting for the "hearts and minds" of the decolonizing peoples of Africa and Asia. For such officials, civil rights for African Americans became a cold war imperative, helping push Washington along as it slowly inched toward the progress in race relations that would culminate with the civil rights legislation of the mid-1960s.

But the impact of the cold war and decolonization on race relations within the United States was by no means simple. Carol Anderson, in *Eyes off the Prize* (2003), focuses on the ways shifting international circumstances shaped the African-American freedom struggle. She shows how the early postwar effort to deploy the discourse of human rights, which reached a high point with the United Nations' promulgation of the Universal Declaration of Human Rights in 1948, was effectively stifled by segregationists who, at the height of the McCarthy Era, tarred those who demanded full human rights for African Americans as traitorous "reds." This, in turn, caused a split within the African-American community between the "moderates," including the leadership of the NAACP, who were willing to downplay demands for social and economic rights in the pursuit of political or civil rights, and the "radicals," such as W.E.B. Du Bois and Paul Robeson, who continued to demand full human rights for African Americans and found themselves hounded and marginalized. Thus the cold war context and the fight for the "hearts and minds" of postcolonial peoples made racial discrimination in U.S. society less tenable, but the trope of anticommunism served as a potent weapon for those who sought to undermine the campaign for equality.

Exploring the importance of African Americans in the history of the United States in the world, recent scholarship has made it clear that the history of U.S. race relations often intersected with the history of foreign relations and must therefore be seen in its full transnational context—just as many saw it at the time. Marc Gallicchio's *The African American Encounter with Japan and China* (2000) showed how black Americans in the first half of the twentieth century explicitly linked their own struggle to the efforts of emerging nations of color to attain equality in international society and tried, though largely unsuccessfully, to forge transnational alliances in a common cause. Penny M. Von Eschen's *Race against Empire* (1997) traced the efforts of African-American activists in the mid-twentieth century to advocate for African independence and locate their own struggle within the global struggle for black liberation. And when, in the 1950s, the State Department recruited African-American jazz musicians, including the great Louis Armstrong, to tour Africa as part of the struggle for third world "hearts and minds," the effort to foster good will for the United States often faltered on the shoals of America's domestic record on civil rights and its international record of support for European imperialists and postcolonial autocrats. In sum, paying attention to racial discourses and to African-American actors has helped to transform our view of the history of U.S. foreign relations as well as that of the civil rights struggle.

Gender analysis, too, has generated new perspectives and explanations of U.S. foreign relations. Kristen L. Hoganson's *Fighting for American Manhood* (1998) showed the significance of the language of masculinity in the public debates that led up to the wars against the Spanish and the Filipinos in 1898. She argued that the desire of a new generation of leaders, such as Theodore Roosevelt, who had not taken part in the Civil War, to find proving grounds for their manliness was among the factors that pushed the United States into these conflicts. Robert D. Dean's *Imperial Brotherhood* (2001) similarly used gender analysis to dissect the worldview of U.S. policy makers in the early cold war era, arguing that the American elites, reared in private academies and Ivy League universities within a "culture of masculinity" and sexual orthodoxy, formed an "imperial brotherhood" in which foreign policy reflected norms of tough, virile masculinity, helping, among other things, to propel the United States into the Vietnam War. And, in a series of innovative articles, Frank Costigliola has shown how gendered anxieties shaped the thinking and policies of such figures as Franklin D. Roosevelt and the architect of containment, George F. Kennan.

Beyond introducing new interpretive lenses into the field, the cultural turn has also shaped it in more literal ways. It has encouraged scholarship on U.S. cultural diplomacy, or the conscious efforts to promote U.S. culture abroad, as a component of the nation's diplomatic efforts, as well as on the broader impact of American cultural forms and productions on the wider world. Pioneering works such as Frank Ninkovich, *The Diplomacy of Ideas* (1981), and Frank Costigliola, *Awkward Dominion* (1984), which between them covered the period from the Versailles Treaty to the early cold war, traced the ways in which American ideas and cultural productions helped to facilitate the rise of U.S. influence in Europe and became fixtures of U.S. "cultural diplomacy" in the cold war. More recently, work such as Christopher Endy's on American tourism in France during the cold war showed how both the U.S. and foreign governments worked to promote leisure travel as part of their foreign relations agenda. On a broader canvas, Richard Pells, *Not like Us* (1997), placed the "Americanization" of Europe—in consumption, entertainment, fashion, youth culture—at the center of the relationship between Americans and Europeans after World War II, while Victoria de Grazia, *Irresistible Empire* (2005), refined that argument even further, positing the triumph of American-style consumer society in Europe as the driving force in the rise of U.S. hegemony over Europe in the last century.

The title of de Grazia's book reminds us that, in recent years, the idea of empire has been front and center in the writing on the history of the United States in the world, used to describe the entire expanse of that history and not solely or even primarily the U.S. experience in formal overseas colonialism. This idea is not new, of course, and has long been deployed by critics of American foreign relations (and occasionally by its supporters as well). But the wars in Afghanistan and Iraq have brought it back to the fore with a vengeance after the brief post–cold war interlude of the 1990s, when international cooperation seemed the order of the day. Charles S. Maier, for example, explored the rise of U.S. global hegemony in *Among Empires* (2006), identifying the prodigiousness of American consumption as well as production as the engine of U.S. global power in the twentieth century. Indeed, the imperial framework often mixes easily with another recently popular concept, globalization, as they converge around the influence of American production, consumption, and culture across the globe. These trends are exemplified in recent work by Walter LaFeber on the worldwide impact of an American icon such as Michael Jordan. And finally, Jeremi Suri has sought to connect cultural revolutions with international politics by exploring the intersection of the upheavals of the 1960s around the globe with the great power politics of the era, viewing the turn toward détente in the early 1970s as at least partially the result of efforts of great power leaders—Nixon, Brezhnev, Mao—to regain a semblance of control in the face of domestic challenges from disaffected youth.

The Transnational Turn: The United States in International Society

The cultural turn, then, has advanced our understanding of the ways in which cultural factors have shaped the history of the United States in the world. But tools borrowed from cultural history also helped historians to see interrelationships, as in the "cold war civil rights" literature, between transnational contexts and "domestic" developments, putting the historiography of the United States in the world at the forefront of the transnational turn in the field of American history as a whole. The move toward the internationalization of the history of the United States in the world has also been driven by a growing sense that, despite the welcome thematic expansion that the cultural turn brought, the study of U.S. relations with the world was still constrained by its very definition as a subfield of American history and the corresponding emphasis on understanding the domestic determinants—whether political, economic, or cultural—of American foreign policy. After all, to study the foreign relations of one nation in isolation is to listen for the sound of one hand clapping.

To some extent, the move toward internationalization is a return to an older mode of scholarship. Prior to the rise of the revisionist school in the 1960s, most historians of American diplomacy included non-U.S. perspectives, actors, and sources as a matter of course, and work in archives outside the United States and in languages other than English was viewed as a sine qua non among practitioners in the field. This scholarship, however, was Eurocentric, focused on elites (overwhelmingly white, male, and powerful), and methodologically conservative, forever documenting, in the words of one famous critique, what one clerk said to another. The challenge of the new international history, then, has been to bring that broad international perspective back into focus while preserving and developing the rich methodological and thematic advances that have accumulated in the decades of scholarship since the 1960s.

The new work in this vein, it should be said, is not evenly distributed across the chronological span of U.S. history. Much of it is concentrated in the twentieth century, and even more so in the post–World War II period. Still, there has been some important new work on earlier periods. Historians have always understood, of course, that the events of the American Revolution could not be studied without reference to the broader contexts—ideological, political, military—in which they unfolded, and U.S. relations with the world in the early republic have long been studied as part of the epic conflict between the British and French empires for what could only be described as world domination. But in his global history of the Declaration of Independence, David Armitage has shown not only that the American founding was embedded in global contexts, tracing how the transnational flow of ideas shaped the declaration, but also how, in subsequent decades and centuries, the ideas articulated by the Founders reverberated across space and time, serving as a model for independence movements throughout the nineteenth century and well into the twentieth—in Latin America and the Caribbean, then in East-Central Europe, and finally across Asia and Africa.

It is not only American ideas, however, that have come to encircle the globe, but also American military power. The recent escalation of U.S. military involvement in the Middle East has rekindled some interest among both academic and popular historians in the Barbary Wars (the first fought from 1801 to 1805 and the second in 1815). Privateers from the North African principalities of Algiers, Tunis, and Tripoli (in present-day Libya) had long attacked commercial traffic in the Mediterranean, and, if before the Revolution American shipping was protected under British treaties with the pirates, by the 1780s the United States was on its own. Despite early attempts at accommodation, the Jefferson administration in the end opted for war. The ensuing battles created the new nation's first naval hero, Steven Decatur, and became enshrined in the official hymn of the U.S. Marine Corps (which begins "From the Halls of Montezuma, To the shores of Tripoli"—the first line refers, of course, to the U.S.-Mexico War). Nevertheless, the history of the Barbary Wars still awaits a deeper historical treatment, one that would probe its lasting impact on U.S. culture, not least military culture, and also locate it in the broader context of international affairs in the Mediterranean and integrate the perspectives of the North African actors into the narrative.

A good model for such work is new scholarship on the U.S.–Mexico War of 1846–1848, which helps us see it not only through the eyes of Americans—not simply as "Mr. Polk's War"—but also through those of other participants, including Mexicans and Native Americans. The former perspective is highlighted in Timothy J. Henderson, *A Glorious Defeat* (2007), which approaches the story of the war from the Mexican side and argues that, in order to understand both the outbreak and the outcome of the war we must consider not only the expansionist urges of the James K. Polk administration and the U.S. public's faith in its "Manifest Destiny," but also the condition of the Mexican state, divided as it was along lines of race, class, and region, which helped propel its political class, determined to rise in defense of Mexico's honor after the loss of Texas, into a conflict that most Mexicans knew they could not win. And in *War of a Thousand Deserts* (2008), Brian Delay has excavated fascinating new sources to illuminate the role of "independent Indians"—Apaches, Navajos, and especially Comanches—in shaping the contours of the conflict during an era in which, most historians have hitherto assumed, Native Americans were no longer an independent force in the international affairs of North America.

No event in American history has produced more historical output than the Civil War, and perhaps no event has been so insistently if understandably studied within the confines of national rather than transnational history. But that is now beginning to change. Sven Beckert's recent work on the global history of cotton has shed light on the Civil War as an event of global consequences in the political economy of the nineteenth century and beyond. He shows that, outside the United States, the main immediate significance of the great conflict between the Union and the Confederacy was the deep and sudden disruption it caused in the global supply of cotton, the raw material that powered the engine of the Industrial Revolution. This disruption in turn spurred, almost immediately, huge spikes in cotton cultivation elsewhere, especially in Egypt and India. With the end of American slavery in the wake of the war the main mode of antebellum cotton production was dead. Capitalists and governments—British first and foremost, but also Germans, Japanese, and others—launched a frenzied search for alternative sources and modes for producing cotton, with far-reaching consequences for global regimes of agricultural labor and industrial production.

If Beckert's work shows how a global perspective can shed new light on a well-known event, other recent work on the nineteenth century has focused on events largely forgotten or ignored by previous historians. Gordon Chang has reminded us of the significance of the U.S. war against Korea—not the one that took place in the early 1950s but rather the conflict of 1871, sparked as the U.S. Navy sought to force open the societies of northeast Asia to American trade—using that episode to explore the two sides' divergent discourses of "civilization" and "barbarism" and show how they shifted to accommodate changing interests and strategic requirements. And the work of Ussama Makdisi on the mid-nineteenth century peregrinations of American missionaries in Ottoman-ruled Lebanon explores their complex relationships with the surrounding society as they sought to "civilize" members of one of the world's oldest Christian communities. This work, part of a growing wave of scholarship on the role of religion in U.S. relations with the world, reminds us of the multiple actors and modalities involved in the interactions between Americans and other peoples and of the multifaceted role that religion has played in the history of U.S. foreign relations. It is a story that, partly under the influence of events since 2001 that have brought to the fore the role of religion in international affairs, is only now beginning to be told more fully.

Still, much of the recent scholarship in the history of the United States in the world has focused on the twentieth century. New work on the U.S. colonial empire in the Pacific and the Caribbean in the early twentieth century has not only expanded our understanding of that central chapter in U.S. history but also shown how it can illuminate many other aspects of American history, such as race relations. If until recently most of the historiographical interest in the U.S. occupation of the Philippines concentrated on the debate over empire at the turn of the century rather than on its actual practice on the ground over the next five decades, we now have substantial work on diverse aspects of U.S. colonial rule there, much of it conveniently summarized in *Colonial Crucible* (2009), edited by Alfred W. McCoy and Francisco A. Scarano. Recent work by Patricio N. Abinales, Warwick Anderson, Anne L. Foster, Paul A. Kramer, and others on this subject means that we now have a much more detailed and textured story. It helps us better understand the complex interactions between Americans and Filipinos and also places the ideology and practice of the United States as an imperial power in relation to other imperial powers, such as the British and the French, and more generally in the context of the broader culture of empire in international society at the time.

World War I and the Paris Peace Conference have long been viewed as major turning points in the history of the United States in the world, but here, too, new scholarship has illuminated these events from fresh perspectives. President Woodrow Wilson, who committed Americans to fight overseas on a scale far beyond anything that came before, wanted the extent of the war aims to match the scale of the sacrifice and so outlined a radical vision for the postwar reordering of international affairs. Building on the work of previous generations of scholars, Thomas J. Knock, *To End All Wars* (1993) showed how the idea of a League of Nations came to form the core of Wilson's vision for a peaceful postwar order, illuminating especially the extent to which activists and intellectuals from the left helped to shape Wilson's ideas. Knock also showed that the struggle in the United States over the League was not between internationalists and isolationists, as many previously thought, but between two distinct visions of internationalism. One was Wilson's "liberal internationalism, which focused on the right of all peoples to self-determination and the empowerment of an inclusive League of Nations as an arbiter of international affairs. The other, the "conservative internationalism" advocated by Wilson's opponents, including Henry Cabot Lodge and Theodore Roosevelt, prioritized close collaboration among the great powers and saw the League as primarily an instrument for the Anglo-American management of world affairs. The outcome of the struggle between these to camps was not preordained, and John Milton Cooper has argued persuasively that the incapacitating stroke that Wilson suffered in October 1919 was crucial in dooming the chances for a compromise over Senate ratification of the Treaty of Versailles, and thus for U.S. membership in the League of Nations.

Despite Wilson's spectacular failure in his own time, many historians now consider the vision he articulated as one of singular importance in the subsequent history of the United States in the world. In U.S. foreign policy, Frank Ninkovich has argued, the twentieth century was the "Wilsonian century." In the aftermath of the cold war in 1991, and even more so after the events of 9/11, a heated argument raged over the precise content and the suitability of the Wilsonian vision as a guide to the U.S. role in the world. But while there has been a tendency, occasionally evident even among professional historians, to reduce Wilson's views to a handful of (in)famous snippets—"making the world safe for democracy," "teaching Latin Americans to elect good men"—recent scholarship has made a compelling case that it was the establishment of multilateral international institutions, rather than the spreading of democracy as such, that stood at the center of Wilson's vision. Still, my own book, *The Wilsonian Moment* (2007), showed that Wilson's ringing wartime rhetoric had far-flung unintended audiences and, therefore, far-reaching unintended consequences, helping to mobilize colonial peoples against the system of imperial rule. Even as Wilson himself soon disappeared from the international arena, replaced in many cases by Lenin as an inspiration for anticolonial struggles, the momentum unleashed in the colonial world in 1919 continued to gain force, helping to shape the eventual process of decolonization and the recasting of international society that came in its wake.

Another aspect of the U.S. role in the world that has roots in Progressive Era politics as well as in America's imperial projects is the ideology and practice of what Emily Rosenberg has called "liberal developmentalism." The burgeoning literature on the history of U.S. development programs abroad brings together a number of historiographical strands that run through the history of American interactions with the world. It connects the "civilizing mission" of nineteenth-century missionaries, the push for overseas empire in the early twentieth century, and the massive public works programs of the New Deal to a central element of U.S. foreign policy after 1945, namely, the pursuit and advocacy of "modernization" around the world, especially in what was then known as the third world. This theme also, and not at all incidentally, carries distinct echoes of the ideologies of Manifest Destiny, racial and civilizational hierarchies, and an American mission to recast world order. It also bears important connections to central themes in domestic U.S. history, from westward expansion through progressivism and the New Deal to the Great Society and beyond.

An important advantage of thinking about the history of the United States in the world through the lens of modernization and development is that it highlights continuities in U.S. attitudes toward and relations with the rest of the world across the traditional divide of 1945, illuminating the myriad ways in which the policies and actions of the cold war era were connected to earlier American ideas, views, and practices. Thus, Michael A. Latham's pioneering work on the Kennedy administration's ideology of modernization tied its development initiatives in Latin America, Africa, and Southeast Asia—the Alliance for Progress, the Peace Corps, the Strategic Hamlet Program in Vietnam—to the tradition of ideologies of civilization and empire that guided earlier U.S. interactions with nonwhite peoples. David C. Engerman has explored the ways in which early American views of Russian modernization and economic development shaped U.S. policies toward the Soviet Union, while David Ekbladh has shown how the domestic development experiments of the Tennessee Valley Authority in the 1930s later became the basis for American modernization programs in Vietnam's Mekong Valley and elsewhere.

While World War II remains one of the defining events in the history of the United States in the world, recent work, rather than viewing the Japanese attack on Pearl Harbor as a radical break, has tended to see the entire period from 1917 to the 1945 as the era in which the United States emerged as the preeminent world power, and in which the European imperium was gradually but inexorably replaced with an American one. The emerging pillars of U.S. world power no doubt included the military-industrial complex, the national security state, and the vast network of military bases in Europe and the Pacific Rim, on which excellent scholarship has been and continues to be written—Michael J. Hogan, *A Cross of Iron* (1998), on the origins of the national security state, is but one example. Increasingly, however, historians are recognizing the extent to which the U.S. vision for the new world order included the construction of international institutions and reshaping of international norms. Townsend Hoopes and Douglas Brinkley, *FDR and the Creation of the United Nations* (1997), show the central role that the establishment of international structures played in

Washington's wartime planning, though much work remains to be done on the rather tumultuous history of relations between the United States and the United Nations. Elizabeth Borgwardt, *A New Deal for the World* (2005), traces central normative aspects of the new American internationalism forged during the war years, reflected not only in declarations of principle such as the Atlantic Charter but also in the institution building that took place at Bretton Woods and San Francisco and the internationalization of justice that occurred at Nuremberg.

Borgwardt's work is a prime example of the work in the new but already substantial field of human rights history, a field that is now at the center of historiographical (not to mention moral) debates about the U.S. role in the world and which, not coincidentally, intersects with the greater attention now paid to international organizations in the making of the contemporary world. Frank Ninkovich has recently delved back into the Gilded Age to show how the crystallization of a set of views on global interconnectedness in the late nineteenth century fostered the emergence of a global consciousness among American elites that underpinned the rise of both imperialism and internationalism, setting the stage for an international politics of human rights. And Mary Ann Glendon has carefully reconstructed the creation of the United Nations' 1948 Universal Declaration of Human Rights, locating Eleanor Roosevelt, who chaired the committee that wrote the declaration, at the center of the multinational group of intellectuals that included the French jurist René Cassin, the Lebanese philosopher Charles Malik, and the Chinese scholar P. C. Chang. Indeed, numerous historians have now begun to trace the rise of international rights regimes, first concerned with the rights of minorities within national polities and then, after World War II, focused on the universal human rights of individuals, uncovering the complex web of interests and motivations involved and exposing the hypocrisies and failed promises. In the process, they are elucidating the growing role of international norms and institutions in the postwar world.

The New Cold War History, and Beyond

Notwithstanding the rich, important scholarship already outlined on the pre-1945 history of the United States in the world, much of the new work published in the last two decades in the field has focused on the period following the end of World War II that saw the advent of the global conflict known as the cold war. Partly, this prodigious output was the result of the flood of new sources that, for a while in the 1990s, came gushing out of previously inaccessible archives in former Soviet bloc countries, as well as from the new (though still very partial) liberality of the Chinese archives. But though most (though by no means all) of these newly available sources have come from Europe, some of the most important work to emerge from them has actually nudged the historiography of the cold war away from its old Eurocentric focus and toward a growing recognition of the importance of third world countries, both as arenas and as actors, in shaping international affairs in the postwar era. A leading example of such work is Odd Arne Westad, *The Global Cold War* (2005), which mined a vast trove of new documents in numerous languages to lay out in great detail how the intersection of postcolonial conflict and superpower competition meant that, in much of the Global South, the "cold war" was in fact a very hot one. For Westad, it is the third world, rather than Europe, that should be viewed as the central arena of cold war conflict.

Another important insight to emerge from recent work on Washington's relations with Third-World countries relates to the impact of the often irreconcilable conflict between anti-imperialism and anticommunism that plagued U.S. policy. The work of Salim Yaqub, for example, explored the efforts of the Eisenhower administration to craft a Middle East policy that would contain communism and replace retreating British and French influence with U.S. power while at the same time fostering good will among the region's newly independent states. But the attempts to convince leaders such as Egypt's Gamal Abdel Nasser (or, for that matter, India's Jawaharlal Nehru) that the United States supported their right to self-determination while also demanding that they declare allegiance to the United States did not usually go very well, to the great frustration of Einsehower and his fiercely anticommunist secretary of state, John Foster Dulles. The United States, as Matthew Connelly, *A Diplomatic Revolution* (2002) has shown, was operating in a changed international environment and had to contend with new norms, forums, and actors in international society. In this new order, Algerian freedom fighters could challenge, and eventually defeat, their militarily far stronger French overlords by leveraging support in sympathetic forums such as the UN General Assembly and plugging into global revolutionary networks that stretched from Cuba to Vietnam.

Indeed, historians using newly available materials from the Cuban archives have been able to shed new light on central episodes in cold war history. Thus, Alexander Fursenko and Timothy Naftali, *One Hell of a Gamble* (1997) integrated Havana's perspective into the history of the Cuban Missile Crisis while Piero Gleijeses, *Conflicting Missions* (2002) outlined the central role of Cuban advisers, aid workers, and soldiers in postcolonial conflicts in sub-Saharan Africa in the 1960s and 1970s. Among other things, such work has highlighted the independent agency of Third-World actors in the postwar world, showing how they were often able to shape in decisive ways the international contexts that decision makers in Washington and Moscow faced. During the cold war era, U.S. officials commonly had to choose between what they saw as the imperative of containing communism and the demands of peoples in the Global South for self-determination. And quite often during this period, the perceived need to bolster European allies or to counter real or imagined communist threats won out over any inclination to support the claims of colonial or postcolonial peoples. The classic case study and (at least from the American perspective) the most tragic one was the U.S. decision, in the late 1940s, to support the desperate French efforts to retake its colonial possessions in Indochina, a decision that, as Mark Atwood Lawrence has recently reminded us, led directly to the U.S. war in Vietnam.

The Vietnam War has long fascinated historians of the United States in the world and it has remained a major topic of interest, though here, too, scholars have recently explored some new themes and perspectives. The attention to the role of culture in foreign relations, as well as the new concern with the role of religion, is evident in the work of Seth Jacobs, who has argued that South Vietnamese president Ngo Dinh Diem's Catholicism helped him gain support among U.S. elites, who tended to view non-Christian Vietnamese as passive and untrustworthy—in essence, as uncivilized. Such cultural analysis of foreign policy is illuminating but has its limits, which are apparent when we recall that it was President John F. Kennedy, a Catholic, who acquiesced in the 1963 coup against Diem once it was deemed that he had become more of a threat than an asset to U.S. goals in Southeast Asia. Another cultural perspective on the U.S.-Vietnam relationship is offered in the work of Mark Philip Bradley, *Imagining Vietnam and America* (2000), which shows how understanding the history of mutual perceptions between the two peoples can help us make sense of their subsequent interactions.

An important feature of new work on the Vietnam War is the move toward seeing the war as more than simply an American event. This has meant, among other things, contextualizing U.S. decisions leading to the war within the broader interplay of international politics at the time, as the work of Mark Atwood Lawrence and Fredrik Logevall has done. And it has also, and no less importantly, meant using Vietnamese-language sources to integrate the various Vietnamese actors into the narrative, as in the work of Robert K. Brigham on the South Vietnamese army or Lien-Hang Nguyen on the policy debates within the North Vietnamese leadership. This shift in the scholarship has now begun to filter into general classroom texts. If one of the most popular of the previous generation of surveys on the Vietnam War, George Herring's *America's Longest War* (1979), was written primarily from the perspective of U.S. history, more recent efforts by Lawrence (*The Vietnam War: A Concise International History*) and Bradley (*Vietnam at War*) remind us that the war must also be understood as international history, and as Vietnamese history.

Perhaps the single most important feature of recent writing on the history of the cold war is that, in the last two decades, historians have been able to glimpse it in the rearview mirror. What was so shocking about the end of the cold war was not so much that it came relatively peacefully (the violence that tore up Yugoslavia was, of course, a glaring exception), but rather that it ended so definitively, with one of the two major antagonists, the Soviet Union, simply disintegrating into thin air. Great empires have fallen before, but typically as a result of war or invasion; one is hard pressed to think of a historical precedent for a major world power simply willing itself out of existence. Unsurprisingly, the debate over the explanation for this puzzling denouement has been vigorous. Some historians, such as John Lewis Gaddis, have awarded substantial credit for the collapse of the Soviet bloc, if not the Soviet Union itself, to Ronald Reagan and Pope John Paul II, while others have highlighted the role of Mikhail Gorbachev and of the unintended consequences of his efforts to reform the Soviet system. But despite the outpouring of excellent new scholarship—the year 2009, the twentieth anniversary of the dramatic events of 1989, saw numerous volumes published on this subject—the debate over the causes and consequences of the end of the cold war is still far from over.

In the context of this chapter, however, perhaps the most interesting consequence of the end of the cold war is not historical but historiographical. Namely, it is the conviction among a growing number of historians that the concept of the "cold war" no longer offers the only or the most compelling framework for understanding the history of the United States in the world between 1945 and 1991. One problem with viewing postwar history through the cold war lens, as already noted, is that it lends excessive importance to 1945 as a bright dividing line in the history of U.S. relations with the wider world. But more importantly, a focus on the cold war as an interpretive framework tends to efface other, arguably more central themes or processes in the history of the postwar world. Two such themes that have begun to emerge as contenders for framing our study of the postwar era are decolonization and the rise of new nations in Asia and Africa, and globalization and the emergence of new international regimes of global order and disorder.

Building on the seminal work of Akira Iriye, Matthew Connelly has recently called on historians to "take off the cold war lens" and to "see beyond the state" as they reconsider the history of the postwar world, and a new generation of historians has begun to answer that call. Still, recent work has shown that we need not, indeed should not ignore the cold war or the indisputably important role of states and state power in international affairs as we open up new topics and themes for historical investigation. Thus, Nick Cullather and Kristin Ahlberg have highlighted the significance of food aid and agricultural modernization in the history of U.S. foreign relations. Amy L. S. Staples has traced the ways UN specialized agencies, along with the networks of international civil servants that cohered around them, laid the groundwork for regimes and practices of global governance in the fields of economics, food, and health. And Connelly himself has uncovered the history of the global campaign to control world population, tracing the elaborate networks of state and nonstate actors that took part in a struggle that both supporters and opponents saw literally as a matter of life and death, not only for individuals or even nations but for the planet itself, and for humanity's moral and biological fiber.

Some of the most exciting new horizons now appearing in the historiography of the United States in the world, then, combine traditional concerns with new approaches and themes. The resulting work gives us a better sense of the roles of non-Western peoples, not merely as objects of

U.S. perceptions and policies but as active agents that have played an important part in shaping the history of U.S. interactions with the world. It also pays greater attention to nonstate actors—not just international organizations, which have emerged as increasingly important, but also missionaries and religious organizations, businesspeople and multinational corporations, philanthropists and activist lobbies, immigrants and diasporic networks, and transnational "epistemic communities" of experts that cohered around shared knowledge, norms, and practices. In short, this new work seeks to write the history of the United States in the world not only as a chapter within U.S. history but also as a central component of the history of international society. And even as the field remains committed to traditional concerns with military conflict, diplomacy, and economic interests it is also paying greater attention to such themes as the development of international norms and institutions, humanitarian interventions, and global campaigns against hunger and disease, among others. From our twenty-first-century perspective, conscious as we are of living in a global era, it seems only fitting that the history of the United States in the world should have this breadth.

BIBLIOGRAPHY

This bibliography lists some of the most important recent works on the history of the United States in the world. The two volumes of Robert L. Beisner, ed., *American Foreign Relations since 1600: A Guide to the Literature* (Santa Barbara, CA: ABC-Clio, 2003) provide a useful guide to earlier work.

Anderson, Carol. *Eyes off the Prize: The United Nations and the African American Struggle for Human Rights, 1944–1955*. New York: Cambridge University Press, 2003.

Armitage, David. *The Declaration of Independence: A Global History*. Cambridge, MA: Harvard University Press, 2007.

Beckert, Sven. "Emancipation and Empire: Reconstructing the Worldwide Web of Cotton Production in the Age of the American Civil War," *The American Historical Review*, December 2004.

Borgwardt, Elizabeth. *A New Deal for the World: America's Vision for Human Rights*. Cambridge, MA: Harvard University Press, 2005.

Borstelmann, Thomas. *The Cold War and the Color Line: American Race Relations in the Global Arena*. Cambridge, MA: Harvard University Press, 2001.

Bradley, Mark Philip. *Imagining Vietnam and America: The Making of Postcolonial Vietnam, 1919–1950*. Chapel Hill: University of North Carolina Press, 2000.

Chang, Gordon H. "Whose 'Barbarism'? Whose 'Treachery'? Race and Civilization in the Unkown United States-Korea War of 1871" *The Journal of American History*, March 2003.

Cobbs Hoffman, Elizabeth. *All You Need Is Love: The Peace Corps and the Spirit of the 1960s*. Cambridge, MA: Harvard University Press, 1998.

Connelly, Matthew. *Fatal Misconception: The Struggle to Control World Population*. Cambridge, MA: Harvard University Press, 2008.

Cooper, John Milton, Jr., ed. *Reconsidering Woodrow Wilson: Progressivism, Internationalism, War, and Peace*. Baltimore: Johns Hopkins University Press, 2008.

Cullather, Nick. The *Hungry World: America's Cold War Battle against Poverty in Asia*. Cambridge, MA: Harvard University Press, 2010.

Delay, Brian. *War of a Thousand Deserts: Indian Raids and the U.S.-Mexican War*. New Haven, CT: Yale University Press, 2008.

Dudziak, Mary L. *Cold War Civil Rights: Race and the Image of American Democracy*. Princeton, NJ: Princeton University Press, 2000.

Ekbladh, David. *The Great American Mission: Modernization and the Construction of an American World Order*. Princeton, NJ: Princeton University Press, 2010.

Endy, Christopher. *Cold War Holidays: American Tourism in France*. Chapel Hill: University of California Press, 2004.

Engerman, David C. *Modernization from the Other Shore: American Intellectuals and the Romance of Russian Development*. Cambridge, MA: Harvard University Press, 2003.

Gaddis, John Lewis. *The Cold War: A New History*. New York: Penguin Press, 2005.

Go, Julian, and Anne L. Foster, eds. *The American Colonial State in the Philippines: Global Perspective*. Durham, NC: Duke University Press, 2003.

Herring, George C. *From Colony to Superpower: U.S. Foreign Relations since 1776*. New York: Oxford University Press, 2008.

Hogan, Michael J., and Thomas G. Paterson, eds. *Explaining the History of American Foreign Relations*, 2nd ed. New York: Cambridge University Press, 2004.

Hoganson, Kristin L. *Fighting for American Manhood: How Gender Politics Provoked the Spanish-American and Philippine-American Wars*. New Haven, CT: Yale University Press, 1998.

Iriye, Akira. *Global Community: The Role of International Organizations in the Making of the Contemporary World*. Berkeley: University of California Press, 2002.

Jacobs, Seth. *America's Miracle Man in Vietnam: Ngo Dinh Diem, Religion, Race, and U.S. Intervention in Southeast Asia, 1950–1957*. Durham, NC: Duke University Press, 2004.

Knock, Thomas J. *To End All Wars: Woodrow Wilson and the Quest for a New World Order*. New York: Oxford University Press, 1992.

Kramer, Paul A. *The Blood of Government: Race, Empire, the United States, and the Philippines*. Chapel Hill: University of North Carolina Press, 2006.

Latham, Michael E. *Modernization as Ideology: American Social Science and "Nation Building" in the Kennedy Era*. Chapel Hill: University of North Carolina Press, 2000.

Lawrence, Mark Atwood. *Assuming the Burden: Europe and the American Commitment to Vietnam*. Berkeley: University of California Press, 2005.

Leffler, Melvyn P. *For the Soul of Mankind: The United States, the Soviet Union, and the Cold War*. New York: Hill and Wang, 2007.

Logevall, Fredrik. *Choosing War: The Lost Chance for Peace and the Escalation of War in Vietnam*. Berkeley: University of California Press, 1999.

Maier, Charles S. *Among Empires: American Ascendancy and Its Predecessors*. Cambridge, MA: Harvard University Press, 2006.

———. "Marking Time: The Historiography of International Relations." In Michael Kammen, ed., *The Past Before Us: Contemporary Historical Writing in the United States*. Ithaca, NY: Cornell University Press, 1980.

Makdisi, Ussama. *Artillery of Heaven: American Missionaries and the Failed Conversion of the Middle East*. Ithaca, NY: Cornell University Press, 2008.

Manela, Erez. *The Wilsonian Moment: Self-Determination and the International Origins of Anticolonial Nationalism*. New York: Oxford University Press, 2007.

Ninkovich, Frank. *Global Dawn: The Cultural Foundations of American Internationalism, 1865–1890*. Cambridge, MA: Harvard University Press, 2009.

Parker, Jason C. *Brother's Keeper: The United States, Race, and Empire in the British Caribbean, 1937–1962*. New York: Oxford University Press, 2008.

Renda, Mary A. *Taking Haiti: Military Occupation and the Culture of U.S. Imperialism*. Chapel Hill: University of North Carolina Press, 2001.

Roorda, Eric Paul. *The Dictator Next Door: The Good Neighbor Policy and the Trujillo Regime in the Dominican Republic, 1930–1945*. Durham, NC: Duke University Press, 1998.

Rosenberg, Emily S. *Financial Missionaries to the World: The Politics and Culture of Dollar Diplomacy, 1900–1930*. Durham, NC: Duke University Press, 2003.

Schwartz, Thomas Alan. *Lyndon Johnson and Europe: In the Shadow of Vietnam*. Cambridge, MA: Harvard University Press, 2003.

Staples, Amy L. S. *The Birth of Development: How the World Bank, Food and Agriculture Organization, and World Health Organization Changed the World, 1945–1965*. Kent, OH: Kent State University Press, 2006.

Stephanson, Anders. *Manifest Destiny: American Expansion and the Empire of Right*. New York: Hill and Wang, 1995.

Suri, Jeremi. *Power and Protest: Global Revolution and the Rise of Détente*. Cambridge, MA: Harvard University Press, 2003.

Von Eschen, Penny M. *Satchmo Blows up the World: Jazz Ambassadors Play the Cold War*. Cambridge, MA: Harvard University Press, 2004.

Westad, Odd Arne. *The Global Cold War*. New York: Cambridge University Press, 2005.

Yaqub, Salim. *Containing Arab Nationalism: The Eisenhower Doctrine and the Middle East*. Chapel Hill: University of North Carolina Press, 2004.

Zeiler, Thomas W. "The Diplomatic History Bandwagon: A State of the Field." *The Journal of American History* 95 (March 2009): 1053–1073.

10
The "Cultural Turn"

LAWRENCE B. GLICKMAN

Cultural historians of the United States find themselves in an unusual position. On the one hand, they are part of a uniquely popular, exciting, and encompassing field of historical inquiry. On the other hand, the remarkable growth of the field in the twenty-first century has rendered it less distinctive than in its incarnation in the 1980s and 1990s as the up-and-coming "new cultural history." Cultural history has triumphed; it is everywhere in the historiography of the United States. Between 1990 and 2005 the number of historians claiming this label doubled, and, by the latter date, nearly 60 percent of American history departments had at least one self-identified cultural historian. As the concerns of cultural history have diffused throughout the profession—as James Vernon announced in 2001, "we are all cultural historians now"—it has become difficult to determine what makes it a unique field.

At the same time, cultural history has benefited from the infusion of new methods and approaches. Some of these—such as disability history, visual studies, and sensory history—while initially associated with the field, have become distinct areas of inquiry. Many other fields have been reinvigorated by their engagement with cultural approaches. (Indeed, many of the topics treated in this chapter of necessity blend into the subjects of the other topical chapters of this volume.) If we have all become culturalists, the forms and practices of this cultural turn in the United States have varied dramatically. However widespread and diverse, the cultural turn has not been directionless, and this chapter will map the growth of the field and tease out its definitional cornerstones. The map, as we will see, tracks a balance between cultural history's new materiality—highlighted by a focus on structures, places, movements, and the senses—combined with a wider range of sources, a deemphasis on purity of methods and approaches, and a growing infiltration of culturalism into other branches of U.S. history.

One could begin a discussion of the gains of cultural history by examining the evolution of this book. The inaugural 1990 version of *The New American History* included a chapter on "social history" but not on cultural history, which was already being invigorated by the broad interest in the "new cultural history" practiced especially by leading Europeanists. Reflecting trends in historical practices—but lagging behind them—the updated 1997 edition dropped the chapter on social history and added a new chapter, "Intellectual and Cultural History," which focused far more on the former than the latter. In this current iteration, which does not contain essays on either social or intellectual history, cultural history stands alone, reflecting its central place in contemporary scholarship. This is the only chapter highlighting an approach instead of an era or a topic. Cultural history is not limited to the history of "culture" but suggests a way of approaching any topic; this is a key reason for the field's persistence and largely why it has overtaken social history, the great growth field of the 1970s and 1980s. Environmental history is perhaps the closest to cultural history in this sense. But in an excellent analysis of how environmental historians have moved beyond their traditional range of topics—especially Western history and "nature"—to make their field a lens for examining multiple issues, Richard White ascribes that transformation to the field's "cultural turn."

If older fields have made a cultural turn in recent years, the category of cultural history has also become something of a placeholder for emerging approaches, some of which have split off to form their own independent identity. Emergent topics such as food studies, disability history, consumer history, and sensory history are often categorized under the rubric of cultural history. And even established categories such as visual culture, environmental history, gender and sexuality studies, and family history are still sometimes grouped under this category.

A key to the success of cultural history has been its healthy balance of trade. It has been an early historical adapter, importing ideas and methods from anthropology, literary theory, geography, and ethnic, gender, and African-American studies, and exporting them to the other branches of history. It is hard to imagine a topic, approach, or narrative style that has not been assimilated into cultural history. In order to catalog some of the most important tendencies and directions in contemporary cultural history, it is necessary to examine the factors leading to the field's emergence.

As James W. Cook and I have argued, the conventional story, in which modern U.S. cultural history emerged in the late 1980s as Americans imported the methods of the "new cultural history" from their Europeanist colleagues, is incomplete. In fact, many vectors of American history scholarship, some going back several generations, contributed to the late-twentieth-century cultural turn.

Once upon a time, the meaning of cultural history seemed straightforward and relatively narrow. Until the 1970s at least, many scholars thought of that rubric as demarcating the history of American high culture: its art, music, and literature. Kenneth Silverman's 1976 cultural history of the American Revolution, for example, examines painting, music, literature, and the theater. American thought was reserved for intellectual historians and American studies scholars, and as a rule historians stayed away from the analysis of popular culture. Scholars who studied American popular culture from a historical perspective—including Russell Nye, Henry Nash Smith, and John Cawelti, authors of pioneering works in the 1950s and 1960s that innovatively used dime novels, success manuals, and popular fiction—found their academic homes in departments of English, or, in the case of Russell Lynes, the scholar of popular taste and cultural hierarchies who was a columnist for *Art in America*, were unaffiliated with academe. Other studies were carried out by sociologists of "mass culture," such as Robert K. Merton, or, by members of the Frankfurt School, such as Leo Lowenthal. The influential 1957 book *Mass Culture: The Popular Arts in America* contained not a single essay by a historian.

But it is inaccurate to view cultural analysis as alien to American historians or to see it as emerging only in the late 1980s. Indeed, as Cook and I have demonstrated, from the founding of the American historical profession in the late nineteenth century through World War II, what Harry Elmer Barnes in 1922 called the "cultural element" was one of the marks of the "New History," practiced by a number of the country's leading scholars. When Caroline Ware's book *The Cultural Approach to History* appeared in 1940, it was widely praised as pointing the way for a new approach. Kolb's review of Ware's book from 1942 noted, in a claim that could have been repeated a half century later, that "many of the writers view this approach as nothing more than what has previously gone under the name social history. This consists of the belief that history should concern itself with the inarticulate masses, their lives, languages, loves, etc." Many years later, one contributor to Ware's book, the business historian Thomas Cochran, expressed surprise and disappointment that this approach had not become "synonymous with history." One of the themes of this chapter is that, after many iterations and infusions, mainstreaming the cultural approach has come to pass.

Many sources, especially the increasingly prominent discipline of American studies and the increasingly popular "new social history," provided these iterations and infusions. American studies scholars pioneered the examination of popular culture. The "new social history" that first emerged in the 1960s sparked a revolution in American historiography with its emphasis on those left out of previous historical narratives and its method of "history from the bottom up." In their attempts to understand the full lives of their subjects, the new social historians paid considerable attention to culture, understood by Herbert Gutman as a "resource" for subaltern groups. As a result, many of the community studies that were a hallmark of the new social history highlighted "working-class culture," "African-American culture," and various forms of immigrant culture.

For a variety of reasons, in the 1980s and 1990s many pioneering new social historians began to redefine themselves as cultural or "social-cultural" historians. Among these reasons were the increasingly important role of culture in their analysis, a loss of faith in the powers of quantification, and a recognition that storytelling—the "narrative history" that the first generation of social historians dismissed as frivolous and even conservative—could be successfully married with analysis. These scholars were joined by many others who came of age in the era of the new cultural history. By the 1990s there was an intergenerational melding, and U.S. cultural history began to be recognized as new, although it drew on earlier incarnations and contemporary models, especially from scholars of Europe and South Asia.

Of course, to say that cultural history has bypassed social history is not strictly accurate because, as with so many other approaches and subject matters, cultural history has absorbed it. When the new cultural history was first proclaimed in the late 1980s, scholars embracing this approach naturally emphasized their differences in method and subject matter from social historians. According to this framework, social historians used the metaphor of "listening" to ordinary people; cultural historians preferred to "read" texts. Social historians were quantifiers, who counted and measured; cultural historians preferred narrative approaches. Social historians preferred community studies, while cultural historians preferred discourse analysis. Social historians understood categories such as class, race, and gender as fixed and sought to explain how they operated as both sources of oppression and avenues of "agency," while cultural historians tended to interrogate the construction of such categories themselves. Social historians practiced history from the bottom up, while cultural historians often examined the powerful. Over time, however, these theoretical distinctions, never particularly descriptive of the actual practice in these fields, lessened. As fields mature, they tend to be less orthodox in their methods and approaches, and cultural historians began to draw from rather than rejecting the methods of social history. At the same time, many new social historians became increasingly attracted to the methods of cultural history, and over time their work came to reflect its markings. Despite the fact that cultural history has moved in so many directions, a few defining characteristics are worthy of comment. Perhaps most important has been the rejection of a sharp separation between culture and other realms of life. Although historians still occasionally juxtapose the material world or the on-the-ground realm of politics with culture, a growing number of historians have blurred this distinction. (It should be noted that there was a noticeable concern with culture or discourse in works by an earlier generation of political historians, including Bernard Bailyn, Gordon Wood, and Eric Foner, who often used the term "ideology" to suggest the cultural and discursive—but decisive—element of politics. And the influential anthropologist Clifford Geertz discussed ideologies as "cultural systems.") Similarly, early debates about the relative importance of experience and agency of ordinary people versus the power of category making—once a hallmark of the social/cultural history divide—have declined in importance.

Cultural history represents a unique category because it is both a method (the cultural history of *x*, *y*, or *z*) and a subject matter (the history of culture). Given the breadth of the method (what topic is immune from cultural analysis?) and the subject matter (culture has come to encompass far more than its earlier meanings of first, the arts, and, later, popular systems of belief) and the increasing legitimacy of both, it is not surprising that it has become such a diverse field, penetrating many aspects of the profession. In recent years, we have seen cultural histories of, to sample only a small percentage, Richard Nixon, Chinese food, blue jeans, the weather, hillbillies, funeral homes, automobiles, Yiddish radio, and the American wind band, not to mention Eric Schatzberg's article "The Cultural History of Aluminum as an Industrial Material," which appeared in *Enterprise and Society* in 2003. This set of topics shows the blending between culture as an analytical framework and as the subject matter of history. Such a list might also suggest that the idea of "cultural history" has become so distended as to lose any clear meaning. (In order to keep the focus on recent trends, this chapter and its bibliography highlight work published since the year 2000.)

As it has gained popularity, the meaning of cultural history has been transformed. The category of "cultural" contains a much larger set of topics and approaches than it did a generation ago. Critics have explained this transformation in two seemingly mutually exclusive ways, as representing either its triumph or its disappearance. Some see the cultural approach as hegemonic, replacing traditional explanatory devices. David Steigerwald offers perhaps the most forceful explication of this view: "Sometime in the last quarter of the twentieth century, the developed world slipped from the Age of Materialism to the Age of Culture. Culture has become in our time what religion was to the early modern period and what science to the Enlightenment. Economic Man of the nineteenth and twentieth centuries had abdicated in favor of Cultural Person, and the new regime has replaced Class Consciousness with Cultural Consciousness." In this understanding, cultural interpretations have triumphed not merely by competing with previous interpretative frameworks but by replacing them.

Others, however, reject this interpretation of the triumph of cultural history and instead see a turn away from culture as traditionally understood, or at least as articulated by earlier social and cultural historians. "The vast majority of American historians no longer regard American culture—whether high culture or mainstream popular culture—as an essential area of study," complained Richard Pells in 2007, who interpreted this as evidence that the "much-vaunted cultural turn in the humanities has run its course." For Pells cultural history is defined by a subject matter with clear parameters—what he calls "American culture"—and his belief in the slighting of that subject matter leads him to view the field as declining.

Both explanations are partially correct: Steigerwald rightly notes the increasing prominence of cultural frameworks for historical examinations of all kinds, including of seemingly noncultural topics, and Pells is on the mark in suggesting that American culture as he defines it is a less common topic than it once was. But these interpretations are also limited: Steigerwald does not recognize that, as we will see, the cultural approach has not so much displaced materialism as incorporated and modified it. Pells is thus correct to the extent that conceptions of cultural history have changed but incorrect to equate this with the death of the cultural turn. At one time, cultural historians concerned themselves primarily with "the best that has been thought and said." Even during this period, other historians—still under the rubric of social history, labor history, or African-American history—put forward a more anthropological conception of culture. An examination of the second category he mentions, popular culture, did define a later generation of pioneering culturalists.

Indeed, work on topics within the parameters approved by Pells continues to flourish and remain very much central to cultural historiography. Recent work on a variety of topics—such as minstrelsy, W. T. Lhamon's *Raising Cain: Blackface Performance from Jim Crow to Hip Hop* (2000); ethnic celebrations, Matthew Jacobson's *Roots Too: White Ethnic Revival in Post-Civil Rights America* (2006); popular music, David Suisman's *Selling Sounds: The Commercial Revolution in American Music* (2009); literary culture, Alice Fahs's *The Imagined Civil War: Popular Literature of the North and South, 1861–1865* (2001); and social thought, Howard Brick's *Transcending Capitalism: Visions of a New Society in Modern American Thought* (2006)—examines aspects of both literary and popular culture in fascinating ways. A shared premise of these diverse works is that culture must be understood in a broad economic and social context. Despite different topics and time periods, all these works share an understanding that cultural products—whether performance, music, literature, ethnicity, or intellectual discourse—cannot be divorced from the economic markets that help create them. Cultural historians have sought to expand their terrain, not only by culturalizing seemingly noncultural topics, but also by blurring the boundaries between culture and other seemingly more institutional, political, or economic categories.

The new cultural history of the 1980s and 1990s was deeply influenced by poststructuralist thought, especially the writings of the French social theorist Michel Foucault. A particular inspiration was the historicization of the concepts of nature and tradition. Rather than asking how medicine changed its approach to treating mental illness, for example, Foucault asked how the category of mental illness was created in the first place. In addition, Foucault's notion "power is everywhere because it comes from everywhere," as he put it in *The History of Sexuality: An Introduction*, reinforced the growing conviction among historians that culture as much as economics or politics is central to maintaining power. Foucault's rejection of what he called "juridical" power, forces that run neatly from state institutions to individuals, provided an important opening for the examination of cultural practices as sites of both repression and agency. In recent years, however, notwithstanding the recognition that power has diffuse sources, cultural historians have sought to identify and analyze particular sites of power. In practice, this trend has led to a search for institutionally grounded forms of discourse analysis. While retaining a belief in the importance of the cultural construction of reality, cultural historians have rejected the antifoundational essence of postmodernism, defined by the literary theorist Jean-Francois Lyotard as "incredulity toward metanarratives."

Cultural history, in short, has become more material, by which I do not mean simply that it focuses more on economics than previous generations of cultural historians or that it has imported a neo-Marxist materialist framework. The materialist turn in cultural history is best understood as an emphasis on a wide variety of concrete manifestations of culture—culture inside of rather than outside of institutions. This is not to say that cultural historians have elided the distinction between culture and other social forces. They have not rejected the need to tease out and recognize the plurality of cultures, and they have not abandoned social history's notion of culture as a resource and political weapon.

To take one example, cultural historians have long been concerned with the process of category creation. Whereas the new social history focused on empathic understandings of those groups—women, slaves, workers, sexual minorities, Native Americans—largely omitted from traditional historiography and emphasized their agency, the first generation of new cultural historians tended to stress the construction of such categories such as whiteness, free laborer, masculinity, and heterosexuality. Another way of discussing this change is that cultural history has shifted from what Daniel Wickberg has called "sympathetic and recuperative histories of the oppressed" to the largely top-down process of category creation. In this view, historians have moved from studying the subjectivities of the subaltern to the ways in which the categories of the dominant are as much cultural processes as the activism of the oppressed.

The method most common in analyzing the creation of such binaries was a generalized discourse analysis, usually, in new historicist fashion, based on an eclectic variety of literary sources. Cultural historians have maintained their interest in the construction of norms and have continued to analyze language carefully, but in the last decade or so they have focused more on the ways in which institutions, such as the state, fundamentally shape this process. They are continuing to interrogate the category of the "natural" but are using a far wider range of sources and perspectives, putting the meat of the state and other institutions on the bones of the process of cultural construction. Peggy Pascoe's *What Comes Naturally*

(2008), provides a good example of this concrete form of cultural analysis. By Pells's definition, Pascoe's subject matter—the history of miscegenation law—does not qualify as cultural at all, since it is not centrally an aspect of high or popular culture. Although race mixing certainly figures in the latter, and such references occasionally are mentioned, Pascoe keeps her focus on the hard surface of the law. Yet the law of miscegenation, she notes, was rooted in a cultural system in which conceptions of nature were central. Her work examines the contingent category of the natural in legislation and judicial opinions. Furthermore, she demonstrates the concrete impact that such conceptions and laws had on real individuals involved in interracial relationships, whose particular plight she traces in each of her chapters. In *Public Vows* (2001), a history of marriage in the United States, Nancy Cott follows a similar strategy of "reading the legal record for cultural and social insights."

Similarly, Margot Canaday's *The Straight State* (2009) has demonstrated a close relation between category production and state power. "The best work on the state by historians takes state institutions seriously, but incorporates rather than jettisons the society and culture side of the binary, blending social and cultural with legal and political history," Canaday writes. Canaday shows that conceptions of sexuality shaped determinations of what the fruits of citizenship should be. The result of these determinations for gay veterans was not merely disrespect in the realm of attitudes but material deprivation of rights accorded to their fellow returning soldiers. Mae Ngai's examination of illegal aliens, *Impossible Subjects* (2004), provides another example of category creation as a political-legal process. Ngai shows how quickly the legislative creation of the "illegal alien" came to be seen as a "normative feature of immigration policy." A generation ago, it is doubtful that either the sources or the topics selected by Pascoe, Cott, Canaday, and Ngai would have been understood as suitable for cultural history. But with the incorporation of the materialist turn, these works provide models for expanding the range of sources and approaches in cultural analysis.

Another example of category creation is Sarah Igo's *The Averaged American* (2007), which examines what we might call the norm of norms, as constructed by scientists of public opinion. Igo shows that social scientists, pollsters, and sex researchers constructed the concept of mass society and also the norms to which members of mass society adhered. Even the most intimate and personal details of one's life became the subject of intensive research, which sought to define a standard of norms and which in turn allowed Americans to determine how they ranked in comparison to the average.

A key element of the expansion of cultural history is precisely its refusal to limit the meaning of the cultural to what is left over after politics and economics. This has manifested itself especially in an interest in reconsidering the relationship among social, political, and economic structures. Part of this is doubtless motivated by the recognition that contemporary politics often lags behind the culture in areas like gay rights, and often seems shaped by cultural forces rather than the reverse. Scholars of the branch of recent cultural history that focuses on the history of capitalism have been particularly attuned to the dialectic between culture and structure. "There can be no capitalism," write Joyce Appleby in *The Relentless Revolution* (2010), "without a culture of capitalism." Thus the emphasis on structure does not mean that cultural historians are interested only in top-down approaches or in stories of hegemony and triumph. Sympathy for outsiders and those left behind and a desire to chart the mainstream from the periphery—long hallmarks of the cultural turn and, before that, the new social history—characterize the cultural history of capitalism. A series of brilliant books about illicit economic actors, the culture of the new urban workplace (the office), and business failures in the nineteenth century have illuminated not just oddballs, losers, and the prehistory of the man in the gray flannel suit, but also the essence of mainstream American identity. Michael Zakim has shown in *Ready-Made Democracy* (2003) that men's fashion was an activity of "acute political significance" and an excellent "vantage point for examining some of the central themes of the times." The studies by Scott A. Sandage on business failures, Stephen Mihm on counterfeiters, and Jane Kamensky on speculators all shed light on the center by focusing on the periphery, in large measure by showing the affiliations and connections between these outsiders and the mainstream economy. Moving into the late twentieth century, Bethany Moreton, in *To Serve God and Wal-Mart* (2009), has shown how the culture of evangelical Christianity became wedded to free-market economics, largely through the example of Sam Walton's largely white, female workforce. Vicki Howard's *Brides, Inc.* (2008) places a potentially narrow cultural topic in the context of business history, producing a study of symbols and discourse rooted in the material base of the multibillion dollar wedding industry.

Another important reflection of the increasing materiality of cultural history is a new emphasis on place, often aligned with the study of memory, as in Kirk Savage's *Monument Wars* (2009) on the history of memorials on the National Mall in Washington, DC. Just as the process of cultural construction has materialized through an emphasis on institutions, so too has place provided concrete sites to observe it. Historians should "reinsert the dimension of space" into their analysis argues Anthony G. Kaye in *Joining Places* (2007), a study of slave communities; similarly, Matthew Klingle has observed that the spatial dimension of history is "commonly reduced to discourse." Many have taken up this call by addressing the community study, the quintessential tool of the new social history, with the tools of the cultural turn. They have often combined the community study with the process of memorialization to better explain what David Blight in *Race and Reunion* (2001) calls "depoliticized memory," in which the gritty realities of injustice and racism are ignored in local instances of memorialization. In *Whitewashed Adobe* (2004), for example, William Deverell explores "the construction of cultural categories in which ethnic others get placed" though an examination of particular moments and places in Los Angeles history. Similarly, Phoebe Kropp argues in *California Vieja* (2006), whose subtitle is *Culture and Memory in a Modern American Place*, that the seemingly "traditional" Southern California aesthetic arose only in the early twentieth century, when Anglo residents recast the region's Mexican past as a nostalgic golden age. In recent years, the community study itself has been reborn, with the community understood not only as a site of working-class culture but also as a site of popular culture. Laurie Green's study of Memphis, *Battling the Plantation Mentality* (2007), for example, emphasizes youth culture, movies, radio, and what she calls "the struggle for a new public sphere," a culturally inflected politicized space that involves struggles for identity and civil rights.

The focus on place has given rise to its opposite: an emphasis on movement and the interactions of previously distant peoples, ideas, and commodities that mix up and transform places and cultures. Scholars have examined in different ways and for different eras the ways in which modernity has transformed time and space by conquering distance through technology, migrations, and an infrastructure of print and commerce. This focus on encounters, diasporas, empire, borderlands, and transnationalism marks a change from the community-based model of social history and from the sometimes placeless discourse analysis characteristic of an earlier generation of cultural history. Becky Nicolaides's charge—aimed particularly at labor historians—that they have "abandon[ed] the community perspective," has been remedied in part by the efforts of historians to follow migrations through space. Historians have accessed these foci through a series of approaches and sources, including print culture, medical discourse, legislative debates, and military communication. In addition, by showing the characteristic collapsing of time and space in the modern world, they have emphasized that diasporas are often the most effective framing for local histories. Diasporic histories take the movement of peoples and commodities as the basis for their cultural investigations. Stephanie Smallwood's study of the middle passage, *Saltwater Slavery* (2007), shows that the history of diasporas can at the same time be attuned to place. Smallwood follows 300,000 captives taken from what is now Ghana between 1675 and 1725 to "widening circles of the diaspora in the Americas."

The emphasis on movement and the global constitution of places has also encouraged American cultural historians to look beyond the nation-state as a natural, necessary, or useful boundary. In her study of consumer culture on the Mexican-American border, *Land of Necessity* (2009), Alexis McCrossen has shown that such "zones of contact" are an important node in cultural history and that understanding commerce in these regions requires understanding of state policy, economic conditions, and marketing advances on both sides of the border. McCrossen reminds us, as Lhamon points out in *Raising Cane*, that marketplaces, far from being stable, are "edgy areas, contact zones between cultures." In *Coyote Nation* (2006), Pablo Mitchell argues that examination of race relations among Native

Americans, those of Mexican descent, and Euro-Americans is better compared with an American colony, Puerto Rico, than with other parts of the West. In *Buffalo Bill's America* (2005) and *Satchmo Blows Up the World* (2004), Louis Warren and Penny M. Von Eschen examine American performers abroad in two different eras in order to shed light on how popular culture ties into the process of commercial and diplomatic expansion. Similarly, many studies of Americanization, such as Uta G. Poiger's, *Jazz, Rock, and Rebels* (2000), which focuses on Germany, and Victoria de Grazia's *Irresistible Empire* (2005), on the ways in which the United States altered Europe's business practices and mass culture, while not strictly U.S. history, should be considered part of the study of transnational American culture. Finally, Kristin Hoganson's *Consumers' Imperium* (2007), on the "global production of American domesticity," shows that Americans often "staged the world" in their households through foreign fashions and furnishings, including "Turkish curtains, French styles of furniture and knick-nacks from around the globe."

Cultural historians, following scholars of various borderlands regions, have embraced the concept of what Pekka Hämäläinen in *The Comanche Empire* (2008) calls "cultural interpenetration." Such a view takes into account the movement of "goods, ideas and people across ecological, ethnic and political boundaries." Native American historians, in particular, have encouraged scholars to examine this process as imperial in nature. For Hämäläinen, this not only was a two-way process but, for a time, constituted a "reverse empire," characterized by Indian "expansion, resistance, conquest, and loss, but with a reversal of usual historical roles." By incorporating empire into borderlands history, scholars have also made clear that imperialism should not be limited to, say, the Spanish-American War and its aftermath, too often seen, as Paul A. Kramer writes in *The Blood of Government* (2006), as one of "a set of exceptional and unrepeatable events in a distant past."

One growth area closely related to the concern about place is sensory history, especially work on how the senses can be tricked in an urbanizing, industrializing society, in which anonymity reigned and sites of production were increasingly separated from sites of consumption. James Cook has highlighted "the chronic semiotic confusion sparked by rapid demographic mobility, market expansion, and urbanization across the nineteenth century: a brave new world in which traditional systems of visual identification (based, for example, on dress or bodily comportment) no longer seemed to signify in consistent and reliable ways." Cook notes that the "perceptual challenges of reading the city" is a major theme in recent U.S. history. In *The Arts of Deception* (2001), on "playing with fraud in the Age of Barnum," Cook wonderfully captures the concern with the relationship between representation and reality in popular and visual culture in the nineteenth century. Building on Cook's concept of playful deception, Warren in *Buffalo Bill's America* (2006) has examined a similar development in the Wild West Show, which was designed to foster rather than repress curiosity about the line between authenticity and artifice. Indeed, many of the historians of capitalism mentioned previously focus on precisely these concerns, highlighting the search for semiotic markers that would help citizens interpret the codes of a market culture. My own book, *Buying Power* (2009), argues that consumer activists encouraged Americans to distrust their instincts, since the fine looks of a prettily packaged good might often hide the exploitation that led to its production. Consumer activists also emphasized what I call "long distance solidarity," the idea that consumers could aid distant people whom they never encountered through the nexus of print and commerce.

Closely related to the history of the senses, two other emerging branches of cultural history include the history of emotions and sensibility, especially as they relate to social and political life. Mark M. Smith's examination of the "visceral, emotional aspect of racial construction and racism" in *How Race Is Made* (2006) provides a good example of the ways in which "manufactured sensory stereotypes" can have concrete manifestations. "Emotions are a slippery topic," admits Nicole Eustace. Yet she, as she demonstrated in *Passion Is the Gale* (2008), the expression of emotions is also an exercise in public power. Wealthy Pennsylvanians complained about the unbridled passions of Native Americans and those in the lower orders, while priding themselves on their ability to constrain their emotions. At the same time, they praised the emotion of sympathy. This latter point brings us back to place and is especially important for scholars of the late eighteenth and early nineteenth centuries, who highlight the era's concern with finding the social glue that could unite a far-flung country. Scholars of the late nineteenth and twentieth centuries continue this line of questioning and extend it to a nascent empire. According to Jose Torre in *The Political Economy of Sentiment* (2007), insecure individuals in a growing market economy sought refuge in the idea of good feelings toward others, as a way of limiting self-seeking behavior. Similarly in *Sensibility and the American Revolution* (2009), Sarah Knott shows how the celebration of the human capacity for sympathy—"fellow feeling"—helps explain the course of the American Revolution.

The search for "ballast" has also taken another form, which perhaps has less to do with method than with temperament: namely, a seeking of a middle ground between familiar binaries, such as top down and bottom up, accommodation and resistance, local and global, agency and oppression. If cultural history has become more eclectic in its use of sources and theories, and more focused on inter-relationships between culture and political economy, it has also become more suspicious of metanarratives. Walter Johnson's critique of the concept of agency, which he calls "the master trope of the New Social History," offers one example of this temperament. Claiming that the "humanity/agency circuit formulates enslaved people's actions in much too abstract a manner" and conflates activity with "resistance," Johnson reinforces cultural history's increased materialism and also its complication of the meaning of politics. A book that would seem to work around this problem, Daniel R. Mandell's *Tribe, Race, and History* (2008), narrates the story of the Native Americans of southern New England neither as tragedy nor as a story of heroism. Instead, Mandell emphasizes the persistence of Native American culture as part of a blending process involving whites and African Americans. Another work in this vein is Phillip Deloria's *Indians in Unexpected Places* (2004), which argues that Native Americans "engaged the same forces of modernization that were making non-Indians reevaluate their own expectation of themselves and their society." Deloria's analysis of the inter-relationship between Indians and popular culture points to a bidirectionality, without in any way underestimating the overwhelming power of American colonialism. Erica Bsumek's *Indian-Made* (2008) on the production, advertising and sales of Navajo arts and crafts similarly captures "the complexity of the marketplace and the ubiquity of culture."

As several of the preceding comments suggest, history's cultural turn has been inextricably connected with a redefinition of politics. This has been a two-way process in which the cultural has been seen as political and in which politics has been addressed as a cultural category. Writing of the American, French, and English political upheavals, Leora Auslander in *Cultural Revolutions* (2009) writes that "radical cultural transformations emerged as instruments of political revolution, and together they challenge us to rethink the place of culture and emotion in the political." Such a trend has been particularly noticeable in the area of consumer history. T. H. Breen's *The Marketplace of Revolution* (2004) draws on Albert Hirschman's conception of the "public citizen who slumbers within the private consumer" to show how boycotts of British goods forged a new imagined community made up of formerly "distant strangers" who resided throughout the Atlantic coast of Britain's North American empire.

Historians have connected culture not only to revolutions, but also to quotidian forms of politics. In *The Big Vote* (2004), Liette Gidlow examines "Get Out the Vote" campaigns in the 1920s, placing them in the context both of the nascent business of marketing research and the efforts of women and African Americans to carve out a new place for themselves in the public sphere. At the same time, she shows how the "civic" became something of a synonym for the white middle class. Outside of the electoral arena, cultural historians have also sought to redefine the meaning of politics, largely by showing the role of culture in the operations of power in all its manifestations. Jackson Lears's *Rebirth of a Nation* (2009), for example, connects an elite longing for regeneration—born of fears of the lower classes, of a new consumerist effeteness, and of the immigration wave that was transforming "Anglo-Saxon" society—not only to the culture of the Gilded Age, but also to a martial spirit that culminated in America's nascent emergence as a military-industrial power. A similar approach for a more recent period can be found in Alan Petigny's *The Permissive Society* (2009), in which cultural matters such as a more relaxed style of child rearing, the rising status of women both inside and outside the home, the increasing reluctance of Americans to regard alcoholism as a sin, loosening sexual attitudes, the increasing influence of modern psychology, and the declining influence of religion in the personal lives of most Americans inform the book's political analysis. In Petigny's interpretation, cultural matters are political not only on their own terms, but also because they in part shape political discourses and practices. In *Dancing in the Street*, Suzanne E. Smith reconstructs various levels of African-American cultural politics, "which took many forms in Detroit," as journalists, poets, musicians, recording studios, and churches "all worked to promote the talents and to articulate the needs of the black community." This cultural "infrastructure" provided a base for grassroots and electoral politics, the preservation of black history, the celebration of black art, and unionization efforts. Along these lines, in *Black Culture and the New Deal* (2009), Lauren Rebecca Sklaroff argues that a struggle for the recognition and dissemination of African-American cultural productions in the Depression era played a key role in the long civil rights movement.

In addition to internal developments and expansions, cultural history has grown in two significant external directions. Many practitioners of other branches of historical inquiry have taken the "cultural turn." Fields that were previously contrasted with cultural history have become far more culturalist in their approach. For example, many histories of U.S. foreign policy and politics routinely offer cultural interpretations, marking a sharp break with their traditional approach. In the early 2000s, Liette Gidlow argued that "political historians have generally dismissed the cultural turn as lightweight at best, fundamentally misguided at worst, with the result that U.S. political history, in particular the new political history, remains largely untouched by these important intellectual developments." Not that long ago, noted Byron A. Shafer and Anthony J. Badger in 2001, a sense of separation and an implicit division of labor dominated in which cultural historians were "more likely to talk about washing machines and cinema than elections and public policy" and political historians were likely to consider the latter but not the former. Their suggestion that these cultural topics reflect a cultural bias to the exclusion of politics is evocative of the criticism a decade or so earlier of the pioneering cultural historian, Warren Susman, for his comment in *Culture as History* (1984) that it might be more important to understand Mickey Mouse than Franklin Roosevelt in explaining the Depression decade. By this time, however, a growing number of historians were rejecting the separation between culture and politics. Shafer and Badger recognized that there is a search for "political history in unusual places," and David Waldstreicher, a pioneering scholar of political culture, claimed that cultural and political approaches should not be seen as "mutually exclusive." Evidence of this transformation can be found in Bruce Kuklick's recent survey text, *A Political History of the USA* (2009), which treats cultural politics and cultural imperialism as integral aspects of U.S. history.

In recent years, topics that were out of fashion a generation ago, including the United States and the world and religious history, have reemerged as seeming threats to the hegemony of cultural history. Especially since the terrorist attacks of September 11, 2001, interest in these themes has been driven in large measure by current concerns, particularly the belief that it is essential to understand America's foreign policy, diplomacy, and military actions in historical perspective, and the realization that religious motivations can be as important a force in world history as economics and politics. In 2009 religious history surpassed cultural history, which had been the most popular subject category among members of the American Historical Association since the mid-1990s, as the most popular specialization. For a time, diplomatic history seemed moribund. But United States and the world is now a leading growth field.

But diplomatic history, once considered the antithesis of cultural history in sources, methods, and approaches, now absorbs it. Building on the pioneering work of Emily Rosenberg, an increasing number of scholars in diplomatic history have examined what David Zietsma has called "the powerful role of culture in structuring U.S. approaches to the world." In an innovative article on the "foreign policy of the calorie," Nick Cullather has applied cultural analysis to the science of development in international relations. Wayne Lee's recent overview of military history shows that issues first raised by cultural historians—including discourse analysis and memory—have moved to the forefront of analysis. One example of such an approach is David Serlin's examination of how U.S. military culture "has exploited and reinforced conceptions of both heteronormative masculinity and able-bodiedness from the late eighteenth century through the mid-1940s." Using military records in much the same way that Pascoe used legal materials, Serlin explores the ways in which the army constructed norms of masculinity and disability.

These trends challenge the conventional view that cultural history is the enemy and opposite of military/political history both in subject matter and approach. Patricia Cohen's 2009 study of history courses in the *New York Times* claimed that cultural history that offered "bottom up history" and "fresh subjects" had supplanted "traditional specialties like economic, military and constitutional history." According to Cohen, scholars in these fields, in contrast to cultural history, "generally work from the top down, diving into official archives and concentrating on people in power, an approach often tagged as elitist and old-fashioned." Trends in American history over the last two decades have made such binaries obsolete, since both cultural history and traditional specialities come in top-down and bottom-up forms. The same is true of dividing lines between cultural history and other fields. If the diffusion has gone in both directions, there is no question that culturalists have provided the spark for the majority of historiographical innovations over the last decades. This has been cultural history's blessing and its curse, since the gains have concomitantly reduced the field's uniqueness. All in all, however, the diffusion of the cultural turn in U.S. history has been one of the signal triumphs of recent historiography.

BIBLIOGRAPHY

Alvarez, Luis. *The Power of the Zoot: Youth Culture and Resistance during World War II*. Berkeley: University of California Press, 2008.

Appleby, Joyce. *The Relentless Revolution: A History of Capitalism*. New York: W. W. Norton, 2010.

Auslander, Leora. *Cultural Revolutions: Everyday Life and Politics in Britain, North America, and France*. Berkeley: University of California Press, 2009.

Avila, Eric. *Popular Culture in the Age of White Flight: Fear and Fantasy in Suburban Los Angeles*. Berkeley: University of California Press, 2004.

Axelrod, Jeremiah B. C. *Inventing Autopia: Dreams and Visions of the Modern Metropolis in Jazz Age Los Angeles*. Berkeley: University of California Press, 2009.

Badger, Tony, and Byron Shafer. *Contesting Democracy: The Substance and Structure of American Political History*. Lawrence, KS: University of Kansas Press, 2002.

Baldwin, Davarian. *Chicago's New Negroes: Modernity, the Great Migration, and Black Urban Life*. Chapel Hill: University of North Carolina Press, 2007.

Bender, Thomas. ed. *Rethinking American History in a Global Age*. Berkeley: University of California Press, 2002.

Blight, David W. *Race and Reunion: The Civil War in American Memory*. Cambridge, MA: Harvard University Press, 2001.

Blum, Edward J. *Reforging the White Republic: Race, Religion, and American Nationalism, 1865–1898*. Baton Rouge: Louisiana State University Press, 2007.

Bradley, Patricia. *Making American Culture: A Social History, 1900–1920*. New York: Palgrave MacMillan, 2009.

Breen, T. H. *The Marketplace of Revolution: How Consumer Politics Shaped American Independence*. New York: Oxford University Press, 2004.

Brick, Howard. *Transcending Capitalism: Visions of a New Society in Modern American Thought*. Ithaca, NY: Cornell University Press, 2006.

Brooks, James F. *Captives and Cousins: Slavery, Kinship, and Community in the Southwest Borderlands*. Chapel Hill: University of North Carolina Press, 2002.

Brown, Vincent. *The Reaper's Garden: Death and Power in the World of Atlantic Slavery*. Cambridge, MA: Harvard University Press, 2008.

Brundage, Fitzhugh, ed. *Where These Memories Grow: History, Memory, and Southern Identity*. Chapel Hill: University of North Carolina Press, 2000.

Bsumek, Erika Marie. *Indian-Made: Navajo Culture in the Marketplace, 1868–1940*. Lawrence: University Press of Kansas, 2008.

Burgos, Adrian, Jr. *Playing America's Game: Baseball, Latinos, and the Color Line*. Berkeley: University of California Press, 2007.

Canaday, Margot. *The Straight State: Sexuality and Citizenship in Twentieth-Century America*. Princeton, NJ: Princeton University Press, 2009.

Cawelti, John G. *Adventure, Mystery, and Romance: Formula Stories as Art and Popular Culture*. Chicago: University of Chicago Press, 1976.

Cohen, Patricia. "Great Caesar's Ghost! Are Traditional History Courses Vanishing?" *New York Times*, June, 10, 2009.

Cook, James W. *The Arts of Deception: Playing with Fraud in the Age of Barnum*. Cambridge, MA: Harvard University Press, 2001.

Cook, James W., and Lawrence B. Glickman. "Twelve Propositions for a History of U.S. Cultural History." In James W. Cook, Lawrence B. Glickman, and

Michael O'Malley, eds. *The Cultural Turn in U.S. History: Past, Present, and Future*, 3–57. Chicago: University of Chicago Press, 2008.
Cook, James W., Lawrence B. Glickman, and Michael O'Malley, eds. *The Cultural Turn in U.S. History: Past, Present, and Future.* Chicago: University of Chicago Press, 2008.
Cott, Nancy F. *Public Vows: A History of Marriage and the Nation.* Cambridge, MA: Harvard University Press, 2001.
Cullather, Nick. "The Foreign Policy of the Calorie." *American Historical Review* 112 (April 2007): 337–364.
Davis, Rebecca L. *More Perfect Unions: The American Search for Marital Bliss.* Cambridge, MA: Harvard University Press, 2010.
de Grazia, Victoria. *Irresistible Empire: America's Advance through Twentieth-Century Europe.* Cambridge, MA: Belknap/Harvard University Press, 2005.
Deloria, Philip J. *Indians in Unexpected Places.* Lawrence: University Press of Kansas, 2004.
Deverell, William. *Whitewashed Adobe: The Rise of Los Angeles and the Remaking of Its Mexican Past.* Berkeley: University of California Press, 2004.
Dickstein, Morris. *Dancing in the Dark: A Cultural History of the Great Depression.* New York: W. W. Norton, 2009.
Eley, Geoff. *A Crooked Line: From Cultural History to the History of Society.* Ann Arbor: University of Michigan Press, 2005.
Eustace, Nicole. *Passion Is the Gale: Emotion, Power, and the Coming of the American Revolution.* Chapel Hill: University of North Carolina Press, 2008.
Fahs, Alice. *The Imagined Civil War: Popular Literature of the North and South, 1861–1865.* Chapel Hill: University of North Carolina Press, 2001.
Faust, Drew Gilpin. *This Republic of Suffering: Death and the American Civil War.* Cambridge, MA: Harvard University Press, 2008.
Feimster, Crystal N. *Southern Horrors: Women and the Politics of Rape and Lynching.* Cambridge, MA: Harvard University Press, 2010.
Foucault, Michel. *The History of Sexuality: An Introduction.* New York: Vintage, 1990.
Geertz, Clifford. *The Interpretation of Cultures: Selected Essays.* New York, Basic Books 1973.
Gidlow, Liette. *The Big Vote: Gender, Consumer Culture, and the Politics of Exclusion, 1890s–1920s.* Baltimore: Johns Hopkins University Press, 2007.
———. "Delegitimizing Democracy: 'Civic Slackers,' the Cultural Turn, and the Possibilities of Politics." *Journal of American History* 89 (June 2002): 922–957.
Giggie, John M. *After Redemption: Jim Crow and the Transformation of African American Religion in the Delta, 1875–1915.* New York: Oxford University Press, 2007.
Glickman, Lawrence B. *Buying Power: A History of Consumer Activism in America.* Chicago: University of Chicago Press, 2009.
———. "The Impact of the Culture Concept on Social History." In Halttunen, *A Companion to American Cultural History*, 396–405.
Green, Laurie B. *Battling the Plantation Mentality: Memphis and the Black Freedom Struggle.* Chapel Hill: University of North Carolina Press, 2007.
Gutman, Herbert G. *Work, Culture, and Society in Industrializing America: Essays in American Working-Class and Social History.* New York: Vintage, 1976.

Halttunen, Karen, ed. *A Companion to American Cultural History*. Malden, MA: Blackwell, 2008.

Hämäläinen, Pekka. *The Comanche Empire*. New Haven, CT: Yale University Press, 2008.

Harvey, Paul, and Phillip Goff, eds. *Themes in Religion and American Culture*. Chapel Hill: University of North Carolina Press, 2004.

Hirschman, Albert O. *Shifting Involvements: Private Interest and Public Action*. Princeton NJ: Princeton University Press, 1982.

Hoffer, Peter Charles. *Sensory Worlds in Early America*. Baltimore: Johns Hopkins University Press, 2003.

Hoganson, Kristin. *Consumers' Imperium: The Global Production of American Domesticity, 1865–1920*. Chapel Hill: University of North Carolina Press, 2007.

Howard, Vicki. *Brides, Inc.: American Weddings and the Business of Tradition*. Philadelphia: University of Pennsylvania Press, 2008.

Igo, Sarah. *The Averaged American: Surveys, Citizens, and the Making of a Mass Public*. Cambridge, MA: Harvard University Press, 2007.

Iton, Richard. *In Search of the Black Fantastic: Politics and Popular Culture in the Post–Civil Rights Era*. New York: Oxford University Press, 2008.

Jacobson, Matthew Frye. *Roots Too: White Ethnic Revival in Post–Civil Rights America*. Cambridge, MA: Harvard University Press, 2006.

Jacoby, Karl. *Shadows at Dawn: A Borderlands Massacre and the Violence of History*. New York: Penguin, 2008.

Johnson, Paul E. *Sam Patch, the Famous Jumper*. New York: Hill and Wang, 2003.

Johnson, Walter. "On Agency." *Journal of Social History* 37 (2003): 113–124.

Kamensky, Jane. *The Exchange Artist: A Tale of High-Flying Speculation and America's First Banking Collapse*. New York, Viking, 2008.

Kaye, Anthony G. *Joining Places: Slave Neighborhoods in the Old South*. Chapel Hill: University of North Carolina Press, 2007.

Klingle, Matthew W. "Spaces of Consumption in Environmental History." *History and Theory* 42 (December 2003): 94–110.

Knott, Sarah. *Sensibility and the American Revolution*. Chapel Hill: University of North Carolina Press, 2009.

Kolb, William. "The Cultural Approach to History" (Review). *American Sociological Review* 7 (February 1942): 122–125.

Kramer, Paul A. *The Blood of Government: Race, Empire, the United States, and the Philippines*. Chapel Hill: University of North Carolina Press, 2006.

Kropp, Phoebe S. *California Vieja: Culture and Memory in a Modern American Place*. Berkeley: University of California Press, 2006.

Kuklick, Bruce. *A Political History of the USA: One Nation under God*. New York: Palgrave Macmillan, 2009.

Kuznick, Peter J., and James Gilbert, eds. *Rethinking Cold War Culture*. Washington, DC: Smithsonian Institution Press, 2001.

La Chapelle, Peter. *Proud to Be an Okie: Cultural Politics, Country Music, and Migration to Southern California*. Berkeley: University of California Press, 2007.

Landsberg, Alison. *Prosthetic Memory: The Transformation of American Remembrance in the Age of Mass Culture*. New York: Columbia University Press, 2004.

Lears, Jackson. *Rebirth of a Nation: The Making of Modern America, 1877–1920*. New York: Harper, 2009.

Lee, Wayne E. "Mind and Matter—Cultural Analysis in American Military History: A Look at the State of the Field." *Journal of American History* 93 (March 2007): 1116–1142.

Lhamon, W. H. *Raising Cain: Blackface Performance from Jim Crow to Hip Hop.* Cambridge, MA: Harvard University Press, 2000.

Lim, Shirley Jennifer. *A Feeling of Belonging: Asian American Women's Public Culture, 1930–1960.* New York: New York University Press, 2006.

Lyotard, Jean-Francois. *The Postmodern Condition: A Report on Knowledge.* Minneapolis: University of Minnesota Press, 1984.

Mandell, Daniel R. *Tribe, Race, History: Native Americans in Southern New England, 1780–1880.* Baltimore: Johns Hopkins University Press, 2008.

McCrossen, Alexis, ed. *Land of Necessity: Consumer Culture in the United States-Mexico Borderlands.* Durham NC: Duke University Press, 2009.

Meyerowitz, Joanne. *How Sex Changed: A History of Transsexuality in the United States.* Cambridge, MA: Harvard University Press, 2002.

Mihm, Stephen. *A Nation of Counterfeiters: Capitalists, Con Men, and the Making of the United States.* Cambridge, MA: Harvard University Press, 2008.

Moreton, Bethany. *To Serve God and Wal-Mart: The Making of Christian Free Enterprise.* Cambridge, MA: Harvard University Press, 2009.

Ngai, Mai M. *Impossible Subjects: Illegal Aliens and the Making of Modern America.* Princeton, NJ: Princeton University Press, 2004.

Nicolaides, Becky M. *My Blue Heaven: Life and Politics in the Working-Class Suburbs of Los Angeles, 1920–1965.* Chicago: University of Chicago Press, 2002.

Ninkovich, Frank A., and Liping Bu. *The Cultural Turn: Essays in the History of U.S. Foreign Relations.* Chicago: Imprint Publications, 2001.

Nye, Russell B. *The Unembarrassed Muse: The Popular Arts in America.* New York: Dial Press, 1970.

Ogbar, Jeffrey O. G. *Hip-Hop Revolution: The Culture and Politics of Rap.* Lawrence: University Press of Kansas, 2009.

Pascoe, Peggy. *What Comes Naturally: Miscegenation Law and the Making of Race in America.* New York: Oxford University Press, 2008.

Pells, Richard. "History Descending a Staircase: American Historians and American Culture." *Chronicle of Higher Education*, August 3, 2007, B6.

Petigny, Alan. *The Permissive Society: America, 1941–1965.* New York: Cambridge University Press, 2009.

Renda, Mary. *Taking Haiti: Military Occupation and the Culture of US Imperialism, 1915–1940.* Chapel Hill: University of North Carolina Press, 2001.

Rosenberg, Emily S. "Turning to Culture." In Gilbert M. Joseph, Catherine C. LeGrand, and Ricardo D. Salvatore, eds., *Close Encounters of Empire: Writing the Cultural History of U.S.–Latin American Relations*, 497–514. Durham, NC: Duke University Press, 1998.

Rozario, Kevin. *The Culture of Calamity: Disaster and the Making of Modern America.* Chicago: University Of Chicago Press, 2007.

Sandage, Scott A. *Born Losers: A History of Failure in America.* Cambridge, MA: Harvard University Press, 2008.

Sandweiss, Martha. *Passing Strange: A Gilded Age Tale of Love and Deception across the Color Line.* New York: Penguin, 2009.

Savage, Kirk. *Monument Wars: Washington, D.C., the National Mall, and the Transformation of the Memorial Landscape.* Berkeley: University of California Press, 2009.

Serlin, David. "Crippling Masculinity: Queerness and Disability in U.S. Military Culture, 1800–1945." *GLQ: A Journal of Lesbian and Gay Studies* 9 (2003): 149–179.

Shah, Nayan. *Contagious Divides: Epidemics and Race in San Francisco's Chinatown*. Berkeley: University of California Press, 2001.

Silverman, Kenneth. *A Cultural History of the American Revolution: Painting, Music, Literature, and the Theatre in the Colonies and the United States from the Treaty of Paris to the Inauguration of George Washington, 1763–1789*. New York: T. Y. Crowell, 1976.

Simon, Bryant. *Everything but the Coffee: Learning about America from Starbucks*. Berkeley: University of California Press, 2009.

Singh, Nikhil Pal. *Black Is a Country: Race and the Unfinished Struggle for Democracy*. Cambridge, MA: Harvard University Press, 2005.

Sklansky, Jeffrey. *The Soul's Economy: Market Society and Selfhood in American Thought, 1820–1920*. Chapel Hill: University of North Carolina Press, 2002.

Sklaroff, Lauren Rebecca. *Black Culture and the New Deal: The Quest for Civil Rights in the Roosevelt Era*. Chapel Hill: University of North Carolina Press, 2009.

Smallwood, Stephanie. *Saltwater Slavery: A Middle Passage from Africa to American Diaspora*. Cambridge, MA: Harvard University Press, 2007.

Smith, Henry Nash. *Virgin Land: The American West as Symbol and Myth*. Cambridge, MA, Harvard University Press, 1950.

Smith, Mark M. *How Race Is Made: Slavery, Segregation, and the Senses*. Chapel Hill: University of North Carolina Press, 2006.

———. *Sensing the Past: Seeing, Hearing, Smelling, Tasting, and Touching in History*. Berkeley: University of California Press, 2008.

Smith, Suzanne E. *Dancing in the Street: Motown and the Cultural Politics of Detroit*. Cambridge, MA: Harvard University Press, 1999.

Steigerwald, David. "All Hail the Republic of Choice: Consumer History as Contemporary Thought." *Journal of American History* 93 (September 2006): 385–403.

———. *Culture's Vanities: the Paradox of Cultural Diversity in a Globalized World*. Lanham, MD: Rowman and Littlefield, 2004.

Stott, Richard. *Jolly Fellows: Male Milieus in Nineteenth-Century America*. Baltimore: Johns Hopkins University Press, 2009.

Streeby, Shelley. *American Sensations: Class, Empire, and the Production of Popular Culture*. Berkeley: University of California Press, 2002.

Sturken, Marita. *Tourists of History: Memory, Kitsch, and Consumerism from Oklahoma City to Ground Zero*. Durham, NC: Duke University Press, 2007.

Suisman, David. *Selling Sounds: The Commercial Revolution in American Music*. Cambridge, MA: Harvard University Press, 2009.

Susman, Warren. *Culture as History: The Transformation of American Society in the Twentieth Century*. New York: Pantheon Books, 1985.

Torre, Jose R. *The Political Economy of Sentiment:Paper Credit and the Scottish Enlightenment in Early Republic Boston, 1780–1820*. London: Pickering and Chatto, 2006.

Vernon, James. "What Is a Cultural History of Politics?" *History Workshop Journal* 52 (Autumn 2001): 261–265.

Von Eschen, Penny M. *Satchmo Blows Up the World: Jazz Ambassadors Play the Cold War*. Cambridge, MA: Harvard University Press, 2004.

Ware, Caroline F., ed. *The Cultural Approach to History*. New York: Columbia University Press, 1940.

Warren, Louis. *Buffalo Bill's America: William Cody and the Wild West Show*. New York: Knopf, 2005.

White, Richard. "From Wilderness to Hybrid Landscapes: The Cultural Turn in Environmental History." *Historian* 66 (2004): 557–564.

Wickberg, Daniel. "Heterosexual White Male: Some Recent Inversions in American Cultural History." *Journal of American History* 92 (2005): 136–157.

Zakim, Michael. *Ready-Made Democracy: A History of Men's Dress in the American Republic, 1760–1860*. Chicago: University of Chicago Press, 2003.

Zietsma, David. "Building the Kingdom of God: Religious Discourse, National Identity, and the Good Neighbor Policy, 1930–1938." *Rhetoric and Public Affairs* 11 (Summer 2008).

11
American Religion

JOHN T. McGREEVY

That more historians now identify themselves as historians of religion than as social historians, cultural historians, or even political historians qualifies as an unanticipated episode in the sociology of the discipline. The number of historians in the past eighteen years willing to type "religion" next to their name when queried by the American Historical Association has doubled. Forty percent of these historians work in North American history.

Just skimming the titles pouring out from the best university and trade presses, let alone reading the acknowledgments, or even, dare I say, the occasional book, exhilarates those toiling in the religious history vineyard and produces dread for the writer of the historiographical essay. Smart journals such as *Religion and American Culture* and the *Journal of Southern Religion* are thriving, in print and online. Blogs such as Religion in American History, moderated by Paul Harvey and at http://usreligion.blogspot.com/, steer the scholarly conversation. Books on religious topics—by Christine Heyrman, George Marsden, Erskine Clarke, and others—triumph in once inaccessible prize competitions.

The task of summarizing this work seemed more manageable even a decade ago when Jon Butler rightly lamented the inability of modern American historians, particularly those working in the period after 1865, to conceptualize theirs as a religious nation. But more American historians now do so conceptualize their nation. Why this is so—the triumph of cultural history, the importance of religion in the contemporary world, dismay at the emergence of "red-state" America—is not obvious, and may also reflect professional imperatives, with historians of the United States catching up to historians of Europe and Latin America, where books about priests, miracles, and revivals have shaped main historiographical currents for the past thirty years.

The sheer sprawl of the field—from formal doctrine to lived experience, from Native Americans encountering Jesuit missionaries in the seventeenth century to evangelicals recruiting Guatemalan Christians to work at Wal-Mart—defies easy summary. And summary becomes even more challenging when you add to conventional history the excellent work done in once sleepy allied areas of inquiry such as religion and sociology, religion and literature, religion and film, religion and photography, religion and architecture, religion and music, and religion and American art. (This last subject now includes major books by Sally Promey and David Morgan on topics as diverse as John Singer Sargent's portraits and mass distributed religious images.)

The term "field" may in fact be a misnomer. Fields mean coverage, certainly, but at a practical level fields are defined by arguments as much as by the day-to-day trudge of the survey course. And in American religious history courses, and the scholarly literature upon which they rest, arguments are elusive. This absence of historiographical dispute makes it difficult to orient newcomers, to identify where one author vigorously disputes the claim of another. Patrick Allitt and Thomas Paterson's helpful compilation—*Major Problems in American Religious History*—is in this sense mistitled. Allitt and Paterson dutifully listed topics—from European-Indian encounters to assimilation of religious groups after 1945—but the absence of scholarly disagreement made it difficult for Allitt to identify genuine historical problems.

Instead, the field's organizing principle is diversity. Precisely because the array of actors and goods in the religious marketplace is so vast, historians can find plenty of work without cultivating another's garden. If a fault line exists, and it has blurred over the past decade, it is methodological, between historians aiming to insert religion into the main narratives of American history and those less interested in those narratives and more attuned to the nuances of religious experience.

The leading figure of the second type remains Robert Orsi, whose *The Madonna of 115th Street* is, deservedly, the field's most influential monograph of the past quarter century. Orsi tapped into excitement among anthropologists (notably Clifford Geertz and William Christian) studying the role of religion in structuring the lives of the devout. Orsi then transferred these concerns from Indonesia and medieval Spain onto the streets of twentieth-century Manhattan. Sensitive, especially, to the ways in which power structured faith—the book began with an arresting description of a woman dragged down the main aisle of the church, tongue dragging on the ground—Orsi spun the religious experience of his Italian American subjects into a powerful meditation on the shifting contours of immigration, faith and family.

Orsi's second book, *Thank You, St. Jude*, studied devotees of the patron saint of hopeless causes on Chicago's South Side. Like *The Madonna of 115th Street*, it was elegantly composed and reached a wide audience. Each book required considerable archival research, but much of the most compelling evidence came from interviews. (For the St. Jude project, Orsi established an 800 number in order to facilitate these conversations.)

More recently, Orsi has published a stimulating collection of essays on method, urging scholars not to judge certain religious practices as good or bad, mature or infantile. Better simply to "understand particular religious ways of living and thinking." Sensible advice, certainly, although Orsi's own influence, as well as that of other ethnographers with whom he can claim scholarly kinship, does not make it a daring strike against orthodoxy. Still, Orsi's willingness to move between theory and ethnographic and archival evidence distinguishes him from less adventurous colleagues, and his influence extends across the field, from David Hall's "Lived Religion" project to recent work on Latino/a religion.

The same impulse to better understand religious experience is also evident in Ann Taves's remarkable dual history of nineteenth-century religious enthusiasms and the modern scholarly study of those same enthusiasms, a topic that takes her from Methodist camp meetings to Emile Durkheim and William James. Even more directly in this line is Marie Griffith's examination of contemporary Pentecostal women in the Women's Aglow Fellowship, as they tack back and forth between biblical texts urging submissiveness and their own experience in relationships, family life, and the workforce.

That work focusing on religious experience will continue, perhaps even accelerate, over the next decade seems clear. At the same time, political theorists and philosophers, not anthropologists, may push the field in a new direction. Charles Taylor's *Sources of the Self* inspired some historians with an interest in American religion a decade ago, notably those, such as James Kloppenberg, pondering the meaning of republicanism in the American context. More recently, Taylor authored a short study of William James. But it is Taylor's *A Secular Age* that has become the twenty-first century's most talked about book in religious studies. Taylor's argument, developed over 776 intermittently brilliant but meandering pages, cannot be condensed here. His central claim can: we have moved from "a society in which belief in God is unchallenged and indeed unproblematic, to one in which it is understood to be one option among others, and frequently not the easiest option."

Taylor's title, *A Secular Age*, itself challenges historians of American religion. Determined to present their topic in its most alluring light, they have skirted ways in which the American experience of religion and secularization is one variant on the North Atlantic norm. Instead they have emphasized an American religious exceptionalism, a conviction that American religiosity defies Weberian predictions of disenchantment in modern, industrial societies. Two editors (Micklethwait and Wooldridge) of *The Econo-*

mist—surveying religion across the globe—make this case in the baldest terms, describing a "European Way" or "the necessity of Atheism" and an American way where religion is "surviving the acids of modernity." And this American way, they maintain, is the norm, not the exception, when scholars take their eyes off Europe and pivot toward the global South.

The success of religion, especially evangelical and Pentecostal Christianity in the United States, is undoubtedly remarkable when compared to most of Europe and Japan. (China, by contrast, may have seen the most rapid growth of Christianity of any nation over the past thirty years.) The vibrancy of religion in the United States would also puzzle Max Weber. But Weber would not be surprised to discover, along with Taylor and recent public opinion surveys, that secularism, too, is thriving side by side with religion. Indeed, as Robert Putnam and David Campbell have explained, contemporary secularism flourishes in part *because* of American religiosity, as Americans annoyed or appalled by the religious right distance themselves from churches, ministers, and creeds.

The fastest-growing group within American society, after all, according to the Pew Religious Landscape Survey of 2008, is those claiming no affiliation with any church or religious tradition, a full 16.1 percent of the population, more than double twenty years ago. These Americans may in fact be religious, but they are certainly disengaged from traditional religious institutions. The number of mainline Protestants is steadily declining, and the number of evangelicals is at best steady. Fully one-third of American Catholics are lapsed, or at least not regular churchgoers, and one in ten American citizens is a lapsed Catholic. (Only high numbers of Catholic immigrants keep the total Catholic population from decreasing.) Europeans, Islamic and Christian, moreover, are also less secular than the quick contrast between a bursting megachurch in Colorado Springs and an empty cathedral in France might suggest.

One consequence, then, of historians emphasizing American religious exceptionalism has been an absence—studies of secularism and de-Christianization. The topic has not been entirely neglected. James Turner in his important *Without God, Without Creed* and Michael Buckley, S.J., working on a wider canvas, anticipated some of Taylor's claims about the emergence of unbelief. David Hollinger traced secularization within the university, as has, less admiringly, Christian Smith. Susan Jacoby has contributed an engaging if boosterish history of a surprisingly neglected topic, free thought, and Jon Butler transferred a rich tradition of European writing on magic and spirituality to American soil in his *Awash in a Sea of Faith*.

But in part because American historians have struggled to imagine a society simultaneously more secular and more religious, no American equivalents exist to Callum Brown's bracing *The Death of Christian Britain*, which posits secularization less as a process than an explosive shift in the 1950s and 1960s. The path forward may lie in the work of historians of American Jewish life, for whom Judaism—that is, active participation in a synagogue community—has long been a vital but still modest part of the Jewish experience. Jonathan Sarna has recently published an overview of Jewish history focusing on the religious end of this spectrum, while Andrew Heinze's examination of how Jews shaped popular psychology in the mid-twentieth century, as well as popular understandings of the good life for Jews and Christians, pushes toward broader interpretive questions. Lila Corwin Berman's *Speaking of Jews*, too, investigates the line between religious expression and a broader Jewish identity.

A second consequence of American religious exceptionalism is less obvious. Taylor's *A Secular Age* asks how faith has assimilated to and shaped modernity, primarily in its North Atlantic context. The nation-state plays a cameo role. Yet even as the study of United States history becomes more anchored in global history, a theme of every chapter in this volume, much of the best recent work on American religious history remains framed around questions of national identity.

Four recent books make the point. Mark Noll's magisterial *America's God* provides an incisive coda to the long-running debate over religion and republicanism, marching from Jonathan Edwards and the founders to Abraham Lincoln. Catherine Albanese's *A Republic of Mind and Spirit: A Cultural History of American Metaphysical Religion* knits together (at times improbably) Paracelsus, Mary Baker Eddy and Father Divine into a single-history "metaphysical religion," or the "evolution of the national religiosity." Richard Wightman Fox's *Jesus in America* offers a shrewd capsule history of "four centuries of Jesus in America; so many Christs, so many cultural incarnations." Leigh Schmidt's *Restless Souls* describes the making of "American spirituality."

Major achievements by major historians all, and navigating these surveys will preoccupy the next generation of scholars. The broad scope of all four books, in fact, indirectly recognizes the increasing sophistication of the monographic literature. But their shared emphasis on an American religion—often across denomination, time, and space—may have inadvertently had two other effects. The first is to deflect attention from the more precise question of the relationship of religion to the nation-state. Robert Bellah's essay on civil religion set off a torrent of commentary in the now distant antinationalist moment of the late 1960s, but never inspired detailed follow-up on how a religious sense of purpose shapes the consciousness of a people and the actions of its political leaders. Bogged down in polemics over whether the founders were or were not orthodox Christians, the relationship between religion and the early political history of the United States, for example, remains vexed. George McKenna's *The Puritan Origins of American Patriotism* is unconvincing in its architecture, but asks the right questions, attempting to sort out the ways in which religion, even a religious affection for the United States among disaffected radicals, has undergirded reaction and reform. Harry Stout's thoughtful (if at times unwieldy) *Upon the Altar of the Nation* is more encouraging, offering the most compelling account of a crucial moment in the link between religion and the nation-state, its "incarnation" on the battlefields of Antietam and Shiloh, and in the pulpits of the northern Protestant ministers who made the Union's cause their own.

More progress has been made on religion and constitutional questions. Scholars interested in the history of religious freedom have begun to trace the meaning of the "separation of church and state" beneath the level of legal platitude. Philip Hamburger's sweeping history of the nineteenth-century ideal of strict separation, a separation driven by anti-Catholicism, is compelling, if written in the mode of a legal brief. Sarah Barringer Gordon's shrewd history of anti-Mormon agitation in the late nineteenth century extends the history of Reconstruction and its egalitarian ethos into questions of religious freedom, and Tisa Wenger explores the meaning of religious freedom in a different key in her history of the Pueblo Indian Dance controversy of the 1920s.

A second effect of American religious exceptionalism may have been to obscure the emergence of a more global literature. This effect is surely temporary, since the transmission of religious ideas, objects, songs, and architectural drawings is more likely than most subjects to resist national frames. In fact, in each of these four survey texts, one can glimpse a global narrative unlocking itself from nationalist handcuffs. Noll followed *America's God* with a determinedly transnational study of theological opinion on the Civil War, and he has long argued for a global understanding of evangelicalism. (Noll's recent work is nicely complemented by Brooks Holifield's erudite history of theology in the antebellum United States, which effortlessly sets antebellum American theologians into contexts as diverse as English Deism and German Lutheran Pietism.) The most absorbing section of Albanese's study identifies the international crosscurrents shaping religion among such diverse actors as Puritans and Spanish missionaries in the Southwest. Fox's Jesus is American, yes, but a Jesus "in America" not wholly of it, shaped by Mexican immigrants along with Ralph Waldo Emerson. Schmidt's history of American spirituality is less capacious than its subtitle, more a probe into one species of liberal Protestantism and its offshoots than a survey of spirituality *tout court*, but even Schmidt is impressively attuned to the ways in which foreign imports, including yoga and Zen, blended with domestic spiritual traditions.

In retrospect, the massive fundamentalism project sponsored by the American Academy of Arts and Sciences served as a sophisticated example of comparative inquiry, even if its direct influence on the field is difficult to ascertain. Individual monographs—ranging from James Campbell's *Songs of Zion: The African Methodist Episcopal Church in the United States and South Africa*, Timothy Matovina's *Guadalupe and Her Faithful*, Thomas Tweed's *Our Lady of Exile*, to Jon Gjerde's *The Minds of the West*—offered models of tracing religious ideas and people across national borders. Gjerde, in particular, with his rich comparison of the religious meanings of migration and nationalism for Dutch Calvinists, Missouri Synod Lutherans, and German Catholics, opened up the history of an entire region, the Upper Midwest, with implications for issues as diverse as land tenure, state politics, and educational policy.

The deepest integration with events beyond the United States has occurred in the early modern period, as for American history more generally. Working under the rubric of the Atlantic World, and spurred by the obvious fact that crucial actors such as George Whitefield, Francis Asbury, and John Wesley worked on both sides of the Atlantic, a cluster of historians have recently connected their American history narratives to the long history of the Reformation and the subsequent Catholic and Protestant missionary effort.

George Marsden's Jonathan Edwards, for example, in contrast to Perry Miller's, is less a symbol of America than a minister of extraordinary ability on the periphery of the British Atlantic world, working with Indians in Stockbridge, awaiting the latest issue of *The Spectator* from London, and conversant with details of the pietistic revival in Germany. New England religion generally now seems less isolated than it once did, certainly by the eighteenth century, and more attuned, as Thomas Kidd outlines, to its allegiance to a British Empire and partisan role in a global struggle between Catholics and Protestants.

David Hempton's *Methodism: Empire of the Spirit* is at once the most old-fashioned and the most revealing of these projects. Hempton takes a fusty genre, the denominational history, and transforms it, making us see eighteenth- and nineteenth-century Methodism as less a part of American or English national histories than an independent force, pushed by John Wesley there, Francis Asbury here. Research in Methodist sources on six continents allows Hempton to flatly claim Methodism as the "most important Protestant religious development since the Reformation" and the forerunner of today's Pentecostalism. Reading Hempton places superb, influential studies such as Nathan Hatch's *The Democratization of American Christianity* and Christine Heyrman's *Southern Cross* in a more provincial light, forcing us to ask just what it was that held Methodism together, and what it was about the American context, in the South for Heyrman and across the nation for Hatch, that permitted it to flourish.

The international integration is perhaps even more vivid in a cluster of recent eighteenth-century case studies. John Fea's biography of Philip Vickers Fithian shows this New Jersey minister melding his Christian beliefs with the classical texts he first encountered as a student at Princeton, an example at ground level of what Henry May once described as the harmonious blend of Enlightenment thought and Christianity evident in the British colonies and then the new United States. Emily Clark's history of Ursuline nuns moving to New Orleans integrates her subjects into both the Spanish and French colonial empires, as well into an occasionally anti-Catholic early American republic. Thomas Slaughter's biography of John Woolman inserts the first American abolitionist into not just the history of slave emancipation, but also the longer narrative of Christian mysticism.

Three other eighteenth-century studies depend upon both missionary documents and ethnographic evidence, providing new analyses, in an almost offhanded way, of the difficult question of how to assess the agency of Native Americans and African Americans in the formation of new Christian communities. Allen Greer's *Mohawk Saint* demonstrates how European theological ideas played out in confrontations with Mohawk and Algonquian understandings of the sacred. Jon Sensbach's *Rebecca's Revival* sketches the life of one woman, Rebecca Protten, her conversion to Christianity, and her journey from slavery to a career as an evangelist in the British Caribbean and Europe. Rachel Wheeler compares the work of Moravian and Reformed missionaries in Connecticut and Massachusetts and, in so doing, reconstructs plausible origins for a distinctive Native American Christianity among the Mohicans.

The same global impulse is evident in at least two other subfields. The first is the history of Catholicism. Early-twentieth-century historians of Catholicism, usually priests and nuns, knew theirs was an international church, with direct ties to Roman authorities. Laypeople, especially women, appeared only in the margins of their narratives, organized around episcopal appointments made, churches founded, and schools begun. The next generation of scholars of Catholicism turned the topic around, focusing more on the laity (although still insufficiently on women) and pondering whether and how the American experience produced an American Catholicism.

Now, the current has again reversed, with Catholicism in the United States understood as one branch of the church universal. The international history of the Second Vatican Council, for example, the single most important religious event of the twentieth century, is as yet at the beginning stage, with John O'Malley's survey offering a clear, if contested, intellectual history, but one can imagine comparative studies tracing the effects of the council in various locales. Peter D'Agostino's beautifully researched transnational history of Italian immigrants, Vatican officials, and American bishops, all shifting their attention back and forth between Rome and America, set a new standard for integration. My own *Catholicism and American Freedom* attempted to insert Catholicism into American intellectual and political history. Recently, work by Michael Hochgeschwender, Stephen Schloesser, S.J., Florian Michel, Luca Condignola, Matteo Sanfilippo, Gerald McKevitt, and others on topics as diverse as the parish trustee controversies of the early nineteenth century, the Catholic response to antebellum slavery, Italian Jesuits in the Southwest, and the migration of French Catholic intellectuals to the United States in the 1930s and 1940s all rest upon a transatlantic frame. These scholars, unusually for American history, write in German, French, and Italian as well as English, and make use of Roman archives, shedding a more cosmopolitan light on what were once understood as strictly American dilemmas. Even old theological controversies, such as the modernist debate of the late nineteenth and early twentieth centuries, are newly illuminated when viewed from beyond the United States.

A second increasingly international subfield is eighteenth- and nineteenth-century African-American religious history. Oddly somnolent for much of the 1980s and 1990s, and still understudied, African-American religious history tagged onto and informed new work on slavery and its development in the United States. Sylvia Frey and Betty Wood's *Come Shouting to Zion* summarized the state of the field in a deceptively matter-of-fact way, emphasizing a gradual religious fusion of evangelical Christianity and African religious forms such as ecstatic performance into a new Christian blend, which in turn influenced Southern religion, black and white. Vincent Brown's intriguing history of death and burial in Jamaica shows white Christian missionaries competing with and eventually supplementing African traditions in the "mortuary politics" of an island famed for its high mortality rate. Death haunts Erskine Clarke's *Dwelling Place*, too, but only because Clarke's history of two antebellum families, one white, one black, is so attuned to the ways in which churches and beliefs organized the signal moments—from birth to marriage to death—of family life. His measured assessment of the ways in which religion for the masters channeled benevolent impulses into deep oppression, and religion for the slaves became part of both resistance and acculturation, is unusual in its ability to evoke the lived experience of all parties working out their destiny on the Georgia coast. James Bennett's study of gilded age New Orleans, and Paul Harvey's survey of southern religion, from slavery to civil rights, are also distinguished by this ability to think about whites and blacks in the South building a shared, if distinct, religious culture.

A third more internationalist literature—subfield is the wrong term since the authors would not consider themselves a cohort—includes scholars committed to demonstrating the international influence of their American subjects. Just as historians of the eighteenth century track European missionaries coming to the United States, an unexpected pleasure of recent work on religion in the United States is its alertness to opposite currents. Books by Steven Miller and James McCartin on topics as diverse as Billy Graham and Catholic piety sketch the work of American religious actors moving outside the United States. McCartin notes that some of the largest religious gatherings in the world, 600,000 in Caracas in 1968, even more in Manila a year later, were organized by the now forgotten American priest, Fr. Patrick Peyton, who founded the Catholic rosary crusade. Miller observes that in 1988 Billy Graham attracted a crowd of one million people in Seoul.

Grant Wacker's study of early Pentecostalism only touches on the role of Pentecostals outside the United States. And he, too, discusses influences from abroad such as the English "higher life" movement. But Wacker's ability to immerse his readers in the waters of early Pentecostalism, with vivid disputes on matters as diverse as raising tobacco and attending amusement parks, has the ring of a Pauline letter, a window onto the early days of an obscure sect in Kansas and Los Angeles, gathering steam before heading across the globe. More than anything else, early Pentecostal texts reveal a faith in personal autonomy—a "jut-jawed stress," in Wacker's phrasing, on personal and occupational mobility. Wacker is less certain that this stress led to economic prosperity, as is frequently claimed, but this focus on the individual must help explain Pentecostalism's power in a global South pockmarked by failed states and mass migrations. In 2000, demographers estimated that there were 525 million Pentecostals across the globe, the largest group of Christians outside of Roman Catholicism. This movement's origins—whether in the United States or, as suggested by David Martin and Ogbu Kalu, outside the United States as well—demands further study.

That much work in American religious history now takes an internationalist cast does not mean all work does, or even should. Three subfields, women and religion, Mormonism, and religion and politics, seem less driven by an international imperative. Women, after all, may become even less visible in a wider global frame likely to be dominated by institutions and prominent (male) religious leaders. In addition, historians of women long kept a measured distance from religious history, a distance occasionally reciprocated by their counterparts working on religious topics. Still, Ann Braude's provocative 1997 essay "Women's History *Is* American Religious History" challenged historians to place women at the center of the field, and a cluster of fine books on women and religion appeared over the past decade, with work on Catholic and evangelical women, surprisingly, in the vanguard. Catherine Brekus's important collection provides a snapshot of the field. Evelyn Brooks Higginbotham and Anthea Butler have established the centrality of women to African-American congregational life, and Jane Addams, as seen in Victoria Brown's biography, is now rightly understood as an important exemplar of liberal Protestant religious thought, not simply a Progressive reformer. Richard Fox's history of the Henry Ward Beecher adultery trial is notable for its ingenious structure, but also for its careful dissection of women's and men's piety in Gilded Age New York. Maureen Fitzgerald has demonstrated the importance of Catholic nuns for the American social welfare system, and Amy Koehlinger and Kathleen Cummings place nuns into the histories of both the turn-of-the-century "new woman" and the 1960s.

Given the topic's importance, surprisingly little scholarship has appeared on the allied subject of religion and sexuality, and we should anticipate more work on topics ranging from gay and lesbian religious communities, contemporary divides over gay marriage, and clergy sex abuse. An important exception to this generalization is Leslie Tentler's remarkable *Catholics and Contraception*, which despite its modest title, offers insights based on unusually rich sources for the history of how not just priests, but also married couples, thought about sex and family for a huge swath of the twentieth century. The best historical study of the contemporary struggle over abortion remains Cynthia Gorney's account of conflicts in St. Louis, where she adroitly knits together religious and secular, pro-choice and pro-life. Mathew Connelly's global history of population control is not religious history, but here too is a subject in the history of sexuality with immense religious consequences, a subject coming into sharper relief as demographics (in the West) now place a greater premium on fertility than control.

That recent histories of Mormonism—from Richard Bushman's elegant biography of Joseph Smith to Kathleen Flake's savvy study of the protracted confirmation hearings of Senator Reed Smoot—rest on an American frame makes sense for this most American of modern religious traditions. (Although even here John Brooke's study of early Mormonism is, in its way, a primer on the exotic fringes of the English Reformation.) But an international vantage point will doubtless soon emerge. Members of the Church of Latter-day Saints outside the United States now outnumber American members—yet another example of American religion circumnavigating the globe.

Political history is the subfield most tied (for understandable reasons) to the nation-state. And work on religion and politics is flourishing. Both Allen Guelzo and Richard Carwardine convincingly describe Abraham Lincoln and the early Republican Party in religious terms, and Lincoln's own rhetoric, notably the Second Inaugural Address, shaped American nationalism into the late nineteenth century and beyond. The long-standing wisdom that religion was central to party identification in the nineteenth century still holds, as confirmed by the centrality of religion in a first-rate survey such as Daniel Walker Howe's *What Hath God Wrought.* The tight link between evangelicals and social reform, once assumed in much of this literature, is slightly frayed, with more recognition from Matthew Grow and others that some Democrats, too, often unorthodox but themselves religious, favored various social reforms. The role of Catholics in urban political machines is receiving its first sustained attention from historians such as Eve Sterne and Mary Wingerd, and Joe Creech's claim that Populists worked from religious motives touches on an important theme in the recent literature. Michael Kazin's reintegration of William Jennings Bryan into both the religious and political histories of the late nineteenth and early twentieth centuries may signal a new synthesis. Even historians of foreign policy, if Andrew Preston's and Willi Inboden's new studies are harbingers, now see the cold war and American policy in the Middle East through a more religious lens.

The most dramatic changes in the discussion of religion and politics have come in the post–World War II period. Two topics touched on in any U.S. history survey course—the civil rights movement and the emergence of the New Right—are now inextricably intertwined with core themes in American religious history. That Martin Luther King, Jr., achieved what he did as an African-American minister is the central claim of Taylor Branch's magnificent three-volume narrative, but the King papers project at Stanford has also revealed to us King's indebtedness to the liberal social gospel tradition and his self-understanding as a liberal Protestant. By contrast, David Chappell's provocative assessment of King and the civil rights movement acknowledges this aspect of King's intellectual biography, but stresses instead King's reliance on Reinhold Niebuhr and an enduring prophetic tradition within Christianity. In Chappell's view, only the solidarity provided by the African-American church, along with the ineffectiveness of white liberals unable to actually effect change, enabled civil rights activists to take the first, dangerous steps against an entrenched apartheid system in the South.

Chappell further posits that white segregationists in the South failed precisely because they could not muster sufficient religious solidarity and self-sacrificial devotion. (He contrasts this failure with the remarkable religious solidarity exhibited during the Civil War.) The claim is contested, with Joseph Crespino, Jane Dailey, Charles Marsh, and others viewing religion as near the core of not only white resistance to racial intermarriage, but also white resistance to desegregation. And even when white Christians distanced themselves from violent opposition to desegregation, as they did in the mid-1960s, Crespino sees the sharp reaction by evangelicals against theological and political liberalism as setting the stage for the emergence of the modern Republican Party in the South.

In the North, too, race relations and the civil rights movement now seem more tightly bound to religious actors. The history of African-American religious life in the North remains unwritten, certainly when compared to what we know of African-American religious life in the South. But several recent studies offer insight into the relationship between religious institutions and community identity, notably Wallace Best's careful examination of Chicago. A variant of the long-running discussion assessing the relative importance of King and fellow Christian ministers in the South versus less self-consciously religious activists in the Student Nonviolent Coordinating Committee may be emerging among scholars interested in African-American religion in the North, where religious leaders were at once key to local civil rights struggles, but also, often, conservative in their instincts, and already enmeshed in and even dependent on local political machines. Barbara Savage cautions against seeing churches and ministers as inevitably voicing the aspirations of African-American communities, especially after passage of the Voting Rights Act. Curtis Evans persuasively sketches the varied ways in which a "natural" African-American religiosity not only led abolitionists to trumpet African-American humanity, but also brought twentieth-century social scientists to bemoan the "escapism" they judged endemic to African-American congregations.

The religious motivations of many civil rights activists are now obvious. Thomas Sugrue shows how religious liberals (African Americans, certainly, but also white Quakers and Jews) played a decisive role in the first campaigns for integrated public facilities and housing in the North, and Beryl Satter identifies white and African-American Catholics as decisive in the effort against contract home sales. At the same time, my own work and that of Gerald Gamm suggest that white Catholics were disproportionately likely to resist African-American entrance into particular urban neighborhoods, even as their presence helped stabilize urban neighborhoods, while other whites quickly moved to the suburbs. Jordan Stanger-Ross's comparative study of Italians in Toronto and Philadelphia argues that the pattern of Euro-American Catholics "defending" their neighborhoods rested less upon timeless patterns of community organization and more upon the suburbanization and deindustrialization characteristic of the postwar United States.

Religion is even more significant in the emergence of modern conservatism. Lisa McGirr's illuminating study of Orange County conservatives included a chapter on the religious orientation of these activists, but in retrospect, McGirr's book only opened the door for a wave of work moving back to the 1920s and 1930s, demonstrating even deeper political and religious connections binding the first generation of movement conservatives. Darren Dochuk points to Christian roots in Arkansas, Oklahoma, and Texas for the religious conservatism underpinning Ronald Reagan's success. Michelle Nickerson analyzes the work of conservative religious women, and a cluster of biographical studies demonstrates the importance of figures as diverse as Aimee Semple McPherson, Phyllis Schlafly, and Bill Bright.

Bethany Moreton's *To Serve God and Wal-Mart*—subtitled *The Making of Christian Free Enterprise*—links this political history to the history of political economy. The lines Moreton draws between contemporary Christian conservatives and nineteenth-century Christian Populists are tenuous, but she clearly registers the importance of the particular Christian ethos at Wal-Mart, an ethos tied to the evangelical and Pentecostal religious culture of the Ozarks region. One in five American women shops in Wal-Mart each week, and the company is not only the largest employer and corporation in the United States, but also the largest employer in Mexico. These Wal-Mart workers and Wal-Mart shoppers disproportionately favor a Christianity allied to the outcomes and discipline of the free market, and remain suspicious of a federal state willing, in their eyes, to impose alien cultural values and redistribute the wealth of its citizens. (In 2004, 76 percent of regular Wal-Mart shoppers voted for George Bush, not John Kerry.)

This vision of Christian free enterprise is as important to this century as the more social vision of, say, the Congress of Industrial Organizations for the last, even though historians of labor have been slow to pick up on the religious dimensions of the mid-twentieth-century labor movement and its opponents, with James Fisher's recent study of the New York waterfront a welcome exception. Wal-Mart is perhaps even more important for the twenty-first century, as Moreton and Nelson Lichtenstein demonstrate, because it carries its vision of Christian free enterprise around the world, and indeed has developed training programs for Guatemalans, Chinese, and others, often themselves Christians, to propagate the Wal-Mart gospel.

The most remarkable fact about Moreton's study is not its (high) quality but its matter-of-fact linking of religion to central themes of American history. The same is true of almost all the books mentioned in this essay, virtually all published within the past fifteen years. And even these books are a partial sample. What they demonstrate is the promise of contemporary religious history, more fully realized in this scholarly generation than any other, and its increasingly successful effort to shape the broad direction of the wider U.S. history field. Let's hope that these historians and their successors become even more adept at probing the religious roots of some of our deepest social and cultural divides.

BIBLIOGRAPHY

Albanese, Catherine. *A Republic of Mind and Spirit: A Cultural History of American Metaphysical Religion.* New Haven, CT: Yale University Press, 2007.

Allitt, Patrick, and Thomas Paterson. *Major Problems in American Religious History.* Florence, KY: Wadsworth, 1999.

Bellah, Robert N. "Civil Religion in America." *Daedalus, Journal of the American Academy of Arts and Sciences* 96 (Winter 1967): 1–21.

Bennett, James B. *Religion and the Rise of Jim Crow in New Orleans.* Princeton, NJ: Princeton University Press, 2005.

Berman, Lila Corwin. *Speaking of Jews: Rabbis, Intellectuals, and the Creation of an American Public Identity.* Berkeley: University of California Press, 2009.

Best, Wallace D. *Passionately Human, No Less Divine: Religion and Culture in Black Chicago, 1915–1952.* Princeton, NJ: Princeton University Press, 2005.

Branch, Taylor. *Parting the Waters: America in the King Years, 1954–63.* New York: Simon and Schuster, 1988.

———. *Pillar of Fire: America in the King Years, 1963–65.* New York: Simon and Schuster, 1998.

———. *At Canaan's Edge: America in the King Years, 1965–68.* New York: Simon and Schuster, 2006.

Braude, Ann. "Women's History *Is* American Religious History." In Thomas Tweed, ed., *Narrating American Religious History*, 87–107. Berkeley: University of California Press, 1996.

Brekus, Catherine A., ed. *The Religious History of American Women: Reimaging the Past.* Chapel Hill: University of North Carolina Press, 2007.

Brooke, John L. *The Refiner's Fire: The Making of Mormon Cosmology, 1644–1844.* New York: Cambridge University Press, 1996.

Brown, Callum G. *The Death of Christian Britain: Understanding Secularisation, 1800–2000.* New York: Routledge, 2009.

Brown, Victoria Bissell. *The Education of Jane Addams.* Philadelphia: University of Pennsylvania Press, 2007.

Brown, Vincent. *The Reaper's Garden: Death and Power in the World of Atlantic Slavery.* Cambridge, MA: Harvard University Press, 2008.

Buckley, Michael J., S.J. *At the Origins of Modern Atheism.* New Haven, CT: Yale University Press, 1990.

———. *Denying and Disclosing God: The Ambiguous Progress of Modern Atheism.* New Haven, CT: Yale University Press, 2004.

Bushman, Richard L. *Joseph Smith: Rough Stone Rolling.* New York: Knopf, 2005.

Butler, Anthea D. *Women in the Church of God in Christ: Making a Sanctified World.* Chapel Hill: University of North Carolina Press, 2007.

Butler, Jon. *Awash in a Sea of Faith: Christianizing the American People*. Cambridge, MA: Harvard University Press, 1990.

———. "Jack-in-the-Box Faith: The Religion Problem in Modern American History." *Journal of American History* 90 (March 2004): 1357–1378.

Campbell, James T. *Songs of Zion: The African Methodist Episcopal Church in the United States and South Africa*. New York: Oxford University Press, 1995.

Carson, Clayborne, ed. *The Papers of Martin Luther King, Jr.*, Vol. 6: *Advocate of the Social Gospel, September 1948–March 1963*. Berkeley: University of California Press, 2007.

Carwardine, Richard. *Lincoln: A Life of Purpose and Power*. New York: Knopf, 2006.

Chappell, David L. *A Stone of Hope: Prophetic Religion and the Death of Jim Crow*. Chapel Hill: University of North Carolina Press, 2003.

Clark, Emily. *Masterless Mistresses: The New Orleans Ursulines and the Development of a New World Society, 1727–1834*. Chapel Hill: University of North Carolina Press, 2007.

Clarke, Erskine. *Dwelling Place: A Plantation Epic*. New Haven, CT: Yale University Press, 2005.

Codignola, Luca. "Roman Catholic Conservatism in a New North Atlantic World 1760–1829." *William and Mary Quarterly*, ser. 3, 64 (October 2007): 717–756.

Connelly, Matthew. *Fatal Misconception: The Struggle to Control World Population*. Cambridge, MA: Harvard University Press, 2009.

Creech, Joe. *Righteous Indignation: Religion and the Populist Revolution*. Champaign: University of Illinois Press, 2006.

Crespino, Joseph. *In Search of Another Country: Mississippi and the Conservative Counterrevolution*. Princeton, NJ: Princeton University Press, 2007.

Critchlow, Donald T. *Phyllis Schlafly and Grassroots Conservatism: A Woman's Crusade*. Princeton, NJ: Princeton University Press, 2007.

Cummings, Kathleen Sprows. *New Women of the Old Faith: Gender and American Catholicism in the Progressive Era*. Chapel Hill: University of North Carolina Press, 2009.

D'Agostino, Peter R. *Rome in America: Transnational Catholic Ideology from the Risorgimento to Fascism*. Chapel Hill: University of North Carolina Press, 2004.

Dailey, Jane. "Sex, Segregation, and the Sacred after *Brown*," *Journal of American History* 91 (June 2004): 119–144.

Dochuk, Darren. *From Bible Belt to Sunbelt: Plain-Folk Religion, Grassroots Politics, and the Rise of Evangelical Conservatism*. New York: W. W. Norton, 2010.

Evans, Curtis J. *The Burden of Black Religion*. New York: Oxford University Press, 2008.

Fea, John. *The Way of Improvement Leads Home: Philip Vickers Fithian and the Rural Enlightenment in Early America*. Philadelphia: University of Pennsylvania Press, 2009.

Fisher, James Terence. *On the Irish Waterfront: The Crusader, the Movie, and the Soul of the Port of New York*. Ithaca, NY: Cornell University Press, 2009.

Fitzgerald, Maureen. *Habits of Compassion: Irish Catholic Nuns and the Origins of New York's Welfare System, 1830–1920*. Urbana: University of Illinois Press, 2006.

Flake, Kathleen. *The Politics of American Religious Identity: The Seating of Senator Reed Smoot, Mormon Apostle.* Chapel Hill: University of North Carolina Press, 2004.

Fox, Richard Wightman. *Jesus in America: Personal Savior, Cultural Hero, and National Obsession.* New York: HarperOne, 2005.

———. *Trials of Intimacy: Love and Loss in the Beecher-Tilton Scandal.* Chicago: University of Chicago Press, 1999.

Frey, Sylvia R., and Betty Wood. *Come Shouting to Zion: African American Protestantism in the American South and British Caribbean to 1830.* Chapel Hill: University of North Carolina Press, 1998.

Gamm, Gerald H. *Urban Exodus: Why the Jews Left Boston and the Catholics Stayed.* Cambridge, MA: Harvard University Press, 1999.

Gjerde, Jon. *The Minds of the West: Ethnocultural Evolution in the Rural Middle West, 1830–1917.* Chapel Hill: University of North Carolina Press, 1999.

Gordon, Sarah Barringer. *The Mormon Question: Polygamy and Constitutional Conflict in Nineteenth-Century America.* Chapel Hill: University of North Carolina Press, 2002.

Gorney, Cynthia. *Articles of Faith: A Frontline History of the Abortion Wars.* New York: Simon and Schuster, 2000.

Greer, Allan. *Mohawk Saint: Catherine Tekakwitha and the Jesuits.* New York: Oxford University Press, 2005.

Griffith, R. Marie. *God's Daughters: Evangelical Women and the Power of Submission.* Berkeley: University of California Press, 2000.

Grow, Matthew J. *"Liberty to the Downtrodden": Thomas L. Kane, Romantic Reformer.* New Haven, CT: Yale University Press, 2009.

Guelzo, Allen C. *Abraham Lincoln: Redeemer President.* Grand Rapids, MI: Wm. B. Eerdmans, 2003.

Hall, David D., ed. *Lived Religion in America: Toward a History of Practice.* Princeton, NJ: Princeton University Press, 1997.

Hamburger, Philip. *Separation of Church and State.* Cambridge, MA: Harvard University Press, 2004.

Harvey, Paul. *Freedom's Coming: Religious Culture and the Shaping of the South from the Civil War through the Civil Rights Era.* Chapel Hill: University of North Carolina Press, 2007.

Hatch, Nathan O. *The Democratization of American Christianity.* New Haven, CT: Yale University Press, 1989.

Heinze, Andrew R. *Jews and the American Soul: Human Nature in the Twentieth Century.* Princeton, NJ: Princeton University Press, 2006.

Hempton, David. *Methodism: Empire of the Spirit.* New Haven, CT: Yale University Press, 2005.

Heyrman, Christine Leigh. *Southern Cross: The Beginnings of the Bible Belt.* New York: Knopf, 1997.

Higginbotham, Evelyn Brooks. *Righteous Discontent: The Women's Movement in the Black Baptist Church, 1880–1920.* Cambridge, MA: Harvard University Press, 1994.

Hochgeschwender, Michael. *Wahrheit, Einheit, Ordnung: Die Sklavenfrage und der Amerikanische Katholizismus, 1835–1870.* Paderborn: Ferdinand Schöningh, 2006.

Holifield, E. Brooks. *Theology in America: Christian Thought from the Age of the Puritans to the Civil War.* New Haven, CT: Yale University Press, 2003.

Hollinger, David A. *Science, Jews, and Secular Culture: Studies in Mid-Twentieth-Century American Intellectual History*. Princeton, NJ: Princeton University Press, 1998.

Howe, Daniel Walker. *What Hath God Wrought: The Transformation of America, 1815–1848*. New York: Oxford University Press, 2007.

Inboden, William. *Religion and American Foreign Policy, 1945–1960: The Soul of Containment*. New York: Cambridge University Press, 2008.

Jacoby, Susan. *Freethinkers: A History of American Secularism*. New York: Metropolitan Books, 2004.

Kalu, Ogbu. *African Pentecostalism: An Introduction*. New York: Oxford University Press, 2008.

Kazin, Michael. *A Godly Hero: The Life of William Jennings Bryan*. New York: Random House, 2007.

Kidd, Thomas. *The Protestant Interest: New England after Puritanism*. New Haven, CT: Yale University Press, 2004.

Kloppenberg, James T. *The Virtues of Liberalism*. New York: Oxford University Press, 2000.

Koehlinger, Amy L. *The New Nuns: Racial Justice and Religious Reform in the 1960s*. Cambridge, MA: Harvard University Press, 2007.

Lichtenstein, Nelson. *The Retail Revolution: How Wal-Mart Created a Brave New World of Business*. New York: Metropolitan Books, 2009.

Marsden, George M. *Jonathan Edwards: A Life*. New Haven, CT: Yale University Press, 2003.

Marsh, Charles. *God's Long Summer: Stories of Faith and Civil Rights*. Princeton, NJ: Princeton University Press, 1997.

Martin, David. *Pentecostalism: The World Their Parish*. Oxford, U.K.: Blackwell Publishers, 2001.

Marty, Martin, and R. Scott Appleby, eds. Vol. 1: *Fundamentalisms Observed* (1991). Vol. 2: *Fundamentalisms and Society: Reclaiming the Sciences, the Family, and Education* (1993). Vol. 3: *Fundamentalisms and the State: Remaking Polities, Economies, and Militance* (1993). Vol, 4: *Accounting for Fundamentalisms: The Dynamic Character of Movements* (1994). Vol. 5: *Fundamentalisms Comprehended* (1995). Chicago: University of Chicago Press.

Matovina, Timothy. *Guadalupe and Her Faithful: Latino Catholics in San Antonio from Colonial Origins to the Present*. Baltimore: Johns Hopkins University Press, 2005.

Matovina, Timothy M., and Gary Riebe-Estrella. *Horizons of the Sacred: Mexican Traditions in U.S. Catholicism*. Ithaca, NY: Cornell University Press, 2002.

McCartin, James P. *Prayers of the Faithful: The Shifting Spiritual Life of American Catholics*. Cambridge, MA: Harvard University Press, 2010.

McGirr, Lisa. *Suburban Warriors: The Origins of the New American Right*. Princeton, NJ: Princeton University Press, 2001.

McGreevy, John T. *Catholicism and American Freedom: A History*. New York: W. W. Norton, 2003.

———. *Parish Boundaries: The Catholic Encounter with Race in the Twentieth-Century Urban North*. Chicago: University of Chicago Press, 1996.

McKenna, George. *The Puritan Origins of American Patriotism*. New Haven, CT: Yale University Press, 2009.

McKevitt, Gerald. *Brokers of Culture: Italian Jesuits in the American West, 1848–1919*. Palo Alto, CA: Stanford University Press, 2007.

Michel, Florian. *La pensée catholique en Amérique du Nord: Réseaux intellectuels et échanges culturels entre l'Europe, le Canada, et les Etats-Unis (années 1920–1960)*. Paris: Desclée de Brouwer, 2010.
Micklethwait, John, and Adrian Wooldridge. *God Is Back: How the Global Revival of Faith Is Changing the World*. New York: Penguin Press, 2009.
Miller, Perry. *Jonathan Edwards*. The American Men of Letters Series. New York: W. Sloane Associates, 1949.
Miller, Steven P. *Billy Graham and the Rise of the Republican South*. Philadelphia: University of Pennsylvania Press, 2009.
Moreton, Bethany. *To Serve God and Wal-Mart: The Making of Christian Free Enterprise*. Cambridge, MA: Harvard University Press, 2009.
Morgan, David. *Icons of American Protestantism: The Art of Warner Sallman*. New Haven, CT: Yale University Press, 1996.
Morgan, David, and Sally Promey. *The Visual Culture of American Religions*. Berkeley: University of California Press, 2001.
Nickerson, Michelle. *Mothers of Conservatism: Women and the Postwar Right*. Princeton, NJ: Princeton University Press, 2010.
Noll, Mark A. *America's God: From Jonathan Edwards to Abraham Lincoln*. New York: Oxford University Press, 2002.
———. *The Civil War as a Theological Crisis*. Chapel Hill: University of North Carolina Press, 2006.
O'Malley, John W. *What Happened at Vatican II*. Cambridge, MA: Harvard University Press, 2008.
Orsi, Robert A. *Between Heaven and Earth: The Religious Worlds People Make and the Scholars Who Study Them*. Princeton, NJ: Princeton University Press, 2006.
———. *The Madonna of 115th Street: Faith and Community in Italian Harlem, 1880–1950*. New Haven, CT: Yale University Press, 1985.
———. *Thank You, St. Jude: Women's Devotion to the Patron Saint of Hopeless Causes*. New Haven, CT: Yale University Press, 1996.
Preston, Andrew. "Bridging the Gap between the Sacred and the Secular in the History of American Foreign Policy." *Diplomatic History* 30 (November 2006): 783–812.
Putnam, Robert, and David Campbell. *American Grace: How Religion Divides and Unites Us*. New York: Simon and Schuster, 2010.
Promey, Sally M. *Painting Religion in Public: John Singer Sargent's Triumph of Religion at the Boston Public Library*. Princeton, NJ: Princeton University Press, 2001.
Sanfilippo, Matteo. *L'Affermazione de Cattolicesimo nel Nord America: Elite Emigranti e Chiesa Cattolica Negli Stati Uniti e in Canada, 1750–1920*. Viterbo, Italy: Sette Città, 2003.
Sarna, Jonathan D. *American Judaism: A History*. New Haven, CT: Yale University Press, 2004.
Satter, Beryl. *Family Properties: Race, Real Estate, and the Exploitation of Black Urban America*. New York: Metropolitan Books, 2009.
Savage, Barbara Dianne. *Your Spirits Walk beside Us: The Politics of Black Religion*. Cambridge, MA: Harvard University Press, 2008.
Schloesser, Stephen, S. J. "Vivo ergo cogito: Modernism as Temporalization and Its Discontents." In David G. Schultenover, ed., *The Reception of Pragmatism in France and the Rise of Roman Catholic Modernism*. Washington, DC: Catholic University of America Press, 2009.

Schmidt, Leigh Eric. *Restless Souls: The Making of American Spirituality*. New York: HarperOne, 2005.

Sensbach, Jon F. *Rebecca's Revival: Creating Black Christianity in the Atlantic World*. Cambridge, MA: Harvard University Press, 2006.

Slaughter, Thomas P. *The Beautiful Soul of John Woolman, Apostle of Abolition*. New York: Hill and Wang, 2009.

Smith, Christian, ed. *The Secular Revolution: Power, Interests, and Conflict in the Secularization of American Public Life*. Berkeley: University of California Press, 2003.

Smith, Christian, and Patricia Snell. *Souls in Transition: The Religious and Spiritual Lives of Emerging Adults*. New York: Oxford University Press, 2009.

Stanger-Ross, Jordan. *Staying Italian: Urban Change and Ethnic Life in Postwar Toronto and Philadelphia*. Chicago: University of Chicago Press, 2010.

Sterne, Evelyn. *Ballots and Bibles: Ethnic Politics and the Catholic Church in Providence*. Ithaca, NY: Cornell University Press, 2010.

Stout, Harry S. *Upon the Altar of the Nation: A Moral History of the American Civil War*. New York: Viking, 2006.

Sugrue, Thomas J. *Sweet Land of Liberty: The Forgotten Struggle for Civil Rights in the North*. New York: Random House, 2008.

Sutton, Matthew Avery. *Aimee Semple McPherson and the Resurrection of Christian America*. Cambridge, MA: Harvard University Press, 2009.

Taves, Ann. *Fits, Trances, and Visions: Experiencing Religion and Explaining Experience from Wesley to James*. Princeton, NJ: Princeton University Press, 1999.

Taylor, Charles. *A Secular Age*. Cambridge, MA: Harvard University Press, 2007.

———. *Sources of the Self: The Making of the Modern Identity*. Cambridge, MA: Harvard University Press, 1992.

———. *Varieties of Religion Today: William James Revisited*. Cambridge, MA: Harvard University Press, 2003.

Turner, James. *Without God, Without Creed: The Origins of Unbelief in America*. Baltimore: Johns Hopkins University Press, 1985.

Turner, John G. *Bill Bright and Campus Crusade for Christ: The Renewal of Evangelicalism in Postwar America*. Chapel Hill: University of North Carolina Press, 2008.

Tweed, Thomas A. *Our Lady of the Exile: Diasporic Religion at a Cuban Shrine in Miami*. New York: Oxford University Press, 1998.

Wacker, Grant. *Heaven Below: Early Pentecostals and American Culture*. Cambridge, MA: Harvard University Press, 2001.

Wenger, Tisa. *We Have a Religion: The 1920s Pueblo Indian Dance Controversy and American Religious Freedom*. Chapel Hill: University of North Carolina Press, 2009.

Wheeler, Rachel. *To Live upon Hope: Mohicans and Missionaries in the Eighteenth-Century Northeast*. Ithaca, NY: Cornell University Press, 2008.

Wingerd, Mary Lethert. *Claiming the City: Politics, Faith, and the Power of Place in St. Paul*. Ithaca, NY: Cornell University Press, 2001.

Woodcock, Leslie Tentler. *Catholics and Contraception: An American History*. Ithaca, NY: Cornell University Press, 2009.

12

Frontiers, Borderlands, Wests

STEPHEN ARON

"Americans have never had much use for histories," quipped historian Richard White, "but we do like anniversaries." For confirmation of White's aphorism, we need look no further than the hoopla surrounding the bicentennial of the Lewis and Clark expedition in 2004–2006. Commemorations included museum exhibitions, television documentaries, an Imax film, plays, musicals, and even an opera. Consumers could choose from an array of Lewis and Clark products, including Corps of Discovery cards and coins, "authentic" foods, puzzles, games, and action figures. The "LewisNClark" company marketed an array of gadgets for travelers. Scores of books appeared. There were Lewis and Clark cookbooks (presumably essential for those who purchase Lewis and Clark foods) and guidebooks (for wilderness enthusiasts eager to follow the Lewis and Clark Trail and put to use their LewisNClark gadgets). New biographies of the cocaptains, the other members of the corps, and the Indians they encountered spilled off the shelves. Lest animal lovers feel left out, Lewis's dog, Seaman, was the subject of a couple of tomes. Two hundred years after Thomas Jefferson instructed Meriwether Lewis and William Clark to go forth "for the purposes of commerce," they fulfilled that part of their mission.

To be sure, the anniversary produced plenty of serious scholarship, some of which ran against the grain of bicentennial enthusiasm by questioning the success and significance of the expedition. Chief among the party crashers was Thomas Slaughter. In his *Exploring Lewis and Clark*, he deplored the excessive credit now given to a mission that had failed in most of its major objectives, was "irrelevant" to the subsequent history of American westward expansion, and was rightly forgotten for much of the nineteenth century.

The resurrection of Lewis and Clark occurred in the twentieth century, boosted, as several studies have pointed out, when the centennial of their journey coincided with World Fairs in St. Louis in 1904 and Portland in 1905. As presented in St. Louis and Portland, the Lewis and Clark expedition at one hundred looked very different than it did a century later, differences that speak to decisive shifts in the prevailing interpretations of the history of the American West. The expedition turned one hundred not long after Frederick Jackson Turner delivered his paper "The Significance of the Frontier in American History." Centennial commemorations celebrated along with Turner the victorious march of American expansion. By the Lewis and Clark bicentennial, however, the course of American expansion and empire no longer generated such good feelings, at least among the vast majority of academic historians. Instead, a "new western history," most fully framed in the texts of Patricia Nelson Limerick and Richard White, had come to the fore. This new western history made the ethnic diversity of the West its centerpiece. It also inverted Turner's triumphant progression into a tragic procession through a land scarred by the legacy of blood-splattering, people-scattering, world-shattering conquests. All of which, its critics contended, left Americans not feeling good, but feeling guilty.

The latest round of Lewis and Clark remembrances reflected the impact of the new western history, promoting the Indian woman Sacagawea and Clark's African-American slave York to costarring roles and moving ecological concerns into the spotlight. Still, most bicentennial versions banished the darker vision of new western histories, emphasizing instead the amicable relations that Lewis and Clark fashioned with Indian peoples. Tellingly, the general public embraced the sunnier side of western history, even as a few scholars and a number of American Indians took issue with the ways in which the expedition had been turned into a tour of Kumbaya colonialism.

For the purposes of this survey of the field of western history, the shifting presentations and the most recent set of commemorations reveal much about changing interpretations of the history of the American West. Overrated though the expedition may be in the eyes of myth-breaking historians, tracking Lewis and Clark from centennial to bicentennial helps to distill the historiographic distance from Frederick Jackson Turner to Patricia Limerick and Richard White. Here, the connections between historical anniversaries that stimulate scholarship and heighten public awareness come clearly into view, as does the gap between what scholars deliver and what the public prefers.

In the last two decades, a number of anniversaries have similarly enlivened the field of western history and illuminated its evolutions. Along with the Lewis and Clark bicentennial, the quincentennial of Columbus's "discovery," the centennial of Turner's "frontier thesis," and the sesquicentennials of the Mexican-American War and California Gold Rush spoke to the concerns of western historians, and resulting publications speak to the currents of scholarship in the field. The productive inquiries these anniversaries generated show us how scholars have put new faces into the western past and changed the complexion of that history. We can take in the West, as historians have increasingly done, in overlapping subregional, regional, national, transnational, and international contexts. These anniversaries also prompted a rethinking of the chronologies we employ to divide the history of the West and the constructs we deploy to makes sense of it. Three terms—"frontier," "borderland," and "West" itself—have been instrumental to the history of the West, and each has been the subject of much debate in recent scholarship. In the case of all three, the plural form has become more proper, a revision with profound implications for how we comprehend what came before and after Lewis and Clark and for how we appraise the significance that frontiers, borderlands, and Wests hold for our histories.

Revising and Reviving Terms

Of all the recent anniversaries, the centennial of Frederick Jackson Turner's "The Significance of the Frontier in American History" least directly engaged a nonscholarly audience. Yet, it was this anniversary that sparked the most ardent debate among western historians. The arguments went to the heart of the field. At stake were the terms upon which the history of the American West had long been constructed and the terrain on which it played out.

Turner had first set those terms in an address to the fledgling American Historical Association in the summer of 1893. That conference, held in Chicago, also coincided with a grand world's fair, the Columbian Exposition, which was itself tied to a major historical anniversary, the quadricentennial of Christopher Columbus's discovery of the Americas. Challenging then-prevailing notions, Turner argued that the course of American development owed less to European foundations than to "American factors." What explained the course of American history and what distinguished Americans from Europeans was "the existence of an area of free land, its continuous recession, and the advance of American settlement westward." In the "colonization of the Great West," Turner claimed, could be found the seed of American democracy and the soil of American distinction.

Although Turner's talk went unnoticed by the millions of people who attended the nearby exposition, his frontier thesis soon became the most influential interpretation of American history; it would remain the reigning paradigm of western American history for a good part of the twentieth century. Key to Turner's framework was the concept of frontier, a word whose meaning Turner defined by making clear what it was not. It was "not the European frontier—a fortified boundary line running through dense populations." What it was Turner left more vague, or at least more varied: "the meeting point between savagery and civilization," "the hither edge of free land," "the Indian country and the outer margin of the 'settled area,'" "the line of most rapid and effective Americanization." Turner also differentiated between the frontier of the fur trader, the miner, the cattle raiser, and the farmer, though he discerned a recurring pattern in how these occupational stages filed across the continent. So while Turner assigned the word many meanings, recognized it to have several phases, and acknowledged numerous geographic chapters as it shifted westward, the essential repetition of the process of settlement and development unified the frontier experience, making it appropriate for Turner and his disciples to speak and write about *the American frontier.*

For Turner, the West, like the frontier, was hard to confine and thus difficult to define. Almost always when Turner referred specifically to "the West" in "The Significance of the Frontier in American History," he was discussing the lands between the Appalachian Mountains and the Mississippi River. Throughout that essay, he distinguished between "the West" and the "Far West," the region from the Mississippi to the Pacific, including the Louisiana Purchase and the territory through which Lewis and Clark traveled. In a subsequent volume published in 1906, Turner christened the region that encompassed the Ohio Valley and reached across to the west bank of the Mississippi "the New West." This, though, added to the confusion, for what Turner deemed the New West was, in regard to American occupation, older than the Far West, which Americans were coming to view nostalgically as the "Old West." But fixing boundaries and naming regions (or what he called sections) was not really Turner's objective. Sometimes, he erased the divisions between one West and another entirely, subsuming the parts under "the Great West," a nineteenth-century designation for the territory that stretched from the Appalachians to the Pacific. In fact, Turner's chief concern was not with "the West" but with westward expansion, with when, how, and to what effect the frontier had passed across the Great West.

The third vital construct, borderland, did not appear at all in Turner's most celebrated essay; its introduction into the lexicon of western historians came a few decades later in the work of Herbert Eugene Bolton. Bolton had briefly been a student of Turner, but he disputed his teacher's singular angle of vision. Where Turner made the westward march of Anglo-Americans the explanation for American development, Bolton maintained that the northward movement of the Spanish had also decisively shaped the colonization of the Great West. Dedicating much of his career to the study of "the Spanish borderlands" (the title of his seminal 1921 book on the subject), Bolton collected a trove of documents, published scores of books and articles, and sent hundreds of students to work in the field. In contrast to Turner's imprecision when it came to setting parameters, Bolton and his students were clearer about the limits of their terrain. In the "Boltonian" vision, the "Spanish Borderlands" extended to meet and attempted to defeat European imperial rivals' ambitions in western and southeastern

North America, running principally across the lowest tier of the current states of the United States from California to Florida.

During the twentieth century, the study of the Spanish borderlands took hold at universities in that vast region, but the construct did not attain the national and popular reach of the frontier. Borderlands, by and large, remained an academic pursuit and a subfield of western history. By contrast, the frontier enjoyed a long run at the center of both academic inquiries and public understandings of American history. True, beginning during Turner's lifetime and intensifying after his death in 1932, scholars chipped away at the frontier edifice. By midcentury, most historians rejected the frontier as *the* explanation for American development. Lacking an alternative paradigm, historians of the American West were more reluctant to dismiss the frontier thesis, though this doggedness contributed to the disdain in which the field was held by more cutting-edge colleagues.

By the time the centennial of the "Significance of the Frontier" essay arrived in 1993, many western historians had separated themselves from Turner. Leading the charge was Patricia Limerick, whose 1987 book *The Legacy of Conquest* prodded western historians to finalize their divorce from Turner. The "f-word," she maintained, was "nationalistic and often racist (in essence, the area where white people get scarce)." Allegiance to it and to Turner trapped western historians in a nostalgic mythology that treated the West before its American colonization as "virgin land" in which the presence of Indian peoples mattered little. Adherence to the frontier also closed the western past at the passing of the frontier, which Turner, following the United States Census, dated to 1890. To confront the West's multiethnic past and its more recent history, Limerick urged western historians to abandon the outmoded, ethnocentric frontier concept and turn away from the process of westward expansion across the continent. In contrast with Turner, who put "the West" east of the Mississippi (at least for a time), Limerick and like-minded new western historians concentrated on the place that is the West today and set out to write its history as a region.

Demonstrating the possibilities of a regional approach, Richard White's 1991 textbook, *"It's Your Misfortune and None of My Own,"* surveyed the history of the American West without indexing the frontier of Frederick Jackson Turner. Further distancing his synthesis from Turner's notion that "the frontier was productive of individualism," White emphasized the essential role of the federal government in the making of the West. In turn, the West acted as the "kindergarten of the American state," for its exploration, conquest, colonization, economic development, and political incorporation required that the capacities of the national government be expanded. Dependence on (and resentment of) the federal government, White maintained, continued to shape the region through the twentieth century, an era to which *"It's Your Misfortune"* devoted almost half its pages.

If regionalists were ready to erase the frontier, they were less certain about where to place the West and what characteristics held it together.

Clyde Milner wrote of the "psychological fault line" that separated westerners from other Americans, while Donald Worster, who identified aridity as the region's defining characteristic, described how his "bones" told him when he had entered the dry lands of the "true West." Aridity also led the editors of *The Atlas of the New West* to distinguish between the West and the West Coast, leaving the western parts of California, Oregon, and Washington beyond the region's boundaries. White settled on the northward bend of the Missouri River for his West's east and took the rest of the western United States in, but he conceded that the lines he drew around the region, on its east as well as on its north, south, and west, were "not naturally determined, they were politically determined." These borders, both internal and international, were just "a series of doors pretending to be walls." Ultimately, too, they made the West nothing more (or less) than what are now the western states of the United States. That seemed to shorten the West's history to the period after it became these (hence, the focus on the twentieth century), and it provided no grander explanation for regional coherence. Indeed, in a valuable collection of essays that examined subregional identities, editors David Wrobel and Michael Steiner concluded that "the West probably does have certain defining characteristics, but they are not readily and evenly applicable to all [its] parts." Better, perhaps, to acknowledge that there were and are "many Wests."

The hundredth anniversary of the frontier thesis roused a vigorous debate among western historians frequently characterized as pitting "place versus process." From the late 1980s through much of the 1990s, academic journals (and sometimes general newspapers and magazines) ran scores of articles that attacked or defended Turner and that disputed the merits of a place-based regional approach and a process-oriented frontier one. Against Limerick's indictment, an assortment of historians sought to salvage at least some of Turner's insights and to save the frontier, which they claimed was too deeply embedded in the public's consciousness to be jettisoned. Rather than a drastic amputation, a more surgical revision could remove the racist taint of a "meeting point between savagery and civilization" and leave the frontier more simply as a "meeting point," a cultural contact zone in which no single polity had established political hegemony.

This was the approach Robert Hine and John Mack Faragher chose for their 2000 survey *The American West: A New Interpretive History*. That text made frontier—or more accurately *frontiers* (which fittingly became the title of the 2007 brief edition of the book)—the foundation for their interpretation of a western history that, like Turner's, spanned the continent. Certainly, though, Hine and Faragher's frontiers were not Turner's. In keeping with new trends in early American history (ably synthesized by Alan Taylor in his 2001 book *American Colonies*), Hine and Faragher adopted a polycolonial vision that decentered the Anglo-Americans' westward gaze. Comparing French, Spanish, and British colonial projects, Hine and Faragher highlighted how different were the frontiers that emerged between these newcomers and the diverse native people they encountered. In place of Turner's predictable procession from one social stage to the next, Hine and Faragher substituted a messier history of frontiers, which was especially attentive to the blending of ways that occurred where peoples met and mingled. To greater and lesser extents, "cultural fusion" characterized the various frontiers that Indians, Europeans, and Africans created across North America from the fifteenth to the nineteenth century, and it remained a hallmark of the West, with its entangled multiethnic population, through the twentieth century.

The fight between place and process produced no knockout blows, nor even a clear winner on points. As the centennial of Turner's "Significance of the Frontier" faded into the past, advocates for each side belatedly realized that the terms of their debate had been mischaracterized and had devolved into what David Hackett Fischer has described as the "fallacy of the false dichotomy." To be for place did not mean to be against process—and vice versa. Conquest, after all, was a process too. Moreover, as Hine and Faragher's text demonstrated, a focus on frontiers and earlier American Wests need not neglect the postfrontier history of the place that is now the West.

Amid the clamor about the frontier and the West in the 1980s and 1990s, what was happening to borderlands slipped by with less fanfare. To be sure, Bolton and the tradition of borderlands studies that he founded did not escape criticism from a new generation of scholars that derided the Eurocentrism and "Hispanophilia" of Boltonians. These batterings, however, did not capture much attention outside the field, and, unlike opponents of Turner, critics of Bolton never suggested that the term "borderlands" be excised. Quite the contrary, they sought to expand the reach of the term and the terrain of the field. In this they succeeded spectacularly.

Here, too, a historical anniversary played a role. The sesquicentennial of the war between Mexico and the United States served as a reminder of how the southern boundary of the American West had been politically (really militarily) determined. It also acted as a stimulus to new scholarship, not just about the war, but about its impact on the peoples of the United States and Mexico. In that spirit, recent work has enlarged the geography of the borderlands to encompass the territories on both sides of the redrawn border. It has also extended the chronology. Where Bolton's borderlands closed with the collapse of the Spanish empire in the early nineteenth century, new studies pushed the borderlands construct to the present. And where Bolton and his disciples tended to spotlight the interests and actions of Europeans, scholars now accented the diversity and dynamism of borderland cultures.

In an even greater departure from earlier studies in the Boltonian tradition, it has become impossible to speak about "the" borderlands as denoting a single zone. In fact, scholars working far from the Mexico–U.S. line have unfurled the banner of borderlands. Indeed, in this era of globalization, borderlands seem to be everywhere. A perusal of recent literature turns up scores of books and articles that employ the construct of borderlands to interpret the histories of central and eastern Europe and the territories where Europe and Asia bleed together.

In the last few decades, not only has the concept gone global, but it has also become a catchall for any kind of border crossing. Thus the review of recent literature turns up explorations of "sexual borderlands" and "surfing borderlands" that seem a long way from Bolton's borderlands. The dangers of such promiscuous usages should be clear in light of the battles over frontier, which suggest a backlash against the "b-word" may be brewing—and perhaps before the 2021 centennial of the publication of Bolton's *The Spanish Borderlands*?

The Deeper Past Recast

While the Turner centennial and, to a lesser extent, the sesquicentennial of the Mexican-American War provoked debates that reworked the terms of western history and the terrain of the field, several other anniversaries served as principal agents for the recasting of that past. As noted, the Lewis and Clark bicentennial made stars of Sacagawea and York and made starkly apparent that the West they explored was no "virgin land." Even more dramatic for the repeopling and rewriting of histories of the West before Lewis and Clark was the fallout from the Columbian quincentennial. No anniversary changed public perceptions so deeply, principally by amplifying the voices and histories of Native Americans. This has also transformed scholarly interpretations, which now delve into pre-Columbian histories of North America, make the "Columbian exchange" the starting point for understanding the conquest and colonization of the continent, and take Indian power and prerogatives seriously in sorting the outcomes of imperial ventures in the centuries after 1492. For what happened after Lewis and Clark, the Gold Rush and the Golden State have taken a turn in the scholarly spotlight. To be sure, the sesquicentennial of the California Gold Rush lacked the public drama sparked by the Columbian quincentennial. But its scholarly impact has been considerable, reconfiguring the Gold Rush's place in nineteenth-century history and underscoring the significance of California to the history of the West and the nation. Before, during, and after the Gold Rush, as new scholarship has elaborated, the Golden State exemplified, magnified, and prefigured the history of the West. Taken together, these recastings have enlarged the company, extended the run, and altered the arc of western history.

Conspicuous as the changes were between the centennial and bicentennial interpretations of the Lewis and Clark expedition, this swing did not compare with the fall suffered by Christopher Columbus between 1892 and 1992. At the four hundredth anniversary, the Columbian Exposition made Columbus synonymous with progress and promise, and his champions in the Catholic Church campaigned for his canonization. A century later, big plans were announced for quincentennial celebrations, but almost all of these were canceled in the face of fierce opposition, the most aggrieved being American Indians. Rather than a candidate for sainthood or the avatar of human progress, protesters blamed Columbus for having ushered the genocide of Native Americans, the enslavement of Africans, and the destruction of the global environment. While scholarly treatments of Columbus did not hold him personally culpable for all the evils that ensued from his voyages, they, too, tarnished the Columbian legacy. The excavation of pre-Columbian histories has given us a better sense of the worlds we have lost. And the more we learn about the decimation of Indian peoples in the centuries after 1492, the more we grasp how European colonists in North America were, in John Murrin's phrase, the "beneficiaries of catastrophe."

The first impact of this scholarship on western history is to deepen its chronology. Not that long ago, western historians might commence their courses with Lewis and Clark or perhaps reach a couple of centuries back for a lecture or two on the Spanish exploration and invasion of lands north of Mexico. What came before the coming of Europeans was dismissed as "prehistory," with pre-Columbian Indians consigned to static worlds. No more, for recent scholarship has recovered a past filled with peoples in motion, societies in flux, cultures entangling, and polities expanding and contracting. Frontiers and borderlands, in short, did not await the arrival of Europeans, and pre-Columbian developments shaped the course of subsequent encounters with Europeans and Africans as much as did progress across the Atlantic.

Nothing in their prior histories, though, could prepare American Indians for the devastation wrought by imported diseases. Back in 1893, Turner had declared that "our early history is the study of European germs developing in an American environment." He did not realize how right he was, because the "germs" to which he referred were just a metaphor for the European ideas and institutions that were transplanted to and then transformed by the American frontier. But, as Alfred Crosby first elucidated in the 1970s, the microbes that Europeans brought with them proved deadly agents of conquest when unleashed upon people who lacked immunities to these diseases. In the years since Crosby first brought "virgin soil epidemics" into the Columbian conversation, historical demographers and epidemiologists have tussled over how large the pre-1492 census of the Americas was and how much of the decline after that should be attributed to diseases (as opposed to the demoralization that followed epidemics and the immiseration that accompanied European takeover of their lands). As Jared Diamond's 1997 best seller proclaimed, Indians also suffered because Europeans possessed guns and steel, and Indians did not before 1492. Yet it was germs, the middle element in Diamond's title, that should have been placed first. These precipitated the worst demographic calamity in human history, and these best explain why Europeans were able to conquer the Americas and where they were able to establish "neo-Europes."

Pathogens, Crosby recognized, were only part of the package of animals, plants, people, and products that passed between Old and New

Worlds after 1492. Because so much of the flow of the first three moved from Europe and Africa to the Americas and because the "Columbian exchange" so clearly enabled the European exploitation and occupation of the Americas, Crosby labeled the process "ecological imperialism." But this did not mean that Indians reaped no benefit from the ecological invasion, as was most obvious in the interior grasslands of North America. There, the introduction of the horse and the spread of imported trade goods (including guns) enhanced the material cultures of Plains peoples and augmented the wealth and power of some of them.

Some, but not all. As works by Elliott West, Richard White, Colin Calloway, and Pekka Hämäläinen have detailed, in the eighteenth century, many of those who were most enriched and empowered were newcomers to the grasslands. From different directions, the Cheyennes, the Lakotas, and the Comanches moved onto the Plains, where horses allowed them to hunt more bison, control more territory, and take captives from people with fewer horses and fewer guns. From James Brooks's *Captives and Cousins* and Ned Blackhawk's *Violence over the Land*, we have learned how far the dominoes from the "contested Plains" toppled, as those pushed off the grasslands turned their violence and captive taking against Great Basin peoples who had fewer (if any) horses and guns. Even among the Indians whom White characterized as the "winners of the West" in the eighteenth century, the unequal distribution of wealth (translated into horses and wives) meant that some Plains men won more than others. For Plains women, in general, the "equestrian revolution" brought more work (as more skins needed to be dressed) and less power (as the growing of crops, which had been women's domain, lost importance).

On the Plains and across the continent, taking the wealth and power of Indian societies seriously has remapped the history of post-Columbian North America. Again, not very long ago (and, in fact, still too often), American history textbooks typically featured maps that erased the presence of Indians and carved up the continent according to the claims of European powers. Based on imperial projections, such maps bore little relation to the actual situation on the ground in the seventeenth and eighteenth centuries. If British colonists gradually extended their exclusive occupation inland from the Atlantic coast, elsewhere most colonial settlements in North America existed as islands amid oceans of Indian countries. The presence and security of these enclaves and the fate of European empires rested on a variety of negotiated arrangements and cultural mixing with native peoples.

Richard White's enormously influential book *The Middle Ground* made famous (at least among academic historians) one such arrangement. Born, in this instance, of mutual weakness and fortuitous misunderstandings, White's middle ground was at once a diplomatic alliance fashioned by French and Algonquian Indians around the Great Lakes and a broader blurring of European and Indian ways. As his book detailed, the middle ground endured (if often tenuously) through much of the eighteenth century and extended (if often tentatively) around the Great Lakes and into the Ohio Valley.

The Middle Ground gave rise to middle grounds, as historians, following White, found (or claimed to find) similar intercultural compositions in other places at other times. Rather than a landscape dominated by Europeans, the "middle grounding" of early American history emphasized the power that native peoples exercised and their ability to compel accommodations from colonial intruders. This situation, Jeremy Adelman and I posited, most often emerged in the interior of the continent where the claims of European empires overlapped. In these borderlands during the eighteenth century, Indians successfully "played imperial rivals off against one another," a practice that allowed them to negotiate more favorable terms of trade and sustain more inclusive frontiers.

Beyond middle grounds, the latest western history has affirmed the existence and persistence of "native grounds," zones where Europeans remained subordinated to Indians. Consider, for example, eighteenth-century Texas, where, Juliana Barr has shown, Indians "dictated the rules and Europeans were the ones who had to accommodate, resist, and persevere." Barr's remapping of these colonial borderlands accented the centrality of gender to Texas Indians' constructions of power relations within and between societies. To be sure, Spanish and French intruders, with their preference for race-based classifications of difference, often misunderstood the alternative systems among the Indians they encountered. Yet, through a "diplomacy of gender," tentative truces and trade relations were established, and women, as captives, slaves, and emissaries, emerged as crucial brokers of the more enduring connections that took root in eighteenth-century Texas.

The apotheosis of Indian power was the "Comanche Empire," a designation that has as yet found its way onto few maps of colonial North America, but soon should, thanks to pathbreaking books by Pekka Hämäläinen and Brian Delay. In giving his book that title, Hämäläinen challenged the convention that reserved empire building to Europeans, at least north of Mexico. But as *The Comanche Empire* explicated, on the southern Plains "European imperialism not only stalled in the face of indigenous resistance, it was eclipsed by indigenous imperialism." "Comancheria" continued to expand well into the nineteenth century. As Delay has detailed, the raiding of Comanches (as well as Kiowas, Apaches, and Navajos) nearly depopulated parts of northern Mexico, weakened the inhabitants' attachment to the Mexican nation, and contributed to the loss of the territory to the United States. That territorial transfer came about in 1848 and included much of the Comanches' realm. But whether the United States would be able to restrain the "incursions" of Indians into Mexico, as required by Article 11 of the Treaty of Guadalupe Hidalgo, remained to be seen.

Included in the territorial handover from Mexico to the United States was California, where the discovery of gold that same year set off an unprecedented rush. One hundred fifty years later and in the decade since the sesquicentennial of the Gold Rush, California, which sometimes fell outside the new West's "true West," has regained its position in western history. California has been and remains "fundamentally western," in Walter Nugent's view, "at the edge of the West and at its center, all at once."

Like other histories in the era of the Columbian quincentennial, new California histories have sometimes simply inverted older understandings. Like Columbus, Father Junipero Serra has seen his reputation plummet. Once he and fellow missionaries were venerated for the souls they saved and the colony they opened; now the missionary regime has been recast as a reign of terror. More nuanced are the interpretations offered by James Sandos, Kent Lightfoot, and Steven Hackel, whose books demolish the former view that the Spaniards dominated California Indians completely. Instead, these studies detail how California Indians, like their counterparts to the east, rebuilt communities in the face of significant population declines and colonial demands. Within the missions, Indians and Spanish engaged one another on unequal terms, but even there Spanish authority depended on a stratum of native officials largely drawn from the ranks of traditional Indian leaders.

The economy, society, and culture of Mexican California have also received a makeover, often harsh, but one that has better connected the regime to broader developments across North America associated with the "market revolution." Albert Hurtado's illumination of the more "intimate frontiers" between men and women, for example, has pretty much drained the romance from oft-told tales of life in "Old California." In keeping with studies of interethnic mixing across the West, Hurtado's research has pointed out how marital and sexual unions both engraved and effaced boundaries between peoples. At the same time, Californios have taken on a more energetic and entrepreneurial face; works by Louise Pubols and David Igler have exhibited how landed elites seized opportunities for profit from commerce that increasingly crossed the Pacific and tied California into an emerging Pacific world system. These deepening trading ties and the migration of people before the Gold Rush from across the continent and across the Pacific made Mexican California in its final years a far more cosmopolitan place than contemporary Anglo-American observers and generations of historians appreciated. Nowhere was this cosmopolitanism better displayed than around the polyglot settlement of New Helvetia established by John Sutter (and featured in several of Hurtado's books).

It was, of course, the discovery of gold on land that Sutter claimed that truly opened the floodgates into California. The scale and global scope of this population movement dwarfed any previous migration to California or into the West, and its extremely unbalanced character—being almost entirely male—made the gold fields a fascinating laboratory in which to examine the collisions of cultures and the constructions of racial and gender relations. These, as Susan Johnson has uncovered, were closely related, for in the nearly all-male diggings, the reassessment of notions about gender and sexuality were entwined with ideas about race and ethnicity. In this and so many other ways, the California experience heralded developments in subsequent mining rushes. Indeed, a hallmark of scholarship that appeared around the sesquicentennial is its recognition that what happened in California did not stay in California. To that point, books by Malcolm Rohrbough, Brian Roberts, Yong Chen, and Aims McGuinness call attention to the impact of the Gold Rush on those left behind and on the places they passed through. Rohrbough and Roberts, in particular, stake the claim that the Gold Rush transformed the American nation more than any event in the first half of the nineteenth century, to which Leonard Richards would add that it was also a critical precipitant to the Civil War.

The connections between California, the West, and the nation grew even more pronounced after the Civil War, a period typically referred to as the Era of Reconstruction. Until relatively recently, historians of Reconstruction usually concentrated on the fate of freed people in the American South and closed their studies in 1877. Now, however, Reconstruction has taken on a broader meaning, a wider scope, and a longer chronology, with the West acknowledged as an integral component in the struggles to remake race relations, establish the primacy of the federal government, and consolidate an industrial capitalist order. No longer distracted by a handful of famous gunfights, historians have now more thoroughly exposed the ethnic and economic roots of most of the violence that occurred during what Richard Maxwell Brown has called the "western Civil War of incorporation." They have brought to light the devices by which forms of unfree labor persisted across the West long after the Civil War, as well as the biases and laws that sought to keep peoples apart—or at least put them in their place.

Chief among these place putters, and now a prime focus of scholarship about California, the West, and the United States, were the shifting boundaries of "whiteness." In the second half of the nineteenth century, the dynamics of whiteness exercised considerable control over the opportunities of life in California—over where individuals resided and worked, what they were paid, with whom they associated, and even whether they could enter California at all. For Mexicans, the shift seemed to push them out of the circle of those considered white. By contrast, the trajectory for European immigrants generally moved in the other direction, and, as the privileges of whiteness opened up to them, the roles and rights granted to Indians, Mexicans, Chinese, and African Americans narrowed. In California and the West, then, the postbellum reordering of race relations closed off countless opportunities. Still, reconstructions were ongoing, even if many breaches did not become visible until well into the twentieth century.

The West "Belongs to All of Us"

One significant anniversary that went entirely unmarked and unremembered was the centennial of the 1903 movie *The Great Train Robbery*. Shot in New Jersey, that twelve-minute film gave birth to the genre that defined and dominated American cinema for a good part of the twentieth century. The thousands of westerns that followed *The Great Train Robbery* did more to shape public perceptions of the West and its history than any scholarly statement. Nor was the impact of westerns limited to the United States. Indeed, when the genre lost favor in Hollywood, foreigners revised and revived it. Most famous perhaps were the "Spaghetti westerns" of Italian director Sergio Leone, which were filmed in Spain, based on Japanese movies, and starred a cast of American, Italian, and Yugoslav actors. In Frayling's *Once Upon a Time in Italy*, Leone states, "the western belongs to all of us. . . . It belongs to the world now."

The lack of interest of western historians in the centennial of *The Great Train Robbery* comes as no surprise in light of scholarly trends. To be sure, historians continue to nod to the power of the "imagined West." At its simplest, this involves pointing out how images and representations from paintings, photography, dime novels, films, and television shows have distorted what really happened. More sophisticated are acknowledgments of the inseparability of "western myth" and western history. In fact, though, most historians pay only lip service to the West of the imagination, leaving its study and its ties to the history of the West to scholars in other disciplines. Notable anomalies include Martha Sandweiss's book on photography and the American West, which elucidates how the medium and the region developed together, and Louis Warren's biography of Buffalo Bill, which presents a compelling portrait of the person and the persona he (and others) created and of the culture in which the man and his myth operated. But these and a handful of other exceptions prove the rule identified by Ryan Carey and Flannery Burke: "Western historians tend to assert the intertwined nature of myth and reality more than they explore it."

While western historians have of late paid little heed to westerns, they have taken up Leone's maxim in other ways. First, they have made western history for all of us by being far more inclusive about who has made that history. Second, they have brought the history of the West to everyone by breaking through the barrier that the closing of the frontier once imposed. Rather than a history trapped "back then" (essentially ending one hundred plus years ago) or confined to places "out there" (meaning those parts of the West where its open spaces still endured), newer western histories have brought the past to the "here and now." Thus have the twentieth-century West and its urban "oases" gained primacy. Third, along with other American historians, western historians have adopted Leone's globalized lens, moving beyond the nation as the sole container in which to fit their histories. Instead, the latest scholarship has accented the transnational and international dimensions of western history and has explored the connections and comparisons that have linked the West to the world.

Through the nineteenth century, the frontiers and borderlands of North America were crossroads for people from diverse places at the intersections of nations and empires, but the worldliness of the West became even more evident during the twentieth century. Its resources were then pulled more deeply into the global economy and its population was further augmented by flows from afar. As Walter Nugent has pointed out, the number of homesteaders, a movement long associated with the 1862 act that encouraged settlement of the Great Plains in the late nineteenth century, did not actually peak until early in the twentieth century. Recent syntheses about the peopling of the West by Nugent and Elliott Barkan attend to this continuation and then the collapse of homesteading, while also explaining how and why the West remained a colossal magnet for both internal migrants and immigrants. To be sure, the magnetism was not spread equally across the region, and legal restrictions and extralegal pressures often redirected and for several decades interrupted the influx of foreigners. Nonetheless, nothing distinguishes the twentieth-century West or its new histories so much as the recognition of the region's demographic diversity. Absent this multiethnic complexion, the West, Richard White remarked, "might as well be New Jersey with mountains."

As in earlier times, the mix was a combustible one. Most of the conflicts that bedeviled the West during Reconstruction carried over into the twentieth century. As new books by Thomas Andrews and Katherine Benton-Cohen eloquently attest, the labor strife and eruptions of violence at Ludlow in 1914 and Bisbee in 1917 continued the struggles over racial boundaries and industrial capitalist supremacy that had characterized earlier chapters in the western war of incorporation.

The volume of newcomers, especially those moving north from Mexico during and after the Mexican Revolution, reshuffled the ethnic profile of the West in the twentieth century, particularly across the Southwest and in no place more dramatically than Los Angeles. Through the first third of the twentieth century, Los Angeles was the "whitest" of major American cities. That situation changed, however, when Mexican immigrants were joined by what James Gregory has called the "Southern Diaspora," which brought significant numbers of African Americans to California during and after World War II. A "second gold rush" was how Marilynn Johnson has described the impact of World War II on California, though in terms of ethnic diversity, the real tidal wave followed major immigration reform in 1965. That reopened Los Angeles, California, and the West to substantial immigration from Asia, which together with ongoing immigration from Mexico and Central America, thoroughly changed the demographic complexion of Los Angeles by century's end—as it has the rest of the nation. In fact, at the start of the twenty-first century, New Jersey, now boasting growing Latin American and Asian American populations, has come to look more like the West—though still without the mountains.

Destructive riots in Los Angeles in 1965 and 1992 showed that race relations remained a trigger for violence in the incorporated West, much as it had been in the incorporating one. Historians of Los Angeles and other western cities have probed these urban conflagrations, the most prescient and darkest account being Mike Davis's *City of Quartz*. More surprising and certainly more uplifting are studies by Scott Kurashige, George

Sanchez, Allison Varzally, and Mark Wild that revisited Los Angeles's multiethnic neighborhoods in the middle decades of the twentieth century and recovered social networks fashioned in streets, shops, and schools that, to borrow Varzally's phrase, "colored" across ethnic lines. From these associations, at first fleeting and fragile, these authors have traced the emergence of more lasting bonds that translated into joint political action. In Los Angeles and across the region, struggles for civil rights and efforts to undo the legal privileges afforded to whiteness ended up taking many forms and brought together shifting coalitions, but at bottom all shared the premise that the American West belongs to everyone who lives there.

For Leone, the "we" in "West" was wider still, taking in not only all who lived there but also all who imagined themselves there. Admittedly, historians have not done much of late for the latter category of inhabitants. They have, however, been actively engaged in bringing the history of the West into conversation with the rest of the world. For western historians, this global turn has meant a further renunciation of the legacy of Frederick Jackson Turner. Turner, after all, had encouraged American historians to look away from foreign "germs" and focus on the frontier, where, he contended, the "really American" part of American history was to be found. Yet historians have now recast the frontiers of North America as multinational before they became national and have determined that the West, even after its incorporation into the United States, continued to be decisively shaped by immigrant chains and commodity flows that moved across borders and oceans.

By no means is this global turn an entirely new development. Three-quarters of a century ago, Herbert Bolton devoted his presidential address to the American Historical Association to a call for an "epic of greater America" that would cultivate a common and comparative history of the Americas. Few, however, answered Bolton's call, and parallel efforts to build "comparative frontiers" into a vibrant field also languished—until recently, when suddenly transnational connections and global comparisons emerged as a signature of the newest western histories.

Fittingly, historians of borderlands have taken the lead. The border provides an ideal vantage point to assess the power of empires and nation-states to enforce territorial claims, while also exposing the limits of that power at the periphery. The border is the place, in Elliott Young's words, where "the nation continues to be made, but it is also the place where it is unmade." The latter fact has especially impressed itself in recent studies, which have emphasized the permeability of borders and the weakness of empires and nation-states at their perimeters. What has become most obvious to historians of borderlands is the necessity of crossing borders. Understanding what happened on one side requires knowing what occurred on the other, and it also now increasingly entails research in archives on both sides of the border. A sterling example of this is Kelly Lytle Hernández's history of the U.S. Border Patrol, which uses both American and Mexican sources to recover the confrontations and collaborations between American and Mexican officials that together shaped the policing of people moving across the U.S.-Mexico border.

In the spirit of Bolton's "Epic of Greater America," historians of borderlands have also taken on comparative projects. Because the concept of borderlands has gone global, there is now much to compare. Within North America, the boundary between the United States and Canada has received much less attention than the line between the United States and Mexico, but a collection of essays edited by Benjamin Johnson and Andrew Graybill opens a stimulating discussion about the similarities and differences between those borders and the borderlands that surround them.

Comparisons tend to unsettle assumptions about American exceptionalism, and, in the particular case of western American history, they often invoke discomforting parallels. Around the time of the Columbian quincentennial, protesters talked of "genocide" and "holocaust" to capture the correspondences between the extermination of American Indians and European Jews. For the most part, historians employed these words more cautiously, maintaining a distinction between the unwitting spread of diseases and the deliberate, state-sponsored eradications pursued by the Nazis. But the terms that have lately gained favor among western historians are hardly more comforting. John Mack Faragher and Gary Anderson, for example, have borrowed the concept of "ethnic cleansing," which was invented in the 1990s to describe the contemporary horrors in the Balkans, and applied it to the deliberate, state-sponsored expulsion of French Acadians and Texas Indians from their respective homelands. Historians have also increasingly used the lens of colonialism or, more specifically, "settler colonialism" to set expansion across North America in a worldwide framework and to bring insights from similar situations into the newest histories of the West.

As an example of "ethnic cleansing" and "settler colonialism," the history of the West has come a long way from the triumphant trail of Frederick Jackson Turner's frontier and the good feelings of the Lewis and Clark bicentennial. The view gets even nastier when we consider who drew inspiration from the American model of spatial expansion and economic development. As Charles Bright and Michael Geyer have pointed out, in the twentieth century the most obvious candidates were the Germans and the Japanese, who "imagined themselves doing in the twentieth century what they thought Americans had done in the nineteenth: conquering a territorial hinterland" while purging it of "savage inhabitants" to transform it into "a source of food and resources, a controllable inland market, and a homeland for a growing population organized for maximum production."

We should beware, however, of allowing our perspective on westward expansion and its aftermath to go too far or too exclusively to the dark side. As the bicentennial celebrated (sometimes excessively), Lewis and Clark did generally get along with the Indians they encountered. Moreover, from middle grounds in the eighteenth century to multiethnic neighborhoods in the twentieth, historians have recovered episodes of concord, times and places in which people overcame their differences, at least temporarily, as opposed to being overcome by them. These, too, are part of the history of frontiers, borderlands, and Wests, and they at least suggest that the West could and still might belong to all of us.

BIBLIOGRAPHY

Abbott, Carl. *Frontiers Past and Future: Science Fiction and the American West.* Lawrence: University Press of Kansas, 2006.

———. *How Cities Won the West: Four Centuries of Urban Change in Western North America.* Albuquerque: University of New Mexico Press, 2008.

Adelman, Jeremy, and Stephen Aron. "From Borderlands to Borders: Empires, Nation-States, and the Peoples in Between in North American History." *American Historical Review* 104 (June 1999): 814–841.

Anderson, Gary. *The Conquest of Texas: Ethnic Cleansing in the Promised Land, 1820–1875.* Norman: University of Oklahoma Press, 2005.

Andrews, Thomas. *Killing for Coal: America's Deadliest Labor War.* Cambridge, MA: Harvard University Press, 2008.

Aron, Stephen. *American Confluence: The Missouri Frontier from Borderland to Border State.* Bloomington: Indiana University Press, 2006.

Avila, Eric. *Popular Culture in the Age of White Flight: Fear and Fantasy in Suburban Los Angeles.* Berkeley: University of California Press, 2004.

Barkan, Elliott. *From All Points: America's Immigrant West, 1870–1952.* Bloomington: Indiana University Press, 2007.

Barr, Juliana. *Peace Came in the Form of a Woman: Indians and Spaniards in the Texas Borderlands.* Chapel Hill: University of North Carolina Press, 2007.

Benton-Cohen, Katherine. *Borderline Americans: Racial Division and Labor War in the Arizona Borderlands.* Cambridge, MA: Harvard University Press, 2009.

Blackhawk, Ned. *Violence over the Land: Indians and Empires in the Early American West.* Cambridge, MA: Harvard University Press, 2006.

Blodgett, Peter J. *Land of Golden Dreams: California in the Gold Rush Decade, 1848–1858.* San Marino, CA: Huntington Library Press, 1999.

Bogue, Allan G. *Frederick Jackson Turner: Strange Roads Going Down.* Norman: University of Oklahoma Press, 1998.

Bolton, Herbert E. "The Epic of Greater America," *American Historical Review,* 38 (April 1933): 448–474.

———. *The Spanish Borderlands: A Chronicle of Old Florida and the Southwest.* New Haven, CT: Yale University Press, 1921.

Bowes, John. *Exiles and Pioneers: Eastern Indians in the Trans-Mississippi West.* New York: Cambridge University Press, 2007.

Bright, Charles, and Michael Geyer. "Where in the World Is America? The History of the United States in the Global Age." In Thomas Bender, ed., *Rethinking American History in a Global Age,* 63–99. Berkeley: University of California Press, 2002.

Brooks, James. *Captives and Cousins: Slavery, Kinship, and Community in the Southwest Borderlands.* Chapel Hill: University of North Carolina Press, 2002.

Brown, Richard Maxwell. *No Duty to Retreat: Violence and Values in American History and Society.* New York: Oxford University Press, 1991.

Burke, Flannery. *From Greenwich Village to Taos: Primitivism and Place at Mabel Dodge Luhan's*. Lawrence: University Press of Kansas, 2008.

Calloway, Colin G. *One Vast Winter Count: The Native American West before Lewis and Clark*. Lincoln: University of Nebraska Press, 2003.

Carey, Ryan, and Flannery Burke. "Corralling the Real and Imagined West: A Review Essay." Unpublished paper presented to Autry Western History Workshop, 2003.

Cayton, Andrew, and Fredrika Tuete, eds. *Contact Points: American Frontiers from the Mohawk Valley to the Mississippi, 1750–1830*. Chapel Hill: University of North Carolina Press, 1998.

Chan, Sucheng, ed. *Chinese American Transnationalism: The Flow of People, Resources, and Ideas between China and America during the Chinese Exclusion Era*. Philadelphia: Temple University Press, 2006.

Chavez, John R. *Beyond Nations: Evolving Homelands in the North Atlantic World, 1400–2000*. New York: Cambridge University Press, 2009.

Chavez-Garcia, Miroslava. *Negotiating Conquest: Gender and Power in California, 1770–1880*. Tucson: University of Arizona Press, 2004.

Chen, Yong. *Chinese San Francisco 1850–1943: A Transpacific Community*. Stanford, CA: Stanford University Press, 2000.

Cronon, William. *Nature's Metropolis: Chicago and the Great West*. New York: W. W. Norton, 1991.

Cronon, William, George Miles, and Jay Gitlin, eds. *Under an Open Sky: Rethinking America's Western Past*. New York: W. W. Norton, 1992.

Crosby, Alfred W., Jr. *The Columbian Exchange: Biological and Cultural Consequences of 1492*. Westport, CT: Greenwood Press, 1972.

———. *Ecological Imperialism: The Biological Expansion of Europe, 900–1900*. New York: Cambridge University Press, 1986.

Culver, Lawrence. *The Frontier of Leisure: Southern California and the Shaping of Modern America*. New York: Oxford University Press, 2010.

Davis, Mike. *City of Quartz: Excavating the Future in Los Angeles*. London: Verso, 1990.

Delay, Brian. *War of a Thousand Deserts: Indian Raids and the U.S.-Mexican War*. New Haven, CT: Yale University Press, 2008.

Deloria, Philip J. *Indians in Unexpected Places*. Lawrence: University Press of Kansas, 2004.

Deverell, William, ed. *A Companion to the American West*. Boston: Blackwell, 2004.

———. *Whitewashed Adobe: The Rise of Los Angeles and the Remaking of Its Mexican Past*. Berkeley: University of California Press, 2004.

Deverell, William, and David Igler, eds. *A Companion to California History*. Boston: Blackwell, 2008.

Diamond, Jared. *Guns, Germs, and Steel: The Fates of Human Societies*. New York: W. W. Norton, 1997.

DuVal, Kathleen. *The Native Ground: Indians and Colonists in the Heart of the Continent*. Philadelphia: University of Pennsylvania Press, 2006.

Elliott, J. H. *Empires of the Atlantic World: Britain and Spain in America, 1492–1830*. New Haven, CT: Yale University Press, 2006.

Faragher, John Mack. *A Great and Noble Scheme: The Tragic Story of the Expulsion of the French Acadians from Their American Homeland*. New York: W. W. Norton, 2005.

Fischer, David Hackett. *Historians' Fallacies: Toward a Logic of Historical Thought*. New York: Harper & Row, 1970.

Flores, Dan L. *The Natural West: Environmental History in the Great Plains and Rocky Mountains*. Norman: University of Oklahoma Press, 2001.

Foley, Neil. *The White Scourge: Mexican, Blacks, and Poor Whites in Texas Cotton Culture*. Berkeley: University of California Press, 1997.

Frayling, Christopher. *Once Upon a Time in Italy: The Westerns of Sergio Leone*. New York: Harry N. Abrams, 2005.

Fresonke, Kris, and Mark Spence, eds. *Lewis and Clark: Legacies, Memories, and New Perspectives*. Berkeley: University of California Press, 2004.

Furstenberg, Francois. "The Significance of the Trans-Appalachian Frontier in Atlantic History." *American Historical Review* 113 (June 2008): 647–677.

Gordon, Linda. *Dorothea Lange: A Life beyond Limits*. New York: W. W. Norton, 2009.

———. *The Great Arizona Orphan Abduction*. Cambridge, MA: Harvard University Press, 1999.

Graybill, Andrew. *Policing the Plains: Rangers, Mounties, and the North American Frontier, 1875–1910*. Lincoln: University of Nebraska Press, 2007.

Greenberg, Amy. *Manifest Manhood and the Antebellum American Empire*. New York: Cambridge University Press, 2005.

Gregory, James N. *The Southern Diaspora: How the Great Migrations of Black and White Southerners Transformed America*. Chapel Hill: University of North Carolina Press, 2005.

Grossman, James, ed. *The Frontier in American Culture*. Berkeley: University of California Press, 1994.

Gutiérrez, David. *Walls and Mirrors: Mexican Americans, Mexican Immigrants, and the Politics of Ethnicity*. Berkeley: University of California Press, 1995.

Gutiérrez, Ramon. *When Jesus Came, the Corn Mothers Went Away: Marriage, Sexuality, and Power in New Mexico, 1500–1846*. Stanford, CA: Stanford University Press, 1991.

Gutiérrez, Ramon, and Richard J. Orsi, eds. *Contested Eden: California before the Gold Rush*. Berkeley: University of California Press, 1998.

Haas, Lisbeth. *Conquests and Historical Identities in California, 1769–1936*. Berkeley: University of California Press, 1995.

Hackel, Steven. *Children of Coyote, Missionaries of St. Francis: Indian-Spanish Relations in Colonial California, 1769–1850*. Chapel Hill: University of North Carolina Press, 2005.

Hämäläinen, Pekka. *The Comanche Empire*. New Haven, CT: Yale University Press, 2008.

———. "The Rise and Fall of Plains Horse Cultures." *Journal of American History* 90 (December 2003): 833–862.

Harmon, Alexandra. *Indians in the Making: Ethnic Relations and Indian Identities around Puget Sound*. Berkeley: University of California Press, 1998.

Hernández, Kelly Lytle. *Migra! A History of the U.S. Border Patrol*. Berkeley: University of California Press, 2010.

Hinderaker, Eric, and Peter Mancall. *At the Edge of Empire: The Backcountry in British North America*. Baltimore: Johns Hopkins University Press, 2003.

Hine, Robert V., and John Mack Faragher. *The American West: A New Interpretive History*. New Haven, CT: Yale University Press, 2000.

Hsu, Madeline. *Dreaming of Gold, Dreaming of Home: Transnationalism and Migration between the United States and South China, 1882–1943*. Stanford, CA: Stanford University Press, 2000.

Hurtado, Albert. *Border Lord: Herbert Bolton, the West, and American History.* Berkeley: University of California Press, 2011.

———. *Intimate Frontiers: Sex, Gender, and Culture in Old California.* Albuquerque: University of New Mexico Press, 1999.

———. *John Sutter: A Life on the North American Frontier.* Norman: University of Oklahoma Press, 2006.

Hyde, Anne F. *An American Vision: Far Western Landscape and American Culture, 1820–1920.* New York: New York University Press, 1990.

Igler, David. "Diseased Goods: Global Exchanges in the Eastern Pacific Basin, 1770–1850." *American Historical Review* 109 (June 2004): 693–719.

———. *Industrial Cowboys: Miller and Lux and the Transformation of the Far West, 1850–1920.* Berkeley: University of California Press, 2001.

Jacobs, Margaret D. *White Mother to a Dark Race: Settler Colonialism, Maternalism, and the Removal of Indigenous Children in the American West and Australia, 1880–1940.* Lincoln: University of Nebraska Press, 2009.

Jacoby, Karl. *Shadows at Dawn: A Borderlands Massacre and the Violence of History.* New York: Penguin, 2008.

Jameson, Elizabeth, and Susan Armitage, eds. *Writing the Range: Race, Class, and Culture in the Women's West.* Norman: University of Oklahoma Press, 1997.

Johnson, Benjamin H. *Revolution in Texas: How a Forgotten Rebellion and Its Bloody Suppression Turned Mexicans into Americans.* New Haven, CT: Yale University Press, 2003.

Johnson, Benjamin H., and Andrew R. Graybill, eds. *Bridging National Borders in North America: Transnational and Comparative Histories.* Durham, NC: Duke University Press, 2010.

Johnson, Marilynn S. *The Second Gold Rush: Oakland and the East Bay in World War II.* Berkeley: University of California Press, 1993.

Johnson, Susan L. *Roaring Camp: A Social History of the California Gold Rush.* New York: W. W. Norton, 2000.

Josephy, Alvin M., Jr., ed. *Lewis and Clark through Indian Eyes.* New York: Knopf, 2006.

Keirnan, Ben. *Blood and Soil: A World History of Genocide and Extermination from Sparta to Darfur.* New Haven, CT: Yale University Press, 2007.

Klein, Kerwin L. *Frontiers of Historical Imagination: Narrating the European Conquest of Native America, 1890–1990.* Berkeley: University of California Press, 1997.

Kropp, Phoebe S. *California Vieja: Culture and Memory in a Modern American Place.* Berkeley: University of California Press, 2006.

Kurashige, Scott. *The Shifting Grounds of Race: Black and Japanese Americans in the Making of Multiethnic Los Angeles.* Princeton, NJ: Princeton University Press, 2008.

Lightfoot, Kent G. *Indians, Missionaries, and Merchants: The Legacy of Colonial Encounters on the California Frontier.* Berkeley: University of California Press, 2005.

Limerick, Patricia N. *The Legacy of Conquest: The Unbroken Past of the American West.* New York: W. W. Norton, 1987.

Limerick, Patricia, Clyde Milner, and Charles Rankin, eds. *Trails: Toward a New Western History.* Lawrence: University Press of Kansas, 1991.

Lotchin, Roger. *The Bad City in the Good War: San Francisco, Los Angeles, Oakland, and San Diego.* Bloomington: Indiana University Press, 2003.

Mann, Charles C. *1491: New Revelations of the Americas before Columbus.* New York: Knopf, 2005.

McGuinness, Aims. *Path of Empire: Panama and the California Gold Rush.* Ithaca, NY: Cornell University Press, 2008.

Merrill, Karen R. *Public Lands and Political Meaning: Ranchers, the Government, and the Property between Them.* Berkeley: University of California Press, 2002.

Milner, Clyde, Carol O'Connor, and Martha Sandweiss, eds. *The Oxford History of the American West.* New York: Oxford University Press, 1994.

Mitchell, Lee C. *Westerns: Making the Man in Fiction and Films.* Chicago: University of Chicago Press, 1996.

Monroy, Douglas. *Thrown among Strangers: The Making of Mexican Culture in Frontier California.* Berkeley: University of California Press, 1990.

Montoya, Maria. *Translating Property: The Maxwell Land Grant and the Conflict over Land in the American West, 1840–1900.* Berkeley: University of California Press, 2002.

Murrin, John. "Beneficiaries of Catastrophe: The English Colonies in America." In Eric Foner, ed., *The New American History,* 3–23. Philadelphia: Temple University Press, 1990.

Nicolaides, Becky M. *My Blue Heaven: Life and Politics in the Working-Class Suburbs of Los Angeles, 1920–1965.* Chicago: University of Chicago Press, 2002.

Nobles, Gregory H. *American Frontiers: Cultural Encounters and Continental Conquest.* New York: Hill and Wang, 1997.

Nugent, Walter. *Habits of Empire: A History of American Expansion.* New York: Knopf, 2008.

———. *Into the West: The Story of Its People.* New York: Knopf, 1999.

Ostler, Jeffrey. *The Plains Sioux and U.S. Colonialism from Lewis and Clark to Wounded Knee.* New York: Cambridge University Press, 2004.

Pascoe, Peggy. *What Comes Naturally: Miscegenation Law and the Making of Race in America.* New York: Oxford University Press, 2009.

Peck, Gunther. *Reinventing Free Labor: Padrones and Immigrant Workers in the North American West, 1880–1930.* New York: Cambridge University Press, 2000.

Pomeroy, Earl. *The American Far West in the Twentieth Century.* New Haven, CT: Yale University Press, 2008.

Prescott, Cynthia C. *Gender and Generation on the Far Western Frontier.* Tucson: University of Arizona Press, 2007.

Pubols, Louise. *The Father of All: The de la Guerra Family, Power, and Patriarchy in Mexican California.* Berkeley: University of California Press, 2010.

Reséndez, Andrés. *Changing National Identities at the Frontier: Texas and New Mexico, 1800–1850.* New York: Cambridge University Press, 2005.

Richards, Leonard L. *The California Gold Rush and the Coming of the Civil War.* New York: Knopf, 2007.

Richter, Daniel. *Facing East from Indian Country: A Native History of Early America.* Cambridge, MA: Harvard University Press, 2001.

Robb, James J., and William E. Riebsame, eds. *Atlas of the New West: Portrait of a Changing Region.* New York: W. W. Norton, 1997.

Roberts, Brian. *American Alchemy: The California Gold Rush and Middle Class Culture.* Chapel Hill: University of North Carolina Press, 2000.

Roche, Jeff, ed. *The Political Culture of the New West.* Lawrence: University Press of Kansas, 2008.

Rohrbough, Malcolm J. *Days of Gold: The California Gold Rush and the American Nation*. Berkeley: University of California Press, 1997.

———. *Trans-Appalachian Frontier: People, Societies, and Institutions, 1775–1850*. Bloomington: Indiana University Press, 2008.

Ronda, James P. *Lewis and Clark among the Indians*. Lincoln: University of Nebraska Press, 1984.

Rothman, Hal K. *Devil's Bargains: Tourism in the Twentieth-Century American West*. Lawrence: University Press of Kansas, 1998.

Sanchez, George J. *Becoming Mexican American: Ethnicity, Culture, and Identity in Chicano Los Angeles, 1900–1945*. New York: Oxford University Press, 1993.

Sandos, James A. *Converting California: Indians and Franciscans in the Missions*. New Haven, CT: Yale University Press, 2008.

Sandweiss, Martha A. *Print the Legend: Photography and the American West*. New Haven, CT: Yale University Press, 2002.

Scharff, Virginia. *Twenty Thousand Roads: Women, Movement, and the West*. Berkeley: University of California Press, 2002.

Scharff, Virginia, and Carolyn Brucken. *Home Lands: How Women Made the West*. Berkeley: University of California Press, 2010.

Self, Robert O. *American Babylon: Race and the Struggle for Postwar Oakland*. Princeton, NJ: Princeton University Press, 2003.

Slaughter, Thomas P. *Exploring Lewis and Clark: Reflections on Men and Wilderness*. New York: Knopf, 2003.

Slotkin, Richard. *Gunfighter Nation: The Myth of the Frontier in Twentieth-Century America*. New York: Athaneum, 1992.

Smith, Sherry L. *Reimagining Indians: Native Americans through Anglo Eyes, 1880–1940*. New York: Oxford University Press, 2000.

Starr, Kevin. *California: A History*. New York: Modern Library, 2005.

Tate, Michael L. *Indians and Emigrants: Encounters on the Overland Trail*. Norman: University of Oklahoma Press, 2006.

Taylor, Alan. *American Colonies: The Settling of North America*. New York: Penguin, 2001.

Taylor, Quintard. *In Search of the Racial Frontier: African Americans in the American West, 1528–1990*. New York: W. W. Norton, 1998.

Truett, Samuel. *Fugitive Landscapes: The Forgotten History of the U.S.-Mexico Borderlands*. New Haven, CT: Yale University Press, 2006.

Truett, Samuel, and Elliott Young, eds. *Continental Crossroads: Remapping U.S.-Mexico Borderlands History*. Durham: Duke University Press, 2004.

Turner, Frederick Jackson. *The Frontier in American History*. New York: Henry Holt, 1920.

———. *Rise of the New West, 1819–1829*. New York: Harper and Brothers, 1906.

Unruh, John D. *The Plains Across: The Overland Emigrants and the Trans-Mississippi West, 1840–1860*. Champaign: University of Illinois Press, 1979.

Varzally, Allison. *Making a Non-White America: Californians Coloring outside Ethnic Lines, 1925–1955*. Berkeley: University of California Press, 2008.

Warren, Louis. *Buffalo Bill's America: William Cody and the Wild West Show*. New York: Knopf, 2005.

Weber, David J. *Barbaros: Spaniards and Their Savages in the Age of Enlightenment*. New Haven: Yale University Press, 2005.

———. *The Spanish Frontier in North America*. New Haven, CT: Yale University Press, 1994.

West, Elliott. *The Contested Plains: Indians, Goldseekers, and the Rush to Colorado*. Lawrence: University Press of Kansas, 1998.

White, Richard. *"It's Your Misfortune and None of My Own": A New History of the American West*. Norman: University of Oklahoma Press, 1991.

———. *The Middle Ground: Indians, Empires, and Republics in the Great Lakes Region, 1650–1815*. New York: Cambridge University Press, 1991.

Wild, Mark. *Street Meeting: Multiethinic Neighborhoods in Early Twentieth-Century Los Angeles*. Berkeley: University of California Press, 2005.

Worster, Donald. *Under Western Skies: Nature and History in the American West*. New York: Oxford University Press, 1992.

Wrobel, David, and Michael Steiner, eds. *Many Wests: Place, Culture, and Regional Identity*. Lawrence: University Press of Kansas, 1997.

13

Environmental History

SARAH T. PHILLIPS

Environmental history is a relatively new field, little older than a generation. In a very short period it has grown enormously and earned a respectable institutional foothold. Yet environmental historians have always struggled to acknowledge the field's obvious alliance with contemporary, even activist, concerns while maintaining the appropriate scholarly distance. No development appears more critical to understanding humanity's global prospects than environmental change, but environmental history is not necessarily concerned with charting the mistakes of the past or offering clear lessons for the future. Though the point is often made, it bears repeating: environmental history is not environmentalist history. Nor is it solely or even primarily the study of environmental movements or environmental policy.

This is not to say that environmental historians avoid somber conclusions about unhealthy ecosystems, polluted locations, or resource profligacy; they certainly tell those stories, and they should. But that is not all they do. Environmental history is committed, most broadly, to studying the relations between a changing nature and a changing society. It examines how people have lived in natural systems; what they have thought about them; how they have shaped those surroundings; and how in turn the transformations of nature have catalyzed new conflicts over economy, society, governance, culture, and ideology. Because the subject matter is not always easily accessible in the archives, environmental historians often develop interdisciplinary skills and seek out new kinds of data and interpretive frameworks. In this respect they have followed the lead of the social historians of the 1960s and 1970s.

Still, there have been some significant shifts of emphasis within these general continuities. For example, many of the scholars investigating human/nonhuman relations today often begin with concerns about the societal distribution of resources and risk, or with questions about the natural or environmental determinants of social and political authority. In addition, many now accept a model of "nature" so contingent and culturally constructed as to make it almost impossible to extricate any purely natural agents from human relations or environs. People are themselves part of nature, subject to its physical and biological laws, and relentlessly mixing with it their labor, technologies, and ideas. It is not so easy, in other words, to remove ourselves from the picture and to say with certainty what nature *is* or what it *should* be.

Even with a less judgmental approach to the commingling of nature and culture, however, it is still possible to build a case for environmental "agency": nonhuman (or human-manipulated) nature's independence, its unmanageability, and its ability to exert causal influence. Because such influence can occur in almost any historical context, environmental historians police few disciplinary borders and resist strict definitions. They also generate an abundant supply of new questions. But if one belief could unify what is now a sprawling, heterogeneous field, it might be this: while environmental conditions alone do not determine the course of human affairs, there never has existed a stable or "postenvironmental" stage for solely anthropogenic players. Nature and culture are always entangled. Previous generations of historians may have assumed that with the right technology or application of ingenuity environmental obstacles could be surmounted; environmental historians hold that any such attempts always create new entanglements and usually constrain future action in unforeseen ways. Whether or not the idea fits easily into established historical frameworks, nonhuman actors shape historical outcomes, and they will never permit the frictionless unfolding of human events.

This chapter will describe some of the primary contributions in American environmental history since its emergence in the late 1970s and early 1980s. The field is now an international discipline that brings together scholarship on every part of the globe, and environmental historians often take up local, regional, and transnational topics—agriculture, water, climate, demography, technology, markets, energy, consumption, waste, health, ideas about nature, and environmental management—that only sometimes intersect with the more established questions of national histories in general and U.S. national history in particular. That said, the themes here are selected to interest historians of colonial America and the United States.

Conquest and Commodities

Studies of colonial settlement, western expansion, and the spread of capitalistic values and institutions formed the backbone of American environmental history as it originally developed and continue to shape it today.

A deeply rooted skepticism toward celebratory accounts of such topics is not unique to the field. But the frenetic pace at which the continent was conquered and its native inhabitants subdued, combined with the relentless drive to submit land, woods, water, and wildlife to the discipline of profit-hungry markets—all this altered ecological conditions and created new forms of power and authority.

The European conquest of the New World and its native people was from the first an environmental event. Only geographical and biological explanations suffice, Alfred Crosby has argued, if we want to answer why Europeans so quickly established dense settlements and abundant food surpluses in those "neo-European" regions of the world with similar climates and in similar latitudes. In North America, the swift advance of the European agricultural frontier resulted from a team of imported weeds, animals, and ills that worked together as a "portmanteau biota." The immune systems of Native Americans had for millennia been isolated from Old World pathogens, and the bulk of the continent's large mammals had become extinct thousands of years before. The first condition led to an epidemiological disaster: widespread native depopulation and illness from virgin-soil epidemics, the exact numbers dead and percentages affected still a matter of dispute. The second condition ensured the rapid proliferation of European livestock in a land with essentially no competition.

While Crosby provided a sweeping, even deterministic, global perspective on ecological imperialism, others had already begun to investigate specific conditions in colonial New England. For William Cronon, the replacement of Indians by European populations was both an ecological and a cultural revolution that took concrete shape as an unequal contest over economic values. The colonists perceived a land of limitless plenty and a population of Indians who paradoxically refused to make productive use of that plenty. Native Americans were not passive players; they actively managed hunting, foraging, and farming grounds, but kept populations low and probably maintained species diversity and soil health. These practices had developed within a context of purposeful mobility that took advantage of seasonal variations and within a cultural mindset that expected occasional food shortages.

The Indians' mobility and their toleration of scarcity contrasted with English notions of fixity, of improved property, and of storable surpluses—notions that justified the expropriation of native lands and the refusal to acknowledge native use rights. The Indian system of local and regional exchange also contrasted with the colonists' economic practices. The Europeans viewed the environment as a compilation of discrete "resources" such as fish, furs, and timber, ripe for entry into the Atlantic market and ready to be pegged to prices that fluctuated according to its abstract dictates. The market, of course, took no account of the complex ecological relations in which a certain species of tree, fish, or animal was embedded; indeed, it was the process of commodification that set the protocapitalist New England economy on an environmentally transformative path.

Carolyn Merchant added the category of gender to her analysis of New England to account for the colonial ecological revolution and the nineteenth-century industrial revolution, which emerged, she argued, from demographic and ecological pressures on patriarchal inheritance patterns. Timothy Silver extended Cronon's analysis to the South Atlantic region, examining the ecological effects of commodity markets in animal skins, timber and naval stores, and tobacco. The establishment of these markets and the expansion of commercial agriculture required first the work of Native Americans, who were unevenly affected by disease epidemics, and then the labor of skilled African slaves. Mart Stewart's work on coastal Georgia made even clearer that the colonial agricultural world involved an ongoing (and never fully successful) struggle for social as well as environmental control. Intending to build a community of equal producers and well-ordered plots of mulberry trees, royal planners had not anticipated how environmental conditions would instead foster a landscape of low-country rice plantations whose complex hydraulic maintenance depended on power over slaves and over the unpredictable environments that slave labor made profitable. Furthermore, as Judith Carney has argued, slaves brought with them from West Africa an intimate familiarity with rice cultivation, suggesting that environmental entanglements also involved the integration and exploitation of alternate knowledge bases.

More recently, Virginia Anderson directed attention back to the domestic livestock of the colonial period. If in Crosby's story all the Old World livestock moved inexorably across the land, in Anderson's hands these domestic animals are more devious "creatures of empire," purposely deployed for political aims. The colonists originally hoped that Native Americans would imitate the settled and civilized lifestyle associated with proper animal husbandry. But the colonists were too consumed by cash cropping to practice what they preached and set most livestock free to roam and forage. The troublesome beasts, especially the feral pigs, caused no end of mischief, and Indians complained bitterly of ravaged fields and damaged property. Social relations might have been mended had the colonists more speedily recognized damages, or if they had recognized Indian property rights in pigs, which many Indians had incorporated into their own economies and cultures. Instead, they rigged livestock markets against Native Americans and set loose ever more animals as the shock troops of western expansion.

As Virginia Anderson's pig-raising Indians suggest, Native Americans proved adaptive amid wrenching change. But cultural adjustments also meant the renegotiation of social and environmental relationships and often resulted in dispossession and dependency. Native Americans could also make errors of environmental judgment. As Andrew Isenberg argued, when Plains Indians used horses to specialize in buffalo hunting to the exclusion of other activities they put their subsistence at risk in a drought-prone region. This would have been the case even if market hunting, railroads, and the U.S. Army had not delivered the final blow to the bison. Such dynamic models of adaptation and agency are useful in countering popular perceptions of Native Americans as the original environmentalists. By no means, as Shepard Krech has detailed, did European settlers encounter an untouched or primeval wilderness. Some agricultural practices certainly depleted soils, and other activities reduced the populations of certain species of plants and animals. Indians also made extensive use of fire, as Stephen Pyne has documented. So anthropogenic and cultural was the landscape, in fact, that it probably makes little sense to divide North American ecological time into neat precontact and postcontact periods, or even to employ precontact nature as a sure baseline for determining normative models of ecological health.

Still, it is clear that Native Americans really did not exploit resources to the fullest extent possible. Guiding this restraint were moderating forms of cultural management and an animistic cosmology stressing dependence on gracious spirits. In his study of the salmon fisheries of the Pacific Northwest, for example, Joseph Taylor argued that Indians influenced fish populations; sophisticated technologies and extensive trade patterns meant that they consumed an enormous share of the regular salmon runs and possessed the capacity to collect much more salmon than they did. But a variety of beliefs, rituals, taboos, and sanctions limited catches and created a "sustainable tension" between nature and aboriginal society. Euro-American settlement of the Oregon country toppled these culturally specific forms of conservation. The traders and settlers introduced capitalist markets for a variety of commodities, all affecting the fish: mining disturbed streambeds and spawning grounds; farming and grazing damaged riparian areas and sent debris into waterways; lumbering choked up the rivers with logs and milldams. And last but not least, industrial fishers and canners frenetically packed salmon for markets around the world.

All this extractive activity gave rise to questions about whether Western religious or scientific culture prepared Euro-Americans to view the earth as a mere storehouse of resources for profit and pleasure. An influential essay by Lynn White traced environmental decline to a Judeo-Christian tradition whose God gave humankind dominion over nature. Carolyn Merchant called attention to the European scientific revolution as the moment when capitalism joined forces with a newly "mechanistic" view of the world to justify the unchecked manipulation of nature's constituent parts. Western history, Merchant even suggested, is mostly a story of "reinventing Eden": establishing anew the productive garden from which Adam and Eve were ejected. Finding accounts of Christianity too one-sided, however, Mark Stoll identified within American Protestantism a corresponding and no less biblical tradition of wonder, care, and stewardship—a tradition, he argues, that helped to shape the modern conservationist and environmentalist ethic.

Whatever the role of religious thinking, these studies of the colonial and early national periods illustrate how for environmental history the concept of *commodification* has remained portable across much time and space. No other process explains as well the modern unraveling of ecological relationships (or the unraveling of entire societies' basis of subsistence and identity, in the case of many Native American groups). And no other process explains as well the new nation's comparatively prosperous economic history. It is true that the geological and climatic forces shaping North America had created a unique abundance of biological and mineral resources. But it should also be kept in mind that "abundance" acquired concrete economic meaning only through the institutional structures of market exchange and capitalist relations. To take the most celebrated example of New World abundance, "land" was indeed more plentiful in the American colonies than in Europe; but the widespread availability of freehold land ownership and the authority to divide, parcel, and sell it at will—in short, to turn land into an unencumbered commodity—was no more a "natural" fact than any other legal or social practice.

Nor were the water resources powering industrialization a straightforward natural endowment, as Ted Steinberg has explained. Factories needed complex networks of locks and dams to drive the industrial machinery. Investors also needed to dispense with practices that had previously guided New Englanders' relationship to water. Common law tradition had meant that landowners along rivers did not *own* water; they had certain rights to use the water as long as they did not impair its use by others. But factory owners needed more precise accounting of water*power* units so that water itself could be packaged and sold. Waterpower became a valuable commodity, and corporate bodies acquired control of water resources on a regional scale through land purchases and additional dam building. The permanent structures provoked protests from a variety of affected users—from farmers whose fields were flooded, and from local people accustomed to more plentiful fish or to unimpeded logging runs—but the courts gradually ruled in favor of the parties (the manufacturers) who generated the most economic return from the rivers. Courts also began to erode older conceptions of public trust doctrine and nuisance law by applying the same economic logic to early forms of industrial pollution, as John Cumbler and Christine Rosen have shown. These rulings established long-standing precedents for legally externalizing the costs of waste and sewage.

In the South, what some scholars have identified as a sustainable pattern of shifting cultivation was supplanted in the late eighteenth century by more ecologically damaging and territorially expansive methods of growing tobacco and cotton. It is not quite clear to what extent distinctive soils, soil exhaustion, and soil erosion shaped a unique southern agricultural history, or how exactly the plantation system and its legacies affected the southern landscape over the nineteenth century and beyond. These are long-standing questions, and there is a rich tradition of southern agricultural history (and indeed, of agricultural history more generally) that has only recently begun to merge with environmental history. But it is probably safe to conclude that the combination of slavery and monocultural crop production pushed investment in directions other than land stewardship. After the Civil War, as the region became locked even further into single-crop cotton production, soils suffered enormous damage, and southern farms became voracious consumers of fertilizer. As a densely populated colonial economy, the New South and its common people suffered both from increased commercial pressures on land, forests, and minerals, and from high levels of outside control over those resources. Many of these developments are deftly explored in Jack Temple Kirby's history of the region's ecological landscapes.

Turning some parts of nature into commodities—goods traded for a profit, accountable in units of abstract wealth—was very much the environmental mechanism of western conquest as well. Western history has long nurtured environmental approaches, and environmental historians, like their western counterparts, have cut conceptual teeth on the question of the frontier in shaping a distinctive American past. In popular mythology and in Frederick Jackson Turner's famous frontier thesis, western expansion had proceeded in an evolutionary manner: first the trader, the "pathfinder of civilization," supplanted the savage Indian and Indian-like hunter; they in turn were replaced by the rancher; then came intensive farm settlement; and finally manufacturing and cities. But in America's "Great West," as William Cronon argued, the industrial city created the countryside—not vice versa. We can only account for Chicago's explosive nineteenth-century growth by understanding how its markets linked eastern capital to the grain, lumber, and meat extracted from the fertile prairies and abundant forests of the city's vast hinterlands. It was the heretofore untapped "wealth of nature," the stored sunshine accumulated over millennia, that so rewarded the comparatively limited applications of human labor. In this formulation Turner was partly correct: the frontier may indeed have created an exceptional American history, but not one premised on "free land" as much as one arising from abundant natural resources that could release stores of untapped energy simply not available in more long-settled parts of the world.

But the wealth of nature could not bankroll forever such levels of extraction. Chicago's stockyards felt the decline; so too did its surrounding grassland ecosystems and the cutover pinelands to the north. And off went the capital to pursue more distant natural quarry while the city stayed put. Evoking a lament that has become quite prominent both in the field and in popular writing, Cronon reminded his readers that the habits of modern American life separate consumption from production. The problem of "distancing" is not solely an environmental myopia, of course, but it is a fact that nature and culture are being constantly reworked in distant locations to generate goods for American consumers unaware of their ecological footprints.

On this theme, Jennifer Price has explored the extinction of the passenger pigeon and the moral distance between the flocks in the forests and the sauced meat on stylish restaurant plates. "Martha," the very last passenger pigeon, died in 1914. Richard Tucker and John Soluri have described a few of the unfortunate environmental and social consequences of Americans' "insatiable appetite" for tropical products such as coffee and bananas. E. Melanie DuPuis and Steven Stoll have also helped to illuminate how the year-round availability of standardized fresh foods—the overcoming of seasonality for urban consumers, in other words—involved, respectively, the environmental and economic restructuring of New York City's rural "milkshed" and the fruit-growing regions of California. Agricultural intensification—increased applications of capital and technology—offered no more protection from ecologically questionable methods of food production than did extensive methods. The subordination of plant and animal biology to industrial logic furthermore created new system-wide risks, because simplified fields and confined bodies are inherently weak, vulnerable to pests and disease, and reliant on problematic inputs like insecticides and antibiotics that threaten ecosystems and public health. The uninvited organisms also develop resistance over time, and methods meant to conquer and control them eventually do neither. "Nature fights back," Rachel Carson famously declared in *Silent Spring*. William Boyd's examination of the poultry industry and James McWilliams's work on insect fighting are just two of the many works that confirm her thesis.

Environment and Temporality

Though the term "commodification" is both too broad and too narrow to encompass the widely diverse methods of making a living and a profit from the "wealth of nature," the concept's centrality to American environmental history has consistently presented difficulties for incorporating the field's primary topics into American history more generally. Chronologies of markets and commodities—the engines of production and consumption that drive environmental change and vice versa—do not map easily onto political timelines. The challenge of integration will loom just as large if environmental history jettisons market-system models and more fully embraces "bioregional" approaches. However, it might be a fair price to pay if, as Dan Flores holds, such "place-based" stories of ecological and cultural adaptation better reflect the common patterns of humans' long evolutionary past and their common biological, even *animal*, drives.

This is not to say that environmental historians have skipped over more familiar historical fare. Two works in the growing field of southern environmental history, for example, speak directly to established lines of inquiry, namely, the question of the southern market revolution and yeoman culture. An examination of antebellum fish petitions confirmed for Harry Watson that the upcountry residents of South Carolina made purposeful choices to resist a growing plantation and commercial economy embodied in mills that blocked rivers, prevented shad migrations, and processed lumber for export and food for slaves. For the New South period, Claire Strom investigated the environmental contours of yeomen's resistance to the spread of commercial agriculture and to the national government's imposition of burdensome stock-raising regulations. The cattle tick is not yet as well known to southern historians as the boll weevil, but it should be. For western and labor history, Thomas Andrews has offered an environmental interpretation of the Colorado coalfield struggles that culminated with the infamous Ludlow massacre of 1914. The violence of the ensuing coalfield war was traceable to a dangerous, underground "workscape" ecology that unfolded within a regional, urban-industrial economy newly dependent on fossil fuels.

Still, competing temporalities are probably inevitable even if environmental history occasionally contributes important perspectives on more established topics. The articulation of alternative chronologies, after all, is fundamental to the field's raison d'être. Environmental history, like social and cultural history, is partly indebted to the French *Annales* school, with its emphasis on long-term historical structures and attention to social, demographic, and geographical change. Most American environmental historians do not exclusively pursue the *longue durée*, to be sure, but they share a desire to analyze transformations and processes that might otherwise remain unseen and unacknowledged.

Topping that list of topics is the relationship between nature and capitalism. As detailed previously, environmental historians mostly tell this story through the lens of commodification. But a rich debate is developing over the timing and extent of commodification and market mentalities at any one period or in any one place. Take, for example, colonial Concord, Massachusetts. By the revolutionary era it was packed with farms whose crop yields were declining and whose children were departing for points west. Surely, historians have agreed, this was the inevitable result of a destructive and extensive agricultural system—clearing fresh land, exhausting its fertility, and then hitting up against New England's stony, unforgiving soils. But what if you discovered that mid-eighteenth century Concord was actually still full of trees? Colonial farmers, Brian Donahue found, actually practiced a sustainable form of common-field mixed husbandry. The division of fields, pastures, and woodlots, and the attentive recycling of nutrients originating in meadow grass, revealed to Donahue a culture and an agroecology oriented toward permanence. Capitalist pressures eventually precipitated unfortunate environmental consequences, but not before the system confronted the same internal force that had always destabilized European agrarian societies: demographic growth.

Discoveries of ecological restraint might appear unremarkable, except for the fact that such stories help dissipate the lines of inevitability that often flow through the field's "degradation narratives." It is also possible to sidestep the usual narratives of conquest and commodification altogether. For example, Thomas Dunlap, Aaron Sachs, and Conevery Valenčius have offered genuinely novel perspectives on continental exploration, environmental change, and environmental perception by means of histories of natural science and bodily health. Still, while environmental history has embraced alternative topical, temporal, and methodological frameworks, the field is unlikely to abandon debate on the chronology and natural implications of a capitalist political economy. These original concerns remain deeply ingrained, largely because environmental historians have mostly believed that American political ideology has operated quite cohesively when it comes to questions of natural conquest and commercial development, and they purposely constructed timelines separate from the usual political chronologies and categories.

No scholar has been more influential in establishing and defending this line of reasoning than Donald Worster, who has maintained that Americans primarily approached the environment with "instrumental reason." A thoroughgoing business culture meant that most Americans viewed nature only as capital—the source of profit and personal wealth—to be mined for all its worth. At a time when social, cultural, and labor historians were busily uncovering numerous political traditions and alternative moral worlds, environmental history appeared to move in the opposite direction. If for an observer like Louis Hartz the liberal tradition in America was a very narrow debate over the ideal distribution of private property (a position besieged from all sides by the 1970s and 1980s), for an environmental historian like Worster there was little debate at all. Liberalism meant a culture largely unified in its determination to take from nature its means to independence; and corporate liberalism meant a culture on the brink of destroying its foundation and structures of support.

Worster has most influentially explored the environmental and social consequences of the American capitalist ethos for the distinctive environments of the West. Jeffersonian and agrarian ideals entailed geographical expansion—why limit desires, share resources, or exercise entrepreneurial restraint when the acquisition of more land can beget more property? But western conditions threw up unexpected and unique roadblocks to the empire of liberty. Living in balance with the region's aridity and climatic volatility, its limited and unpredictable rainfall, would have required revisions to the capitalist mindset that Americans were unwilling to imagine. When a speculative business culture encountered the southern plains, for example, the result was not a slow-moving series of environmental ills, but one enormous ecological disaster in real time: the Dust Bowl. New agricultural technology played a part in the great plow-up; so too did a booming international market for wheat. But at bottom, Worster argues, the tragedy was caused by the culture's failure to adapt to drought and wind as the grasslands had done. And furthermore, despite some farsighted proposals, Franklin Roosevelt's New Deal propped up crop farming in the region and made every American taxpayer a shareholder of that risk.

Indeed, according to Worster, no region more adeptly compelled the rest of the nation to finance its environmental conquest than the West. An arid land on the "raw edge of scarcity," the modern West developed as a hydraulic society, utterly dependent on the unified control of every river and the storage and manipulation of every drop of water. But despite this dependence, Worster maintained, the West is actually an *empire* where neither nature nor society is free. The history of all past hydraulic societies reveals one inescapable fact: feats of environmental control necessitate both the centralization of power and the subjugation of people. Every large-scale irrigation society requires a rural proletariat, that is, and the fate of the American West was no different, particularly California's, whose ascent to world agricultural preeminence was piloted by a state-capitalist "power elite" who directly controlled the fate of the migrant labor force and indirectly held sway over the remaining herd of westerners.

The irony is that over the course of the twentieth century so many genuinely democratic voices supported the U.S. reclamation program begun in 1902 and expanded every decade thereafter until the 1970s. Irrigation, the reasoning went, would reclaim the West from land monopolists like the cattle and wheat barons. Family farms would thrive and freedoms would multiply if resources were more fairly divided and collectively governed. But populists and Democrats, according to Worster, and indeed all subsequent leftists and liberals, were really no different from the capitalists and their trusty engineer servants. The do-gooders assumed that the ultimate problem was concentrated land ownership, not the concentration of power—technical, economic, and political—that followed *inevitably* from environmental conquest. Never would such expensive water have supported an equitable agrarian landscape: to make that water *pay*, landowners planted high-value crops and demanded wage laborers for the harvest, and only for the harvest. Little wonder the democratic theorists and reformers never successfully limited large growers' access to subsidized water or to exploitable workers, or understood that, like all empires, the hydraulic West too would decline.

Worster has not been allowed the last word on either the Dust Bowl or western reclamation. R. Douglas Hurt and Pamela Riney-Kehrberg, for example, have drawn different conclusions about the Dust Bowl's causes and significance. Geoff Cunfer found that land use patterns on the Great Plains were relatively stable over the twentieth century, with the period from 1925 and 1940 containing not an ecological disaster, but a relatively mild course correction when crop farmers pushed a little too far onto marginal land and pulled back slightly. The factors of low rainfall and very high temperatures may have been more critical in triggering dust storms than the amount of plowed acreage. About western water in general and the Bureau of Reclamation in particular there is a head-spinning number of works, but Norris Hundley and Donald Pisani have contributed useful counterweights. Their studies undercut any notion of a unified "power elite" with complicated portraits of shifting political alliances and cross-cutting interests, especially the West's voracious urban consumers of water and electric power. And on the question of whether nature itself was conquered, Mark Fiege strongly demurred. The irrigated landscape was a dynamic entity in which elements of the wild certainly endured. What is more, unruly waterways and a "hybrid biota" consistently foiled attempts at control.

But Worster's scholarship remains enormously influential. Perhaps its influence remains strong because his frameworks transcend their topics, arguing defiantly for the ultimate historical irrelevance of political divisions that contest the distribution of wealth and not its environmental foundation or unavoidable depreciation. In a recent biography of John Muir (the most important forerunner of American environmentalism), Worster even found a branch of the liberal tradition he deemed more democratic and morally advanced than any of the other economic reform programs or redistributive schemes of the Gilded Age and Progressive Era. John Muir believed that a love of wild nature—indeed, a *need* for it—dwelled equally in every man and woman. The fullest expression of religious, social, and economic freedom was to exult in nature's beauty and to extend both empathy and justice, even *rights*, to nature's nonhuman creatures. While Muir often expressed sympathy with efforts to regulate the influence of concentrated wealth, he believed that such reform would never address the root problem: a poor man was just as capable of plundering nature's riches as a corporation. If part of Muir's material legacy can be gleaned from the country's extensive system of national forests, parks, wildlife refuges, and wilderness areas, his philosophical and political legacy might be understood as the contemporary commitment, however faint, to halting the global destruction of an environment upon which everyone's liberty ultimately depends.

The Nature of Power and the Power of Nature

The reader might be forgiven if American environmental history still sounds like environmental*ist* history. At one level, the field must plead guilty. Its practitioners are obviously troubled by environmental degradation and want to account for it. But they should not be charged with unreflective biocentrism or social reductionism. Especially since the mid-1990s, environmental historians have largely jettisoned holistic accounts of American capitalist culture and more deftly explored the social-historical categories of class, race, and gender. Works on conservation and environmental policy have multiplied voluminously, also positioning those movements within broad political, legal, and cultural contexts. The field never ignored cities entirely, but not until recently has urban environmental history come of age. An interest in sustainability has led back to agricultural history and to the cultivated fields. Environmental history has grown still further to merge with histories of public health, science, and technology. Transnational and comparative approaches are thriving; cultural and intellectual approaches abound. In short, as some of the works cited earlier already suggest, environmental history is globally oriented, attentive to inequity, alert to competitions for knowledge and power, and concerned with what changing environments have meant and will mean for the *people* who inhabit them.

What might explain some of these shifts? At the risk of oversimplifying a complicated and ongoing debate, it appears that the field's original orientation toward capitalist conquest and commodities masked a few problems. One concerned the standard against which settlement and expansion was most often measured: wilderness. The portrait of the wasteful pioneers (and their corporate and state successors) chopping, plowing, mining, and river-pushing their way through the land had often called forth stories that chronicled the awakening of appreciation for that lost wilderness. Protection, in other words, was the historiographical flip side of pioneering, and unspoiled Eden was usually the normative counterpoint to conquest. But environmental historians started to interrogate more critically the assumptions and assertions of authority that lay behind protectionist feelings and protectionist measures. They began to ask, "Protection in whose interest, and for what ends?"

William Cronon famously suggested that the conceptual distinction between conquered and wild nature had prevented Americans from developing healthy and sustainable relationships with the nature at their doorsteps. While the hypothesis may or may not be open to empirical testing, he detected a real problem: the historiographical dualism that he found so worrisome had no doubt stymied more subtle explorations of labor and work, as well as more critical investigations of leisure and recreation. "Are You an Environmentalist or Do You Work for a Living?" read the backlash bumper sticker that Richard White so provocatively used to title an essay reflecting upon some of these themes in Cronon's *Uncommon Ground.* Given the "trouble with wilderness," as Cronon put it, more environmental historians turned their attention to sites of work and class divisions, to landscapes of hybridity, and to the construction of "organic machines," to use White's now famous phrase. Everywhere they looked they discovered more artifice in the natural, and more nature in the artificial. The recognition, acceptance even, of hybrid landscapes and "second" natures has created some tension in the field between those who seek to understand the power of discourse and narrative in shaping both environmental perception and nature itself, and those who worry that such approaches might deflect the field from its materialist origins and foster a disengaged relativism about environmental change.

But environmental historians were not only building bridges to social history, and they were not simply taking the cultural turn. Nature was still *there.* It was (and is) a set of actual, material facts. But what set of facts? These questions point to environmental history's complicated relationship with science in general and with ecology in particular. Ecologists study biological interdependence—how solar energy and chemical nutrients flow through plant and animal communities called ecosystems (a term coined in the 1930s). Because ecology and the biological sciences provided postwar environmentalists (and environmental historians) with hard data about how environments respond to disturbance, they freed both activists and analysts from the sentimentality that had so often underlay previous defenses of beauty, scenery, and natural integrity. An environmental approach to history was in fact proposed by one of the earliest American popularizers of ecological concepts. In 1949, Aldo Leopold suggested that most events were not the outcomes of human enterprise alone, but of the "biotic interactions" between people and land.

Like any scholarly discipline, however, ecological science is not fixed or unchanging. There is a popular conception of ecosystems, for example, largely deriving from texts like Leopold's, that views them as stable, permanent webs of perfectly evolved biological and chemical teams. Contemporary ecologists, however, do not hold these views, and no one has known this better than environmental historians. For some time, models of "normal" or even "healthy" ecosystems have emphasized disturbance and change, not stasis and permanence. But incorporating whole models of disturbance or chaos within historical narratives (as opposed to more issue-specific data) is exceedingly tricky. What is a healthy ecosystem? When are people and their poisons greater disturbers than other natural events? And how should we write scientifically informed stories about nature (and hybrid natures) given that scientific theories are themselves open to scrutiny and revision? The notion of an unstable, and perhaps unknowable, nature has created considerable intellectual turmoil within the field. It is less tempting now to blame everything on human disturbance. More troubling, though, at least from the viewpoint of environmental historians who would prefer an increase in scientific literacy, it is more tempting to devalue scientific approaches altogether.

The intellectual turmoil, however, has not slowed the field's expansion or prevented the proliferation of new work. On one front, many environmental historians choose to sidestep the scientific arena and to revisit intellectual, political, and social topics, mainly the evolution of protectionist attitudes and the formation of conservation and environmental policy. Questions of American environmental sentiment and politics are longstanding to the field, predating it even, and any newcomer should be aware of two influential books written several decades ago. Roderick Nash first asked how a society premised on environmental conquest could hatch a movement for wilderness and declare it a civilizational requirement. Nature appreciation, Nash argued, first arose in the cities and from men of artistic and literary talents who perceived in wildness a necessary complement to the stultifying requirements of modern life. From this romantic seed grew a more widespread wilderness cult, which eventually joined forces with the ecology minded to demand the setting aside of vast wilderness areas in the post–World War II era.

A key moment in Nash's history took place during the Progressive Era. Then, the wilderness advocates battled not only the usual economic interests opposed to preservation; they also had to contend with the newest iteration of the pioneering spirit: conservationists such as chief forester Gifford Pinchot who also demanded economic returns from the nation's resources, even if over the long term, and who too cast a long shadow over the twentieth century. The pivotal standoff was the fight over Hetch Hetchy in the 1910s: conservationists may have won the battle—they succeeded in damming this picturesque valley in the Yosemite National Park—but over the long term the preservationists would win the war. Nash bequeathed to environmental history an influential chronology; a cast of character-heroes; and a dualist conceptual framework (the pioneer versus the romantic, the utilitarian conservationist versus the preservationist-ecologist). Subsequent historians have remained in Nash's debt even as they revise many of these contributions. One can find a more nature-loving Gifford Pinchot, for example, in Char Miller's biography; and one will discover few champions of untouched wilderness in Robert Righter's recent history of Hetch Hetchy.

A few years before Nash, Samuel Hays provided an equally enduring portrait of the turn-of-the-century conservationists. The first large areas of public land reserved from private entry and managed directly by the federal government were the national forests—a system that now covers one-tenth of the country's surface area, mostly in the West. Because a Progressive-Era luminary like Theodore Roosevelt had defended such conservationist policies as a victory for common Americans, it had been easy for historians to accept this rhetoric at face value and to conclude that conservation was no doubt a victory for "the people" over greedy industrial interests. Hays argued instead that the conservationists were motivated not by their desire to rein in the power of the trusts, but by their loyalty to the ideals of the emerging scientific professions. This new spirit of efficiency required expert personnel with administrative discretion: executive power independent of Congress and the courts. Furthermore, the conservationists promised *expansion*, not limits; they believed that the woods and rivers were *under*utilized, not overused! This is why in Hays's account the conservation crusade actually formed first around concerns over the long-term control, storage, and distribution of water. The reclamation program begun in 1902 flowed from these concerns, as did the national forests that were established to protect the headwaters of major Western rivers. Indeed, over the twentieth century, issues of multiple-purpose water management in both the West and the East probably exerted more influence over national conservation governance than did forest policy.

While Hays's interpretation remains influential, it is not invulnerable. William Robbins depicted forestry and forest policy as almost completely dominated by private and industrial interests. Other scholars, attentive to Hays's contribution to the political history of the Progressive Era, have returned to the themes of national state building and administration. Donald Pisani found that neither "science" nor "efficiency" shaped a reclamation program that basically failed during the first three decades of its existence; explaining this history requires a grasp of political divisions rooted in nineteenth-century ideologies and congressional prerogatives. In a similar vein, Brian Balogh downplayed the novelty of Gifford Pinchot's administrative strategies, highlighting instead the forester's "half-baked" professional training, his support for patronage networks, and the fuzzy accounting meant to convince proper businessmen that conservation was profitable.

Despite such examples of administrative underdevelopment, Bruce Schulman has argued that Progressive-Era conservationists nonetheless established enough bureaucratic and managerial autonomy to send American government on an internationally distinct path focused on the exploitation and management of natural resources. One reason why this path may have been taken is suggested in Karen Merrill's history of western ranchers and the public lands: because the federal government claimed ownership over vast amounts of territory, it was able to join an established moral and legal discourse on property rights. Taking the state-building story forward in time, my own work has shown that conservationist ideas pursued after the Progressive Era, and much more oriented toward questions of distributive justice, underlay New Deal strategies of rural rehabilitation and national economic recovery in the 1930s. While I concluded that American political institutions ultimately proved incapable of reconciling the competing tensions among sustainability, efficiency, and equity, Neil Maher found in the New Deal era the more hopeful mainstreaming of ecological understandings and the grassroots origins of postwar environmentalism.

There are other works that broaden the history of conservation. Richard Judd and Steven Stoll pushed the story further back into the nineteenth century, uncovering agrarian conservationist traditions in which the maintenance of soils, forests, and farm landscapes nurtured a genuinely local and not necessarily elitist appreciation for natural balance and environmental harmony. Ian Tyrrell analyzed agrarian reform as a transnational conservationist tradition, finding that both Australians and Californians shared a garden and horticultural aesthetic intended to redeem and renovate vast landscapes maimed by mining and ranching. Moving back East, John Cumbler looked at how the first steps of conservation in the Connecticut River Valley emerged from efforts to regulate fisheries and control water pollution.

Cumbler is not the only historian to draw attention to the urban and industrial origins of environmentalism in the conservation era. City dwellers and civic reformers demanded a clean, healthful environment and a certain measure of environmental equity well before the modern environmental movement. In fact, sensitive to modern-day charges that environmentalists have always valued wild nature more than people, Robert Gottlieb included in his overview of the American environmental movement a chapter on the Progressive-Era municipal and workplace roots of what we now might call environmental justice. Women such as Alice Hamilton and Jane Addams emerged as key players in this early history. More recently, David Stradling also identified a strain of grassroots civic environmentalism in the activism of many lesser-known but no less engaged Progressive-Era clubwomen who fought coal smoke pollution. His work even suggested that the larger antismoke campaign was ultimately unsuccessful because the women's concerns were supplanted by a less effective and more industry-friendly approach dominated by professional male engineers. Sylvia Hood Washington has looked at immigrant and African-American responses to environmental marginalization in Chicago. Moving into the factory, Christopher Sellers analyzed the workplace origins of industrial toxicology, the first science to grapple in the laboratory with the health effects of airborne poisons and contaminants rather than bacteria.

Returning to rural areas, a different revisionist direction has been taken by those historians interested in examining the social groups at whose expense and against whose welfare new conservationist policies were usually enacted and sustained. The clearest instances of outright dispossession involved Native Americans. As Mark Spence has shown, Americans justified the creation of new national park boundaries and the abrogation of clear treaty rights on the false ideas that these lands were never occupied and that they should remain in a purely virgin, untouched state. Louis Warren explored how the Anglo settlers of southern Arizona uncharacteristically welcomed public conservationist supervision over game animals largely owing to their desire to restrict and control Indian hunters. Aiming straight at the heart of the national park mystique with an analysis of the Grand Canyon, Karl Jacoby has detailed how the annual subsistence rhythms of the Havasupai Indians were needlessly undermined by the establishment of a national forest reserve on the canyon's rim. A variety of struggles over native rights continues to this day in many regions of the country, but in most others Americans have concocted a variety of stories to explain and give meaning to dispossessed landscapes. In Utah, Jared Farmer found that settlers not only ejected native people from the well-watered lowlands, but also, over time, invented false histories of mountain-dwelling Indians and wove myths about native princesses doomed to die.

But the social critique extends beyond cases of Native American dispossession. Many studies have pointed out the considerable class, racial, ethnic, and gender biases among conservationists and preservationists. In Ian Tyrrell's cross-Pacific history, for example, the ideal agrarian landscape is—in a word—white. Peter Coates has examined links between nativist efforts to restrict immigration and attempts to exclude nonnative, *alien*, species of flora and fauna, though he finds no evidence for the material continuity of these connections after the 1950s despite the continuity of rhetoric. Adam Rome has convincingly proposed that the marginalization of women's groups and women's activism narrowed the environmental agenda between the Progressive Era and the 1960s.

Environmental historians have also explored the erosion of local subsistence strategies and the moral economies of resource use that governed communities before the imposition of outside and often elite control. One early pioneer here was Arthur McEvoy, who included in his history of the California fisheries sympathetic portraits of nineteenth-century Chinese and Italian fishermen, and suggested that the elimination of their operations had adverse environmental consequences. In their study of New York

City's Central Park, Roy Rosenzweig and Elizabeth Blackmar did not celebrate the park as a premier example of landscape architecture, but instead embedded its history within contentious debates over how *public* this parcel of public land really should be, and in whose interest it should be managed. Acquiring land for the park, for example, required the expulsion of stable communities of African Americans and immigrants, disparagingly called "squatters" by wealthier people who did not understand or appreciate the resourceful ways these pre-park residents gathered food and made use of the city's debris.

An interest in social history and moral economy has assisted the discovery of resistance to conservationist authority, a methodological development that aligned American environmental history more closely with the environmental histories of other parts of the world. Louis Warren uncovered how Italian immigrants who hunted songbirds to provide meat for family tables resisted regulations directed at them by the elite members of Pennsylvania's sporting clubs. In the Adirondack preserve in upstate New York, Karl Jacoby described locals who well understood the threat to their subsistence posed by new forest rules and by the expansion of vast, privately owned hunting estates. While many of these stories can be understood as revisionist descriptions of upper-class sportsmen, who had formerly been considered uncomplicated conservationist forerunners, much of this scholarship makes a further point: working landscapes often became landscapes of commodified leisure and wage labor, and it is not at all certain that the rewards of these changes outweighed the costs. For the best example of how an enclosure movement voided alternative and perhaps more sustainable working landscapes, one need only look to the post–Civil War South. There, as Steven Hahn and Jack Temple Kirby have shown, the closing of the open range and new restrictions on hunting and fishing circumscribed the economic and subsistence possibilities of blacks and poorer whites. Reflecting upon some of these lost freedoms, Mart Stewart has even imagined a different trajectory for American environmentalism, one that might have developed had John Muir turned south instead of west, and had he become more engaged by the region's occupied lands, its diverse people, and its agrarian traditions.

There are further reasons why American environmental history has embraced attempts to locate past examples of sustainability and community. Simply put, it appears that the revolutionary new efforts begun around the turn of the twentieth century to protect large parcels of land, certain forms of wildlife, and scenic places from short-term development may not only have foreclosed genuinely alternative working landscapes, but also may have done nothing to prevent the maturation of a voracious and environmentally predatory consumer economy. In fact, the two developments went hand in hand: consumers demanded environmental access and recreational amenities. Linking modern consumers to nature, of course, was the automobile. As Paul Sabin has explored, government policy between 1900 and 1940—not the free market—established the legal and institutional framework for the cheap oil that first fueled Americans' car-crazy ways and their petroleum-dependent economy.

Concerns about the consumer society, in fact, have led some scholars back into the wilderness. While certainly aware of "the trouble with wilderness," Paul Sutter determined that none of the revisionist social critiques applied to the men who, between the World Wars, developed the specific proposals that culminated in the Wilderness Act of 1964. Expecting to find the influence of ecological thinking, Sutter instead discovered that the founders of the Wilderness Society really came together over a different set of concerns: road building and the troubling expansion of motorized recreation that roads suddenly allowed. "Roadlessness," after all, is the functional definition of a wilderness area. Such attention to timing allowed Sutter to defend the modern wilderness idea as a needed brake on modern consumer behavior.

While all these works complicate and deepen our understanding of the history of conservation, they rely heavily on the tools and methods of social, cultural, and political history to do so. But environmental historians also employ scientific and ecological concepts to make sense of the landscapes and organisms that conservationists so hopefully intended to manage and control. One might assume that, once initiated, professional and public-spirited management ensured the longevity and ecological health of wildlife and forests. But public management has had a very poor ecological track record, and officials have all too frequently needed to address unforeseen problems caused by past actions. In his history of salmon, for example, Joseph Taylor explained how fish propagation and hatcheries, methods originally intended to protect and even increase the supply of salmon, actually directed the species onto a different evolutionary path, one much more ecologically vulnerable than before. Nancy Langston has deftly explored the ideological assumptions and scientific blinders that handicapped foresters and wildlife managers, whether they were trying to "grow" trees or ducks.

Environmental history has also become more urban in orientation. For quite some time, rural and wild places remained the primary areas of analysis because the field was mostly concerned with the immediate locations of production and preservation—nature was something "out there." In a general sense, however, the field has always been aware that cities, with their spatial concentrations of population and industry, were entities with crucial environmental ramifications for both residents and hinterlands. Important tributaries to urban environmental history were the investigations of disease, sanitation, and municipal reform undertaken by public health scholars like Charles Rosenberg. A related stream flowed from the technological and political histories of sanitary services—water supply, sewerage, and solid-waste removal—pioneered by Joel Tarr and Martin Melosi. This infrastructure was undoubtedly a major accomplishment that created more healthful and livable cities, but these systems also "outsourced" urban problems, drawing water from distant locations and sending ever-increasing amounts of garbage, pollution, and sewage far beyond the city limits. Infrastructure meant to "wrest" a city from nature also generated new geographies of risk and environmental instability, as Craig Colten's studies of New Orleans have shown.

Many observers have perceived within the field a decidedly antiurban bias. There are grounds for these assertions: environmental historians have depicted modern cities as growth machines and parasites. Urban development and expansion are predicated upon increasing levels of consumption and energy use, and cities gather up resources from distant locations and expel their wastes, trash, and poisons far and wide. But these are not the only stories about cities one can tell. Ari Kelman's work on New Orleans and Matthew Klingle's on Seattle illustrate how urban environmental history has been at the forefront of the field's recent attention to hybridity, cultural formation, and social division. Cities do not eradicate nature, nor do their residents lose contact with the environment or fail to develop a sense or ethic of place. Cities are in fact sites of a new synthesis—"metropolitan nature," in Matthew Gandy's phrase—that emerges from the creation and remixing of environmental amenities, public space, and public services. Still, environmental quality is unequally distributed, and urban environments both reflect and reify the city's architecture of power.

Something New under the Sun

The twentieth century presents environmental history with its greatest opportunity as well as its greatest challenge. On the one hand, the period witnessed the unprecedented intensification of resource use and the rapid acceleration of ecological degradation. As J. R. McNeill put it, there indeed was "something new under the sun." Perhaps a quarter of the world's people—and almost all Americans—now live and eat in ways that unwisely assume the infinite existence of cheap water, cheap energy, and a stable climate. For U. S. history, it is possible to argue that this fossil-fuel-based society, and the entirely new oil economy, changed almost every aspect of American life, from farming to pharmaceuticals, housing to foreign policy. What is more, petroleum-derived products and compounds also created vast new waste streams, poisoned wildlife and ecosystems, and became endemic menaces to human health and reproductive functions. Such obvious and fundamental change should be at the center of how we write and teach the twentieth century; energy, plastics, and petrochemicals are just a few examples, even though they are probably the most important. But the environmental perspective has not really altered primary historical approaches to the twentieth century, nor have environmental historians pushed it too hard onto their colleagues in other fields. The declensionist teleology is just too destabilizing, particularly on the questions of economic expansion, immigration and population growth, and the consumer society.

What environmental history has explored, within a voluminous literature, is the relation between the accelerated pace of environmental change since 1945 and the concomitant rise of modern environmentalism, or the impulses meant to constrain damaging behaviors and mitigate the effects of developmental practices. The postwar economic boom, in other words, created both skyrocketing demand for material goods and the desire to enjoy the environmental amenities (and physical well-being) that the production of these goods put in jeopardy. Just as he did for the conservationist period, Samuel Hays produced the most influential historical treatment of the environmental era. With Barbara Hays, he argued that postwar environmental engagement arose from rising incomes, which meant that Americans were expanding their definition of the quality of life to include more "beauty, health, and permanence." The Hayses surveyed the contours of environmental politics and administration between 1955 and 1985, describing regional distinctions, interscientific controversies, and the environmental opposition. Most important, they drew a sharp distinction between the newer environmental impulses, part of the history of consumption, and the previous conservation movement, which had stressed efficiencies of production.

Postwar activists specifically targeted the developmental direction of older conservationist programs. In the mid-1950s, as Mark Harvey has shown, a reinvigorated Sierra Club led by David Brower inspired a broad movement in opposition to the Bureau of Reclamation's plans to flood the Dinosaur National Monument. Such instances of revived preservationist agitation drew strength and national support from an expanding and prosperous middle class, many of them new suburbanites. After the war, the federal government had underwritten a surge to the suburbs, where a majority of the population lived by 1970. Upon relocation, as Adam Rome described, these pioneers of the crabgrass frontier discovered they had purchased front-row seats to watch the bulldozers tear up the meadows, trees, marshes, and orchards that had originally lured them beyond the city limits. Thus primed, many Americans supported more vigorous efforts to protect parks and open space, and to regulate the pace and character of new development. Rome's analysis of suburbanization as an environmental process on the scale of the Dust Bowl also breaks down any sharp distinctions between production-driven and consumer-driven politics.

The environmental consequences of the post–World War II boom could also be measured in the astounding amount of raw sewage flowing untreated into the nation's rivers and lakes, the clouds of poisonous exhaust fumes gathering over new roads and expressways, and the industrial waste lurking beneath vacant and soon-to-be-developed land. Perhaps most important, the postwar era saw an abrupt technological shift in the composition and use of persistent synthetic and chlorine-based chemicals that do not naturally degrade. Chemical companies involved in government-sponsored research on products like DDT during World War II, for example, were quick to establish both agricultural and home-and-garden markets for highly toxic pesticides and herbicides. Production was expanded, Edmund Russell discovered, not because everyone believed such compounds were safe; the chemical industry grew despite the wartime objections of federal wildlife biologists and public health scientists.

No wonder, then, that Rachel Carson's *Silent Spring* shot to the best-seller list when it appeared in 1962. Carson gracefully introduced the basic concepts of ecological science, synthesized the existing research on DDT and other synthetics, and argued that humans could not presume to poison parts of the environment without also poisoning themselves. This message reached an audience more prepared to receive it because of debates over radioactive fallout from nuclear testing—biologist and environmental activist Barry Commoner believed, in fact, that the Nuclear Test Ban Treaty of 1963 was the first accomplishment of the environmental era. Commoner, as Michael Egan has explored, held that the chemical and physical sciences had sped too far ahead of the "life sciences" after the war, subjecting Americans to dangerous threats against their knowledge. A functioning democracy required public and participatory discussions of science and risk.

The environmental impulses that began to gather strength in the 1960s included a wide range of concerns and a diverse set of adherents. Women in particular responded to Rachel Carson's message, and middle-class mothers, housewives, and professionals were often the first to organize. But environmental critique also emanated from the era's more emblematic ideological battlefields. Radical political critics, often veterans of the New Left, traced environmental despoilation to the interlocked hierarchies of capitalist, political, and military power, and countercultural critics attempted to build antimaterialist alternatives to mainstream American society. Such diversity was on full display across the country during the first Earth Day in April 1970.

Recent scholarship has also revealed a story in which the seemingly new discourse of environmentalism overlapped and resonated with more long-standing traditions of economic development and resource utilization. Paul Milazzo drew attention to policy entrepreneurs in Congress, many of them "unlikely environmentalists," who helped to usher in the era of environmental governance with arguments that would have been quite familiar to earlier conservationists: that the potential for economic expansion ultimately depended on the availability of abundant and unspoiled natural resources. Pointing to a similar continuity between the early postwar and environmental eras, Karl Brooks has argued that the primary features of environmental law (such as citizen participation and court review of administrative decisions) emerged well before 1970, mainly at the local and state levels.

At the national level, the movement achieved its most prominent successes in the late 1960s and early 1970s. A far-reaching series of legislative and administrative changes required the national government to set and enforce minimum water and air quality standards. These would not be the cooperative-style compliance schedules drawn up in cozy meetings between state agencies and industrial leaders; they would be "technology forcing" standards based on the needs of human health and determined without regard to cost. Furthermore, all government projects themselves would be subject to environmental assessments. The puzzle of why such legislation had the support of Republican Richard Nixon has been resolved by J. Brooks Flippen: the president wanted to be kept out of trouble on an issue he knew was actively pursued by his Democratic rivals and feared was embraced by the general public. Whatever the role of the chief executive, however, environmental legislation had bipartisan support through the 1970s; Congress not only set goals for clean air and water; it also passed new regulations covering pesticides, toxic substances, solid and hazardous waste, coastal zones, endangered species, and the public lands and forests.

Environmental historians have not just charted the variety of environmentalist activity and legislation, however; they have also examined how environmental benefits fell unequally along the lines of race and class. Andrew Hurley's study of Gary, Indiana, from 1945 to 1980 showed not only that African Americans and working-class whites bore the brunt of industrial pollution, but also that environmentalist reform had similar consequences. Waste and toxins were not reduced after 1970; they were mainly *transferred* to the land from water and air. Collected at point sources, the pollution was dumped into the ground in the poorer areas of town that put up the least political resistance. Children in those neighborhoods swam in toxic lagoons and played in waste dumps. Ellen Stroud has drawn similar conclusions about Portland, Oregon, where one toxic-ridden zone appears to have been sacrificed for environmental improvements elsewhere.

There is perhaps nothing more important for understanding the ecological and social limitations of modern environmentalism than the fact that pollution is rarely reduced, only reallocated. This reallocation occurs on local, regional, national, and international scales, and is the basis for a rapidly growing movement of environmental justice that is calling attention to disparities in health, opportunity, and environmental quality. The literature on this subject is now unmanageably large, but a few points emerge clearly. First, the radicalism of environmental justice tests the capacity of a liberal political system to respond to redistributive demands: environmental justice requires more than the provision of public goods and the mild regulation of business and industry. In this respect the challenges are similar to those posed by climate change. Second, environmental justice is the basis for a universally just and sustainable world where pollution and risk are reduced, not merely shifted around. This remains the movement's primary objective even though, as Eileen McGurty has argued, activists initially focused their energies on issues of procedural equity rather than on the restructuring of industrial production processes. And finally, because environmental health science will never be able to "prove" a direct connection between physical harm and any one agent or contaminant in isolation from all others, environmental justice is the political foundation for a much-needed precautionary policy with regard to new technologies and chemicals. Otherwise, as Gerald Markowitz and David Rosner have concluded, powerful industrial interests will continue to exploit scientific uncertainties and turn them to their regulatory advantage.

Environmental justice is not the only way of narrating the limits of the modern environmental era. Across the board, commentators have found environmental commitments broadly but only shallowly rooted in American society. According to Hal Rothman, Americans are half-hearted about the whole affair, embracing environmentalism only when it is easy and inexpensive. Other scholars have begun to put much more emphasis on the organized opposition, spotlighting the political and economic interests that obstruct or dilute environmental initiatives, and highlighting especially the pervasive devotion to property rights and the speculative advantages that inhere in property ownership. Shifting variants of populist outrage, for example, drove the Republican Party's increasingly antienvironmental positions, as James Turner's examination of modern wilderness politics has revealed. However, a key dimension of modern environmental politics is one that environmental history has mainly left to other analysts: the administration and implementation of policy. With a few exceptions, such as Paul Hirt's study of the national forests, the field has not begun a thorough exploration of the evolution of environmental governance since 1970 and the overarching institutional, not to mention constitutional, limitations on its successful articulation. Environmental historians would do well to investigate bureaucratic and governing structures more thoroughly, especially the courts, which have exercised enormous power over modern environmental affairs.

While histories of environmentalism and environmental policy predominate among twentieth-century topics, the field has broadened beyond those initial focal points. Linda Nash, Gregg Mitman, and Nancy Langston have written innovative and fused histories of health, the environment, medical science, and the body, and such scholarship certainly demonstrates that there are alternatively fruitful ways of narrating the twentieth century. Environmental history is also more transnational than originally. Markets and commodities radiate far beyond national boundaries, as do environmental processes. Nature itself respects few borders, and environmental topics are excellent exhibits for the merits of transnational approaches. In the twentieth century, American global power was accompanied by the country's disproportionate influence over international development methods, environmental management, and environmental science, within both the governmental and nongovernmental realms. Fittingly, environmental perspectives are beginning to influence diplomatic history and the history of international relations. Yet the national perspective will retain relevance and importance. As American environmental history expands into unpredictable methodological territory and spills across borders, it is still likely to remain grounded in the country's distinctive governing and constitutional structures, as well as in discussions of the environmental rules and rights created by the nation-state.

BIBLIOGRAPHY

Reference Works

Andrews, Richard N. L. *Managing the Environment, Managing Ourselves: A History of American Environmental Policy.* New Haven, CT: Yale University Press, 2006.

Black, Brian. *Nature and the Environment in American Life.* Westport, CT: Greenwood Press, 2006.

Merchant, Carolyn. *American Environmental History: An Introduction.* New York: Columbia University Press, 2007.

Steinberg. Ted. *Down to Earth: Nature's Role in American History.* New York: Oxford University Press, 2009.

Wellock, Thomas R. *Preserving the Nation: The Conservation and Environmental Movements.* Wheeling, IL: Harlan Davidson, 2007.

Works Cited

Anderson, Virginia DeJohn. *Creatures of Empire: How Domestic Animals Transformed Early America.* New York: Oxford University Press, 2006.

Andrews, Thomas G. *Killing for Coal: America's Deadliest Labor War.* Cambridge, MA: Harvard University Press, 2008.

Balogh, Brian. "Scientific Forestry and the Roots of the Modern American State." *Environmental History* 7 (2002): 198–225.

Boyd, William. "Making Meat: Science, Technology, and American Poultry Production." *Technology and Culture* 42 (2001): 631–664.

Brooks, Karl B. *Before Earth Day: The Origins of American Environmental Law, 1945–1970.* Lawrence: University Press of Kansas, 2009.

Carney, Judith A. *Black Rice: The African Origins of Rice Cultivation in the Americas.* Cambridge, MA: Harvard University Press, 2001.

Carson, Rachel. *Silent Spring.* Boston: Houghton Mifflin, 1962.

Coates, Peter. *American Perceptions of Immigrant and Invasive Species: Strangers on the Land.* Berkeley: University of California Press, 2007.

Colten, Craig E. *An Unnatural Metropolis: Wresting New Orleans from Nature.* Baton Rouge: Louisiana State University Press, 2005.

Cronon, William. *Changes in the Land: Indians, Colonists, and the Ecology of New England.* New York: Hill and Wang, 1983.

———. *Nature's Metropolis: Chicago and the Great West.* New York: W. W. Norton, 1991.

———, ed. *Uncommon Ground: Rethinking the Human Place in Nature.* New York: W. W. Norton, 1996.

Crosby, Alfred W., Jr. *Ecological Imperialism: The Biological Expansion of Europe, 900–1900.* New York: Cambridge University Press, 1986.

Cumbler, John T. *Reasonable Use: The People, the Environment, and the State, New England, 1790–1930.* New York: Oxford University Press, 2001.

Cunfer, Geoff. *On the Great Plains: Agriculture and Environment.* College Station: Texas A&M University Press, 2005.

Donahue, Brian. *The Great Meadow: Farmers and the Land in Colonial Concord.* New Haven, CT: Yale University Press, 2004.

Dunlap, Thomas R. *Nature and the English Diaspora: Environment and History in the United States, Canada, Australia, and New Zealand.* New York: Cambridge University Press, 1999.

DuPuis, E. Melanie. *Nature's Perfect Food: How Milk Became America's Drink.* New York: New York University Press, 2002.

Egan, Michael. *Barry Commoner and the Science of Survival: The Remaking of American Environmentalism.* Cambridge, MA: MIT Press, 2009.

Farmer, Jared. *On Zion's Mount: Mormons, Indians, and the American Landscape.* Cambridge, MA: Harvard University Press, 2010.

Fiege, Mark. *Irrigated Eden: The Making of an Agricultural Landscape in the American West.* Seattle: University of Washington Press, 1999.

Flippen, J. Brooks. *Nixon and the Environment.* Albuquerque: University of New Mexico Press, 2000.

Flores, Dan. *The Natural West: Environmental History in the Great Plains and Rocky Mountains.* Norman: University of Oklahoma Press, 2001.

Gandy, Matthew. *Concrete and Clay: Reworking Nature in New York City.* Cambridge, MA: MIT Press, 2003.

Gottlieb, Robert. *Forcing the Spring: The Transformation of the American Environmental Movement.* Washington, DC: Island Press, 1993.

Hahn, Steven. "Hunting, Fishing, and Foraging: Common Rights and Class Relations in the Postbellum South." *Radical History Review* 26 (1982).

Hartz, Louis. *The Liberal Tradition in America.* New York: Harcourt, Brace, 1955.

Harvey, Mark W. T. *A Symbol of Wilderness: Echo Park and the American Conservation Movement.* Albuquerque: University of New Mexico Press, 1994.

Hays, Samuel P. *Conservation and the Gospel of Efficiency: The Progressive Conservation Movement, 1890–1920.* Cambridge, MA: Harvard University Press, 1959.

Hays, Samuel P., and Barbara Hays. *Beauty, Health, and Permanence: Environmental Politics in the United States, 1955–1985.* New York: Cambridge University Press, 1987.

Hirt, Paul W. *A Conspiracy of Optimism: Management of the National Forests since World War II.* Lincoln: University of Nebraska Press, 1994.

Hundley, Norris, Jr. *The Great Thirst: Californians and Water, 1770s–1990s.* Berkeley: University of California Press, 1992.

Hurley, Andrew. *Environmental Inequalities: Class, Race, and Industrial Pollution in Gary, Indiana.* Chapel Hill: University of North Carolina Press, 1995.

Hurt, R. Douglas. *Dust Bowl: An Agricultural and Social History.* Chicago: Nelson-Hall, 1981.

Isenberg. Andrew C. *The Destruction of the Bison.* New York: Cambridge University Press, 2000.

Jacoby, Karl. *Crimes against Nature: Squatters, Poachers, Thieves, and the Hidden History of American Conservation.* Berkeley: University of California Press, 2001.

Judd, Richard W. *Common Lands, Common People: The Origins of Conservation in Northern New England.* Cambridge, MA: Harvard University Press, 1997.

Kelman, Ari. *A River and Its City: The Nature of Landscape in New Orleans.* Berkeley: University of California Pres, 2003.

Kirby, Jack Temple. *Mockingbird Song: Ecological Landscapes of the South.* Chapel Hill: University of North Carolina Press, 2006.

Klingle, Matthew. *Emerald City: An Environmental History of Seattle.* New Haven, CT: Yale University Press, 2007.

Krech, Shepard, III. *The Ecological Indian: Myth and History.* New York: W. W. Norton, 1999.

Langston, Nancy. *Forest Dreams, Forest Nightmares: The Paradox of Old Growth in the Inland West.* Seattle: University of Washington Press, 1995.

———. *Toxic Bodies: Hormone Disrupters and the Legacy of DES.* New Haven, CT: Yale University Press, 2010.

———. *Where Land and Water Meet: A Western Landscape Transformed.* Seattle: University of Washington Press, 2006.

Leopold, Aldo. *A Sand County Almanac, and Sketches Here and There.* New York: Oxford University Press, 1949.

Maher, Neil M. *Nature's New Deal: The Civilian Conservation Corps and the Roots of the American Environmental Movement.* New York: Oxford University Press, 2009.

Markowitz, Gerald, and David Rosner. *Deceit and Denial: The Deadly Politics of Industrial Pollution.* Berkeley: University of California Press, 2003.

McEvoy, Arthur F. *The Fisherman's Problem: Ecology and Law in the California Fisheries.* New York: Cambridge University Press, 1986.

McGurty, Eileen. *Transforming Environmentalism: Warren County, PCBs, and the Origins of Environmental Justice.* New Brunswick, NJ: Rutgers University Press, 2007.

McNeill, J. R. *Something New under the Sun: An Environmental History of the Twentieth-Century World.* New York: W. W. Norton, 2000.

McWilliams, James E. *American Pests: The Losing War on Insects from Colonial Times to DDT.* New York: Columbia University Press, 2008.

Melosi, Martin V. *The Sanitary City: Urban Infrastructure in America from Colonial Times to the Present.* Baltimore: Johns Hopkins University Press, 2000.

Merchant, Carolyn. *Ecological Revolutions: Nature, Gender, and Science in New England.* Chapel Hill: University of North Carolina Press, 1989.

———. *Reinventing Eden: The Fate of Nature in Western Culture.* New York: Routledge, 2003.

Merrill, Karen. *Public Lands and Political Meaning: Ranchers, the Government, and the Property between Them.* Berkeley: University of California Press, 2002.

Milazzo, Paul. *Unlikely Environmentalists: Congress and Clean Water, 1945–1972.* Lawrence: University Press of Kansas, 2006.

Miller, Char. *Gifford Pinchot and the Making of Modern Environmentalism.* Washington, DC: Island Press, 2001.

Mitman, Gregg. *Breathing Space: How Allergies Shape Our Lives and Landscapes.* New Haven, CT: Yale University Press, 2007.

Nash, Linda. *Inescapable Ecologies: A History of Environment, Disease, and Knowledge.* Berkeley: University of California Press, 2006.

Nash, Roderick. *Wilderness and the American Mind.* New Haven, CT: Yale University Press, 1967.

Phillips, Sarah T. *This Land, This Nation: Conservation, Rural America, and the New Deal.* New York: Cambridge University Press, 2007.

Pisani, Donald J. *Water and American Government: The Reclamation Bureau, National Water Policy, and the West, 1902–1935.* Berkeley: University of California Press, 2002.

Price, Jennifer. *Flight Maps: Adventures with Nature in Modern America.* New York: Basic Books, 1999.

Pyne, Stephen J. *Fire in America: A Cultural History of Wildland and Rural Fire.* Seattle: University of Washington Press, 1997.

Righter, Robert. *The Battle over Hetch Hetchy: America's Most Controversial Dam and the Birth of Environmentalism*. New York: Oxford University Press, 2005.

Riney-Kehrberg, Pamela. *Rooted in Dust: Surviving Drought and Depression in Southwestern Kansas*. Lawrence: University Press of Kansas, 1994.

Robbins, William G. *Lumberjacks and Legislators: Political Economy of the U.S. Lumber Industry*. College Station: Texas A&M University Press, 1982.

Rome, Adam. *The Bulldozer in the Countryside: Suburban Sprawl and the Rise of American Environmentalism*. New York: Cambridge University Press, 2001.

———. "'Political Hermaphrodites': Gender and Environmental Reform in Progressive America." *Environmental History* 11 (2006): 440–463.

Rosen, Christine M. "'Knowing' Industrial Pollution: Nuisance Law and the Power of Tradition in a Time of Rapid Economic Change." *Environmental History* 8 (2003): 565–597.

Rosenberg, Charles E. *The Cholera Years: The United States in 1832, 1849, and 1866*. Chicago: University of Chicago Press, 1963.

Rosenzweig, Roy, and Elizabeth Blackmar. *The Park and the People: A History of Central Park*. Ithaca, NY: Cornell University Press, 1998.

Rothman, Hal K. *The Greening of a Nation? Environmentalism in the United States since 1945*. Fort Worth, TX: Harcourt Brace, 1998.

Russell, Edmund. *War and Nature: Fighting Humans and Insects with Chemicals from World War I to Silent Spring*. New York: Cambridge University Press, 2001.

Sabin, Paul. *Crude Politics: The California Oil Market, 1900–1940*. Berkeley: University of California Press, 2005.

Sachs, Aaron. *The Humboldt Current: Nineteenth-Century Exploration and the Roots of American Environmentalism*. New York: Penguin, 2007.

Schulman, Bruce J. "Governing Nature, Nurturing Government: Resource Management and the Development of the American State." *Journal of Policy History* 17 (2005): 375–403.

Sellers, Christopher H. *Hazards of the Job: From Industrial Disease to Environmental Health Science*. Chapel Hill: University of North Carolina Press, 1997.

Silver, Timothy. *A New Face on the Countryside: Indians, Colonists, and Slaves in South Atlantic Forests, 1500–1800*. New York: Cambridge University Press, 1990.

Soluri, John. *Banana Cultures: Agriculture, Consumption, and Environmental Change in Honduras and the United States*. Austin: University of Texas Press, 2005.

Spence, Mark David. *Dispossessing the Wilderness: Indian Removal and the Making of the National Parks*. New York: Oxford University Press, 1999.

Steinberg, Ted. *Nature Incorporated: Industrialization and the Waters of New England*. New York: Cambridge University Press, 1991.

Stewart, Mart A. "If John Muir Had Been an Agrarian: American Environmental History West and South." *Environment and History* 11 (2005).

———. *"What Nature Suffers to Groe": Life, Labor, and Landscape on the Georgia Coast, 1680–1920*. Athens: University of Georgia Press, 1996.

Stoll, Mark. *Protestantism, Nature, and Capitalism in America*. Albuquerque: University of New Mexico Press, 1997.

Stoll, Steven. *The Fruits of Natural Advantage: Making the Industrial Countryside in California*. Berkeley: University of California Press, 1998.

———. *Larding the Lean Earth: Soil and Society in Nineteenth-Century America.* New York: Hill and Wang, 2002.

Stradling, David. *Smokestacks and Progressives: Environmentalists, Engineers, and Air Quality in America, 1881–1951.* Baltimore: Johns Hopkins University Press, 1999.

Strom, Claire. *Making Catfish Bait out of Government Boys: The Fight against Cattle Ticks and the Transformation of the Yeoman South.* Athens: University of Georgia Press, 2009.

Stroud, Ellen. "Troubled Waters in Ecotopia: Environmental Racism in Portland, Oregon." *Radical History Review* 74 (1999): 65–95.

Sutter, Paul. *Driven Wild: How the Fight against Automobiles Launched the Modern Wilderness Movement.* Seattle: University of Washington Press, 2002.

Tarr, Joel A. *The Search for the Ultimate Sink: Urban Pollution in Historical Perspective.* Akron, OH: University of Akron Press, 1996.

Taylor, Joseph E., III. *Making Salmon: An Environmental History of the Northwest Fisheries Crisis.* Seattle: University of Washington Press, 1999.

Tucker, Richard P. *Insatiable Appetite: The United States and the Ecological Degradation of the Third World.* Berkeley: University of California Press, 2000.

Turner, James Morton. "'The Specter of Environmentalism': Wilderness, Environmental Politics, and the Evolution of the New Right." *Journal of American History* 96 (2009): 123–148.

Tyrrell, Ian. *True Gardens of the Gods: Californian-Australian Environmental Reform, 1860–1930.* Berkeley: University of California Press, 1999.

Valenčius, Conevery Bolton. *The Health of the Country: How American Settlers Understood Themselves and Their Land.* New York: Basic Books, 2002.

Warren, Louis S. *The Hunter's Game: Poachers and Conservationists in Twentieth-Century America.* New Haven, CT: Yale University Press, 1997.

Washington, Sylvia Hood. *Packing Them In: An Archaeology of Environmental Racism in Chicago, 1865–1954.* Lanham, MD: Lexington Books, 2005.

Watson, Harry L. "'The Common Rights of Mankind': Subsistence, Shad, and Commerce in the Early Republican South." *Journal of American History* 83 (1996): 13–43.

White, Lynn, Jr. "The Historical Roots of Our Ecological Crisis." *Science* 155 (1967): 1203–1207.

White, Richard. *The Organic Machine: The Remaking of the Columbia River.* New York; Hill and Wang, 1995.

———. *The Roots of Dependency: Subsistence, Environment, and Social Change among the Choctaws, Pawnees, and Navajos.* Lincoln: University of Nebraska Press, 1983.

Worster, Donald. *Dust Bowl: The Southern Plains in the 1930s.* New York: Oxford University Press, 1979.

———. *A Passion for Nature: The Life of John Muir.* New York: Oxford University Press, 2008.

———. *Rivers of Empire: Water, Aridity, and the Growth of the American West.* New York: Pantheon, 1985.

14
History of American Capitalism

SVEN BECKERT

The United States has been the preeminent capitalist economy for more than a century. By any measure—aggregate output, per capita GNP, labor productivity, and innovation—it ranks at or near the top globally. Indeed, the United States has emerged as a symbol for capitalism as such, drawing to it the sharpest critics of capitalism as well as its most enthusiastic admirers. Such diverse Europeans as Karl Marx, Joseph Schumpeter, Antonio Gramsci, and Friedrich von Hayek have all chimed in. American observers ranging from Richard Hofstadter and Arthur Schlesinger, Jr., to Ronald Reagan hold entrepreneurship to be a defining trait of their nation, believing that the business activities of private citizens set the United States apart from the rest of the world. Indeed, discourses of American exceptionalism, especially outside academia, often take inspiration from a particular reading of the nation's economic history. Consequently, the nation's political debates are singularly focused on economic growth. Indeed, for better or for worse capitalism has come to define the United States. While Athens had its Parthenon and Rome its Colosseum, the United States had its River Rouge Factory in Detroit, the stockyards of Chicago, and the World Trade Center in New York City.

Thus it is somewhat ironic that, until recently, professional historians have largely underemphasized the history of capitalism. To be sure, in an academic ocean as large as that of the United States, there are islands on which many strands of research survive, and even in history departments Lou Galambos, Peter Coclanis, Naomi Lameraux, and others have published a steady stream of works on the history of capitalism. Moreover, capitalism cannot but be present as a background to many stories authors want to tell—a part of the local scenery not in need of explanation. Still, historians have largely ceded interpretative hegemony when it comes to matters of economic change to economists, political scientists, sociologists, and a host of popular writers. This lack of interest has not only limited our understanding of American history, but also impoverished public debate. As capitalism in the United States and its history has been increasingly interpreted from the narrow theoretical vantage point of neoclassical economics or by a deeply ideological popular press that freely mixes fact with fiction, historians' particular perspective is often sorely lacking. The historical dimensions of capitalism—close attention to change over time, an emphasis on path dependency (in which capitalism is identified as a particular moment in the very long history of economic change), and the embedding of economic change in accounts of society, culture, institutions, and the state—is often missing. Ceding that interpretative territory has had significant political implications.

Lately, however, the history of American capitalism has attracted growing interest among historians. Building upon, but also disagreeing with, Alfred D. Chandler, Jr.'s "managerial capitalism," Thomas McCraw's "modern capitalism," and Joyce Appleby's "revolutionary capitalism," some scholars now identify themselves as historians of capitalism, a new subfield in the professional roster. Courses on the history of American capitalism have emerged at various universities, and conferences on the theme have been organized. And if contemporary events in the global economy are any guide, it is safe to predict that the history of capitalism will emerge as an even more important field in the next decade or so.

Why this recent and sudden interest in the history of economic change? Some of the reasons for this reorientation are external to the discipline, and others internal. Clearly, the world has changed: Historians—ever sensitive like bards of earlier ages to the environment they live in—witness the massive economic upheavals that are recasting our contemporary world and wonder about their origins. Moreover, a powerful current in contemporary politics has made a particular set of economic arrangements out to be "natural" and inevitable. Many historians bridle at such claims with an instinctual dislike of the naturalization of any social reality and a mix of distress and pity for triumphalist claims of an end of history. They see capitalism as a particular moment of human history, and believe that the social and geographic spread of capitalist social relations in the United States and elsewhere is a problem to be investigated, not simply assumed. Yet beyond such easily identifiable external factors, the fresh interest in the history of American capitalism is equally motivated by a sense among economic, labor, and business historians that their fields—once fascinating if narrow—had reached an impasse and were in need of new perspectives. By embracing the history of American capitalism, they can now link their work on business, labor, and economic change to the concerns of a broader field that is, arguably, central to the American historical profession. By doing so, they can also tap into a popular demand for explanation of crucial contemporary political issues, such as global financial crisis, resource politics, and labor migration. Such a departure gains further impetus from the newfound interest in global and transnational history, which is almost always accompanied by an interest in economic change.

As difficult as it is to imagine, during the 1960s and 1970s economic history was considered one of the most exciting fields in the study of American history. Armed with new methods of quantification, some of its most gifted practitioners promised, in effect, to finally resolve some of the more puzzling questions in American history. Was slavery rational and profitable? Did shifting regional economic links spark the Civil War? What was the impact of gender discrimination on women's wages? Did railroads stimulate economic growth in the nineteenth century? Were state investments in infrastructure good for economic growth? Uncovering fresh historical data and subjecting it to rigorous analysis promised an entirely new mode of historical argumentation. The signal contribution here was *Time on the Cross: The Economics of American Negro Slavery* by Stanley Engerman and Robert Fogel, which showed that slavery, indeed, was a profitable institution for planters and created a thriving regional economy in the American South. Nobel prize winner Douglass North, in an equally important contribution, asserted the importance of interregional trade in general, and the southern slave economy in particular, to the early-nineteenth-century United States. North and Engerman and Fogel, along with Claudia Goldin, Gavin Wright, and others, produced works that self-consciously tried to connect the quantitative methods of economics with the broader qualitative concerns of historians and for a time strongly influenced a number of core debates in the history of the United States.

The honeymoon of economists and historians practicing the "new economic history" was short-lived. By the 1980s, historians became progressively less interested in the work of their historically minded colleagues in economics departments. Economic history largely migrated from history into economics departments, where it thrives to this day. Stanley Engerman, for example, continued to write and organize massive studies, especially the multivolume *Cambridge Economic History of the United States* with Robert Gallman; while Gavin Wright, Kenneth L. Sokoloff, Ronald Findlay, Kevin O'Rourke, Claudia Goldin, and Lawrence Katz, among others, contributed major new interpretations of core questions in the development of the American economy.

History departments, moreover, experienced a backlash against the new economic history. As the mathematical tools needed to master the discipline moved beyond the course offerings of most history graduate programs, history departments lost candidates to economics programs and increasingly went without economic historians. Moreover, with the rise of cultural history during the 1980s and 1990s, a sharper, more foundational rejection of "scientific" history won converts among the growing number of historians who lost faith in the conceit of cumulative knowledge production that was at the heart of economic history and the broader enlightenment project itself. The stigma attached to "master narratives" further undermined the analytical project of economic history. As a result, by 2005, only 2 percent of historians in American history departments listed economic history as their area of special expertise, down from 5 percent in 1975.

The fate of economic historians—becoming marginal to most history departments—also affected another field: labor history. In its heyday during the 1970s and 1980s, graduate students and professors produced myriad studies on nearly every conceivable aspect of the history of labor in the United States. Inspired by European historians such as E. P. Thompson and Eric Hobsbawm—the new labor historians sought to write the history of labor in the United States "from the bottom up"—setting themselves apart from an older labor history that had focused mostly on the white, skilled, male, and organized working class. They expanded the reach of labor history to include the history of all workers irrespective of their affinity to trade unions or socialist political projects. The typical mode of inquiry was to focus on an industrializing town, trace the origins of the local working class, and investigate their cultural proclivities, identities, beliefs, and politics, usually ending with an account of dramatic working-class collective action. For example, Alan Dawley studied the shoe workers in Lynn, Massachusetts, famously concluding that their inclusion in electoral politics was ironically the "coffin of class consciousness." Mary Blewett brought activist women into the new labor history. Sean Wilentz traced the fortunes of artisan workers in New York, while Roy Rosenzweig investigated the leisure culture of workers in nineteenth-century Worchester and Herbert Gutman provided fascinating glimpses into the Old World origins of nineteenth-century American working-class culture.

While impressively diverse in time, location, and perspective, many of these historians were still explicitly or implicitly informed by one question, namely, Werner Sombart's famous "Why is there no Socialism in the United States?" With the labor movement found wanting, workers' collective identities, especially as expressed in the realm of culture, increasingly moved to the center of attention. The inability to find a socialist project among the American working class that matched, a cynic might say, the perhaps exaggerated expectations of historians, led scholars ultimately to make do with collective picnics in the park. Labor historians, as an unintended result, became ever more removed from economic analyses—the firms, the state, and the evolution of capitalism. By the 1980s and 1990s, labor history wandered even further afield, to investigate other, perhaps even competing "identities," analyzing how class was reflected and often deflected by gender, ethnic, and race identities—examples include Teresa Amott's, Julie Matthaei's, and Neil Foley's studies. Their work for the first time brought women, African Americans, and others—not to mention workers in the union-resistant South and West—into the story of American labor, a seminal and vital contribution. Unfortunately, these rich new perspectives were often wedded to the rather weak conceptual tool of identity, whose connection to structural elements of these workers' historical context, the state, and the global economy was hard to map. It was perhaps not surprising that by the 2000s, graduate students and their mentors had lost enthusiasm for the history of workers and their institutions.

Students of the other side of the social divide, namely, business historians, went through a parallel process, though in greater isolation from the mainstream of the historical profession. Business history has a long and distinguished pedigree. Since the 1920s, practitioners often celebrated the American entrepreneurs who time and again heroically recast the American economy. Entrepreneurs, they implied or argued outright, were the central actors in American history. Alan Nevins's *Study in Power: John D. Rockefeller, Industrialist and Philanthropist* exemplified the best of that school. A competing set of historians made similar arguments, though with the opposite political spin: Informed by Progressive-Era muckraking journalism, they presented entrepreneurs as the principal villains of U.S. history—rapacious men whose scheming designs threatened to undermine all that was good about the American republic. Matthew Josephson's *The Robber Barons* was the most important contribution in this genre. Nonetheless, both groups cast charismatic business leaders—whether "robber barons" or "industrial statesmen"—in leading roles.

By the 1970s, business historians became less concerned with individual entrepreneurs and more focused on firms as institutions. This literature was crowned by the brilliant works of Alfred D. Chandler, Jr., whose *Visible Hand* and, later, *Strategy and Structure* fundamentally recast the field. Sidestepping the issue of entrepreneurs as heroes or villains, Chandler delineated radical changes in the structure of America businesses in the course of the nineteenth and twentieth centuries and wondered why these changes had taken place. Chandler found that structural and especially technological pressures were fueling a quite unstoppable wave of consolidation that tore asunder existing relationships between merchants, manufacturers, and financiers and recreated them in the form of "big business." To be sure, important challenges to his accounts have emerged—Philip Scranton, in *Endless Novelty*, for example, argued that much of American business did not follow the Chandlerian model. William Roy and Martin Sklar contended that Chandler had left out politics and the state and thereby fundamentally distorted the real process by which these firms emerged. Gerald Berk's history of late-nineteenth-century railroad regulation confirmed that critique, showing effectively how constitutional choices determined the shape of the industrial order, not simply technological imperatives. And taking a slightly different but nonetheless crucial critical approach, a group of business historians have challenged the Chandlerian paradigm by including a different set of characters, including, for example, women, African Americans, and Latinos in the story, as in the work of Angel Kwolek-Folland, Juliet Walker, and Maureen Gilligan. Yet all agree that Chandler's work was a turning point for business history.

Despite vibrant debate, business historians, like labor and economic historians, complained of a sense of impasse and isolation during the 1980s and 1990s. Moreover, in the wake of the social history revolution of the 1970s and the turn to cultural history during the 1990s, studying businesses and the white men who ran most of them was perceived to be somewhat retrograde. Business historians were not content to be perceived as part of a relatively narrow subfield: In 2008, the Business History Conference summed up the collective mood by urging participants to "expand . . . the field's connection across disciplines and perspectives, [and] demonstrate the relevance of business history to other fields of history."

The History of Capitalism

By the 1990s, economic, business, and labor historians to various extents began to reach out to the rest of the discipline and, especially, to one another. Integrating economic, labor, and business history into a larger history of capitalism promised to open vital questions about the connections between economic change, the evolution of firms, and the agency and shifting nature of labor. While at its most superficial simply a rebranding campaign, at its best it marks the exciting dawn of a genuinely fresh approach. The new historians of American capitalism combine many of the approaches of economic, business, and labor history, but enmesh those familiar narratives into a story of fundamental economic, social, and political change. These works trace how economic and political forces influence one another, without treating the sociopolitical and economic worlds as discrete and intrinsically separate entities. They make questions of economic change central to the history of North America, but embed into that account the complexity and diversity of American politics, society, and culture.

These historians of capitalism argue that states and markets, politics and business, cannot be understood separately from one another. For them, the history of American capitalism is deeply embedded in the history of the American state and American politics. They study the political economy of the United States and are critical of approaches that privilege the internal logic of firms, markets, and capital. Even property rights, the quintessential foundational category of capitalism—as Morton Horwitz has shown in *The Transformation of American Law*—are conventions formed by rules that are often articulated by the law, and thus the state. Historians of capitalism study the particular ways in which the market and the state interact, how this interaction is influenced by the shifting power relations of various social groups, and how the rules of exchange are set politically. In short, they do not study capital as such, but instead the political economy of capitalism, and this political economy is not exclusively constituted by capital and capitalists.

Moreover, historians of capitalism see the "economy" as a category that cannot be isolated analytically or historically from the rest of American history. Obviously, economic change had a huge impact on all aspects of

American society. But fundamental features of American society also affected the development of capitalism. Racism, for example, was a persistent feature throughout American history, and it radically altered the involvement of black Americans, among others, within particular markets. As Gavin Wright argued in *Old South, New South: Revolutions in the Southern Economy since the Civil War*, racism helped foster and stabilize segmented labor markets. It also created huge differences in access to credit based upon skin color, religion, and national origin. And long after slavery was abolished, it continued to confine particular groups of American capitalists to particular markets, as Louis Hyman has shown in connection to housing policies.

Furthermore, historians of capitalism portray businesspeople not as atomized individuals in search of profit but as complete social actors embedded within particular social, cultural, and political networks, networks that at times solidify into organizations and institutions and even into collective political mobilization. Their work on American capitalism is therefore an implicit if not explicit critique of neoclassical model building, and is analytically close to various forms of heterodox economics. Sanford Jacoby's work on anti–New Deal businessmen, Jeffrey Haydu's comparative history of the late-nineteenth-century bourgeoisie of Cincinnati and San Francisco, and Olivier Zunz's work on corporate executives have revealed parts of that story. These are fresh perspectives for a generation of historians whose exposure to the social history of the 1970s and 1980s had taught them to associate collective action with striking workers, protesting farmers, and activist women. But, as historians of capitalism are increasingly demonstrating, the market, as a social entity, has been created, among other things, by elite collective action as well.

Historians of capitalism also have shown that businesspeople, consumers, workers, and others embed their economic actions within networks and institutions. These networks can be based on common class backgrounds, but also on shared political interests, national origins, and religious beliefs. All these networks, however, have in common that they can effectively enforce trust, and trust is a key category for understanding markets and thus capitalism. Charles Tilly has written on trust in broad conceptual terms in his *Trust and Rule*, and Pierre Bourdieu's *Distinction* explains how financial capital is linked to cultural and social capital, but these themes are also important to Rowena Olegario's work on the history of credit reporting, Edward Balleisen's and Scott Sandage's books on the history of failure, David Hancock's writings on the transatlantic market in Madeira wine, and Sally Clarke's monograph on the importance of trust in the automobile market. These historians of capitalism, quite typically, tend to focus less on firms—the quintessential unit of analysis of earlier forms of business history—or towns—the preferred unit of analysis of earlier forms of labor history—but instead on the emergence of markets constructed by a whole range of social actors and deeply embedded within traditions, institutions, beliefs, and networks.

This approach denaturalizes particular economic arrangements and emphasizes the historical and regional diversity of capitalism in the United States. There are, in fact, many different kinds of capitalism, as Walter Licht in his *Industrializing America*, William Cronon in his *Nature's Metropolis*, and Richard White in his *"It's Your Misfortune and None of My Own"* have shown. Such sensitivity for diverse outcomes over time and space offers fertile possibilities—not yet realized—for links to the emerging studies of global capitalism of which Peter Hall's *Varieties of Capitalism* is a prominent example. They also pose the question of whether there was a transition to capitalism in North America, and if so, how, when, and why it took place in particular regions.

Last but not least, such historicizing of economic change and the denaturalizing of the economic order support the view that economic theorizing is not just a scientific endeavor, but also a production of ideology, related to political conflicts and interests. Important examples of such histories include Philip Mirowski's work on how the epistemology of physics has influenced that of economics; Michael A. Bernstein's tracing of the history of economic thought in the twentieth-century United States; Howard Brick's work on the history of postcapitalist thinking in the United States; S. M. Amadae's exploration of how rational choice theory originated in the RAND Corporation's project to develop a "scientific" approach to the social sciences suitable for planning; Walter Friedman's fascinating charting of the dubious history of economic forecasting; and Dieter Plehwe's and Bernard Walpen's important histories of the origins of neoliberalism in a globe-spanning network of economists, politicians, and business leaders focused on the activities of the Mont Pèlerin Society.

This "new" history of American capitalism is, of course, not without its own distinguished antecedents. After all, a small but productive cohort of scholars had never given up on writing on the political economy of American capitalism. From Eric Foner's work on Reconstruction, which traces among other things the emergence of new labor regimes in a core sector of the American economy, to Richard White's work on the history of the American West and the federal government's role in making it accessible and productive to private capital, political economy was alive and well. Others have grappled with core issues in the history of American capitalism as well, including Steven Hahn in his work on the (economic) origins of southern Populism, Elizabeth Blackmar's writing on the social history of housing in New York, Thomas McCraw's history of twentieth-century business, and Barbara Fields's account of the transition from slavery to freedom in Maryland. In many ways the questions they identified are the ones that are still very much at the center of debates on the history of American capitalism.

Building on such works, historians of capitalism also draw into the discussion several other strands of research. Two "schools" of political history are particularly relevant here. In one, political scientists interested in political economy often look at the interactions of economic interests and preferences—individual, institutional, or regional—and relate them to particular forms of political organization, political interests, and political outcomes. Heavily quantitative, this research, which includes Jeff Frieden's work on the history of globalization, borrows many of its methods as well as its epistemological principles from economics. Engaged with a similar set of questions, but starting from very different methodological premises are scholars working in the field of American Political Development. They are interested in state structures and their role in economic change. Important works in this tradition are Richard Bensel's books on the political economy of the United States in the nineteenth century, especially his *Yankee Leviathan: The Origins of Central State Authority in America, 1859–1877.* Julian Zelizer, Daniel Carpenter, Elizabeth Sanders, Meg Jacobs, Brian Balogh, and William Novak, dealing with a wide range of topics and time periods but united in their interest in political economy, also have provided significant interventions into this debate.

Perhaps the most important contribution of this strand of research to the history of American capitalism is its novel way of thinking about the relationship between the state and economic development. This strand was long suppressed by the assumption of many American historians that the United States was exceptional because of its allegedly weak, even insignificant, state. But in the 1980s, historians and sociologists rediscovered the state—most self-consciously in Charles Tilly's *Coercion, Capital, and European States* and Theda Skocpol's call "to bring the state back in." Political scientist Steven Skowronek took up some of these ideas in his important work *Building a New American State*, which charts the transition from a state of courts and parties to one with greater administrative capacities (with obvious effects on economic regulation, for example) as did Skocpol in her rewriting of the history of the American welfare state, linking its origins to the emergence of the post–Civil War soldiers' pensions.

This rediscovery of the state was an essential step for the writing of the history of the political economy of capitalism in the United States. A number of books go so far as to argue for the political origins of American capitalism, echoing in interesting ways an earlier generation of progressive historians. A special issue of the *Journal of Policy History* brought researchers together in 2006 to explore what Richard R. John has called particular "regulatory regime[s]." In his own work on the postal service and on telecommunications, which is sympathetic to a political economy approach, John also emphasized the political nature of the construction of markets. Among the more recent important works in this genre are David Moss's study on the origins of protective labor legislation and, in a different volume, his history of how the United States government became an important risk manager, and why such government activities became popular despite widespread antistatist sentiments. In a related vein, Robin Einhorn linked the policy goal of a weak state to the political interests of American slaveholders; L. Ray Gunn demonstrated how the political nature of the corporation changed in the course of the nineteenth century;

Steven Usselman gave the state an important role in facilitating innovations in railroads; and Jason Scott Smith's excellent work on the New Deal showed the long-term importance of public works programs to the shape of the American economy. Colleen Dunlavy's comparative study of railroads in the United States and Prussia also analyzed the importance of the state, demonstrating that American state governments were more active in formulating railroad policies than the quintessential strong state of Prussia. These more recent books follow the trail originally cleared by post–New Deal historians who unsurprisingly grasped the importance of public policy to the economic history of the United States, including Oscar Handlin, Harry Scheiber, Clifton K. Yearley, and Irvin Unger.

Near cousins to this historiographical tradition on political economy, legal historians have created an important body of work on the economic role of law. They needed little persuading, of course, that the state mattered to economic change. To this day, the seminal work in this field is Morton Horwitz's two-volume study *The Transformation of American Law*, which showed in great detail how markets, and even the very conception of property, were legally constructed. Going far beyond the often-superficial search for precedent, Horwitz brought to life the living history of the law in America, showing how particular legal definitions and outcomes were the result of particular sets of interests and particular distributions of power in American society. These basic insights were subsequently applied by a new school of legal historians, who looked at different realms of economic activities. Christine Desan developed the notion that money is a complex institution made of a variety of collective determinations and thus subject to the interests and inclinations of the weak and the powerful. William Forbath showed how labor law shaped the ability of organized labor to articulate its collective interests. Robert Steinfeld investigated the legal construction of "free" labor, a field also fruitfully investigated by Amy Dru Stanley. John Witt, in the same tradition, investigated the changing notions of risk in tort and the rise of workers' compensation. In less obvious, but nonetheless revealing ways, Rebecca McLennan examined the history of the prison-industrial complex, and Roy Kreitner disentangled the history of contract.

The recent flourishing of the history of American capitalism was fed from these varied intellectual and institutional sources. Ironically, it might have also benefited from the demise of economic history in history departments during prior decades, effectively giving historians working in other traditions the opportunity to reinvent the field.

Debates

Today, the history of capitalism has become a broad and thriving field, dealing with a vast range of questions, indeed, too many to discuss in this essay. Here, by way of example, are some of the more important contemporary debates.

One of the most compelling mysteries about the history of the world since 1800 is how a numerically and geographically marginal part of the globe became spectacularly wealthier than people in other parts of the world or any other period in human history. The question has been labeled the "Great Divergence," and the most important contribution to this debate is Kenneth Pomeranz's book by the same title. Comparing the economic situation of a southern Chinese region to the economically most advanced parts of England, Pomeranz finds that in many ways they were quite similar as late as the eighteenth century. A hundred years later, however, their economic fortunes diverged drastically. Pomeranz argues that this divergence occurred because some Europeans were lucky to find coal near the most important manufacturing regions, which enabled them to overcome energy constraints, and because they were able to draw upon the resources of the New World, such as sugar. While North America does not figure dominantly in Pomeranz's account, it would soon come to matter a great deal, since North America turned into the supplier of cotton—the most important ingredient for industrial production by around 1800. Joseph Inikori, building on Eric Williams's *Capitalism and Slavery*, has added to this argument by emphasizing the importance of access to African markets and African labor as an important determinant of Europe's economic success. While historians of North America have not widely contributed to this discussion, it is a crucial chapter in the history of American capitalism, since the incorporation of large parts of the United States into the global economy played a decisive role in the Great Divergence.

Second, some of the most exciting work in the history of American capitalism of recent years has tried to embed the history of American capitalism in the broader course of global history of which the Great Divergence is just one chapter. Here we have both traditional comparative and network histories. Cyrus Veeser's work on the Santo Domingo Improvement Association shows how American capitalists cooperated with the American state to incorporate one Caribbean island into the circuits of capital and American power. Mira Wilkins's work on multinational firms, Peter Coclanis's writings on the history of rice, and Sven Beckert's study of the history of cotton embed U. S. capitalism into global history in distinct ways. Looking at the world more than a century later, Nelson Lichtenstein's publications on the history of Wal-Mart trace how a modern retailer integrates Chinese and American capitalism.

Global perspectives naturally tend to stress the spatial dimensions of economic change, a theme that is also important to understanding the internal history of the United States. Often, the links between territorial expansion and economic change have been treated as separate stories, but the history of American capitalism, perhaps more so than that of other national capitalisms, is bound up with the incorporation of new territories. Adam Rothman highlights this marriage of territorial expansion and economic incorporation well for the slave economy of the South, a theme also represented by the writings of Eugene Genovese and Ira Berlin. Bill

Cronon's *Nature's Metropolis* and Richard White's "*It's Your Misfortune and None of My Own*" did the same for the incorporation of the trans-Mississippi West.

The territorial scope of the American nation eventually would set the United States apart from its main nineteenth- and twentieth-century capitalist competitors, giving its economy a unique dynamic. In that story, the interaction with native people is of great importance, as the dynamism of American capitalism was very much built upon the incorporation and destruction of Native America economies and the expropriation of their resources. For the connection between territory, expropriation, economic growth, and Indians' engagement with the expanding capitalist economy, see especially the work of Alexandra Harmon, Brian Hosmer, and Jessica Cattelino. The diverse forms of political incorporation of territory into the national political economy are also at the core of Tami Friedman's book on the relocation of industry from the urban Northeast into the low-wage, nonunionized South, an issue also taken up by Jeffery Cowie in his history of the relocations of RCA and their impact on working-class communities.

It is not without irony that slavery—the purported antithesis of free labor, free soil, and free markets—is increasingly becoming an essential ingredient in the study of American capitalism. In the past, histories of slavery and the economic development of the American Northeast have been told as two separate stories, with a more rapidly growing manufacturing sector eventually overtaking slavery and subduing it. This story of antagonism has recently been subverted from many quarters. Historians have shown that every aspect of the slave economy of the South depended on northern or European support, most especially the flow of capital and the provision of markets. For their part, historians of northern economic development have been ever more attuned to how important the slave South was to the development of the North: Capital accumulated in the slave trade and the trade in slave-grown agricultural commodities was invested in northern manufacturing. Southern markets proved exceedingly important to many northern manufacturers. Indeed, the core raw material of the American industrial revolution—cotton—was grown by slaves, and the South pioneered many institutional innovations in finance, insurance, and bookkeeping techniques that Chandler would rediscover in America's quintessential modern corporations. Seth Rockman's writings on the dependence of some New England manufacturers on southern markets, Craig Wilder's book on the link between northern educational institutions and slavery, and David Waldstreicher's investigation of the importance of slavery to the Constitution are some of the important contributions to this debate. And slavery studies have also contributed tremendously to the study of the diverse ways in which markets have been constructed—as exemplified by Walter Johnson's study of the slave market in New Orleans.

This integration of the history of slavery into the history of the national and global economy has also had an impact on labor history, the fourth vibrant field in capitalism studies. In contrast to earlier labor history, questions of identity have moved to the sidelines, and larger structural concerns have become more prevalent: the patterns of work at particular sites, the distribution of social power in particular locations between a whole range of actors, and the role of the natural environment, for example. Workers are seen as much less autonomous and powerful than in the accounts of an earlier generation of labor historians, perhaps expressing among other things the much darker prospects of labor in the twenty-first century. Excellent examples of this genre are Seth Rockman's work on early-nineteenth-century Baltimore laborers, Thomas G. Andrews's book on coal workers, Gunther Peck's study of immigrant workers in the American West, and Susan O'Donovan's writings on cotton workers in reconstruction Georgia. Historians also tend to deromanticize labor, as shown especially in the work of Peter Way, which depicts the limited cultural, social, and especially economic space enjoyed by unskilled wage workers in the early nineteenth century, a world entirely different from that of Sean Wilentz's artisan workers. This new labor history has simultaneously broadened by seeing all forms of commodified labor, not just wage labor, as the work of capitalism. Slavery, indentured servants, women's domestic labor, and other productive activities all now fit into the story. The story of labor has also become much more global, as exemplified in the work of Leon Fink tracing the international composition of the working class in one community. The most innovative rethinking of global labor history, however, comes from Amsterdam's International Institute for Social History and especially here from the works of Marcel van der Linden.

Fifth, in recent histories of capitalism, businesspeople have become important political actors, and both their forms of collective action and their efforts at political mobilization have moved to the fore. Sanford Jacoby has written two exceedingly important books on the politics of capital, stretching over many decades. For the nineteenth century, Noam Maggor's work on Boston, Sven Beckert's book on New York City, and Robert Johnston's study of Portland are all accounts of how the collective action of businesspeople has shaped the political economy of the United States. Many essays in Steve Fraser and Gary Gerstle's *Ruling America* on the United States' economic elite explore this issue as well.

Most of the work on businesspeople's collective action, however, has focused on the late twentieth century and most particularly on the global rise of neoliberalism during the 1970s and thereafter. This is the sixth lively debate among historians of capitalism. As the 1970s are beginning to emerge in historical analysis as one of the most important turning points of the twentieth century and as the moment of origin of many of our current dilemmas, historians of capitalism have made important efforts to come to terms with the decade. Ben Waterhouse traces businesspeople's collective action during the 1970s, Bethany Moreton charts the peculiar intersection of religion and business strategy, Kimberly Phillips-Fein investigates the rise of neoliberalism, and Judith Stein shows how policy choices of the 1970s left the United States on a path of rapid deindustrialization and a concurrent rise of the financial services industry, with devastating effects for America's working class and, ultimately, for the United States' position in the global economy.

These are just a few examples of the innovative work being done right now on the history of American capitalism. Other issues up for debate are just as important: Interesting books have been written on the politics of different forms of capital, from Nelson Lichtenstein's new work on the transition from industrial to merchant capital in the late twentieth century, to Pierre Gervais's work on the persistence of merchant capital and its relationship to early industrialization. Julia Ott, Richard Sylla, Kenneth Lipartito, Mary O'Sullivan, and Jonathan Levy have all done important new work on financial history. Michael Zakim has studied the figure of the nineteenth-century clerk as a way of tracing the revolutionary social, cultural, and political upheavals generated by the rise of capitalism. Kathy Peiss has analyzed the cultural history of the American beauty industry. Biography is another genre used to explore the history of American capitalism, ranging from David Farber's recent work on Alfred P. Sloan to T. J. Stiles's biography of Cornelius Vanderbilt. The spread of capitalist social relations, or the question whether there was a transition to capitalism in the United States, and if so, when and why it occurred, is still a thriving field, with some classic works by Christopher Clark, Winifred Rothenberg, and Charles Sellers. Finally, the history of consumption also has been a subject of a number of excellent recent monographs, among them works by Larry Glickman, Liz Cohen, William Leach, Regina Lee Blaszczyk, and Pamela Laird. Many more issues could be mentioned, addressed by dozens if not hundreds of important studies.

Perspectives

As a relatively young field, albeit one deeply indebted to some of its precursors, there are plentiful avenues for further research. Indeed, because many American historians for all too long have taken capitalism as part of the natural scenery in which American history unfolded, the history of American capitalism still poses many questions. For example, the recent recognition of the diversity of capitalism in the United States at any given point raises a further interesting issue: How does this diversity relate to the whole? Moreover, if markets are not only embedded, but also socially and politically constituted, then the distribution of social power in society matters a great deal. There is still too little known about how particular political economies were constituted, though we do know from existing studies that change within capitalism does not follow some universal logic of capital. In this contest, the history of labor deserves new emphasis, including the institutions that workers have built over the past two hundred years, since they played a significant role in the shaping of capitalism at any given point. Moreover, as the story of American capitalism was part of a much larger, global story of the social and geographic spread of capitalist social relations, there are many questions about how the United States fits into this larger story that are worth exploring. And, last but not least, the new history of American capitalism could deploy its conceptual and methodological insights to pick up once again some of the issues that have kept prior generations of historians busy: the history of the firm, for example; the logic of the American Industrial Revolution; the transition from an agricultural to an industrial economy; accounts of and explanations for economic growth; class itself. There are many other such issues, but in all of them it is important to link investigations of local cases, certain industries, and particular subsets of people to the big-picture history of American capitalism.

There has never been a better time for telling the history of American capitalism. Economists have cloaked themselves in the mantle of science, and their discourse and their interpretations have become truly hegemonic. Historians, on the other side, have been too absent from much of that debate. Yet in the wake of the global economic crisis a growing number of historians have discovered their ability to provide an alternative reading—namely, a deeply contextual and indeterminate one—of the history of American capitalism. In the process they have offered insights—from the importance of politics to the construction of markets to the socially embedded nature of the economy—that have great relevance to understanding our contemporary dilemmas as well.

BIBLIOGRAPHY

Adams, Sean. *Old Dominion, Industrial Commonwealth: Coal, Politics, and Economy in Antebellum America.* Baltimore: Johns Hopkins University Press, 2004.

Amadae, S. M. *Rationalizing Capitalist Democracy: The Cold War Origins of Rational Choice Liberalism.* Chicago: Chicago: University of Chicago Press, 2003.

Amott, Teresa, and Julie Matthaei. *Race, Gender, and Work: A Multicultural Economic History of Women in the United States.* Boston: South End Press, 1991.

Andrews, Thomas G. *Killing for Coal: America's Deadliest Labor War.* Cambridge, MA: Harvard University Press, 2008.

Appleby Joyce. *The Relentless Revolution: A History of Capitalism.* New York: W. W. Norton, 2010.

Bailyn, Bernard. *The New England Merchants in the Seventeenth Century.* Cambridge, MA: Harvard University Press, 1955.

Balleisen, Edward J. *Navigating Failure: Bankruptcy and Commercial Society in Antebellum America*, Chapel Hill: University of North Carolina Press, 2001.

Balogh, Brian. *Chain Reaction: Expert Debate and Public Participation in American Commercial Nuclear Power, 1945–1975.* New York: Cambridge University Press, 1991.

Beckert, Sven. *The Empire of Cotton: A Global History.* New York: Knopf, forthcoming.

———. *Monied Metropolis: New York and the Formation of the American Bourgeoisie, 1850–1896.* New York: Cambridge University Press, 2001.

Bender, Thomas. *A Nation among Nations: America's Place in World History.* New York: Hill and Wang, 2006.

Bensel, Richard. *The Political Economy of American Industrialization, 1877–1900.* New York: Cambridge University Press, 2000.

———. *Yankee Leviathan: The Origins of Central State Authority in America, 1859–1877.* New York: Cambridge University Press, 1990.

Berk, Gerald. *Alternative Tracks: The Constitution of American Industrial Order, 1865–1917.* Baltimore: Johns Hopkins University Press, 1994

Berlin, Ira. *Many Thousands Gone: The First Two Centuries of Slavery in North America.* Cambridge, MA: Belknap/Harvard University Press, 1998.

Bernstein, Michael A. *A Perilous Progress: Economists and Public Purpose in Twentieth-Century America.* Princeton, NJ: Princeton University Press, 2001.

Blackmar, Elizabeth. *Manhattan for Rent: 1785–1850.* Ithaca, NY: Cornell University Press, 1991.

Blaszczyk, Regina Lee. *Imagining Consumers: Design and Innovation from Wedgwood to Corning.* Baltimore: Johns Hopkins University Press, 200.

Blewett, Mary. *Men, Women, and Work: Class, Gender, and Protest in the New England Shoe Industry, 1780–1910.* Urbana: University of Illinois Press, 1988.

Bourdieu, Pierre. *Distinction: A Social Critique of the Judgment of Taste.* London: Routledge and Kegan Paul, 1986.

Brick, Harold. *Transcending Capitalism: Visions of a New Society in Modern American Thought.* Ithaca, NY: Cornell University Press, 2006.

Business History Conference. Annual Meeting. Sacramento: California State University. April 10–12, 2008.

Carpenter, Daniel. *The Forging of Bureaucratic Autonomy: Reputations, Networks, and Policy Innovation in Executive Agencies, 1862–1928.* Princeton, NJ: Princeton University Press, 2001.

Cattelino, Jessica. *High Stakes: Florida Seminole Gaming and Sovereignty.* Durham, NC: Duke University Press, 2008.

Chandler, Alfred D. *Strategy and Structure: Chapters in the History of the Industrial Enterprise.* Cambridge, MA: MIT Press, 1962, 1975, 1990.

———. *Visible Hand: The Managerial Revolution in American Business.* Cambridge, MA: Belknap/Harvard University Press, 1977.

Clark, Christopher. *The Roots of Rural Capitalism: Western Massachusetts, 1780–1860.* Ithaca, NY: Cornell University Press, 1990.

Clarke, Sally. *Trust and Power: Consumers, the Modern Corporation, and the Making of the United States Automobile Market.* New York: Cambridge University Press, 2007.

Cochran, Thomas. *Frontiers of Change: Early Industrialism in America.* New York: Oxford University Press, 1981.

Coclanis, Peter. "Distant Thunder: The Creation of a World Market in Rice and the Transformations It Wrought." *American Historical Review* 98 (October 1993): 1050–1078.

Cohen, Liz. *A Consumer's Republic: The Politics of Mass Consumption in Postwar America.* New York: Knopf, 2003.

Cowie, Jefferson. *Capital Moves: RCA's Seventy-Year Quest For Cheap Labor,* Ithaca, NY: Cornell University Press, 1999.

Cronon, William. *Nature's Metropolis: Chicago and the Great West.* New York: W. W. Norton, 1991.

Dawley Alan. *Class and Community: The Industrial Revolution in Lynn.* Cambridge, MA: Harvard University Press, 2000.

Desan, Christine. "The Market as a Matter of Money: Denaturalizing Economic Currency in American Constitutional History." *Law and Social Inquiry* 30 (Winter 2005): 1–60.

Dunlavy, Colleen. *Politics and Industrialization: Early Railroads in the United States and Prussia*. Princeton, NJ: Princeton University Press, 1994.

Einhorn, Robin. *American Taxation, American Slavery*. Chicago: University of Chicago Press, 2006.

Engerman, Stanley, and Robert Fogel. *Time on the Cross: The Economics of American Negro Slavery*. New York: W. W. Norton, 1974.

Farber, David. *Sloan Rules: Alfred P. Sloan and the Triumph of General Motors*. Chicago: University of Chicago Press, 2002.

Fields, Barbara Jeanne. *Slavery and Freedom on the Middle Ground: Maryland during the Nineteenth Century*. New Haven, CT: Yale University Press, 1987.

Findlay, Ronald, and Kevin O'Rourke. *Power and Plenty*. Princeton, NJ: Princeton University Press, 2007.

Fink, Leon. *The Maya of Morganton: Work and Community in the Nuevo New South*. Chapel Hill: University of North Carolina Press, 2003.

Fogel, Robert. *Without Consent or Contract: The Rise and Fall of American Slavery*. New York: W. W. Norton, 1989.

Foley. Neil. *The White Scourge: Mexicans, Blacks, and Poor Whites in Texas Cotton Culture*. Berkeley: University of California Press, 1997.

Foner, Eric. *Reconstruction: America's Unfinished Revolution, 1863–1877*. New York: Harper and Row, 1988.

Forbath, William. *Law and the Shaping of the American Labor Movement*. Cambridge, MA: Harvard University Press, 1991.

Fraser, Steve, and Gary Gerstle, eds. *Ruling America: A History of Wealth and Power in Democracy*. Cambridge, MA: Harvard University Press, 2005.

Frieden, Jeff, with David A. Lake, eds. *International Political Economy: Perspectives on Global Power and Wealth*. New York: St. Martin's Press, 1987.

Friedman, Tami. *Communities in Competition: Capital Migration and Plant Relocation in the U.S. Carpet Industry, 1929–1975*. New York: Columbia University Press, 2001.

Friedman, Walter. *Prophets of Boom: America's First Generation of Economic Forecasters*. Forthcoming.

Galambos, Lou. *Competition and Cooperation: The Emergence of a Modern Trade Association*. Baltimore: Johns Hopkins University Press, 1966.

Galambos, Lou, and Barbara Barrow Spence. *The Public Image of Big Business in America, 1880–1940: A Quantitative Study in Social Change*. Baltimore: Johns Hopkins University Press, 1975.

Gallman, Robert. *Cambridge Economic History of the United States*. New York: Cambridge University Press, 2008.

Genovese, Eugene. *The Political Economy of Slavery: Studies in the Economy and the Society of the Slave South*. New York: Vintage Books, 1965.

Gervais, Pierre. *Les origines de la révolution industrielle aux Etats-Unis: Entre économie marchande et capitalisme industrielle, 1800–1850*. Paris: Editions EHESS, 2004.

Gilligan, Maureen Carroll. *Female Corporate Culture and the New South: Women in Business between the World Wars*. New York: Taylor & Francis, 1999.

Glickman, Lawrence B. *Buying Power: A History of Consumer Activism in America*. Chicago: University of Chicago Press, 2009.

Goldin, Claudia. *Understanding the Gender Gap: An Economic History of American Women*. New York: Oxford University Press, 1990.

Goldin, Claudia, and Larry Katz. *The Race between Education and Technology*. Cambridge, MA: Belknap/Harvard University Press, 2008.

Gunn, L. Ray. *The Decline of Authority: Public Economic Policy and Political Development in New York, 1800–1860*. Ithaca, NY: Cornell University Press, 1988.

Gutman, Herbert. *Work, Culture and Society*. New York: Vintage, 1977.

Hahn, Steven. *The Roots of Southern Populism: Yeoman Farmers and the Transformation of the Georgia Upcountry*. New York: Oxford University Press, 1983.

Hall, Peter. *Varieties of Capitalism: The Institutional Foundations of Comparative Advantage*. New York: Oxford University Press, 2001.

Hancock, David. *Oceans of Wine: Madeira and the Emergence of American Trade and Taste*, New Haven, CT: Yale University Press, 2009.

Handlin, Oscar. *Commonwealth: A Study of the Role of Government in the American Economy: Massachusetts, 1774–1861*. Cambridge, MA: Belknap/Harvard University Press, 1969.

Harmon, Alexandra. *Rich Indians: Native People and the Problem of Wealth in American History*. Chapel Hill: University of North Carolina Press, 2010.

Hartmann, Susan. *The Home Front and Beyond: American Women in the 1940s*. Boston: Twayne, 1982.

Haydu, Jeffrey. *Citizen Employers: Business Communities and Labor in Cincinnati and San Francisco, 1870–1916*. Ithaca, NY: ILR Press, 2008.

Horwitz, Morton. *The Transformation of American Law, 1780–1860*. Cambridge, MA: Harvard University Press, 1977.

———. *The Transformation of American Law, 1870–1960: The Crisis of Legal Orthodoxy*. New York: Oxford University Press, 1992.

Hosmer, Brian. *American Indians in the Marketplace: Persistence and Innovation among the Menominees and Metlakatlans, 1870–1920*. Lawrence: University Press of Kansas, 1999.

Hyman, Louis. *Debtor Nation: The History of America in Red Ink*. Princeton, NJ: Princeton University Press, 2011.

Inikori, Joseph. *Africans and the Industrial Revolution in England: A Study in International Trade and Economic Development*. New York: Cambridge University Press, 2002.

Jacobs, Meg. *Pocketbook Politics: Economic Citizenship in Twentieth Century America*. Princeton, NJ: Princeton University Press, 2005.

Jacobs, Meg, William Novak, and Julian Zelizer, eds. *The Democratic Experiment: New Directions in American Political History*. Princeton, NJ: Princeton University Press, 2003.

Jacoby, Sanford, ed. *Masters to Managers: Historical and Comparative Perspectives on American Employers*. New York: Columbia University Press, 1991.

———. *Modern Manors: Welfare Capitalism since the New Deal*. Princeton, NJ: Princeton University Press, 1997.

John, Richard. *Network Nation: Inventing American Telecommunications*. Cambridge, MA: Belknap/Harvard University Press, 2010.

———. *Spreading the News: The American Postal System from Franklin to Morse*. Cambridge, MA: Harvard University Press, 1995.

Johnson, Walter. *Soul by Soul: Life inside the Antebellum Slave Market*. Cambridge, MA: Harvard University Press, 1999.

Johnston, Robert. *The Radical Middle Class: Populist Democracy and the Question of Capitalism in Progressive Era Portland, Oregon*. Princeton, NJ: Princeton University Press, 2003.

Josephson, Matthew. *The Robber Barons: The Great American Capitalists*. New York: Harcourt, Brace, 1934.

Kreitner, Roy. *Calculating Promises: The Emergence of Modern American Contract Doctrine*. Stanford, CA: Stanford University Press, 2007.

Kwolek-Folland, Angel. *Incorporating Women: A History of Women in Business in the United States*. New York: Twayne, 1998.

Laird, Pamela Walker. *Advertising Progress: American Business and the Rise of Consumer Marketing*, Baltimore: Johns Hopkins University Press, 1998.

Lamoureux, Naomi R. *The Great Merger Movement in American Business, 1895–1904*. New York: Cambridge University Press, 1985.

Leach, William. *Land of Desire: Merchants, Power, and the Rise of a New American Culture*. New York: Pantheon, 1993.

Lears, Jackson. *Fables of Abundance: A Cultural History of Adverstising in America*. New York: Basic, 1995.

Levy, Jonathan. *The Ways of Providence: Capitalism, Risk, and Freedom in America*. Cambridge, MA: Harvard University Press, 2011.

Licht, Walter. *Industrializing America: The Nineteenth Century*. Baltimore: John Hopkins University Press, 1995.

Lichtenstein, Nelson. *Investing for Middle America: John Elliott Tappan and the Origins of American Express Financial Advisors*. New York: Palgrave/ St. Martin's Press, 2001.

———. *The Retail Revolution: How Wal-Mart Created a Brave New World of Business*. New York: Henry Holt, 2009.

———. *Wal-Mart: The Face of Twenty-First-Century Capitalism*. New York: New Press, distributed by W. W. Norton, 2006.

Lipartito. Kenneth. *Constructing Corporate America: History, Politics, Culture*. New York: Oxford University Press, 2004.

Maggor, Noam. "Politics of Property: Urban Democracy in the Age of Capital, Boston 1865–1900." Ph.D. thesis, Harvard University, 2010.

McCraw, Thomas. *Creating Modern Capitalism: How Entrepreneurs, Companies, and Countries Triumphed in Three Industrial Revolutions*. Cambridge, MA: Harvard University Press, 1997.

———. *Prophets of Regulation: Charles Francis Adams, Louis D. Brandeis, James M. Landis, Alfred E. Kahn*. Cambridge, MA: Belknap/Harvard University Press, 1984.

McLennan, Rebecca. *The Crisis of Imprisonment: Protest, Politics, and the Making of the American Penal State, 1776–1941*. New York: Cambridge University Press, 2008.

Mirowski, Philip. *More Heat Than Light: Economics as Social Physics, Physics as Nature's Economics*. New York: Cambridge University Press, 1989.

Mirowski, Philip, and Dieter Plehwe. *The Road from Mont Pèlerin: The Making of the Neoliberal Thought Collective*. Cambridge, MA: Harvard University Press, 2009.

Moreton, Bethany. *To Serve God and Wal-Mart: The Making of Christian Free Enterprise*. Cambridge, MA: Harvard University Press, 2009.

Moss, David. *Socializing Security: Progressive-Era Economists and the Origins of American Social Policy*. Cambridge, MA: Harvard University Press, 1996.

———. *When All Else Fails: Government as the Ultimate Risk Manager*. Cambridge, MA: Harvard University Press, 2002.

Nevins, Alan. *Study in Power: John D. Rockefeller: Industrialist and Philanthropist*. New York: Scribner's, 1953.

Niethammer, Lutz. *"Kollektive Identität": Heimliche Quellen einer unheimlichen Konjunktur*. Reinbek, Germany: Rowolt, 2000.

Noble, David. *America by Design: Science, Technology, and the Rise of Corporate Capitalism*. New York: Knopf, 1979.

North, Douglass. *The Economic Growth of the United States, 1790–1860*. Englewood Cliffs, NJ: Prentice Hall, 1961.

———. *Structure and Change in Economic History*. New York: W. W. Norton, 1981.

O'Donovan, Susan. *Becoming Free in the Cotton South*. Cambridge, MA: Harvard University Press, 2007.

Olegario, Rowena. *A Culture of Credit: Embedding Trust and Transparency in American Business*. Cambridge, MA: Harvard University Press, 2006.

O'Sullivan, Mary. *Contests for Corporate Control: Corporate Governance and Economic Performance in the United States and Germany*. New York: Oxford University Press, 2000.

Ott, Julia. "When Wall Street Met Main Street: The Quest for an Investors' Democracy and the Emergence of the Retail Investor in the United States, 1890–1930." *Enterprise and Society* 9 (2008): 619–630.

Peck, Gunther. *Reinventing Free Labor: Padrones and Immigrant Workers in the North American West, 1880–1930*. New York: Cambridge University Press, 2000.

Peiss, Kathy L. *Hope in a Jar: The Making of America's Beauty Culture*. New York: Henry Holt, 1999.

Phillips-Fein, Kimberly. *Invisible Hands: The Making of the Conservative Movement from the New Deal to Reagan*. New York: W. W. Norton, 2010.

Pomeranz, Kenneth. *The Great Divergence: China, Europe, and the Making of the Modern World Economy*. Princeton, NJ: Princeton University Press, 2000.

Rockman, Seth. *Landscape of Industry: An Industrial History of the Blackstone Valley*. Lebanon, NH: University Press of New England, 2009.

———. *Scraping By: Wage Labor, Slavery, and Survival in Early Baltimore*. Baltimore: Johns Hopkins University Press, 2009.

Rosenzweig, Roy. *Eight Hours for What We Will*. New York: Cambridge University Press, 2002.

Rothenberg, Winifred B. *From Market-Places to a Market Economy: The Transformation of Rural Massachusetts, 1750–1850*. Chicago: University of Chicago Press, 1992.

Rothman, Adam. *Slave Country: American Expansion and the Origins of the Deep South*. Cambridge, MA: Harvard University Press, 2005.

Roy, William. *Socializing Capital: The Rise of the Large Industrial Corporation in America*. Princeton, NJ: Princeton University Press, 1997.

Sandage, Scott. *Born Losers: A History of Failure in America*. Cambridge, MA: Harvard University Press, 2005.

Sanders, Elizabeth. *Roots of Reform: Farmers, Workers, and the American State, 1877–1917*. Chicago: University of Chicago Press, 1999.

Scheiber, Harry. *Ohio Canal Era: A Case Study of Government and the Economy, 1820–1861*. Athens: Ohio University Press, 1987.

Scranton, Philip. *Endless Novelty: Specialty Production and American Industrialization, 1865–1925*. Princeton, NJ: Princeton University Press, 1997.

Sellers, Charles. *The Market Revolution: Jacksonian America, 1815–1846*. New York: Oxford University Press, 1994.

Sklar, Martin. *The Corporate Reconstruction of American Capitalism, 1890–1916: The Market, the Law, and Politics*. New York: Cambridge University Press, 1988.

Skocpol, Theda. *Protecting Soldiers and Mothers: The Political Origins of Social Policy in the United States*. Cambridge, MA: Belknap/Harvard University Press, 1992.

Skowronek, Stephen. *Building a New American State: The Expansion of National Administrative Capacities, 1877–1920*. New York: Cambridge University Press, 1982.

Smith, Jason Scott. *Building New Deal Liberalism: The Political Economy of Public Works, 1933–1956*. New York: Cambridge University Press, 2006.

Sokoloff, Kenneth L. *Slavery in the Development of the Americas*. New York: Cambridge University Press, 2004.

Sombart, Werner. *Warum gibt es in den Vereinigten Staaten keinen Sozialismus?* Tübingen, Germany: Mohr, 1906.

Stanley, Amy Dru. *From Bondage to Contract: Wage Labor, Marriage, and the Market in the Age of Slave Emancipation*. New York: Cambridge University Press, 1998.

Stein, Judith. *Pivotal Decade: How the United States Traded Factories for Finance in the Seventies*. New Haven, CT: Yale University Press, 2010.

———. *Running Steel, Running America: Race, Economic Policy, and the Decline of Liberalism*. Chapel Hill: University of North Carolina, 1998.

Steinfeld, Robert. *Invention of Free Labor: The Employment Relation in English and American Law and Culture, 1350–1870*. Chapel Hill: University of North Carolina Press, 1991.

Stiles, T. J. *The First Tycoon: The Epic Life of Cornelius Vanderbilt*. New York: Knopf, 2009.

Sylla, Richard. *The Evolution of the American Economy: Growth, Welfare, and Decision Making*. New York: Basic Books, 1979.

———. *A History of Interest Rates*. New Brunswick, NJ: Rutgers University Press, 1991.

Tilly, Charles. *Coercion, Capital, and European States, AD 990–1990*. Oxford, U.K.: B. Blackwell, 1990.

———. *Trust and Rule*. New York: Cambridge University Press, 2005.

Unger, Irwin. *The Greenback Era: A Social and Political History of American Finance, 1865–1879*. Princeton, NJ: Princeton University Press, 1964.

Usselman, Steven. *Regulating Railroad Innovation: Business, Technology, and Politics in America, 1840–1920*. New York: Cambridge University Press, 2002.

Van der Linden, Marcel. *Workers of the World: Essays towards a Global Labor History*. Leiden: Brill, 2008.

Veeser, Cyrus. *A World Safe for Capitalism: Dollar Diplomacy and America's Rise to Global Power*. New York: Columbia University Press, 2002.

Waldstreicher, David. *Slavery's Constitution: From Revolution to Ratification*. New York: Hill and Wang, 2009.

Walker, Juliet. *The History of Black Business in America: Capitalism, Race, Entrepreneurship*. New York: Macmillian/Prentice Hall International, 1998.

Walpen, Bernard. *Die offenen Feinde und Ihre Gesellschaft: Eine Hegemonietheoretische Studie zur Mont Pelerin Society*. Hamburg: VSA Verlag, 2004.

Waterhouse, Ben. *Lobbying America's Business Leaders in an Age of Conservatism, 1969–1994*. Forthcoming.

Way, Peter. *Common Labor: Workers and the Digging of North American Canals, 1780–1860*. Baltimore: Johns Hopkins University Press, 1997.

White, Richard. *"It's Your Misfortune and None of My Own": A History of the American West*. Norman: University of Oklahoma Press, 1991.

Wilder, Craig Steven. *In the Company of Black Men: The African Influence on African American Culture in New York City*. New York: New York University Press, 2001.

Wilentz, Sean. *Chants Democratic: New York City and the Rise of the American Working Class, 1788–1850*. New York: Oxford University Press, 1984.

Wilkins, Mira. *The Emergence of Multinational Enterprise: American Business from the Colonial Era to 1914*. Cambridge, MA: Harvard University Press, 1970.

Williams, Eric. *Capitalism and Slavery*. Chapel Hill: University of North Carolina Press, 1944.

Witt, John. *The Accidental Republic: Crippled Workingmen, Destitute Widows, and the Remaking of American Law*. Cambridge, MA: Harvard University Press, 2004.

Wright, Gavin. *Old South, New South: Revolutions in the Southern Economy since the Civil War*. New York: Basic Books, 1986.

———. *The Political Economy of the Cotton South: Households, Markets, and Wealth in the Nineteenth Century*. New York: W. W. Norton, 1978.

Yearley, Clifton K. *The Money Machines: The Breakdown and Reform of Governmental and Party Finance in the North, 1860–1920*. Albany: State University of New York Press, 1970.

Zelizer, Julian. *Taxing America: Wilbur D. Mills, Congress, and the State, 1945–1975*. New York: Cambridge University Press, 1998.

Zunz, Olivier. *Making America Corporate, 1870–1920*. Chicago: University of Chicago Press, 1990.

15

Women's and Gender History

REBECCA EDWARDS

Emerging from feminist inquiries in the 1960s and 1970s, women's history has become one of the most prolific and creative fields in U.S. history. Before the mid-1980s, scholars treated it as a branch of social history, whose goal was to illuminate the experiences of ordinary women and the sources of their oppression *as women*. Early historians in the field emphasized the rise and fall of Victorian domesticity, with its attention to women's "separate sphere" in the home. Scholars sought particularly to understand women's organizing efforts on their own behalf—notably, through the suffrage movement—and their entry into public life. Those stories pointed, rather heroically, toward the feminist movement of the 1960s, from which the field itself had emerged.

In the past quarter century, most of the preceding assumptions have been seriously challenged or discarded. This transformation began with the appearance of two key articles. Joan Scott's "Gender: A Useful Category of Historical Analysis," published in 1986, helped introduce historians of women to what is widely known as the "cultural turn." Scott showed how historians could draw on insights from anthropology, postcolonial studies, and other emerging fields to illuminate the ways in which gender categories shaped knowledge, identities, and power relations. In an essay published two years later, Linda Kerber raised questions about the metaphor of separate spheres. Among its many limitations, she suggested, was that it "helped historians avoid thinking about race" by keeping their focus on the alleged sphere of white middle-class women.

At the time Kerber wrote, scholars were already beginning to grasp the multiplicity of women's experiences. Rural women were receiving new attention, as in Laurel Thatcher Ulrich's brilliant reconstruction of a midwife's life and work on the Maine frontier. Historians such as Jacqueline Jones were publishing groundbreaking work on African-American women. Through scholarship on Native American, Asian American, Latina, and other women of color, also, it became clear that gender and race were not independent categories. Some women of color described race, not gender, as the most powerful defining factor in their experience. They rejected the idea that women's oppression *as women* should be their paramount concern.

Both the rise of gender history and the new emphasis on differences among women have reshaped—even fragmented—historians' understanding of women as historical subjects. Such insights have fueled a tremendous burst of scholarly creativity over the past two decades, accompanied by a (generally) cheerful sense of chaos. Women's history is no longer solely a branch of social history. It treats, among other things, electoral politics, economics, intellectual life, and popular culture. At the same time, gender history offers a set of lenses through which scholars in *all* subfields need to peer. Historians of law, technology, and foreign relations—to name just a few—now routinely recognize gender as a category of analysis. Important findings are coming from researchers who do not consider themselves historians of women at all. It is hardly possible, today, to identify any single, central conversation that is taking place among historians of women and gender. To paraphrase Walt Whitman, the field "contradicts itself; it contains multitudes."

The real triumph of women's history, then, can be found elsewhere in this volume: almost every author, whether writing on a specific period or a major theme in American history, incorporates findings in women's and gender history. Nonetheless, women's and gender history continues to thrive, though in certain ways the field no longer belongs distinctly to itself. One recent bibliography, focusing solely on the history of women, lists more than a thousand books and articles. This chapter faces, then, the daunting task of surveying that field while also noting broader trends in gender history, with at least a nod to the emerging fields of queer history and the history of masculinity. Clearly, what follows will be suggestive rather than comprehensive.

I explore in this chapter four broad areas in which historians have reshaped the field since 1990: scholarship on gender, race, and empire; on women's economic roles; on sexuality, public space, and consumer culture; and on citizenship, politics, and the state. These have no claim to being the most important areas, much less the *only* areas, of recent work. Each overlaps with the others and with additional fields, such as the history of gender and religion, barely touched on here. The areas covered here do, however, illustrate some of the most dramatic ways in which earlier assumptions have been overturned.

Gender, Race, and Empire

One of the most important findings of recent decades is that women's oppression *as women* cannot be untangled from other forms of oppression, especially on the basis of race. The two have been mutually constituted. Historians of slavery were among the first to powerfully show how race and gender are intertwined categories. In the seventeenth and eighteenth centuries, Europeans changed their views of sexual difference from a one-sex model, in which the female body was seen as an inverted form of the male body, to a two-sex model that viewed women as inherently different beings. This dualistic ideology developed alongside the equally new notion that "black" and "white" were fixed and opposite categories, with these definitions of gender and race informing each other.

Kathleen Brown, for example, shows how the colony of Virginia gradually passed laws that marked racial difference through women's bodies. In 1643 the colony began to levy a tithe on "negro women" held as servants or slaves, holding them equivalent to men as field laborers. By 1668, the tax was extended to include African-American wives and daughters. Meanwhile, in 1662, another law classified all children as "bond or free . . . according to the condition of the mother." Since, under English law, a child ordinarily followed the condition of the father, this law made the sexual exploitation of black women a central feature of slavery. The same law doubled the fine for any "christian" convicted of fornicating with a "negro man or woman," showing how religious and racial definitions intertwined. Black women's enslavement defined their children as slaves for life.

Sharon Block explores racialized legal patterns in the eighteenth and early nineteenth centuries, again demonstrating the interplay of race and gender. Block finds that courts defined consent not so much by evidence of a woman's wishes (to the extent that they acknowledged that she had a rational will) but by hierarchies of power within and beyond the household, including gender, age, economic status, and particularly race. In 95 percent of prosecuted cases, victims were white women, while the vast majority of men sentenced to death for rape were African American. The resulting "racialization of rape" was reinforced "every time a black man was convicted of rape and a white man was not." A sexualized set of racial prejudices emerged that profoundly shaped future law and racial violence in the United States.

Historians are still untangling the complicated skeins of race, class, gender, and legal status. In a study of sexual contacts between white women and black men in the nineteenth century, Martha Hodes finds that, remarkably, whites often tolerated such contacts during slavery days but became far more hostile and punitive after Emancipation. Other historians have pursued related questions in the twentieth century. Lisa Lindquist Dorr, for example, shows that responses to alleged sexual crime by African-American men were shaped by gender and class. This was true even in Jim Crow Virginia, where it might be assumed that a black man accused of rape had little or no chance of acquittal. Studying 271 cases of alleged black-on-white rape, Dorr finds wildly varied results: 17 alleged perpetrators were lynched, but in another 35 cases all charges were dismissed, with the perceived character of the white female victim playing a significant role in the outcome. The work of historians such as Block, Hodes, and Dorr, taken together, suggests that more work needs to be done on the intersections of gender and race.

Nowhere has scholarly conversation been richer than in studies of the slave family. Such work was originally stimulated by fierce debates over the 1965 Moynihan Report, which justified government programs for the African-American family by pathologizing it as matriarchal. For a generation, historians refuted that slur by arguing that slave families were "normal": they fit the white patriarchal model of a stable, nuclear family with a strong husband and father. Historians of women have, in the past twenty years, substantially complicated this thesis. Surveying the domestic arrangements of slaves in Virginia, Brenda Stevenson finds not only "monogamous marriages and co-residential nuclear families" but also, among other arrangements, "matrifocality, polygamy, single parents, abroad spouses, [and] one-, two-, and three-generation households." As Ann Paton Malone reports, most historians now reject both the "myth of matriarchy" and the claim that slave families were homogeneous. "The real strength of the slave family," Malone writes, "was its multiplicity of forms, its tolerance for a variety of families and households, its adaptability, and its acceptance of all types of families and households as functional and contributing." As such work shows, claims about the historical "norm" for American families must henceforth take diversity strongly into account.

Scholars of frontiers and empire building have also shown how race and gender are intertwined. As with slavery, an important component of imperial conquest has been white men's appropriation of the bodies of women of color. In the imperial imagination, territorial and sexual domination have often been linked. Historians have documented not only figurative desire of native women, but also sexual liaisons that ranged from consensual interracial marriage to brutal rape. In North Carolina, Kirsten Fischer shows that European colonists justified theft of native lands by claiming that Indian women were "drudges" for their men and preferred white men as partners. The same patterns held true in other sites of empire building. Amy Greenberg finds that in the Mexican-American War, Anglo men coveted the "beautiful and available women" of Mexico and Central America as the "greatest of all natural resources."

White women have also had important racial identities, though that has not always been obvious to historians. Elizabeth Jameson, writing about the American West, observes that "in practice, it has often been as hard to decenter white women as to decenter the story of westward expansion." Frontiers and zones of conquest are particularly useful places to study gender and racial privilege. In a pattern that repeated itself in many places and eras, the arrival of Anglo women transformed interethnic and interracial marriage into a marker of low class status and disrespectability, causing it to become less frequent. Reporting on Arizona mining towns in the late nineteenth century, for example, Linda Gordon notes that Anglo women's advent "challenged Anglo men's patriarchal colonial privilege to marry and make 'white' their Mexican wives." It was Anglo women who "fully spliced class status to whiteness."

As Anglo women redefined relationships of gender, race, and class, their presence increased the vulnerability and dependency of women of color. In the Southwest, Anglo intrusion forced many Mexican-American women into poverty and domestic service, where they labored under the direction of Anglo female employers. Under such circumstances, women of color faced difficult choices. Some worked as negotiators across cultural boundaries; Theda Perdue and Michelene Pesantubbee have uncovered, for instance, the roles of Cherokee and Choctaw women as decision makers and intermediaries. Other women withdrew, insofar as possible, from interactions with the conquerors and worked to sustain and strengthen their own communities.

In the nineteenth and twentieth centuries, white women shaped race relations not only by their presence but also through conscious efforts to "civilize" women of color. Believing white women should take a special role in such work, they embarked on what Peggy Pascoe describes as a racialized quest for "female moral authority." This search for public power, with its central emphasis on cultivating Anglo-style domesticity, was especially prominent in the trans-Mississippi West, and it also extended beyond U.S. borders. By the late 1800s and early 1900s, many single and married female missionaries served in China, India, and other "heathen lands." American women—Protestant and Catholic, white and black—supported this work in enormous numbers, building missionary societies into the largest grassroots women's movement of the era.

Historians such as Thomas Winter have begun to explore how ideals of manhood also shaped mission and uplift activities, like those of the Young Men's Christian Association. Conceptions of masculinity also played an obvious role in empire building overseas. To date, much work has focused on the era between the 1890s and the 1920s, when, as Glenda Gilmore, Gail Bederman, and others have shown, appeals to "Anglo-Saxon manhood" helped construct the political frameworks for both segregation at home and imperialism abroad. Kristin Hoganson's influential book *Fighting for American Manhood* demonstrates that widespread fears of male weakness helped fuel America's entry into the Spanish-American War.

In the twentieth century, imperial projects often took more secular and state-directed forms. Doctors and social workers of the 1920s and 1930s, for example, justified Puerto Ricans' exclusion from full citizenship by pointing to prostitution and allegedly immoral sexual relations on the island. "Puerto Rican difference," Laura Briggs writes, "has been produced and located in women's sexuality and reproduction." Naoko Shibusawa and other scholars have carried this story into other parts of the world where the United States asserted its power. Meanwhile, Robert Dean offers a sophisticated reading of the class and gender compulsions that drove elite cold war policy makers—in Dean's phrase, an "imperial brotherhood"—to persist in escalating the Vietnam War.

Women's Economic Roles

Recent studies of gender and labor also complicate our view of women as historical subjects. In some ways, industrialization and the rise of modern capitalism helped free women from patriarchal legal structures; at the same time, these processes introduced new forms of domination. Nowhere is this clearer than in a rich body of recent scholarship on marriage law, which figured centrally in the construction of citizenship, property rights, and public policy. Lawmakers and courts long viewed the husband and father as the family's unitary sovereign; upon marriage, a woman endured "coverture," or legal death. The first married women's property acts in the United States, enacted between the 1830s and the 1850s, were largely designed to protect men from creditors. During the same years, a widow's traditional right to a "dower third" of her husband's estate was eroded by new rulings that gave creditors access to all assets. While historians such as Nancy Cott emphasize women's gains in this period, Henrik Hartog argues that the erosion of dower rights, along with the abandonment of other laws that spelled out husbands' obligations, made wives and widows more vulnerable. Norma Basch finds a similar complexity in nineteenth-century debates over the rising incidence of divorce. Did liberal divorce laws liberate women? Or did they allow husbands to act irresponsibly and abandon faithful wives?

Amy Dru Stanley shows how such questions emerged, in part, in the context of slavery's demise. She explores interrelated ideas about several types of contracts—especially marriage and labor contracts—in the postbellum era of "free labor." Americans argued in these decades over "the limits of commodity exchange," Stanley writes, as they debated marriage and labor law. These conversations "revealed deep ambiguities concerning self ownership in a free market society as well as relations of dependence and dominion both at work and at home." Stanley finds that prostitution—the selling of sex—remained the one type of contract that was almost universally condemned, as Americans "valoriz[ed] sex rather than labor as the essence of selfhood."

As such work shows, historians are raising complex questions about how women's labor—productive and reproductive, paid and unpaid—has shaped class identities. As early as 1981, Mary Ryan observed that the definition of "middle class" in the United States centered on the family, and that women's work in the household fueled the success of "self-made" men. In an influential study of women's labor in the early republic, Jeanne Boydston argued that a wife's economic role often determined whether a family was working class or middle class. If a woman could devote her energies to managing household resources, rather than to wage labor outside the home, the family could accumulate property. Such work was, however, largely invisible to men, and middle-class women came to be classified as "not working." Women's reproductive labor (or lack thereof) also played a profound role in shaping a family's class status, especially in urban areas. A couple with two children could invest more resources in their education and training; in an industrial economy, those children had better odds for upward mobility. Fertility and family limitation, then, must be treated as central aspects of women's work.

Emerging from the field of women's history, such insights are reshaping how other historians of the United States think about industrialization and class formation. In the meantime, they have undercut historians' earlier assumption that nineteenth-century women inhabited a separate sphere in the private home. "Surveying the terrain of antebellum America today," reports Catherine Kelly, "we no longer see separate spheres, but the broad and sweeping transformation of the household economy. . . . It is no longer possible to imagine that women's work, whether performed in factory or household, whether paid or unpaid, was isolated from the social and economic processes that transformed men's work."

As they negotiated their place in the industrial economy, working-class women faced distinct challenges. Women's paid labor has often occurred *within* the home, as married women took in laundry or boarders or engaged in low-wage, subcontracted "homework," completed within the household and paid by the piece. This phenomenon began in the nineteenth-century shoemaking and garment trades and has, as Eileen Boris has shown, reemerged with a vengeance since the 1970s.

But it is clear that, despite their frequent segregation in the labor market and the hostility they faced from male labor unions, working-class women played central roles in labor activism and state building. Nancy Gabin demonstrates this point in her study of women in the United Auto Workers, while Dorothy Cobble and Karen Sacks, among others, find that wage-earning women in the post–World War II era developed distinctive forms of working-class feminism, focused on community building, economic self-help, and activism on such issues as pay inequity and sexual harassment. Latina women played an important role in these developments, and other immigrant women also took up the cause. Xiaolan Bao, for example, finds that in the 1980s female Chinese garment workers in New York City organized strikes and negotiations around the issue of daycare. As family breadwinners, these women gained considerable authority in their households in relation to male kin, but the dual pressures of work and family left them, like millions of wage-earning women, frustrated and exhausted. Much labor activism in recent decades, like these garment workers' strike, has been female-led and driven by working-class feminist concerns.

Men have also had gendered identities in the workplace, as well as at home. In 1991, Ava Baron proposed that historians rethink class and gender as distinct categories, questioning "a whole series of conceptual dualisms—

capitalism/patriarchy, public/private, production/reproduction, men's work/women's work—which assume that class issues are integral to the first term of each pair and gender is important only to the second." Scholars like Mary Blewett have responded to this challenge, focusing attention on working-class masculinity. But in analyzing the gendered history of labor, much remains to be done.

Sexuality, Public Space, and Consumer Culture

In 1629, a court in Virginia made an unusual decision about a colonist known as both Thomas and Thomasine Hall. At the behest of colonial officials, an employer, and a neighbor, Hall's genitals had been examined several times, but no one could agree on Hall's sex. Hall was therefore proclaimed to be both "a man and a woeman" and instructed to wear men's clothing, but with an apron and a woman's "Coyfe and Crosecloth" on his head. More than two centuries later, in the 1850s, the U.S. surgeon general encountered intersex individuals when he visited pueblos in the Southwest. At Acoma, one traditional healer declared that "he had nursed several infants whose mothers had died, and that he had given them plenty of milk from his breasts"; at the same time, he said, he "had a large penis and his testicles were *grandes como huevos*—as large as eggs." Such evidence of intersexualism—an emerging area of historical research—blurs the boundary between male and female, undermining not only the notion of "separate spheres" but even the idea of distinct sexes. It also shows that sexual identities have rarely been a private matter; instead, they have been publicly performed and defined.

As they explore such sites of gendered discourse and conflict, scholars have focused on struggles over public space. In an imaginative study of enslaved women, Stephanie Camp uses Edward Said's term "rival geography" to describe how they, like other peoples who resisted colonial oppression, created "alternative ways of knowing and using plantation and southern space that conflicted with planters' ideals and demands." Camp finds that women, in comparison with men, more often employed their cabins and nearby locations to carry out short-term negotiations over their conditions of servitude. They also constructed alternative spaces, such as illegal celebrations, where the body became "an important site not only of suffering but also . . . of enjoyment and resistance."

Despite creative work such as Camp's, the bulk of scholarship on gender and public space has focused on the city. In *Sex among the Rabble*, Clare Lyons traces distinctive patterns of urban sexuality in Philadelphia as early as the pre-Revolutionary years, including marked female independence, casual sexual relationships, a thriving erotic print culture, and commercial sex. Patricia Cline Cohen and Amy Gilman Srebnick explore public discourses surrounding sex, crime, and commerce in New York City by studying the murders of sex worker Helen Jewett in 1836 and the "Beautiful Cigar Girl" Mary Rogers in 1841. By the post–Civil War period, Sarah Deutsch shows how women reshaped Boston's public spaces, asserting a place for themselves in streets and polling places and developing kitchen bars and other semipublic ventures. In a study of Davenport, Iowa, in the 1880s, Sharon Wood offers a rich account of women's public activities, driven especially by their entry into paid employment.

Private businesses had a strong interest in making commercialized public sphere safe and accessible for middle-class women. Amy Richter documents the rise of "public domesticity," as railroads created Pullman cars and waiting rooms that seemed safe and homelike. "Originally considered a moral haven from the competitive world of business," Richter writes, "the private sphere came to connote comfort, convenience, and social respectability." Following this story into the legal realm, Barbara Welke reveals how wide acceptance of women's railroad travel gradually altered court awards to compensate for injuries and emotional distress from railroad accidents, as well as creating the context in which African-American plaintiffs—overwhelmingly women—sued for equal access to the protection of "ladies' cars."

Historians have paid a great deal of attention to gender, leisure, and consumer culture. Though few dispute the power of advertisers to serve corporate purposes and reinforce gender norms, some, including Tera Hunter, Vicki Ruíz, Kathy Peiss, and Susan Douglas, see women's appropriations of consumer culture as also serving their own ends. These include entry into public spaces like dance halls, which posed sexual dangers but permitted greater freedom than the workplace or home. Historians of the Progressive Era have shown, for example, that ready-made fashions, popular novels, movies, and magazines such as *True Confessions* helped wage-earning women build a working-class feminist sensibility.

While some historians are exploring conflicts over public space, others have studied different realms of sexual behavior. Some have challenged the idea that Victorian women internalized the idea of female "passionlessness." Helen Lefkowitz Horowitz documents the persistence of an early "vernacular sexual culture" in the nineteenth century, as well as new scientific ideas that celebrated "the naturalness of the body's sexual appetites." Other historians have uncovered a lively conversation among nineteenth-century sex reformers, who sought to promote birth control. In the 1870s and 1880s, the supposed heyday of antivice crusader Anthony Comstock, Andrea Tone documents a flourishing commercial birth control industry that served a national market of mail-order customers. Much more needs to be known about how nineteenth-century couples purchased and used cervical caps, condoms, and "douching powders." But recent research decisively disproves the assumption that sexual abstinence was the primary method of fertility control.

The fields of queer theory and queer history, which hardly existed in 1990, have played a central role in reshaping the history of sexuality.

George Chauncey's pathbreaking book *Gay New York*, perhaps the most influential work in this field, uncovers an exuberant urban gay world in the late nineteenth and early twentieth centuries. Chauncey finds that sexual identities were flexible—homosexual activity did not necessarily mark a person as having a fixed homosexual *identity*—and that commercial venues such as cabarets, boardwalks, dance halls, and bathhouses became convenient sites for sexual encounters. Relationships between middle-class "queers" and working-class "fairies" often crossed class lines. Chauncey finds that World War II and the cold war ushered in new heterosexual norms; gradually, after the end of Prohibition, gay New Yorkers were stigmatized and forced into the closet by prosecution and violence.

Citizenship, Politics, and the State

As earlier sections of this chapter illustrate, historians have focused considerable attention lately on gender and the law. They have also investigated women's role in politics, in ways that range far beyond the field's early emphasis on the suffrage movement. As Americans embarked on their experiment in self-government, citizens of the new republic needed to assert their "civic virtue," which most political leaders defined as male. Joanne Freeman, among others, has shown that an aggressive code of masculine honor lay at the heart of political culture. Nonetheless, women claimed an early role as republican mothers who would educate their sons for citizenship. Historians such as Catherine Allgor find that, as far back as the Revolutionary era, elite, well-connected women wielded political influence through skillful adaptations of "private" space. By the early 1800s, some women claimed a more direct role as "female politicians," engaging in partisan debate. Rosemarie Zagarri identifies a backlash by the 1820s and 1830s: the rise of universal white male suffrage and mass-based political parties, she argues, worked to exclude women who had asserted political claims. In these same years, however, republican womanhood clearly offered a basis for women's broader public role.

These decades witnessed the rise of a dizzying number of women's reform organizations. In a meticulously researched study of Boston and New York between 1797 and 1840, Anne Boylan describes women's participation in diverse public projects, ranging from the Abyssinian Benevolent Daughters of Esther to the Society for the Relief of Respectable, Aged, Indigent Females. With the rising influence of evangelical Protestantism, women gradually combined republican motherhood with powerful claims to Christian womanly action. Boylan also finds that Catholic and Jewish women in the two cities engaged in public activism earlier than historians had once believed. Catherine Brekus, meanwhile, focuses on female preaching between the mid-eighteenth century and 1845, finding an array of women who offered public spiritual testimony. She argues that such speakers, unlike the far smaller number of women's rights advocates, were "active participants in the public sphere, but they never challenged the political structures that enforced their inequality in family, church, and state."

The rise of mass-based political parties offered new opportunities for women, while also reflecting contested ideals of manhood. A self-conscious middle-class began, in the antebellum years, to reject patriarchal models of household order, which were grounded in a vigorous defense of white men's prerogatives as citizens and heads of households. They promoted, instead, an ideal of piety, self-discipline, and domesticity for both sexes. The leading political parties squared off over these competing ideals: Democrats tended to defend patriarchal family models (including slavery), while Whigs, and later Republicans, promoted domesticity. In Amy Greenberg's apt formulation, Jacksonian Democrats' "aggressive manhood" stood in opposition to a "restrained manhood" rooted in temperance, self-control, and recognition of female influence, including a limited political role for women.

The rise of the Republican Party, a political agent of domesticity and bourgeois values, intensified the gendered basis of party politics. Race was, again, a central factor. Stephanie McCurry finds that in the secession crisis, elite South Carolinians warned other men of threats to patriarchy: if Republicans could interfere with slavery, they could invade the home and transform the nature of marriage, perhaps even liberating women. "The legitimacy of [white] male authority over women within the household," writes McCurry, "was the cornerstone of the slavery edifice." At the same time, abolitionists denounced slavery for making family life impossible for the enslaved, giving white men tyrannical power over their households, and destroying the sexual purity of both black and white Americans.

The story of women's partisan activities now extends from the antebellum period all the way through 1920, when the achievement of full voting rights reshaped women's place in the electoral arena. My own work, for example, traces women's partisan activism in the post–Civil War era and its relationship to competing Republican and Democratic models of gender behavior. Throughout the nineteenth century, new upstart parties proved particularly receptive to women's involvement. Michael Pierson finds women playing prominent roles in the antislavery Liberty Party of the 1840s. Bruce Dorsey, describing the gendered contours of public activism in Philadelphia, shows that male domesticity and women's political activism lent themselves easily to a range of causes, including nativism and the American (or "Know Nothing") Party of the 1850s. After the Civil War, the same relative openness to women's participation characterized the Prohibitionist and Populist Parties.

The crucible of the Civil War transformed women's political goals. A number of studies have focused on the war itself as a catalyst for change, while in the Reconstruction era, historians such as Carole Faulkner describe cooperative projects launched by black and white women. Along with these have come a plethora of state and regional studies of the suffrage movement and allied causes, most of which bridge the traditional divide between the so-called Gilded Age (circa 1877–1900) and the Progressive Era (circa 1900–1920). These include work by Marjorie Spruill Wheeler on the South, Rebecca Mead on the West, and Gayle Gullett on California. Their findings suggest that we need to rethink the origins of women's modern political activism, which had roots well before the arrival of familiar social settlements like Hull House.

Though prosperous African Americans were not middle class in the same sense as white women, they shared many of the same values and commitments in the post–Civil War decades. As Evelyn Higginbotham has written, black women who sought to make cross-racial alliances engaged in a "politics of respectability" that operated as a "bridge discourse." One of the most influential studies in this field is Glenda Gilmore's *Gender and Jim Crow*, which emphasizes the key political roles of African-American women in the era of segregation and black men's disfranchisement. "By embracing a constellation of Victorian middle-class values," Gilmore writes, "—temperance, thrift, hard work, piety, learning—African Americans believed that they could carve out space for dignified and successful lives and that their examples would wear away prejudice." Lisa Materson extends this insight beyond the South. She finds that politically engaged African-American women in Chicago, between the 1870s and the 1930s, not only addressed local issues but also used their voting power on behalf of southern blacks, pressuring national legislators to fight disfranchisement and lynching.

For historians of the twentieth century, one of the most energetic areas of research has been the gendered basis of government welfare policies. In her pathbreaking book *Pitied but Not Entitled*, Linda Gordon showed how public officials retained many of the gendered assumptions held by their predecessors in private charities: both groups conducted home visits to make sure that the conduct of women who received state aid was "respectable." Such restrictions were rarely placed on workmen's compensation and other forms of aid to men, which were viewed as outright entitlements. Jennifer Mittelstadt, exploring similar issues between the New Deal of the 1930s and the Great Society of the 1960s, also finds that policy makers lacked a basic understanding of the causes of women's poverty. As a result, they repeatedly passed laws that proved ineffective or detrimental.

A number of studies, including those by Premilla Nadasen, Annalise Orleck, and Rhonda Williams, have examined the influence of government welfare policies on African-American and working-class women, and vice versa. In general, historians of the welfare rights movement find that federal programs worked, but only when women at the grassroots "forced responsiveness," in Williams's phrase, to meet their needs. Rickie Solinger illustrates some of the formidable obstacles faced by black women in the early cold war era. In her study of illegal abortions before *Roe v. Wade*, she finds that social workers and government agencies encouraged pregnant, unmarried white women to give up babies for adoption, but since no "market" existed for African-American babies, single black women were expected to keep and raise their children. White single motherhood was thus largely invisible to the public eye, while black single motherhood became stigmatized and defined as a political problem.

In the past few years, historians have built on such insights to ask sweeping questions about the gendered basis of citizenship and government. Alice Kessler-Harris's *In Pursuit of Equity* documents the stubborn persistence, throughout the twentieth century, of policies designed to shore up the legal, economic, and cultural authority of male breadwinners. By contrast, Linda Kerber explores women's exemption from such citizens' responsibilities as taxation, jury service, and military conscription. "Rights and obligations are reciprocal elements of citizenship," Kerber observes; women's exclusion from certain obligations, such as military service, diminishes their claim to equal political rights. In *The Straight State*, Margot Canaday carries such inquiries in a different direction, showing how, from the early twentieth century through the cold war, the category "homosexual" became recognized by lawmakers and the general public. She demonstrates how U.S. military, immigration, and social welfare policies created new categories of deviance and a definition of citizenship as heterosexual.

Canaday's story ends with the emergence of the gay rights movement; it thus echoes, in some ways, the earlier story of Reconstruction, when lawmakers first put the word "male" in the Constitution (in the Fourteenth Amendment), at the very moment when an independent women's rights movement arose. On each occasion, the identification of a new interest group precipitated its formal, political exclusion by lawmakers; in both cases, exclusion itself seems to have helped generate a movement for equal rights. This observation perhaps confirms Linda Kerber's insight about how articulating goals may be the most essential step in working to achieve them. She writes, second wave feminists of the 1960s and 1970s "were as much the *namers* of change as the *makers* of change"; what they named was "hypocrisy."

The history of second wave feminism remains a lively field of research. Sara Evans's *Tidal Wave*, perhaps the most important recent history of modern feminism, recovers in rich detail the diverse perspectives of women in the movement, especially women of color. Evans emphasizes the achievements of liberal feminists, with their concrete policy goals, over radical feminists who, in her view, misdirected their political energies in matters of personal lifestyle. Other historians, though, are busy critiquing the limits of liberal feminists' achievement, noting how many of their goals—such as equal pay in the workplace and access to safe contraception and abortion—have stalled in subsequent decades. The extent of what we still do not know about the second wave is suggested by the fact that a new generation of historians is just beginning to trace how feminism arose and evolved in places as diverse as Seattle, Denver, Minneapolis, Dayton, and Durham, North Carolina.

Most historians of modern feminism depict it as *the* watershed moment in U.S. women's history. Evans, for example, argues that second wave feminists presented "a far more radical challenge" to male power than earlier movements for women's rights had been able to do. Before 1920, Evans argues, women supposedly focused all their attention on the "single, symbolic issue" of voting rights. For Ruth Rosen, in another recent history, second wave feminism was the moment when *The World Split Open*. Equally revealing is the title of Gail Collins's popular account of the second wave, *When Everything Changed: The Amazing Journey of American Women from 1960 to the Present.*

Recent scholarship glaringly undermines this simplistic view of events before the 1960s. It is clear now that if a first wave did exist, its origins lay further back, in the 1790s, when Americans read and debated the work of Mary Wollstonecraft and property-owning New Jersey women briefly won the vote. Yet the climate for women's-rights activism in this era differed substantially from that of the antebellum decades of antislavery and women's rights conventions, much less the era of imperialism and Jim Crow. It is hard to think of any nuanced way to narrate women's political struggles over thirteen decades as a single "wave." By focusing on suffrage, the wave theory ignores major transformations in women's lives, before and after 1920. And while suffrage was, indeed, an important goal from the 1840s onward, activism was hardly limited to that one issue; instead, women advanced an array of legal, intellectual, economic, religious, political, and other claims.

A keener understanding of racial, class, religious, and other forms of diversity among women disproves the wave theory even more dramatically, calling into question what counts as a gain or loss in any given era. During the era of imperialism and Jim Crow, for example, white women managed to advance women's rights through racialized claims that excluded women of color; at the same time, some of their work built new legal protections for working-class women. Who achieved progress, and at what cost? Consider the conflicting experiences of American women in 1848, when the Seneca Falls convention supposedly launched the first wave. In that year, thousands of desperate Irish women were fleeing a horrific famine and taking up low-wage work in New England textile mills. Northern Mexican women, their nation defeated in a humiliating war, were facing colonization by the United States through the Treaty of Guadalupe Hidalgo. Millions of African-American women lived in slavery, while native women (including the Seneca for whom the Falls were named) were coping with the aftermath of conquest: ravaging diseases, land loss, and economic marginalization.

As a way of periodizing U.S. women's history, the "first wave, second wave" model is no longer tenable. As yet, however, there has been little conversation on whether or how to replace it. Some creative attempts have been made; Sandra VanBurkleo, for example, divides U.S. constitutional culture into three successive "settlements"—decided during the Revolution, the Civil War, and the era of civil rights—and explores how each legal framework was contested, afterward, by both advocates and opponents of women's rights. Such analyses may provide the basis for a new understanding of the relationship between the changing nature of women's rights advocacy, in various political contexts, and the goals and the achievements of twentieth-century feminism. The work of the past twenty years makes that task a challenge; even more formidable is the idea of constructing any overarching narrative of U.S. women's and gender history or calculating gains and losses for diverse groups of women in particular eras.

These are important tasks for the future. In the meantime, historians of women and gender are moving beyond the boundaries of the nation-state, recognizing that the tenacious, commanding narrative of America's national development still shapes—and perhaps warps—our understanding of women's history. Bonnie Anderson and Margaret McFadden, among others, have explored transatlantic connections among women's rights advocates before the Civil War. Historians of the Progressive Era are comparing gendered welfare policies in various countries and reconstructing conversations among women reformers in the United States and Europe. As this chapter goes to press, several historians are working on books that will place the women's suffrage and feminist movements in global perspective. These developments suggest that, while the field of women's and gender history may no longer own itself, its horizons will continue to expand.

BIBLIOGRAPHY

Note: In earlier editions of *The New American History*, Linda Gordon elegantly recounted the rise of U.S. women's history, and Estelle Freedman surveyed work on sexuality and family history. Both these articles remain valuable, and readers are encouraged to consult them.

Allgor, Catherine. *Parlor Politics: In Which the Ladies of Washington Help Build a City and a Government*. Charlottesville: University Press of Virginia, 2000.

Anderson, Bonnie S. *Joyous Greetings: The First International Women's Movement, 1830–1860*. New York: Oxford University Press, 2000.

Armitage, Susan, and Elizabeth Jameson, eds. *Writing the Range: Race, Class, and Culture in the Women's West*. Norman: University of Oklahoma Press, 1997.

Bailey, Beth, and David Farber. *The First Strange Place: The Alchemy of Race and Sex in World War II Hawai'i*. New York: Free Press, 1992.

Baker, Jean H., ed. *Votes for Women: The Struggle for Suffrage Revisited*. New York: Oxford University Press, 2002.

Bao, Xiaolin. "Chinese Mothers in New York City's Sweatshops." In Alexis Jetter, Annelise Orleck, and Diana Taylor, eds. *The Politics of Motherhood: Activist Voices from Left to Right*, 127–137. Hanover, NH: University Press of New England, 1997.

Baron, Ava, ed. *Work Engendered: Toward a New History of American Labor*. Ithaca, NY: Cornell University Press, 1991.

Barr, Juliana. *Peace Came in the Form of a Woman: Indians and Spaniards in the Texas Borderlands*. Chapel Hill: University of North Carolina Press, 2007.

Basch, Norma. *Framing American Divorce: From the Revolutionary Generation to the Victorians*. Berkeley: University of California Press, 1992.

Bederman, Gail. *Manliness and Civilization: A Cultural History of Gender and Race in the United States, 1880–1917.* Chicago: University of Chicago Press, 1995.

Blee, Kathleen. *Women of the Klan: Racism and Gender in the 1920s.* Berkeley: University of California Press, 1991.

Blewett, Mary H. *Men, Women, and Work: A Study of Class, Gender, and Protest in the Nineteenth-Century New England Shoe Industry, 1780–1910.* Urbana: University of Illinois Press, 1998.

Block, Sharon. *Rape and Sexual Power in Early America.* Chapel Hill: University of North Carolina Press, 2006.

Boris, Eileen. *Home to Work: Motherhood and the Politics of Industrial Homework in the United States.* New York: Cambridge University Press, 1994.

Boydston, Jeanne. *Home and Work: Housework, Wages, and the Ideology of Labor in the Early Republic.* New York: Oxford University Press, 1990.

Boylan, Anne M. *The Origins of Women's Activism: New York and Boston, 1797–1840.* Chapel Hill: University of North Carolina, 2002.

Brekus, Catherine A. *Strangers and Pilgrims: Female Preaching in America, 1740–1845.* Chapel Hill: University of North Carolina Press, 1998.

Briggs, Laura. *Reproducing Empire: Race, Sex, Science, and U.S. Imperialism in Puerto Rico.* Berkeley: University of California Press, 2002.

Brodie, Janet. *Contraception and Abortion in Nineteenth-Century America.* Ithaca, NY: Cornell University Press, 1994.

Brown, Kathleen. *Good Wives, Nasty Wenches, and Anxious Patriarchs: Gender, Race, and Power in Colonial Virginia.* Chapel Hill: University of North Carolina Press, 1996.

Cahn, Susan K. *Coming on Strong: Gender and Sexuality in Twentieth-Century Women's Sport.* New York: Free Press, 1994.

Camp, Stephanie M. H. *Closer to Freedom: Enslaved Women and Everyday Resistance in the Plantation South.* Chapel Hill: University of North Carolina Press, 2004.

Canaday, Margot. *The Straight State: Sexuality and Citizenship in Twentieth-Century America.* Princeton, NJ: Princeton University Press, 2009.

Celello, Kristin. *Making Marriage Work: A History of Marriage and Divorce in the Twentieth Century United States.* Chapel Hill: University of North Carolina Press, 2008.

Chauncey, George. *Gay New York: Gender, Urban Culture, and the Making of a Gay Male World, 1890–1940.* New York: Basic Books, 1994.

Choy, Catherine Ceniza. *Empire of Care: Nursing and Migration in Filipino American History.* Durham, NC: Duke University Press, 2003.

Cobble, Dorothy Sue. *Dishing It Out: Waitresses and Their Unions in the Twentieth Century.* Urbana: University of Illinois Press, 1991.

Cohen, Miriam. *Workshop to Office: Two Generations of Italian Women in New York City, 1900–1950.* Ithaca, NY: Cornell University Press, 1992.

Cohen, Patricia Cline. *The Murder of Helen Jewett.* New York: Vintage, 1999.

Coontz, Stephanie. *The Way We Never Were: American Families and the Nostalgia Trap.* New York: Basic Books, 1992.

Cott, Nancy. *Public Vows: A History of Marriage and the Nation.* Cambridge, MA: Harvard University Press, 2002.

Cox, Karen. *Dixie's Daughters: The United Daughters of the Confederacy and the Preservation of Confederate Culture.* Gainesville: University Press of Florida, 2003.

Davis, Flora. *Moving the Mountain: The Women's Movement in America since 1960.* Urbana: University of Illinois Press, 1999.

Dayton, Cornelia Hughes. *Women before the Bar: Gender, Law, and Society in Connecticut, 1639–1789.* Chapel Hill: University of North Carolina Press, 1995.

Dean, Robert D. *Imperial Brotherhood: Gender and the Making of Cold War Foreign Policy.* Amherst: University of Massachusetts Press, 2001.

D'Emilio, John, and Estelle B. Freedman. *Intimate Matters: A History of Sexuality in America*, 2nd ed. Chicago: University of Chicago Press, 1997.

Deslippe, Dennis A. *Rights, Not Roses: Unions and the Rise of Working-Class Feminism, 1945–1980.* Urbana: University of Illinois Press, 2000.

Deutsch, Sarah. *Women and the City: Gender, Space, and Power in Boston, 1870–1940.* New York: Oxford University Press, 2000.

Dorr, Lisa Lindquist. *White Women, Rape, and the Power of Race in Virginia, 1900–1960.* Chapel Hill: University of North Carolina Press, 2004.

Dorsey, Bruce. *Reforming Men and Women: Gender in the Antebellum City.* Ithaca, NY: Cornell University Press, 2002.

Douglas, Susan. *Where the Girls Are: Growing Up Female with the Mass Media.* New York: Times Books, 1994.

Duggan, Lisa. *Sapphic Slashers: Sex, Violence, and American Modernity.* Durham, NC: Duke University Press, 2000.

Edwards, Laura. *Gendered Strife and Confusion: The Political Culture of Reconstruction.* Chicago: University of Illinois Press, 1997.

Edwards, Rebecca. *Angels in the Machinery: Gender in American Party Politics from the Civil War to the Progressive Era.* New York: Oxford University Press, 1997.

Enstad, Nan. *Ladies of Labor, Girls of Adventure: Working Women, Popular Culture, and Labor Politics at the Turn of the Twentieth Century.* New York: Columbia University Press, 1999.

Estes, Steve. *I Am a Man! Race, Manhood, and the Civil Rights Movement.* Chapel Hill: University of North Carolina Press, 2005.

Evans, Sara. *Tidal Wave: How Women Changed America at Century's End.* New York: Free Press, 2004.

Faulkner, Carole. *Women's Radical Reconstruction: The Freedmen's Aid Movement.* Philadelphia: University of Pennsylvania Press, 2004.

Faust, Drew Gilpin. *Mothers of Invention: Women of the Slaveholding South in the American Civil War.* Chapel Hill: University of North Carolina, 2004.

Finnegan, Margaret. *Selling Suffrage: Consumer Culture and Votes for Women.* New York: Columbia University Press, 1999.

Fischer, Kirsten. *Suspect Relations: Sex, Race, and Resistance in Colonial North Carolina.* Ithaca, NY: Cornell University Press, 2002.

Foster, Thomas A., ed. *Long before Stonewall: Histories of Same-Sex Sexuality in Early America.* New York: New York University Press, 2007.

Freeman, Joanne. *Affairs of Honor: National Politics in the New Republic.* New Haven, CT: Yale University Press, 2001.

Gabin, Nancy F. *Feminism in the Labor Movement: Women and the United Auto Workers, 1935–1975.* Ithaca, NY: Cornell University Press, 1990.

Gilmore, Glenda. *Gender and Jim Crow: Women and the Politics of White Supremacy in North Carolina, 1986–1920.* Chapel Hill: University of North Carolina Press, 1996.

Ginzberg, Lori D. *Women and the Work of Benevolence: Morality, Politics, and Class in the Nineteenth-Century United States*. New Haven, CT: Yale University Press, 1990.

Glenn, Susan. *Female Spectacle: The Theatrical Roots of Modern Feminism*. Cambridge, MA: Harvard University Press, 2000.

González, Deena. *Refusing the Favor: The Spanish-Mexican Women of Santa Fe, 1820–1880*. New York: Oxford University Press, 1999.

Gordon, Linda. *The Great Arizona Orphan Abduction*. Cambridge, MA: Harvard University Press, 1999.

———. *Pitied but Not Entitled: Single Mothers and the History of Welfare*. New York: Free Press, 1994.

Gordon, Sarah Barringer. *The Mormon Question: Polygamy and Constitutional Conflict in Nineteenth Century America*. Chapel Hill: University of North Carolina Press, 2001.

Greenberg, Amy. *Manifest Manhood and the Antebellum American Empire*. New York: Cambridge University Press, 2005.

Grossberg, Michael. *Governing the Hearth: Law and the Family in Nineteenth-Century America*. Chapel Hill: University of North Carolina, 1985.

Gullett, Gayle. *Becoming Citizens: The Emergence and Development of the California Women's Movement, 1880–1911*. Urbana: University of Illinois Press, 2000.

Gustafson, Melaine, Kristie Miller, and Elisabeth Israels Perry, eds. *We Have Come to Stay: American Women and Political Parties, 1880–1960*. Albuquerque: University of New Mexico Press, 1999.

Gutiérrez, Ramón. *When Jesus Came, the Corn Mothers Went Away: Marriage, Sexuality, and Power in New Mexico, 1500–1846*. Stanford, CA: Stanford University Press, 1991.

Hartog, Hendrik. *Man and Wife in America: A History*. Cambridge, MA: Harvard University Press, 2000.

Hewitt, Nancy A., ed. *A Companion to American Women's History*. Malden, MA: Blackwell, 2005.

———. *Southern Discomfort: Women's Activism in Tampa, Florida, 1880s–1920s*. Urbana: University of Illinois Press, 2001.

Hewitt, Nancy A., and Suzanne Lebsock, eds. *Visible Women: New Essays on American Activism*. Urbana: University of Illinois Press, 1993.

Higginbotham, Evelyn Brooks. *Righteous Discontent: The Women's Movement in the Black Baptist Church, 1880–1920*. Cambridge, MA: Harvard University Press, 1993.

Hodes, Martha. *Black Women, White Men: Illicit Sex in the Nineteenth-Century South*. New Haven, CT: Yale University Press, 1997.

Hoganson, Kristin. *Fighting for American Manhood: How Gender Politics Provoked the Spanish-American and Philippine-American Wars*. New Haven, CT: Yale University Press, 1998.

Horowitz, Helen Lefkowitz. *Rereading Sex: Battles over Sexual Knowledge and Suppression in Nineteenth-Century America*. New York: Knopf, 2002.

Hunter, Jane. *How Young Ladies Became Girls: The Victorian Origins of American Girlhood*. New Haven, CT: Yale University Press, 2002.

Hunter, Tera. *To 'Joy My Freedom: Southern Black Women's Lives and Labors after the Civil War*. Cambridge, MA: Harvard University Press, 1997.

Isenberg, Nancy. *Sex and Citizenship in Antebellum America*. Chapel Hill: University of North Carolina Press, 1998.

Jameson, Elizabeth. "Toward a Multicultural History of Women in the Western United States." *Signs* 13 (Summer 1988): 761–791.

Jeansonne, Glen. *Women of the Far Right: The Mother's Movement and World War II.* Chicago: University of Chicago Press, 1996.

Jeffrey, Julie Roy. *The Great Silent Army of Abolition: Ordinary Women in the Antislavery Movement.* Chapel Hill: University of North Carolina Press, 1998.

Jensen, Kimberly. *Mobilizing Minerva: American Women in the First World War.* Urbana: University of Illinois Press, 2008.

Johnson, David K. *The Lavender Scare: The Cold War Persecution of Gays and Lesbians in the Federal Government.* Chicago: University of Chicago Press, 2004.

Jones, Jacqueline. *Labor of Love, Labor of Sorrow: Black Women, Work, and the Family, from Slavery to the Present*, 2nd ed. New York: Basic Books, 2009.

Kelly, Catherine. "Gender and Class Formations in the Antebellum North." In Nancy A. Hewitt, ed., *A Companion to American Women's History*, 100–116. Malden, MA: Blackwell, 2005.

Kerber, Linda K. *No Constitutional Right to Be Ladies: Women and the Obligations of Citizenship.* New York: Hill and Wang, 1998.

———. "Separate Spheres, Female Worlds, Woman's Place: The Rhetoric of Women's History." *Journal of American History* 75 (1988): 9–39.

Kessler-Harris, Alice. *In Pursuit of Equity: Women, Men, and the Quest for Economic Citizenship in 20th-Century America.* New York: Oxford University Press, 2001.

Kunzel, Regina. *Fallen Women, Problem Girls: Unmarried Mothers and the Professionalization of Social Work, 1890–1945.* New Haven, CT: Yale University Press, 1993.

Kwolek-Folland, Angela. *Engendering Business: Men and Women in the Corporate Office, 1870–1930.* Baltimore: John Hopkins University Press, 1994.

Ladd-Taylor, Molly. *Mother-work: Women, Child Welfare, and the State, 1890–1930.* Urbana: University of Illinois Press, 1994.

Ling, Huping. *Surviving on the Gold Mountain: A History of Chinese American Women and Their Lives.* Albany: State University of New York Press, 1998.

Little, Ann M. *Abraham in Arms: War and Gender in Colonial New England.* Philadelphia: University of Pennsylvania Press, 2007.

Lovett, Laura L. *Conceiving the Future: Pronatalism, Reproduction, and the Family in the United States, 1890–1938.* Chapel Hill: University of North Carolina Press, 2007.

Lyons, Clare A. *Sex among the Rabble: An Intimate History of Gender and Power in the Age of Revolution, Philadelphia, 1730–1830.* Chapel Hill: University of North Carolina Press, 2006.

Malone, Ann Paton. *Sweet Chariot: Slave Family and Household Structure in Nineteenth-Century Louisiana.* Chapel Hill: University of North Carolina Press, 1996.

Materson, Lisa G. *For the Freedom of Her Race: Black Women and Electoral Politics in Illinois, 1877–1932.* Chapel Hill: University of North Carolina Press, 2009.

McCurry, Stephanie. *Masters of Small Worlds: Yeoman Households, Gender Relations, and the Political Culture of the Antebellum South Carolina Low Country.* New York: Oxford University Press, 1995.

McFadden, Margaret. *Golden Cables of Sympathy: The Transatlantic Sources of Nineteenth-Century Feminism.* Lexington: University Press of Kentucky, 1999.

Mead, Rebecca. *How the Vote Was Won: Woman Suffrage in the Western United States, 1868–1914*. New York: New York University Press, 2004.

Meyerowitz, Joanne, ed. *Not June Cleaver: Women and Gender in Postwar America, 1945–1960*. Philadelphia: Temple University Press, 1994.

Michel, Sonya. *Children's Interests/Mothers' Rights: The Shaping of America's Child Care Policy*. New Haven, CT: Yale University Press, 1999.

Mink, Gwendolyn. *The Wages of Motherhood: Inequality in the Welfare State, 1917–1942*. Ithaca, NY: Cornell University Press, 1995.

Mittelstadt, Jennifer. *From Welfare to Workfare: The Unintended Consequences of Liberal Reform, 1945–1965*. Chapel Hill: University of North Carolina Press, 2005.

Morantz-Sanchez, Regina. *Conduct Unbecoming a Woman: Medicine on Trial in Turn-of-the-Century Brooklyn*. New York: Oxford University Press, 1999.

Morgan, Francesca. *Women and Patriotism in Jim Crow America*. Chapel Hill: University of North Carolina Press, 2005.

Muncy, Robyn. *Creating a Female Dominion in American Reform, 1890–1935*. New York: Oxford University Press, 1991.

Nadasen, Premilla. *Welfare Warriors: The Welfare Rights Movement in the United States*. New York: Routledge, 2005.

Namias, June. *White Captives: Gender and Ethnicity on the American Frontier*. Chapel Hill: University of North Carolina Press, 1993.

Newman, Louise M. *White Women's Rights: The Racial Origins of Feminism in the United States*. New York: Oxford University Press, 1990.

Norton, Mary Beth. *Founding Mothers and Fathers: Gendered Power and the Forming of American Society*. New York: Knopf, 1996.

Odem, Mary. *Delinquent Daughters: Protecting and Policing Adolescent Female Sexuality in the United States, 1885–1920*. Chapel Hill: University of North Carolina Press, 1995.

Orleck, Annelise. *Common Sense and a Little Fire: Women and Working-class Politics in the United States, 1900–1965*. Chapel Hill: University of North Carolina Press, 1995.

———. *Storming Caesar's Palace: How Black Mothers Fought Their Own War on Poverty*. Boston: Beacon Press, 2006.

Pascoe, Peggy. *Relations of Rescue: The Search for Female Moral Authority in the American West, 1874–1939*. New York: Oxford University Press, 1990.

Passet, Joanne E. *Sex Radicals and the Quest for Women's Equality*. Urbana: University of Illinois Press, 2003.

Peiss, Kathy. *Hope in a Jar: The Making of America's Beauty Culture*. New York: Metropolitan Books, 1998.

Perdue, Theda. *Cherokee Women: Gender and Culture Change, 1700–1835*. Lincoln: University of Nebraska Press, 1998.

Pesantubbee, Michelene. *Choctaw Women in a Chaotic World: The Clash of Cultures in the Colonial Southeast*. Albuquerque: University of New Mexico Press, 2005.

Peterson, Carla L. *"Doers of the Word": African-American Women Speakers and Writers in the North, 1830–1880*. New York: Oxford University Press, 1995.

Pierson, Michael D. *Free Hearts and Free Homes: Gender and American Antislavery Politics*. Chapel Hill: University of North Carolina Press, 2003.

Plane, Ann Marie. *Colonial Intimacies: Indian Marriage in Early New England*. Ithaca, NY: Cornell University Press, 2000.

Regan, Leslie J. *When Abortion Was a Crime: Women, Medicine, and Law in the United States, 1867–1973.* Berkeley: University of California Press, 1997.

Richter, Amy G. *Home on the Rails: Women, the Railroad, and the Rise of Public Domesticity.* Chapel Hill: University of North Carolina Press, 2005.

Rosen, Ruth. *The World Split Open: How the Modern Women's Movement Changed America.* New York: Viking, 2000.

Rosenberg, Emily. "'Foreign Affairs' after World War II: Connecting Sexual and International Politics," *Diplomatic History* 18 (1994): 59–70.

Rotundo, E. Anthony. *American Manhood: Transformations in Masculinity from the Revolution to the Modern Era.* New York: Basic Books, 1993.

Ruíz, Vicki L. *From Out of the Shadows: Mexican Women in Twentieth-Century America.* New York: Oxford University Press, 1998.

Rupp, Leila. *Worlds of Women: The Making of an International Women's Movement.* Princeton, NJ: Princeton University Press, 1997.

Ryan, Mary P. *Cradle of the Middle Class: The Family in Oneida County, New York, 1780–1865.* New York: Cambridge University Press 1981.

Rymph, Catherine E. *Republican Women: Feminism and Conservatism from Suffrage through the Rise of the New Right.* Chapel Hill: University of North Carolina, 2006.

Sacks, Karen B. *Caring by the Hour: Women, Work and Organizing at Duke Medical Center.* Urbana: University of Illinois Press, 1988.

Schwalm, Leslie. *A Hard Fight for We: Women's Transition from Slavery to Freedom in South Carolina.* Urbana: University of Illinois Press, 1997.

Scott, Joan C. "Gender: A Useful Category of Historical Analysis." *American Historical Review* 91 (1986): 1053–1075.

Shaw, Stephanie J. *What a Woman Ought to Be and Do: Black Professional Women Workers during the Jim Crow Era.* Chicago: University of Chicago Press, 1996.

Shibusawa, Naoko. *America's Geisha Ally: Reimagining the Japanese Enemy.* Cambridge, MA: Harvard University Press, 2006.

Shoemaker, Nancy, ed. *Negotiators of Change: Historical Perspectives on Native American Women.* New York: Routledge, 1995.

Silber, Nina. *Daughters of the Union: Northern Women Fight the Civil War.* Cambridge, MA: Harvard University Press, 2005.

Smith, Susan L. *Japanese American Midwives: Culture, Community and Health Politics, 1880–1950.* Urbana: University of Illinois Press, 2004.

Sneider, Allison L. *Suffragists in an Imperial Age: U.S. Expansion and the Woman Question, 1870–1929.* New York: Oxford University Press, 2008.

Solinger, Rickie. *Wake up Little Susie: Single Pregnancy and Race before* Roe v. Wade. New York: Routledge, 1992.

Srebnick, Amy Gilman. *The Mysterious Death of Mary Rogers: Sex and Culture in Nineteenth-Century New York.* New York: Oxford University Press, 1995.

Stanley, Amy Dru. *From Bondage to Contract: Wage Labor, Marriage, and the Market in the Age of Slave Emancipation.* New York: Cambridge University Press, 1998.

Stevenson, Brenda E. *Life in Black and White: Family and Community in the Slave South.* New York: Oxford University Press, 1996.

Summers, Martin. *Manliness and Its Discontents: The Black Middle Class and the Transformation of Masculinity, 1900–1930.* Chapel Hill: University of North Carolina Press, 2004.

Tannenbaum, Rebecca. *The Healer's Calling: Women and Medicine in Early New England.* Ithaca, NY: Cornell University Press, 2002.

Tone, Andrea. *Devices and Desires: A History of Contraceptives in America*. New York: Hill and Wang, 2001.

Ullman, Sharon R. *Sex Seen: The Emergence of Modern Sexuality in America*. Berkeley: University of California Press, 1998.

Ulrich, Laurel Thatcher. *A Midwife's Tale: The Life of Martha Ballard, Based on Her Diary, 1785–1812*. New York: Vintage, 1991.

VanBurkleo, Sandra F. *"Belonging to the World": Women's Rights and American Constitutional Culture*. New York: Oxford University Press, 2001.

Varon, Elizabeth. *We Mean to Be Counted: White Women and Politics in Antebellum Virginia*. Chapel Hill: University of North Carolina Press, 1998.

Weiss, Jessica. *To Have and to Hold: Marriage, the Baby Boom, and Social Change*. Chicago: University of Chicago Press, 2000.

Welke, Barbara Young. *Recasting American Liberty: Gender, Race, Law, and the Railroad Revolution, 1865–1920*. New York: Cambridge University Press, 2001.

Wellman, Judith. *The Road to Seneca Falls: Elizabeth Cady Stanton and the First Woman's Rights Convention*. Urbana: University of Illinois Press, 2004.

Wheeler, Marjorie Spruill. *New Women of the New South: The Leaders of the Woman's Suffrage Movement in the Southern States*. New York: Oxford University Press, 1993.

White, Debora Gray. *Too Heavy a Load: Black Women in Defense of Themselves, 1894–1994*. New York: W. W. Norton, 1999.

Williams, Rhonda Y. *The Politics of Public Housing: Black Women's Struggles against Urban Inequality*. New York: Oxford University Press, 2004.

Wilson, Lisa. *Ye Heart of a Man: The Domestic Life of Men in Colonial New England*. New Haven, CT: Yale University Press, 1999.

Winter, Thomas. *Making Men, Making Class: The YMCA and Workingmen, 1877–1920*. Chicago: University of Chicago Press, 2002.

Wood, Sharon. *The Freedom of the Streets: Work, Citizenship, and Sexuality in a Gilded Age City*. Chapel Hill: University of North Carolina Press, 2005.

Yung, Judy. *Unbound Feet: A Social History of Chinese Women in San Francisco*. Berkeley: University of California Press, 1995.

Zagarri, Rosemarie. *Revolutionary Backlash Women and Politics in the Early American Republic*. Philadelphia: University of Pennsylvania Press, 2007.

Zaretsky, Natasha. *No Direction Home: The American Family and the Fear of National Decline, 1968–1980*. Chapel Hill: University of North Carolina Press, 2007.

16

Immigration and Ethnic History

MAE M. NGAI

The field of immigration and ethnic history has changed over time, from a study of European immigration to one defined by increasingly broad concepts. It is now popular, for example, to present immigration history under the rubric of "the peopling of America." That phrase is used as the name of the National Park Service's new national immigration museum, scheduled to open in 2011 on Ellis Island, adjacent to the Statue of Liberty in New York harbor. At some colleges, courses formerly listed as immigration history now appear as "The Peopling of America." The expansive notion of "peopling" often includes the first humans who came to North America from across the Bering Strait 12,000 years ago; European colonial settlers in the sixteenth and seventeenth centuries; and the involuntary migration of enslaved people from Africa—in addition to voluntary immigrants who have come to the United States since the early nineteenth century. Such a broad framework recognizes that migration is a fundamental human experience and expresses an inclusive sensibility; but, because there remain important analytical distinctions between indigeneity and conquest, between coerced and voluntary migrations, a tension exists between "peopling" and "immigration." The concept of "ethnicity" also bears close examination. It is often used to suggest a cultural, rather than racial, identity, but sometimes at the cost of reifying culture or eliding questions of race and racism in the history of immigration. For purposes of this chapter, immigration and ethnic history refers to the history of voluntary migrations from foreign countries to the United States (and its colonial antecedents) and the group-based communities and identities created by those migrants and their descendants. It does not, in the main, include Native American Indian or African-American history, which are not centrally about immigration; it does include the conquest and annexation of the present-day American Southwest because of its connection to later migrations from Mexico and the role of both in the historical formation of the U.S.-Mexico borderlands; and it does include discussion of race and racism as critical to the history of immigration and ethnicity.

Emigration and Immigration

Before the late nineteenth century, despite two centuries of migration and settlement, the word "immigrant" was rarely used by Americans. The first arrivals from Europe called themselves settlers and colonists, identifying with their respective empires—New England, New Spain, New France, and so on. They did not see themselves "assimilating" to their new environment but, rather, as transplanting Europe's civilization to the lands of "savages." From the sixteenth to the mid-eighteenth century, some 9,600 Spanish colonials settled the present-day U.S. Southwest, the northern frontier of New Spain (Mexico); 70,000 French the Great Lakes region and New Orleans; and one and a half million the English colonies along the eastern seaboard. Of the latter, more than half were English and Scottish. During the colonial period, the English brought some 312,000 enslaved Africans to North America, mostly to the tobacco-growing Chesapeake and rice plantations in South Carolina, a relatively small number compared to the 5.38 million slaves brought by Europeans to Caribbean and Brazilian plantation colonies. The precontact population of North America declined from four or five million to between 600,000 and one million by 1800 as a result of disease and war.

During the period of national settlement and continental expansion, 1820 to 1880, the United States attracted ten million migrants from diverse origins and conditions in their homelands, resulting in diverse migration experiences and identities. Germans and Scandinavians who settled the upper Midwest in the 1840s and 1850s, generally of the middling strata displaced by the commercialization of agriculture and manufacture, tended to come in family units and typically worked in America as farmers, artisans, or shopkeepers. They identified as "emigrants," again connoting acts of pioneering, colonizing, and settlement. By contrast, most Irish who emigrated in the nineteenth century came as young single men and women laborers. British colonial domination and capitalist agriculture in Ireland, which turned the potato blight of the late 1840s into a great famine, gave Irish migration a sense of exile and banishment more than self-improvement.

The annexation of the northern half of Mexico after the U.S.-Mexico war (1846–1848) completed the project of the United States' continental expansion and brought some 75,000 Mexican nationals living in the ceded territory under the jurisdiction of the United States. They were not "migrants" (for they had not moved anywhere) but subjects of conquest. The

Chinese laborers who migrated to California in the decades after the Civil War were but a small proportion of the three million people who emigrated from southern China in the nineteenth century as a result of European colonial penetration of China, including indentured laborers to Southeast Asia and voluntary migrants to the Anglo-American settler colonies in North America, Hawaii, and Australia. Notably, the native-born typically called them neither German, Irish, nor Chinese "immigrants" but "foreigners"—and worse, if they were Catholics or Chinese. An anti-Catholic nativist party (the "Know Nothings") made a splash in the 1850s but achieved only modest electoral victories. Congress passed legislation barring Chinese immigration in 1882, as anti-Chinese racism on the Pacific coast found support in the national parties during the reversal of Reconstruction and the federal government's turn away from racial equality. Otherwise, there was little regulation of immigration.

It was not until the surge of mass migration from Europe to the United States in the late nineteenth century that it became common to speak of "immigrants." The earlier "emigrants" were now, retrospectively, called the "old immigrants," in order to distinguish them from these "new immigrants." The distinction was not a function of academic periodization (in fact, Germans continued to be one of the largest migrant groups through the 1890s) but an expression of contemporary politics. The "new" immigrants were those from eastern and southern Europe—Italy, Russia, Poland, Hungary, Greece—more than twenty million people who provided the unskilled-labor power that fueled the nation's industrial and urban growth between 1880 and 1920. Religious and cultural difference, combined with an association of immigrants with industrial strife and urban poverty, provoked anxiety and opposition among the native-born, many of them descendants of the "old" immigrants. In the context of late-nineteenth- and early-twentieth-century nativism, the "old" immigrants were mythologized for their hardiness, independence, and assimilability—traits seemingly lacking in the new arrivals. It was during this time of controversy over immigration, from the 1890s to World War I, that the first academic studies of American immigration were produced.

Social scientists, especially economists, and not historians, generated these first studies, which sought to explain immigration as a social problem. Many, informed by social Darwinism and scientific racism, found the mass immigration of Europe's "degraded races" to be a threat to American society. These views permeated the forty-one-volume report of the United States Immigration Commission, chaired by Senator William Dillingham, published in 1911. On the other side of the debate were a few political thinkers and social scientists, many of them women, associated with the urban-settlement-house and sweatshop-reform movements. They also compiled data about immigrants' living and working conditions, but in order to advocate for housing and industrial regulation, not immigration restriction. Historical works written in this period were not scholarly studies but instead were produced by leaders of immigrant-ethnic groups, who countered racial nativism with celebratory accounts of their peoples' cultures and their positive contributions to American life. This tradition of filiopietism established an emphasis on immigrant assimilation that would long endure in the historical literature.

Anti-immigrant sentiment gathered steam during the first decades of the century but prevailed only with the advent of World War I and the politics of war nationalism. The Immigration Act of 1917 was the most stringent to date, establishing a literacy test, aimed at excluding east and south Europeans, and a "barred Asiatic zone," excluding all of Asia save for Japan. After the war, there were renewed calls for restriction: A strong antiradical current merged with nativism; in the economic realm, the country simply no longer needed the same levels of mass immigration. In 1924, Congress legislated, for the first time, numerical limits on immigration from Europe, set at 15 percent of prewar levels, distributed in quotas according to a hierarchy of desirability based on national origin, and excluded Asians altogether. Western hemisphere migration was exempt from numerical restriction, in deference to foreign policy and southwestern agricultural interests. The Immigration Act of 1924 turned U. S. policy from one that was normatively open—that is, open with some exceptions—to one that was normatively closed. With it came a regime of modern immigration restriction based on quotas and documents, and the advent of illegal immigration as a mass phenomenon.

The Uprooted and the Transplanted

The first academic histories of immigration—interpretive analyses grounded in historical research—were not written until the decades surrounding World War II. Formerly treated as objects of study (i.e., problems), immigrants were now the subjects of historical inquiry. More than any other scholar, Oscar Handlin established immigration as a legitimate subfield of American history. Handlin's famous first lines in *The Uprooted* (1951)—"Once I thought to write a history of the immigrants in America. Then I discovered that the immigrants *were* American history"—carried a double meaning: that immigrants made up the nation and that their process of assimilation was the same as Americans' transition to modern urban and industrial society. The latter insight was indebted to the work of the interwar generation of sociologists at the University of Chicago, who had first conceptualized immigrant adaptation as a process of modernization.

The first idea, that the United States was a "nation of immigrants," blossomed in the post–World War II years as a rebuke to the remainders of nativism. John Higham's classic study of nativism, *Strangers in the Land* (1955), was inspired by the same impulse for democratic inclusion. Their pluralism reflected the coming of age of the children of the "new immigrants" of the early twentieth century and their aspirations for political inclusion, to establish ethnic groups as legitimate interest groups in a democratic polity. The ethos of the era also encouraged a resurgence of filiopietistic histories and grand popular narratives that universalized "immigration" as the "American experience." John F. Kennedy's *A Nation of Immigrants* (1958), the paradigmatic postwar work in this regard, read the founding colonists as America's first immigrants and American history as a succession of immigrations from Europe, with each wave assimilating to and revitalizing the nation's core values of individualism and democracy. Both academic and popular histories entrenched a nationalist framework, which posited the telos of assimilation as evidence of America's exceptional history and character. The founding historiography had established a normative theory of American immigration based on a model of European assimilation and American exceptionalism.

If economists provided the statistical rationalizations for immigration restriction in the early twentieth century, historians established the intellectual framework for immigration reform in the post–World War II period. Writing American history as a progression of inclusions, the historians imagined immigration reform as a cousin to African-American civil rights. The same principles of formal equal rights guided the Immigration Act of 1965, which abolished the discriminatory national-origin quotas in favor of a system of global restriction based on family reunification, high skills, and a uniform numerical limit for all countries. The policy was an inclusive reform for Europeans and Asians but a regressive one for western hemisphere countries, which had never before had numerical quotas. But few noticed this latter aspect, which was overshadowed by the politics of liberal inclusion that surrounded the law and its history.

Scholars of the next generation, those who received their Ph.D.'s in the late 1970s and 1980s, challenged and revised immigration history in significant ways. Handlin's uprooted and alienated peasants were displaced by self-directed migrants already familiar with capitalist market relations. Instead of assimilation and Anglo cultural conformity, historians emphasized communal identities—"ethnicities"—that were amalgams of cultural persistence and acculturation. The making of ethnic identities was seen as a complex process, both imposed on the migrants by outsiders and constructed by them, often in defiance of Anglo Protestant nativism. The shift in analysis was aptly captured in titles such as John Bodnar's *The Transplanted* (1985). Like the previous generation, the new scholars of ethnicity were claiming their own citizenship, but the political culture had moved from pluralist consensus to civil rights and a budding multiculturalism. Other major revisions came from the field of labor history, where the move from institutional to social history included a new appreciation of the role of immigrants in the development of the working class and the role of class in the formation of ethnic identities. Herbert Gutman's classic study *Work, Culture, and Society in Industrializing America* (1976), which argued that working-class formation was a recurring process of acculturating successive waves of immigrants to the rhythms and prerogatives of industrial discipline, showed how the new labor and immigration histories were entwined. Still, there were continuities, notably the emphasis on geographic communities and ethnic institutions. The focus also remained largely on European immigrants. Moreover, the turn to ethnicity was not entirely a repudiation of the assimilation paradigm. There remained an assumption of inclusion as a progressive and normative process.

Asian-American and Chicano/a and Latino/a studies emerged in the 1970s as distinct fields, aligning more with African-American studies and its thematics of racial subordination and resistance than with European immigration history. In addition to writing their own ethnic histories, their scholarship on subjects such as conquest, exclusion, and wartime internment contributed new knowledge to established fields of American history, such as nineteenth-century western expansion and World War II. Yet there was a consistency in the emphasis on building America and becoming American, largely to counter the view that non-European immigrant groups were marginal to American society. For the same reason, Asian-American and Chicano/a studies resisted both historiographic and professional association with Asian studies and Latin American studies.

The Transnational Turn

Since the mid-1990s, the frameworks and methodologies guiding American immigration history have undergone a sea change. The multidisciplinary field of migration studies has been at the forefront of the so-called transnational turn that has swept the humanities and social sciences. Human migration, along with the movement of commodities, currencies, and information, highlights the phenomenon of "globalization," a multivalent concept referring generally to the interconnectedness of the world in our time (defined by communications technology, supranational organization, neoliberal market policy, etc.). In a related vein, scholars have historicized the nation, in Benedict Anderson's famous phrase, as an "imagined community," not a timeless or natural entity. With that insight also came recognition of nationalism's abiding influence on the practice of history. With much greater sensitivity to the constructedness of the American nation and the place of that nation in the world, scholars have critically reconceived immigration history in both domestic and global contexts. The normative assumptions that previously underlay immigration history—unidirectional migration, permanent settlement, and eventual inclusion, if not full assimilation and citizenship—have virtually collapsed in the face of alternate frameworks of analysis: transnationalism, diaspora, borderlands, colonialism and postcolonialism, hybridity. These concepts inform not only the study of contemporary immigration, but also a reconsideration of earlier periods, which has reshaped historical analysis. By showing that national boundaries have always been porous and that immigration patterns have always been diverse, these histories establish a critical position against nationalist history. They also serve as a corrective to the tendency among social scientists to treat globalization as a new phenomenon.

Transnational migration histories emphasize ongoing influence and a mixture of politics and culture in both the sending and receiving nations, often supported by circular or multiple migration patterns. Based on deep empirical research, often in non-English language materials and in non-U.S. archival sources, this body of work reflects in part a transnational trend within the discipline of history itself: some of the best work on immigration to the United States has been done by scholars trained in non-U.S. fields of history.

We now have really new portraits of migrants and migrant communities in dynamic and fluid "regional worlds"—Atlantic, Pacific, western hemispheric—that are highly nuanced and complex, sympathetic while not idealized, replete with novel insight. Alison Games's *Migration and the Origins of the English Atlantic World* (1999) used port registries and colonial records to track emigrants, both freeholders and indentured servants, who left England in a single year (1635) for colonies in the Caribbean, the Chesapeake, and New England. The discrete findings may be familiar, but by viewing colonial settlement in a single, larger frame, Games found remarkable fluidity in seventeenth-century English migrations, with multiple moves, family dispersals and reunifications, and connected experiences across the colonies that constituted England's Atlantic empire.

Transnational migration scholarship in Asian-American and Latino/a history has been particularly innovative. A paradigmatic work is Madeline Y. Hsu's *Dreaming of Gold, Dreaming of Home* (2000), which showed how the practice of Chinese male sojourning sustained a single transpacific culture of dependence and obligation, shaping the nature of homosocial Chinatown communities in California and villages of remittance-dependent "gold-mountain widows" in southern China. Scholarship on the Mexican agricultural guest-worker (*bracero*) program of the post–World War II era has been transformed by transnational research in the U.S. and Mexico. Formerly a literature emphasizing structural dynamics, a new generation of *bracero* scholarship emphasizing *braceros*' agency is emerging, as seen in Deborah Cohen's work on *braceros*' constructions of modern and masculine identities and Ana Rosas's study of *braceros*' flexible family strategies. These transnational works give a new angle on the histories of male labor migrations, showing the connections of "single" men to families and villages left behind and the changes in gender, family, and social relations wrought by migration in both sending and receiving communities.

Prior studies recognized migration as a product of uneven development between agricultural and industrializing areas primarily within the Atlantic world. Now, empire, colonialism, and imperialism are common thematics in transnational histories. Eiichiro Azuma's *Between Two Empires* (2005) analyzed the American West as a kind of double borderlands that was not only understood as a frontier in U.S. history making but also believed to be the far eastern frontier of Japan's expansionist ambition, making Japanese immigrants' dualism oppositional but complementary. Jesse Hoffnung-Garskof's *A Tale of Two Cities* (2008) considered migration from Santo Domingo to New York City in the post–World War II era as a product of and response to United States economic, political, and military interventions in the Dominican Republic. Resentment and desire stoked migrants' ambitions, as captured in the phrase "Yankee go home—and take me with you." Catherine Ceniza Choy's *Empire of Care* (2003) put the practice of Filipina nurse migration to the United States in the context of the Philippines' colonial history, from its import of American nursing education to its development of nursing as an export industry.

Closely related to transnational histories but bearing a different analytic emphasis are diasporic studies, which take the United States as one of many destinations from a region of origin and compare and contrast migration experiences across the world. Initially a referent to premodern and early-modern dispersals resulting from forced expulsions—Jewish, African, and Armenian—with their themes of banishment, alienation, and longings for home—diaspora has assumed a more capacious meaning with regard to period and volition. Diasporas may be created by migrations driven by economic factors (labor and trade), as shown in Donna Gabaccia and Fraser Ottanelli's *Italian Workers of the World* (2001) and Philip Kuhn's *Chinese among Others* (2008); or by combinations of political exile and economic opportunity, as discussed in Rebecca Kobrin's *Jewish Bialystok and its Diaspora* (2010).

Transnational and diasporic methodologies each resituate the nation-state in global frameworks, but from different angles. Kevin Kenny, a historian of Irish immigration, has urged historians to combine the two in order to broaden our view beyond the single nation-state, while not losing the nation-state as a useful unit of analysis. The nation-state, he argues, still exerts powerful influence on the experience of migrants and remains a basis for comparison when considering global migrations from a single source country.

Borderlands

The United States and Mexico share in the history of the region that is now the southwestern United States: colonization of the area and conquest of indigenous peoples, war and annexation, migration and settlement by both Euro-Americans and Mexicans. Through the late twentieth century, the southwest and California remained the place of residence for 83 percent of all ethnic Mexicans in the United States.

Formerly the study of the American southwest was part of the western frontier history defined by Frederick Jackson Turner, concerned mainly with white settlement and national transformation. A new borderlands history emerged in the 1970s and 1980s, influenced by both the new western history and Chicano/a history. Recent borderlands scholarship has emphasized cross-cultural exchange, conflict, and change along shifting lines of power. Unlike transnational studies that consider movement between two places at some distance from each other, and diasporic histories that follow a global dispersal from a single source, borderlands history focuses on the dynamics of a contact zone that overlaps the jurisdictions of neighboring nation-states. Here, two or more cultures meet, mix, and struggle, creating a hybrid social world across borders. Some scholars argue that borderlands exist only in the absence of strong states, usually at the periphery of empires; others treat the dynamics of modern state authority as a constitutive element of borderland culture and politics. The U.S.-Mexico borderland might be understood as having been forged in both historical contexts.[1]

Some of the most provocative recent work has recentered indigenous people in the region's history. Using anthropology and history, James Brooks's *Captives and Cousins* (2002) examined captive taking, ransoming, enslavement, and adoption among native peoples and between native peoples and European colonists and settlers to show how ritual practices of gender and family built trade networks, political alliances, and interethnic communities. Pekka Hämäläinen's *Comanche Empire* (2008) argued that the Comanche exercised extraordinary power over Euro-Americans in New Mexico and Texas by deploying such typically imperial strategies as control over trade routes, diplomacy, and war.

The social and political upheavals surrounding the U.S. annexation of Texas and the U.S.-Mexico war are another area of renewed interest. From different angles, Andrés Reséndez's *Changing National Identities at the Frontier* (2005) and Benjamin H. Johnson's *Revolution in Texas* (2003) explored the cultural and political processes of national-identity formation among Mexicans, Texans, and Americans. Historians writing on the period after the U. S. conquest have created a rich body of work about the dynamics of American power and Mexican subordination. Maria Montoya's *Translating Property* (2002) tracked the legal and political means by which Anglos dispossessed Mexican land-grantees in Colorado after the U.S.-Mexico War. Linda Gordon's *Great Arizona Orphan Abduction* (1999) used the case of Irish orphans sent by the Catholic Church from New York City to Mexican families in the copper mining town of Bisbee, Arizona, at the turn of the twentieth century to examine the constructions of racial and gender difference among Anglos and Mexicans. A new book by Kelly Lytle Hernandez, *Migra!* (2010), based on research in United States and Mexican sources, tells the history of border surveillance and regulation from both sides of the border.

Ethnicity and Race

Implicit in the older literature on immigration (and in American history generally) was the notion that Euro-American immigrants possessed "ethnic" identities but had no meaningful relation to "race." Immigrants suffered from nativism, whereas race and racism were understood as questions of black-white ("American," not immigrant) relations. In short, the assimilation paradigm marginalized the question of race in immigration studies. If some groups (Asians, Latinos) seemed slow to assimilate, the reasons for their intractability were found in deep cultural difference (with the onus implicitly placed upon the immigrants), not in structures of racial subordination.

As Asian-American and Latino/a studies grew—and as their populations in the United States grew—many historians of European immigration welcomed their addition to the field. But were non-European migration histories to be simply "added" to the existing framework of immigration and ethnic history, with its basic assumptions of eventual inclusion and full citizenship—or did those assumptions need rethinking and revision? One way that this tension was expressed was in a growing divide between those advocating for "ethnicity" and those favoring "race" as their analytic of choice. Even though both ethnicity and race posed similarly complicated problems—a tendency to essentialize identity, an obscuring of differences within ethnic/racial communities, a neglect of gender and other categories of difference—the division bespoke a certain epistemological crisis. The intellectual questions that had framed the field for a generation (cultural persistence versus Anglo conformity) held little purchase for those pursuing newer themes and methods (race, gender, colonialism, law). Historian George Sánchez, in an influential essay written in 1999, declared that the field was at an impasse.

A decade later, the field is no longer deadlocked. In part this result follows from the generally transformative transnational turn. But recent scholarship on race and racism had proved powerful, finally even irresistible, to immigration history. One source of new scholarship was a trend in labor history, which advanced a critical appraisal of the effects of white racism on American working-class formation and labor politics. This line of inquiry had a direct bearing on immigration history because European immigrant workers posed particularly interesting cases for the labor question: Irish immigrants in the nineteenth century and the "new immigrants" at the turn of the twentieth were themselves considered by nativists to come from inferior races, yet over time they came to identify (and be identified) as white. David Roediger, James Barrett, Matthew Jacobson, and others argued that for European immigrants, the process of becoming "American" and becoming "white" were inextricably linked. They and other historians have shown that this process was never a simple matter but a complex and contingent one involving many factors ranging from domestic and imperial politics to material and psychological advantage. Recent work has parsed these questions with increasing subtlety. Russell Kazal's *Becoming Old Stock* (2004) showed how diverse German Americans in Philadelphia wrestled with their identity in the wake of World War I's anti-German hysteria and 1920s immigration restrictionism. Among German Americans whose families immigrated in the late nineteenth century, working-class Catholics, Kazal argues, increasingly identified as part of a white ethnic working class, whereas middle-class Lutherans appropriated as their forebears the eighteenth-century "Pennsylvania Dutch" in order to align themselves with "native" white Americans.

Much of the work on race in Asian-American and Latino/a studies has sought to understand the racialization of foreignness, that is, the ways in which Chinese, Japanese, Mexican, Puerto Rican, and other non-European migrant groups have been classified in official, academic, and popular knowledge as unassimilable to American society. This form of racism combines ideas about physiognomic difference and national origin, and treats the cultures of non-Europeans as especially unchanging and unchangeable. From David Gutiérrez's *Walls and Mirrors* (1995) to Stephen Pitti's *The Devil in Silicon Valley* (2003), historians have shown how people of Mexican descent in the United States—those with family histories predating the American conquest, naturalized citizens, the U.S.-born children of immigrants, legal immigrants, and those whose presence is unauthorized—have been racialized through both law and the labor market simply as "Mexicans," all deemed foreign to the United States regardless of their citizenship or immigration status, and creating lines of both solidarity and tension within their ethnic group.

Literary scholar Lisa Lowe's influential book *Immigrant Acts* (1996) paved the way for historical investigation of race and colonialism in Asian-American studies. Lowe drew attention to "Asia" as a double problem for the United States, as an enemy in military and economic wars and as a source of racialized migrant labor. Lowe's work not only reshaped Asian-American literary studies but also prompted historians, many not particularly interested in literary theory, to pursue research that gave archival-based historical specificity to those themes. Notably, Asian-American historical work on race has intersected with gender and sexuality analysis. Mary Lui's *Chinatown Trunk Mystery* (2005) showed how ideas about Chinese as racial and sexual menace to whites informed whites' perception of urban space, specifically in their view of New York's "Chinatown" as a noncontiguous space that included Chinese laundrymen living and working in other neighborhoods. Karen Leong's *The China Mystique* (2005) offered a gendered analysis of the transformation in American Orientalism during World War II through the careers of three women: Pearl S. Buck, Anna May Wong, and Soong Mei-ling (Madame Chiang Kai-shek).

These histories do far more than "add" Asian and Latino experiences to the history of immigration; they have changed our view of the entire American racial landscape. This change is most evident in work that is comparative and relational. Neil Foley's *The White Scourge* (1997) studied the relations among black, white, and Mexican cotton workers in Texas, at the intersection of the South and the Southwest, with their respective legacies of slavery and conquest. Moon-Ho Jung's *Coolies and Cane* (2006) offered two related triangulations, one about ideas and practices with regard to Chinese "coolie" labor, enslaved African-American labor, and free labor in the nineteenth century, and a second as those ideas played out according to American ambitions in the U.S. South, the Caribbean, and China. Writing on a later period, Scott Kurashige's *The Shifting Grounds of Race* (2008) analyzed Japanese Americans' and African Americans' changing racial and social status in Los Angeles during the first half of the twentieth century, showing that city's multiracial problematic as a foreshadowing of the nation's.

The new immigration and ethnic histories are less likely to be about "identity" per se but are interested in hetereogeneity within descent groups and treat identity as a "process," not as a "thing." That process, moreover, is informed by myriad factors, including changing gender relations, generational dynamics, and class conflict both within ethnic groups and from without. These histories have struck important blows to the lingering influences of filiopietism, with its idealized portrayals of homogeneous ethnic groups with strong nuclear families and respected leaders, and modernization theory, which treated conflict as a stage in the assimilation process.

Finally, the new immigration history includes an emphasis on comparative and multigroup works. In addition to scholarship on the production of racial difference mentioned previously, other comparative studies focus on how the boundaries of national belonging and citizenship have been drawn. From different angles, Amy Fairchild, Alexandra Stern, and Natalia Molina have explored the role of medical science and public health in the construction of knowledge about different immigrant groups. Focusing on law, Mae Ngai's *Impossible Subjects* (2004) and Aristide Zolberg's *A Nation by Design* (2006) analyzed differential policy treatments of Europeans and non-European immigrants, showing how these differences led to different prospects for national inclusion. Gunther Peck's *Reinventing Free Labor* (2000) compared the experiences of Italian, Greek, and Mexican labor contractors and workers in the North American west and the legal and cultural associations made between immigrants and unfree labor. Joan M. Jensen's *Calling this Place Home* (2006), a social history of women in late-nineteenth-century Wisconsin, shows how a "place" became defined through European immigrant and Native American women's respective relationships to the land and to each other. The trend toward multigroup studies is particularly salutary, as these both broaden our knowledge about specific groups as they compare and relate to one another and direct attention to thematic questions of American national development. Immigration and ethnic histories are offering revealing insights about citizenship, capitalism, gender and sexuality, mass culture, state formation, and empire—in short, the multiple facets of nation making.

Immigration and Immigration History in the Twenty-First Century

As with previous generations, the new immigration history is shaped by immigration in our own time. The percentage of foreign-born in the U.S. population has risen from a historical low of 4.7 percent in 1970 to 12 percent in 2010 (approaching the historical high of 15 percent in the early 1910s). Unlike previous waves, immigration today is both lawful and unauthorized.

Over 80 percent comes from Mexico, Latin America, and Asia; and immigrants now live and work in all areas of the country, including regions that previously saw very few, such as the South. They are both unskilled and highly educated. Public sentiment is sharply divided between those favoring inclusion (including a growing Latino electorate) and nativist reaction, and, especially since September 11, 2001, there has been a heightened association of immigration with threats to national security. Among the nation's estimated twelve million unauthorized immigrants, more than two-thirds are from Mexico and Central America. Among the adult unauthorized population, 37 percent live in "mixed status" families, that is, in households with family members who are U.S. citizens and legal immigrants. Contemporary globalization, including the western hemispheric free-trade agreements, has led to greater prosperity in parts of the developing world but also greater inequalities, which drive migration. These trends prompt us to ask questions of the past about the patterns of global inequalities, the power of law and the state, the dynamism of transnational cultures, and the conditions that enable political change within the United States.

What the first two generations of historiography crafted as a normative theory of immigration now can be seen, with historical distance, as the product of a specific moment in U.S. history: the assimilation of the second generation of "new immigrants" in the post–World War II era made possible by unprecedented American economic growth and global power, a steady decline in wealth inequality (1947–1974), and the generosity of the American welfare state, in particular, higher education and homeownership for World War II veterans. The theme of universal inclusion and citizenship could be read back onto the nineteenth century only by bracketing slavery, southwestern annexation, Asiatic exclusion, Jim Crow, and the nation's imperial projects in the history of the development of the American nation. In fact, the experience of the "new immigrants" at the turn of the twentieth century, as well as that generally of non-European migrants throughout American history, was marked by exploitation in a segmented labor market, political exclusion, social isolation, and nativist opposition. Even the Fourteenth Amendment's provision of birthright citizenship to all persons born in the United States, including the children of immigrants—the foundation for the second generation's access to the polity—has proved viable only under favorable conditions that are at once economic (expansion not contraction), demographic (concentration of voters), and political (foreign relations, domestic labor movement, civil rights movement, etc.). Perhaps, as historian David Gutiérrez suggests, immigration in the early twenty-first century, with its high incidence of labor exploitation and political exclusion, is the "new normal."[2] From this angle, the prospects for democratic inclusion—now as in the past—are certainly not foreclosed, but must be understood not as organic or inevitable, but as residing in conditions of possibility that are chiefly political, domestic, and global. As long as this remains the case, current trends in the historical study of immigration and ethnicity are likely to continue.

NOTES

1. On the former view, Jeremy Adelman and Stephen Aron, "From Borderlands to Borders: Empires, Nation-States, and the People in Between in North American History." *American Historical Review* 104 (June 1999): 814–841; on the latter view, David Gutiérrez, "Migration, Emergent Ethnicity, and the 'Third Space': The Shifting Politics of Nationalism in Greater Mexico." *Journal of American History* 86 (September 1999): 481–517.

2. On economic stagnation of Mexican Americans from 1965 to 2000, despite marked trends of acculturation (English-language acquisition), see Edward Telles and Vilma Ortez, *Generations of Exclusion: Mexican Americans, Assimilation, and Race*. New York: Russell Sage, 2008. Telles and Ortiz's findings implicate failing urban public schools and persistent segmentation in the labor market as key reasons for Mexican Americans' lack of socioeconomic mobility.

BIBLIOGRAPHY

General Histories, Surveys, and Document Collections

Bayor, Ronald H., ed. *Race and Ethnicity in America: A Concise History*. New York: Columbia University Press, 2003.

Gabaccia, Donna R., and Vicki Ruíz, eds. *American Dreaming, Global Realities: Rethinking U.S. Immigration History*. Urbana: University of Illinois Press, 2006.

Hoerder, Dirk. *Cultures in Contact: World Migrations in the Second Millennium*. Durham, NC: Duke University Press, 2002.

Ngai, Mae M., and Jon Gjerde, eds. *Major Problems in American Immigration and Ethnic History*, 2nd ed. Boston: Cengage Learning, 2010.

Zolberg, Aristide R. *A Nation by Design: Immigration Policy in the Fashioning of America*. Cambridge, MA: Russell Sage Foundation of Harvard University Press, 2006.

Historiography and Method

Anderson, Benedict. *Imagined Communities*. New York: Verso, 1991.

Duara, Prasenjit. *Rescuing History from the Nation: Questioning Narratives of Modern China*. Chicago: University of Chicago Press, 1995.

Gabaccia, Donna. "Great Migration Debates: Keywords in Historical Perspective," July 28, 2006, in Social Science Research Council, *Border Battles: The U.S. Immigration Debates*, http://borderbattles.ssrc.org/Gabaccia/ (accessed Dec. 16, 2009).

Kenny, Kevin. "Diaspora and Comparison: The Irish as a Case Study." *Journal of American History* 90 (June 2003): 134–162.

Park, Robert S. *Race and Culture*, Glencoe, IL: Free Press, 1950.

Sánchez, George J. "Race, Nation, and Culture in Recent Immigration Studies." *Journal of American Ethnic History* 18 (1999): 66–84.

Group, Multigroup, and Thematic Studies

Abelmann, Nancy, and John Lie. *Blue Dreams: Korean Americans and the Los Angeles Riots*. Cambridge, MA: Harvard University Press, 1995.

Alba, Richard D., and Victor Nee. *Remaking the American Mainstream: Assimilation and Contemporary Immigration*. Cambridge, MA: Harvard University Press, 2003.

Anbinder, Tyler. *Five Points: The 19th-Century New York City Neighborhood That Invented Tap Dance, Stole Elections, and Became the World's Most Notorious Slum*. New York: Plume, 2001.

Arredondo, Gabriela. *Mexican Chicago: Race, Identity, and Nation, 1916–1939*. Urbana: University of Illinois Press, 2008.

Azuma, Eiichiro. *Between Two Empires: Race, History, and Transnationalism in Japanese America*. New York: Oxford University Press, 2005.

Barrett, James R., and David Roediger. "In-Between Peoples: Race, Nationality, and the 'New Immigrant' Working Class." *Journal of American Ethnic History* (Spring 1997): 3–47.

Benton-Cohen, Katherine. *Borderline Americans: Racial Division and Labor War in the Arizona Borderlands*. Cambridge, MA: Harvard University Press, 2009.

Bodnar, John E. *The Transplanted: A History of Immigrants in Urban America*. Bloomington: Indiana University Press, 1985.

Bosniak, Linda. *The Citizen and the Alien: Dilemmas of Contemporary Membership*. Princeton, NJ: Princeton University Press, 2006.

Brooks, Charlotte. *Alien Neighbors, Foreign Friends: Asian Americans, Housing, and the Transformation of Urban California*. Chicago: University of Chicago Press, 2009.

Brooks, James. *Captives and Cousins: Slavery, Kinship, and Community in the Southwest Borderlands*. Chapel Hill: University of North Carolina Press, 2002.

Choy, Catherine Ceniza. *Empire of Care: Nursing and Migration in Filipino American History*. Durham, NC: Duke University Press, 2003.

Cohen, Deborah. *Transnational Subjects: Braceros, Nation, and Migration (United States and Mexico, 1942–1964)*. Chapel Hill: University of North Carolina Press, 2010.

Fairchild, Amy L. *Science at the Borders: Immigrant Medical Inspection and the Shaping of the Modern Industrial Labor Force*. Baltimore: Johns Hopkins University Press, 2003.

Fink, Leon. *The Maya of Morganton: Work and Community in the Nuevo New South*. Chapel Hill: University of North Carolina Press, 2003.

Foley, Neil. *The White Scourge: Mexicans, Blacks, and Poor Whites in Texas Cotton Culture*. Berkeley: University of California Press, 1997.

Foner, Nancy. *From Ellis Island to JFK: New York's Two Great Waves of Immigration*. New Haven, CT: Yale University Press, 2000.

Gabaccia, Donna R., and Fraser M. Ottanelli. *Italian Workers of the World: Labor Migration and the Formation of Multiethnic States*. Urbana: University of Illinois Press, 2001.

Games, Alison. *Migration and the Origins of the English Atlantic World*. Cambridge, MA: Harvard University Press, 1999.

García, Matt. *A World of Its Own: Race, Labor, and Citrus in the Making of Greater Los Angeles, 1900–1970*. Chapel Hill: University of North Carolina Press, 2001.

Gerstle, Gary. *American Crucible: Race and Nation in the Twentieth Century*. Princeton, NJ: Princeton University Press, 2001.

Gualteri, Sarah M. *Between Arab and White: Race and Ethnicity in the Early Syrian American Diaspora*. Berkeley: University of California Press, 2009.

Guglielmo, Thomas A. *White on Arrival: Italians, Race, Color, and Power in Chicago, 1890–1945*. New York: Oxford University Press, 2003.

Gutiérrez, David R. "The 'New Normal?' Reflections on the Shifting Politics of the Immigration Debate." *International Labor and Working Class History* 78 (Fall 2010): 118–122.

———. *Walls and Mirrors: Mexican Americans, Mexican Immigrants, and the Politics of Ethnicity*. Berkeley: University of California Press, 1995.

Gutiérrez, Ramón A. *When Jesus Came, the Corn Mothers Went Away: Marriage, Sexuality, and Power in New Mexico, 1500–1846*. Palo Alto, CA: Stanford University Press, 1991.

Gutman, Herbert. *Work, Culture, and Society in Industrializing America*. New York: Knopf, 1976.

Handlin, Oscar. *The Uprooted: The Epic Story of the Great Migrations That Made the American People*. New York: Grossett and Dunlap, 1951.

Hattam, Victoria. *In the Shadow of Race: Jews, Latinos, and Immigrant Politics in the U.S.* Chicago: University of Chicago Press, 2007.

Hayashi, Brian M. *Democratizing the Enemy: The Japanese Internment*. Princeton, NJ: Princeton University Press, 2004.

Hernandez, Kelly Lytle. *Migra!* Berkeley: University of California Press, 2010.

Higham, John. *Strangers in the Land: Patterns of American Nativism, 1860–1925*. New Brunswick, NJ: Rutgers University Press, 1955.

Hoffnung-Garskof, Jesse. *A Tale of Two Cities: Santo Domingo and New York after 1950*. Princeton, NJ: Princeton University Press, 2008.

Hsu, Madeline Yuan-yin. *Dreaming of Gold, Dreaming of Home: Transnationalism and Migration between the United States and South China, 1882–1943*. Palo Alto, CA: Stanford University Press, 2000.

Jacobson, Matthew. *Special Sorrows: The Diasporic Imagination of Irish, Polish, and Jewish Immigrants in the United States*. Cambridge, MA: Harvard University Press, 1995.

———. *Whiteness of a Different Color: European Immigrants and the Alchemy of Race*. Cambridge, MA: Harvard University Press, 1998.

Jensen, Joan M. *Calling This Place Home: Women on the Wisconsin Frontier, 1850–1925*. St. Paul: Minnesota Historical Society Press, 2006.

Johnson, Benjamin Heber. *Revolution in Texas: How a Forgotten Rebellion and Its Bloody Suppression Turned Mexicans into Americans*. New Haven, CT: Yale University Press, 2003.

Jung, Moon-Ho. *Coolies and Cane: Race, Labor, and Sugar in the Age of Emancipation*. Baltimore: Johns Hopkins University Press, 2006.

Kazal, Russell A. *Becoming Old Stock: The Paradox of German-American Identity*. Princeton, NJ: Princeton University Press, 2004.

Kennedy, John F. *A Nation of Immigrants*. New York: Anti-Defamation League of B'nai B'rith, 1958; Harper and Row, 1964, 2008.

Kenny, Kevin. *Making Sense of the Molly Maguires*. New York: Oxford University Press, 1998.

Kobrin, Rebecca. *Jewish Bialystok and Its Diaspora: Between Exile and Empire*. Bloomington: Indiana University Press 2010.

Kuhn, Philip. *Chinese among Others: Emigration in Modern Times*. Lanham, MD: Rowman and Littlefield, 2008.

Kurashige, Lon. *Japanese American Celebration and Conflict: A History of Ethnic Identity and Festival, 1934–1990*. Berkeley: University of California Press, 2002.

Kurashige, Scott. *The Shifting Grounds of Race: Blacks and Japanese Americans in the Making of Multi-ethnic Los Angeles.* Princeton, NJ: Princeton University Press, 2008.

Lederhendler, Eli. *Jewish Immigrants and American Capitalism: From Caste to Class.* New York: Cambridge University Press, 2009.

Lee, Erika. *At America's Gates: Chinese Immigration during the Exclusion Era, 1882–1943.* Chapel Hill: University of North Carolina Press, 2003.

Leong, Karen. *The China Mystique: Pearl S. Buck, Anna May Wong, Mayling Soong, and the Transformation of American Orientalism.* Berkeley: University of California Press, 2005.

Lowe, Lisa. *Immigrant Acts: On Asian American Cultural Politics.* Durham, NC: Duke University Press, 1996.

Lui, Mary Ting Yi. *The Chinatown Trunk Mystery: Murder, Miscegenation, and Other Dangerous Encounters in Turn-of-the-Century New York City.* Princeton, NJ: Princeton University Press, 2005.

McKeown, Adam. *Chinese Migrant Networks and Cultural Change: Peru, Chicago, Hawaii, 1900–1936.* Chicago: University of Chicago Press, 2001.

Meagher, Timothy J. *Inventing Irish America: Generation, Class, and Ethnic Identity in a New England City, 1880–1928.* Notre Dame, IN: University of Notre Dame Press, 2001.

Miller, Kerby. *Emigrants and Exiles: Ireland and the Irish Exodus to North America.* New York: Oxford University Press, 1985.

Molina, Natalia, *Fit to Be Citizens? Public Health and Race in Los Angeles, 1879–1939.* Berkeley: University of California Press, 2006.

Montejano, David. *Anglos and Mexicans in the Making of Texas, 1836–1986.* Austin: University of Texas Press, 1987.

Montoya, María E. *Translating Property: The Maxwell Land Grant and the Conflict over Land in the American West, 1840–1900.* Berkeley: University of California Press, 2002; Lawrence: University Press of Kansas, 2005.

Ngai, Mae M. *Impossible Subjects: Illegal Aliens and the Making of Modern America.* Princeton, NJ: Princeton University Press, 2004.

Peck, Gunther. *Reinventing Free Labor: Padrone and Immigrant Workers in the North American West, 1880–1930.* New York: Cambridge University Press, 2000.

Pitti, Stephen. *The Devil in Silicon Valley: Northern California, Race, and Mexican Americans.* Princeton, NJ: Princeton University Press, 2003.

Reséndez, Andrés. *Changing National Identities at the Frontier: Texas and New Mexico, 1800–1850.* New York: Cambridge University Press, 2005.

Roediger, David R. *The Wages of Whiteness: Race and the Making of the American Working Class.* New York: Verso, 1991.

Rosas, Ana. "Flexible Familias." Ph.D. dissertation, University of Southern California, 2008.

Ruíz, Vicki. *From Out of the Shadows: Mexican Women in Twentieth-Century America.* New York: Oxford University Press, 1998.

Ruíz, Vicki, and John Chavez, eds. *Memories and Migrations: Mapping Boricua and Chicana Histories.* Urbana: University of Illinois Press, 2008.

Salyer, Lucy E. *Law Harsh as Tigers: Chinese Immigrants and the Shaping of Modern Immigration Law.* Chapel Hill: University of North Carolina Press, 1995.

Sánchez, George J. *Becoming Mexican American: Ethnicity, Culture, and Identity in Chicano Los Angeles, 1900–1945.* New York: Oxford University Press, 1995.

Schmidt Camacho, Alicia R. *Migrant Imaginaries: Latino Cultural Politics in the U.S.-Mexico Borderlands.* New York: New York University Press, 2008.

Shah, Nayan. *Contagious Divides: Epidemics and Race in San Francisco's Chinatown.* Berkeley: University of California Press, 2001.

Shukla, Sandhya Rajendra. *India Abroad: Diasporic Cultures of Postwar America and England.* Princeton, NJ: Princeton University Press, 2003.

Smith, Robert C. *Mexican New York: Transnational Lives of New Immigrants.* Berkeley: University of California Press, 2006.

Soyer, Daniel. *A Coat of Many Colors: Immigration, Globalism, and Reform in the New York City Garment Industry.* New York: Fordham University Press, 2005.

Stern, Alexandra Minna. *Eugenic Nation: Faults and Frontiers of Better Breeding in Modern America.* Berkeley: University of California Press, 2005.

Street, Richard Steven. *Beasts of the Field: A Narrative History of California Farmworkers, 1769–1913.* Palo Alto, CA: Stanford University Press, 2004.

Tchen, John Kuo Wei. *New York before Chinatown: Orientalism and the Shaping of American Culture, 1776–1882.* Baltimore: Johns Hopkins University Press, 1999.

Thomas, William, I., and Florian Znaniecki. *The Polish Peasant in Europe and America,* 5 vols. Chicago: University of Chicago Press and Boston: Gorham Press, 1918–1920.

Vargas, Zaragosa. *Labor Rights Are Civil Rights: Mexican American Workers in Twentieth-Century America.* Princeton, NJ: Princeton University Press, 2005.

Weber, David J. *Bárbaros: Spaniards and Their Savages in the Age of Enlightenment.* New Haven, CT: Yale University Press, 2005.

———. *The Mexican Frontier, 1821–1846: The American Southwest under Mexico.* Albuquerque: University of New Mexico Press, 1982.

Whalen, Carmen. *From Puerto Rico to Philadelphia: Puerto Rican Workers and Postwar Economies.* Philadelphia: Temple University Press, 2001.

Yung, Judy. *Unbound Feet: A Social History of Chinese Women in San Francisco.* Berkeley: University of California Press, 1995.

17

American Indians and the Study of U.S. History

NED BLACKHAWK

It goes without saying that American Indians maintain a deeper history upon the North American continent than any other people, but American historians have only recently engaged the long-standing and often traumatic tale of indigenous struggle and survival found throughout our nation's past. As a growing body of scholarship over the past three decades has revealed, American Indian history not only predates the colonial and national periods but also exposes critical dynamics within every temporal and geographic field of American history. Indian histories now routinely garner professional historical prizes and have particularly reoriented the fields of early American, U.S. western, and comparative history. By all professional measures the field has now arrived.

Such ascendancy stands in marked contrast to the preceding generations of historical inquiry. In fact, one would be hard pressed to find another field of historical study that has witnessed more dramatic reversals of scholarly fortune than has American Indian history. Throughout most of U.S. history, historians generally considered American Indians either too culturally different or too unimportant for rigorous historical investigation. The ethnographic, cultural, linguistic, and political distinctions that have characterized American Indian societies for millennia seemingly prohibited historical inquiry while broader venues of U.S. popular culture reinforced timeless, negative, and one-dimensional portraits of Native people.

Because historians generally failed to investigate the complexities inherent in the Native American past, anthropologists and scholars working on the so-called frontiers of historical inquiry developed a new field of study in the 1950s called ethnohistory. Designed partly to assist in adjudicating postwar Indian land claims cases, this field deploys both anthropological and historical methods, and it generated heightened study of American Indian historical experiences, culminating in the landmark series *Handbook of North American Indians.* Published by the Smithsonian Institution, this twenty-volume reference set includes a thousand essays and is generally divided by regional culture areas—for example, the Northwest Coast, Northeast, or Southwest—each of which is largely subdivided by tribal nations, such as the Makah, Mohawk, or Mohave. Unlike any other scholarly resource, the *Handbook* provides comprehensive ethnographic as well as bibliographic information on American Indians.

Historiographically, American Indians occupy an iconic but underinterrogated place in the nation's past. As American history became increasingly professionalized in the nineteenth century, historians often crafted narratives in contradistinction to those of European nations, and American Indians figure prominently (if problematically) in these late-nineteenth-century studies. Most notably, American western historians, particularly Frederick Jackson Turner, examined processes of national self-definition that attended the expansion of the nation across the continent. In such "frontier" narratives, Indians became antitheses of American subjectivity and modernism, either tragic victims of an increasingly industrializing society or uncultured impediments incapable of inclusion in the nation. As Robert Berkhofer suggests in *The White Man's Indian*, such binary representations predate the national period. As Philip Deloria has similarly shown in *Playing Indian*, Euro-American fascination with, and mimicry of, Indian dress and presumed behaviors grew heightened during moments of social transformation and modernization.

Studies of the American West, propelled by Turner's frontier thesis, not only celebrated the nineteenth-century expansion of the United States, but also helped to institutionalize the larger field of American history. Barely more than a century old, American history has now become the world's most researched national history, and after a century of neglect, the American Indian past has now emerged as a flourishing field of academic inquiry. Across the lands that would become the United States, American Indians developed complex societies that, starting in the sixteenth century, increasingly came into deep and deadly conflict with European newcomers.

The American West and Spanish Borderlands

Worried that the closing of the "frontier" in the 1890s would deprive millions of non-Anglophone immigrants access to the quintessential processes of settlement and Americanization, Turner identified the expansion of Euro-American communities across Indian homelands as the defining feature of American history. Like leading intellectuals of his time, he worked during a period in which American Indians appeared doomed by history; not coincidentally, he delivered his "frontier thesis" in 1893 upon the four-hundredth anniversary of the Columbian encounter. He did so in Chicago, host to the world's fair known as the Columbian Exposition. Like Turner, the fair's organizers believed that American Indians represented not only antitheses of modernity, but that they also constituted a "vanishing race," one whose cultural forms needed to be both archived and exhibited. Practicing early versions of ethnographic research known as "salvage anthropology," fair organizers like the German ethnologist Franz Boas undertook massive campaigns of American Indian object collecting and also staged exhibitions of American Indians at the fair. Living for months within the fairgrounds and spectrally posed to elicit fairgoers' reactions, hundreds of American Indians were so represented. At few times in American history have such powerful cultural currents converged in a single space for such an extended period.

As Paige Raibmon has explored in *Authentic Indians*, American Indian communities in Chicago—some of whom Turner may have seen—came from societies under multiple forms of colonial surveillance. Missionaries, governmental officials, and anthropologists all targeted Indians, but did so differently. Viewing, for example, the cultural practices of communal wealth redistribution (known as the potlatch) as hindrances to assimilation, governmental officials in the United States and Canada policed Northwest Coast Indian mobility, outlawing their communal giveaways for decades. Communal giveaways, officials believed, hampered assimilation into property-owning societies. As Raibmon highlights, anthropologists, like Boas, thus enabled select community members to continue their cultural practices not only outside the region and for wages but also in ways that allowed them to critique the prohibition of the potlatch. To understand American Indian community participation within such staged exhibitions requires consideration of the multiple colonial contexts structuring their participation.

Raibmon's work on Northwest Coast Indian communities provides a model not only for better understanding American Indian cultural history, but also for gauging the dramatic changes in the overlapping historiographies of the American West and American Indians. The majority of American Indian reservations and community members are found in the West, and unlike other subfields of American historical inquiry, the West has generated countless assessments of Indian histories. How dramatically different, then, are twenty-first-century histories like Raibmon's from those of Turner and his many disciples?

Like many studies in the field, Raibmon's work does not self-consciously engage the history of the West. A comparative study of Northwest Coast communities astride the U.S.-Canadian border, *Authentic Indians* also does not limit itself to the history of a single nation. In such departures from region and nation, Raibmon and other scholars of North American indigenous history transcend many of the binary limits and residual prejudices of American western history, the birth field of many American Indian histories. Attuned to contemporary indigenous social and political concerns, studies of the Northwest have particularly re-centered the region's history. Coll Thrush's *Native Seattle*, Alexandra Harmon's *Indians in the Making*, and Cole Harris's *The Resettlement of British Columbia* and *Making Native Space* are a few works from the past generation that speak more to transnational and contemporary intellectual currents than they engage historiographical concerns rooted in studies of the American West.

The American West, however, still remains a powerful field of historical analysis, and the celebrated paradigm of "New Western History" of the early 1990s initiated multiple studies in which issues of race relations, state power, and unresolved American Indian treaty rights resonated. Patricia Nelson Limerick in *The Legacy of Conquest* and Richard White in *It's Your Misfortune and None of my Own* produced field-shaping overviews that highlighted Indian-white relations as defining and enduring features of western history.

Many recent studies of western Indian history are also deeply concerned with indigenous experiences prior to American settlement. Interestingly, a range of scholars have reengaged another, century-old paradigm for understanding the West, one developed by one of Turner's students, Herbert Eugene Bolton. Bolton's *The Spanish Borderlands* and subsequent exhaustive research established an alternative vision of the West rooted not in Anglo-American expansion but in the presence of the continent's oldest imperial power, Spain.

Like Turner, Bolton celebrated European colonization, but did so with a regional emphasis upon "the Spanish Borderlands," a realm larger than British North America reaching from Florida to California and with centuries-old influences on both American coastlines. Unlike Turner's, Bolton's studies did little to shape the larger development of American historiography; his work, for example, on Spanish influences in colonial Georgia, let alone his mammoth studies of California mission history, barely appeared on the radar of U.S. colonial history. Turner, essentially, established an exceptionalist claim about American history, one rooted in encounters between a singular imperial and national power, not a multiplicity of European powers and resident Native Americans. Conversely, Boltonian studies examined processes of European expansion in which American Indians remained central to the course of empire. As hosts, guides, converts, laborers, subjects, adversaries, and diplomats, American Indians played crucial roles in the development of Spain's flagship colony, New Spain. Studies of British North America have only recently paid comparable attention to such dynamics.

While less recognizable than Turner and his disciples, Bolton nonetheless reigned over portions of western historiography, particularly California history, influencing the direction of hundreds of graduate students at Berkeley and establishing the Bancroft Library as the premier archive for western Americana. Whereas many of his students continued excavating the Spanish colonial experience in North America, scholars after World War II increasingly began refashioning Bolton's visions of the borderlands. In a series of important studies, Jack D. Forbes, David J. Weber, Elizabeth John, and Edward Spicer recast the celebratory emphasis of Bolton's work, laying the foundations for more recent interpretations. In *The Mexican Frontier* and *The Spanish Frontier in North America*, Weber invoked the nomenclature of Turner's West but adopted regional analyses rooted in Spanish and Mexican historical dynamics. In *Storms Brewed in Other Men's Worlds*, John analyzed sets of Indian-imperial relations, including those between French imperial agents and Native Americans, but did so in a vast, multipolar area ranging from California to Louisiana. Similarly, Forbes reoriented studies of the Southwest prior to Anglo-American influence in *Apache, Navaho, and Spaniard* and *Warriors of the Colorado*, while Spicer provided a rich overview in *Cycles of Conquest*. Their insights have been particularly influential in recent works.

Since 1991, dozens have published works that refashion aspects of Borderlands and Native American history. Utilizing sometimes French, Spanish, Mexican, English, Canadian, and American archival source materials, these new "borderlands" historians examine the continent's earliest colonial dynamics. Whereas Limerick and White devote nearly the entirety of their respective overviews to the U.S. national period, more recent studies probe the complexities of imperial encounters and indigenous adaptations found before Anglo-American settlement. The results have been impressive and defy easy summation. Collectively, borderland histories have recast the history of the American West prior to the U.S.-Mexican War.

For example, as Brian Delay, Gary Anderson, and Pekka Hämäläinen emphasize, Indians decisively shaped Mexico's diplomacy following its independence in 1821. Rather than seeing, for example, the struggle for Texas as solely between Anglo-American settlers and Mexican nationals, these scholars emphasize the centrality of indigenous communities in the unmaking of Mexican rule, highlighting how equestrian Indians, particularly the Comanche, disrupted northern Mexican communities. As each shows, U.S. military forces literally followed equestrian raiding paths into Mexico during the war, and the subsequent U.S. conquest of the Southwest is best viewed in a multinational as well as indigenous context.

As in any field of inquiry, recent work offers divergent accounts of this and other subjects. Delay, James F. Brooks, and Ramón A. Gutiérrez, for example, often ascribe indigenous behavior to cultural motivations, whereas Hämäläinen and others draw from economic studies, particularly Thomas Hall's *Social Change in the Southwest*, and emphasize more structural and material forces. Colin Calloway's *One Vast Winter Count* provides a rich and moderating overview. All agree that the aftermath of the U.S.-Mexican War precipitated increased conflicts between Indian and U.S. communities, the roots of which predate the establishment of Anglo-American sovereignty west of the Mississippi, while the legacies of such nineteenth-century wars reverberate to the present.

Indians and Empires in Eastern North America

While studies in and of the West most regularly expose the vibrancy of American Indian history, studies of Indian-imperial relations in eastern America accelerated the current borderlands paradigm and initated the field's overall ascendancy. Retrospectively, it appears that only through engagement with dominant assumptions within the national historiographical tradition could such seismic scholarly shifts occur. Whereas studies of Indians and empires now routinely garner recognition, such was not the case on the eve of the Columbian quincentenary when Indian history remained largely a subfield of western history, and when countless textbooks, university graduate programs, and professional associations routinely dismissed this field of study.

The year 1991 challenged and ultimately changed such exclusion. The year not only witnessed the publication of Gutiérrez's award-winning, if controversial, study of colonial New Mexico, *When Jesus Came, the Corn Mothers Went Away*, but also the arrival of a book subtitled *Indians, Empires, and Republics in the Great Lakes Region, 1650–1815*. Like few books in American history, this study offered an unprecedented reconceptualization of early American history.

Richard White's *The Middle Ground* broke open the geographic and temporally bounded field of U.S. colonial history. By extension, it recast the narrative of American history. Despite several lucid and compelling Indian colonial histories from the 1980s, including *Manitou and Providence* by Neil Salisbury and *The Indians' New World* by James Merrell, the field of U.S. colonial history largely focused on British North America and its diverse social, economic, and religious communities. Prominent works in African-American and southern history had dislodged the field's once exclusive focus on New England, while many studies had exposed the phases of Indian dispossession within Puritan and Chesapeake societies. By and large, however, colonial history remained synonymous with the Anglo-American world. The field, as Fred Anderson suggests, often served as a prologue to the American Revolution, devaluing in his words "the most important war of the 18th century," the Seven Years War, also known as the French and Indian War.

Anderson's confident and assured insights from 2000 remain indebted to the dramatic transitions from the early 1990s, particularly to *The Middle Ground* and studies of the powerful Iroquois Confederacy. The convergence of White's work on the Great Lakes with those by Daniel Richter, Matthew Dennis, and Francis Jennings on the Iroquois ultimately cast asunder the Anglocentric vision of early America, exploding the field to include multiple regional, indigenous, linguistic, and imperial communities. How did such a dramatic development occur?

It began in diaspora, a concept then rarely applied to American Indians. Starting in the midst of fur-trading wars initiated in the 1600s, *The Middle*

Ground traced continent-wide changes attending the seventeenth-century arrival of European colonists. Whereas U.S. colonies once remained geographically and hermetically bound to the Atlantic, White's study revealed the effects of European trade, warfare, and diseases on Algonquin communities throughout the continent. Such communities had become "refugees" as a result of the unprecedented disruptions brought to their villages by the Iroquois, themselves coping with the growth of Anglo, Francophone, and Dutch colonies on their many borders.

Rather than focusing upon the pre-Columbian nature of Indian societies, White's study opens with linguistically related indigenous communities coping with the grim realities of European contact. It subsequently traces their relations not only with respective imperial powers, but also importantly with each other. Newcomers themselves to portions of the western Great Lakes, many Algonquin villagers struggled to reestablish social and political cohesion, while also competing with resident indigenous peoples over land and resources. Into this chaotic and violent world entered Francophone missionaries, traders, and officials, and through their relations with France's many agents of empire, these village communities both reorientated themselves and also constructed a colonial world that bore little resemblance to either New Spain or New England. In the vast realm of New France, distinctions between Indians and Europeans were often less apparent than their commonalities. The French, according to White, provided "an imperial glue" that held this world together, as mutuality both characterized and determined the region's identity.

Restoring, then, multiple Indian as well as European actors to the narrative of early America, *The Middle Ground* helped to decenter, if not provincialize, the Anglo-American experience. While small demographically, French settlements on the St. Lawrence as well as Dutch settlements on the Hudson sent shockwaves into interior worlds, refashioning landscapes and indigenous communities long before they directly encountered Europeans. Comparatively, the struggle of English colonists remains but one of many within the vast and bewildering seventeenth-century colonial world. Synthesizing the field a decade after *The Middle Ground*, Alan Taylor in *American Colonies* extends such analyses, suggesting for instance how before 1650 the British colony of Barbados had as many English settlers as did England's North American colonies. The seventeenth century has thus now become an undetermined world of multiple colonial spheres, providing a much richer as well as more sobering historical universe.

The Middle Ground, along with Richter's *The Ordeal of the Longhouse*, also centers on the eighteenth century, which witnessed not only the ascension of Anglo America but also the dissolution of the shared forms of mutuality between European and Indian peoples in New France. For the Iroquois and numerous southern Indian nations, the century brought the demise of the multilateral "play-off system," a complex diplomatic practice that Indian communities effectively deployed within overlapping colonial spheres. As many studies have examined, such transformations remade indigenous diplomacy, economics, and politics across both the Ohio River Valley and the Southeast, foreshadowing these regions' nineteenth-century histories. Claudio Saunt, Robbie Ethridge, and Theda Perdue have all exposed the importance of interior southern Indian societies to the development of British North America, linking their insights with those of Merrell, Peter Wood, and Alan Gallay on the centrality of Indians to the making of the colonial South.

The results of such analysis have yielded fundamentally new understandings of the eighteenth century's two most dramatic conflicts, the Seven Year's War and the American Revolution. Whereas previous U.S. colonial histories often traced the shifting historical forces that ultimately brought independence, studies of Indians and empires have complicated the once teleological direction of the field. As Anderson reveals in *Crucible of War*, the unprecedented expenditures, logistical organization, and complex legacies of the clash between France and England both originated in conflicts between Indians and English settlers in the Ohio River Valley and fueled subsequent tensions between settlers and English authorities. The Treaty of Paris of 1763 formally ended the conflict, and that year also witnessed the last theater of the war, one not between French and English forces but between unconquered Algonquin villagers and English authorities attempting to rule from forts inherited from the French. This "rebellion" led by the Ottawa leader Pontiac ultimately restored patterns of mutuality essential to Great Lakes villagers but also further divided English settlers from the crown. As England's Parliament increasingly passed the economic burdens of the war onto its colonists, the crown also moved to quell costly Indian conflicts in the "backcountry," many of which required the British to police the behavior as well as the ambitions of their colonial subjects. White characterizes such initial compromise as the "restoration of the middle ground," while underscoring the impossibilities of coexistence within these contested lands. Collectively, his and other studies have now made the region's Indian affairs essential factors in the calculus of the American Revolution.

The U.S. Constitution, Indian Removal, and America's Many Indian Wars

Paradigm shifts in scholarly fields are uncommon, and while Indian histories have recast the paradigm of early American history, post-Revolutionary and nineteenth-century U.S. historiography remains less affected. Notwithstanding a profusion of scholarship on "the American Revolution in Indian Country," the evolution of federal Indian policy in the new republic, and the constitutional crisis brought by Indian removal, studies of antebellum America still frequently elide these central dimensions of the national experience.

Such elision is both ironic and debilitating. As Colin Calloway, Woody Holton, Michael Green, Gary Nash, and Anthony Wallace have highlighted, American Indians centrally influenced both the American Revolution and early republic. A foundational text in ethnohistory, Wallace's *The Death and Rebirth of the Seneca* examines the cultural revitalization movement of the Seneca prophet Handsome Lake and underscores the multiple forms of devastation sown by Revolutionary forces upon Iroquois villages. Coping with the disintegration of their once extensive political orbit, Iroquois community members developed religious and cultural traditions that reordered their village societies torn asunder by the Revolution. Such military and political relations powerfully influenced the Revolution and its aftermath. Indian conflicts after 1783, for example, exposed many of the weaknesses of the Articles of Confederation and helped to inspire the shift to a more powerful, centralized federal system. The Constitution of 1787 specifically locates authority over Indian affairs with the federal government in the Commerce Clause, lodging the five pivotal words—"and with the Indian tribes"—in our nation's founding document.

While American Indian legal history has become a growing field of inquiry, American constitutional historians rarely include federal Indian law in their work. The headwaters from which federal Indian law flows, the Commerce Clause has been interpreted by the Supreme Court as recognition of the inherent, if circumscribed, sovereignty of tribal nations, particularly vis-à-vis the authority of state governments. Lindsay Robertson, Sidney Harring, C. Blue Clark, David Wilkins, K. Tsianina Lomawaima, Christian McMillen, and Lisa Ford have all examined the evolution of federal Indian law as well as the results of particularly influential rulings of the Supreme Court. Their combined efforts build upon the classic works of federal Indian legal scholars, including John Reid's *A Law of Blood* and Felix Cohen's *Handbook of Federal Indian Law* that established the parameters of the field. Within these studies, congressional statutes, ratified treaties, Supreme Court rulings, and presidential executive orders provide the sinews that bind the field, linking the applied practice of American Indian law with historical studies of its origins.

Notwithstanding such insights, broader surveys of the Constitution and the Supreme Court often fail to engage this long-standing field of American jurisprudence. Peter Irons, for example, examines eighty-five Supreme Court rulings in his *People's History of the U.S. Supreme Court*, a volume in the social-history inspired *People's History Series*, edited by Howard Zinn. Of the eighty-five cases featured in Irons's overview, none involve American Indians; a cryptic paragraph on one of Chief Justice John Marshall's three Indian legal rulings—which scholars refer to as the Marshall Trilogy and generally analyze in sequence—constitutes the entirety of the federal government's legal relationship with the nation's most federally subordinated communities.

In fact, not only did federal-Indian relations become one of the early republic's most vexing moral concerns, but Indian legal challenges also provoked constitutional dilemmas regarding the nature of federal authority within and across newly acquired territories. As Francis Paul Prucha, Theda Perdue, and Tiya Miles have demonstrated, Indian affairs in Jeffersonian and Jacksonian America remained fraught with painful ambiguities as well as irreconcilable visions. The forced removal of America's eastern Indians during the half century following independence has generated intense scholarly interest, and highlighting the contingency and contestation of removal characterizes recent works on this era.

The Louisiana Purchase of 1803 and Trail of Tears of the 1830s are generally not viewed in tandem. And, while scholars have highlighted the centrality of American Indians to the ultimate course of America's empire, until recently few studies attempted to gauge American Indian experiences within the rapid processes of U.S. expansion. An unexpected consequence arising in the aftermath of the Haitian Revolution, the Louisiana Purchase both doubled the size of the United States and also placed hundreds of different Indian communities under American jurisdiction. It also provided many federal policy makers with a renewed faith that an ultimate refuge for America's Indian peoples was indeed possible, a final solution for America's growing "Indian problem."

As Reginald Horsman, Richard Drinnon, Anders Stephanson, and Amy Kaplan have suggested, racial and cultural motivations fueled U.S. expansion, justifying the forced removal of indigenous communities from within the American body politic. "Manifest Destiny" was, however, not just an ideology but also a practice, one most painfully experienced as well as contested by Indian communities. Whereas many Ohio River Valley Indians, as John Bowes shows, realized that autonomous life was rapidly diminishing after the War of 1812 and consequently migrated west, others, notably the Cherokee, attempted legal challenges to their dispossession. The Cherokee did so in two Supreme Court cases in 1831 and 1832. The first, *Cherokee Nation v. Georgia*, was not heard by the Marshall Court, which ruled that the Cherokee did not constitute a separate foreign nation, as they maintained, but rather comprised "a domestic dependent nation" within the federalist system entitled to certain but not complete forms of political sovereignty. The subsequent case, *Worcester v. Georgia*, clarified Marshall's intentions while also questioning the constitutionality of the centerpiece legislative effort of the Jackson presidency, the 1830 Removal Act.

Andrew Jackson's presidency not only inaugurated the "second party system" in American politics, but also brought into office the first American leader from neither Massachusetts nor Virginia, a frontiersman intimately familiar with Indian warfare. And, while scholars since the nineteenth century have questioned the morality of Indian removal, few have recalibrated larger understandings of Jacksonian Democracy to include Indian removal and the constitutional crisis inherent in Marshall's decision. As McMillen suggests in *Making Indian Law* and Ford reveals in *Settler Sovereignty*, the Marshall court's ruling in favor of Samuel Worcester—who had been illegally imprisoned by the state of Georgia for working on Cherokee lands—not only laid the foundations for late-nineteenth- and twentieth-century articulations of American Indian land rights but also challenged the state of Georgia's assertion of its "perfect settler sovereignty."

As Marshall's biographers have highlighted for generations, Marshall's ruling—which declared both Worcester's imprisonment illegal and, notably, upheld the sovereign rights of tribes outside the laws of state governments—stood little chance of enforcement in the political climate of Jacksonian Washington. Adam Rothman has highlighted the centrality of Indian lands to the rise of the cotton South during this period, and a potential constitutional crisis was thus averted by Jackson's simple but unconstitutional disavowal of Marshall's majority court opinion. Not enough historians, however, have probed the dimensions of this violation of the Constitution's "separations of powers doctrine," which holds—based on Marshall's most famous decision, *Madison v. Marbury*—that the Supreme Court determines the constitutionality of congressional statues. Unlike studies of early American history, then, studies of the Age of Jackson have yet to take full account of the tensions and contradictions brought by Indian resistance to the expansion of state and settler authority.

West of the Mississippi, historians have fully probed the multiple phases of military conflict between American Indians and the U.S. government, particularly after the California Gold Rush. For four decades following 1848, military affairs dominated the nation's relationships with western Indian communities; after the Civil War, the Union Army's primary antagonists were Indians. Rich overviews on America's many western Indian wars are found in Robert M. Utley's *The Indian Frontier of the American West, 1846–1890*, Alvin M. Josephy, Jr.'s *The Civil War in the American West*, and most popularly Dee Brown's *Bury My Heart at Wounded Knee.* Studies of particular battles or U.S. Army campaigns against Indian communities constitute a nearly endless field of study, and there are rich biographies of Indian military leaders from the era. As with the Age of Jackson, however, general works on the Civil War and Reconstruction often fail not only to include analyses of the Civil War's many western theaters, but also to see the war's course and aftermath from a continental perspective. Amy Kaplan and I have each examined, for example, how Samuel Clemens fled his divided Missouri homeland in the summer of 1861 and developed a literary career and pseudonym in Nevada during the war; subsequently, at the dawn of Reconstruction, he journeyed to Hawaii to cover the growth of U.S. plantation economies in the Pacific at a time when an indigenous monarchy, the Hawaiian Kingdom, governed a diverse community of Native and non-Native Hawaiian peoples. Such "imperial routes" are thus constitutive of Twain's earliest writings. As Noenoe K. Silva has further emphasized through an impressive engagement with Native Hawaiian newspapers and political petitions, Native Hawaiian monarchists and their supporters resisted American efforts to topple their internationally recognized government, with thousands petitioning the U.S. Senate to support the monarchy in the 1890s.

Military affairs between Indians and the U.S. government often frame the context and contours of western history. Several recent studies have examined such military relations within larger regional and historic dynamics. Jeffery Ostler's *The Plains Sioux and U.S. Colonialism from Lewis and Clark to Wounded Knee*, Elliot West's *Contested Plains*, Hämäläinen's *The Comanche Empire*, Jacoby's *Shadows at Dawn*, and my own *Violence over the Land* expose deeper origins of Indian battles and massacres than are usually found in broader surveys. These studies also engage their subjects within broader historiographical terms and do so for larger purposes. *Shadows at Dawn*, for example, views settler violence against Indians as the most familiar but overlooked feature of American history, while *The Comanche Empire* sees indigenous military relations as part of a larger imperial project, one initiated by the southern Plains' most powerful equestrians, the Comanche. As with the more developed historiography on the Lakota of the northern Plains, powerful equestrian powers now figure prominently in assessments of American expansion, while collectively, studies of America's many Indian wars provide fruitful avenues for further studies of the nineteenth-century American West.

The Reservation Era and the Campaigns of Assimilation

Following America's many Indian wars, the federal government organized the confinement of American Indian communities upon legally recognized reservations. Created by treaties before 1871 and executive orders thereafter, reservations, however, rarely became the refuges initially intended. Instead, continued government and external campaigns targeted Indian communities and resources. Such campaigns and reservation histories now constitute a growing realm of inquiry.

The reservation experience frames much of nineteenth- and twentieth-century American Indian history. In the western Great Lakes, for example, large reservations were created in the 1840s and 1850s, while subsequent ones became established throughout the Southwest, Northwest, and northern Plains in the 1850s and 1860s, making the "Reservation Era" a largely western field of inquiry. However, Turnerian legacies still structure much of western historiography, limiting interrogation of the aftermath of U.S. expansion for those most adversely affected by it. Reservation and tribal histories, thus, often work against such patterns of historiographic exclusion. As Frederick Hoxie bluntly begins his history of Montana's Crow Indian Nation, *Parading through History*, "Why are there no Indians in the twentieth century?" And, while his pointed query has been partly answered by many scholars, many reservation histories remain unincorporated into broader narratives of the United States.

Reservation histories are in many ways national histories of their own. Geographically and temporally focused around the cultural and political boundaries of an identified community, tribal histories provide valuable chronological, ethnographic, and empirical details and often do so for communities not only overlooked by national historians but also often engaged in long-standing resource and political conflicts. Such investigations can provide evidentiary findings for ongoing land claims, treaty rights, and related legal concerns, while collectively reservation histories highlight the diverse but shared experiences of Indian communities across nearly all American regions.

In the Upper Midwest, for example, the phases of Indian removal that dispersed tens of thousands of Ohio River Valley community members generally affected northern "woodlands" villages less severely. In northern Michigan, Wisconsin, and Minnesota, for example, Algonquian-speaking Ojibwe communities signed treaties in the 1840s and 1850s that recognized Ojibwe claims to large reservation lands. Indian tribes in the southern, more agrarian-suited portions of each of these states faced more aggressive settler communities, and the 1840s, 1850s, 1860s, and even 1870s witnessed multiple conflicts, such as the 1862 Dakota War, as well as campaigns of forced removal of Indian peoples.

As Melissa Meyer shows in *The White Earth Tragedy*, while circumscribed, Minnesota's White Earth Ojibwe reservation possessed bountiful acres of lands from which to harvest traditional foods. The reservation also provided for the continued economic exchange between "mixed-blood" entrepreneurs within the reservation's towns and more traditional gatherers who migrated seasonally harvesting wild rice, game, and other resources. As with Hoxie's study of the Crow, Meyer's work highlights the continuity of indigenous social and economic forms into the reservation era as well as the dramatic changes subsequently initiated by external corporate and political interests. In her work, the tragedy that beset White Earth derived not from the establishment of the reservation itself but from the assaults upon the reservation community thereafter, as a series of land acts, particularly the 1887 Dawes Act and 1904 Clapp and Steenerson Acts, eroded the tribe's communally regulated lands.

Of the many tragedies endured by American Indian communities, the dramatic shifts in federal Indian policy remain among the most studied. While reservations, like White Earth, were established across the American landscape through bilateral treaty negotiations, such efforts as the installation of reservation agents, the construction of boarding schools for Indian children, and the movement to subdivide reservation lands into plots known as allotments received little input from tribal members. As Francis Paul Prucha demonstrates in *American Indian Policy in Crisis*, such policies were often initiated by "friends" of American Indians—Progressive-Era reformers who believed that they were acting in the best interests of Native peoples. Among the Ojibwe of Minnesota, the Crow of Montana, the Ute of Colorado, the Comanche of Oklahoma, indeed throughout Indian Country, such federal policy changes undercut the autonomy of tribal communities while also targeting available resources for external development. Had the 150 million acres of reservation lands established by the federal government for Indian tribes—roughly 8 percent of the entire continental United States—been allowed to remain under tribal control, the history of American Indians as well as modern America would be different. Instead, such practices as the erosion of reservation lands, the curtailment of tribal cultural practices, the deportation of reservation children to boarding schools, and the imposition of autocratic political institutions became the hallmarks of the federal government's Indian policy following the Indian wars.

While scholars highlight the forms of autonomy available to reservation communities as well as the surprising methods of adaptation initiated by tribal leaders, such works nonetheless support the broader consensus regarding the oppressive nature of federal policy. Indeed, the dialectics of indigenous resistance in the face of external impositions characterize most studies of federal Indian policy from this era; the adaptive abilities of some tribal leaders and communities reinforce rather than undermine the relational aspects of the subject. As Thomas Biolsi and Jeffrey Ostler have shown, the growing institutional constraints used to subordinate Lakota Sioux autonomy across South Dakota's once massive Great Sioux Reservation undercut Lakota efforts to maintain social cohesion, while federal educational policies aimed at Indian children constituted, in David Wallace Adams's work, a program of "education for extinction," whose supporters, according to Andrea Smith, "advocated cultural rather than physical genocide."

Dozens of scholars have now analyzed how young Indian children adapted to such institutions of social engineering. K. Tsianina Lomawaima, Brenda Child, John Troutman, and Matthew Sakiestewa Gilbert highlight the forms of adaptation and agency deployed by Native children without losing sight of the challenging nature of being away from home. These recent works extend as well as modify the earlier insights of Robert Trennert and Prucha, who often focused more on those who developed Indian educational policies than on the creative adaptations required by Native students within boarding schools. In more recent studies, Indian dress patterns, musical and athletic programs, and intertribal romances form the basis for exploring the complexities of American Indian educational history.

From 1880 to 1930, federal policy makers debated various efforts aimed at assimilating American Indians, at times supporting the redistribution of reservation lands and the forced removal of Indian children from their families. American Indians not only resisted such assimilation efforts within their tribal communities, but also actively organized broader political associations aimed at reforming federal law. Often educated within boarding school environments, many critics became national spokespeople and reformers, and biographies of Sarah Winnemucca, Carlos Montezuma, and Henry Roe Cloud have helped to illuminate the political strategies developed by these reformers. Intertribal political associations, including the Society of American Indians founded in 1911 and California's Mission Indian Federation founded in 1919, have also been featured in recent works.

The Indian New Deal, Termination Era, and Contemporary Indian Sovereignty

The presence of hundreds of federally controlled Indian reservations presents incongruous counterpoints to broader and often celebratory narratives of twentieth-century American history, and only recently have scholars begun to link more fully American Indian experiences with the nation's modern history. Charles Wilkinson's *Blood Struggle: The Rise of Modern Indian Nations* provides an accessible, legally informed narrative of twentieth-century Indian history. Beginning in the Reservation Era, a period he terms "the Deadening Years," Wilkinson charts the slow but then explosive growth of tribal sovereignty efforts in the mid-twentieth century. Like all legal scholars, he remains deeply attuned to the changing dimensions of federal Indian affairs, particularly to the reforms initiated in the 1930s that are generally characterized as "the Indian New Deal." In this period, land allotment was formally ended and new educational and legal programs adopted, as culturally sensitive educational programs attempted to codify Indian languages and new legal structures were developed for most of the nation's Indian tribes. Championed by Bureau of Indian Affairs Commissioner John Collier and culminating in the Indian Reorganization Act of 1934, these statutes and legal codifications created new constitutional forms for many tribal governments.

As Wilkinson and biographers of Collier and his able Department of Interior solicitor Felix Cohen have highlighted, Indian New Deal reforms both moved unevenly and encountered resistance, not only from tribal communities long suspicious of promises from Washington, but also from congressional representatives uncomfortable with new government programs. After World War II, such senators and representatives reversed many New Deal efforts. In the process, they enacted what Wilkinson terms "the most extreme Indian program" in U.S. history, the 1953 Termination laws, a set of congressional statutes aimed at "terminating" the federal government's recognition of tribal communities, extending state jurisdiction over many Indian reservations, and federally subsidizing the one-way migration, or "relocation," of American Indians to urban areas for job-training and placement programs.

As Donald Fixico has emphasized in *Termination and Relocation*, the immediate results of Termination approached the catastrophic, as state governments lacked the requisite will and resources to take on reservation needs, while more than a hundred thousand reservation members took part in urbanization efforts, often exchanging reservation for urban poverty. Within such relocation centers, as Paul Chaat Smith and Robert Allen Warrior detail in *Like a Hurricane*, new forms of political activism developed among Indian youth, veterans, and activists, culminating in the rise of the American Indian Movement (AIM). Part of three dramatic sieges and occupations from 1969 to 1973 and led by a cadre of charismatic spokespeople, AIM became the contemporary face of Indian America for much of American society.

While iconic and the subject of multiple films and biographies, AIM's legacy, according to Wilkinson, overshadows the more transformative efforts of reservation leaders to reverse Termination and establish modern Indian nations. While influenced by AIM and earlier pan-Indian political associations, the struggle of Indian reservation leaders to ward off and eventually reverse Termination inaugurated the modern era of "self-determination." This era, codified in the mid-1970s, has continued to the present, and *Blood Struggle* synthesizes not only much of post–World War II Indian history but does so in the aftermath of the advent of Indian gaming, one of the most visible economic developments in American Indian history.

Unlike scholars like Wilkinson, few U.S. historians possess sufficient knowledge to explain the phenomenon of Indian gaming, which received congressional regulation in 1988 with the passage of the Indian Gaming and Regulatory Act (IGRA). Since federally recognized tribes possess sovereign rights and jurisdiction over their reservation lands, state authorities cannot prohibit tribal communities from initiating federally sanctioned enterprises, and many studies of contemporary Indian history contend with this recent, fast-moving development. Wilkinson's study, then, locates the rise of Indian gaming within the larger dynamics of Termination-era policies and finds the origins of gaming within the "self-determination," or sovereignty movement.

Barely two decades old, IGRA has led to powerful changes not only for select tribal communities but also in popular conceptions of American Indians. As Jessica Cattelino highlights in *High Stakes*, American Indian economic development often confounds larger societal perceptions of American Indians, perceptions often rooted in polarities and binaries regarding Indian "authenticity." Building upon Raibmon's *Authentic Indians* and Philip Deloria's *Indians in Unexpected Places*, Cattelino underscores how gaming has in fact enabled the Seminole Nation of Florida to more fully express aspects of their "traditional" culture. From housing to dress and from language revitalization to art, gaming has accelerated processes of cultural development. Such processes remain vexed not only by outside perceptions but also by internal challenges regarding resource allocations and ultimately cultural identity, as membership within many tribal communities has become an increasingly fraught process.

Given the recentness of such developments, few comprehensive histories have been written on "gaming tribes," but studies of American Indian museums and arts communities, as well as sociological analyses, have all identified the transformative effects catalyzed by gaming. For example, studies of the National Museum of the American Indian, which opened in 2004 on the National Mall in Washington, DC, analyze the powerful cultural and economic currents that emerged in the 1980s and 1990s that fostered the museum's development. Amy Lonetree and Amanda Cobb's edited volume, *The National Museum of the American Indian: Critical Conversations*, assesses the celebratory as well as contested nature of the museum's opening and exhibitions. Several essays trace the museum's initial difficulties with the Smithsonian Institution, which, like the Bureau of Indian Affairs, has often held tightly onto its proprietary role over the millions of ethnographic and artistic objects within its vast domain.

Conclusion

With a national museum located on the National Mall, with many gaming communities powering regional economies, and following the 2007 passage of the United Nations Declaration on the Rights of Indigenous Peoples, the first decade of the twenty-first century provides a stark contrast to its twentieth-century counterpart. Indeed, as Taiaike Alfred has suggested, despite the fact that "North American history from the Native perspective . . . is a tragedy with a continuing legacy of social pathology shadowing the existence of every Native person . . . there is a growing conviction among Native peoples that the Dark Ages are over. Some are even venturing to celebrate."

Contemporary American Indian historiography reflects such cautious optimism. The capacity of Native peoples to not only endure but also establish autonomous, self-governing spaces out of generations of subordination and impoverishment informs many studies in the field. The celebratory and once exclusive Anglocentric vision of U.S. history no longer holds, and many recent studies embrace broader comparative and transnational concerns rooted in less nationalistic historiographies. Winner of the 2010 Bancroft Prize, for example, Margaret Jacobs' *White Mother to a Dark Race* analyzes the gendered dynamics of the forced assimilation campaigns of American Indian and Australian Aboriginal children and highlights the congruence of numerous forms of shared historical experiences and oppression.

Once an afterthought within a broader intellectual horizon, American Indian history has emerged from the shadows of neglect and reclaimed a central place in the cannon of U.S. history. Future studies in the field will likely continue to expose the centrality of Native peoples to the establishment of American history as well as continue to highlight the distinctiveness of that lived experience.

BIBLIOGRAPHY

General Surveys, Anthologies, and Reference Works

Calloway, Colin G. *First Peoples: A Documentary Survey of American Indian History*, 3rd ed. Boston: Bedford/St. Martin's, 2008.

Deloria, Philip J., and Neal Salisbury, eds. *A Companion to American Indian History*. Malden, MA: Blackwell, 2002.

Hoxie, Frederick E., et al., eds. *American Nations: Encounters in Indian Country, 1850 to the Present*. New York: Routledge, 2001.

Jennings, Francis. *The Founders of America: From the Earliest Migrations to the Present*. New York: W. W. Norton, 1993.

Mancall, Peter C., and James H. Merrell. *American Encounters: Natives and Newcomers from European Contact to Indian Removal*, 2nd ed. New York: Routledge, 2007.

Oberg, Michael Leroy. *Native America: A History*. Malden, MA: Wiley-Blackwell, 2010.

Shoemaker, Nancy, ed. *Negotiators of Change: Historical Perspectives on Native American Women*. New York: Routledge, 1995.

Sturtevant, William C., ed. *Handbook of North American Indians*. Washington, DC: Smithsonian Institution Press, 1978–2008.

Thorton, Russell, ed. *Studying Native America: Problems and Prospects*. Madison: University of Wisconsin Press, 1998.

Trigger, Bruce G., and Wilcomb E. Wasburn, eds. *North America*. Vol. 1 of *The Cambridge History of the Native Peoples of the Americas*. New York: Cambridge University Press, 1996.

The American West and Spanish Borderlands

Anderson, Gary Clayton. *The Conquest of Texas: Ethnic Cleansing in the Promised Land, 1820–1875*. Norman: University of Oklahoma Press, 2005.

———. *The Indian Southwest: Ethnogenesis and Reinvention*. Norman: University of Oklahoma Press, 1999.

Barr, Julianna. *Peace Came in the Form of a Woman: Indians and Spaniards in the Texas Borderlands*. Chapel Hill: University of North Carolina Press, 2007.

Blackhawk, Ned. *Violence over the Land: Indians and Empires in the Early American West*. Cambridge, MA: Harvard University Press, 2006.

Bolton, Herbert E. *The Spanish Borderlands: A Chronicle of Old Florida and the Southwest*. New Haven, CT: Yale University Press, 1921.

Brooks, James F. *Captives and Cousins: Slavery, Kinship, and Community in the Southwest Borderlands*. Chapel Hill: University of North Carolina Press, 2002.

Calloway, Colin G. *One Vast Winter Count: The Native American West before Lewis and Clark*. Lincoln: University of Nebraska Press, 2003.

Delay, Brian. *War of a Thousand Deserts: Indian Raids and the U.S.-Mexican War*. New Haven, CT: Yale University Press, 2008.

Forbes, Jack D. *Apache, Navaho, and Spaniard*. Norman: University of Oklahoma Press, 1961.

———. *Warriors of the Colorado: The Yumas of the Quechan Nation and Their Neighbors*. Norman: University of Oklahoma Press, 1965.

Gutiérrez, Ramón A. *When Jesus Came the Corn Mothers Went Away: Marriage, Sexuality and Power in New Mexico, 1500–1846*. Palo Alto, CA: Stanford University Press, 1991.

Hackel, Steven W. *Children of Coyote, Missionaries of St. Francis: Indian-Spanish Relations in Colonial California, 1769–1850*. Chapel Hill: University of North Carolina Press, 2005.

Hall, Thomas D. *Social Change in the Southwest, 1350–1880*. Lawrence: University Press of Kansas, 1989.

Hämäläinen, Pekka. *The Comanche Empire*. New Haven, CT: Yale University Press, 2008.
Harmon, Alexandra. *Indians in the Making: Ethnic Relations and Indian Identities around Puget Sound*. Berkeley: University of California Press, 2000.
Harris, Cole. *Making Native Space: Colonialism, Resistance, and Reserves in British Columbia*. Vancouver: University of British Columbia Press, 2003.
———. *The Resettlement of British Columbia: Essays on Colonialism and Geographic Change*. Vancouver: University of British Columbia Press, 1997.
Hurtado, Albert. *Indian Survival on the California Frontier*. New Haven, CT: Yale University Press, 1988.
John, Elizabeth A. H. *Storms Brewed in Other Men's Worlds: The Confrontation of Indians, Spanish, and French in the Southwest, 1540–1795*. College Station: Texas A&M University Press, 1975.
Limerick, Patricia Nelson. *The Legacy of Conquest: The Unbroken Past of the American West*. New York: W. W. Norton, 1988.
Raibmon, Paige. *Authentic Indians: Episodes of Encounter from the Late-Nineteenth-Century Northwest Coast*. Durham, NC: Duke University Press, 2005.
Spicer, Edward H. *Cycles of Conquest: The Impact of Spain, Mexico, and the United States on the Indians of the Southwest, 1533–1960*. Tucson: University of Arizona Press, 1962.
Thrush, Coll. *Native Seattle: Histories from the Crossing-Over Place*. Seattle: University of Washington Press, 2007.
Turner, Frederick Jackson. *The Frontier in American History*. New York: Henry Holt, 1920.
Weber, David J. *The Mexican Frontier, 1821–1846*. Albuquerque: University of New Mexico Press, 1982.
———. *The Spanish Frontier in North America*. New Haven, CT: Yale University Press, 1992.
West, Elliot. *Contested Plains: Indians, Goldseekers, and the Rush to Colorado*. Lawrence: University Press of Kansas, 1998.
White, Richard. *"It's Your Misfortune and None of My Own": A New History of the American West*. Norman: University of Oklahoma Press, 1991.

Indians and Empires in Eastern North America

Anderson, Fred. *Crucible of War: The Seven Years' War and the Fate of Empire in British North America, 1754–1766*. New York: Knopf, 2000.
Axtell, James. *The European and the Indian: Essays in the Ethnohistory of Colonial North America*. New York: Oxford University Press, 1981.
Calloway, Colin G. *New Worlds for All: Indians, Europeans, and the Remaking of Early America*. Baltimore: Johns Hopkins University Press, 1997.
Cronon, William. *Changes in the Land: Indians, Colonists, and the Ecology of New England*. New York: Hill and Wang, 1983.
Demos, John. *The Unredeemed Captive: A Family Story from Early America*. New York: Knopf, 1994.
Dennis, Matthew. *Cultivating a Landscape of Peace: Iroquois-European Encounters in Seventeenth-Century America*. Ithaca, NY: Cornell University Press, 1993.
Dowd, Gregory Evans. *War under Heaven: Pontiac, the Indian Nations, and the British Empire*. Baltimore: Johns Hopkins University Press, 2002.

Duval, Kathleen. *The Native Ground: Indians and Colonists in the Heart of the Continent*. Philadelphia: University of Pennsylvania Press, 2006.

Ethridge, Robbie. *Creek Country: The Creek Indians and Their World*. Chapel Hill: University of North Carolina Press, 2003.

———. *From Chicaza to Chickasaw: The European Invasion and the Transformation of the Mississippian World, 1540–1715*. Chapel Hill: University of North Carolina Press, 2010.

Ethridge, Robbie, and Sheri M. Shuck-Hall, eds. *Mapping the Mississippian Shatter Zone: The Colonial Indian Slave Trade and Regional Instability in the American South*. Lincoln: University of Nebraska Press, 2009.

Gallay, Alan. *The Indian Slave Trade: The Rise of the English Empire in the American South, 1670–1717*. New Haven, CT: Yale University Press, 2002.

Greer, Allan. *Mohawk Saint: Catherine Tekakwitha and the Jesuits*. New York: Oxford University Press, 2004.

Jennings, Francis. *The Ambiguous Iroquois Empire: The Covenant Chain Confederation of Indian Tribes with English Colonies from Its Beginnings to the Lancaster Treaty of 1744*. New York: W. W. Norton, 1984.

Kupperman, Karen Ordahl. *Indians and English: Facing Off in Early America*. Ithaca, NY: Cornell University Press, 2000.

Lepore, Jill. *The Name of War: King Philip's War and the Origins of American Identity*. New York: Knopf, 1998.

Merrell, James. *The Indians' New World: Catawbas and Their Neighbors from European Contact through the Era of Removal*. Chapel Hill: University of North Carolina Press, 1989.

———. *Into the American Woods: Negotiators on the Pennsylvania Frontier*. New York: W. W. Norton, 1999.

Merritt, Jane. *At the Crossroads: Indians and Empires on a Mid-Atlantic Frontier, 1700–1763*. Chapel Hill: University of North Carolina Press, 2003.

Norton, Mary Beth. *In the Devil's Snare: The Salem Witchcraft Crisis of 1692*. New York: Knopf, 2002.

O'Brien, Jean M. *Dispossession by Degree: Indian Land and Identity in Natick, Massachusetts, 1650–1790*. New York: Cambridge University Press, 1997.

Richter, Daniel K. *Facing East from Indian Country: A Native History of Early America*. Cambridge, MA: Harvard University Press, 2001.

———. *The Ordeal of the Longhouse: The Peoples of the Iroquois League in the Era of European Colonization*. Chapel Hill: University of North Carolina Press, 1992.

Salisbury, Neal. *Manitou and Providence: Indians, Europeans, and the Making of New England, 1500–1643*. New York: Oxford University Press, 1982.

Saunt, Claudio. *A New Order of Things: Property, Power, and the Transformation of the Creek Indians, 1733–1816*. New York: Cambridge University Press, 1999.

Silver, Peter. *Our Savage Neighbors: How Indian War Transformed Early America*. New York: W. W. Norton, 2008.

Taylor, Alan. *American Colonies: The Settling of North America*. New York: Viking-Penguin, 2001.

———. *The Divided Ground: Indians, Settlers, and the Northern Borderland of the American Revolution*. New York: Knopf, 2006.

Trigger, Bruce G. *Natives and Newcomers: Canada's "Heroic Age" Reconsidered*. Montreal: McGill-Queen's University Press, 1985.

White, Richard. *The Middle Ground: Indians, Empires, and Republics in the Great Lakes Region, 1650–1815*. New York: Cambridge University Press, 1991.

Wood, Peter H., et al., eds. *Powhatan's Mantle: Indians in the Colonial South*, 2nd and rev. eds. Lincoln: University of Nebraska Press, 2006.

The U.S. Constitution, Indian Removal, and America's Many Indian Wars

Banner, Stuart. *How the Indians Lost Their Land: Law and Power on the Frontier*. Cambridge, MA: Harvard University Press, 2005.

Bowes, John P. *Exiles and Pioneers: Eastern Indians in the Trans-Mississippi West*. New York: Cambridge University Press, 2007.

Brown, Dee. *Bury My Heart at Wounded Knee: An Indian History of the American West*. New York: Holt, Reinhart and Winston, 1970.

Calloway, Colin G. *The American Revolution in Indian Country: Crisis and Diversity in Native American Communities*. New York: Cambridge University Press, 1995.

Clark, C. Blue. *Lone Wolf v. Hitchcock: Treaty Rights and Indian Law at the End of the Nineteenth Century*. Lincoln: University of Nebraska Press, 1994.

Cohen, Felix S. *Handbook of Federal Indian Law with Reference Tables and Index*. Washington, DC: U.S. Government Printing Office, 1942.

Dowd, Gregory Evans. *A Spirited Resistance: The North American Indian Struggle for Unity, 1745–1815*. Baltimore: Johns Hopkins University Press, 1992.

Drinnon, Richard. *Facing West: The Metaphysics of Indian-Hating and Empire-Building*. Minneapolis: University of Minnesota Press, 1980.

Edmunds, R. David. *The Shawnee Prophet*. Lincoln: University of Nebraska Press, 1983.

Ford, Lisa. *Settler Sovereignty: Jurisdiction and Indigenous People in America and Australia, 1788–1836*. Cambridge, MA: Harvard University Press, 2010.

Green, Michael D. *The Politics of Indian Removal: Creek Government and Society in Crisis*. Lincoln: University of Nebraska Press, 1982.

Harring, Sidney. *Crow Dog's Case: American Indian Sovereignty, Tribal Law, and United States Law in the Nineteenth Century*. New York: Cambridge University Press, 1994.

Holton, Woody. *Forced Founders: Indians, Debtors, Slaves, and the Making of the American Revolution in Virginia*. Chapel Hill: University of North Carolina Press, 1999.

Horsman, Reginald. *Expansion and American Indian Policy, 1783–1812*. East Lansing: Michigan State University Press, 1967.

Hoxie, Frederick E., et al., eds. *Native Americans and the Early Republic*. Charlottesville: University of Virginia Press, 1999.

Irons, Peter. *A People's History of the U.S. Supreme Court*. New York: Penguin, 1999.

Jacoby, Karl. *Shadows at Dawn: A Borderlands Massacre and the Violence of History*. New York: Penguin Press, 2008.

Josephy, Alvin M. *The Civil War in the American West*. New York: Knopf, 1991.

Kaplan, Amy. *The Anarchy of Empire in the Making of U.S. Culture*. Cambridge, MA: Harvard University Press, 2002.

Konkle, Maureen. *Writing Indian Nations: Native Intellectuals and the Politics of Historiography, 1827–1863*. Chapel Hill: University of North Carolina Press, 2004.

McMillen, Christian W. *Making Indian Law: The Hualapai Land Case and the Birth of Ethnohistory*. New Haven, CT: Yale University Press, 2007.

Miles, Tiya. *Ties That Bind: The Story of an Afro-Cherokee Family in Slavery and Freedom*. Berkeley: University of California Press, 2005.

Nash, Gary B. *Race and Revolution*. Madison, WI: Madison House, 1990.

Ostler, Jeffrey. *The Plains Sioux and U.S. Colonialism from Lewis and Clark to Wounded Knee*. New York: Cambridge University Press, 2004.

Perdue, Theda. *Cherokee Women: Gender and Culture Change, 1700–1835*. Lincoln: University of Nebraska Press, 1998.

Prucha, Francis Paul. *The Great Father: The United States Government and the American Indians*, 2 vols. Lincoln: University of Nebraska Press, 1984.

Reid, John Phillip. *A Law of Blood: The Primitive Law of the Cherokee Nation*. New York: New York University Press, 1970.

Robertson, Lindsay G. *Conquest by Law: How the Discovery of America Dispossessed Indigenous Peoples of Their Lands*. New York: Oxford University Press, 2005.

Rothman, Adam. *Slave Country: American Expansion and the Origins of the Deep South*. Cambridge, MA: Harvard University Press, 2005.

Satz, Ronald N. *American Indian Policy in the Jacksonian Era*. Norman: University of Oklahoma Press, 2002.

Silva, Noenoe K. *Aloha Betrayed: Native Hawaiian Resistance to U.S. Colonialism*. Durham, NC: Duke University Press, 2004.

Stephanson, Anders. *Manifest Destiny: American Expansion and the Empire of Right*. New York: Hill and Wang, 1995.

Utley, Robert M. *The Indian Frontier of the American West, 1846–1890*. Albuquerque: University of New Mexico Press, 1984.

Wallace, Anthony. *The Death and Rebirth of the Seneca*. New York: Knopf, 1972.

———. *Jefferson and the Indians: The Tragic Fate of the First Americans*. Cambridge, MA: Harvard University Press, 1999.

———. *The Long, Bitter Trail: Andrew Jackson and the Indians*. New York: Hill and Wang, 1993.

Whaley, Gray H. *Oregon and the Collapse of Illahee: U.S. Empire and the Transformation of an Indigenous World, 1792–1859*. Chapel Hill: University of North Carolina Press, 2010.

Wilkins, David E., and K. Tsianina Lomawaima. *Uneven Ground: American Indian Sovereignty and Federal Law*. Norman: University of Oklahoma Press, 2001.

Wishart, David J. *An Unspeakable Sadness: The Dispossession of the Nebraska Indians*. Lincoln: University of Nebraska Press, 1994.

Wunder, John R. *"Retained by the People": A History of American Indians and the Bill of Rights*. New York: Oxford University Press, 1994.

The Reservation Era and the Campaigns of Assimilation

Adams, David Wallace. *Education for Extinction: American Indians and the Boarding School Experience, 1875–1928*. Lawrence: University Press of Kansas, 1995.

Bauer, William J. *We Were All Like Migrant Workers Here: Work, Community, and Memory on California's Round Valley Reservation, 1850–1941*. Chapel Hill: University of North Carolina Press, 2009.

Berkhofer, Robert F., Jr. *The White Man's Indian: Images of the American Indian from Columbus to the Present*. New York: Knopf, 1978.

Biolsi, Thomas. *Deadliest Enemies: Law and the Making of Race Relations on and off Rosebud Reservation.* Berkeley: University of California Press, 2001.

Burton, Jeffrey. *Indian Territory and the United States, 1866–1906: Courts, Government, and the Movement for Oklahoma Statehood.* Norman: University of Oklahoma Press, 1995.

Chang, David A. *The Color of the Land: Race, Nation, and the Politics of Landownership in Oklahoma, 1832–1929.* Chapel Hill: University of North Carolina Press, 2010.

Child, Brenda J. *Boarding School Seasons: American Indian Families, 1900–1945.* Lincoln: University of Nebraska Press, 1998.

Crum, Steven J. "Henry Roe Cloud, a Winnebago Indian Reformer: His Quest for American Indian Higher Education." *Kansas History: A Journal of the Central Plains* 11 (Autumn 1988): 171–184.

Deloria, Philip J. *Indians in Unexpected Places.* Lawrence: University Press of Kansas, 2004.

———. *Playing Indian.* New Haven, CT: Yale University Press, 1998.

Fowler, Loretta. *Arapahoe Politics, 1851–1978: Symbols in Crises of Authority.* Lincoln: University of Nebraska Press, 1982.

Gilbert, Matthew Sakiestewa. "Hopi Footraces and American Marathons, 1912–1930." *American Quarterly* 62 (March 2010): 77–101.

Hoxie, Frederick E. *A Final Promise: The Campaign to Assimilate the Indians, 1880–1920.* New York: Cambridge University Press, 1984.

———. *Parading through History: The Making of the Crow Nation in America, 1805–1935.* New York: Cambridge University Press, 1995.

Iverson, Peter. *Carlos Montezuma and the Changing World of the American Indian.* Albuquerque: University of New Mexico Press, 1982.

Jacobs, Margaret D. *White Mother to a Dark Race: Settler Colonialism, Maternalism, and the Removal of Indigneous Children in the American West and Australia, 1880–1940.* Lincoln: University of Nebraska Press, 2009.

Lewis, David Rich. *Neither Wolf nor Dog: American Indians, Environment, and Agrarian Change.* New York: Oxford University Press, 1994.

Lomawaima, K. Tsianina. *They Called It Prairie Light: The Story of the Chilocco Indian School.* Lincoln: University of Nebraska Press, 1994.

Lowery, Melinda Maynor. *Lumbee Indians in the Jim Crow South: Race, Identity, and the Making of a Nation.* Chapel Hill: University of North Carolina Press, 2010.

Meyer, Melissa. *The White Earth Tragedy: Ethnicity and Dispossession at a Minnesota Anishinaabe Reservation.* Lincoln: University of Nebraska Press, 1994.

Miner, Craig H. *The Corporation and the Indian: Tribal Sovereignty and Industrial Civilization in Indian Territory, 1865–1907.* Columbia: University of Missouri Press, 1976.

Prucha, Francis Paul. *American Indian Policy in Crisis: Christian Reformers and the Indian, 1865–1900.* Norman: University of Oklahoma Press, 1976.

Shepherd, Jeffrey P. *We Are an Indian Nation: A History of the Hualapai People.* Tucson: University of Arizona Press, 2010.

Smith, Andrea. *Conquest: Sexual Violence and American Indian Genocide.* Boston: South End Press, 2005.

Trennert, Robert A. *The Phoenix Indian School: Forced Assimilation in Arizona, 1891–1935.* Norman: University of Oklahoma Press, 1988.

Troutman, John W. *Indian Blues: American Indians and the Politics of Music, 1879–1934.* Norman: University of Oklahoma Press, 2009.

Warren, Kim Cary. *The Quest for Citizenship: African American and Native American Education in Kansas, 1880–1935*. Chapel Hill: University of North Carolina Press, 2010.

Zanjani, Sally. *Sara Winnemucca*. Lincoln: University of Nebraska Press, 2001.

The Indian New Deal, Termination Era, and Contemporary Indian Sovereignty

Alfred, Gerald R. (now Taiaike Alfred). *Heeding the Voices of Our Ancestors: Kahnawake Mohawk Politics and the Rise of Native Nationalism*. New York: Oxford University Press, 1995.

Biolsi, Thomas. *Organizing the Lakota: The Political Economy of the New Deal on Pine Ridge and Rosebud Reservations*. Tucson: University of Arizona Press, 1992.

Cattelino, Jessica R. *High Stakes: Florida Seminole Gaming and Sovereignty*. Durham, NC: Duke University Press, 2008.

Cornell, Stephen. *The Return of the Native: American Indian Political Resurgence*. New York: Oxford University Press, 1988.

Deloria, Vine, Jr., and Clifford Lytle. *The Nations Within: The Past and Future of American Indian Sovereignty*. New York: Pantheon, 1984.

Fixico, Donald L. *Termination and Relocation: Federal Indian Policy, 1945–1960*. Albuquerque: University of New Mexico Press, 1986.

Frank, Gelya, and Carol Goldberg. *Defying the Odds: The Tule River Tribe's Struggle for Sovereignty in Three Centuries*. New Haven, CT: Yale University Press, 2010.

Kelly, Lawrence C. *The Assault on Assimilation: John Collier and the Origins of Indian Policy Reform*. Albuquerque: University of New Mexico Press, 1983.

Lonetree, Amy, and Amanda J. Cobb, eds. *The National Museum of the American Indian: Critical Conversations*. Lincoln: University of Nebraska Press, 2008.

Mitchell, Dalia Tsuk. *Architect of Justice: Felix S. Cohen and the Founding of American Legal Pluralism*. Ithaca, NY: Cornell University Press, 2007.

Nagel, Joane. *American Indian Ethnic Renewal: Red Power and the Resurgence of Identity and Culture*. New York: Oxford University Press, 1997.

Nesper, Larry. *The Walleye War: The Struggle for Ojibwe Spearfishing and Treaty Rights*. Lincoln: University of Nebraska Press, 2002.

Smith, Paul Chaat, and Robert Allen Warrior. *Like a Hurricane: The Indian Movement from Alcatraz to Wounded Knee*. New York: New Press, 1996.

Wilkinson, Charles F. *American Indians, Time, and the Law: Native Societies in a Modern Constitutional Democracy*. New Haven, CT: Yale University Press, 1987.

———. *Blood Struggle: The Rise of Modern Indian Nations*. New York: W. W. Norton, 2005.

———. *Messages from Frank's Landing: A Story of Salmon, Treaties, and the American Indian Way*. Seattle: University of Washington Press, 2000.

18

African-American History

KEVIN GAINES

Academic historians have no monopoly on the production of historical narratives. Historians engage in lively public debates about the meaning of the past with many actors, including journalists, politicians, political and religious leaders, and members of civic associations. History is, thus, produced in a set of overlapping sites, including those outside of academia. History is also, as Michel-Rolph Trouillot observed, laden with silences. Academic historians and others with a stake in the matter are often selective in their interests, and not immune to blind spots.

Such overlapping sites of production and silences have shaped the field of African-American history. In its formative period, the history of African Americans was written against the silences, evasions and propaganda of a U.S. historical profession that, until the mid-twentieth century, was dominated by those who had little regard for the humanity of blacks. Early historians of the African-American experience, including W.E.B. Du Bois, Carter G. Woodson, and Benjamin Quarles, confronted either negative depictions of black people or their outright erasure from narratives about the American past. Excluded from the white-dominated academy, these historians recorded the integral contributions of African Americans to the development of constitutional freedom and democracy in the United States. Gaining a doctorate in history at Harvard in 1912, Woodson, the son of former slaves, assumed the vital task of building an infrastructure and audience for African-American history, founding the Association for the Study of Negro Life and History in 1915 and the *Journal of Negro History* the following year, as well as a publishing company. In 1926, Woodson founded Negro History Week, initially celebrated during February, now expanded to the entire month. "Negro history," as promoted by Woodson and others, and taught almost exclusively in black schools and colleges, had a dual character as both a public and academic endeavor, taking aim at racial prejudice in American society and the historical profession. The efforts of Woodson and countless others have paid off today, in the transformative impact of African-American history on the writing of U.S. history and through the field's strong global presence within college and university curricula.

The past is always with us, though we often fail to notice. Occasionally it resurfaces, tangibly. In 1991, construction work uncovered the graves of 427 enslaved Africans at the site of a planned 34-story federal office building in Lower Manhattan. The graves were just a portion of what has become known as the African burial ground, a graveyard of approximately 10,000 to 20,000 people paved over as the city expanded northward.

Forensic archaeologists' examination of the skeletal remains suggests the physical suffering of the slaves. In many of the adult skeletons, hollow lesions in the legs, arms, and shoulders offer mute testimony that in life the strain of hard labor severed ligaments and muscle from bone. As Brent Staples wrote in the *New York Times*, "The brutality etched on these skeletons easily matches the worst of what we know of slavery in the South."

Another recent encounter with the past involves the amateur Historian in Chief, Barack Obama, who in July 2009, during a state visit to Ghana, visited the Cape Coast Castle, a massive seaside fortress that served as the seat of Britain's Gold Coast colony and a major transit point for the Atlantic slave trade. Extensive media coverage of the visit of the first African-American president to a major slave-trading fort brought worldwide attention to a place and a history invisible to many Americans. Obama acknowledged the "evil" of the trade, and the tragically double-edged meaning of the place for African Americans, who, like many Caribbean and Latin American people of African descent (but not Obama himself), can trace their origins to places like Cape Coast Castle.

These two events were emblematic of the development of the field of African-American history since the 1990s. Studies of the slave trade and of slavery in the Northern colonies and states have addressed silences in the historical record and in public awareness. These works present U.S. slavery, North and South, as a global system of market relations integral to the development of the American nation-state. Recent scholarship on slavery is noteworthy for its shift away from a prior emphasis on the autonomy of slave culture and on slave "agency" in favor of an emphasis on exploitation and its consequences, including psychological ones, analyzing the impact of slavery's market-driven commodification on the lives of its victims and enslavers alike.

Amid growing public awareness of the foundational significance of Africa and the slave trade, historians have extended their gaze beyond U.S. boundaries, making the African diaspora the key unit of analysis. Moreover, just as the history of slavery in colonial New York disrupts the idea of slavery as a uniquely southern institution, historians of the civil rights movement have expanded their attention to black struggles for equality in the North, as well as those in the South. In this chapter, I will offer an overview of three main periods that reflect significant developments in the writing of African-American history over roughly the last twenty years: slavery and the slave trade; the era of segregation, in both the North and South; and "the long civil rights movement."

Slavery

Slavery was the source of unrivaled political and economic power in the antebellum United States. On the eve of the Civil War, the economic value of slaves in the United States was $3 billion in 1860 currency, a sum that exceeded the combined value of all the factories, railroads, and banks in the country. Members of the merchant and political class in New York City were actively involved in the domestic slave trade, and gleaned profits from the cotton trade as well. Not surprisingly, staunch defenders of the institution could be found among their ranks. According to an 1852 report to Congress, the maritime shipment of the cotton crop was a vast enterprise, with 1.1 million tons of American-bound shipping to eastern and southern gulf ports, employing upward of 55,000 American maritime workers.

An appreciation of the vast profitability of the domestic slave trade and slave-produced cotton is essential for students of U.S. history. But there is another dimension of this history. Inspired by the historian Nell Painter's call for a "fully loaded cost accounting" of slavery, scholars have assessed the psychological toll of slavery's physical and sexual abuse on its victims. Painter challenged historians to ponder slavery's impact as a defining feature of American society, politics, and nation building, past and present. Recent scholars have answered the call by foregrounding the subjectivity and actions of the enslaved, and the impact of slavery's routine violence on its victims, on slave owners, and on American society. They have interrogated the conditions of life within a system of domination that Orlando Patterson has termed "social death."

This scholarship shows how far the field has come since the late 1960s. Then, almost without exception, male historians studied male slaves. And the question of that generic male slave's personality loomed large, as historians shied away from issues of political economy raised by Eric Williams in *Capitalism and Slavery* (1944). Stanley Elkins set the terms of debate in 1959, when, in describing the crippling impact of slavery, he portrayed slaves as too traumatized to resist their lot. Elkins's view of the slaves' childlike, compliant personality was based on studies of the inmates of Nazi concentration camps. To be sure, Elkins's account of the brutality of slavery and its traumatized victims countered enduring myths of the plantation legend that portrayed slavery as a benevolent institution. At that time, by a similar logic of paternalism, segregationists parried rising demands for equality by asserting that Jim Crow society bestowed upon African Americans a higher standard of living than most of the world's peoples. The damage-victimization thesis invoked by Elkins and others was subjected to critical analysis by Daryl Michael Scott's study *Contempt and Pity* (1997), but in Elkins's time the idea of blacks damaged by racial segregation was a staple of liberal demands for civil rights and was endorsed by black and white scholars alike. No less than E. Franklin Frazier and Howard Zinn lauded Elkins's account of the crippling impact of the "closed system" of plantation slavery on the personality of the slaves.

The most influential challenge to Elkins came from Sterling Stuckey's 1968 essay "Through the Prism of Folklore: The Black Ethos in Slavery." Stuckey's essay called for more rigorous investigation of African-American culture as a site of resistance. Stuckey's subsequent work on the salience of the African past for the study of African-American history and culture helped inspire among scholars of slavery an increased emphasis on the African diaspora as the central unit of analysis. Over the past twenty years, Michael A. Gomez, Dylan Penningroth, Sharla Fett, Stephanie Smallwood, and others explored the West African social and cultural roots of the Afro-American experience of slavery.

Rejecting Elkins's thesis of slave docility, such scholars as John Blassingame, Herbert Gutman, Stuckey and others emphasized the survival of family, community and autonomous cultural identities, and practices of resistance. But claims of community strength and resistance, and an emphasis on Africanity, while important in their time, deferred consideration of slavery as a sociopolitical and legal system with gender as a defining feature of its power relationships. The pioneering work of Deborah Gray White and subsequent studies of slavery informed by women's and gender history, including the work of Stephanie Camp, Thavolia Glymph, and Stephanie McCurry, have deepened our understanding of resistance, moving away from the limited, all-or-nothing, male-centered image of slave revolts at the heart of the dispute between Elkins, on one side, and his critics, on the other.

Jennifer Morgan has been especially influential in employing gender analysis to complicate issues of resistance. In *Laboring Women*, Morgan writes of the intolerable burden of enslaved women forced to bear children in addition to the agricultural labor they performed. Slave owners in the colonial Bahamas referred to their female slaves as "increasors." Besides physical and sexual abuse, these women endured the constant threat of separation from their offspring through sale. Morgan warns us of the difficulty of defining resistance in this degrading situation rife with contradictions. Enslaved women enriched their captors while at the same time playing a vital role in creating the communities that would foster a complex dynamic of opposition to and compliance with racial slavery. Under such abject conditions, the meanings enslaved women might ascribe to their fertility or infertility defy generalization. Morgan cautions historians against imposing modern assumptions about resistance or motherhood in assessing the behavior of enslaved women.

While historians have written extensively about the slaves' culture and resistance, some have focused their attention on the slave trade. Since the publication of Philip Curtin's classic study *The Atlantic Slave Trade*, historians have debated estimates of the number of Africans caught up in this forced mass migration. In *Saltwater Slavery*, Stephanie Smallwood goes beyond this quantitative approach by focusing on the experience of the captives. Inventively mining the records of the Royal African Company, Smallwood follows the captives from enslavement on the Gold Coast in Africa and detention in the dungeons of Cape Coast and Elmina to the crossing of the ocean in the so-called Middle Passage and, finally, to sale in the British colonies of the Americas. Smallwood describes how the Atlantic slave trade and forced migration across the water transformed people into commodities. Smallwood not only attends to the subjectivity and actions of enslaved Africans, but also seeks to understand the traders themselves, along with the world that produced them. Smallwood demonstrates how African captives made meaning of the terror, death, and suffering that underwrote the destruction of the bonds of community and kinship, in sum, their social annihilation. In so doing, she succeeds in bringing the captives aboard slave ships to life as subjects of American social history.

Focusing on a different site of commodification, the antebellum slave market, Walter Johnson examines the internal slave trade in his influential work *Soul by Soul*. Johnson lays bare the dehumanizing market logic of slavery and the racial and ideological assumptions, transmogrified into notions of value and worthlessness, that underlay its mundane transactions. He writes vividly of the moral, spiritual, and physical annihilation of the bodies and souls of the enslaved that took place in the slave pen. The negotiations between traders and buyers and the inspections of the bodies of the enslaved enacted racial theories positing the disobedience of slaves as evidence of biological depravity and reinforcing invidious distinctions between blackness and whiteness. Johnson, like Morgan, writes of the limits of notions of agency and resistance for those subject to the violent logic of the slave market. Johnson nevertheless shows the slaves as thinking, even calculating, beings, who sought to gain whatever leverage they could, attempting to manipulate the decisions of buyers and sellers to their potential advantage.

In addition to work that reads the records of slave traders and planters against the grain to recover the experience of those reduced to property by the market relations of slavery, recent studies have expanded our understanding of the scope of the institution. Tiya Miles's groundbreaking *Ties That Bind*, a study of an Afro-Cherokee family shaped by antebellum slaveholding among Native Americans, challenges popular assumptions about race, exploitation, and community. Writing the largely untold history of black slaves in Cherokee country, Miles pieces together the story of Doll, the African-American concubine of the Cherokee war hero Shoe Boots. Mobilizing secondary literature on the sexual oppression of enslaved women, Miles writes with sensitivity about Doll's likely feelings regarding the narrow range of choices she faced as Shoe Boots's slave and mother of his children.

Miles's study locates the genesis of present-day conflict between the Cherokee nation and Afro-Cherokees in the nineteenth-century trauma of removal from Georgia. The forced separation from Cherokee ancestral lands destroyed a shared past of personal and communal ties between native and black Cherokees. Miles foregrounds the "psychological and spiritual reverberations" of Indian removal. She contends that it "was more than the relocation of bodies and possessions. It was the tearing of the flesh of the people from the same flesh of the land, a rupture of soul and spirit. . . . [R]emoval created a legacy of detachment between Cherokees and blacks that would lessen potential for cross-racial alliances and narrow the possibility of subverting racial hierarchies."

Annette Gordon-Reed provides still another rich portrait of enslaved women's experience in her magisterial work the *Hemingses of Monticello: An American Family*, the definitive history of the Hemings family *and* the family of Thomas Jefferson, whose blood ties to the Hemingses belie the racial fiction of separateness. Making a powerful case for Hemings's historical importance, Gordon-Reed ultimately provides an account of American slavery worthy of Painter's injunction to study the inner lives of the enslaved, in Gordon-Reed's words, "to see slavery through the eyes of the enslaved." At the same time, Gordon-Reed's study of the Hemings family breaks with Patterson's view of slavery as social death, a view which, while theoretically compelling, is also challenged by Penningroth's study of property ownership among slaves and Fett's book on slave healing practices, both of which suggest that the lives of slaves were defined by creativity and resiliency as much as social and spiritual annihilation. It does not mitigate the horror of slavery to write, as Gordon-Reed does, "That the Hemingses were enslaved did not render them incapable of knowing who they were, of knowing their mothers, fathers, sisters and brothers. Slavery did not destroy their ability to observe, remember and reason."

Gordon-Reed's chapters on the genesis of the relationship between Sally Hemings, a girl of sixteen, and the widowed Jefferson, thirty years her senior, while the latter was on a diplomatic mission in France, are a tour de force. Seeking to unlock the "mystery" of what transpired between them from the record of Jefferson and Hemings's five years in Paris, Gordon-Reed mines numerous sources, including the vast biographical record of Jefferson's actions and temperament, the historiography of courtship and marriage in early America (whose legal status and protections were unavailable to Hemings), and the reminiscences of Madison Hemings, the son of Jefferson and Hemings.

The work of Leslie Harris, Joanne Melish, and others reminds us that slavery, though largely domestic in the North, was hereditary and permanent. As Melish shows for New England and Harris for New York City, the racial and gendered hierarchies at the core of the system survived its abolition in northern states, constraining the lives of emancipated and free blacks. As a buffer against this stark prejudice and discrimination, free blacks in the antebellum North and many areas of the South developed vibrant communities of their own, replete with churches, schools, and mutual aid institutions. By 1830, America's free black population had grown to almost a quarter of a million. Roy E. Finkenbine and Richard S. Newman have written of the outspoken leadership of "black founders" of the early republic, who condemned slavery and the exclusion of blacks from northern white churches, schools, and civic organizations, laying a solid foundation for the abolitionist and civil rights movements of the nineteenth and twentieth centuries. As the work of Julius Scott and Maurice Jackson has shown, the Haitian Revolution loomed large in the political imagination of these "black founders," enslaved and free persons throughout the Atlantic world, and less renowned African-American seamen.

After Slavery: African-American Political Behavior in the Era of Segregation

As W.E.B. Du Bois wrote of emancipation and Reconstruction in 1935, "The slave went free, stood a brief moment in the sun, then moved back again towards slavery. The whole weight of America was thrown to color caste." Reconstruction revolutionized the South's and the nation's politics, outlawing slavery and enfranchising black male citizens. Black men were elected to office in substantial numbers, serving in Congress, state legislatures, and municipal governments throughout the South. African-American elected officials, in tandem with white Republicans, redefined the scope of government for the South and the entire nation, enacting a broader vision of freedom. Reconstruction state governments throughout the South supported free public education and universal male suffrage, outlawed racial discrimination, and expanded the public infrastructure.

But the defeated slave owners and their political representatives waged incessant war against Reconstruction governments and the voting rights of blacks. With the withdrawal of federal troops from the South in 1877, antiblack violence escalated in the region. Blacks were deprived of the suffrage and barred from juries, police forces, and electoral offices. Silences and willful acts of forgetting continue to define the violent legacy of post-Reconstruction. In recent years, some states have conducted official investigations into atrocities of the era of segregation and disfranchisement, seeking some measure of civic healing. In 2006, the 1898 Wilmington Riot Commission appointed by the state of North Carolina concluded that the overthrow of Wilmington's Republican interracial "fusion" government was an insurrection planned for months by white supremacists. Following a spate of inflammatory newspaper articles demonizing black political power as a threat to white womanhood, an unknown number of blacks were killed in broad daylight, in the words of the report, as "part of a state-wide effort to put white supremacist Democrat[ic Party members] in office and stem the political advances of black citizens." After the violence, white Democrats enacted laws that disfranchised blacks until the Voting Rights Act of 1965. Noting the continuing debate over voting rights in Congress and the courts, the state archivist who helped research the report noted, "More than a hundred years later, we're still trying to resolve the issues."

Investigative commissions on events like the Wilmington massacre are much-needed attempts to educate the public. It is also true that African Americans were not simply the passive victims of the post-Reconstruction onslaught against their political and civil rights, a period termed "the Nadir" by historian Rayford Logan. Following Logan, scholars often centered their accounts on the rise of segregation, the coerced labor of the sharecropping system, disfranchisement, and lynching. Sexual violence against women, neglected until recently, has been studied by Darlene Clark Hine, Hannah Rosen, and Crystal Feimster. If works on slavery have moved from highlighting agency to a recent concern with exploitation, since the late 1990s the trend seems to have gone in the opposite direction for historians of the era of segregation. Their earlier narratives of antiblack oppression have given way to accounts of agency, resistance, grassroots organization, and mass activism.

Over the last three decades, historians have grappled with the problem of defining the political behavior of African Americans reduced to statelessness by the systematic repeal of their civil and political rights. Shane and Graham White have explored the bodily displays and comportment of African Americans in urban public spaces as acts of individual and collective transgression of white expectations of deference under slavery and Jim Crow. "From Reconstruction through the early decades of the twentieth century," they write, "African-American parades became an established feature of the southern urban landscape," with a plethora of black civic associations staging processions on Emancipation Day and the Fourth of July, using these occasions to express a sense of unity and pride. But such manifestations were impossible for African Americans in besieged rural areas. Under such dire conditions, migration to southern cities, and later, to the relative freedom of the urban North during World War I, constituted the most viable means of escape from poverty and the constant threat of violence through lynching and rape.

Nell Painter's *Exodusters*, a study of the mass migration of some five to seven thousand blacks from the Louisiana and Mississippi Delta to Kansas in 1879, enriched our understanding of the political behavior of poor and working African-American people. The immediate causes of the Kansas Exodus were chronic poverty and a surge of political violence against rural blacks in Louisiana. But the Exodus also reflected the freedpeople's enduring aspirations for economic independence and freedom from white dominance. Painter's study highlighted the importance of emigration and an African diaspora perspective, along with the black folk religion derived from the Old Testament Exodus story, for blacks in the rural South. The initial destination of the migrants had been Liberia, which soon proved beyond their resources.

For impoverished African Americans, migration—voting with one's feet—was their strongest collective protest against exploitation and terror. The journalist and antilynching activist Ida B. Wells understood this fact when she convinced many blacks in Memphis to punish white civic and business leaders who condoned lynching by leaving the city, taking with them their labor and purchasing power. Equally aware of the stakes for employers, Booker T. Washington rejected migration, famously urging the southern black masses in 1895 to "cast down your bucket where you are." Painter contrasts grassroots black leaders such as Henry Adams and Joseph "Pap" Singleton, both of whom supported the Exodus, with Frederick Douglass and less renowned "representative colored men" who implored would-be migrants to stand their ground against rampant political terror, lest the depletion of their numbers erode the strength of the Republican Party.

Painter's study, along with subsequent scholarship on the era of Jim Crow segregation, brought into focus an indigenous black politics as a defining feature of African-American life. In much of this work, the class dynamics of African-American leadership and politics are a central concern. All told, recent scholarship on the Nadir points to a varied repertoire of African-American political activism, both within and outside the formal domains of party, electoral, and trade union politics, and reflecting assertions of economic and cultural citizenship that were often inseparable from the quest for political and civil rights.

A Nation under Our Feet, Steven Hahn's study of the grassroots thought and politics of southern African Americans from Emancipation to the Great Migration to the North during World War I, builds on Painter's work and Robin D. G. Kelley's study of African-American Communists in Alabama during the 1930s. For Hahn, emancipation and aspirations for economic independence and the redistributive justice of "forty acres and a mule" were integral to African-American politics over generations. Labor concerns were at the core of black aspirations, nurtured despite the constant threat of white violence within a vibrant black civil society. During the late 1880s and 1890s, after the violent ouster of Reconstruction and fusion interracial coalitions, populist and labor challenges to white landowners reached a crescendo throughout the region. Excluded from white agrarian organizations, African Americans organized Colored Farmer's Alliance locals all over the Deep South. The Knights of Labor, which recruited blacks, spread from such cities as Richmond, Raleigh, Birmingham, and Little Rock to nearly two thousand local assemblies in small towns, more than two-thirds in rural counties in the former Confederacy. These organizations "appear to have tapped and fed on an institutional infrastructure of benevolent, church, and political associations commonly known to African Americans as 'secret societies,' which had been developing in the countryside for years." Secrecy was essential, as landowners and authorities organized white militias and "regulators" with the aim of intimidating black labor insurgencies and their leaders into submission.

Undaunted, African Americans demanded justice at public assemblies, with black women often playing prominent roles. The assault on black electoral politics and labor insurgency led to the rise of separate black neighborhoods and enclaves and the rise of an extensive black civil society, with scores of benevolent societies, schools, churches, and associations, and an explosion of black newspapers in cities and towns across the South. "It may well have been," writes Hahn, "that the exclusion of black men from the official arenas of politics in the 1890s and early 1900s" helped give "new voice and authority . . . to black women who, for years had been actively involved in community mobilizations through churches, schools, charitable organizations, and auxillaries, not to mention Union Leagues, Republican Parties, and benevolent societies."

The prominence of African-American women within the intraracial politics of class, gender, and sexuality is an even more central theme in Michele Mitchell's analysis of the discourse of racial destiny of African Americans, from the post-Reconstruction South to the Garvey movement of the 1920s. Racial destiny was the preoccupation of black reformers and spokespersons of middle- and striving-class status. In a bid for cultural citizenship, these reformers voiced an intense concern with the race's biological reproduction, viewed as synonymous with its social well-being. Mitchell analyzes a neglected archive of frank public discussions of sexuality and hygiene. Breaking with late Victorian norms of reticence about sexuality, these "race activists" opposed the ubiquitous racial and sexual stereotypes that justified the oppression of black men and women, while openly confronting threats to the community's well-being posed by a lack of instruction in sexual matters and by self-destructive sexual behaviors. Mitchell surveys their efforts in a number of gendered sites: late-nineteenth-century emigrationist movements, scientific and popular discourses on eugenics, anthologies of race progress, "better baby" contests, conduct manuals, tracts asserting the importance of homes for black progress, and black nationalist discourses of motherhood and child rearing. For Mitchell, the activities of domestic reformers, particularly women, constituted an ephemeral grassroots politics. Mitchell's study illuminates how perennial concerns about sexuality, well-being, and the role of patriarchy mitigated an effective response to public health problems in African-American communities.

Taken together, these studies expand the purview of black politics during the ordeal of racial segregation, North and South, indicating a departure from narratives about the integration of black people into the U.S. nation. Instead of a focus on black participation in the mainstream areas of electoral politics, civil rights activism, the labor movement, and military service in domestic and foreign wars, with pride of place given to the thought and actions of educated elites, the work of Painter, Hahn, and Mitchell, among others, offers examples of indigenous and grassroots politics emerging from a black civil society suffused with the long memory of postemancipation struggles for economic independence and full citizenship. In these accounts, African Americans confront the barriers of segregation by seeking inclusion into the American nation on their own terms.

Just as one almost suspects that all the stories have been researched and told, one is startled by the seeming infinity of the past and its enduring silences. Mary Frances Berry tells the remarkable story of an indigenous black mass movement led by an unlettered black woman who petitioned the U.S. government for ex-slave pensions and was undone by federal agencies in her quest for justice. In recounting the activism of the former slave and Nashville washerwoman Callie House, Berry recovers a neglected strain of grassroots politics that illustrates the simultaneous production of scholarship and silences. Inspired by the payment of pensions to Civil War veterans and a pamphlet and proposed legislation for a pension for ex-slaves during the 1890s, House and others organized the Ex-Slave Mutual Relief, Bounty, and Pension Association, backing legislation proposed in Congress that would provide pensions for former slaves. As one of the officers of the organization, House traveled throughout the South, gaining the support and dues of thousands of former slaves and their relatives. As House and others gathered names on petitions in support of the ex-slave pension bill, the association provided mutual aid for its impoverished members and held national conventions. But House ran afoul of the Justice Department, which enlisted the Post Office to seek the destruction of the organization through accusations of mail fraud. Despite the lack of support, if not outright contempt, of middle-class black leaders and journalists, House and her organization withstood the hostility of the federal government for years, a testament to the popularity of the cause with southern blacks. House was released from federal prison in 1918, and the association was largely forgotten at the time of her death in 1928. But elderly ex-slaves had not forgotten, writing letters to Presidents Herbert Hoover and Franklin D. Roosevelt inquiring about pensions for ex-slaves. Berry views Callie House and her movement as a precursor for the contemporary reparations movement.

Berry's study, along with other studies of the era of segregation, suggests the varied nature of black struggles, often against difficult odds. Diverse expressions of indigenous politics, including migration and emigration, civil society reform efforts, parades and public commemorations, and claims for reparations, defy normative generalizations or teleological assumptions about integration into the U.S. nation. Of course, state-centered approaches have generated much important work on the legal, constitutional, and legislative dimensions of the struggle for equality, and much more work remains to be done in these areas. But what seems to have emerged is a composite view of black struggles that foregrounds the economic and cultural dimensions of the struggle for full citizenship and views internationalism and "overlapping black diasporas," in Earl Lewis's phrase, as resources for African Americans against the constraints imposed by the U. S. government and civil society.

For example, Beth Bates's study of A. Philip Randolph and the Brotherhood of Sleeping Car Porters reminds us that the brotherhood's conception of "manhood rights" was more than a struggle for the suffrage, but held at its core a vision of economic justice dating back to Reconstruction. Winston James's *Holding Aloft the Banner of Ethiopia*, a study of Caribbean radicalism in the early twentieth century, highlights the diasporic cosmopolitanism of black public culture, particularly in a Harlem shaped by immigration from the West Indies as well as urban migration from the South. Brenda Gayle Plummer produced the first comprehensive study of African Americans' engagement with foreign affairs over the course of the twentieth century. African Americans across the political spectrum, from civil rights leaders and organizations to left-wing activists and grassroots nationalist groups, were intensely engaged in foreign affairs, seeking to influence U.S. policy toward Africa and Haiti, forging alliances between anticolonial movements and U.S. black struggles for equality, and using the United Nations as a forum for crafting a vision of global order that would encompass the democratic aspirations of blacks and colonized peoples. More recently, Clare Corbould has argued that a central theme in black public life in Harlem during the interwar years was a formative engagement with African art, history, and expressive cultures. The search for a usable African past and present was manifested in the New Negro Renaissance, the Garvey movement, protests against the U.S. occupation of Haiti, and Italy's invasion of Ethiopia in 1935.

The Long Civil Rights Movement

The outpouring of work over the past three decades on the history of the black freedom struggle defies easy summation. Scholars in the last decade have adopted the term "the long civil rights movement," to describe this proliferation of scholarship, but also to register qualms about mass-media representations of the movement. Nikhil Singh and Jacquelyn Hall use the phrase to refer to the blossoming of studies whose overall impact challenges a narrow master narrative of the movement. That narrative chronicles a "short" civil rights movement beginning with the 1954 *Brown v. Board of Education* decision and concluding with the passage of the Civil Rights Act of 1964 and the Voting Rights Act of 1965. Subsequent events—urban riots, the Vietnam war, black militancy, feminism, student revolts, busing, and affirmative action—signal the unraveling of America and the decline of the movement. Martin Luther King, Jr., remains fixed at the Lincoln Memorial in 1963, his dream of a color-blind America endlessly replayed while his opposition to the Vietnam War and support of campaigns for economic justice are expunged from popular memory.

This triumphant but diminished image of the movement prevents it, Hall writes, "from speaking effectively to the challenges of our time." Against this distortion of the movement, Hall emphasizes "a more robust, more progressive and truer story" of a "long civil rights movement" that took root during the New Deal and the Popular Front, accelerated during World War II, extended far beyond the South, was hotly contested, and persisted with considerable force into the 1970s. By situating the post-*Brown* struggle for civil rights legislation within that longer story, Hall not only reinforces the moral authority of those who fought for change, but also seeks to "make civil rights harder. . . . [H]arder to simplify, appropriate and contain."

But the "long civil rights movement" thesis has not gone unchallenged. Sundiata K. Cha-Jua and Clarence Lang argue that the thesis expands the time period and regional scope of the movement beyond all recognition. These critics seem most concerned with the potential marginalization of the southern struggle for civil and voting rights during the 1960s, which for many Americans retains an unquestioned moral authority. As the work of John Dittmer, Tim Tyson, and others has shown, however, the southern freedom movement encompassed the local and the global, and rested on the shoulders of traditions of black resistance that predate the modern civil rights movement. It did not burst onto the scene, sui generis, in splendid historical or regional isolation. Rather, its possibilities were forged in the immediate aftermath of the eclipse of a wartime liberal-left alliance between labor, civil rights, and anticolonial activists.

Several influential studies viewing the southern movement from the vantage point of indigenous and grassroots politics have challenged accounts centered on high-level administration officials and such national civil rights leaders as King. Taking issue with the view of the 1954 *Brown* decision as the catalyst for the movement, Aldon Morris emphasized the indigenous resources that gave rise to the modern struggle for equality, with the black church supplying crucial leadership, organization, and fundraising. Breaking from top-down approaches to the movement, Clayborne Carson's book on the Student Nonviolent Coordinating Committee (SNCC) foregrounded the southern movement's radical wing, with SNCC organizers Robert Moses, John Lewis, and Fannie Lou Hamer, under the inspiration of veteran civil rights organizer Ella Baker, adopting the strategy of grassroots organizing for voting rights in Mississippi. Laboring in rural communities far from the media spotlight and facing the constant threat of violence, SNCC sought to empower the most downtrodden blacks in the Deep South. In a somewhat different vein, Charles Payne's magisterial study of the "organizing tradition" in Mississippi recounts the deep egalitarian and democratic structures of black southern life that informed SNCC's ethos and efforts, rooted in generations of struggle. Through their voter education efforts, the young activists in SNCC "were bringing back to the rural Black South a refined, codified version of something that had begun there, an expression of the historical vision of ex-slaves, men and women who understood that, for them, maintaining a deep sense of community was itself an act of resistance." Eschewing triumphalism, Payne explores the limits of liberal consensus. He notes SNCC's fraught relationship with liberalism and the Democratic Party. The activists' faith in government as an ally and their own ideals of interracial cooperation were tested by their mounting frustration at the nation's apparent indifference to the loss of black life. Particularly telling is Payne's discussion of the impact of the news media, which, by focusing on Dr. King's nonviolent direct action campaigns and largely ignoring SNCC's undramatic grassroots organizing, set the tone for histories of the movement that rendered indigenous mass activism invisible.

A similar interest in recovering traditions of resistance and struggle obscured by "mainstream" perspectives has guided the efforts of scholars working at the juncture of African-American, southern, and labor history, focusing on what Robert Korstad has called civil rights unionism. As Patricia Sullivan has shown, the New Deal's federal relief programs and pro-labor policy opened the solid South to labor organizing and voting rights campaigns mounted by black labor and civil rights activists and southern liberals and progressives. This revival of mass activism shocked those convinced of black acquiescence to Jim Crow. In Theodore Rosengarten's *All God's Dangers*, Ned Cobb, an Alabama sharecropper and organizer with the Southern Tenant Farmer's Union, recalled a white employer's alarmed response to the union's popularity among blacks: "The Lord is bringing down the world." Whether or not African-American workers believed their fight against workplace discrimination enjoyed a divine sanction, the wartime mood of antiracism and rights consciousness fueled the alliance between civil rights organizations and the Congress of Industrial Organizations (CIO). The vibrant labor–civil rights pact recounted by Sullivan, Korstad, Michael Honey, and others became a casualty of the red scare's campaign against liberal-left unionism in northern bastions such as Detroit and southern cities including Memphis and Winston-Salem. While the Supreme Court's majority opinion in *Brown v. Board of Education* (1954) cited the importance of desegregation as an asset in the cold war struggle against the Soviet Union, cold war anticommunism also provided segregationists with a formidable weapon in their opposition to Court-ordered desegregation. The cold war consensus in national politics pressured civil rights leaders to jettison demands for economic justice for the pursuit of formal equality through legal and legislative remedies.

Martha Biondi's *To Stand and Fight* brings together several aspects of the approach to the long civil rights movement, writing the history of the movement from the standpoint of postwar northern liberalism. Moving beyond an exclusive emphasis on the Jim Crow South, Biondi shows that discrimination in public accommodations, housing, and the workplace, as well as police brutality, were deeply entrenched in New York City. Biondi's account of racial apartheid in the North leads her to debunk the notion of "de facto segregation," an argument reinforced by the work of Matthew Countryman on Philadelphia and Thomas Sugrue on Detroit. Public policies of real estate, banking, and insurance companies; federal, state, and local governments; and members of the judiciary promoted and upheld segregation in New York and other northern cities. Black mobilizations against discriminatory practices and policies gained momentum from the antiracist thrust of wartime popular sentiment and from a vibrant liberal-left political culture that Biondi terms a "Black popular front." These mobilizations, in which trade unions played a crucial role, influenced the national Democratic Party and served as incubators for political leadership and legal support for the southern civil rights movement. Although the movement in New York and many of its left-wing and labor activists were casualties of the cold war, Biondi concludes that their campaigns against discrimination in housing and employment were influential in providing the basis for such national reforms as affirmative action and the Great Society. Biondi highlights the global consciousness of local black activists, some of them products of multiple histories of racism and colonialism, migrating from the Caribbean and the Panama Canal Zone to societies differently structured in racial dominance in Harlem and New York City.

Indeed, African Americans' interactions with the broader colonial world has been an important dimension of African-American historiography as well as politics, stretching back to the early work of W.E.B. Du Bois, Carter Woodson, and C.L.R. James, to name just a few. As Nikhil Singh has shown, black radical and liberal intellectuals responded to the crises of segregation, depression, and war with a critical discourse of "Black worldliness" that framed U.S. black demands for equality within the democratic aspirations of colonized and oppressed peoples on a global scale. As Rayford Logan phrased the issue in *What the Negro Wants* (1944), a collection of essays by fourteen black intellectuals, "We want the Four Freedoms to apply to black Americans as well as to the brutalized peoples of Europe and to other underprivileged peoples of the world."

Since the mid-1990s, such scholars as Brenda Gayle Plummer, Penny Von Eschen, and James Meriwether have explored the fluid wartime order defined by the collapse of Europe's colonial empires, decolonization, and African and Asian nonaligned movements. What Von Eschen has termed "the politics of the African Diaspora," took shape in the form of African-American activists' linkage of their struggle against U.S. racism with accelerating anticolonial movements in Africa and Asia. Led by stalwarts of the black left—W.E.B. Du Bois, Paul Robeson, and Alphaeus Hunton—the broad-based advocacy of African anticolonial struggles and international labor was grounded in such institutions as the nationally circulated black press, labor unions, and churches, and attracted broad support from African Americans of all political persuasions. As civil rights organizations and black civil society institutions sought representation at the United Nations to lobby on behalf of anticolonial causes, and amid the global war against fascism, internationalism seemed to be a viable strategy for opposing Jim Crow and campaigning for political and economic rights. However, with the advent of the cold war, such figures as Rayford Logan, Walter White, and A. Philip Randolph opposed discrimination within the framework of anticommunism, rather than anticolonialism. Cold war ideology demanded that African Americans limit their political and civic affiliations to the American nation, discrediting wartime expressions of solidarity with African and Asian anticolonial struggles.

Although the cold war's rollback of progressive labor–civil rights–anticolonial projects blocked hopes for a more democratic global order, a dissident black worldliness persisted among a younger generation of black radicals critical of cold war liberalism and U.S. foreign policy toward Africa. Such diverse figures as Du Bois, James Baldwin, Lorraine Hansberry, Malcolm X, and others wondered how African Americans on the threshold of full citizenship would define themselves in relation to political change in Africa and the colonized world. In 1959, while visiting India, Martin Luther King himself declared that "the strongest bond of fraternity was the common cause of minority and colonial peoples in America, Africa, and Asia struggling to throw off racism and imperialism." Whether as expatriates in Ghana or as part of the Harlem-based activist community, some African Americans reserved the right to define their U.S. citizenship in affiliation with Africa and its diaspora, breaking from the ideological tenets of U.S. cold war liberalism. As hopes for nonviolent change in the United States and Africa yielded to the bloodshed that in the minds of many would join Mississippi and Birmingham with South Africa and the Congo, black Americans critical of cold war liberalism declared themselves Afro-American nationalists, fending off reflexive accusations of communism. The former Nation of Islam minister Malcolm X's meeting with voting rights activists in Selma, Alabama, signaled, according to Clayborne Carson, a transformation of his politics from racial-religious separatism to militant political engagement. Malcolm's interactions with young SNCC activists and the high esteem in which they held him indicate the growing influence of his radical pan-African internationalism.

To date, the scholarship produced under the banner of the long civil rights movement tends to cluster around locating the movement's origins in the decades spanning the New Deal and World War II. But the long civil rights movement also includes a growing number of studies of the black power movement. Some of this scholarship challenges the master narrative's declension story by blurring the line between civil rights and black power. Such a view can be seen in Tim Tyson's study of Robert F. Williams, the militant North Carolina NAACP official whose advocacy of armed self-defense during the late 1950s led to his ouster from that organization and his increasingly radical critique of cold war liberalism. Recent scholarship on northern struggles for equality, such as Matthew Countryman's work on Philadelphia, views black power activism in that city not as a rupture, but as an outgrowth of the limited gains of civil rights organizations in the face of persistent discrimination in the workplace and public schools. Historian Peniel Joseph has been a leading contributor to the emerging field of "Black Power studies." The work of Joseph, William Van Deburg, and Jeffrey Ogbar has emphasized the transformative cultural significance of black power. Though not focused on black power per se, Rhonda Williams, Premilla Nadasen, and Annelise Orleck have studied black women's involvement in public housing and welfare rights activism, both key expressions of black power's shift to struggles for economic and social justice after the passage of civil rights reforms. Komozi Woodard's groundbreaking study of Amiri Baraka and black power politics in Newark suggests the need for more local studies of black power.

Scholarship on black power faces its sternest challenge not from the "normative" studies of liberal consensus historians of the "short civil rights movement," but from such scholars of the southern movement as Clayborne Carson and Charles Payne. Carson notes a deep disconnect between black power leaders and mass mobilizations. In his view, black power spokespersons gained national status through media coverage, but they could only react to spontaneous urban rebellions and were unable to deliver any tangible results to the masses they purported to lead. For his part, Payne views the "radical-nationalist thrusts" after the mid-1960s as diametrically opposed to the nonhierarchical assumptions of the organizing tradition. "While their analysis was in fact growing sharper in many ways," according to Payne, "movement activists lost the ability to relate to one another in human terms." The growing number of studies of local black struggles during the 1960s and 1970s that might perhaps be grouped under the heading of Black Power studies seems analogous to the aforementioned trend of scholarship on grassroots black struggles during the era of segregation, more legible as an efflorescence of local struggles rather than as a full-fledged national movement with dedicated leadership.

As with studies of slavery, a focus on women, gender, and sexuality has transformed the study of the civil rights movement. Barbara Ransby's *Ella Baker and the Black Freedom Movement: A Radical Democratic Vision*, along with other studies of women in the movement, greatly enhances our understanding of the movement's gendered dimension. Ransby grounds Baker's long career as an activist for civil and women's rights, from the Popular Front era to the 1970s, in her rural North Carolina origins and the traditions of black southern resistance that were bequeathed to her and many others. Baker, who had contended with the sexism of male-dominated leadership during her brief tenure as executive director of the Southern Christian Leadership Conference, inspired SNCC workers with her democratic vision of grassroots organizing and an ideal of social change that transcended struggles for civil and political rights. Biography appears to be a fruitful means of exploring issues of gender and sexuality. Like Ransby's book on Ella Baker, John D'Emilio's biography of Bayard Rustin complicates triumphalist narratives of the movement, illuminating the dilemma of Rustin, the African-American pacifist and gifted organizer of the 1963 March on Washington, whose homosexuality made him a convenient target of segregationists and often estranged him from his ostensible allies in the movement.

African-American history continues to thrive as a vital subfield of U.S. history. Its subject matter continues to provide occasions for scholarly and public debate, some measured, others strident, on the nation's tortured history of racial and social conflict. In a nation that continues to be afflicted by racial segregation, scholarship outstrips understanding. Many continue to deny the wide gulf separating America's promises and its practices, resulting, for example, in cumulative wealth disparities between blacks and whites. African-American history offers all Americans a unique opportunity for understanding past and present inequalities and ultimately, reconciling differences. Indeed, reconciliation and humanism are central themes of the African-American story. That much is illustrated by those who have experienced the worst treatment at the hands of whites in Jim Crow Mississippi and yet concluded, as did Lou Emma Allen, "Of course there is no way I can hate anybody and hope to see God's face." In addition, one cannot fail to notice African Americans' unmatched fidelity to ideals of freedom and citizenship, grounded in a long memory of generations of struggle and the sacrifices of millions. Darrell Kenyatta Evers once argued with his mother, claiming that he did not see the point of voting. Myrlie Evers ended the discussion by showing her son the bloodied poll-tax receipt his father, Medgar Evers, had been carrying when he was gunned down in his driveway in 1963. At a moment when the progress and legacy of the civil rights movement remain hotly contested, a final lesson that we can derive from African-American history is the extent to which past social and political advances of African Americans have been subject to backlash and reversal by the forces of reaction. That final lesson raises the stakes for the production of future scholarship that advances the field and meaningfully engages public audiences.

BIBLIOGRAPHY

Bates, Beth. *Pullman Porters and the Rise of Protest Politics in Black America, 1925–1945.* Chapel Hill: University of North Carolina Press, 2001.

Berry, Mary Frances. *My Face Is Black Is True: Callie House and the Struggle for Ex-Slave Reparations.* New York: Knopf, 2005.

Biondi, Martha. *To Stand and Fight: The Struggle for Civil Rights in Postwar New York City.* Cambridge, MA: Harvard University Press, 2003.

Blassingame, John. *The Slave Community: Plantation Life in the Antebellum South.* New York: Oxford University Press, 1972.

Camp, Stephanie. *Closer to Freedom: Enslaved Women and Everyday Resistance in the Plantation South.* Chapel Hill: University of North Carolina Press, 2004.

Carson, Clayborne. "African American Leadership and Mass Mobilization." *The Black Scholar* 24 (Fall 1994): 2–7.

———. *In Struggle: SNCC and the Black Awakening of the 1960s.* Cambridge, MA: Harvard University Press, 1981.

Cha-Jua, Sundiata Keita, and Clarence Lang. "The 'Long Movement' as Vampire: Temporal and Spatial Fallacies in Recent Black Freedom Studies." *Journal of African American History* 92 (Spring 2007): 265–288.

Corbould, Clare. *Becoming African Americans: Black Public Life in Harlem, 1919–1939.* Cambridge, MA: Harvard University Press, 2009.

Countryman, Matthew. *Up South: Civil Rights and Black Power in Philadelphia.* Philadelphia: University of Pennsylvania Press, 2006.

Curtin, Philip. *The Atlantic Slave Trade: A Census*. Madison: University of Wisconsin Press, 1969.

D'Emilio, John. *Lost Prophet: The Life and Times of Bayard Rustin*. New York: Free Press, 2003.

Dittmer, John. *Local People: The Struggle for Civil Rights in Mississippi*. Urbana: University of Illinois Press, 1995.

Du Bois, W.E.B. *Black Reconstruction*. New York: Oxford University Press, 2007 [1935].

Elkins, Stanley M. *Slavery: A Problem in American Institutional and Intellectual Life*. Chicago: University of Chicago Press, 1959.

Feimster, Crystal. *Southern Horrors: Women and the Politics of Rape and Lynching*. Cambridge, MA: Harvard University Press, 2009.

Fett, Sharla. *Working Cures: Healing, Health, and Power on Southern Slave Plantations*. Chapel Hill: University of North Carolina Press, 2002.

Finkenbine, Roy E., and Richard S. Newman, "Black Founders in the New Republic: Introduction." *William and Mary Quarterly* 64 (January 2007): 83–94.

Frazier, E. Franklin. *Black Bourgeoisie*. New York: Collier, 1962.

Glymph, Thavolia. *Out of the House of Bondage: The Transformation of the Plantation Household*. New York: Cambridge University Press, 2008.

Gomez, Michael A. *Exchanging Our Country Marks: The Transformation of African Identities in the Colonial and Antebellum South*. Chapel Hill: University of North Carolina Press, 1998.

Gordon-Reed, Annette. *The Hemingses of Monticello: An American Family*. New York: W. W. Norton, 2008.

Gutman, Herbert. *The Black Family in Slavery and Freedom*. New York: Pantheon, 1976.

Hahn, Steven. *A Nation under Our Feet: Black Political Struggles in the Rural South, from Slavery to the Great Migration*. Cambridge, MA: Belknap/Harvard University Press, 2003.

Hall, Jacquelyn. "The Long Civil Rights Movement and the Political Uses of the Past." *Journal of American History* 91 (March 2005): 1233–1263.

Harris, Leslie. *In the Shadow of Slavery: African Americans in New York City, 1626–1863*. Chicago: University of Chicago Press, 2003.

Hine, Darlene Clark. "Rape and the Inner Lives of Black Women in the Middle West: Preliminary Thoughts on the Culture of Dissemblance." In Beverly Guy-Sheftall, ed., *Words of Fire: An Anthology of African-American Feminist Thought*, 380–388. New York: New Press, 1995.

Honey, Michael. *Southern Labor and Black Civil Rights: Organizing Memphis Workers*. Urbana: University of Illinois Press, 1993.

Jackson, Maurice. "'Friends of the Negro! Fly with Me, the Path Is Open to the Sea': Remembering the Haitian Revolution in the History, Music, and Culture of the African American People." *Early American Studies* 6 (Spring 2008): 59–103.

James, Winston. *Holding Aloft the Banner of Ethiopia: Caribbean Radicalism in Early Twentieth-Century America*. London: Verso, 1998.

Johnson, Walter. *Soul by Soul: Life inside the Antebellum Slave Market*. Cambridge, MA: Harvard University Press, 1999.

Joseph, Peniel. *Waiting 'til the Midnight Hour: A Narrative History of Black Power in America*. New York: Henry Holt, 2006.

Kelley, Robin D. G. *Hammer and Hoe: Alabama Communists during the Great Depression*. Chapel Hill: University of North Carolina Press, 1990.

Korstad, Robert. *Civil Rights Unionism: Tobacco Workers and the Struggle for Democracy in the Mid-Twentieth-Century South*. Chapel Hill: University of North Carolina Press, 2003.

Lewis, Earl. "'To Turn as on a Pivot': Writing African Americans into a History of Overlapping Diasporas." *American Historical Review* 100 (June 1995): 765–787.

Logan, Rayford. *The Betrayal of the Negro, from Rutherford B. Hayes to Woodrow Wilson*. New York: Da Capo Press, 1997.

———. *What the Negro Wants*. Notre Dame, IN: University of Notre Dame Press, 1944.

McCurry, Stephanie. *Masters of Small Worlds: Yeoman Households, Gender Relations, and the Political Culture of the Antebellum South Carolina Low Country*. New York: Oxford University Press, 1995.

Melish, Joanne Pope. *Disowning Slavery: Gradual Emancipation and "Race" in New England, 1780–1860*. Ithaca, NY: Cornell University Press, 1998.

Meriwether, James. *Proudly We Can Be Africans: Black Americans and Africa, 1935–1961*. Chapel Hill: University of North Carolina Press, 2002.

Miles, Tiya. *Ties That Bind: The Story of an Afro-Cherokee Family in Slavery and Freedom*. Berkeley: University of California Press, 2005.

Mitchell, Michele. *Righteous Propagation: African Americans and the Politics of Racial Destiny after Reconstruction*. Chapel Hill: University of North Carolina Press, 2004.

Morgan, Jennifer. *Laboring Women: Reproduction and Gender in New World Slavery*. Philadelphia: University of Pennsylvania Press, 2004.

Morris, Aldon. *The Origins of the Civil Rights Movement: Black Communities Organizing for Change*. New York: Free Press, 1984.

Nadasen, Premilla. *Welfare Warriors: The Welfare Rights Movement in the United States*. New York: Routledge, 2005.

Ogbar, Jeffrey. *Black Power: Radical Politics and African American Identity*. Baltimore: Johns Hopkins University Press, 2005.

Orleck, Annelise. *Storming Caesar's Palace: How Black Mothers Fought Their Own War on Poverty*. Boston: Beacon Press, 2005.

Painter, Nell Irvin. *Exodusters: Black Migration to Kansas after Reconstruction*. New York: W. W. Norton, 1977.

———. "Soul Murder and Slavery: Toward a Fully Loaded Cost Accounting." In *Southern History across the Color Line*, 15–39. Chapel Hill: University of North Carolina Press, 2002.

Patterson, Orlando. *Slavery and Social Death: A Comparative Study*. Cambridge, MA: Harvard University Press, 1982.

Payne, Charles. *I've Got the Light of Freedom: The Organizing Tradition and the Mississippi Freedom Struggle*. Berkeley: University of California Press, 1995.

Penningroth, Dylan. *The Claims of Kinfolk: African American Property and Community in the Nineteenth Century South*. Chapel Hill: University of North Carolina Press, 2003.

Plummer, Brenda Gayle. *Rising Wind: Black Americans and U.S. Foreign Affairs, 1935–1960*. Chapel Hill: University of North Carolina Press, 1996.

Quarles, Benjamin. *Black Mosaic: Essays in Afro-American History and Historiography*. Amherst: University of Massachusetts Press, 1988.

Ransby, Barbara. *Ella Baker and the Black Freedom Movement: A Radical Democratic Vision*. Chapel Hill: University of North Carolina Press, 2003.

Rosen, Hannah. *Terror in the Heart of Freedom: Citizenship, Sexual Violence, and the Meaning of Race in the Postemancipation South*. Chapel Hill: University of North Carolina Press, 2009.

Rosengarten, Theodore. *All God's Dangers: The Life of Nate Shaw*. New York: Knopf, 1974.

Scott, Daryl Michael. *Contempt and Pity: Social Policy and the Image of the Damaged Black Psyche*. Chapel Hill: University of North Carolina Press, 1997.

Scott, Julius. "'Negroes in Foreign Bottoms': Sailors, Slaves, and Communication." In Laurent Dubois and Julius Scott, eds., *Origins of the Black Atlantic: Rewriting Histories*, 69–98. New York: Routledge, 2010.

Singh, Nikhil Pal. *Black Is a Country: Race and the Unfinished Struggle for Democracy*. Cambridge, MA: Harvard University Press, 2004.

Sitkoff, Harvard. *A New Deal for Blacks: The Emergence of Civil Rights as a National Issue*. New York: Oxford University Press, 1978.

Smallwood, Stephanie. *Saltwater Slavery: A Middle Passage from Africa to American Diaspora*. Cambridge, MA: Harvard University Press, 2007.

Staples, Brent. "History Lessons Learned from the Slaves of New York." *New York Times*, January 9, 2000.

Stuckey, Sterling. *Slave Culture: Nationalist Theory and the Foundations of Black America*. New York: Oxford University Press, 1987.

———. "Through the Prism of Folklore: The Black Ethos in Slavery." *Massachusetts Review* 9 (Summer 1968): 417–437.

Sugrue, Thomas. *Sweet Land of Liberty: The Forgotten Struggle for Civil Rights in the North*. New York: Random House, 2008.

Sullivan, Patricia. *Days of Hope: Race and Democracy in the New Deal Era*. Chapel Hill: University of North Carolina Press, 1996.

Trouillot, Michel-Rolph. *Silencing the Past: Power and the Production of History*. Boston: Beacon Press, 1995.

Tyson, Timothy B. *Radio Free Dixie: Robert F. Williams and the Roots of Black Power*. Chapel Hill: University of North Carolina Press, 1999.

Van Deburg, William. *New Day in Babylon: The Black Power Movement and American Culture, 1965–1975*. Chicago: University of Chicago Press, 1992.

Von Eschen, Penny. *Race against Empire: Black Americans and Anticolonialism, 1937–1957*. Ithaca, NY: Cornell University Press, 1997.

White, Deborah Gray. *Ar'n't I a Woman: Female Slaves in the Plantation South*. New York: W. W. Norton, 1985.

White, Shane, and Graham White. *Stylin': African American Expressive Culture from Its Beginnings to the Zoot Suit*. Ithaca, NY: Cornell University Press, 1998.

Williams, Eric E. *Capitalism and Slavery*. New York: Capricorn Books, 1966 [1944].

Williams, Rhonda. *The Politics of Public Housing: Black Women's Struggles against Urban Inequality*. New York: Oxford University Press, 2004.

Wilmington Race Riot Commission. Final Report. May 31, 2006. www.history.ncdcr.gov/1898-wrrc/report/report.htm.

Woodard, Komozi. *A Nation within a Nation: Amiri Baraka (LeRoi Jones) and Black Power Politics*. Chapel Hill: University of North Carolina Press, 1999.

Zinn, Howard. *The Southern Mystique*. New York: Knopf, 1964.

CONTRIBUTORS

STEPHEN ARON is Professor of History at UCLA and Executive Director of the Institute for the Study of the American West at the Autry National Center. He is currently writing a book with the working title *Can We All Just Get Along: An Alternative History of the American West.*

SVEN BECKERT is Professor of American History at Harvard University and author of *The Monied Metropolis: New York City and the Consolidation of the American Bourgeoisie* (2001). He is currently at work on a global history of cotton.

NED BLACKHAWK is Professor of History and American Studies at Yale University. He is the author of *Violence over the Land: Indians and Empires in the early American West* (2006) which won the Frederick Jackson Turner Prize from the Organization of American Historians.

REBECCA EDWARDS is Eloise Ellery Professor of History at Vassar College. She is the author of *Angels in the Machinery: Gender in American Party Politics from the Civil War to the Progressive Era* (1997) and *New Spirits: Americans in the "Gilded Age," 1865–1905* (2nd ed., 2010), and coauthor, with James Henretta and Robert Self, of *America's History* (7th ed., 2011).

ERIC FONER is DeWitt Clinton Professor of History at Columbia University and the author of numerous works of American history. He has served as president of the American Historical Association, the Organization of American Historians, and the Society of American Historians. His most recent book is *The Fiery Trial: Abraham Lincoln and American Slavery* (2010), winner of the Bancroft and Pulitzer prizes.

KEVIN GAINES is the Robert Hayden Collegiate Professor of History and Afroamerican and African Studies at the University of Michigan. He is author of *Uplifting the Race: Black Leadership, Politics, and Culture during the Twentieth*

Century (1996), winner of the John Hope Franklin Book Prize of the American Studies Association, and *American Africans in Ghana: Black Expatriates and the Civil Rights Era* (2006). He was president of the American Studies Association in 2009–2010.

LAWRENCE B. GLICKMAN is Professor of History at the University of South Carolina. He coedited, with James W. Cook and Michael O'Malley, *The Cultural Turn in U.S. History: Past, Present, and Future* (2008). He is the author, most recently, of *Buying Power: A History of Consumer Activism in America* (2009).

WOODY HOLTON is Associate Professor of History and American Studies at the University of Richmond. His books include *Forced Founders: Indians, Debtors, Slaves, and the Making of the American Revolution in Virginia* (1999) and *Abigail Adams* (2009), winner of the Bancroft Prize.

MEG JACOBS is Associate Professor of History at the Massachusetts Institute of Technology and author of *Pocketbook Politics: Economic Citizenship in Twentieth-Century America* (2007). She is currently completing a book on the energy crisis of the 1970s.

ROBERT D. JOHNSTON is Associate Professor of History and director of the Teaching of History program at the University of Illinois at Chicago. He is the author of the award-winning *The Radical Middle Class: Populist Democracy and the Question of Capitalism in Progressive Era Portland, Oregon* (2003) and is working on a book about controversies over vaccination in American history.

EREZ MANELA is Professor of History at Harvard University and the author of *The Wilsonian Moment: Self-Determination and the International Origins of Anticolonial Nationalism* (2007). Most recently, he coedited *Shock of the Global: The 1970s in Perspective* (2010).

LISA McGIRR is Professor of History at Harvard University. Her research focuses on politics and social movements in the twentieth century. The author of the award-winning *Suburban Warriors: Origins of the New American Right* (2001), she is currently working on a book entitled *Prohibition and the Making of Modern America.*

JOHN T. McGREEVY is the I. A. O'Shaughnessy Dean of the College of Arts and Letters and Professor of History at the University of Notre Dame. He is the author of *Parish Boundaries: The Catholic Encounter with Race in the Twentieth Century Urban North* (1996) and *Catholicism and American Freedom: A History* (2003).

MAE M. NGAI is Lung Family Professor of Asian American Studies and Professor of History at Columbia University. She is the author of *Impossible Subjects: Illegal Aliens and the Making of Modern America* (2004) and *The Lucky Ones: One Family and the Extraordinary Invention of Chinese America* (2010).

SARAH T. PHILLIPS is Assistant Professor of History at Boston University and the author of *This Land, This Nation: Conservation, Rural America, and the New Deal* (2007).

KIM PHILLIPS-FEIN is Assistant Professor at the Gallatin School of New York University. Her first book, *Invisible Hands: The Making of the Conservative Movement from the New Deal to Reagan*, was published in 2009.

SETH ROCKMAN is Associate Professor of History at Brown University. He is the author of *Welfare Reform in the Early Republic* (2003) and *Scraping By: Wage Labor, Slavery, and Survival in Early Baltimore* (2009).

ADAM ROTHMAN is Associate Professor of History at Georgetown University. He is the author of *Slave Country: American Expansion and the Origins of the Deep South* (2005).

ALAN TAYLOR is Professor of History at the University of California at Davis, and the author of *William Cooper's Town: Power and Persuasion on the Frontier of the Early American Republic* (1996), which won the Pulitzer Prize for American History. His most recent book is *The Civil War of 1812: American Citizens, British Subjects, Indian Allies and Irish Rebels* (2010).

ADDITIONAL TITLES IN THE SERIES

Critical Perspectives on the Past

Ellen M. Snyder-Grenier, *Brooklyn! An Illustrated History*
William Eric Perkins, ed., *Droppin' Science: Critical Essays on Rap Music and Hip Hop Culture*
Mike Wallace, *Mickey Mouse History and Other Essays on American Memory*
Thomas Dublin, ed., *Becoming American, Becoming Ethnic: College Students Explore Their Roots*
Susan Levine, *Degrees of Equality: The American Association of University Women and the Challenge of Twentieth-Century Feminism*
Hope Cooke, *Seeing New York: History Walks for Armchair and Footloose Travelers*
George Lipsitz, *A Life in the Struggle: Ivory Perry and the Culture of Opposition*
Joanne Meyerowitz, ed., *Not June Cleaver: Women and Gender in Postwar America, 1945–1960*
Leah Levenson and Jerry Natterstad, *Granville Hicks: The Intellectual in Mass Society*
Michael Adas, ed., *Islamic and European Expansion: The Forging of a Global Order*
Alfred F. Young, Terry J. Fife, and Mary E. Janzen, *We the People*
Leonard Wilcox, *V. F. Calverton: Radical in the American Grain*
Elizabeth Fee, Linda Shopes, and Linda Zeidman, eds., *The Baltimore Book: New Views of Local History*
Joshua Brown, Patrick Manning, Karin Shapiro, and Jon Wiener, eds., *History from South Africa: Alternative Visions and Practices*
Robert Sklar and Charles Musser, eds., *Resisting Images: Essays on Cinema and History*
Richard Butsch, *For Fun and Profit: The Transformation of Leisure into Consumption*
Paul Buhle, ed., *History and the New Left: Madison, Wisconsin, 1950–1970*
Bryan D. Palmer, *Descent into Discourse: The Reification of Language and the Writing of Social History*
Kathy Peiss, Christina Simmons, and Robert A. Padgug, eds., *Passion and Power: Sexuality in History*
Susan Porter Benson, Stephen Brier, and Roy Rosenzweig, eds., *Presenting the Past: Essays on History and the Public*